Boyds Tracker Plush

THE WORLD'S MOS

Second Edition - Volume 1
Includes the early pieces & variations
Current secondary market prices
Includes all new releases

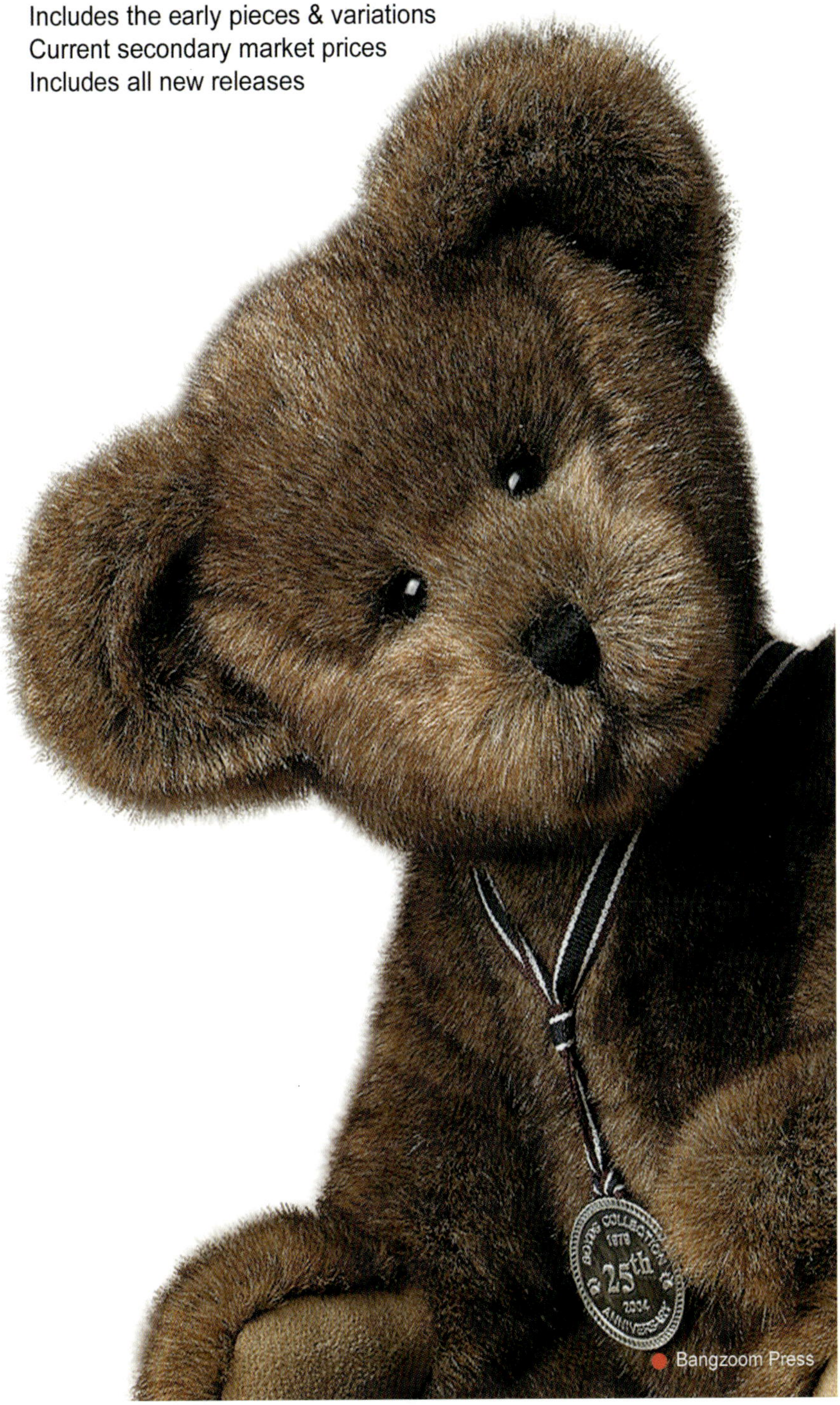

Bangzoom Press

The Boyds Collection Ltd. and associated trademarks, copyrights, and photography are owned by The Boyds Collection Ltd. and used under license. All Rights Reserved. The Boyds Collection Ltd. is not affiliated with Bangzoom Software Inc. nor shares the opinions expressed in this publication.

The staff at Bangzoom wishes to express a special thanks to Capt*n Ron and Kristy Northman, historical consultants and Boyds experts, who generously shared their great knowledge with us in the preparation of our past and current Boyds Tracker guides.

PUBLISHER
Jim Kelley

EDITORIAL
Beth Phillips – Managing Editor
Suzie Hocker – QVC & Exclusive Consultant
Mark & Jean Ann Sovereign – Contributing Consultants
Doug Young - Contributing Editor
Pat Johnson - Contributing Editor

ART & PRODUCTION
Peter Custer – Technical Manager
Lee Sherry – Production Manager
Tom Demeter – Art Director

BUSINESS
Sharen Forsyth – Operations Manager
Chuck Barnard – Service Manager

ACKNOWLEDGEMENTS
Denise Casemier
Janet Earnest
Sharon Everton
Sue and Tony Frank
Becki Freeland
Bev & Frank Freeland
Marcia Haluga
Dee Kahuila
Ilona Williams

ISBN 0-9728646-4-4

Copyright © 2004 by Bangzoom Software, Inc.

All rights reserved. No part of this book may be reproduced or transmitted in any form or by any means, electronic or mechanical, including photocopying, recording, or by any information storage or retrieval system, without the written permission of the publisher.

Bangzoom Publishers
(A Division of Bangzoom Software, Inc.)
14 Storrs Avenue
Braintree, MA 02184
800-589-7333
www.bangzoom.com

CONTRIBUTORS

Thanks to all of you for your great contributions. We couldn't have done it without you!

Jodi Africa	Dwight Davis	Robin Lashley	Lee Robin
Cynthia Algier	Leslie Davis	Brigitte LeJeune	Suzan Rogers
Carolyn Anderson	Julie Debrey	Rachel Lepree	Mary Sabins
Ann from The Doll House	Mary Jean Fasig	Kay Levert	Krys Saldivar
Tiffani Ault	Carol Floyd	Ruth Libey	Rebecca Schiess
Cheryl Barnes	Fran from The Old Blue Barn	Nancy Lind	Brenda Schuett
Marjorie Barnett	Barbara Freeman	Dawn Lowther	Beth Senft
Sally Basiliere	Rosanne Galassi	Maryann Lutz	Valerie Sewell
Beck from Timeless Treasures	Nancy Garavaglia	Joan Markle	Dottie Shattuck
Sheryl Bell	Barbara Aine Gaynor-Ryder	Margaret Celli Martin	Carol Silvia
Missy Bennett	Shannon Gibbons	Coleen Mays	Paula D. Smith
Tara Bentley	Carol Gilmore	Susan McDonald	Mary Snook
Nancy Bitonti	Beverly Goddard	Suzie McKay	Nick Soto
Jennifer Black	Darlene Goldring	Sharon McMillan	Marti Starks
Cindy Blue	Stacie Gorman	Chris Medio	Betsy Stauffer
Dawn Borden	Doreen Gudel	Gerri Michaud	Kathy Stevens
Marlene Bourke	Jennifer Gullings	Michelle's Gifts	Lori Stover
Cheryl Bragg	Heather Haessler	Dianne Miller	Terry Stroh
Linda Brand	Renee Hancotte	Miss Yvonne's	Eileen Suss
Jenny Brennan	Dawn Havard	Temple Moorehead	Pamela Swales
Reta Bush	Joan Higgins	Cheyney Morgan	Connie Tankard
Tammy Catlett	Susan Howe	Roger Munz	Judith Taylor
Melynda Johnson Center	René Hubal	Lesley Nelson	Retta Thayer
Christen from Sarah's Bears	Nancy Huff	Marcie Nye	Rose Tomasov
Heather Christie	Susan Hughes	Janice Oakley	Linda Tuttle
Cindy Christoffel	Stacey Jacoby	Nicole Oertmann	Nicole Vanderzon
Lynda Cicciari	Judi Jamieson	Brenda Ott	Margo Wagner
Lori Clanton	Hazel Jenkins	Tia Pesko	Pamela Waite
Linda Cole	Diane Jones	Eileen Phillips	Jodi Walsh
Lauren Corbin	Emma Jean Juram	Suzette Putman	Jody Weigle
Donna Craiglow	Sherilyn Keck	Donna Ritchie	Tonda Wolfe
Tiffany Crivelli	Frances K. Kuskie	Penny Robbins	

At Bangzoom we're dedicated to creating the most complete and accurate BoydsTracker guides and software in the world! Because you are one of our most important customers, we would like to extend to you a very special invitation to the Bangzoom Contributor Pages.

Help us make the next BoydsTracker the very best guide it can be. If you have any ideas on how to improve the usefulness of our books, want to contribute to the editorial content, can spot omissions or corrections, or can send us an image better than the one we have, we'll proudly list your name in the book as a contributor.

Sign up is free and takes just a few minutes. And to say THANK YOU for just signing up, we'll give you up to 20% off on your BoydsTracker preorder.

To contribute go to http://contribute.bangzoom.com

Table of Contents

Editorials

Welcome to the 2nd Edition 1
The Long & Short of It! 3
Top 5 Boyds Related Websites 4
Boyds 101 - A History 5
The Heart of Boyds 7
Congratulations to the Winners! 9
Those Elusive Exclusives 11
Who Am I? - A Guide to Identification 13
A Bear By Any Other Name 17
Paw Notes Introduction by Kristy Northman 20

Bobby Labonte
Boyds Racing Family

Decoys 21

Early Carver's Choice 32

Boyds Racing Family 40

F.o.B. 44

Bears 50

Sugar Beary Jam
F.o.B.

Critters

Alligators 244
Beavers 244
Camels 244
Cats 245
Cloth Dolls 263
Cows 263
Crows 266
Dogs 266
Donkeys 272
Doves 273
Ducks 273
Elephants 273
Foxes 274
Frogs 275
Geese 276
Giraffes 276
Gorillas 276
Guinea Pigs 277
Hares 277

Americana Angelbear
Bears

Margaret Q. Harington
Hares

Table of Contents

Critters (continued)
Hens 310
Hippos 311
Horses 311
Kangaroos 311
Lambs 311
Lions 314
Llamas 316
Mice 316
Monkeys 318
Moose 320
Owls 329
Pandas 330
Penguins 332
Pigs 332
Raccoons 337
Roosters 337
Skunks 337
Squirrels 338
Tigers 338
Turtles 339
Walruses 339

Muffles P. Mooseltoof
Moose

Farley O'Pigg
Pigs

Others
Ornaments 340
Pins 361
Puppets 363
String Alongs .364
Tree Toppers 364

Future Releases 367

Value Of My Collection 371

Paw Notes by Kristy Northman 379

BoydsTracker Indexes
Alphabetical Index .400
Exclusive Index 432

Philip A. Stocking
Ornaments

Lizzie
Pins

Welcome to the 2nd Edition

Thank you all for your support of our BoydsTracker Plush 2nd Edition. We hope you will be delighted with the new and improved BoydsTracker. We've listened to you and made many improvements.

WHAT'S NEW?
We have doubled the size of this book from the 1st edition! This is by far the most complete Boyds guide ever published. We have reformatted each page so you can keep track of the value of each item or jot down notes and comments. We've added alphabetical and exclusive checklists so you can quickly find items or keep track, at glance, of the items you have or want. We've improved the format of the book to make it easier to read and reference. We've incorporated the "Camera-Shy" sections into the main book and have found the majority of the "Camera-Shy" images. All of the F.o.B. items have been added to both books.

WITH BOYDS SO VAST, WHAT DID WE INCLUDE?
As the Boyds Collection continues to grow and introduce new lines, a distinction between the giftable and collectible lines with new tags and designations is being made. BoydsTracker focuses on the lines that our readers have expressed the most interest in and the items that are most likely to have value on the secondary market.

You may find some items are no longer carried in the books. This is part of an ongoing effort to provide the collector with the best information about the secondary market, while still allowing you the flexibility to add to your book or software any other Boyds items you might collect.

For example, Plush items without formal given names, message mini-bears, Bear and Company items, Baby Boyds, University Bears, and the Thinkin' of Ya Series have been classified as giftables and have not been included. Plush ornaments and non-Bearstone resin ornaments have not been included due to the numbers produced. Exclusive ornaments are listed as they continue to carry interest with collectors.

HOW DID WE GET OUR PRICES?
Questions have been raised about the prices in the Tracker. We are aware that there is disappointment over lower prices than in previous value guides published. Much discussion with long time collectors revealed the need for value guides that are more realistic in terms of the current market. Bangzoom does not arbitrarily decide how to price an item – this information is gathered from collectors, from auction web sites, from many pieces of information available to us. Unfortunately, collectibles are not a static value item – values are driven by two main variables: supply and demand. When demand is high and supply is low, prices go up. When demand is low and supply is high, prices go down. Currently, the overall supply of Boyds

items in the marketplace is greater than the demand for those items; hence, lower values. Anyone who has invested in the stock market knows that stock values have plummeted in recent years. No investment is guaranteed to continue to appreciate in value year after year. One fact is true: an item is worth what someone is willing to pay for it. That amount can vary from week to week, month to month, and year to year. Some items grow in popularity while others may diminish. It is not an easy process to assign values to so many items and expect they will be accurate all of the time.

WHAT ELSE AFFECTS MARKET VALUE?
Other factors affect market value. The condition of an item determines whether or not it will command a high price. A pristine item, showing no wear or fading, with ribbon, hang tag, and tush tag intact and in original packaging where applicable, will command a higher price than an item with rips, stains, wear, odors, faded or missing tags. Early Boyds items were produced in much smaller quantities than more recent items. As the company grew, so did the number of items and the quantities of each. Store and catalog exclusives typically exist in much smaller quantities, even in recent years, and will tend to carry a higher secondary market value than regular line items. QVC exclusives are possibly the most popular group of exclusives and usually sell out very quickly, reaching the secondary market in days. Regular line items generally do not acquire a secondary market value until they have been retired and become difficult to find in retail outlets. This can take a number of years, so do not expect recent releases to increase in value for some time.

WHAT DOES THE OVERALL MARKET LOOK LIKE?
The collectibles market overall has been hit very hard in recent years. The slowing of the economy, the lingering effects of the September 11th tragedy, unemployment, military action overseas, and uncertainty in consumers means fewer dollars are being spent on items that are not necessities. The number of individuals selling their collections has also increased. While making the market for collectibles more global, eBay has also increased the number of sellers who can reach buyers. Buyers are getting more conservative and more patient with the increased supply of old and rare items showing up in the secondary market. It is a great time to buy, but not a great time to sell.

SUMMING IT UP
The market is showing signs of improvement. Bangzoom feels that the values shown in the Tracker are an accurate reflection of current market values. We will continue to monitor those values for any changes. Values should never drive a collector; rather, the love of the item collected should be the deciding factor in a purchase. Our guides are great tools to research, reference, and track the stuff we all love...
The Boyds Collection Ltd!

The Long & Short of It!

You'll notice that we've used abbreviations throughout the book for series, exclusive sources, and pricing.

Abbreviations for Series
Animal Menagerie . . . . .AM
Artisan Series . . . . .AR
Archive Series . . . . .AS
Bears in the Attic . . . . .BA
Bubba Bears . . . . .BB
Bailey & Friends . . . . .BF
Boyds Racing Family . . . . .BR
Choir Bears . . . . .CB
Clinton's Cabinet CC
Cloth Dolls . . . . .CD
Flatties . . . . .FL
Himalayan Dancing Bears . . . . .HD
Holiday Pageant . . . . .HP
Toyland Hares . . . . .HT
ImagineBeary Friends . . . . .IF
J.B. Bean & Associates .JB
Mohair Bears . . . . .MB
Message Bears . . . . .ME
Northern Lights . . . . .NL
Noah's Ark Plush . . . . .NO
Noah's Pageant . . . . .NP
Ornaments . . . . .OR
Snow Bears . . . . .SB
T.F. Wuzzie . . . . .TF
T.J.'s Best Dressed . . . . .TJ
Uptown Bears . . . . .UB
Wool Bear Series . . . . .WB
Wearable Wuzzies . . . . .WW

Abbreviations for Exclusive Sources
Boyds Bear Country . . . . .BBC
Canadian Exclusive . . . . .CAN
Gift Creation Concepts . . . . .GCC
Holiday or Retailer Special Event . . . . .EVENT
Miss Yvonne's & Sarah's Bears . . . . .Miss Yvonne's
Parade of Gifts . . . . .POG
Quality, Value, Convenience . . . . .QVC
San Francisco Music Box . . . . .SFMB
Special Limited Edition .SLE
Syndicated Catalog Groups . . . . .SYN

Other Abbreviations
Current Retail Price . . . .$R/E
Limited Edition . . . . .LE
Not Established . . . . .N/E
Unknown or Missing Information . . . . .unknown

Top 5 Boyds Related Websites

Are you Crazy about Boyds? Whether you are looking for new releases, information, or that one bear that you still haven't hunted down, the internet is a good place to look. You will find a great network of official sources, avid collectors and retailers that are always willing to help each other. Find what you are looking for or just chat with old friends! We were amazed at the number of sites that are out there. Which sites came out on top? We've listed the Top Boyds Related Websites in 5 categories.

Which site would you consider to be the definitive source?

www.boydsstuff.com - The ONLY Official Boyds Website! What's new, what's happening, F.o.B. Membership signup, chats, and a lot more! This should be your first stop when travelin' on the internet!

What site outlines significant recent events?

www.boydsbearcountry.com - Learn about Boyds Bear Country™ from Boyds themselves.

What chat room do you use the most?

www.bearsnbuddies.com - Bulletin boards, news, pictures, classified ads, e-mail newsletter and contests.
(not officially related to Boyds)

Where to go to learn about those really rare bears?

www.bearmuseum.com - Hundreds and hundreds of photos of rare and exclusive bears... growing daily.
(not officially related to Boyds)

Where to go to find more places to go?

www.boydsweb.com - An extensive list of U.S. and Canadian retailers and links to other great sites.
(not officially related to Boyds)

Boyds 101
A History of The Boyds Collection Ltd.®

In the Beginning
The Boyds Collection Ltd.® began back in 1979 as an Antique Shop in the home of G.M. Lowenthal and his partner, (now wife) Justina Unger. Refugees from the "Rat Race," they had been working in management at that "Mecca of Merchandising" known as Bloomingdales, when they chucked it all and moved to rural Boyds, Maryland, to start their own business.

Jeez Antiques are Expensive!
Their great love of antiques outweighed their ability to purchase... sounds familiar, doesn't it? So instead of true antiques with outrageously high costs, G.M. and Tina began to search out and sell antique reproductions, with the look and feel of those *true* antiques but at more affordable prices. Their retail venture proved to be so successful that by 1982 they began to wholesale some of these top-selling antique reproductions.

Duck Decoys to the Rescue...
Some of their most successful wholesale items were their Antique Reproduction Duck Decoys that ranged from a 9" Teal to a giant 3' Whistling Swan. The  wholesale part of The Boyds Collection began to flourish as G.M. designed, painted, antiqued, boxed and sold the Duck Decoys, and Tina handled the customer service, billing, shipping, and accounting aspects of their business. Their expanding wholesale product line soon grew to encompass wool Teddy Bears imported from China.

Hmmm... how about a Bear?
In 1984, G.M. – who was more than just a little tired of painting 20,000 duck decoys until 3 a.m. – turned to resin sculpting with "The Gnomes Homes," extremely detailed miniature houses based on American architecture and his own imagination. About that same time, G.M. designed a fully-jointed 100% Merino Wool Teddy Bear named for his latest "joint venture" with Tina... their newborn son, Matthew. Thus the two partners began what was soon to become a beloved part of The Boyds Collection Ltd. – the Plush designs known far and wide simply as "Boyds Bears."

Boyds 101 (continued)
A History of The Boyds Collection Ltd.®

Weee're Grooowing...
After expanding beyond the Lowenthal's "semi-restored" Victorian home in Boyds to an old Sunday School building down the street, the still-growing company needed even more room! In 1987, the Lowenthals relocated the firm to the Gettysburg, Pennsylvania area. The Boyds Collection Ltd. continued to evolve and to grow in popularity by proverbial leaps and bounds. Today the plush animals known as the "Bears and Hares You Can Trust™" are sold nationwide.

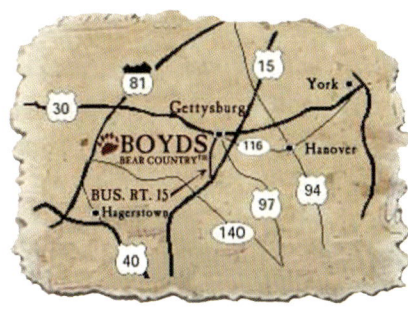

F.o.B. (Friends of Boyds)
In 1996 the enthusiasm of Boyds collectors nationwide resulted in the founding of the fast-growing collectors' club, "The Loyal Order of Friends of Boyds," whose members are proudly know as "Loyal F.o.B's."

Boyds Bear Country™
It was always G.M.'s dream to open a flagship store – a magical place where Boyds bears, hares, and friends could live and play! His dream came true in early 2002 when the Folks at Boyds broke ground and began construction of Boyds Bear Country™. Now open, the World's Most Humongous Teddy Bear Store™, is a definite 'must see' for Bear Lovers young and old. Boyds Bear Country Stores slated for future openings are located in Pigeon Forge, TN and Myrtle Beach, SC.

To The Heart and Soul...
Describing Boyds plush animals is like trying to describe your own kids... each one is unique and irresistible. From a single wool bear in 1984 to the entire collection today, The Boyds Collection Ltd.® has continued to grow by leaps and bounds over the years. As G.M. says, "We're a lot bigger than when we were a 'mom and pop' shop, but, for better or worse, we still run it like a 'mom and pop' shop, only on steroids. We're still a little disorganized and a little off-center, and slightly eccentric... just like our bears!" Boyds has received many awards and a whole lotta recognition from the gift industry and collectors alike. Their whimsical and "Slightly Off-Centered" designs speak to the heart and soul... a bit of Ol' Fashioned Appeal in a slick and fast-moving world.

The Heart of Boyds

Boyds and Charitable Giving by Beth Phillips

One of the many reasons collectors love The Boyds Collection Ltd., is the company's heart for giving. Boyds has given many thousands of dollars to some very special causes and has been the catalyst for other fundraising efforts.

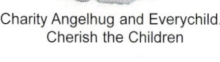
Burke P. Bear

In 1997 Gary Lowenthal learned of a young Boyds collector with cystic fibrosis named Burke Derr. Inspired by this young man's courage, Gary named a bear in his honor: Burke P. Bear. Sadly, Burke lost his life to this disease, spurring a Pennsylvania Boyds dealer to suggest that fellow retailers donate one dollar to Pennsylvania Cystic Fibrosis Inc. for each Burke bear sold. This movement has raised well over $150,000 for research and awareness. With Burke's father and stepmother, the official Burke bear has traveled near and far to help raise funds for this worthy cause.

The Starlight Foundation

Actress Emma Samms began the Starlight Foundation in the 1980's as a way to brighten the lives of youngsters who are in the hospital with serious illnesses. Prolonged hospitalization can be emotionally draining for all family members and take precious "normal" childhood time from those who are ill. Providing televisions, video cassette players, video game players, and other items to hospitals not only helps the children who are hospitalized pass time, but also it is a terrific way to help families continue to interact. Boyds joined this effort in the fall of 2000 by donating the profits from a resin figurine, Charity Angelhug and Everychild... Cherish the Children, and the matching pin. Subsequent years have introduced new Starlight Foundation resins and plush bears.

Joy Angelwish and Everychild... Cherish Small Miracles

Charity Angelhug and Everychild... Cherish the Children

Vanessa R. Angel

In spring 2001 the first Starlight plush, Vanessa R. Angel, was produced. All proceeds from her sale were donated to the Starlight Foundation. Vanessa was named after a very special young lady who lost her life in 2001 to leukemia. Vanessa loved her namesake bear, and her courage and selflessness while battling this disease inspired all those who were privileged to know her story. Subsequent

Starlight Foundation plush are named after children who are fighting serious illnesses. Each year in the spring a new plush bear is released, and a resin figurine is released each fall. All profits from these items go to the Starlight Foundation. To date the Starlight Foundation has received more than one million dollars from the sale of these items.

9-11 Disaster Relief Fund
The Boyds Collection Ltd. also donated $600,000 to the 9-11 Disaster Relief Fund. Part of this amount came from the sale of the October 2001 Event piece, Teddy B. Bear. $450,000 came from the proceeds of two pieces: the Bearstone, Our American Hero, and the Crumpleton, Our American Hero. The response to these items was phenomenal.

Our American Hero

Other Charities
The Boyds Collection Ltd. also donates thousands of items to Toys for Tots and the Today Show Holiday Gift Drive. You can read more about Boyds charitable activities at www.boydsstuff.com.

Which Ones Do You Have?

American Forests
☐ 2001   Fern Woodsbeary

Pennsylvania Cystic Fibrosis Inc.
☐ 1987   Burke P. Bear

Starlight Foundation
☐ 2000   Charity Angelhug and Everychild…Cherish the Children
☐ 2001   Hope Angelwish and Everychild…Bless Our Children
☐ 2001   Vanessa R. Angel
☐ 2002   Alisa R. Angel
☐ 2002   Joy Angelwish and Everychild… Cherish Small Miracles
☐ 2003   Jesselyn R. Angel
☐ 2003   Twinkle Starlight Ornament
☐ 2004   Ashlee R. Angel

9-11 Disaster Relief Fund
☐ 2001   Teddy B. Bear
☐ 2002   Our American Hero… Strength, Dedication and Courage (Bearstone)
☐ 2002   Our American Hero… Strength, Dedication and Courage (Crumpleton)

Congratulations to the Winners!

Award Winning Items by Beth Phillips

In the collectible world, a number of different awards are given out annually in a wide variety of categories.

The TOBY awards, a competition sponsored by *Teddy Bear & Friends* magazine, recognize outstanding achievement in the manufacture, design, and workmanship of teddy bears and other critters. There are a number of categories for bears ranging from miniature to large in size, and from artist "one of a kind" bears to manufactured bears such as Boyds. *Teddy Bear Review* magazine bestows the Golden Teddy Awards. NALED, the National Association of Gift and Collectible Dealers, also awards annual recognition to plush, figurines, dolls, plates, and many other types of collectibles. The DOTY awards, sponsored by *Doll Reader* magazine, recognize the Doll of the Year and highlight outstanding achievement in doll design and manufacture. Gary Lowenthal personally has received numerous awards as an artist and an entrepreneur.

Mr. Noah and Friends
2001 NALED Award Winner

In February 2004, Boyds was pleased to announce they had been nominated for three more Golden Teddy Awards. Polly Peapod was nominated in the over 5 inch/under 14 inch dressed category, Harlan the great big soft huggable bear was nominated in the over 14 inch undressed category, and Moocha Latte, the adorable bean filled cow, was nominated in the Soft Sculpture/Plush Animal category.

Harry and Millie
2001 TOBY Award Winner

The Boyds Collection Ltd. has received numerous awards over the years for their plush, figurines, and dolls. Do you have any of these prizewinners in your collection?

Polly Peapod

Harlan

Moocha Latte

2004 Golden Teddy Award Nominees

Which Ones Do You Have?

1995
- Chanel and Percy (plush), **Golden Teddy**
- Eddie Beanbauer (plush), **TOBY**
- Ms. Bruin & Bailey…the Lesson (resin), **TOBY**
- Eugenia with Apple Crate (plush), **TOBY**

1996
- Collector's Choice Award, **Collector's Jubilee**
- Emma and Bailey…Afternoon Tea (resin), **Golden Teddy**
- Noah & Co…Ark Builders (resin), **TOBY**
- Corinna gold (plush), **TOBY**

Neville…Compubear
1997 TOBY Award Winner

1997
- Emma & Bailey…Afternoon Tea (resin), **Award of Excellence**
- Gary Lowenthal & The Boyds Collection Ltd., **GCC Achievement Award**
- Brittany…Life's Journey (doll), **NALED**
- Neville…Compubear, **TOBY**

1998
- Humboldt (plush), **Award of Excellence**
- Collector's Choice Award, **Collector's Jubilee**
- Grace & Jonathan…Born to Shop (resin), **NALED**

1999
- Amy with Edwin…Momma's Clothes (doll), **NALED**
- Omega T. Legacy & Alpha (plush set), **NALED**
- Flash McBear And The Sitting (resin), **TOBY**
- Roscoe P. Bumpercrop (plush), **TOBY**

2000
- Patches B. Beariluved (plush), **TOBY**

2001
- Mr. Noah & Friends (plush set), **NALED**
- Harry & Millie…Through the Years (resin), **TOBY**
- Graffitie…Put On Your Happy Face (resin), **Golden Teddy**
- Bailey Fall 2001 (plush), **NALED**
- Megan and Faithful…Old and Dear Friends, **DOTY**

Carlie Mae with Ben
2002 DOTY Award Winner

2002
- Slim B. Woodsley (plush), **TOBY**
- Archie Strutencrow (plush), **TOBY**
- Nellie…Baby Buckles (plush), **TOBY**
- Bailey Spring 2002 (plush), **Golden Teddy**
- Sammy Bearmerican…I Pledge Allegiance (resin), **Golden Teddy**
- Carlie Mae with Ben…Bunny Watching (doll), **DOTY**
- Cameron with Zig Zag…Sew Perfect (doll), **DOTY**
- Aubrey With Waddle…Puddle Jumping (doll), **NALED**

2003
- Trevor T. Elfbeary with Giddyup (plush), **TOBY**
- Potsie Daisydew (plush), **TOBY**
- Annie with Tapper…Keeping in Step (doll), **DOTY**
- Krystle B. Bearbright with Joelle & Paz (plush), **Golden Teddy**

Congratulations to the Winners!

Those Elusive Exclusives

A Word on Store Exclusives by Beth Phillips

Exclusives seem to automatically spark interest in collectors. Why are they more valuable? Where do they come from?

Exclusives are Boyds items, either resin or plush, that are created to be sold only through a particular store chain such as Hallmark, Parade of Gifts, and Gift Creations Concepts, or a large catalog/internet retailer like Elder Beerman (a syndicated catalog group), Longaberger, Disney, and QVC. These items become desirable on the secondary market for two prime reasons: they are produced in very limited quantities and for a limited amount of time. Therefore, demand quickly surpasses supply.

Pooh Ornament [Disney]

Over time, Boyds has produced exclusives for a number of different stores. The May Company, Lord & Taylor, Bon Ton, Elder Beerman, and Frederick Atkins all sold Boyds exclusives at one time. You might have found an Elder Beerman exclusive at any Frederick Atkins group store, which includes Bon Ton, Gottschalks, Peebles, and Younkers. Barnes and Noble, the bookstore chain, and Little Debbie had only brief collaborations. Dillards often produced both spring and fall exclusives. Disney has sold a wonderful series of exclusives featuring Pooh and friends in both resin and plush, including mohair Pooh bears.

Twinkle Bear [Macy's East]

More recently, the store exclusives most often mentioned come from Cracker Barrel, Country Clutter, and Kirlins Hallmark. Frequently these exclusives tie into a T.J.'s Best Dressed Series or group for each season with coordinating outfits. Collectors look forward to these seasonal releases with much anticipation.

Catalog groups also have regularly produced exclusives that are sold through subscribers to the catalog. Individual retailers may subscribe to a group like Gift Creations Concepts or the Parade of Gifts catalog and therefore offer those exclusives to their customers. Chain stores like Hallmark, with their quantity buying power, often carry the catalog exclusives if they sell Boyds. A Kirlins Hallmark store might carry the Kirlins exclusives and also the GCC and POG exclusives. Gift Creations Concepts has a web site with a store finder feature to help

Andrea Jane [GCC]

locate stores in your area that carry their exclusives. These gift catalogs produce exclusives with other collectible companies and market them as a group to gift and specialty retailers.

One unique group of exclusives is from the San Francisco Music Box Company. No longer being made, this is a large group of items ranging from plush bears and hares to resin music boxes, musical waterglobes, plush and resin musical ornaments, and even musical dolls.

Lucinda and Dawn...By the Sea [SFMB]

A more recent marriage of concepts that has proven to be a hit with collectors are the Longaberger exclusives. Bear collectors often collect baskets since baskets are great way to display bears. Longaberger makes quality collectible baskets, and not surprisingly, many Boyds collectors are also Longaberger collectors. Longaberger has chosen to carry a fairly extensive selection of both plush and resin items, including a line of bears that have the added feature of helping the fight against breast cancer. Longaberger's Horizon of Hope campaign began in 1995. Longaberger sells baskets, bears, and other items that are earmarked for this campaign. A portion of the proceeds from the sales of these items is donated to the American Cancer Society's breast cancer research, education, and awareness campaign. For the first time in 2004, there is a Horizon of Hope exclusive resin Bearstone. Most plush Longaberger exclusives coordinate with a fabric used in basket liners and other basket accessory items. Frequently, the resin items coordinate with similar plush items and have matching pins. A more recent first for Longaberger has been the production of exclusive Treasure Boxes. The Longaberger Treasure Boxes differ from those in the regular line in that they have a little bear inside instead of a little mouse. Longaberger carries a wide variety of Boyds items, from ornaments and Bearstones to plush bears and hares; a plush tree topper is even part of the line.

Faith Bearywell [Longaberger]

Without a doubt, the largest and most sought after exclusives comes from a single source – QVC. This TV/Internet retailer can lay claim to more than 600 different exclusives for Boyds. Admittedly, often the "limited" sets sold through QVC are not THAT limited in number, but QVC is the only place to find the beautiful groups that often include a family of bears with an accessory item or a matching resin. The shows on QVC used to feature the "Head Bean" himself, Gary Lowenthal. His humor, antics, and costumes converted many a casual observer to avid collector. Liz Smith now carries on as the voice of Boyds on QVC with her wonderful stories of fabrics and items that inspire the designers to create the wonderfully appointed bears and hares.

Uneeda Biggersize [QVC]

WHO AM I?

A Guide To Identification by Beth Phillips

Collectors of Boyds plush know that the early items were made, and often sold, with blank hang tags. The retailers were supposed to write the names on the tags but many did not. As a result, many collectors find themselves with a bear or other critter that they KNOW is a Boyds, but have NO IDEA which one!

Learning to identify your bear begins with some basics of Boyds plush. Identifying your Boyds item accurately will depend on a number of clues. The five keys to identification are Type and/or Series, Production Date, Height, Fur Type, and Color.

Boyds are grouped by type and series. Type refers to the way the bear is stuffed and series refers to the family – Boyds items usually have BOTH a type AND a series designation. The two main types are Archive/poly-fill and J.B. Bean. Archive bears are stuffed with poly-fill/fiber. J.B. Bean are stuffed with pellets. Recently, Boyds began to put some beans in an otherwise poly-filled item to make it sit better or to add some weight. How then to tell the difference? By the tush tag. Archive/poly-fill bears have blue tags with gold letters; bean bears have blue tags with white letters.

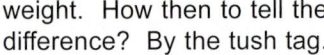

Dabney P. Powderfoot - J.B. Bean

Magillacuddy - Archive Series

Besides type, a number of series, or family names, exists. Often the family is based on a design characteristic, like the Himalayan Dancing Bears with their distinctive curved backs, arms, legs, and a pronounced hump. Others are based on the name or association. For example, Bailey and Friends is the group of 8-inch bears that come out twice a year in different themed outfits. Clinton's Cabinet critters were named after members of President Clinton's Cabinet. The Woolies are a group of bears named for their fabrication – 100% wool. The Bubba Bears have double-jointed faces, and the series includes a couple of lions. Many collectors like to collect by series and will try to complete a series, searching for every member of that group. A series can have items that are different types. For example, the Himalayan Dancing Bears are primarily fiber-filled Archive bears, but there are a few in this family that are bean-filled. T.J.'s Best Dressed critters also can have both Archive and bean-filled critters in their series. Subcategories of the T.J.'s Best Dressed collection, like the Daisy Fields family, are grouped according to the theme or pattern of clothing and usually don't continue for more than a year or two.

Determining the date of production is often key to identification. Examine the tush tag: the most RECENT date on the tush tag is the year of production and like new cars, might have the year before release as the year of production. For example, a bear for Valentine's Day in spring 2003 was actually produced in the year 2002, so it might have a 2002 date on her tag. The hang tag should have 2003 on it. The hang tag, if original, will have a date that will come within a year of the date on the tush tag to confirm the date of issue. The very early white tags can be confusing since they often list a number of critters and dates like Cat 1989, Dog 1987, Lion 1990, and Bear 1989. In this case, the item would be from 1990, regardless if it is a cat, lion, dog or bear. The most recent date is the key date. The exception is the white tag that reads only 1990. This tag was used on items from 1990 through 1993, so an original hang tag is needed to confirm the year of production. These white 1990 tags were also used on plush ornaments for a number of years. Items produced over a number of years can have different dates of production covering those years. A bear made from 1992 through 1998 can have 1992, 93, 94, 95, 96, 97 or 98 as the last date on the tush tag. Remember, Boyds are handmade items so sometimes a tag will turn up that just doesn't match with the date of production.

Tush tags can also help determine series. Critters from the Bears in the Attic or Artisan Series will be blue with red lettering. Very early mohairs had dark red tush tags. Hang tags should also help determine the series if original. The Bailey and Friends group used to have a particular hang tag that was oval in shape but it is no longer used. The Bubba Bears, long retired, DID have a particular hang tag designed just for that series with an image on the front of Bubba. The very early wool bears sold by Boyds (but not produced by Boyds) had a special "storybook" hang tag that was not found on other bears. Hang tags on Archive series bears were flat single tags that early on were almost a pale green in color or a ridged, textured brown tag. J.B. Bean tags are folded storybook tags and also vary in color from pale green to brown.

Zazu - Bears in the Attic

Once you have determined as closely as possible the year of production, measure your critter. Bears are measured from the top of the head to the bottom of the heel. Critters like the snow bears made to stand on all fours should be measured with their legs straight down, as though they were standing, and to the top of the head – not the tip of the nose. Hares and moose are generally measured without ears or antlers. Exceptions are listed as such in this book. Remember again that these items are hand made. Items may be as much as an inch shorter or taller than the listed measurement, particularly with older items. Many of the very early Boyds plush can be as much as two inches shorter than more modern versions of the same item.

The next step in identifying your Boyds is to decide the fur type and color. Regular plush ranges from a very short, smooth, velvety plush to the long, shaggy chenille. Very early critters were made with long, smooth, almost

WHO AM I???

shiny plush that is a different shade and appearance than later critters with the same name. White tag items with very long, smooth, shiny plush are very early versions and may be a slightly different color than later versions. Wool bears have a short, dense nap, and have a tag that reads 100% wool. Some versions of plush, as found on some of the Doodle Bears, McMullen, and Rohley and Pohley, are short, smooth, velvety plush. Individual strands that are short or long but thick are chenille. Chenille can be short or long, curly or straight. Sherpa is a short, nubby fur almost like Berber carpet in appearance. Curly is also a short, nubby, textured fur. Mohair is usually curly, fine and soft to the touch, with longer fibers than the short wool plush. Mohairs are marked as such on their tags.

Color is the next step in identifying your Boyds. As I mentioned before, the color of an item may change during it's lifetime. The early version of J.B. Bean is a pale butter yellow, while later versions are more of a soft white. Early Gordon B. Beans, Speed Poochbergs, and Zenus Grimilkins are a cinnamon, while later versions are tan or British tan. Corinna and Corinna II are different shades – but the same bear. The very first Bailey bear was a dark brown, later changed to the more familiar gold. Most times, a slight color change in early years was not noted with a name change. The easy way to determine color is to pick an item with a known color attached and compare.

COLOR	EXAMPLE
Stark white	Arthur or Pearl Catberg
Butter, off-white, soft white	J.B. Bean or Hillary Bean
Beige (light tan, darker than soft white)	Bupus or Homer
Tan or British tan	Dufus, Otis, Eden or Regina
Taupe (grayish brown)	Janet Hare or Pop Bruin
Mocha (mixture of brown and beige)	Travis or Raleigh
Brown (solid, more chocolate brown)	Malcolm or Winston
Mink (brown and black mix, very dark brown)	Rufus or Siegfried Moose
Chestnut, Cinnamon, Nutmeg or Rust	Cookie Grimilkin, Churchill, Wilson or Eliot B. Bean

Gordon (tan) , Elliot (rust), and Bartholomew B. Bean (mocha)

Sometimes stark white and soft white can only be determined by comparison. With items such as Nod and Nod II, Sinkin and Sinkin II, or Tinkin and Tinkin II, the color is the deciding factor in identification because production dates can overlap. Rufus and Daryl look very much alike but Rufus is mink and Daryl is brown. When they are next to each other, you can see Daryl is lighter and Rufus has the characteristic black hairs mixed with brown that determine the mink color. Bartholomew in mocha can easily be distinguished from the brown Winston when they are side-byside. Many of the J.B. Bean series of naked bears can only be identified by their color and size. Photographs at on-line auction sites like eBay can be misleading so be sure to ask questions of the seller if you are not certain of identification.

Bartholomew B. Bean

Winston

Once you have determined all of these factors, you can begin to compare photos and decide on your bear or hare's identity. Before you start, there are a few more variables to keep in mind. Some items are made for a number of years and over time, modifications may be made to the design. This book illustrates some of the variations that can occur as a piece evolves. Other changes are less dramatic: cats might have stitched toes on their paw pads where early versions had plain unstitched paws. Ribbon colors and paw pad colors frequently changed over the years. Just like with wallpaper and different dye lots, even the same color critter might be slightly lighter or darker than another. Not all items are made at the same factory so these slight differences are of no importance. Now and then you will find that an item like a pillow being held is stitched on upside down or a bow is tied wrong. Again, with handmade items, errors can occur and rarely affect the secondary market value. Some variations are a result of a deliberate change or rectification of an error, as in the two versions of Ms. Rouge Chapeau, the Red Hat Society Bear. Some of the bears were produced and sold with no insignia on the paw. Later versions have the Red Hat label. Early Cracker Barrel exclusives did not have a special marking, while more recent Cracker Barrel exclusives have that designation on a paw.

Early J.B. Bean critters have very flat profiles to their faces and are almost primitive looking. As time went on, the faces changed, ears changed shape and location, noses grew, cheeks filled out. I really enjoy seeing the variations of items that were made for a long time like Ernest the cat or Amelia the hare. The Tracker illustrates many of these known variations. Some of the cats were made in two or three different face styles in regards to the amount and location of white on their faces. Sweetpea was made both in a bluish gray color and a darker pewter color, as was Grayson Hare. Some cows were made in an early "pig nose" version and also the more familiar stitched nostrils, like Bessie and Hortense Moostein. Remember, variety is the spice of life, so learn and enjoy!

A Bear By Any Other Name…
The Origin of Critter Names by Beth Phillips

One of the best things about Boyds items is the critter name. Names are often so funny and so perfect for the critters. How on earth does Boyds come up with these names?

I am sure most of us would love to listen in to a session where names are discussed. Boyds characteristic humor is evident in many items like the big pig called "Wille B. Porkroast" or the squirrel named "Grabby Nutcruncher." Who can say Puff and Poof Fuzzibutt without smiling? Other names clearly tied to the critters they belong to are Oda Parfume the skunk, Bowser Barksalot the dog, and Lester McHootle the owl. Professions and hobbies are also the inspiration for names, as in Putter T. Parfore the golfer bear, Sammy Slugger the baseball player bear, or Miss Winsalot who clearly loves Bingo! Most of the mice are named for different kinds of cheese, naturally. How could a mouse not love a name like Stilton, Chedda, Munster, Brie, Gouda, Cottage, Swiss or one of my favorite cheeses: Feta!

Grabby Nutcruncher

Oda Parfume

Other names draw their inspiration from the series to which a bear belongs. The Choir bears are all named after monks, as in John, Joshua, Gabriel, and Sebastian. The Choir hares are named for convent teachers like Margaret Mary, Mary Catherine, or Grace Agnes. The choir bears and hares have bent knees so that they can be posed like they are praying. The early mohair bears were named for Presidents such as Lincoln, Reagan, and Roosevelt, and the early mohair hares were named for president's wives, as in Dolly and Martha. Many of the mohair cats are named after vice presidents, like Mondale and Spiro. The Clinton's Cabinet Series were named for members of President Clinton's Cabinet – how many can you name? There is a group of Canadian exclusives that are all named for Canadian prime ministers or cabinet members; Lester, Pierre, and Joe are just a few. Many of the naked archive bears are named for English prime ministers, such as Addington, Melbourne, Disraeli, Perceval, Asquith, Chamberlain, Atlee, Eden, Heath, Callaghan and Thatcher. Can you identify all of the English prime ministers that have been immortalized as Boyds bears?

Romano B. Grated

Often the names come from the theme of the outfits the bears are wearing. The McRind family wears outfits with a watermelon theme. The Pearsleys have pears as their unifying color scheme. The MacDonalds share a barnyard theme, and the Sugarcones have a real thing for ice cream cones! The Daisydews happily wear their daisy-printed outfits of sunny yellow, sky blue, and white. It's always fun to collect an entire "family" of bears with the same last name.

Shara Sugarcone

Melanie McRind

The Woodsley bears all share a common design heritage – they are artisan bears manufactured from original designs by the Out of the Woods gang, a talented group of individuals with an eye for whimsy. Other bears have gen-yoo-wine celebrity names, like Dick Butkus, Samuel Adams, or Waldo in his distinctive red and white striped "Where's Waldo?" sweater.

The "Wall Street" bears are named for famous firms like Smith Witter, J.P. Huttin, Fidelity B. Morgan, and D.L. Merrill. Besides their distinguished names, they carry a unique characteristic of paw pads that match their bows: plaid, houndstooth or other patterns you might find in a tie or a suit in the financial district. The Country Clutter Exclusive bears all share the last name of "Goodbear" – an easy way to spot these exclusives on eBay (or anyplace you look for your beloved bears.)

Of course no discussion of names would be complete without mentioning the "Bailey and Friends" series. Bailey, first produced in fall 1992, was named for Gary Lowenthal's daughter Bailey, and collectors were touched by such a special tribute. Bailey, who is released twice a year (spring and fall) in new outfits, continues to be an extremely popular and sentimental bear with collectors. Emily Babbit the rabbit, named for a friend of Bailey's, joined her in the spring of 1993. Then the circle grew to include Matthew, who was named for Gary's son (and Bailey's brother) and Edmund. Indy the dog joined them for a few years but has since trotted off to retire in peace and quiet. Bailey and Matthew will hopefully be produced for many more years as tangible proof of a father's love and devotion.

Bailey

Matthew

With thousands of plush bears and hares in the line, it

A Bear By Any Other Name...

should come as no surprise that some names are repeated and repeated and repeated some more. For example, you can look for the bear named Madeline, Madeline or Madeline – not to be confused with Maddison, Madison or Madison! Unlike the Bailey and Friends series, these are NOT the same bears in different clothes. You can also look for Inga, Ingrid, and Ingrid or Jackson, Jackson and Jackson or George, George, George, George and George! Fortunately, you have the Tracker to help you determine which is which!

It's fun to see if you can find bears or other critters to match your children's or your grandchildren's names. If you have a particularly catchy or unusual family name, by all means, send it in to Boyds. You never know when they might use your suggestion.

Dean S. Bearslot

Dean S. Bearslot was named for a very special husband who took such terrific care of his wife through a serious illness that she wrote to Boyds and told them the story. Boyds honored him with a handsome bear that holds a special place in the hearts of collectors who know the story behind him. All of the Starlight Foundation plush bears are named after children who are or have fought serious illnesses like leukemia. The bears remind us of the real children who struggle every day with pain, loneliness, and fear while being treated in hospitals. These very special bears not only help remind us of our priorities in life, but they also make unique keepsakes for any child who is fighting a chronic health problem.

Ashlee R. Angel
Starlight Foundation

A name can remind us of a parent we have lost, a teacher who cared, an old boyfriend, or a new baby. The name might make you smile, make you laugh, or sometimes make you shake your head and wonder what Boyds was thinking that day! I sometimes can't remember the names of my friends but I can walk around my house – filled with more than 600 bears, hares, cats and dogs – and tell you their names because the names are as special as the critters themselves. Would a bear by any other name be as cute? Maybe it would be but I am glad Boyds continues to charm us with names that are as much fun as the bears.

Bart Barkenfarkle

Paw Notes

By Kristy Northman

You may notice in this Plush Boyds Tracker guide that there are a lot of variations in the early plush pieces. If you are seeing these variations for the first time, I hope that you enjoy seeing the differences.

In the early years of Boyds Plush, it was not uncommon to see Boyds restyle a piece by changing the face, the body, the eye color, or the fur. Rather than giving a re-styled critter a new name to avoid confusion, Boyds kept the same name. Unlike the Resin pieces, these evolutionary plush critters were never retired after they were tweaked and generally kept the same item number even though the changes were noticeable. This explains why you can see two bears with the same name that look so completely different that you would swear that they were different pieces. You may have also found two pieces that have different names but look the same. Boyds occasionally gave one critter two different names. Talk about an identity crisis!

In this book, I have been given the opportunity to share some of the fun facts, rumors, and interesting tidbits that Capt*n Ron and I have learned over the years from Gary and other Boyds employees. Boyds is one of my favorite subjects, so I welcomed the opportunity to create "Paw Notes". Paw Notes are brief notes at the end of the book that document information about a particular piece. I have been an avid Boyds collector since the 80s, and have witnessed a lot of evolutionary changes first hand. Fact or legend, these Paw Notes are accurate to the best of my knowledge. I hope that you enjoy reading them as much as I have loved writing them. When you see this symbol 🐾 with a number in it next to a critter, there is a Paw Note that pertains to it in the last section of the book.

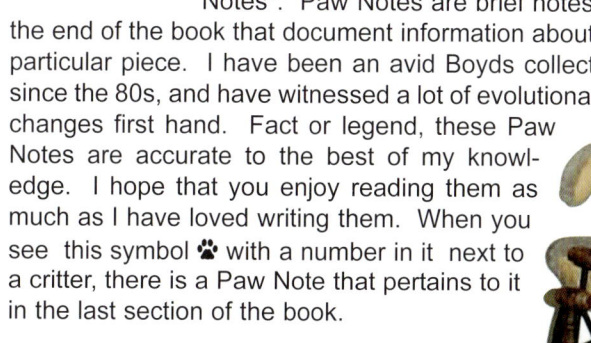

Decoys

Black Hills

1.

Have You Seen Me?

Black Swan (¾ size)
#8006 • 25"
Issued: N/E • Retired: N/E
Original: $N/E • Value: $475

2.

Common Loon
#7015 • 14"
Issued: N/E • Retired: N/E
Original: $50 • Value: $225

3.

Common Loon (superior)
#7016 • 21"
Issued: N/E • Retired: N/E
Original: $100 • Value: $350

4.

Folk Art Loon
#8012 • 21"
Issued: N/E • Retired: N/E
Original: $N/E • Value: $350

5.
Have You Seen Me?
L.S. Black Swan
#8005 • 32"
Issued: N/E • Retired: N/E
Original: $N/E • Value: $700

6.

Have You Seen Me?
L.S. Canada Goose (drake)
#8003 • 25"
Issued: N/E • Retired: N/E
Original: $N/E • Value: $525

7.

L.S. Canada Goose (hen)
#8004 • 27"
Issued: N/E • Retired: N/E
Original: $N/E • Value: $650

8.

L.S. Preening Whistling Swan
#8001 • 27"
Issued: N/E • Retired: N/E
Original: $N/E • Value: $650

BLACK HILLS

	PRICE PAID	VALUE
1.		
2.		
3.		
4.		
5.		
6.		
7.		
8.		
TOTALS		

NOTES

Decoys (Black Hills, Classic Group)

9.

L.S. Whistling Swan
#8000 • 32"
Issued: N/E • Retired: N/E
Original: $N/E • Value: $700

10.

Shorebird (curlew)
#7101 • 13"
Issued: N/E • Retired: N/E
Original: $N/E • Value: $190

11.

Shorebird (snipe)
#7103 • 11"
Issued: N/E • Retired: N/E
Original: $N/E • Value: $180

12.

Have You Seen Me?
Shorebird (stilt)
#7102 • 14"
Issued: N/E • Retired: N/E
Original: $N/E • Value: $190

13.

Special Edition Whistling Swan
(¾ size)
#8002 • 25"
Issued: N/E • Retired: N/E
Original: $N/E • Value: $650

Classic Group

14.

Classic Blue Wing Teal (drake)
#7042 • 16"
Issued: N/E • Retired: N/E
Original: $N/E • Value: $400

15.

Classic Bufflehead (drake)
#7054A • 12"
Issued: N/E • Retired: N/E
Original: $60 • Value: $385

16.
Classic Canvasback (drake)
#7044A • 14"
Issued: N/E • Retired: N/E
Original: $N/E • Value: $375

17.
Classic Canvasback (hen)
#7044A • 14"
Issued: N/E • Retired: N/E
Original: $N/E • Value: $358

18.
Classic Green Wing Teal (drake)
#7040A • 12"
Issued: N/E • Retired: N/E
Original: $60 • Value: $345

19.
Classic Green Wing Teal (hen)
#7041A • 12"
Issued: N/E • Retired: N/E
Original: $60 • Value: $325

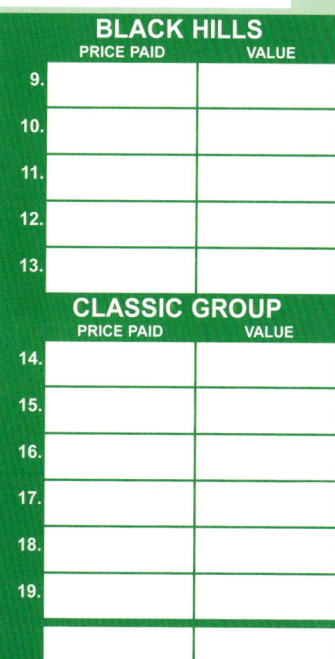

BLACK HILLS	PRICE PAID	VALUE
9.		
10.		
11.		
12.		
13.		

CLASSIC GROUP	PRICE PAID	VALUE
14.		
15.		
16.		
17.		
18.		
19.		
TOTALS		

NOTES

Decoys (Classic Group, Hunter's Group)

Classic Group

20. Classic Mallard (drake)
#7012A • 12"
Issued: N/E • Retired: N/E
Original: $55 • Value: $310

21. Classic Mallard (hen)
#7014A • 12"
Issued: N/E • Retired: N/E
Original: $55 • Value: $300

22. Classic Pintail (drake)
#7048A • 16"
Issued: N/E • Retired: N/E
Original: $60 • Value: $410

23. Classic Puffin
#7056A • 12"
Issued: N/E • Retired: N/E
Original: $55 • Value: $350

Have You Seen Me?

24. Classic Puffin (standing)
#7059A • 8"
Issued: 1987 • Retired: 1990
Original: $60 • Value: $300

25. Classic Redhead (drake)
#7046A • 14"
Issued: 1987 • Retired: 1990
Original: $65 • Value: $275

26. Classic Redhead (hen)
#7047A • 14"
Issued: 1987 • Retired: 1990
Original: $65 • Value: $365

Have You Seen Me?

27. Classic Sleeper Goose
#8015 • 20"
Issued: 1987 • Retired: 1989
Original: $100 • Value: $375

Classic Group

	PRICE PAID	VALUE
20.		
21.		
22.		
23.		
24.		
25.		
26.		
27.		
28.		

Hunter's Group

	PRICE PAID	VALUE
29.		
30.		
TOTALS		

NOTES

28. Classic Widgeon (drake)
#7050A • 14"
Issued: N/E • Retired: N/E
Original: $60 • Value: $350

Hunter's Group

29. Hunter's Blue Wing Teal
#7074 • 16"
Issued: N/E • Retired: N/E
Original: $85 • Value: $450

30. Hunter's Canvasback
#7021 • 15"
Issued: N/E • Retired: N/E
Original: $83 • Value: $435

Decoys (Hunter's Group)

31.
Hunter's Goose
#7018 • 17"
Issued: N/E • Retired: N/E
Original: $80 • Value: $468

32.
Hunter's Green Wing Teal
#7060 • 12"
Issued: N/E • Retired: N/E
Original: $75 • Value: $410

33.
Hunter's Loon
#7072 • 21"
Issued: N/E • Retired: N/E
Original: $100 • Value: $500

34.
Hunter's Loon (open mouth)
#7072 • 21"
Issued: N/E • Retired: N/E
Original: $100 • Value: $525

35.
Hunter's Mallard
#7017 • 17"
Issued: N/E • Retired: N/E
Original: $77 • Value: $440

36.
Hunter's Mallard (sleeper)
#7070 • 12"
Issued: N/E • Retired: N/E
Original: $77 • Value: $405

37.
Hunter's Pheasant
#7022 • 23"
Issued: 1987 • Retired: 1990
Original: $100 • Value: $1260

38.
Hunter's Pintail
#7020 • 21"
Issued: N/E • Retired: N/E
Original: $100 • Value: $495

39.
Hunter's Redhead
#7073 • 16"
Issued: N/E • Retired: N/E
Original: $95 • Value: $375

40.
Hunter's Ruddy Duck
#7076 • 12"
Issued: N/E • Retired: N/E
Original: $75 • Value: $395

41.
Hunter's Wood Duck
#7075 • 16"
Issued: N/E • Retired: N/E
Original: $80 • Value: $475

HUNTER'S GROUP

	PRICE PAID	VALUE
31.		
32.		
33.		
34.		
35.		
36.		
37.		
38.		
39.		
40.		
41.		
TOTALS		

NOTES

Minnesota Flats

42.
Canada Goose (swimmer)
#7092 • 22"
Issued: N/E • Retired: N/E
Original: $30 • Value: $200

43.
Canada Goose (preener)
#7091 • 15"
Issued: 1986 • Retired: 1992
Original: $30 • Value: $225

44.
Canada Goose (sentinel)
#7093 • 17"
Issued: 1986 • Retired: 1992
Original: $30 • Value: $195

45.
Fisher Loon Full Body
#7083A • 25"
Issued: N/E • Retired: N/E
Original: $N/E • Value: $352

46.
Loon (feeder)
#7082 • 17"
Issued: N/E • Retired: N/E
Original: $30 • Value: $195

47.
Loon (preener)
#7080 • 15"
Issued: N/E • Retired: N/E
Original: $30 • Value: $125

48.
Loon (swimmer)
#7081 • 22"
Issued: 1986 • Retired: 1994
Original: $30 • Value: $165

49.
Mallard (preener)
#7096 • 15"
Issued: N/E • Retired: N/E
Original: $30 • Value: $150
(aka sleeper)

50.
Mallard (sentinel)
#7095 • 22"
Issued: N/E • Retired: N/E
Original: $30 • Value: $175
(aka swimmer)

51.
Mallard (swimmer)
#7097 • 17"
Issued: N/E • Retired: N/E
Original: $30 • Value: $160
(aka feeder)

52.
Mini Canada Goose (set of 3)
#7094 • 8"
Issued: N/E • Retired: N/E
Original: $25 • Value: $180

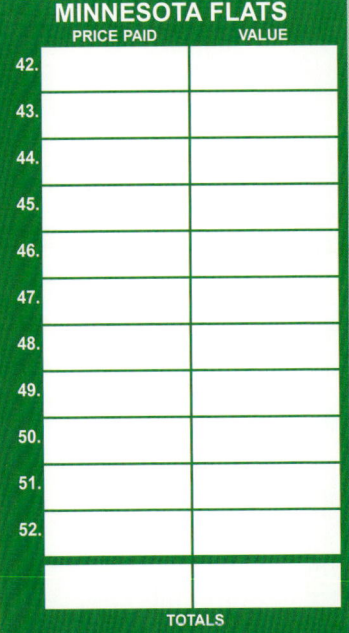

MINNESOTA FLATS

	PRICE PAID	VALUE
42.		
43.		
44.		
45.		
46.		
47.		
48.		
49.		
50.		
51.		
52.		
TOTALS		

NOTES

Decoys (Minnesota Flats)

53.
Mini Loons (set of 3)
#7090 • 8"
Issued: 1986 • Retired: 1995
Original: $25 • Value: $105

54.
Mini Mallards (set of 3)
#7098 • 8"
Issued: N/E • Retired: N/E
Original: $25 • Value: $115

55.
Have You Seen Me?
Mini Minnesota Cats
(black/white - set of 3)
#8003 • 5"
Issued: 1990 • Retired: 1992
Original: $25 • Value: $145

56.
Mini Minnesota Cats
(tiger - set of 3)
#8007 • 5"
Issued: 1990 • Retired: 1992
Original: $25 • Value: $145

57.
Have You Seen Me?
Mini Pintail (set of 3)
#7086 • 8"
Issued: 1990 • Retired: 1991
Original: $25 • Value: $115

58.
Mini Swans (set of 3)
#7307 • 8"
Issued: 1986 • Retired: 1995
Original: $25 • Value: $175

59.
Have You Seen Me?
Mini Wood Duck Flats (set of 3)
#7003 • 8"
Issued: 1990 • Retired: 1991
Original: $25 • Value: $135

60.
Minnesota Cats (b/w jumping)
#8001 • 16"
Issued: 1990 • Retired: 1992
Original: $32 • Value: $222

61.
Minnesota Cats (b/w lying)
#8002 • 7"
Issued: 1990 • Retired: 1992
Original: $32 • Value: $195

62.
Minnesota Cats (b/w sitting)
#8000 • 15"
Issued: 1990 • Retired: 1992
Original: $32 • Value: $245

63.
Have You Seen Me?
Minnesota Cats (tiger jumping)
#8005 • 16"
Issued: 1990 • Retired: 1992
Original: $32 • Value: $214

64.
Minnesota Cats (tiger sitting)
#8004 • 15"
Issued: 1990 • Retired: 1992
Original: $32 • Value: $225

MINNESOTA FLATS

	PRICE PAID	VALUE
53.		
54.		
55.		
56.		
57.		
58.		
59.		
60.		
61.		
62.		
63.		
64.		
TOTALS		

NOTES

Decoys (Minnesota Flats, Museum Series)

65.

Minnesota Cats (tiger stretching)
#8006 • 7"
Issued: 1990 • Retired: 1992
Original: $16 • Value: $219

66.

Pintail (preener)
#7083 • 15"
Issued: 1990 • Retired: 1991
Original: $30 • Value: $205

67.

Pintail (sentinel)
#7085 • 17"
Issued: 1990 • Retired: 1991
Original: $30 • Value: $220

68.

Pintail (swimmer)
#7084 • 22"
Issued: 1990 • Retired: 1991
Original: $30 • Value: $225

69.

Swan (preener)
#7304 • 15"
Issued: 1986 • Retired: 1994
Original: $30 • Value: $165

70.

Swan (sentinel)
#7306 • 17"
Issued: 1986 • Retired: 1994
Original: $30 • Value: $175

71.
Swan (swimmer)
#7305 • 22"
Issued: 1986 • Retired: 1994
Original: $30 • Value: $195

72.

Wood Duck (preener)
#7000 • 15"
Issued: 1991 • Retired: N/E
Original: $30 • Value: $225

73.

Have You Seen Me?

Wood Duck (sentinel)
#7002 • 17"
Issued: 1991 • Retired: 1994
Original: $30 • Value: $250

74.
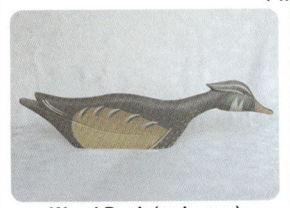
Wood Duck (swimmer)
#7001 • 22"
Issued: 1991 • Retired: N/E
Original: $30 • Value: $270

Museum Series

75.

Have You Seen Me?

Museum Bluebill
#8946 • 14"
Issued: pre-1986 • Retired: 1990
Original: $100 • Value: $305

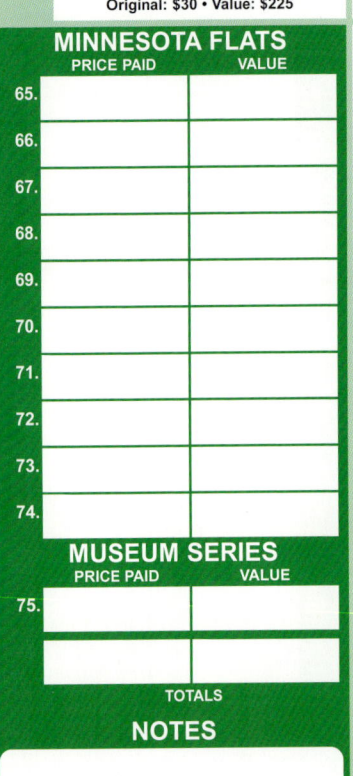

MINNESOTA FLATS

	PRICE PAID	VALUE
65.		
66.		
67.		
68.		
69.		
70.		
71.		
72.		
73.		
74.		

MUSEUM SERIES

	PRICE PAID	VALUE
75.		

TOTALS

NOTES

Decoys (Museum Series, Traditional Group)

76.

Have You Seen Me?

Museum Bufflehead
#8947 • 14"
Issued: pre-1986 • Retired: 1990
Original: $100 • Value: $300

77.

Museum Mallard
#8944 • 16"
Issued: pre-1986 • Retired: 1991
Original: $110 • Value: $325

78.

Museum Pintail
#8944 • 18"
Issued: pre-1986 • Retired: 1990
Original: $100 • Value: $360

79.

Museum Wood Duck
#8945 • 16"
Issued: pre-1986 • Retired: 1990
Original: $110 • Value: $300

Traditional Group

80.

Canada Goose
#7004 • 14"
Issued: N/E • Retired: N/E
Original: $N/E • Value: $325

81.

Canvasback (drake)
#7002 • 14"
Issued: N/E • Retired: N/E
Original: $N/E • Value: $300

82.

Canvasback (hen)
#7003 • 14"
Issued: N/E • Retired: N/E
Original: $N/E • Value: $310

83.

Carvers Goose
#7038 • 20"
Issued: N/E • Retired: N/E
Original: $N/E • Value: $375

84.

Carvers Mallard
#7037 • 17"
Issued: 1987 • Retired: 1989
Original: $N/E • Value: $385

85.

Have You Seen Me?

Carvers Pintail
#7030 • 21"
Issued: 1987 • Retired: 1989
Original: $N/E • Value: $440

86.

Green Wing Teal
#7000 • 9"
Issued: N/E • Retired: N/E
Original: $N/E • Value: $235

MUSEUM SERIES

	PRICE PAID	VALUE
76.		
77.		
78.		
79.		

TRADITIONAL GROUP

	PRICE PAID	VALUE
80.		
81.		
82.		
83.		
84.		
85.		
86.		
TOTALS		

NOTES

Decoys (Traditional Group)

87.

Green Wing Teal (hen)
#7001 • 9"
Issued: N/E • Retired: N/E
Original: $N/E • Value: $248

88.

Mallard (drake)
#7009 • 12"
Issued: N/E • Retired: N/E
Original: $N/E • Value: $300

89.

Have You Seen Me?
Merganser (drake)
#7008 • 14"
Issued: 1986 • Retired: 1991
Original: $N/E • Value: $475

90.

Pintail (drake)
#7005 • 16"
Issued: N/E • Retired: N/E
Original: $N/E • Value: $390

91.

R.B. Merganser (drake - 16")
#7027 • 16"
Issued: N/E • Retired: N/E
Original: $N/E • Value: $540

92.

R.B. Merganser (drake - 18")
#7026 • 18"
Issued: 1987 • Retired: 1989
Original: $N/E • Value: $550

93.

Redhead (drake)
#7010 • 12"
Issued: N/E • Retired: N/E
Original: $N/E • Value: $325

94.

Ruddy Duck (drake)
#7011 • 9"
Issued: 1986 • Retired: 1991
Original: $N/E • Value: $330

95.

Have You Seen Me?
Winter Mallard
#7006 • 16"
Issued: N/E • Retired: N/E
Original: $N/E • Value: $358

96.

Have You Seen Me?
Winter Redhead (drake)
#7007 • 16"
Issued: N/E • Retired: N/E
Original: $N/E • Value: $385

97.

Wood Duck (sentinel)
#7024 • 12"
Issued: N/E • Retired: N/E
Original: $N/E • Value: $500

98.

Wood Duck (sleeper)
#7025 • 11"
Issued: N/E • Retired: N/E
Original: $N/E • Value: $510

TRADITIONAL GROUP

	PRICE PAID	VALUE
87.		
88.		
89.		
90.		
91.		
92.		
93.		
94.		
95.		
96.		
97.		
98.		
TOTALS		

NOTES

White Group

99.
Barnegat Swan
#7301 • 12"
Issued: N/E • Retired: N/E
Original: $40 • Value: $240

100.
Barnegat Swan (large)
#7303 • 14"
Issued: 1987 • Retired: 1991
Original: $55 • Value: $275

101.
Barnegat Swan (preener)
#7302 • 12"
Issued: 1987 • Retired: 1991
Original: $40 • Value: $253

102.
Farmyard Duck
#7201 • 14"
Issued: 1987 • Retired: 1987
Original: $N/E • Value: $295

103.
Farmyard Duckling
#7202 • 9"
Issued: 1987 • Retired: 1991
Original: $35 • Value: $190

104.
Resting Swan
#7203 • 9"
Issued: N/E • Retired: N/E
Original: $35 • Value: $210

Wooden Stained Group

105.
Canada Goose
#6004 • 14"
Issued: N/E • Retired: N/E
Original: $N/E • Value: $240

106.
Have You Seen Me?
Canvasback
#6002 • 14"
Issued: N/E • Retired: N/E
Original: $N/E • Value: $240

107.
Have You Seen Me?
Comfort Bird (gift boxed)
#6204 • 7"
Issued: N/E • Retired: N/E
Original: $N/E • Value: $175

108.
Have You Seen Me?
Loon
#6015 • 14"
Issued: N/E • Retired: N/E
Original: $N/E • Value: $190

WHITE GROUP

	PRICE PAID	VALUE
99.		
100.		
101.		
102.		
103.		
104.		

WOODEN STAINED GROUP

	PRICE PAID	VALUE
105.		
106.		
107.		
108.		
TOTALS		

NOTES

Decoys (Wooden Stained Group)

109.

Have You Seen Me?

Mallard
#6009 • 12"
Issued: N/E • Retired: N/E
Original: $N/E • Value: $215

110.
Have You Seen Me?

Pintail
#6005 • 17"
Issued: N/E • Retired: N/E
Original: $N/E • Value: $235

111.

Have You Seen Me?

Resting Swan
#6203 • 8"
Issued: N/E • Retired: N/E
Original: $N/E • Value: $200

112.
Have You Seen Me?

Ruddy Duck
#6011 • 9"
Issued: N/E • Retired: N/E
Original: $N/E • Value: $195

113.

Teal
#6000 • 9"
Issued: N/E • Retired: N/E
Original: $N/E • Value: $195

114.

Have You Seen Me?

Winter Mallard
#6006 • 16"
Issued: N/E • Retired: N/E
Original: $N/E • Value: $245

WOODEN STAINED GROUP

	PRICE PAID	VALUE
109.		
110.		
111.		
112.		
113.		
114.		
TOTALS		

NOTES

Early Carver's Choice

By popular demand, Boyds Tracker includes this series of wooden carved Ornaments and Produce Stands. Not to be confused with the current Resin Carver's Choice series, Boyds sold this line from 1990 to 1995. All pieces in this series were hand carved of mahogany by Pennsylvania artist Jill Strausbaugh.

Produce Stands

115.
The Apple Harvest Stand
#6525
Issued: 1994 • Retired: 1995
Original: $30 • Value: $125
With accessories.

116.
Bear Hollow Honey Stand
#6522
Issued: 1994 • Retired: 1995
Original: $30 • Value: $85
With accessories.

117.
The Carrot Stand
#6520
Issued: 1994 • Retired: 1995
Original: $30 • Value: $95
With accessories.

118.
Fox Hollow Honey Stand
#6529
Issued: 1994 • Retired: 1995
Original: $20 • Value: $75
Came with no accessories.

119.
Huckleberry Tree Farm
#6523
Issued: 1994 • Retired: 1995
Original: $30 • Value: $200
With accessories.

120.
The Lemonade Stand
#6521
Issued: 1994 • Retired: 1995
Original: $30 • Value: $95
With accessories.

121.
Pumpkin Hollow Stand
#6524
Issued: 1994 • Retired: 1995
Original: $30 • Value: $150
With accessories.

122.
The Watermelon Stand
#6526
Issued: 1995 • Retired: 1996
Original: $30 • Value: $175
With accessories.

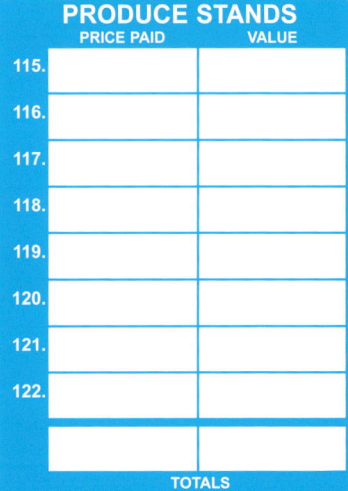

PRODUCE STANDS

	PRICE PAID	VALUE
115.		
116.		
117.		
118.		
119.		
120.		
121.		
122.		
TOTALS		

NOTES

Ornaments

Early Carver's Choice (Ornaments)

123.
Angel Bear (red)
#7116R
Issued: 1990 • Retired: 1995
Original: $8 • Value: $57

124.
Angel Bear (blue)
#7116B
Issued: 1992 • Retired: 1994
Original: $8 • Value: $105

125.
Antique Santa
#7124
Issued: 1990 • Retired: 1995
Original: $8 • Value: $39

126.
Bear Gabriel (angel)
#7111
Issued: 1990 • Retired: 1991
Original: $8 • Value: $105

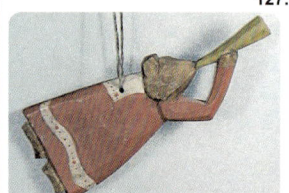

127.
Bear Gabriel (with horn)
#7132
Issued: 1991 • Retired: 1994
Original: $8 • Value: $125

128.

Have You Seen Me?

Bear Gabriel Plaque
#7101
Issued: 1990 • Retired: 1991
Original: $35 • Value: $150

129.
Bear in Basket
#7176
Issued: 1993 • Retired: 1994
Original: $8 • Value: $70

130.
Bear Skater
#7113
Issued: 1990 • Retired: 1995
Original: $8 • Value: $57

131.
Bear Sweep
#7159
Issued: 1993 • Retired: 1995
Original: $8 • Value: $31

132.
Bear with Bunny
#7171
Issued: 1993 • Retired: 1995
Original: $8 • Value: $55

133.
Bear with Tree
#7126
Issued: 1991 • Retired: 1995
Original: $8 • Value: $61

ORNAMENTS

	PRICE PAID	VALUE
123.		
124.		
125.		
126.		
127.		
128.		
129.		
130.		
131.		
132.		
133.		
TOTALS		

NOTES

134.

Bird Bear
#7152
Issued: 1990 • Retired: 1995
Original: $8 • Value: $31

135.
Chimney Santa
#7189
Issued: 1995 • Retired: 1998
Original: $8 • Value: $31

136.

Chimney Santa (stand-up)
#7189A
Issued: 1995 • Retired: 1998
Original: $12 • Value: $39

137.

Choir Boy
#7151
Issued: 1992 • Retired: 1994
Original: $8 • Value: $55

138.

Choir Girl
#7149
Issued: 1992 • Retired: 1994
Original: $8 • Value: $55

139.

Have You Seen Me?
Christmas Goose
#7121
Issued: 1990 • Retired: 1991
Original: $8 • Value: $75

140.

Drummer Bear
#7131
Issued: 1991 • Retired: 1992
Original: $8 • Value: $105

141.

Duffer Bear (golfer)
#7184
Issued: 1995 • Retired: 1998
Original: $8 • Value: $57

142.

Ebony Angel
#7141
Issued: 1992 • Retired: 1994
Original: $8 • Value: $52

143.

Eco Bear
#7150
Issued: 1992 • Retired: 1995
Original: $8 • Value: $60

144.

Eco Bear (stand-up large)
#7150A
Issued: 1992 • Retired: 1995
Original: $16 • Value: $110

145.

Have You Seen Me?
Father Christmas Ornament
#7114
Issued: 1990 • Retired: 1991
Original: $8 • Value: $45

Early Carver's Choice (Ornaments)

ORNAMENTS

	PRICE PAID	VALUE
134.		
135.		
136.		
137.		
138.		
139.		
140.		
141.		
142.		
143.		
144.		
145.		
TOTALS		

NOTES

Early Carver's Choice (Ornaments)

146.
Father Christmas (small)
#7180
Issued: 1993 • Retired: 1995
Original: $8 • Value: $50

147.
Father Christmas (large)
#7180A
Issued: 1993 • Retired: 1995
Original: $16 • Value: $95

148.
Flying Santa
#7156
Issued: 1993 • Retired: 1994
Original: $8 • Value: $57

149.
Folk Art Santa
#7183
Issued: 1995 • Retired: 1998
Original: $8 • Value: $78

150.
Frontier Santa
#7135
Issued: 1991 • Retired: 1995
Original: $8 • Value: $37

151.
Frosty
#7158
Issued: 1993 • Retired: 1995
Original: $8 • Value: $52

152.
Gardner Bear
#7155
Issued: 1992 • Retired: 1994
Original: $8 • Value: $35

153.
Harp Angel
#7146
Issued: 1992 • Retired: 1995
Original: $8 • Value: $55

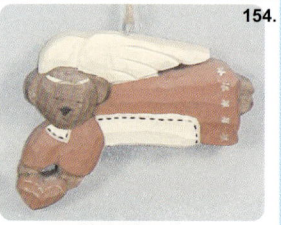

154.
Heart Angel
#7142
Issued: 1992 • Retired: 1995
Original: $8 • Value: $49

155.
Hiking Santa
#7188
Issued: 1995 • Retired: 1998
Original: $8 • Value: $41

156.
Joshua Bear
#7140
Issued: 1992 • Retired: 1995
Original: $8 • Value: $65

157.
Kerchief Bunny (stand-up)
#7174
Issued: 1993 • Retired: 1995
Original: $12 • Value: $70

ORNAMENTS

	PRICE PAID	VALUE
146.		
147.		
148.		
149.		
150.		
151.		
152.		
153.		
154.		
155.		
156.		
157.		
TOTALS		

NOTES

Early Carver's Choice (Ornaments)

158.
Listed Santa
#7134
Issued: 1991 • Retired: 1995
Original: $8 • Value: $50

159.
Little Bear Blue
#7185
Issued: 1995 • Retired: 1998
Original: $8 • Value: $57

160.
Have You Seen Me?
Love Conquers All Plaque
#7102
Issued: 1990 • Retired: 1991
Original: $38 • Value: $150

161.
Magic Santa (green)
#7125G
Issued: 1990 • Retired: 1995
Original: $8 • Value: $75

162.
Magic Santa (red)
#7125R
Issued: 1990 • Retired: 1995
Original: $8 • Value: $40

163.
Magic Santa (blue)
#7125B
Issued: 1993 • Retired: 1995
Original: $8 • Value: $110

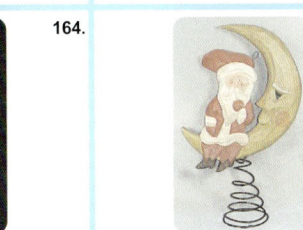
164.
Mistletoe Santa
#7136
Issued: 1991 • Retired: 1992
Original: $8 • Value: $46

165.
Moon Santa (tree topper)
#7139
Issued: 1991 • Retired: 1995
Original: $16 • Value: $85

166.
Mystery Bunny
(Bunny in a Basket)
#unknown
Issued: N/E • Retired: N/E
Original: $N/E • Value: $54

167.
Noel Bear
#7129
Issued: 1991 • Retired: 1995
Original: $8 • Value: $52

168.
Oops Bear
#7148
Issued: 1992 • Retired: 1994
Original: $8 • Value: $55

169.
Patchwork Bunny
#7170
Issued: 1993 • Retired: 1995
Original: $8 • Value: $50

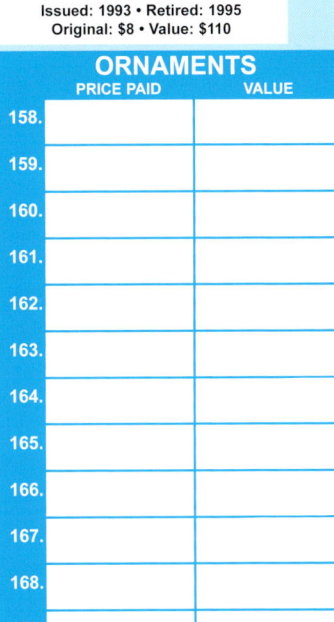

ORNAMENTS

	PRICE PAID	VALUE
158.		
159.		
160.		
161.		
162.		
163.		
164.		
165.		
166.		
167.		
168.		
169.		
	TOTALS	

NOTES

Early Carver's Choice (Ornaments)

170.

Peace Santa
#7186
Issued: 1995 • Retired: 1998
Original: $8 • Value: $33

171.
Rabbit Gabriel
#7110
Issued: 1990 • Retired: 1992
Original: $8 • Value: $110

172.

Have You Seen Me?

Rabbit Gabriel Plaque
#7100
Issued: 1990 • Retired: 1991
Original: $65 • Value: $150

173.

Rag Doll
#7147
Issued: 1992 • Retired: 1995
Original: $8 • Value: $46

174.

Revolutionary Santa
#7181
Issued: 1995 • Retired: 1998
Original: $8 • Value: $44

175.

Sailor Bear
#7130
Issued: 1991 • Retired: 1992
Original: $8 • Value: $50

176.

Santa Gabriel
#7137
Issued: 1991 • Retired: 1992
Original: $8 • Value: $95

177.
Santa Toy (stand-up large)
#7145A
Issued: 1992 • Retired: 1995
Original: $16 • Value: $90

178.

Santa Toy (stand-up medium)
#7145B
Issued: 1993 • Retired: 1995
Original: $12 • Value: $52

179.

Santa Toy Ornament (green sack)
#7145
Issued: 1992 • Retired: 1995
Original: $8 • Value: $35

180.

Have You Seen Me?

Santa with Bag Ornament
#7115
Issued: 1990 • Retired: 1991
Original: $8 • Value: $50

181.

Have You Seen Me?

Santa's Face
#7123
Issued: 1991 • Retired: 1993
Original: $8 • Value: $40

ORNAMENTS

	PRICE PAID	VALUE
170.		
171.		
172.		
173.		
174.		
175.		
176.		
177.		
178.		
179.		
180.		
181.		

TOTALS

NOTES

Early Carver's Choice (Ornaments)

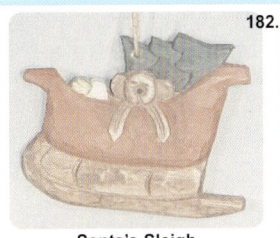

182.
Santa's Sleigh
#7122
Issued: 1990 • Retired: 1991
Original: $8 • Value: $55

183.
Shepard Bear
#7144
Issued: 1992 • Retired: 1994
Original: $8 • Value: $58

184.
Skater Santa
#7133
Issued: 1991 • Retired: 1992
Original: $8 • Value: $39

185.
Skier Bear
#7127
Issued: 1991 • Retired: 1995
Original: $8 • Value: $58

186.
Sledder Bear
#7128
Issued: 1991 • Retired: 1995
Original: $8 • Value: $52

187.
Sledding Santa
#7182
Issued: 1995 • Retired: 1998
Original: $8 • Value: $39

188.
Snow Bear (antique)
#7143
Issued: 1992 • Retired: 1995
Original: $8 • Value: $45

189.
Snow Bear (white)
#7143
Issued: 1992 • Retired: 1995
Original: $8 • Value: $55

190.
Snowball Bear (green)
#7157
Issued: 1993 • Retired: 1995
Original: $8 • Value: $70

191.
Snowball Bear (red)
#7157
Issued: 1993 • Retired: 1995
Original: $8 • Value: $55

192.
Star Santa
#7138
Issued: 1991 • Retired: 1995
Original: $8 • Value: $33

193.
Starstruck Santa
#7187
Issued: 1995 • Retired: 1998
Original: $8 • Value: $39

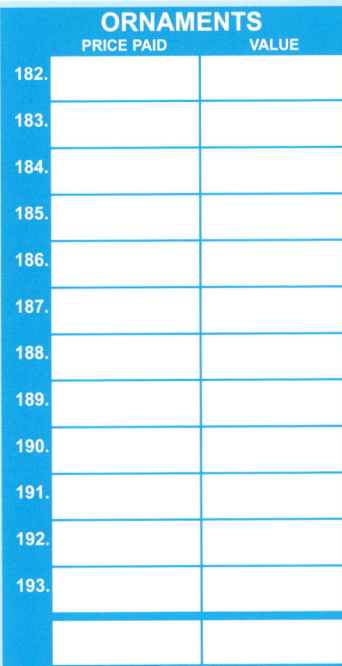

ORNAMENTS

	PRICE PAID	VALUE
182.		
183.		
184.		
185.		
186.		
187.		
188.		
189.		
190.		
191.		
192.		
193.		
TOTALS		

NOTES

Early Carver's Choice (Ornaments)

194.

Ted E. Bear
#7112
Issued: 1990 • Retired: 1994
Original: $8 • Value: $55

195.

Tree Santa
#7120
Issued: 1990 • Retired: 1994
Original: $8 • Value: $39

196.

Walking Bunny (stand-up)
#7172
Issued: 1993 • Retired: 1996
Original: $12 • Value: $85

197.
Have You Seen Me?
Wooden Angel Bear
#7152
Issued: 1990 • Retired: 1991
Original: $30 • Value: $70

198.
Have You Seen Me?
Wooden Momma Cat
#7151
Issued: 1990 • Retired: 1991
Original: $30 • Value: $70

199.
Have You Seen Me?
Wooden Momma Rabbit
#7153
Issued: 1990 • Retired: 1991
Original: $30 • Value: $60

200.
Have You Seen Me?
Wooden Poppa Cat
#7150
Issued: 1990 • Retired: 1991
Original: $30 • Value: $70

201.
Have You Seen Me?
Wooden Poppa Rabbit
#7154
Issued: 1990 • Retired: 1991
Original: $30 • Value: $60

ORNAMENTS

	PRICE PAID	VALUE
194.		
195.		
196.		
197.		
198.		
199.		
200.		
201.		

TOTALS

NOTES

Boyds Racing Family

Bobby Labonte

202.
Bobby Labonte #18
(firesuit)
#919415 • 16" • BR
Issued: 2004 • Current
Original: $51 • Value: $R/E

203.
Bobby Labonte #18
(jacket)
#919416 • 14" • BR
Issued: 2004 • Current
Original: $36 • Value: $R/E

204.
Bobby Labonte #18
(plush ornament)
#919419 • 5½" • BR
Issued: 2004 • Current
Original: $11 • Value: $R/E

205.
Bobby Labonte #18
(resin ornament)
#919418 • 4" • BR
Issued: 2004 • Current
Original: $11 • Value: $R/E

206.
Bobby Labonte #18
(sweatshirt)
#919417 • 10" • BR
Issued: 2004 • Current
Original: $21 • Value: $R/E

Dale Earnhardt

207.
Dale Earnhardt #3
(firesuit)
#919420 • 16" • BR
Issued: 2004 • Current
Original: $51 • Value: $R/E

208.
Dale Earnhardt #3
(jacket)
#919421 • 14" • BR
Issued: 2004 • Current
Original: $36 • Value: $R/E

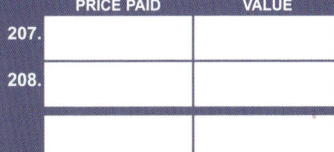

BOBBY LABONTE	PRICE PAID	VALUE
202.		
203.		
204.		
205.		
206.		

DALE EARNHARDT	PRICE PAID	VALUE
207.		
208.		
TOTALS		

NOTES

Boyds Racing Family (Dale Earnhardt...)

209.
Dale Earnhardt #3
(plush ornament)
#919424 • 5½" • BR
Issued: 2004 • Current
Original: $11 • Value: $R/E

210.
Dale Earnhardt #3
(resin ornament)
#919423 • 4" • BR
Issued: 2004 • Current
Original: $11 • Value: $R/E

211.
Dale Earnhardt #3
(sweatshirt)
#919422 • 10" • BR
Issued: 2004 • Current
Original: $21 • Value: $R/E

Dale Earnhardt, Jr.

212.
Dale Earnhardt, Jr. #8
(firesuit)
#919425 • 16" • BR
Issued: 2004 • Current
Original: $51 • Value: $R/E

213.
Dale Earnhardt, Jr. #8
(jacket)
#919426 • 14" • BR
Issued: 2004 • Current
Original: $36 • Value: $R/E

214.
Dale Earnhardt, Jr. #8
(plush ornament)
#919429 • 5½" • BR
Issued: 2004 • Current
Original: $11 • Value: $R/E

215.
Dale Earnhardt, Jr. #8
(resin ornament)
#919428 • 4" • BR
Issued: 2004 • Current
Original: $11 • Value: $R/E

216.
Dale Earnhardt, Jr. #8
(sweatshirt)
#919427 • 10" • BR
Issued: 2004 • Current
Original: $21 • Value: $R/E

Jeff Gordon

217.
Jeff Gordon #24
(firesuit)
#919400 • 16" • BR
Issued: 2004 • Current
Original: $51 • Value: $R/E

218.
Jeff Gordon #24
(jacket)
#919401 • 14" • BR
Issued: 2004 • Current
Original: $36 • Value: $R/E

DALE EARNHARDT		
	PRICE PAID	VALUE
209.		
210.		
211.		

DALE EARNHARDT, JR.		
	PRICE PAID	VALUE
212.		
213.		
214.		
215.		
216.		

JEFF GORDON		
	PRICE PAID	VALUE
217.		
218.		
	TOTALS	

NOTES

Boyds Racing Family (Jeff Gordon...)

219.
Jeff Gordon #24
(plush ornament)
#919404 • 5½" • BR
Issued: 2004 • Current
Original: $11 • Value: $R/E

220.
Jeff Gordon #24
(resin ornament)
#919403 • 4" • BR
Issued: 2004 • Current
Original: $11 • Value: $R/E

221.
Jeff Gordon #24
(sweatshirt)
#919402 • 10" • BR
Issued: 2004 • Current
Original: $21 • Value: $R/E

Jimmy Johnson

222.
Jimmy Johnson #48
(firesuit)
#919405 • 16" • BR
Issued: 2004 • Current
Original: $51 • Value: $R/E

223.
Jimmy Johnson #48
(jacket)
#919406 • 14" • BR
Issued: 2004 • Current
Original: $36 • Value: $R/E

224.
Jimmy Johnson #48
(plush ornament)
#919409 • 5½" • BR
Issued: 2004 • Current
Original: $11 • Value: $R/E

225.
Jimmy Johnson #48
(resin ornament)
#919408 • 4" • BR
Issued: 2004 • Current
Original: $11 • Value: $R/E

226.
Jimmy Johnson #48
(sweatshirt)
#919407 • 10" • BR
Issued: 2004 • Current
Original: $21 • Value: $R/E

Kevin Harvick

227.
Kevin Harvick #29
(firesuit)
#919430 • 16" • BR
Issued: 2004 • Current
Original: $51 • Value: $R/E

228.
Kevin Harvick #29
(jacket)
#919431 • 14" • BR
Issued: 2004 • Current
Original: $36 • Value: $R/E

JEFF GORDON		
	PRICE PAID	VALUE
219.		
220.		
221.		

JIMMY JOHNSON		
	PRICE PAID	VALUE
222.		
223.		
224.		
225.		
226.		

KEVIN HARVICK		
	PRICE PAID	VALUE
227.		
228.		
	TOTALS	

NOTES

Boyds Racing Family (Kevin Harvick...)

229.
Kevin Harvick #29
(plush ornament)
#919434 • 5½" • BR
Issued: 2004 • Current
Original: $11 • Value: $R/E

230.
Kevin Harvick #29
(resin ornament)
#919433 • 4" • BR
Issued: 2004 • Current
Original: $11 • Value: $R/E

231.
Kevin Harvick #29
(sweatshirt)
#919432 • 10" • BR
Issued: 2004 • Current
Original: $21 • Value: $R/E

Tony Stewart

232.
Tony Stewart #20
(firesuit)
#919410 • 16" • BR
Issued: 2004 • Current
Original: $51 • Value: $R/E

233.
Tony Stewart #20
(jacket)
#919411 • 14" • BR
Issued: 2004 • Current
Original: $36 • Value: $R/E

234.
Tony Stewart #20
(resin ornament)
#919414 • 5½" • BR
Issued: 2004 • Current
Original: $11 • Value: $R/E

235.
Tony Stewart #20
(plush ornament)
#919413 • 4" • BR
Issued: 2004 • Current
Original: $11 • Value: $R/E

236.
Tony Stewart #20
(sweatshirt)
#919412 • 10" • BR
Issued: 2004 • Current
Original: $21 • Value: $R/E

KEVIN HARVICK

	PRICE PAID	VALUE
229.		
230.		
231.		

TONY STEWART

	PRICE PAID	VALUE
232.		
233.		
234.		
235.		
236.		

TOTALS

NOTES

F.o.B.

Are you a Friend of Boyds? The Friends of Boyds is a club for Boyds lovers. These items either come with the purchase of a membership or can be purchased only by club members.

F.o.B. (1996 – 1997, 1998)

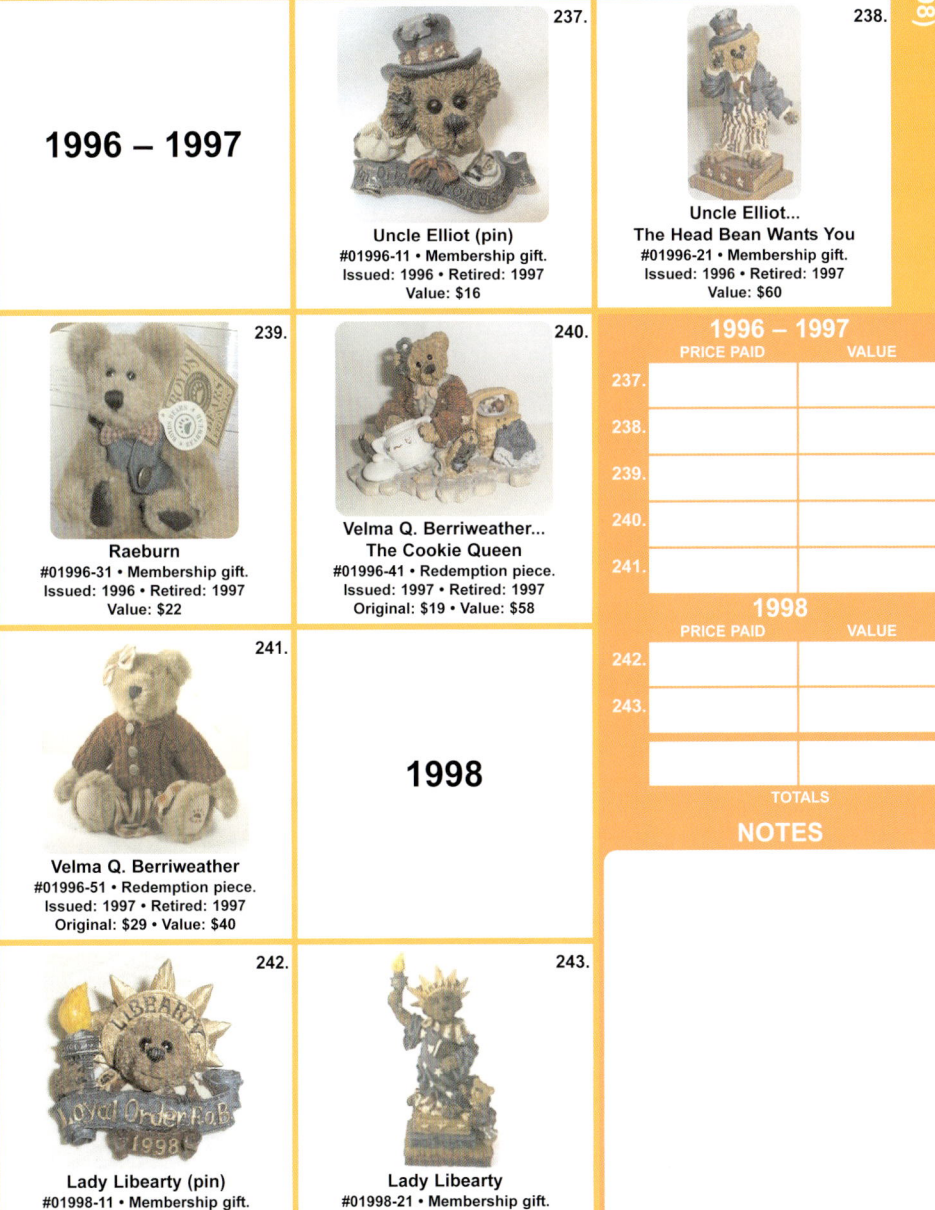

1996 – 1997

237.
Uncle Elliot (pin)
#01996-11 • Membership gift.
Issued: 1996 • Retired: 1997
Value: $16

238.
Uncle Elliot...
The Head Bean Wants You
#01996-21 • Membership gift.
Issued: 1996 • Retired: 1997
Value: $60

239.
Raeburn
#01996-31 • Membership gift.
Issued: 1996 • Retired: 1997
Value: $22

240.
Velma Q. Berriweather...
The Cookie Queen
#01996-41 • Redemption piece.
Issued: 1997 • Retired: 1997
Original: $19 • Value: $58

241.
Velma Q. Berriweather
#01996-51 • Redemption piece.
Issued: 1997 • Retired: 1997
Original: $29 • Value: $28

1998

242.
Lady Libearty (pin)
#01998-11 • Membership gift.
Issued: 1998 • Retired: 1998
Value: $8

243.
Lady Libearty
#01998-21 • Membership gift.
Issued: 1998 • Retired: 1998
Value: $30

1996 – 1997	
	PRICE PAID	VALUE
237.		
238.		
239.		
240.		
241.		

1998	
	PRICE PAID	VALUE
242.		
243.		

TOTALS

NOTES

44

F.o.B. (1998, 1999, 2000)

244.
Eleanor
#01998-31 • Membership gift.
Issued: 1998 • Retired: 1998
Value: $20

245.
Ms. Berriweather's Cottage
#01998-41 • Redemption piece.
Issued: 1998 • Retired: 1998
Original: $21 • Value: $45

246.
Zelma G. Berriweather
#01998-51 • Redemption piece.
Issued: 1998 • Retired: 1998
Original: $32 • Value: $51

1999

247.
Bloomin' F.o.B. (pin)
#01999-11 • Membership gift.
Issued: 1999 • Retired: 1999
Value: $8

248.
Blossom B. Berriweather...
Bloom With Joy!
#01999-21 • Membership gift.
Issued: 1999 • Retired: 1999
Value: $30

249.
Flora Mae Berriweather
#01999-31 • Membership gift.
Issued: 1999 • Retired: 1999
Value: $20

250.
Sunny and Sally Berriweather...
Plant With Hope
#01999-41 • Redemption piece.
Issued: 1999 • Retired: 1999
Original: $23 • Value: $33

251.
Plant With Hope, Grow With
Love, Bloom With Joy
#01999-51 • Redemption piece.
Issued: 1999 • Retired: 1999
Original: $25 • Value: $37

252.
Noah's Genius At Work Table
#2429 • NP • Members Only piece.
Issued: 1999 • Retired: 1999
Original: $12 • Value: $17
Starts at 3E.

2000

253.
Caitlin Berriweather (pin)
#02000-11 • Membership gift.
Issued: 2000 • Retired: 2000
Value: $8

1998	PRICE PAID	VALUE
244.		
245.		
246.		

1999	PRICE PAID	VALUE
247.		
248.		
249.		
250.		
251.		
252.		

2000	PRICE PAID	VALUE
253.		

TOTALS

NOTES

F.o.B. (2000, 2001)

254.
Catherine And Caitlin Berriweather...Fine Cup of Tea
#02000-21 • Membership gift.
Issued: 2000 • Retired: 2000
Value: $28

255.
Caitlin Berriweather
#02000-31 • Membership gift.
Issued: 2000 • Retired: 2000
Value: $23

256.
Catherine And Caitlin Berriweather With Little Scruff... Family Traditions
#02000-41 • Redemption piece.
Issued: 2000 • Retired: 2000
Original: $25 • Value: $38

257.
Catherine Berriweather and Little Scruff
#02000-51 • Redemption piece.
Issued: 2000 • Retired: 2000
Original: $26 • Value: $39

258.
Brewin' F.o.B Mini-Tea Set
#02000-65 • Membership gift.
Issued: 2000 • Retired: 2000
Value: $23

259.
Tea Time Brewin Bubble (pin)
#02000-80 • Redemption piece.
Issued: 2000 • Retired: 2000
Original: $15 • Value: $22

260.
Noah's Toolbox
#2434 • NP • Members Only piece.
Issued: 2000 • Retired: 2000
Original: $12 • Value: $18

2001

261.
Gizmoe...Life's A Juggle
#02001-21 • Membership gift.
Issued: 2001 • Retired: 2001
Value: $23

262.
Greatest F.o.B On Earth (pin)
#02001-11 • Membership gift.
Issued: 2001 • Retired: 2001
Value: $9

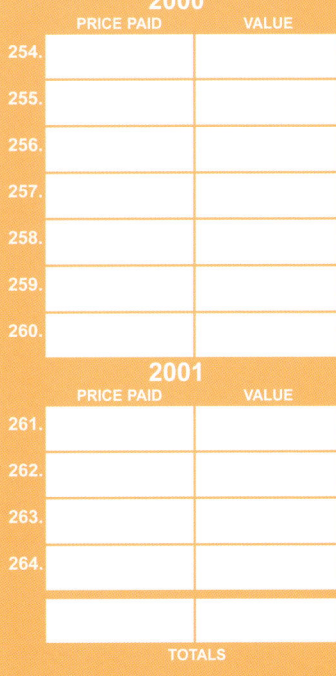

263.
Gadget
#02001-31 • Membership gift.
Issued: 2001 • Retired: 2001
Value: $19

264.
Gussie...Life is a Balancing Act
#02001-41 • Redemption piece.
Issued: 2001 • Retired: 2001
Original: $25 • Value: $30

46

F.o.B. (2001, 2002, 2003)

265.
Melvin Sortalion
#02001-51 • Redemption piece.
Issued: 2001 • Retired: 2001
Original: $30 • Value: $46
♪ The Circus March ♪

266.
Gizmoe's Big Top with Giggle McNibble (box)
#02001-65 • Redemption piece.
Issued: 2001 • Retired: 2001
Original: $13 • Value: $46

267.
Noah's Bookshelf
#2439 • NP • Members Only piece.
Issued: 2001 • Retired: 2001
Original: $12 • Value: $35

2002

268.
Molly B. Beariweather (pin)
#02002-11 • Membership gift.
Issued: 2002 • Retired: 2002
Value: $8

269.
Molly B. Beariweather... Teddy Bear's Picnic
#02002-21 • Membership gift.
Issued: 2002 • Retired: 2002
Value: $18

2001	
PRICE PAID	VALUE
265.	
266.	
267.	

2002	
PRICE PAID	VALUE
268.	
269.	
270.	
271.	
272.	
273.	

2003	
PRICE PAID	VALUE
274.	
TOTALS	

NOTES

270.
Morgan B. Berriweather
#02002-31 • Membership gift.
Issued: 2002 • Retired: 2002
Value: $27
With quilt and basket.

271.
Patti and John Berriweather... Havin' A Wonderful Time
#02002-41 • Redemption piece.
Issued: 2002 • Retired: 2002
Original: $20 • Value: $32

272.
Maggie D. Berriweather
#02002-51 • Redemption piece.
Issued: 2002 • Retired: 2002
Original: $25 • Value: $32
With basket.

273.
Noah's Life Boat
#2444 • NP • Members Only piece.
Issued: 2002 • Retired: 2002
Original: $11 • Value: $25

2003

274.
Aunt Birdie (pin)
#02003-11 • Membership gift.
Issued: 2003 • Retired: 2003
Value: $6

F.o.B. (2003, 2004)

275.

Aunt Birdie Berriweather...
A Sprinkle A Day
#02003-21 • Membership gift.
Issued: 2003 • Retired: 2003
Value: $24

276.

Allison Rose Berriweather
#02003-31 • Membership gift.
Issued: 2003 • Retired: 2003
Value: $21

277.

Gertie Mae Berriweather...
Take Time
#02003-41 • Redemption piece.
Issued: 2003 • Retired: 2003
Value: $18

278.

Petunia P. Berriweather
#02003-51 • Redemption piece.
Issued: 2003 • Retired: 2003
Value: $29

2004

279.

Bearie (pin)
#02004-11 • 2" • Membership gift.
Issued: 2004 • Retired: 2004
Value: $N/E

280.

Frank, Oscar, Barney & Stu
#02004-21 • Membership gift.
Issued: 2004 • Retired: 2004
Value: $N/E

281.

Sugar Beary Jam
with Sugar's Bowl of Berries
#02004-31 • Membership gift.
Issued: 2004 • Retired: 2004
Value: $N/E

282.

Jenny Sweet-Tooth...
It's Dairy To Me
#02004-41 • 2¾" • Redemption piece.
Issued: 2004 • Current
Original: $10 • Value: $R/E

283.
Benjamin
#02004-51 • 17" • Redemption piece.
Issued: 2004 • Current
Original: $25 • Value: $R/E

284.
Minkle B. Beansley
#02004-52 • 10" • Redemption piece.
Issued: 2004 • Current
Original: $9 • Value: $R/E

285.

F.o.B. Exclusive Paw Print Charm
#02004-82 • Membership gift.
Issued: 2004 • Retired: 2004
Value: $22

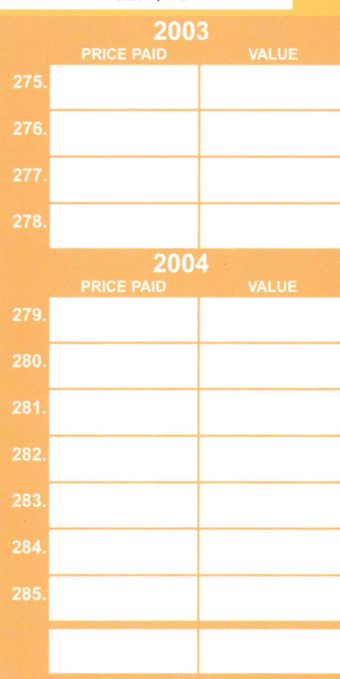

2003	PRICE PAID	VALUE
275.		
276.		
277.		
278.		

2004	PRICE PAID	VALUE
279.		
280.		
281.		
282.		
283.		
284.		
285.		
TOTALS		

NOTES

F.o.B. (2005)

2005

286.
Have You Seen Me?

Bon-Bon Sweetbeary (pin)
#02005-11 • 1¾" • Membership gift.
Issued: 2005 • Retired: N/E
Value: $N/E

287.

**Truffle D. Sweetbeary...
So Much Chocolate, So Little Time**
#02005-21 • Membership gift.
Issued: 2005 • Retired: N/E
Value: $N/E

288.

Have You Seen Me?

Cocoa B. Sweetbeary
#02005-31 • 6" • Membership gift.
Issued: 2005 • Retired: N/E
Value: $N/E

289.
Have You Seen Me?

**Coco's Candy Box
with Morsel McNibble (box)**
#02005-32 • 1" • Redemption piece.
Issued: 2005 • Retired: N/E
Original: $N/E • Value: $N/E

2005

	PRICE PAID	VALUE
286.		
287.		
288.		
289.		
TOTALS		

NOTES

Bears

290.
20th Anniversary Bear [QVC]
#(C56359) • 14"
LE • Issued: 1999 • Retired: 1999
Original: $74 • Value: $110
Justina, Matt, B. Anne, Zuzu.

291.
A. J. Blixen
#917307 • 8" • TJ
Issued: 2000 • Retired: 2000
Original: $14 • Value: $24

292.
Abbott Q. Beanster
#510406 • 16" • JB
Issued: 2003 • Current
Original: $23 • Value: $R/E

293.
Abby & Katie Forever Friends [Carlton Cards]
#919841CA • 6"
Issued: 2002 • Retired: 2002
Original: $25 • Value: $32

294.
Abby Grace [POG]
#94585POG • 6"
Issued: 2000 • Retired: 2000
Original: $15 • Value: $25

295.
Abercrombie B. Beanster
#510400-05 • 16" • JB
Issued: 1999 • Retired: 2001
Original: $21 • Value: $29

Have You Seen Me?

296.
Aberdeen [QVC]
#unknown • 21" • AS
Issued: 1994 • Retired: 1994
Original: $N/E • Value: $165

297.
Abigail [Bon Ton]
#unknown • 12"
Issued: 1996 • Retired: 1996
Original: $30 • Value: $50

298.
Abigail [Elder Beerman]
#unknown • 10"
Issued: 1998 • Retired: 1998
Original: $25 • Value: $47

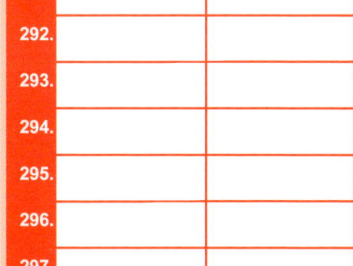

BEARS

	PRICE PAID	VALUE
290.		
291.		
292.		
293.		
294.		
295.		
296.		
297.		
298.		
TOTALS		

NOTES

Bears

299.
Abigail A. Beanster [QVC]
#(C78126) • 10"
Issued: 2000 • Retired: 2000
Original: $11 • Value: $23

300.
Abigail and Beryl Bramblebeary [QVC]
#(C78116) • 6"
Issued: 2000 • Retired: 2000
Original: $19 • Value: $27

301.
Abigail Bramblebeary
#913963 • 6" • TJ
Issued: 2000 • Retired: 2002
Original: $10 • Value: $20

302.
Abigail Rose Primsley
#912645 • 14" • TJ
Issued: 2002 • Retired: 2002
Original: $44 • Value: $44

303.
Ace Bruin
#5122 • 10" • JB
Issued: 1989 • Retired: 1996
Original: $14 • Value: $58

304.
Ace Q. Dooright
#900203 • 12" • UB
LE of 12998 • Issued: 1999 • Retired: 2000
Original: $91 • Value: $103

305.
Adaline Bearett
#918437 • 6" • TJ
Issued: 2000 • Retired: 2002
Original: $10 • Value: $28

306.
Adam Appleton
#904302 • 10" • TJ
Issued: 2004 • Current
Original: $18 • Value: $R/E

307.
Adam [York Fair]
#94182YF • 8"
Issued: 2002 • Retired: 2002
Original: $14 • Value: $18

308.
Adams F. Bearington
#590083-03 • 6" • MB
Issued: 1998 • Retired: 1998
Original: $18 • Value: $39

309.
Addington
#5701-05 • 12" • AS
Issued: 1993 • Retired: 1996
Original: $20 • Value: $55

310.
Adeline B. Appleton
#904301 • 14" • TJ
Issued: 2004 • Current
Original: $26 • Value: $R/E

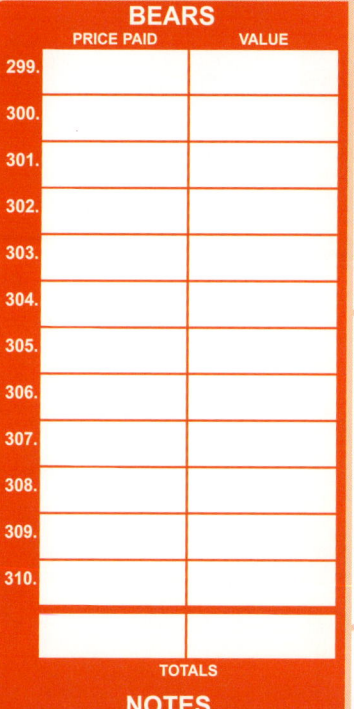

BEARS

	PRICE PAID	VALUE
299.		
300.		
301.		
302.		
303.		
304.		
305.		
306.		
307.		
308.		
309.		
310.		
TOTALS		

NOTES

311.
Adeline LaBearsley
#912657 • 12" • TJ
Issued: 2001 • Retired: 2001
Original: $23 • Value: $35

312.
Adkin [Frederick Atkins]
#unknown • 10"
Issued: 1997 • Retired: 1997
Original: $20 • Value: $35

313.
Agatha B. Bearington [QVC]
#91477V (C0430) • 6" • MB
LE of 1200 • Issued: 2003 • Retired: 2003
Original: $17 • Value: $20

314.
Agatha Snoopstein
#91870 • 8" • TJ
Issued: 2000 • Retired: 2000
Original: $14 • Value: $25

315.
Agnes MacBear [CAN]
#94294PO • 10" • AM
LE of 4800 • Issued: 2002 • Retired: 2002
Original: $26 • Value: $R/E

316.
Aimee Warmheart
#917371 • 10" • ME
Issued: 2001 • Retired: 2001
Original: $20 • Value: $28

317.
Aissa Witebred
#912070 • 12" • TJ
Issued: 2000 • Retired: 2001
Original: $23 • Value: $25

318.
Alabaster B. Bigfoot
#51110-01 • 18" • JB
Issued: 2000 • Current
Original: $37 • Value: $R/E

319.
Alastair
#5725-08 • 5½" • AS
Issued: 1996 • Retired: 1997
Original: $7 • Value: $28

320.
Alastair & Camilla
#98042 • 6" • TJ
Issued: 1996 • Retired: 1997
Original: $10 • Value: $46

321.
Albert B. Bean
#5123-03 • 14" • JB
Issued: 1993 • Retired: 1997
Original: $20 • Value: $38

322.
Albert Merrybeary
#915212 • 8¼" • TJ
Issued: 2001 • Retired: 2001
Original: $14 • Value: $21

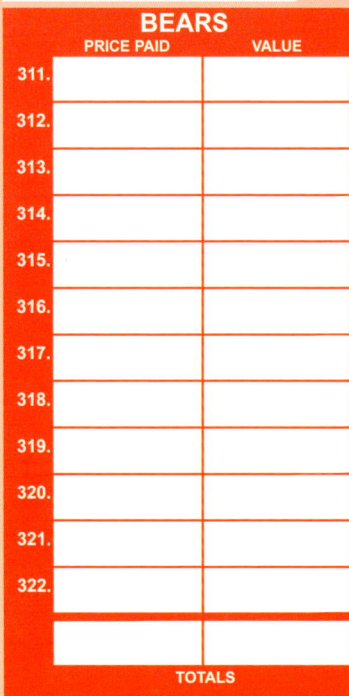

Bears

323.

Al'Berta B. Bear [CAN]
#BC94277 • 10"
LE of 10000 • Issued: 1998 • Retired: 1998
Original: $30 • Value: $43

324.

Albin and Tootie Whizzalong [QVC]
#C100430 • 10"
Issued: 2001 • Retired: 2001
Original: $62 • Value: $75
Sold with sled.

325.

Aldina [Dillards]
#94714DL • 14"
Issued: 1997 • Retired: 1997
Original: $30 • Value: $50

326.

Alec (a.k.a. Alex)
#5711 • 5½" • AS
Issued: 1990 • Retired: 1991
Original: $7 • Value: $84

327.

Aleesha Bearlet [QVC]
#93205V • 12"
Issued: 2001 • Retired: 2001
Original: $23 • Value: $30

328.

Aletha The Bearmaker
#9217 • 14"
LE of 500 • Issued: 1994 • Retired: 1994
Original: $74 • Value: $362

329.

Alex Berriman with Nikita
#900202 • 16" • UB
LE of 12998 • Issued: 1999 • Retired: 1999
Original: $70 • Value: $84

330.

Alex Nicole [Dillards]
#94743DL • 10"
Issued: 1999 • Retired: 1999
Original: $18 • Value: $28

331.

Alexander M. Pattington [QVC]
#93119V (C57540) • 15" • MB
Issued: 1999 • Retired: 1999
Original: $91 • Value: $100

332.

Alexander P. Bearsworth
#510901 • 6" • AS
Issued: 2003 • Current
Original: $7 • Value: $R/E

333.

Alexandra & Jessica Bearyfriends [Carlton Cards]
#919843CA • 8"
Issued: 2003 • Retired: 2003
Original: $23 • Value: $28

334.

Alexandra and Belle [QVC]
#99873V (C78130) • 10"
Issued: 2000 • Retired: 2000
Original: $38 • Value: $65

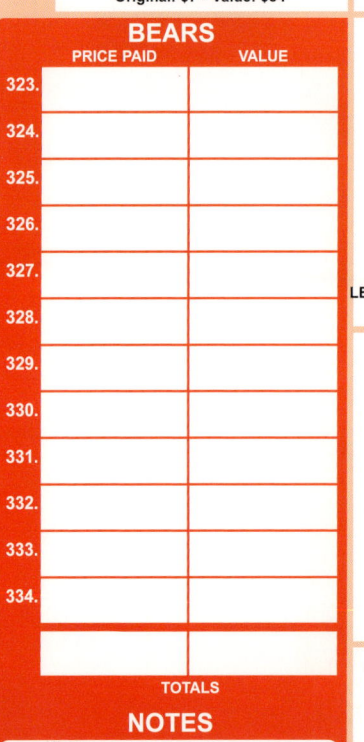

BEARS	PRICE PAID	VALUE
323.		
324.		
325.		
326.		
327.		
328.		
329.		
330.		
331.		
332.		
333.		
334.		
TOTALS		

NOTES

Bears

335.
Alexis Bearinsky [GCC]
#94862GCC • 16"
Issued: 1998 • Retired: 1998
Original: $58 • Value: $89

336.
Alexis Berriman
#912022 • 16" • TJ
Issued: 1998 • Retired: 2000
Original: $53 • Value: $75

337.
Alexis Berriman [SFMB]
#41-72770 • 16"
Issued: 1999 • Retired: 1999
Original: $60 • Value: $80
♫ Lara's Theme ♫

338.
Alfred Q. Rothsbury
#57004-11 • 12" • AS
Issued: 2001 • Retired: 2001
Original: $15 • Value: $18

339.
Ali Marie Beansley
[Country Living]
#(C17721) • 16"
Issued: 2002 • Retired: 2002
Original: $27 • Value: $35

340.
Alice
#1101-08 • 11" • CC
Issued: 1995 • Retired: 1995
Original: $10 • Value: $42

341.
Alice B. Patchbeary
#913978 • 6" • TJ
Issued: 2002 • Retired: 2002
Original: $10 • Value: $10

342.
Alice II
#1101-08 • 11" • CC
Issued: 1995 • Retired: 1998
Original: $12 • Value: $30

343.
Alicia Bearsley [Platinum Paw]
#919817 • 16"
Issued: 2002 • Retired: 2002
Original: $45 • Value: $65

344.
Alisa R. Angel [Starlight]
#51112 • 16"
Issued: 2002 • Retired: 2002
Original: $16 • Value: $21

345.
Alissa Angelhope
#83004 • 12" • AS
Issued: 2000 • Retired: 2000
Original: $20 • Value: $27

346.
Allie Bearington [Welcome Home]
#unknown • 12"
Issued: 1999 • Retired: 1999
Original: $35 • Value: $50

BEARS	PRICE PAID	VALUE
335.		
336.		
337.		
338.		
339.		
340.		
341.		
342.		
343.		
344.		
345.		
346.		
TOTALS		

NOTES

Bears

347.
Allison B. Beansley [QVC]
#93265V (C0543) • 8"
Issued: 2002 • Retired: 2002
Original: $12 • Value: $29

348.
Allison Bearburg [QVC]
#(C76933) • 16"
Issued: 2000 • Retired: 2000
Original: $32 • Value: $56

349.
Ally [Lord & Taylor]
#unknown • 8"
Issued: 1997 • Retired: 1997
Original: $10 • Value: $27

350.
Ally II [Lord & Taylor]
#unknown • 8"
Issued: 1998 • Retired: 1998
Original: $13 • Value: $26

351.
Alouetta de Grizetta
#91842 • 6" • AR
Issued: 1996 • Retired: 1999
Original: $8 • Value: $21

352.
Alouysius Quackenwaddle
#91860 • 10" • TJ
Issued: 2001 • Retired: 2001
Original: $18 • Value: $25

353.
Alvin
#590069 • 8" • MB
Issued: 2004 • Current
Original: $26 • Value: $R/E

354.
Alvis Q. Bearnap with Snoozy T. Puddlemaker
#900208 • 14" • UB
LE of 12998 • Issued: 1999 • Retired: 2002
Original: $39 • Value: $55

355.
Alyssa M. Punkinbeary [GCC]
#94924GCC • 12"
Issued: 2002 • Retired: 2002
Original: $30 • Value: $42

356.
Amanda K. Huntington
#912025 • 16" • TJ
Issued: 1999 • Retired: 2002
Original: $51 • Value: $65

357.
Amber B. Oakley
#904001 • 16" • TJ
Issued: 2002 • Retired: 2002
Original: $45 • Value: $45

358.
Amber Glorybear [QVC]
#93481V • 10"
Issued: 2003 • Retired: 2003
Original: $16 • Value: $27

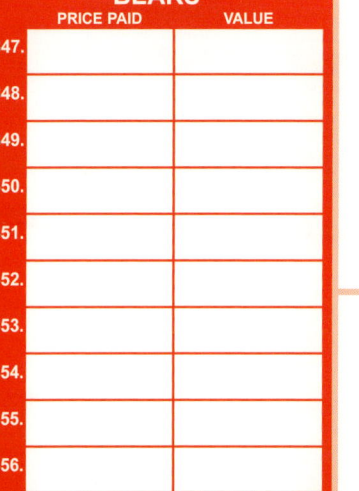

BEARS	PRICE PAID	VALUE
347.		
348.		
349.		
350.		
351.		
352.		
353.		
354.		
355.		
356.		
357.		
358.		
TOTALS		

NOTES

359.

Amber McPunkin
#904326 • 6" • TJ
Issued: 2004 • Current
Original: $11 • Value: $R/E

360.

**Amber Woodsbeary
[Welcome Home]**
#94535WH • 8"
LE of 3600 • Issued: 2001 • Retired: 2001
Original: $15 • Value: $30

361.

Amelia P. Quignapple [QVC]
#(C95006) • 10"
Issued: 1999 • Retired: 1999
Original: $23 • Value: $45

362.

Americana Angelbear [QVC]
#(C02792) • 6"
Issued: 2004 • Retired: 2004
Original: $10 • Value: $11

363.

**Americus P. Bearsley
[Clarion Bear Festival]**
#99098CL • 12"
Issued: 2003 • Retired: 2003
Original: $20 • Value: $24

364.

Amos (a.k.a. MacKenzie)
#5700-03 • 12" • AS
Issued: 1996 • Retired: 1996
Original: $27 • Value: $180

365.

Amos T. Woodsley [QVC]
#93258V • 12"
Issued: 2001 • Retired: 2001
Original: $17 • Value: $130

366.

Amy Lynn Flutterfoot [QVC]
#(C60269) • 8"
Issued: 2002 • Retired: 2002
Original: $11 • Value: $18

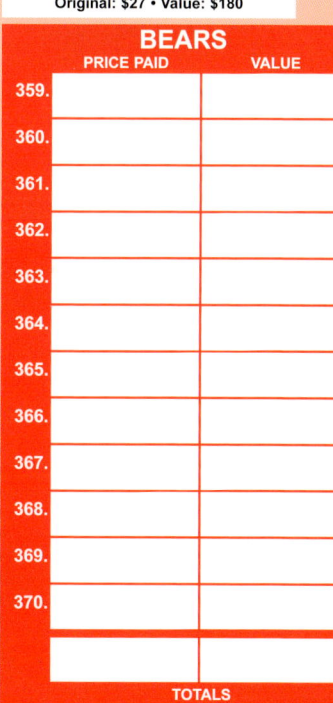

367.

Anastasia [QVC]
#(C12655) • 8"
Issued: 1995 • Retired: 1995
Original: $18 • Value: $75

368.

Anastasia Bearskoff [J.C.Penney]
#94380JCP • 10"
Issued: 2001 • Retired: 2001
Original: $30 • Value: $45

369.

Andrea DeBearvoire
#918102 • 6"
Issued: 2002 • Retired: 2002
Original: $10 • Value: $10

370.

Andrea Jane [GCC]
#94656GCC • 14"
Issued: 2004 • Retired: 2004
Original: $26 • Value: $45

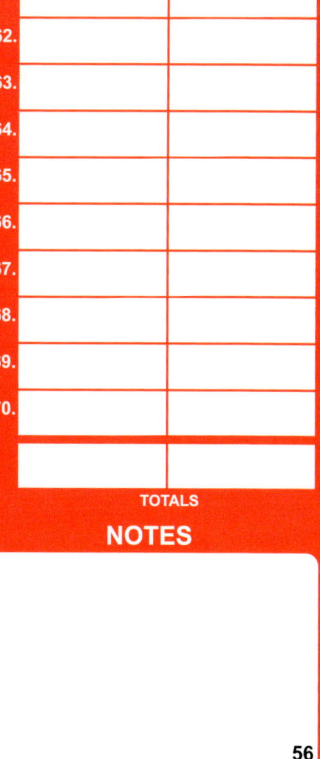

Bears

371.
Andrea Oakley
#904004 • 8" • TJ
Issued: 2002 • Retired: 2004
Original: $14 • Value: $14

372.
Andrei Berriman
#917300-06 • 5½" • TJ
Issued: 1998 • Retired: 2000
Original: $13 • Value: $20

373.
Andrew [Dillards]
#94742DL • 10"
Issued: 1999 • Retired: 1999
Original: $18 • Value: $35

374.
Andrew Huntington
#918053 • 6" • TJ
Issued: 1999 • Retired: 2002
Original: $10 • Value: $18

375.
Andy B. Pattington
#92001-06 • 14" • MB
Issued: 2002 • Retired: 2002
Original: $55 • Value: $85

376.
Angel [GCC]
#94885GCC • 10"
Issued: 2000 • Retired: 2000
Original: $15 • Value: $27

377.
Angela Keepsafe
#903031 • 8" • ME
Issued: 2003 • Current
Original: $10 • Value: $R/E

378.
Angeline [QVC]
#(C36214) • 8"
Issued: 1997 • Retired: 1997
Original: $17 • Value: $25

379.
Anissa Whittlebear
#912650 • 12" • TJ
Issued: 1999 • Retired: 2002
Original: $22 • Value: $30

380.
Anita Lotsalove with Basket [QVC]
#(C01899) • 14"
LE of 1250 • Issued: 2004 • Retired: 2004
Original: $40 • Value: $55

381.
Ann I. Bearsary [BBC]
#918051SM • 12"
LE of 3000 • Issued: 2003 • Retired: 2003
Original: $10 • Value: $35
BBC 1 Year Anniversary item.

382.
Ann Marie
#590066 • 8" • MB
LE of 5000 • Issued: 2004 • Current
Original: $25 • Value: $R/E

BEARS

	PRICE PAID	VALUE
371.		
372.		
373.		
374.		
375.		
376.		
377.		
378.		
379.		
380.		
381.		
382.		
TOTALS		

NOTES

Bears

383.
Anna Belle [POG]
#94581POG • 14" • TJ
Issued: 1999 • Retired: 1999
Original: $30 • Value: $38

384.
Anna Eleanor Bearington [QVC]
#93290V (C60290) • 6" • MB
LE of 2808 • Issued: 2002 • Retired: 2002
Original: $17 • Value: $29

385.
Anna Mae Bakersbear with Li'l Snap [Miss Yvonne's]
#94182PP • 12"
LE of 3600 • Issued: 2002 • Retired: 2002
Original: $26 • Value: $R/E

386.
Anna Manymore
#903102 • 8" • ME
Issued: 2002 • Retired: 2002
Original: $10 • Value: $10

387.
Annabella [GCC]
#912072GCC • 12" • TJ
Issued: 1998 • Retired: 1998
Original: $24 • Value: $38
Same as QVC Annabelle.

388.
Annabelle Dickens
#904222 • 12" • TJ
Issued: 2003 • Current
Original: $30 • Value: $R/E

389.
Annabelle Z. Witebred [QVC]
#(C46244) • 12" • TJ
Issued: 1998 • Retired: 1998
Original: $24 • Value: $38

390.
Annie B. Appleton
#904300 • 16" • TJ
Issued: 2004 • Current
Original: $50 • Value: $R/E

391.

Ansel
#91271 • 6" • TJ
Issued: 1995 • Retired: 1999
Original: $13 • Value: $26

392.

Anthony
#918664 • 10" • TJ
Issued: 2003 • Current
Original: $15 • Value: $R/E

393.
Antoinette de Bearvoire
#918440 • 6" • TJ
Issued: 2001 • Retired: 2002
Original: $13 • Value: $18

394.
Anya Frostfire
#912023 • 16" • TJ
Issued: 1999 • Retired: 1999
Original: $51 • Value: $68

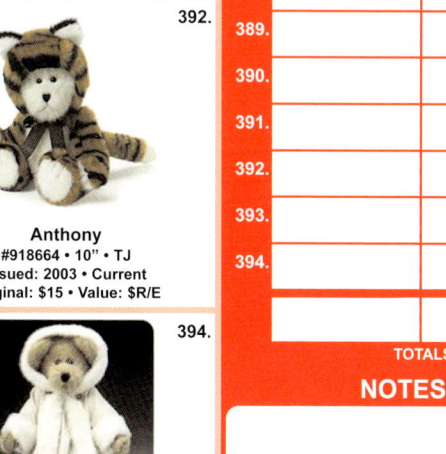

BEARS	PRICE PAID	VALUE
383.		
384.		
385.		
386.		
387.		
388.		
389.		
390.		
391.		
392.		
393.		
394.		
TOTALS		

NOTES

Bears

395.
AP Gold Bear [CAN]
#BC94283 • 10"
LE of 4800 • Issued: 1999 • Retired: 1999
Original: $30 • Value: $40

396.
April Mae
#917445 • 10" • TJ
Issued: 2002 • Retired: 2002
Original: $15 • Value: $15

397.
April Mae McVeggie
#904240 • 16" • TJ
Issued: 2004 • Current
Original: $47 • Value: $R/E

398.
Archibald McBearlie
#91393 • 6" • TJ
Issued: 1998 • Retired: 2000
Original: $11 • Value: $20

399.
Have You Seen Me?
Arctic Bear
#9011P
Issued: 1992 • Retired: 1993
Original: $20 • Value: $405

400.
Ariana Angelwish
#904041 • 14" • TJ
Issued: 2002 • Retired: 2004
Original: $30 • Value: $30

401.
Arlington B. Beanster
#510400-03 • 16" • JB
Issued: 2001 • Retired: 2002
Original: $21 • Value: $38

402.
Arlo (red vest)
#9141 • 8" • TJ
Issued: 1994 • Retired: 1996
Original: $12 • Value: $47

403.
Arlo (pumpkin sweater)
#98040 • 8" • TJ
Issued: 1996 • Retired: 1997
Original: $12 • Value: $45

404.
Artemus
#1003-08 • 8" • CC
Issued: 1997 • Retired: 1999
Original: $7 • Value: $18

405.
Artemus J. Bear (a.k.a John Michael) [Country Living]
#unknown • 16"
LE of 1500 • Issued: 1997 • Retired: 1997
Original: $N/E • Value: $42

406.
Arthur
#5712 • 16" • AS
Issued: 1990 • Retired: 1993
Original: $30 • Value: $171

BEARS	PRICE PAID	VALUE
395.		
396.		
397.		
398.		
399.		
400.		
401.		
402.		
403.		
404.		
405.		
406.		
TOTALS		

NOTES

Bears

407.
Arthur C. Bearington
#590060-03 • 9" • MB
Issued: 1999 • Retired: 2000
Original: $28 • Value: $36

408.
Ashlee R. Angel [Starlight]
#51115 • 14"
Issued: 2004 • Current
Original: $15 • Value: $R/E

409.
Ashley B. Bean
#5109 • 14" • JB
Issued: 1992 • Retired: 1992
Original: $20 • Value: $265

410.
Ashley Huntington
#918054 • 6" • TJ
Issued: 1999 • Retired: 2002
Original: $10 • Value: $18

411.
Ashley Lynn [Elder Beerman]
#unknown • 8"
Issued: 2000 • Retired: 2000
Original: $22 • Value: $30

412.
Ashlyn Bloomengrows
#912653 • 12" • TJ
Issued: 2001 • Retired: 2002
Original: $23 • Value: $35

413.
Ashlyn LaBearsley
#918352 • 8" • TJ
Issued: 2001 • Retired: 2001
Original: $17 • Value: $27

414.
Asquith
#5705-05 • 8" • AS
Issued: 1993 • Retired: 1995
Original: $13 • Value: $33

415.
Astrid
#9137 • 9" • TJ
Issued: 1994 • Retired: 1996
Original: $20 • Value: $41

416.
Attie [Frederick Atkins]
#unknown • 8"
Issued: 1997 • Retired: 1997
Original: $14 • Value: $45

417.
Attlee
#5705B • 8" • AS
Issued: 1992 • Retired: 1993
Original: $12 • Value: $90

418.
Aubrey [Dillards]
#94723DL • 14"
Issued: 1997 • Retired: 1997
Original: $N/E • Value: $38

BEARS

	PRICE PAID	VALUE
407.		
408.		
409.		
410.		
411.		
412.		
413.		
414.		
415.		
416.		
417.		
418.		
TOTALS		

NOTES

Bears

419.
Aubrey [GCC]
#94863GCC • 10"
Issued: 1998 • Retired: 1998
Original: $28 • Value: $42

420.
Aubrey T. Autumnfest
#904150 • 16" • TJ
Issued: 2003 • Current
Original: $45 • Value: $R/E

421.
Aubrey Tippeetoes
#912054 • 12" • TJ
Issued: 2000 • Retired: 2002
Original: $24 • Value: $35

422.
Aubrey T. Tippeetoes [SFMB]
#41-72980 • 12"
Issued: 2000 • Retired: 2000
Original: $35 • Value: $45
♪ Dance of the Sugar Plum Fairy ♪

423.
Aubry T. Autumnfest with Buckeye [QVC]
#99977V (C0540) • 14"
Issued: 2003 • Retired: 2003
Original: $46 • Value: $55

424.
Auggie Bruin
#5125 • 16" • JB
Issued: 1992 • Retired: 1995
Original: $25 • Value: $67

425.
Augusta
#91010 • 14" • TJ
Issued: 1998 • Retired: 1998
Original: $36 • Value: $53

426.
Aunt Bea
#903202 • 8" • ME
Issued: 2002 • Current
Original: $10 • Value: $R/E

427.
Aunt Becky Bearchild
#912052 • 12" • TJ
Issued: 1998 • Retired: 2002
Original: $28 • Value: $35

428.
Aunt Becky Bearchild [SFMB]
#912052SF • 12"
Issued: 1999 • Retired: 1999
Original: $35 • Value: $50
♪ Whistle While You Work ♪

429.
Aunt Bessie Skidoo
#91931 • 9" • TJ
Issued: 1998 • Retired: 2000
Original: $25 • Value: $40

430.
Aunt Fanny Fremont
#918350 • 8" • TJ
Issued: 1999 • Retired: 2001
Original: $19 • Value: $30

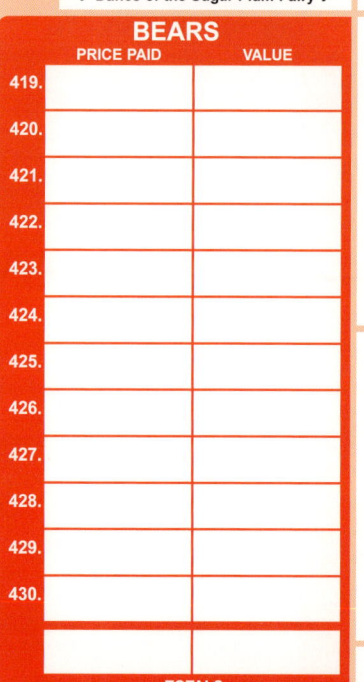

BEARS

	PRICE PAID	VALUE
419.		
420.		
421.		
422.		
423.		
424.		
425.		
426.		
427.		
428.		
429.		
430.		
TOTALS		

NOTES

431.
Aunt Jo Ann O'Beary [Macy's East]
#94168MA • 12"
Issued: 2003 • Retired: 2003
Original: $27 • Value: $R/E

432.
Aunt Mable with Snowy
#90506 • 12" • TJ
Issued: 2002 • Retired: 2002
Original: $38 • Value: $38

433.
Aunt Mamie Bearington
#590104 • 4½" • MB
Issued: 2000 • Retired: 2000
Original: $11 • Value: $16

434.
Aunt Mattie MacDolittle [QVC]
#(C99061) • 16"
Issued: 2000 • Retired: 2000
Original: $33 • Value: $55

435.
Aunt Phiddy Bearburn [J.T. Webb]
#94286JTW • 10"
LE of 3600 • Issued: 1998 • Retired: 1998
Original: $25 • Value: $34

436.
Aunt Yvonne Dubeary
#918450 • 11" • TJ
Issued: 1998 • Retired: 2001
Original: $21 • Value: $35

437.
Auntie Adeline [Carson Pirie Scott]
#unknown • 12"
Issued: 1997 • Retired: 1997
Original: $28 • Value: $54

438.
Auntie Aleena de Bearvoire
#918451 • 10" • TJ
Issued: 1999 • Retired: 2002
Original: $19 • Value: $26

439.
Auntie Alice
#9183 • 10" • TJ
Issued: 1993 • Retired: 1996
Original: $21 • Value: $53

440.
Auntie Autumn and Lil' Harvey [Show Specials]
#919827 • 10" • TJ
Issued: 2003 • Retired: 2003
Original: $49 • Value: $59

441.
Auntie Bearburg
#unknown • 14"
LE of 400 • Issued: 1993 • Retired: 1993
Original: $74 • Value: $350

442.
Auntie Edna with Flora & Tillie [QVC]
#unknown • 14"
LE of 2400 • Issued: 1998 • Retired: 1998
Original: $75 • Value: $135

BEARS

	PRICE PAID	VALUE
431.		
432.		
433.		
434.		
435.		
436.		
437.		
438.		
439.		
440.		
441.		
442.		
	TOTALS	

NOTES

Bears

443.
Auntie Erma
#91832 • 10" • TJ
Issued: 1996 • Retired: 1997
Original: $21 • Value: $42

444.
Auntie Esther and Theona J Doolittle [QVC]
#(C53002) • 16"
LE of 1800 • Issued: 1998 • Retired: 1998
Original: $70 • Value: $115

445.
Auntie Iola
#91612 • 10" • TJ
Issued: 1995 • Retired: 1997
Original: $30 • Value: $50

446.
Auntie Lavonne Higgenthorpe
#918452 • 12" • TJ
Issued: 2000 • Retired: 2002
Original: $21 • Value: $28

447.
Auntie Marguerite, Honeybruin, Beesley Honeybruin, and Topaz F. Wuzzie [QVC]
#(C57691) • 14"
LE of 1800 • Issued: 1999 • Retired: 1999
Original: $60 • Value: $75

448.
Auntie Sheila Bearisch [Peebles/Gottschalks]
#94171PG • 8"
Issued: 2003 • Retired: 2003
Original: $14 • Value: $17

449.
Autumn & Fallston [QVC]
#(C66207) • 14"
LE of 3000 • Issued: 1999 • Retired: 1999
Original: $76 • Value: $100

450.
Autumn Fallsbeary
#91745 • 10" • TJ
Issued: 2000 • Retired: 2000
Original: $15 • Value: $23

451.
Autumn Pumpkin Patch [Longaberger]
#94639LB • 10"
Issued: 2001 • Retired: 2001
Original: $28 • Value: $48

452.
Ava Marie [SYN]
#94586YSN • 12"
Issued: 2000 • Retired: 2000
Original: $18 • Value: $45

453.
Avery B. Bean (open mouth)
#5101 • 14" • JB
Issued: 1989 • Retired: 1989
Original: $20 • Value: $271

454.
Avery B. Bean (smooth fur)
#5101 • 14" • JB
Issued: 1989 • Retired: 1990
Original: $20 • Value: $214

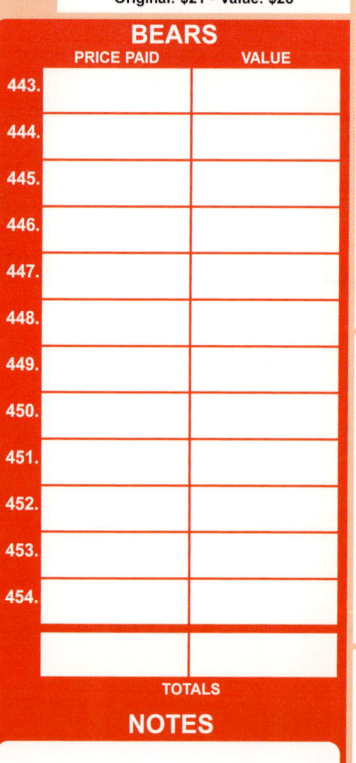

BEARS	PRICE PAID	VALUE
443.		
444.		
445.		
446.		
447.		
448.		
449.		
450.		
451.		
452.		
453.		
454.		
TOTALS		

NOTES

Bears

455.
Avery B. Bean (regular plush)
#unknown • 14" • JB
Issued: 1990 • Retired: 1990
Original: $19 • Value: $180

456.
Azalea & Jordan Rosebeary [QVC]
#99666V (C56959) • 11"
Issued: 1999 • Retired: 1999
Original: $25 • Value: $55

457.
Azure Lee, Ginger C. & Sunbeam P. Snickelfritz [QVC]
#99657V (C56964) • 5½"
Issued: 1999 • Retired: 1999
Original: $18 • Value: $27
Musical.

458.
B. Everluvin
#82019 • 16" • JB
Issued: 2001 • Retired: 2001
Original: $21 • Value: $25

459.
B. Jay Tweeter
#904264 • 6" • TJ
Issued: 2004 • Current
Original: $10 • Value: $R/E

460.
B.A. Bigfoot [QVC]
#93165V (C76775) • 18"
Issued: 2000 • Retired: 2000
Original: $33 • Value: $50

461.
B.A. Blackbelt
#917361 • 10" • ME
Issued: 2000 • Current
Original: $18 • Value: $R/E

462.
B.A. Scholar
#917369 • 10" • ME
Issued: 2001 • Retired: 2004
Original: $22 • Value: $26

463.
B.B. Bugsley with Lil' Lady Bugsley [QVC]
#99953V (C22073) • 6"
Issued: 2003 • Retired: 2003
Original: $29 • Value: $35

464.
B.B. Country Bear [BBC]
#918011SM
Issued: 2002 • Retired: 2002
Original: $15 • Value: $N/E

465.
B.J. Bearricane
#83003 • 12" • TJ
Issued: 2000 • Retired: 2000
Original: $23 • Value: $23

466.
B.Y. Lotsaluck
#917370 • 10" • ME
Issued: 2001 • Retired: N/E
Original: $13 • Value: $16

BEARS

	PRICE PAID	VALUE
455.		
456.		
457.		
458.		
459.		
460.		
461.		
462.		
463.		
464.		
465.		
466.		
	TOTALS	

NOTES

Bears

467.
Baah'b (beige)
#9131 • 8" • TJ
Issued: 1994 • Retired: 1996
Original: $17 • Value: $37

468.
Baah'b (tan)
#9131 • 8" • TJ
Issued: 1994 • Retired: 1996
Original: $17 • Value: $35

469.
Baakins
#91863 • 10" • TJ
Issued: 2002 • Current
Original: $15 • Value: $R/E

470.
Baby
#6105B • 12" • JB
Issued: 1990 • Retired: 1990
Original: $N/E • Value: $245

471.
Baby Mae Wishkabibble
#90503 • 6" • TJ
Issued: 2001 • Retired: 2002
Original: $18 • Value: $24

472.
Baby Mookins
#917820 • 7" • TJ
Issued: 2004 • Current
Original: $20 • Value: $R/E

473.
Baby Noel
#912057 • 12" • TJ
Issued: 2001 • Retired: 2001
Original: $18 • Value: $22

474.
Bailey (Fall 1992)
#9199 • 8" • BF
Issued: 1992 • Retired: 1992
Original: $22 • Value: $644

475.
Bailey (Spring 1993)
#unknown • 8" • BF
Issued: 1993 • Retired: 1993
Original: $23 • Value: $450

476.
Bailey (Fall 1993)
#9170 • 8" • BF
Issued: 1993 • Retired: 1993
Original: $24 • Value: $312

477.
Bailey (Spring 1994 - black)
#9199-01 • 8" • BF
Issued: 1994 • Retired: 1994
Original: $26 • Value: $166

478.
Bailey (Spring 1994 - navy)
#9199-01 • 8" • BF
Issued: 1994 • Retired: 1994
Original: $26 • Value: $235

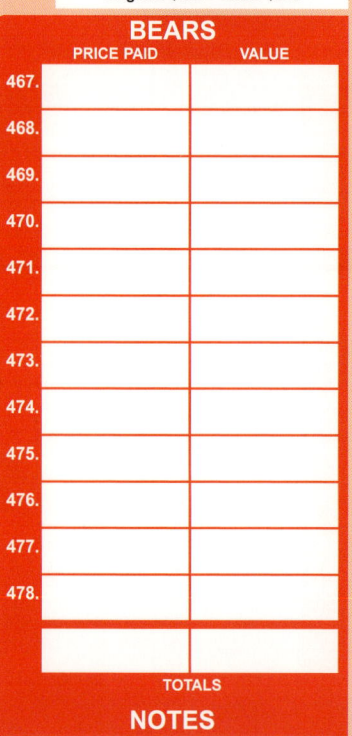

BEARS

	PRICE PAID	VALUE
467.		
468.		
469.		
470.		
471.		
472.		
473.		
474.		
475.		
476.		
477.		
478.		
TOTALS		

NOTES

Bears

479.
Bailey (Fall 1994)
#9199-02 • 8" • BF
Issued: 1994 • Retired: 1994
Original: $26 • Value: $75

480.
Bailey (Spring 1995)
#9199-03 • 8" • BF
Issued: 1995 • Retired: 1995
Original: $26 • Value: $70

481.
Bailey (Fall 1995)
#9199-04 • 8" • BF
Issued: 1995 • Retired: 1995
Original: $26 • Value: $69

482.
Bailey (Spring 1996)
#9199-05 • 8" • BF
Issued: 1996 • Retired: 1996
Original: $26 • Value: $71

483.
Bailey (shiny purple dress) [QVC]
#unknown • 8" • BF
Issued: 1996 • Retired: 1996
Original: $22 • Value: $150

484.
Bailey (Fall 1996)
#9199-06 • 8" • BF
Issued: 1996 • Retired: 1996
Original: $26 • Value: $54

485.
Bailey & Matthew with Resin Ornaments (Fall 1996)
#9224 • BF
Issued: 1996 • Retired: 1996
Original: $70 • Value: $85

486.
Bailey (lilac dress) [QVC]
#(C35666) • 8" • BF
Issued: 1997 • Retired: 1997
Original: $22 • Value: $78

487.
Bailey (Spring 1997)
#9199-07 • 8" • BF
Issued: 1997 • Retired: 1997
Original: $27 • Value: $43

488.
Bailey (Fall 1997)
#9199-08 • 8" • BF
Issued: 1997 • Retired: 1997
Original: $27 • Value: $37

489.
Bailey & Matthew with Resin Ornaments (Fall 1997)
#9225 • BF
Issued: 1997 • Retired: 1997
Original: $70 • Value: $92

490.
Bailey (Spring 1998)
#9199-09 • 8" • BF
Issued: 1998 • Retired: 1998
Original: $27 • Value: $37

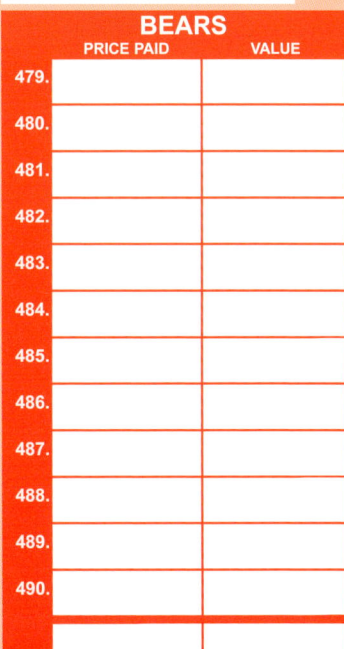

BEARS

	PRICE PAID	VALUE
479.		
480.		
481.		
482.		
483.		
484.		
485.		
486.		
487.		
488.		
489.		
490.		
TOTALS		

NOTES

Bears

491.
Bailey with Squiggles [QVC]
#(C46250) • 8" • BF
Issued: 1998 • Retired: 1998
Original: $27 • Value: $45

492.
Bailey (Fall 1998)
#9199-10 • 8" • BF
Issued: 1998 • Retired: 1998
Original: $27 • Value: $31

493.
Bailey & Matthew with Resin Ornaments (Fall 1998)
#9227 • BF
Issued: 1998 • Retired: 1998
Original: $71 • Value: $85

494.
Bailey (Spring 1999)
#9199-11 • 8" • BF
Issued: 1999 • Retired: 1999
Original: $27 • Value: $35

495.
Bailey with Dottie (Fall 1999)
#9199-12 • 8" • BF
Issued: 1999 • Retired: 1999
Original: $25 • Value: $36

496.
Bailey & Matthew with Resin Ornaments (Fall 1999)
#9228 • BF
Issued: 1999 • Retired: 1999
Original: $70 • Value: $74

497.
Bailey (Spring 2000)
#9199-14 • 8" • BF
Issued: 2000 • Retired: 2000
Original: $23 • Value: $35

498.
Bailey (Fall 2000)
#9199-15 • 8" • BF
Issued: 2000 • Retired: 2000
Original: $25 • Value: $30

499.
Bailey & Matthew with Resin Ornaments (Fall 2000)
#9229 • BF
Issued: 2000 • Retired: 2000
Original: $67 • Value: $80

500.
Bailey (Spring 2001)
#9199-16 • 8" • BF
Issued: 2001 • Retired: 2001
Original: $25 • Value: $32

501.
Bailey (Fall 2001)
#9199-17 • 8" • BF
Issued: 2001 • Retired: 2001
Original: $20 • Value: $60
NALED Award Winner

502.
Bailey (Spring 2002)
#9199-18 • 8" • BF
Issued: 2002 • Retired: 2002
Original: $20 • Value: $28
Golden Teddy Award Winner

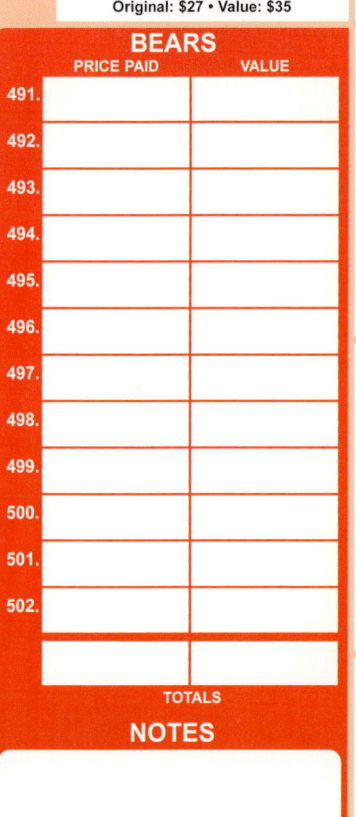

BEARS	PRICE PAID	VALUE
491.		
492.		
493.		
494.		
495.		
496.		
497.		
498.		
499.		
500.		
501.		
502.		
TOTALS		

NOTES

Bears

503.
Bailey (Fall 2002)
#9199-19 • 8" • BF
Issued: 2002 • Retired: 2002
Original: $20 • Value: $28

504.
Bailey (Spring 2003)
#9199-20 • 8" • BF
LE • Issued: 2003 • Retired: 2003
Original: $25 • Value: $R/E

505.
Bailey (Fall 2003)
#9199-21 • 8" • BF
Issued: 2003 • Retired: 2003
Original: $24 • Value: $R/E

506.
Bailey (Spring 2004)
#9199-22 • 8" • BF
Issued: 2004 • Retired: 2004
Original: $20 • Value: $R/E

507.
Bailey (Fall 2004)
#9199-23 • 8" • BF
Issued: 2004 • Retired: 2004
Original: $20 • Value: $R/E

508.
Baldwin (old face)
#5718 • 5½" • AS
Issued: 1992 • Retired: 1993
Original: $7 • Value: $33

509.
Baldwin (new face)
#5718 • 5" • AS
Issued: 1993 • Retired: 1999
Original: $8 • Value: $19

510.
Barbara Mary [Boscovs]
#unknown • 10"
Issued: 1999 • Retired: 1999
Original: $N/E • Value: $50

BEARS

	PRICE PAID	VALUE
503.		
504.		
505.		
506.		
507.		
508.		
509.		
510.		
511.		
512.		
513.		
514.		
	TOTALS	

NOTES

511.
Barnaby B. Bean
#5150-03 • 10" • JB
Issued: 1994 • Retired: 1999
Original: $16 • Value: $30

512.
Barney B. Keeper [Bon Ton]
#unknown • 10"
Issued: 1997 • Retired: 1997
Original: $15 • Value: $34

513.
Barney Bowlsalot
#903501 • 8" • ME
Issued: 2002 • Current
Original: $13 • Value: $R/E

514.
Barrett [SLE]
#unknown • 10"
LE of 1200 • Issued: 1996 • Retired: 1996
Original: $25 • Value: $40

68

Bears

515.
Barston Q. Growler [QVC]
#(C39092) • 16"
Issued: 1997 • Retired: 1997
Original: $32 • Value: $58

516.
Bartholemew B. Bean
#5103 • 10" • JB
Issued: 1992 • Retired: 1998
Original: $13 • Value: $28

517.
Bartholomew [Eddie Bauer]
#unknown • TJ
Issued: 1996 • Retired: 1996
Original: $22 • Value: $45

518.
Bartholomew [J.C.Penney]
#unknown • 10"
Issued: 1995 • Retired: 1995
Original: $21 • Value: $44

519.
Bartlett
#904164 • 6" • TJ
Issued: 2003 • Current
Original: $10 • Value: $R/E

520.
Barton [Alps]
#8712 • 12"
Issued: 1996 • Retired: 1996
Original: $20 • Value: $49

521.
Bashful T. Bearhugs
#82004 • 10" • TJ
Issued: 2000 • Retired: 2000
Original: $19 • Value: $23

522.
Bath & Body Works Bear [Bath & Body Works]
#unknown • 20"
Issued: 1996 • Retired: 1996
Original: $38 • Value: $49

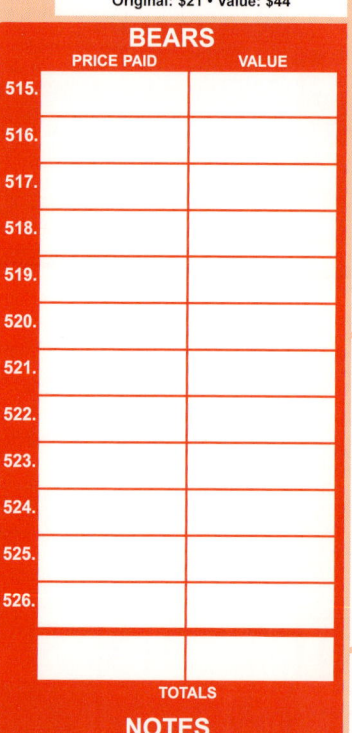

523.
Bauer B. Bear [Eddie Bauer]
#unknown • 12"
Issued: 1998 • Retired: 1998
Original: $26 • Value: $64

524.
Baxter B. Bean
#5151-05 • 8" • JB
Issued: 1994 • Retired: 1999
Original: $12 • Value: $20

525.
Baxter T. Birch [Hallmark]
#9690HM • 8"
Issued: 2002 • Retired: 2002
Original: $15 • Value: $22

526.
Bea Bear
#5061 • 12" • WB
Issued: 1985 • Retired: 1989
Original: $15 • Value: $330

BEARS

	PRICE PAID	VALUE
515.		
516.		
517.		
518.		
519.		
520.		
521.		
522.		
523.		
524.		
525.		
526.		
TOTALS		

NOTES

Bears

527.

Bea Beary [Longaberger]
#94631LB • 10"
Issued: 2000 • Retired: 2000
Original: $32 • Value: $65

528.

**Bear Lee Survivedit
[Boyds Family Reunion]**
#02001-85 • 10"
Issued: 2001 • Retired: 2001
Original: $N/A • Value: $31
Gift Item

529.

Have You Seen Me?
Bear-Among-Bears (brown)
#5051 • 16"
Issued: 1989 • Retired: 1989
Original: $20 • Value: $408

530.

Bear-Among-Bears (tan)
#5052 • 16" • WB
Issued: 1985 • Retired: 1989
Original: $30 • Value: $314

531.

Bear-let (brown)
#5021 • 8" • WB
Issued: 1985 • Retired: 1989
Original: $8 • Value: $240

532.

Bear-let (tan)
#5020 • 8" • WB
Issued: 1985 • Retired: 1992
Original: $8 • Value: $135

533.

Bearlove
#903022 • 6" • ME
Issued: 2002 • Retired: 2002
Original: $15 • Value: $15

534.

Bearly A. Hare [Harry & David]
#94206HD • 8"
Issued: 2003 • Retired: 2003
Original: $25 • Value: $R/E

535.

Have You Seen Me?
Bearly-a-Bear (brown)
#5031 • 10" • WB
Issued: 1986 • Retired: 1991
Original: $13 • Value: $247

536.

Bearly-a-Bear (tan)
#5030 • 10" • WB
Issued: 1986 • Retired: 1991
Original: $13 • Value: $176

537.

Bears' Bear (brown)
#5041 • 12" • WB
Issued: 1985 • Retired: 1992
Original: $17 • Value: $258

538.

Bears' Bear (rust)
#5042 • 12" • WB
Issued: 1985 • Retired: 1986
Original: $17 • Value: $336

BEARS		
	PRICE PAID	VALUE
527.		
528.		
529.		
530.		
531.		
532.		
533.		
534.		
535.		
536.		
537.		
538.		
TOTALS		

NOTES

Bears

539.
Bears' Bear (tan)
#5040 • 12" • WB
Issued: 1985 • Retired: 1992
Original: $17 • Value: $258

540.
The Bearsleys [Show Specials]
#919810 • 14"
Issued: 2001 • Retired: 2001
Original: $59 • Value: $83
Juniper, Joel & Jean

541.
Bearwinkle [Harry & David]
#94205HD
Issued: 2002 • Retired: 2002
Original: $13 • Value: $R/E

542.
Beatrice
#6168H • 14"
LE • Issued: 1991 • Retired: 1991
Original: $70 • Value: $466

543.
Beatrice [Frederick Atkins]
#unknown • 10"
Issued: 1998 • Retired: 1998
Original: $15 • Value: $33

544.
Beatrice Bearyman
[May Company]
#94158MC • 12"
Issued: 2000 • Retired: 2000
Original: $35 • Value: $48

545.
Beatrice Bearymore
[May Company]
#94155MC • 12"
Issued: 1999 • Retired: 1999
Original: $30 • Value: $55

546.
Beauregard [SLE]
#unknown • 10"
Issued: 1996 • Retired: 1996
Original: $N/E • Value: $35

547.
Beauregard [QVC]
#(C48185) • 16" • BB
Issued: 1998 • Retired: 1998
Original: $21 • Value: $95

548.
Bebe Z. Beezley with Bizzybee
[QVC]
#99955V (C22080) • 12"
Issued: 2003 • Retired: 2003
Original: $37 • Value: $44

549.
Becca Bearheart
#904080 • 14" • TJ
Issued: 2003 • Current
Original: $30 • Value: $R/E

550.
Becky (green plaid dress)
#91395 • 6" • TJ
Issued: 1995 • Retired: 1999
Original: $11 • Value: $21

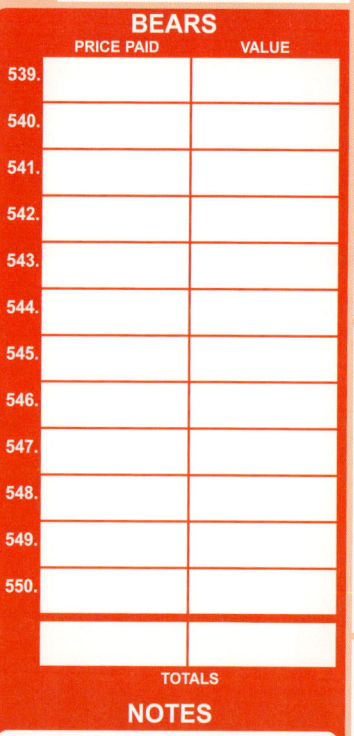

BEARS

	PRICE PAID	VALUE
539.		
540.		
541.		
542.		
543.		
544.		
545.		
546.		
547.		
548.		
549.		
550.		
TOTALS		

NOTES

Bears

551.
Becky (red plaid dress)
#91395-01 • 6" • TJ
Issued: 1996 • Retired: 1999
Original: $11 • Value: $24

552.
Bedford B. Bean
#5121-08 • 10" • JB
Issued: 1995 • Retired: 1996
Original: $14 • Value: $59

553.
Bee Mihoney [POG]
#94602POG • 8"
Issued: 2003 • Retired: 2003
Original: $8 • Value: $16

554.
Beesley Buzzoff [QVC]
#99877V (C107612) • 8"
Issued: 2002 • Retired: 2002
Original: $20 • Value: $30
With iron bucket.

555.
Beezer B. Goodlebear [QVC]
#(C95070) • 16"
Issued: 1999 • Retired: 1999
Original: $26 • Value: $45

556.
Beggin' D. Bones
#918669 • 10" • TJ
Issued: 2004 • Current
Original: $16 • Value: $R/E

557.
Ben Hardley Doinnuttin
#903012 • 10" • ME
Issued: 2002 • Retired: 2002
Original: $15 • Value: $15

558.
Benjamin
#9159 • 10" • TJ
Issued: 1993 • Retired: 1994
Original: $20 • Value: $46

559.
Benjamin [SFMB]
#41-72142 • 12"
Issued: 1998 • Retired: 1998
Original: $25 • Value: $36
♪ Let Me Be Your Teddy Bear ♪

560.
Benjamin Beanbeary [Belks]
#unknown • 8"
Issued: 1998 • Retired: 1998
Original: $N/E • Value: $35

561.
Benjamin F. Almanac with Caroline Mayflower [QVC]
#(C76936) • 6"
Issued: 2000 • Retired: 2000
Original: $10 • Value: $20

562.
Benjamin W. Bear [Barnes & Noble]
#unknown • 12"
Issued: 2000 • Retired: 2000
Original: $31 • Value: $50

BEARS	PRICE PAID	VALUE
551.		
552.		
553.		
554.		
555.		
556.		
557.		
558.		
559.		
560.		
561.		
562.		
TOTALS		

NOTES

Bears

563.
Bennington W. Bruin
#510400-08 • 16" • JB
Issued: 2000 • Retired: 2002
Original: $23 • Value: $30

564.
Bentley B. Woodsley
#92002-11 • 15" • AR
Issued: 2004 • Current
Original: $22 • Value: $R/E

565.
Bernadette B. Bearington [QVC]
#93207V (C40591) • 10" • MB
LE of 2400 • Issued: 2001 • Retired: 2001
Original: $36 • Value: $55

566.
Bernadette Bearbuck [QVC]
#(C22621) • 14"
LE of 3000 • Issued: 2003 • Retired: 2003
Original: $41 • Value: $49
Sold with piggy bank.

567.
Bernadette de Bearvoire
#918443 • 6" • TJ
Issued: 2001 • Retired: 2002
Original: $13 • Value: $16

568.
Bernard B. Bear [Barnes & Noble]
#94165BN • 10"
Issued: 1998 • Retired: 1998
Original: $25 • Value: $35

569.
Bernice B. Bear [Barnes & Noble]
#94166BN • 10"
Issued: 1999 • Retired: 1999
Original: $30 • Value: $40

570.
Berrybear
#5762 • 14" • HD
Issued: 1992 • Retired: 1994
Original: $27 • Value: $340

23

571.
Bess Bearman [Welcome Home]
#94538WH • 8"
Issued: 2002 • Retired: 2002
Original: $16 • Value: $37

572.
Bess W. Pattington
#92001-02 • 14" • MB
Issued: 1999 • Retired: 1999
Original: $39 • Value: $48

573.
Bestest & Buddy Truefriends
#903005 • 6" • ME
Issued: 2001 • Retired: 2001
Original: $15 • Value: $18

574.
Bestest & Buddy Truefriends [SFMB]
#41-72571 • 6"
Issued: 2001 • Retired: 2001
Original: $22 • Value: $29
♪ My Favorite Things ♪

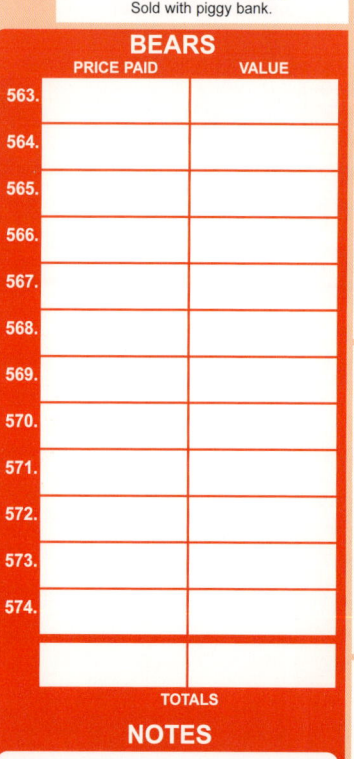

BEARS

	PRICE PAID	VALUE
563.		
564.		
565.		
566.		
567.		
568.		
569.		
570.		
571.		
572.		
573.		
574.		
	TOTALS	

NOTES

Bears

575.

Bethany Bearington
#590053-01 • 8" • MB
Issued: 2000 • Retired: 2001
Original: $26 • Value: $36

576.

Bethany Thistlebeary
#913955 • 6" • TJ
Issued: 1999 • Retired: 2001
Original: $10 • Value: $19
Also with Heidi Thistlebeary as QVC set.

577.

Betsey
#913952 • 6" • TJ
Issued: 1997 • Retired: 2000
Original: $13 • Value: $20

578.

Betsey Lou Bearyproud [QVC]
#99964V • 8"
LE of 2400 • Issued: 2002 • Retired: 2002
Original: $46 • Value: $60
With iron shelf.

579.

Betsie B. Jodibear
#92000-07 • 9" • AR
Issued: 2000 • Retired: 2001
Original: $18 • Value: $28

580.

Betsie L. Steadsbeary [Longaberger]
#94623LB • 10"
Issued: 2003 • Retired: 2003
Original: $27 • Value: $48

581.

Betsy B. Bearyproud [QVC]
#999869V (C22823) • 16"
LE of 4200 • Issued: 2003 • Retired: 2003
Original: $59 • Value: $71
Sold with resin utensil holder.

582.

Betty B. Learnin'
#903103 • 10" • TJ
Issued: 2002 • Current
Original: $25 • Value: $R/E

583.

Betty Fisher [CAN]
#BC94298PO • 10"
Issued: 2003 • Retired: 2003
Original: $31 • Value: $37

584.
Betty Jane Maybeary
#918454 • 6" • TJ
Issued: 2002 • Retired: 2002
Original: $13 • Value: $13

585.

Betty Lou [QVC]
#unknown • 16"
Issued: 1996 • Retired: 1996
Original: $23 • Value: $337

586.

Betty Lou, Clementine & Josie McCoy [Show Specials]
#919808 • 14" • TJ
Issued: 2001 • Retired: 2002
Original: $49 • Value: $68

74

Bears

587.
Bianca T. Witebred
#912076 • 8" • TJ
Issued: 1998 • Retired: 1999
Original: $19 • Value: $28

588.
Biddle Beezley
#904115 • 8" • TJ
Issued: 2003 • Current
Original: $12 • Value: $R/E

589.
Biff Grizzwood
#912617 • 14" • TJ
Issued: 2000 • Retired: 2002
Original: $29 • Value: $33

590.
Big Ben Bearhugs
#500050-05 • 40" • JB
Issued: 2000 • Retired: 2000
Original: $200 • Value: $245

591.
Big Boy
#9108 • 5½" • TJ
Issued: 1995 • Retired: 1997
Original: $12 • Value: $41

592.
Big Harry
#500054 • 40" • AS
Issued: 2004 • Current
Original: $200 • Value: $R/E

593.
Bill [QVC]
#unknown • 14" • JB
Issued: 1995 • Retired: 1995
Original: $36 • Value: $147

594.
Billy Bob Bruin with Froggie
#912622 • 14" • TJ
Issued: 2000 • Retired: 2002
Original: $26 • Value: $31

595.
Billy Ray
#5050 • 9" • BB
Issued: 1992 • Retired: 1997
Original: $13 • Value: $48

596.
Billy Ray Beanster with Petey Porker
#900207 • 16" • UB
LE of 13000 • Issued: 1999 • Retired: 2002
Original: $51 • Value: $60

597.
Bingham [QVC]
#(C4988) • 22"
Issued: 1998 • Retired: 1998
Original: $53 • Value: $75

598.
Bingle Beartoes
#510010 • 8" • JB
Issued: 2002 • Current
Original: $9 • Value: $R/E

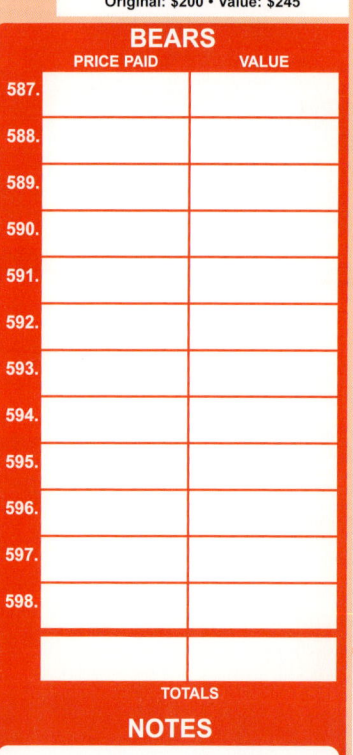

BEARS	PRICE PAID	VALUE
587.		
588.		
589.		
590.		
591.		
592.		
593.		
594.		
595.		
596.		
597.		
598.		
TOTALS		

NOTES

Bears

599.
Bingles [QVC]
#unknown • 12"
Issued: 2002 • Retired: 2002
Original: $24 • Value: $31

600.
Binkie B. Bean (original)
#5115 • 16" • JB
Issued: 1989 • Retired: 1992
Original: $27 • Value: $200

601.
Binkie B. Bean (black nose)
#5115 • 16" • JB
Issued: 1991 • Retired: 1992
Original: $27 • Value: $100

602.
Binkie B. Bean II
#5115 • 16" • JB
Issued: 1994 • Retired: 1992
Original: $27 • Value: $66

603.
Bixby B. Bear [QVC]
#(C02194) • 30"
LE of 1500 • Issued: 2004 • Retired: 2004
Original: $58 • Value: $70

604.
Bixby Trufflebeary
#56390-10 • 12" • BA
Issued: 1999 • Retired: 2002
Original: $14 • Value: $17

605.
Blackstone (small eyes)
#5840-07 • 6" • AS
Issued: 1997 • Retired: 1999
Original: $9 • Value: $24

606.
Blackstone (big eyes) [QVC]
#(C35894) • 6" • AS
Issued: 1997 • Retired: 1997
Original: $9 • Value: $24

607.
Blanche de Bearvoire
#91841 • 6" • TJ
Issued: 1996 • Retired: 1999
Original: $9 • Value: $23

608.
Blessed B. Babybear
#903100 • 8" • ME
Issued: 2002 • Current
Original: $15 • Value: $R/E

609.
Blink, Hush & Shush [QVC]
#(C99856) • 6"
Issued: 2001 • Retired: 2001
Original: $20 • Value: $32

610.
Blinkin
#5807 • 18" • SB
Issued: 1991 • Retired: 1993
Original: $32 • Value: $250

BEARS

	PRICE PAID	VALUE
599.		
600.		
601.		
602.		
603.		
604.		
605.		
606.		
607.		
608.		
609.		
610.		
TOTALS		

NOTES

Bears

611.
Blossom DuBearvoire [QVC]
#93544V (C06193) • 10"
Issued: 2004 • Retired: 2004
Original: $19 • Value: $21

612.
Blossom Monarch [GCC]
#94890GCC • 6"
Issued: 2001 • Retired: 2001
Original: $12 • Value: $20

613.
Bluebeary
#56421-06 • 8" • BA
Issued: 1998 • Retired: 2002
Original: $9 • Value: $15

614.
Bluebeary [Smuckers]
#(CGS0010) • 12" • TJ
Issued: 2000 • Retired: 2000
Original: $44 • Value: $110

615.
Blueberry
#590063 • 10" • MB
Issued: 2003 • Current
Original: $30 • Value: $R/E

616.
Bobbi Frostbeary [SYN]
#94589SYN • 10" • TJ
Issued: 2000 • Retired: 2000
Original: $18 • Value: $35

617.
Bobbi Jo Bearican
#904252 • 12" • TJ
Issued: 2004 • Current
Original: $27 • Value: $R/E

618.
Bobbi McBobble
#510306-01 • 10" • JB
Issued: 2002 • Retired: 2002
Original: $10 • Value: $21

619.
Bobbie Jo
#5853 • 12" • BB
Issued: 1992 • Retired: 1997
Original: $20 • Value: $51

620.
Bobbie Sue Maybeary with Betty Jane [QVC]
#99844V (C100405) • 6"
Issued: 2001 • Retired: 2001
Original: $23 • Value: $25

621.
Bobble B. Beansford [QVC]
#(C98050) • 10"
Issued: 2000 • Retired: 2000
Original: $11 • Value: $20

622.
Bojingles [SFMB]
#91264SF • 12"
Issued: 2002 • Retired: 2002
Original: $45 • Value: $58
♪ Entry of the Gladiators ♪

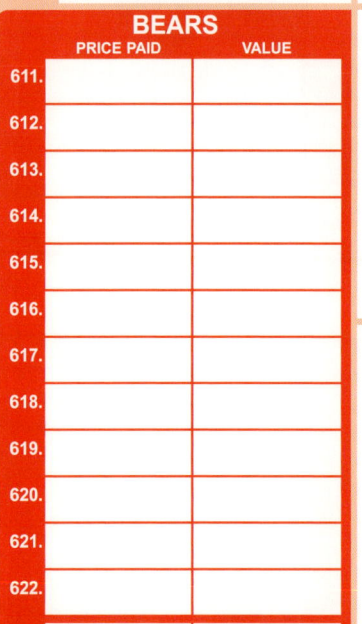

BEARS

	PRICE PAID	VALUE
611.		
612.		
613.		
614.		
615.		
616.		
617.		
618.		
619.		
620.		
621.		
622.		
TOTALS		

NOTES

Bears

623.
Bonnie
#913951 • 6" • TJ
Issued: 1997 • Retired: 2000
Original: $13 • Value: $22

624.
Boo B. Bear [QVC]
#(C41115) • 8"
Issued: 1997 • Retired: 1997
Original: $14 • Value: $32

625.
Boo Bear [Marshall Field's]
#unknown • 16"
Issued: 1994 • Retired: 1994
Original: $N/E • Value: $49

626.
Boo Boo Bear
#903028 • 8" • ME
Issued: 2003 • Current
Original: $10 • Value: $R/E

627.
Boo-Boo [SLE]
#unknown • 5½"
Issued: 1998 • Retired: 1998
Original: $N/E • Value: $25

628.
Boris Berriman
#918021 • 6" • TJ
Issued: 1998 • Retired: 2002
Original: $9 • Value: $24

629.
Bosc P. Pearsley
#904163 • 8" • TJ
Issued: 2003 • Current
Original: $10 • Value: $R/E

630.
Bosley
#91561 • 8½" • TJ
Issued: 1997 • Retired: 1999
Original: $12 • Value: $22
Also with Chadwick as QVC set.

631.
Braden P. Oakley
#904002 • 14" • TJ
Issued: 2002 • Retired: 2004
Original: $30 • Value: $30

632.
Bradford
#57052-08 • 8" • AS
Issued: 2002 • Retired: 2002
Original: $10 • Value: $10

633.
Bradie B. Bearsley
[Clarion Bear Festival]
#99096CL • 10"
LE of 3600 • Issued: 2001 • Retired: 2001
Original: $28 • Value: $35

634.
Bradley Boobear
#919610 • 8" • TJ
Issued: 1998 • Retired: 1999
Original: $13 • Value: $21

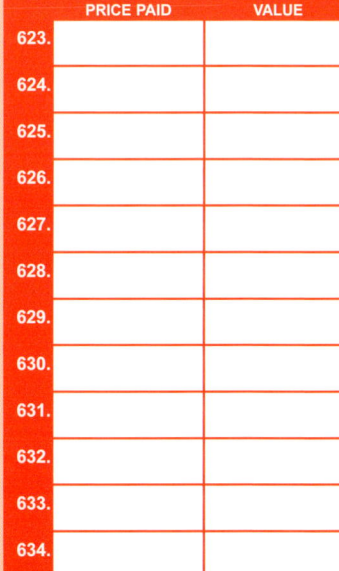

BEARS	PRICE PAID	VALUE
623.		
624.		
625.		
626.		
627.		
628.		
629.		
630.		
631.		
632.		
633.		
634.		
TOTALS		

NOTES

Bears

635.
Bradshaw P. Beansford
#51091-08 • 14" • JB
Issued: 1999 • Retired: 1999
Original: $20 • Value: $24

636.
Brady Bearimore
#918321 • 10" • TJ
Issued: 2000 • Retired: 2002
Original: $24 • Value: $30

637.
Brambley B. Bigfoot [QVC]
#(C80700) • 18"
Issued: 2000 • Retired: 2000
Original: $40 • Value: $55

Have You Seen Me?

638.
Brandie & Madeira [QVC]
#unknown • 10"
Issued: 1998 • Retired: 1998
Original: $20 • Value: $45

639.
Brandon [Dillards]
#94703DL • 7"
Issued: 1996 • Retired: 1996
Original: $10 • Value: $25

640.
Brandon A. Bearski [GCC]
#94886GCC • 16"
Issued: 2000 • Retired: 2000
Original: $38 • Value: $50

641.
Brandon Michael
#510311 • 10" • AS
Issued: 2004 • Current
Original: $10 • Value: $R/E

642.
Brantley B. Beansley [QVC]
#(C21159) • 15"
Issued: 2002 • Retired: 2002
Original: $24 • Value: $31

643.
Braxton B. Bear
#51081-08 • 14" • JB
Issued: 1998 • Retired: 2001
Original: $16 • Value: $25

644.
Braxton B. Bear [SFMB]
#41-72640 • 14" • JB
Issued: 1998 • Retired: 1998
Original: $25 • Value: $35
♪ I Will Always Love You ♪

645.
Breezy T. Frostman
#91522 • 8" • TJ
Issued: 1999 • Retired: 2000
Original: $11 • Value: $18

646.
Brendon B. Beanster [QVC]
#93319V (C20219) • 18"
Issued: 2002 • Retired: 2002
Original: $44 • Value: $58

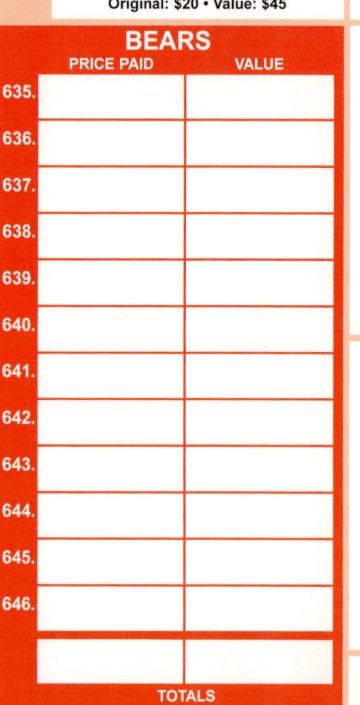

BEARS

	PRICE PAID	VALUE
635.		
636.		
637.		
638.		
639.		
640.		
641.		
642.		
643.		
644.		
645.		
646.		
TOTALS		

NOTES

647.

Brett B. Bearican
#904253 • 10" • TJ
Issued: 2004 • Current
Original: $18 • Value: $R/E

648.

**Breven B. Bearski
with Willie Waddlewalk**
#900206 • 14" • UB
LE of 12998 • Issued: 1999 • Retired: 2002
Original: $49 • Value: $60

649.

Brewin
#5806 • 10" • SB
Issued: 1991 • Retired: 1991
Original: $20 • Value: $70
Brewin had 2 style numbers
by mistake - 5802.

650.

**Brewster McRooster
[QVC]**
#(C63343) • 10" • MB
Issued: 1999 • Retired: 1999
Original: $40 • Value: $70

651.

Brewster T. Bear
#912627 • 14" • TJ
Issued: 2000 • Retired: 2002
Original: $20 • Value: $30

652.

Bria [Frederick Atkins]
#unknown • 10"
Issued: 1998 • Retired: 1998
Original: $22 • Value: $30

653.

Brian [CAN]
#BC100708 • 12"
Issued: 1997 • Retired: 1997
Original: $17 • Value: $28

654.

Briana Bearlov [POG]
#94592POG • 8"
Issued: 2001 • Retired: 2001
Original: $14 • Value: $22

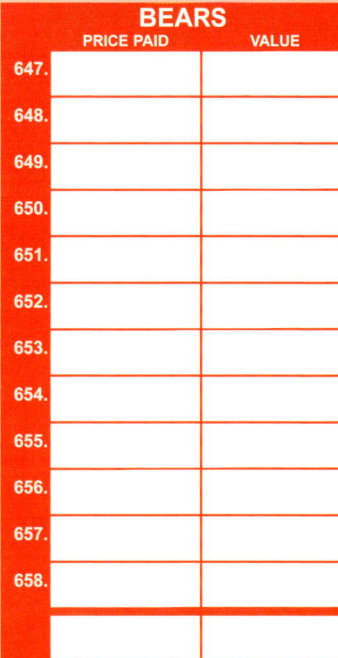

BEARS		
	PRICE PAID	VALUE
647.		
648.		
649.		
650.		
651.		
652.		
653.		
654.		
655.		
656.		
657.		
658.		
	TOTALS	

NOTES

655.

Brianna [Elder Beerman]
#unknown • 11"
Issued: 1999 • Retired: 1999
Original: $N/E • Value: $27

656.

Brianna Angelbless [QVC]
#(C6047) • 10"
Issued: 2003 • Retired: 2003
Original: $15 • Value: $18

657.

Brianna B. Bearican
#919831 • TJ
Issued: 2004 • Current
Original: $23 • Value: $R/E

658.

**Brianna Q. Yachtley with
Mr. Waddlesworth [QVC]**
#unknown • 16"
Issued: 2002 • Retired: 2002
Original: $49 • Value: $75

Bears

659.
Brianna Tippeetoes
#913959 • 6" • ME
Issued: 2000 • Retired: 2002
Original: $10 • Value: $16

660.
Bridgette & Suzanne Dubeary [QVC]
#(C99309) • 6"
Issued: 2001 • Retired: 2001
Original: $25 • Value: $40

661.
Bridgette Beardeaux
#904316 • 9" • TJ
Issued: 2004 • Current
Original: $11 • Value: $R/E

662.
Brighton, Salisbury & Somerset [QVC]
#unknown • 6"
Issued: 1998 • Retired: 1998
Original: $19 • Value: $36

663.
Brinkley Bearsdale
#510811 • 14" • JB
Issued: 2002 • Retired: 2002
Original: $15 • Value: $21

664.
Brinsley Bruin [QVC]
#(C99312) • 10"
Issued: 2001 • Retired: 2001
Original: $16 • Value: $54
Remake of open mouth bear.

665.
Brinton S. Beansford [QVC]
#(C57655) • 14"
Issued: 1999 • Retired: 1999
Original: $16 • Value: $30

666.
Bristol B. Windsor
#57052-03 • 8" • AS
Issued: 2000 • Retired: 2002
Original: $11 • Value: $13
Also with Chelsea, Cornwell as QVC set.

667.
Brittney [York Fair]
#94183YF • 8"
Issued: 2003 • Retired: 2003
Original: $10 • Value: $R/E

668.
Bromley Q. Bear
#5151-03 • 8" • JB
Issued: 1998 • Retired: 1999
Original: $13 • Value: $21

669.
Bronson [SLE]
#unknown • 8"
Issued: 1996 • Retired: 1996
Original: $21 • Value: $50

670.
Brooke B. Bearsley
#917400 • 10" • TJ
Issued: 2000 • Retired: 2002
Original: $16 • Value: $25

BEARS	PRICE PAID	VALUE
659.		
660.		
661.		
662.		
663.		
664.		
665.		
666.		
667.		
668.		
669.		
670.		
TOTALS		

NOTES

Bears

671.
Bruce (nekkid)
#1000-08 • 8" • CC
Issued: 1993 • Retired: 1999
Original: $6 • Value: $22

672.
Bruce (heart sweater)
#9157-08 • 8" • CC
Issued: 1993 • Retired: 1994
Original: $14 • Value: $40

673.
Bruce (Ted sweater)
#98038 • 8" • AS
Issued: 1996 • Retired: 1997
Original: $13 • Value: $36

674.
Bruce (bat costume)
#904346 • 6" • TJ
Issued: 2004 • Current
Original: $11 • Value: $R/E

675.
Bruinhilda Von Bruin
#5010-03 • 6" • WB
Issued: 1994 • Retired: 1995
Original: $12 • Value: $35

676.
Brumley [QVC]
#(C39091) • 12" • AS
Issued: 1997 • Retired: 1997
Original: $18 • Value: $37

677.
Bruno Bedlington [QVC]
#93073V • 11"
Issued: 1998 • Retired: 1998
Original: $23 • Value: $57

678.
Bryson Beansley [QVC]
#93471V (C3017) • 16"
Issued: 2003 • Retired: 2003
Original: $26 • Value: $31

679.
Bubba
#5856 • 16" • BB
Issued: 1992 • Retired: 1997
Original: $27 • Value: $60

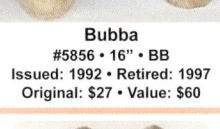

680.
Buchanan J Bearington [QVC]
#(C34962) • 11" • MB
LE of 1700 • Issued: 1998 • Retired: 1998
Original: $43 • Value: $56

681.
Buckingham
#57221 • 21" • AS
Issued: 1997 • Retired: 1999
Original: $55 • Value: $75

Have You Seen Me?

682.
Buckles [Lord & Taylor]
#unknown • 16" • BA
Issued: 1997 • Retired: 1997
Original: $18 • Value: $39

82

Bears

683.
Buckley
#9104 • 8" • TJ
Issued: 1994 • Retired: 1996
Original: $18 • Value: $30

684.
Buckley [QVC]
#93479V (C0383) • 14" • TJ
Issued: 2003 • Retired: 2003
Original: $34 • Value: $47

685.
Buckley the Fireman
#917373 • 10"
Issued: 2001 • Retired: 2002
Original: $25 • Value: $30

686.
Buckley the Fireman [SFMB]
#917373SF • 10"
LE of 801 • Issued: 2002 • Retired: 2002
Original: $34 • Value: $44
♪ William Tell Overture ♪

687.
Buffington Fitzbruin
#912031 • 10" • TJ
Issued: 1997 • Retired: 1998
Original: $20 • Value: $32

688.
Have You Seen Me?
Buffy
#5639-10 • 12" • BA
Issued: 1995 • Retired: 1996
Original: $16 • Value: $35

689.
Buffy [Victoria's Secret]
#unknown • 12"
Issued: 1996 • Retired: 1996
Original: $25 • Value: $52

690.
Buford B. [QVC]
#(C37282) • 12" • BB
Issued: 1997 • Retired: 1997
Original: $18 • Value: $104

691.
Buford B. Beezley
#904112 • 12"
Issued: 2003 • Retired: 2003
Original: $17 • Value: $17

692.
Bumbershoot B. Jodibear
#92000-03 • 8" • AR
Issued: 1999 • Retired: 2000
Original: $17 • Value: $20

693.
Bumble B. Bugsley
#918700 • 8"
Issued: 2003 • Retired: 2003
Original: $17 • Value: $17

694.
Bumble B. Buzzoff
#91773 • 8" • TJ
Issued: 2000 • Retired: 2002
Original: $14 • Value: $17

BEARS

	PRICE PAID	VALUE
683.		
684.		
685.		
686.		
687.		
688.		
689.		
690.		
691.		
692.		
693.		
694.		
TOTALS		

NOTES

Bears

695.
Bumbles S. Beezley [QVC]
#93431V (C22082) • 14"
LE of 4000 • Issued: 2003 • Retired: 2003
Original: $42 • Value: $50
Sold with Beehive Tug Along.

696.
Bumbley B. Bear
#510405 • 16"
Issued: 2003 • Current
Original: $23 • Value: $R/E

697.
Bumpkin…Country Bear [BBC]
#918075SM • 30"
Issued: 2003 • Retired: 2003
Original: $110 • Value: $N/E

698.
Bunker Bedlington [GCC]
#94869GCC • 8"
Issued: 1999 • Retired: 1999
Original: $14 • Value: $25

699.
Burke P. Bear
#5109-05 • 14" • JB
Issued: 1997 • Retired: 2002
Original: $19 • Value: $32

700.
Burl
#91761 • 10" • TJ
Issued: 1996 • Retired: 1998
Original: $20 • Value: $35

701.
Burlington P. Beanster
#510400-07 • 16" • JB
Issued: 1999 • Retired: 2002
Original: $21 • Value: $35

702.
Buster McRind
#915503 • 8" • TJ
Issued: 2001 • Retired: 2001
Original: $13 • Value: $16

703.
Buttercup C. Snicklefritz
#51761-12 • 8" • BA
Issued: 1999 • Retired: 1999
Original: $12 • Value: $18

704.
Buttercup Pufflefluff
#56398-12 • 14" • BA
Issued: 2001 • Retired: 2002
Original: $11 • Value: $13

705.
Butterfly Kisses & Bear Hugs [POG]
#94606POG • 8"
Issued: 2003 • Retired: 2003
Original: $16 • Value: $19

706.
Buxton B. Beansley [QVC]
#93408V (C21159) • 16"
Issued: 2003 • Retired: 2003
Original: $25 • Value: $34

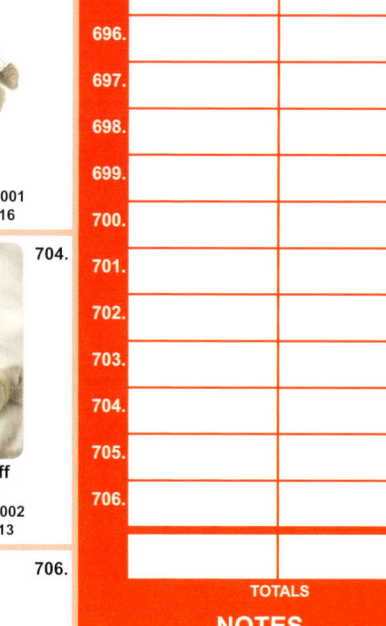

BEARS	PRICE PAID	VALUE
695.		
696.		
697.		
698.		
699.		
700.		
701.		
702.		
703.		
704.		
705.		
706.		
TOTALS		

NOTES

Bears

707.

Buzz B. Bean
#5120 • 10" • JB
Issued: 1989 • Retired: 1990
Original: $13 • Value: $269

708.

Buzzby
#9143 • 8" • TJ
Issued: 1994 • Retired: 1995
Original: $18 • Value: $63

709.

Byron
#unknown • 9"
Issued: 1998 • Retired: 1998
Original: $10 • Value: $19

710.

C. Elbert [Dillards]
#94720DL • 18"
Issued: 1997 • Retired: 1997
Original: $30 • Value: $56

711.

C. Fallin' Leafowitz [QVC]
#93230V (C64870) • 14"
Issued: 2001 • Retired: 2001
Original: $38 • Value: $54

712.

C.B. [QVC]
#93370V (C20972) • 6"
Issued: 2002 • Retired: 2002
Original: $10 • Value: $22

713.

C.C. Beansley [QVC]
#(C20942) • 11"
Issued: 2002 • Retired: 2002
Original: $18 • Value: $23

714.

C.C. Boobear
#904201 • 10" • TJ
Issued: 2003 • Current
Original: $15 • Value: $R/E

715.

C.C. Cocoa Bear [Carlton Cards]
#unknown • 8"
Issued: 2000 • Retired: 2000
Original: $22 • Value: $30

716.

C.C. Goodbear [Country Clutter]
#unknown • 10"
Issued: 1999 • Retired: 1999
Original: $28 • Value: $45

717.

C.C. Peekers
#913984 • 6"
Issued: 2002 • Retired: 2002
Original: $10 • Value: $10

718.

C.J. Cherrybeary
#904092 • 10"
Issued: 2003 • Current
Original: $15 • Value: $R/E

BEARS

	PRICE PAID	VALUE
707.		
708.		
709.		
710.		
711.		
712.		
713.		
714.		
715.		
716.		
717.		
718.		
TOTALS		

NOTES

719.

C.Z. Comet
#917308 • 8" • TJ
Issued: 2000 • Retired: 2002
Original: $16 • Value: $24

720.

C.Z. Sparklefrost Sparkling [QVC]
#(C5128) • 8"
Issued: 2003 • Retired: 2003
Original: $18 • Value: $22
Sold with ceramic mug.

721.

Have You Seen Me?

Cabin Bear
#9013B
Issued: 1992 • Retired: 1993
Original: $25 • Value: $409

722.

Cagney
#9189-01 • 8" • TJ
Issued: 1994 • Retired: 1995
Original: $20 • Value: $61

723.

Caitlin Cherry Berry [Elder Beerman]
#unknown
Issued: 2003 • Retired: 2003
Original: $15 • Value: $18

724.

Caitlynn P.J. Crystalfrost [Cracker Barrel]
#94997CB • 10"
Issued: 2003 • Retired: 2003
Original: $25 • Value: $30

725.

Cal Doubleplay
#917710 • 9" • AR
Issued: 2001 • Retired: 2002
Original: $20 • Value: $24

726.

Caledonia
#5840-01 • 6" • AS
Issued: 1997 • Retired: 2001
Original: $9 • Value: $13
Also with Humboldt, Shasta as QVC set.

727.

Callaghan (old face)
#5704 • 8" • AS
Issued: 1990 • Retired: 1993
Original: $12 • Value: $45

728.

Callaghan (new face)
#5704 • 8" • AS
Issued: 1993 • Retired: 1996
Original: $12 • Value: $24

729.

Calvin Ellis
#91223 • 8" • TJ
Issued: 1996 • Retired: 1997
Original: $18 • Value: $36

730.

Cambridge Q. Bearrister
#57003-08 • 12" • AS
Issued: 2000 • Retired: 2001
Original: $16 • Value: $24

BEARS

	PRICE PAID	VALUE
719.		
720.		
721.		
722.		
723.		
724.		
725.		
726.		
727.		
728.		
729.		
730.		
TOTALS		

NOTES

Bears

731.
Cameron & Deacon Bearsford
with Jameson [QVC]
#(C57654) • 6"
Issued: 1999 • Retired: 1999
Original: $22 • Value: $40

732.
Cameron W. Bearsmark [Hallmark]
#9691HM • 10"
Issued: 2002 • Retired: 2002
Original: $18 • Value: $23

733.
Camille du Bear
#91804 • 6" • TJ
Issued: 1996 • Retired: 1999
Original: $9 • Value: $30

734.
Camryn B. Bear
#510312 • 10" • AS
Issued: 2004 • Current
Original: $11 • Value: $R/E

735.
Camryn B. Pearsley
#904162 • 10" • TJ
Issued: 2003 • Current
Original: $19 • Value: $R/E

736.
Candy B. Corn
#919633 • 6" • TJ
Issued: 2001 • Retired: 2002
Original: $10 • Value: $19

737.
Canute
#9136 • 6" • TJ
Issued: 1994 • Retired: 1996
Original: $12 • Value: $27

738.
Cara Sue [SLE]
#unknown • 14"
Issued: 2004 • Retired: 2004
Original: $20 • Value: $R/E

739.
Caramel, Meringue, Molasses
Bearenburg [QVC]
#(C55533) • 10"
Issued: 1999 • Retired: 1999
Original: $31 • Value: $40

740.
Cari Carrot
#904246 • 5½" • TJ
Issued: 2004 • Current
Original: $10 • Value: $R/E

741.
Carin Angelmom
#903200 • 8"
Issued: 2002 • Current
Original: $10 • Value: $R/E

742.
Carina T. McBeansley
with Bah-Bah [QVC]
#93336V (C20214) • 10"
Issued: 2002 • Retired: 2002
Original: $21 • Value: $27

BEARS

	PRICE PAID	VALUE
731.		
732.		
733.		
734.		
735.		
736.		
737.		
738.		
739.		
740.		
741.		
742.		
	TOTALS	

NOTES

743.
Carlie & Kristen [Profitts]
#unknown • 12"
Issued: 1999 • Retired: 1999
Original: $28 • Value: $49

744.
Carly Bearworth [Show Specials]
#919801 • 6"
Issued: 2000 • Retired: 2000
Original: $9 • Value: $14

745.
Carmela Cocobeary
#904334 • 8" • TJ
Issued: 2004 • Current
Original: $13 • Value: $R/E

746.
Carmella de Bearvoire
#918401 • 6" • TJ
Issued: 1999 • Retired: 2002
Original: $9 • Value: $13

747.
Carol Anne Primsley
#913979 • 6"
Issued: 2002 • Retired: 2002
Original: $10 • Value: $17

748.
Caroline [QVC]
#(C19268) • 11"
Issued: 1996 • Retired: 1996
Original: $18 • Value: $49

749.
Caroline Mayflower
#913958 • 6" • TJ
Issued: 2000 • Retired: 2002
Original: $12 • Value: $24
Also with Benjamin F.
Almanac as QVC set.

750.
Carrie B. Beansley [QVC]
#93331V (C20217) • 8"
Issued: 2002 • Retired: 2002
Original: $12 • Value: $16

751.
Carrie N. Lotsalove
#82518 • 6" • TJ
Issued: 2002 • Retired: 2002
Original: $10 • Value: $10

752.
Carter M. Bearington
#590050-08 • 10" • MB
Issued: 1998 • Retired: 1999
Original: $31 • Value: $43

753.
Casey Renee [SYN]
#94590SYN • 10"
Issued: 2001 • Retired: 2001
Original: $17 • Value: $28

754.
Casimir B. Bean
(with extra sweater) [GCC]
#94858GCC • 10"
Issued: 1998 • Retired: 1998
Original: $26 • Value: $40

BEARS

	PRICE PAID	VALUE
743.		
744.		
745.		
746.		
747.		
748.		
749.		
750.		
751.		
752.		
753.		
754.		
TOTALS		

NOTES

Bears

755.
Cass [SLE]
#unknown • 12"
Issued: 1998 • Retired: 1998
Original: $22 • Value: $35

756.
Cassidy [QVC]
#(C37280) • 16"
Issued: 1997 • Retired: 1997
Original: $37 • Value: $85

757.
Cassidy L. Bearsmark [Hallmark]
#9693HM • 6"
Issued: 2002 • Retired: 2002
Original: $11 • Value: $24

758.
Cavendish
#5701-02 • 12" • AS
Issued: 1994 • Retired: 1996
Original: $20 • Value: $46

759.
CB The Skater [Sparx]
#BC94285PO • 12"
LE of 3600 • Issued: 1999 • Retired: 1999
Original: $35 • Value: $52

760.
Cecelia DeBearvoire
#918101 • 6"
Issued: 2002 • Retired: 2002
Original: $10 • Value: $16

761.
Cecelia T. Bearington
#590056 • 9" • MB
Issued: 2002 • Retired: 2002
Original: $30 • Value: $48

762.
Cecil
#5726 • 5½" • AS
Issued: 1992 • Retired: 1996
Original: $7 • Value: $25

763.
Cecile Bearnet [Carlton Cards]
#unknown • 6"
Issued: 2001 • Retired: 2001
Original: $15 • Value: $30

764.
Cedar T. Woodsley
#92002-08 • 15" • AS
Issued: 2003 • Current
Original: $22 • Value: $R/E

765.
Cela Bration [Carlton Cards]
#91984CA • 8"
Issued: 2003 • Retired: 2003
Original: $13 • Value: $16

766.
Celana Celeste Angelwish
#904043 • 8" • TJ
Issued: 2002 • Retired: 2002
Original: $14 • Value: $22

BEARS	PRICE PAID	VALUE
755.		
756.		
757.		
758.		
759.		
760.		
761.		
762.		
763.		
764.		
765.		
766.		
TOTALS		

NOTES

Bears

767.
Celeste Angeltrust with Hope
#900101
LE • Issued: 2001 • Retired: 2001
Original: $60 • Value: $72

768.
Ceylon Pekoe [QVC]
#(C41092) • 10"
Issued: 1997 • Retired: 1997
Original: $28 • Value: $65

769.
Chadwick with Bosley [QVC]
#(C39076) • 8"
Issued: 1997 • Retired: 1997
Original: $22 • Value: $38

770.
Chamberlain
#5709 • 16" • AS
Issued: 1990 • Retired: 1992
Original: $32 • Value: $150

771.
Chamomille Q. Quignapple
#91004 • 10" • TJ
Issued: 1979 • Retired: 2002
Original: $19 • Value: $35

772.
Chamomille Quignapple [SFMB]
#41-72785 • 10"
Issued: 1998 • Retired: 1998
Original: $27 • Value: $N/E
♪ A Dream is a Wish Your Heart Makes ♪

773.
Chan
#9153 • 6" • TJ
Issued: 1994 • Retired: 1998
Original: $12 • Value: $30

774.
Chance Furgold [Welcome Home]
#94537WH • 10"
Issued: 2002 • Retired: 2002
Original: $16 • Value: $35

775.
Chanceford Q. Beansley [QVC]
#93304V (C107584) • 16"
Issued: 2002 • Retired: 2002
Original: $24 • Value: $30

776.
Chandler [Younker's]
#unknown • 10"
Issued: 1997 • Retired: 1997
Original: $N/E • Value: $35

777.
Chandler Crystalfrost
#904182 • 10" • TJ
Issued: 2003 • Retired: 2003
Original: $20 • Value: $20

778.
Chanel de la Plumtete
#9184 • 6" • TJ
Issued: 1995 • Retired: 1999
Original: $9 • Value: $24

BEARS		
	PRICE PAID	VALUE
767.		
768.		
769.		
770.		
771.		
772.		
773.		
774.		
775.		
776.		
777.		
778.		
TOTALS		

NOTES

Bears

779.
Chanelle Cocobeary
#904330 • 16" • TJ
Issued: 2004 • Current
Original: $50 • Value: $R/E

780.
Chantelle Chapeau
#918448 • 6"
Issued: 2002 • Retired: 2002
Original: $10 • Value: $10

781.
Chardonnay Beardeaux
#904310 • 16" • TJ
Issued: 2004 • Current
Original: $50 • Value: $R/E

782.
Charlotte B. Beezley
#904111 • 14"
Issued: 2003 • Current
Original: $34 • Value: $R/E

783.
Charlotte Tewksbeary with Hobbes [QVC]
#C63356 • 16"
Issued: 1999 • Retired: 1999
Original: $47 • Value: $75

784.
Chase Bearimore
#913930 • 6" • TJ
Issued: 2000 • Retired: 2000
Original: $13 • Value: $22

785.
Chauncey Fitzbruin
#912033 • 6" • TJ
Issued: 1997 • Retired: 1999
Original: $12 • Value: $25

786.
Cheese N. Crackers
#918667 • 10" • TJ
Issued: 2004 • Current
Original: $16 • Value: $R/E

787.
Chelci Robear [Ideation]
#900217IDE • 8"
Issued: 2001 • Retired: 2001
Original: $12 • Value: $30

788.
Chelsea & Cornwell with Bristol B. Windsor [QVC]
#99726V (C98051) • 8½"
Issued: 2000 • Retired: 2000
Original: $31 • Value: $46

789.
Cher N. Hugs
#903024 • 8" • ME
Issued: 2002 • Retired: 2002
Original: $10 • Value: $10

790.
Cherry Blossom Bear [Smithsonian Institute]
#94564SI • 8"
Issued: 2003 • Retired: 2003
Original: $20 • Value: $26

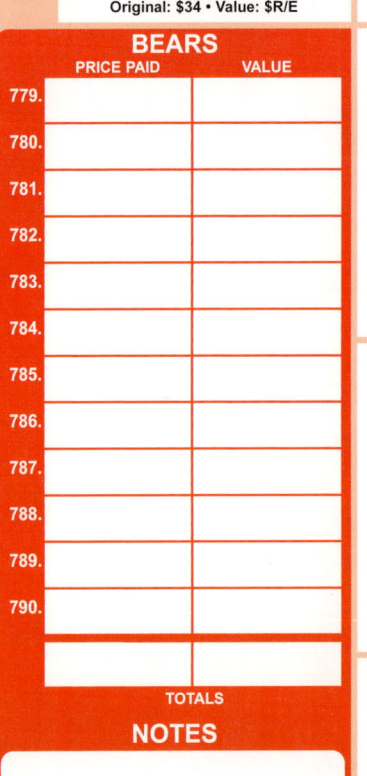

BEARS	PRICE PAID	VALUE
779.		
780.		
781.		
782.		
783.		
784.		
785.		
786.		
787.		
788.		
789.		
790.		
TOTALS		

NOTES

Bears

791.
Cherry Blossom Kimono Bear
[Smithsonian Institute]
#unknown • 8"
Issued: 2004 • Retired: 2004
Original: $15 • Value: $N/E

792.
Cheryl S. Grammykins
#912664 • 12" • ME
Issued: 2002 • Current
Original: $25 • Value: $R/E

793.
Chester B. Bearsworth
#57253-05 • 6" • AS
Issued: 2001 • Retired: 2002
Original: $7 • Value: $8

794.
Chipper
#5642-05 • 8" • BA
Issued: 1996 • Retired: 1997
Original: $11 • Value: $25

795.
Christian (with boat)
#9190 • 8" • TJ
Issued: 1992 • Retired: 2000
Original: $15 • Value: $70

796.
Christian [Dillards]
#94744DL • 12"
Issued: 1999 • Retired: 1999
Original: $32 • Value: $48

797.
Christiana LaBearsley
#918446 • 6" • TJ
Issued: 2001 • Retired: 2001
Original: $10 • Value: $12

798.
Christine P. Plumbeary
#918355 • 8" • TJ
Issued: 2001 • Retired: 2001
Original: $19 • Value: $23

799.
Christmas Bear [QVC]
#(C18106) • 14"
LE of 1200 • Issued: 1995 • Retired: 1995
Original: $70 • Value: $229

800.
Christopher
#9161 • 10" • TJ
Issued: 1993 • Retired: 1998
Original: $20 • Value: $39

801.
Christopher T. Beansley [QVC]
#93219V • 10"
Issued: 2001 • Retired: 2001
Original: $12 • Value: $23

802.
Chuck Woodbeary
#917366 • 10" • TJ
Issued: 2000 • Retired: 2000
Original: $20 • Value: $27

BEARS

	PRICE PAID	VALUE
791.		
792.		
793.		
794.		
795.		
796.		
797.		
798.		
799.		
800.		
801.		
802.		
TOTALS		

NOTES

Bears

803.
Churchill (old face)
#5700 • 12" • AS
Issued: 1990 • Retired: 1990
Original: $20 • Value: $90

804.
Churchill (2nd version)
#5700 • 12" • AS
Issued: 1991 • Retired: 1993
Original: $20 • Value: $52

805.
Churchill (new face)
#5700 • 12" • AS
Issued: 1993 • Retired: 1999
Original: $N/E • Value: $34

806.
Cimmaron [QVC]
#(C45011) • 14"
Issued: 1997 • Retired: 1997
Original: $16 • Value: $35

807.
Cindy [CAN]
#BC94293PO • 6"
LE of 2400 • Issued: 2001 • Retired: 2001
Original: $16 • Value: $24

808.
Cindy Lou Bearican
[Cracker Barrel]
#94998CB • 10"
Issued: 2004 • Retired: 2004
Original: $25 • Value: $27

809.
Cindy McSnoozle
#904064 • 8"
Issued: 2002 • Retired: 2002
Original: $17 • Value: $24

810.
Cindyrella
#91777 • 10" • TJ
Issued: 2001 • Retired: 2001
Original: $25 • Value: $34

811.
Cinnebelle McPunkin
#904320 • 16" • TJ
Issued: 2004 • Current
Original: $50 • Value: $R/E

812.
Cissy [Lord & Taylor]
#unknown • 8"
Issued: 1998 • Retired: 1998
Original: $12 • Value: $22

813.
Claire
#9179 • 10" • TJ
Issued: 1994 • Retired: 1998
Original: $20 • Value: $33

814.
Clara
#911061 • 14" • AR
Issued: 1996 • Retired: 1998
Original: $20 • Value: $33

BEARS

	PRICE PAID	VALUE
803.		
804.		
805.		
806.		
807.		
808.		
809.		
810.		
811.		
812.		
813.		
814.		
TOTALS		

NOTES

Bears

815.
Clara [Kirlins]
#unknown • 14" • AR
LE of 1200 • Issued: 1996 • Retired: 1996
Original: $15 • Value: $43

816.
Clara [Bon Ton]
#unknown • 14"
Issued: 1996 • Retired: 1996
Original: $N/E • Value: $49

817.
Clara B. Bearcountry [QVC]
#93334V (C20181) • 18"
LE of 12500 • Issued: 2002 • Retired: 2002
Original: $35 • Value: $46

818.
Clarissa
#91202 • 16" • TJ
Issued: 1996 • Retired: 1999
Original: $58 • Value: $79

819.
Clarissa [SFMB]
#41-72584 • 15"
Issued: 1998 • Retired: 1998
Original: $57 • Value: $75
♪ Make Someone Happy ♪

820.
Clark [QVC]
#unknown • 10"
Issued: 1998 • Retired: 1998
Original: $16 • Value: $50

821.
Clark II [Platinum Paw]
#918055-01 • 6"
Issued: 2000 • Retired: 2000
Original: $8 • Value: $21

822.
Clark S. Bearhugs
#918055 • 6" • TJ
Issued: 2000 • Retired: 2000
Original: $10 • Value: $15

BEARS

	PRICE PAID	VALUE
815.		
816.		
817.		
818.		
819.		
820.		
821.		
822.		
823.		
824.		
825.		
826.		
TOTALS		

NOTES

823.
Claudette Beardeaux
#904317 • 6" • TJ
Issued: 2004 • Current
Original: $11 • Value: $R/E

824.
Claudius B. Bean [QVC]
#(C45006) • 14"
Issued: 1997 • Retired: 1997
Original: $29 • Value: $45

825.
Claudius B. Bean [Lord & Taylor]
#unknown • 14"
Issued: 1998 • Retired: 1998
Original: $30 • Value: $45

826.
Claus Kringlebeary
#917311-01 • 14" • TJ
Issued: 2001 • Retired: 2001
Original: $35 • Value: $42

Bears

827.
Claus Kringlebeary [SFMB]
#41-72582 • 14"
Issued: 2001 • Retired: 2001
Original: $45 • Value: $59
♪ Greensleeves ♪

828.
Cleason
#5121N • 10" • JB
Issued: 1992 • Retired: 1996
Original: $14 • Value: $42

829.
Clem Cladiddlebear
#500070-08 • 30" • JB
Issued: 2001 • Retired: 2002
Original: $57 • Value: $68

830.
Clement
#5710 • 16" • AS
Issued: 1990 • Retired: 1992
Original: $32 • Value: $155

831.
Clementine [Frederick Atkins]
#unknown • 14"
Issued: 1997 • Retired: 1997
Original: $30 • Value: $45

832.
Clementine
#913953 • 6" • TJ
Issued: 1998 • Retired: 2001
Original: $10 • Value: $20

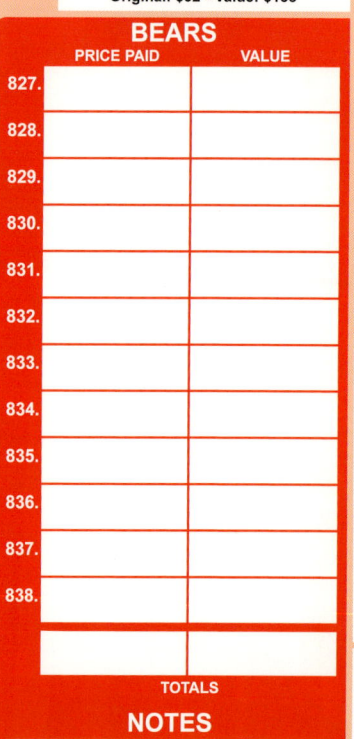

BEARS	PRICE PAID	VALUE
827.		
828.		
829.		
830.		
831.		
832.		
833.		
834.		
835.		
836.		
837.		
838.		

TOTALS

NOTES

833.
Cleveland G. Bearington
#590042-03 • 12" • MB
Issued: 2000 • Retired: 2001
Original: $46 • Value: $55

834.
Clinton B. Bean
#5109 • 14" • JB
Issued: 1993 • Retired: 1995
Original: $20 • Value: $34

835.
Clover I. Buzzoff
#91772 • 10" • TJ
Issued: 1999 • Retired: 2001
Original: $15 • Value: $21

836.
Coach Hayden
#917375 • 10" • ME
Issued: 2001 • Current
Original: $20 • Value: $R/E

837.
Coco Bruin (brown nose)
#5121 • 10" • JB
Issued: 1989 • Retired: 1995
Original: $14 • Value: $100
Black nose worth less.

838.
Coco DeBearvoire
#904075 • 6"
Issued: 2003 • Retired: 2004
Original: $10 • Value: $10

Bears

839.
Colette Dubeary
#918439 • 6" • TJ
Issued: 2000 • Retired: 2002
Original: $11 • Value: $13

840.
Colleen [QVC]
#unknown • 16" • TJ
Issued: 1998 • Retired: 1998
Original: $N/E • Value: $65

841.
Colleen O'Bruin
#91805 • 6" • TJ
Issued: 1995 • Retired: 1997
Original: $12 • Value: $36

842.
Collette [SLE]
#unknown • 11"
Issued: 1997 • Retired: 1997
Original: $15 • Value: $29

843.
Collin Q. Bearsworth [QVC]
#93326V (C19890) • 21"
Issued: 2002 • Retired: 2002
Original: $50 • Value: $65

844.
Comfy B. Bear [QVC]
#(C05175) • 8"
Issued: 2004 • Retired: 2004
Original: $12 • Value: $13

845.
Conner D. Devilbear
#919632 • 10" • TJ
Issued: 2001 • Retired: 2002
Original: $19 • Value: $23

846.
Constance
#91202-01 • 16" • TJ
Issued: 1998 • Retired: 2002
Original: $40 • Value: $53

847.
Constance Bearyfine [GCC]
#94897GCC • 12"
LE of 3800 • Issued: 2001 • Retired: 2001
Original: $30 • Value: $45

848.
Cookie Bearchild
#903009 • 8" • ME
Issued: 2001 • Retired: 2001
Original: $10 • Value: $12

849.
Cooper T. Wishkabibble
#90502 • 8" • TJ
Issued: 2001 • Retired: 2002
Original: $18 • Value: $22

850.
Cora B. Applesmith
#912634 • 16" • TJ
Issued: 2001 • Retired: 2002
Original: $30 • Value: $36

BEARS	PRICE PAID	VALUE
839.		
840.		
841.		
842.		
843.		
844.		
845.		
846.		
847.		
848.		
849.		
850.		
TOTALS		

NOTES

Bears

851.
Corey Allen Bearsmoore
#912616 • 14" • TJ
Issued: 2000 • Retired: 2002
Original: $25 • Value: $26

852.
Cori Beariburg
#915211 • 8½" • TJ
Issued: 2000 • Retired: 2001
Original: $12 • Value: $16

853.
Corinna
#91201 • 16" • TJ
Issued: 1996 • Retired: 1998
Original: $45 • Value: $86
TOBY Award Winner

854.
Corinna II
#912011 • 16" • TJ
Issued: 1997 • Retired: 1999
Original: $45 • Value: $54

855.
Cornelius McPunkin
#904321 • 15" • TJ
Issued: 2004 • Current
Original: $31 • Value: $R/E

856.
Cornwallis (overalls)
#9126 • 16" • TJ
Issued: 1994 • Retired: 1996
Original: $45 • Value: $79

857.
Cornwallis (heart sweater)
#9126-01 • 16" • TJ
Issued: 1996 • Retired: 1997
Original: $53 • Value: $60

858.
Corrine Patchbeary [GCC]
#94901GCC • 6"
Issued: 2002 • Retired: 2002
Original: $14 • Value: $29

859.
Courtney
#912021 • 16" • TJ
Issued: 1997 • Retired: 2000
Original: $45 • Value: $51

860.
Courtney (burgundy plaid) [QVC]
#(C34960) • 16" • TJ
Issued: 1998 • Retired: 1998
Original: $36 • Value: $78

861.
Cousin Marty with Rover
#90508 • 9" • TJ
Issued: 2002 • Retired: 2002
Original: $20 • Value: $26

862.
Cousin Matilda with Ted
#90507 • 8" • TJ
Issued: 2002 • Retired: 2002
Original: $20 • Value: $26

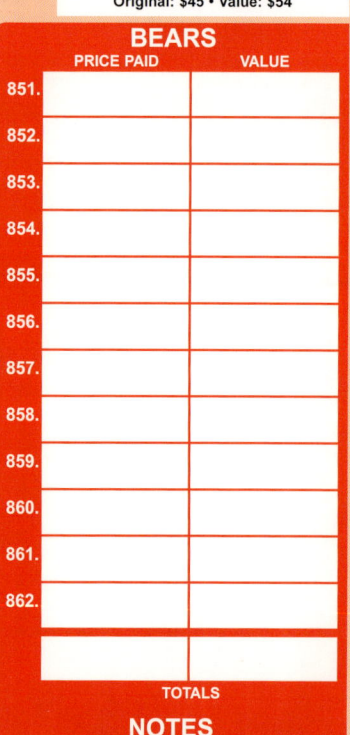

BEARS	PRICE PAID	VALUE
851.		
852.		
853.		
854.		
855.		
856.		
857.		
858.		
859.		
860.		
861.		
862.		
TOTALS		

NOTES

Bears

863.
Cranbeary N. Bear
#500100-02 • 8¼" • JB
Issued: 2000 • Retired: 2002
Original: $9 • Value: $11

864.
Cranston [GCC]
#94855GCC • 8"
Issued: 1997 • Retired: 1997
Original: $12 • Value: $35
Came with earbow, some stores took it off.

865.
Craxton B. Bean
#510300-11 • 10" • JB
Issued: 1998 • Retired: 2001
Original: $11 • Value: $19
Also with Maxton, Paxton as QVC set.

866.
Creme Bearleigh [QVC]
#93228V (C64875) • 14"
Issued: 2001 • Retired: 2001
Original: $17 • Value: $25

867.
Cromwell [QVC]
#(C35263) • 22"
Issued: 1997 • Retired: 1997
Original: $52 • Value: $75

868.
Crystal & Frosty Icebeary [Welcome Home]
#unknown • 8"
Issued: 2000 • Retired: 2000
Original: $21 • Value: $32

869.
Crystal B. Goodbear [Country Clutter]
#94978CC • 10"
Issued: 2003 • Retired: 2003
Original: $25 • Value: $30

870.
Cubby T. Bearington [QVC]
#99874V (C107577) • 9" • MB
LE of 2400 • Issued: 2002 • Retired: 2002
Original: $34 • Value: $50

871.
Cybill Quackenwaddle
#913939 • 8"
Issued: 2002 • Current
Original: $13 • Value: $R/E

872.
Cynthia Berrijam [QVC]
#93106V (C56963) • 16"
Issued: 1999 • Retired: 1999
Original: $32 • Value: $45

873.
D.L. Merrill
#51100-05 • 16" • JB
Issued: 1999 • Retired: 2000
Original: $23 • Value: $28

874.
Dahlia
#590062 • 10" • MB
LE of 5000 • Issued: 2003 • Retired: 2003
Original: $30 • Value: $30

BEARS		
	PRICE PAID	VALUE
863.		
864.		
865.		
866.		
867.		
868.		
869.		
870.		
871.		
872.		
873.		
874.		
TOTALS		

NOTES

Bears

875.
Daisy Anna Goodbear [Country Clutter]
#94977CC • 10"
Issued: 2003 • Retired: 2003
Original: $22 • Value: $35

876.
Daisy Bearylove [Kirlins]
#94530KR • 10"
LE of 7200 • Issued: 2001 • Retired: 2001
Original: $22 • Value: $46

877.
Daisy Bloomengrows
#913964 • 6" • TJ
Issued: 2001 • Retired: 2002
Original: $12 • Value: $19

878.
Dana & Desiree DeBearvoire [QVC]
#99750V (C76784) • 6"
Issued: 2000 • Retired: 2000
Original: $18 • Value: $28

879.
Dana Marie Bearsley [GCC]
#94848GCC • 8"
Issued: 2003 • Retired: 2003
Original: $14 • Value: $21

880.
Dandy B. Doodlebear [QVC]
#93541V (C05838) • 18"
Issued: 2004 • Retired: 2004
Original: $75 • Value: $110
♪ Yankee Doodle Dandy ♪
Musical and animated.

881.
Daniel [Sight & Sound Ministries]
#94914SAS • 10"
Issued: 2002 • Retired: 2002
Original: $22 • Value: $30

882.
Daniel & Darbey Bearimore [QVC]
#(C63355) • 8"
Issued: 1999 • Retired: 1999
Original: $30 • Value: $45

883.
Danielle & Elizabieta de Bearvoire [QVC]
#99528V (C39087) • 11"
Issued: 1997 • Retired: 1997
Original: $26 • Value: $45

884.
Daphne [Elder Beerman]
#8155914EB • 10"
Issued: 1999 • Retired: 1999
Original: $24 • Value: $35

885.
Darby [SLE]
#unknown • 6"
Issued: 1997 • Retired: 1997
Original: $9 • Value: $17

886.
Darby Beariburg
#913960 • 6" • TJ
Issued: 2000 • Retired: 2002
Original: $10 • Value: $15

BEARS

	PRICE PAID	VALUE
875.		
876.		
877.		
878.		
879.		
880.		
881.		
882.		
883.		
884.		
885.		
886.		
TOTALS		

NOTES

Bears

887.
Daria & Dickens Jodibear [QVC]
#(C34955) • 8"
Issued: 1998 • Retired: 1998
Original: $30 • Value: $180

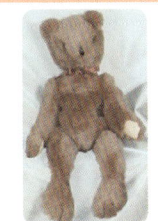

888.
Dark Brown Bean Bear
#unknown • 13" • JB
Issued: 1985 • Retired: 1985
Original: $N/E • Value: $350

889.
Darla May & Ann Marie [QVC]
#99815V (C64860) • 6"
Issued: 2001 • Retired: 2001
Original: $25 • Value: $40

890.
Daryl Bear (old face)
#5114 • 16" • JB
Issued: 1989 • Retired: 1990
Original: $27 • Value: $163

891.
Daryl Bear (new face)
#5114 • 16" • JB
Issued: 1990 • Retired: 1993
Original: $27 • Value: $115

892.
Dawson B. Bearsworth
#57150-08 • 16" • AS
Issued: 2001 • Retired: 2002
Original: $25 • Value: $30

893.
Dazie
#590061 • 10" • MB
LE of 5000 • Issued: 2003 • Retired: 2003
Original: $30 • Value: $30

894.
Dean B. Bearberg [SLE]
#unknown • 8"
Issued: 1998 • Retired: 1998
Original: $10 • Value: $21

895.
Dean S. Bearslot
#510501 • 21" • AS
Issued: 2003 • Current
Original: $53 • Value: $R/E

896.
Debbie Claire [Dillards]
#94741DL • 12"
Issued: 1999 • Retired: 1999
Original: $35 • Value: $51

897.
Debbie M. Dobbsey
[Coach House Gifts]
#unknown • 10"
Issued: 2000 • Retired: 2000
Original: $26 • Value: $40

898.
Deborah Sue Bearington [QVC]
#93470V (C3132) • 6" • MB
LE of 2400 • Issued: 2003 • Retired: 2003
Original: $17 • Value: $26

BEARS		
	PRICE PAID	VALUE
887.		
888.		
889.		
890.		
891.		
892.		
893.		
894.		
895.		
896.		
897.		
898.		
TOTALS		

NOTES

Bears

899.
Deirdre Rose [Bon Ton]
#unknown • 12"
Issued: 1997 • Retired: 1997
Original: $38 • Value: $53

900.
Delaney and the Duffer
#9212 • 13"
LE of 500 • Issued: 1993 • Retired: 1994
Original: $74 • Value: $300

901.
Delanie B. Beansford
#51101-10 • 16" • JB
Issued: 1999 • Retired: 2002
Original: $23 • Value: $33

902.
Delanie B. Beansford [SFMB]
#41-72935
Issued: 2000 • Retired: 2000
Original: $35 • Value: $45
♪ Are You Lonesome Tonight ♪

903.
Delbert Quignapple
#91003 • 10" • TJ
Issued: 1996 • Retired: 2002
Original: $19 • Value: $30

904.
Delilah Higgenthorpe with Twila [QVC]
#(C46245) • 6"
Issued: 1998 • Retired: 1998
Original: $18 • Value: $35

905.
Delmarva V. Crackenpot
#91002 • 10" • TJ
Issued: 1997 • Retired: 1999
Original: $29 • Value: $46
Variation: no pillow.

906.
Delmarva V. Crackenpot [QVC]
#(C41098) • 10" • TJ
Issued: 1997 • Retired: 1997
Original: $29 • Value: $51

907.
Delta [QVC]
#(C98049) • 16"
Issued: 2000 • Retired: 2000
Original: $44 • Value: $69

908.
Denise N. Daisydew
#904070 • 16"
Issued: 2003 • Current
Original: $54 • Value: $R/E

909.
Denise Needsmoreshoes [GCC]
#94655GCC • 8"
LE of 3400 • Issued: 2003 • Retired: 2003
Original: $15 • Value: $26

910.
Denton P. Jodibear
#92000-06 • 9" • AR
Issued: 1999 • Retired: 2002
Original: $17 • Value: $23

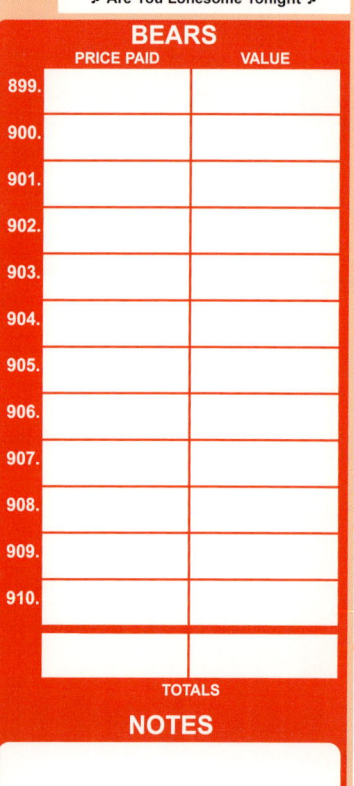

BEARS

	PRICE PAID	VALUE
899.		
900.		
901.		
902.		
903.		
904.		
905.		
906.		
907.		
908.		
909.		
910.		
TOTALS		

NOTES

Bears

911.
Derby Scruffles
#510702 • 8"
Issued: 2003 • Retired: 2003
Original: $9 • Value: $9

912.
Derry O. Beary
#57252-05 • 6½" • AS
Issued: 2000 • Retired: 2000
Original: $7 • Value: $8

913.
Desdomona T. Witebred
#912075 • 10" • TJ
Issued: 1997 • Retired: 1998
Original: $21 • Value: $33

914.
Destiny Angelbear [GCC]
#94893GCC • 10"
LE of 5700 • Issued: 2001 • Retired: 2001
Original: $22 • Value: $37

915.
Devin
#904344 • 6" • TJ
Issued: 2004 • Current
Original: $11 • Value: $R/E

916.
Devin Fallsbeary
#912621 • 14" • TJ
Issued: 1999 • Retired: 2002
Original: $35 • Value: $42

917.
Devon [GCC]
#94859GCC • 8"
Issued: 1998 • Retired: 1998
Original: $40 • Value: $48
Sold as a set with Stafford.

918.
Dexter
#91331 • 8" • TJ
Issued: 1996 • Retired: 1998
Original: $25 • Value: $45

919.
Have You Seen Me?
Diana (with boy cub)
#6102B • 14"
LE • Issued: 1991 • Retired: 1991
Original: $70 • Value: $475

920.
Diana (with girl cub)
#6102B • 14"
LE • Issued: 1991 • Retired: 1991
Original: $70 • Value: $450

921.
Diane Bearyfriend [GCC]
#94654GCC • 8"
Issued: 2003 • Retired: 2003
Original: $15 • Value: $R/E

922.
Diane D. Beansford and Topsey F. Wuzzie [QVC]
#unknown • 12"
Issued: 2000 • Retired: 2000
Original: $23 • Value: $45

BEARS

	PRICE PAID	VALUE
911.		
912.		
913.		
914.		
915.		
916.		
917.		
918.		
919.		
920.		
921.		
922.		
TOTALS		

NOTES

Bears

923.
Dickens
#500051 • 40" • JB
Issued: 2001 • Retired: 2001
Original: $200 • Value: $240

924.
Dingle B. Bumbles
#904116 • 6"
Issued: 2003 • Retired: 2003
Original: $9 • Value: $9

925.
Dingle Beartoes
#510011 • 8" • JB
Issued: 2002 • Retired: 2002
Original: $9 • Value: $9

926.
Dingles [QVC]
#5641 • 12"
Issued: 2002 • Retired: 2002
Original: $24 • Value: $31

927.
Dink (first version)
#5641 • 16" • BA
Issued: 1992 • Retired: 1994
Original: $21 • Value: $52

928.
Dink (chenille)
#5641-08 • 16" • BA
Issued: 1995 • Retired: 1997
Original: $24 • Value: $43

929.
Dion Bearberg [SLE]
#unknown • 12"
Issued: 1998 • Retired: 1998
Original: $N/E • Value: $28

930.
Disraeli
#5716 • 5½" • AS
Issued: 1991 • Retired: 1993
Original: $7 • Value: $73

931.
Dixie Hackett
#918334 • 10" • TJ
Issued: 2001 • Retired: 2001
Original: $20 • Value: $24

932.
Dixie Hackett [SFMB]
#918334SF • 10"
Issued: 2001 • Retired: 2001
Original: $30 • Value: $42
♪ Fascination ♪

933.
Dixon [BBC]
#918019SM • 14"
Issued: 2002 • Current
Original: $35 • Value: $R/E

934.
Doc Bearsley
#903302 • 8" • ME
Issued: 2002 • Retired: 2002
Original: $14 • Value: $14

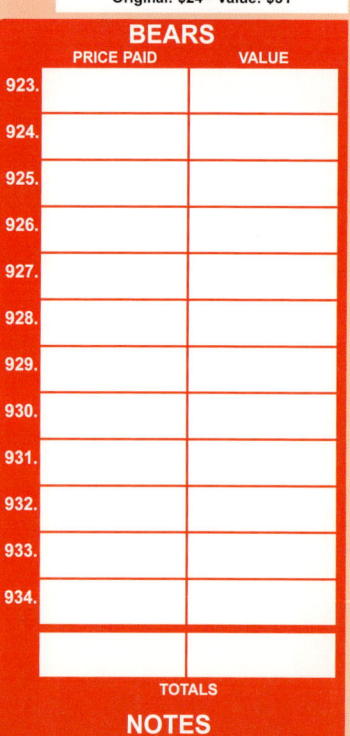

BEARS		
	PRICE PAID	VALUE
923.		
924.		
925.		
926.		
927.		
928.		
929.		
930.		
931.		
932.		
933.		
934.		
	TOTALS	

NOTES

Bears

935.
Dolley M. Jodibear
#92000-23 • 9" • AR
Issued: 2003 • Current
Original: $15 • Value: $R/E

936.
Dolly M. Bearington [QVC]
#93542V (C06198) • 6" • MB
LE of 2000 • Issued: 2004 • Retired: 2004
Original: $17 • Value: $26

937.
Dolly M. Bearsevelt [BBC]
#918012SM
Issued: 2002 • Retired: 2002
Original: $50 • Value: $N/E

938.
Donna Scarvesdale
#918455 • 6"
Issued: 2002 • Retired: 2002
Original: $8 • Value: $8

939.
Donovan B. Bear
#510403 • 16" • JB
Issued: 2002 • Retired: 2002
Original: $23 • Value: $23

940.
Doodle & Dandy [Longaberger]
#94624LB • 6"
Issued: 2003 • Retired: 2003
Original: $17 • Value: $24

941.
Doodle B. Beanster [QVC]
#93388V (C21001) • 10"
Issued: 2002 • Retired: 2002
Original: $18 • Value: $33

942.
Doolittle Buckshot
#51200-08 • 12" • JB
Issued: 1999 • Retired: 2001
Original: $16 • Value: $19

943.
Doomoore Buckshot
#51200-03 • 13" • JB
Issued: 2000 • Retired: 2000
Original: $15 • Value: $16

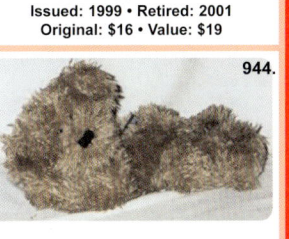

944.
Doonuttin Buckshot [QVC]
#(C76776) • 12"
Issued: 2000 • Retired: 2000
Original: $16 • Value: $25

945.
Doreen Q. Daisydew
#904071 • 14"
Issued: 2003 • Current
Original: $25 • Value: $R/E

946.
Dorinda & Donna [Show Specials]
#unknown • 16"
Issued: 1999 • Retired: 1999
Original: $N/E • Value: $55
Minneapolis Show

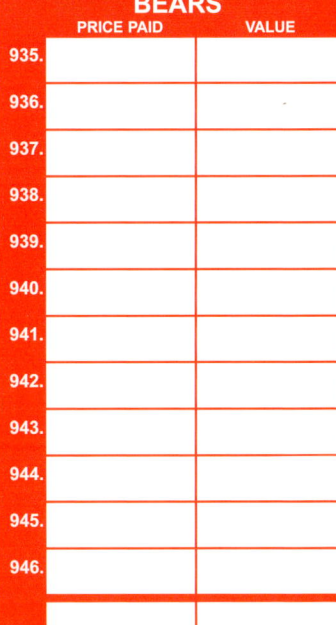

BEARS		
	PRICE PAID	VALUE
935.		
936.		
937.		
938.		
939.		
940.		
941.		
942.		
943.		
944.		
945.		
946.		
	TOTALS	

NOTES

Bears

947.
Dorothea Laceley
#918345 • 10"
Issued: 2002 • Retired: 2002
Original: $17 • Value: $17

948.
Dorothy
#904370 • 7" • TJ
Issued: 2004 • Current
Original: $16 • Value: $R/E

949.
Dorothy B. Beansley
#82525 • 10" • AS
Issued: 2003 • Retired: 2003
Original: $12 • Value: $12

950.
Dottie B. Bug
#913936 • 8" • TJ
Issued: 2002 • Retired: 2004
Original: $13 • Value: $13

951.
Douglas [SLE]
#unknown • 8"
Issued: 1996 • Retired: 1996
Original: $10 • Value: $43

952.
Dover D. Windsor
#57051-03 • 8" • AS
Issued: 2000 • Retired: 2002
Original: $10 • Value: $13

953.
Drema Yawnsalot [GCC]
#94902GCC • 10"
Issued: 2002 • Retired: 2002
Original: $30 • Value: $41

954.
Dubley
#510309 • 10"
Issued: 2003 • Current
Original: $12 • Value: $R/E

955.
Dufus Bear (old face)
#5112 • 16" • JB
Issued: 1989 • Retired: 1990
Original: $27 • Value: $95
Black nose value $75.

956.
Dufus Bear (new face)
#5112 • 16" • JB
Issued: 1990 • Retired: 1997
Original: $27 • Value: $54

957.
Dugan B. Beansley [QVC]
#93446V (C22623) • 14"
Issued: 2003 • Retired: 2003
Original: $18 • Value: $21

958.
Duncan [SLE]
#unknown • 6"
Issued: 1997 • Retired: 1997
Original: $8 • Value: $19

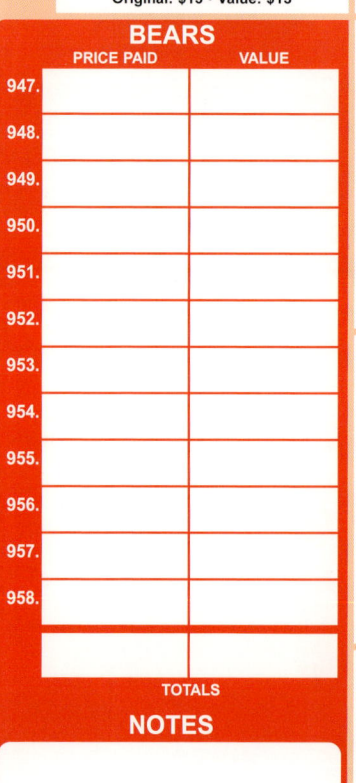

BEARS	PRICE PAID	VALUE
947.		
948.		
949.		
950.		
951.		
952.		
953.		
954.		
955.		
956.		
957.		
958.		
TOTALS		

NOTES

959.

Dunkin'
#917381 • 10" • ME
Issued: 2002 • Retired: 2002
Original: $20 • Value: $20

960.

Dunston J. Bearsford
#57251-07 • 6" • AS
Issued: 1999 • Retired: 2002
Original: $8 • Value: $12

961.

Dustin D. Bearican
#904251 • 16" • AS
Issued: 2004 • Current
Original: $23 • Value: $R/E

962.

Dutch P. Beansford
#510301-08 • 10" • JB
Issued: 2000 • Retired: 2001
Original: $10 • Value: $18

963.

Dwight D. Bearington
#590081-03 • 6" • MB
Issued: 2000 • Retired: 2000
Original: $14 • Value: $24

964.

Dylan T. Beansford
#510402-11 • 16" • JB
Issued: 2002 • Retired: 2002
Original: $23 • Value: $31

965.

Eastwick Bearington
#590101 • 4½" • MB
Issued: 1999 • Retired: 2002
Original: $11 • Value: $21

966.

Ebenezer S. JodiBear
#92000-09 • 9" • AR
Issued: 2000 • Retired: 2000
Original: $20 • Value: $29

967.

**Eddie Bauer Diamond
[Eddie Bauer]**
#(N78 678 6994) • 17"
Issued: 1997 • Retired: 1997
Original: $45 • Value: $75

968.

Eddie Bauer Hunter [Eddie Bauer]
#unknown • 17"
Issued: 1996 • Retired: 1996
Original: $50 • Value: $78

969.

**Eddie Beanberger (red striped
sweater with star)**
#9119 • 10" • TJ
Issued: 1995 • Retired: 1999
Original: $27 • Value: $39
Originally Eddie Beanbauer.

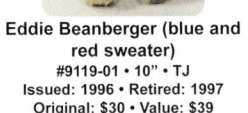

970.

**Eddie Beanberger (blue and
red sweater)**
#9119-01 • 10" • TJ
Issued: 1996 • Retired: 1997
Original: $30 • Value: $39

BEARS		
	PRICE PAID	VALUE
959.		
960.		
961.		
962.		
963.		
964.		
965.		
966.		
967.		
968.		
969.		
970.		
	TOTALS	

NOTES

Bears

971.
Eden (old face)
#5708 • 5½" • AS
Issued: 1991 • Retired: 1993
Original: $7 • Value: $40

972.
Eden (new face)
#5708 • 6" • AS
Issued: 1993 • Retired: 1996
Original: $13 • Value: $30

973.
Eden (red sweater)
#9139 • 6" • TJ
Issued: 1994 • Retired: 1996
Original: $13 • Value: $35

974.
Eden II
#91391 • 6" • TJ
Issued: 1996 • Retired: 1997
Original: $9 • Value: $31

975.
Edgar Eggplant
#904244 • 5½" • TJ
Issued: 2004 • Current
Original: $10 • Value: $R/E

976.
Edith & James Henry Maybeary [QVC]
#(C76785) • 10"
Issued: 2000 • Retired: 2000
Original: $31 • Value: $50

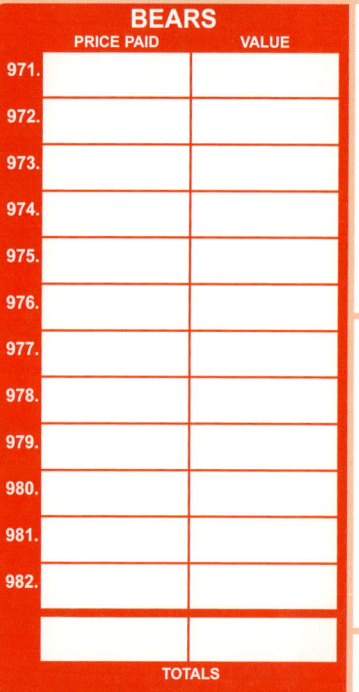

BEARS	PRICE PAID	VALUE
971.		
972.		
973.		
974.		
975.		
976.		
977.		
978.		
979.		
980.		
981.		
982.		
TOTALS		

NOTES

977.
Edith Glorybear
#904196 • 6" • TJ
Issued: 2003 • Current
Original: $10 • Value: $R/E

978. 🐾 37
Edmund (Fall 1993)
#9175 • 8" • BF
Issued: 1993 • Retired: 1993
Original: $22 • Value: $235

979. 🐾 39
Edmund [Eddie Bauer]
#unknown • 8" • BF
Issued: 1994 • Retired: 1994
Original: $25 • Value: $160

980. 🐾 38
Edmund (Spring 1994 - black)
#9175-01 • 8" • BF
Issued: 1994 • Retired: 1994
Original: $26 • Value: $110

981. 🐾 38
Edmund (Spring 1994 - navy)
#9175-01 • 8" • BF
Issued: 1994 • Retired: 1994
Original: $26 • Value: $140
Known as "Confused Edmund".

982.
Edmund (Fall 1994)
#9175-02 • 8" • BF
Issued: 1994 • Retired: 1994
Original: $24 • Value: $125

Bears

983.
Edmund (Spring 1995)
#9175-03 • 8" • BF
Issued: 1995 • Retired: 1995
Original: $24 • Value: $52

984.
Edmund (Fall 1995)
#9175-04 • 8" • BF
Issued: 1995 • Retired: 1995
Original: $24 • Value: $52

985.
Edmund (Spring 1996)
#9175-05 • 8" • BF
Issued: 1996 • Retired: 1996
Original: $26 • Value: $42

986.
Edmund (Fall 1996)
#9175-06 • 8" • BF
Issued: 1996 • Retired: 1996
Original: $24 • Value: $40

987.
Edmund (Spring 1997)
#9175-07 • 8" • BF
Issued: 1997 • Retired: 1997
Original: $24 • Value: $39

988.
Edmund (Spring 1997- big heart)
#9175-07 • 8" • BF
Issued: 1997 • Retired: 1997
Original: $24 • Value: $50

989.
Edmund (Fall 1997)
#9175-08 • 8" • BF
Issued: 1997 • Retired: 1997
Original: $24 • Value: $31

990.
Edmund (Spring 1998)
#9175-09 • 8" • BF
Issued: 1998 • Retired: 1998
Original: $26 • Value: $37

991.
Edmund (Fall 1998)
#9175-10 • 8" • BF
Issued: 1998 • Retired: 1998
Original: $27 • Value: $32

992.
Edmund (Spring 1999)
#9175-11 • 8" • BF
Issued: 1999 • Retired: 1999
Original: $26 • Value: $35

993.
Edmund (Fall 1999)
#9175-12 • 8" • BF
Issued: 1999 • Retired: 1999
Original: $22 • Value: $29

994.
Edmund (Spring 2000)
#9175-14 • 8" • BF
Issued: 2000 • Retired: 2000
Original: $22 • Value: $26

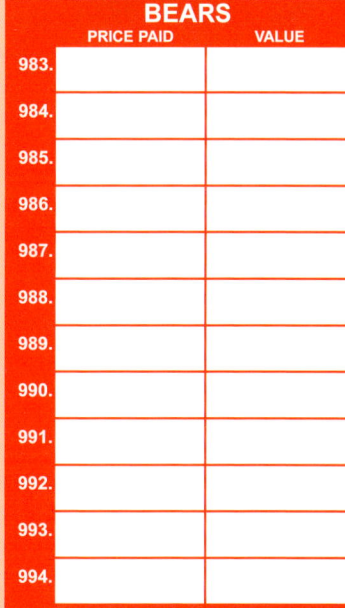

BEARS	PRICE PAID	VALUE
983.		
984.		
985.		
986.		
987.		
988.		
989.		
990.		
991.		
992.		
993.		
994.		
TOTALS		

NOTES

Bears

Edmund (Fall 2000)
#9175-15 • 8" • BF
Issued: 2000 • Retired: 2000
Original: $22 • Value: $26
995.

Edmund (Spring 2001)
#9175-16 • 8" • BF
Issued: 2001 • Retired: 2001
Original: $21 • Value: $25
996.

Edmund (Fall 2001)
#9175-17 • 8" • BF
Issued: 2001 • Retired: 2001
Original: $17 • Value: $20
997.

Edmund (Spring 2002)
#9175-18 • 8" • BF
Issued: 2002 • Retired: 2002
Original: $18 • Value: $18
998.

Edmund (Fall 2002)
#9175-19 • 8" • BF
Issued: 2002 • Retired: 2002
Original: $18 • Value: $18
999.

Edmund (Spring 2003)
#9175-20 • 8" • BF
LE • Issued: 2003 • Retired: 2003
Original: $19 • Value: $19
1000.

BEARS

	PRICE PAID	VALUE
995.		
996.		
997.		
998.		
999.		
1000.		
1001.		
1002.		
1003.		
1004.		
1005.		
1006.		
	TOTALS	

NOTES

Edmund (Fall 2003)
#9175-21 • 8" • BF
Issued: 2003 • Retired: 2003
Original: $18 • Value: $18
1001.

Edmund (Spring 2004)
#9175-22 • 8" • BF
Issued: 2004 • Retired: 2004
Original: $18 • Value: $18
1002.

Edmund (Fall 2004)
#9175-23 • 8" • BF
Issued: 2004 • Retired: 2004
Original: $15 • Value: $15
1003.

Edward & Binkie LE Set [QVC]
#unknown • 10"
LE of 4200 • Issued: 2001 • Retired: 2001
Original: $58 • Value: $75
1004.

Edward Q. Bearston & Apopka [GCC]
#94874GCC • 16"
Issued: 1999 • Retired: 1999
Original: $35 • Value: $56
1005.

Edwin R. Elfstein [Lord & Taylor]
#unknown • 10"
Issued: 1996 • Retired: 1996
Original: $21 • Value: $35
1006.

Bears

1007.
Effie May [Bon Ton]
#unknown • 12"
Issued: 1998 • Retired: 1998
Original: $N/E • Value: $41

1008.
Egbert Q. Bearsford
#81510 • 10" • TJ
Issued: 2001 • Retired: 2001
Original: $20 • Value: $24

1009.
Einstein Q. Scaredybear
#917368 • 10" • TJ
Issued: 2000 • Retired: 2000
Original: $24 • Value: $27

1010.
Elder with Newton [EVENT]
#50011 • 8" • TJ
Issued: 2004 • Current
Original: $11 • Value: $R/E

1011.
Eldora
#91615 • 14" • TJ
Issued: 1996 • Retired: 1998
Original: $31 • Value: $44

Have You Seen Me?

1012.
Eleanor Bear
#6102 • 14" • TJ
Issued: 1990 • Retired: 1990
Original: $70 • Value: $509
Early dressed.

1013.
Eleanore Bearsvelt
#912010 • 16" • TJ
Issued: 2000 • Retired: 2002
Original: $51 • Value: $80

1014.
Elfwood Bearington
#590100 • 4½" • MB
Issued: 1999 • Retired: 2000
Original: $11 • Value: $18

1015.
Elgin (elf bear)
#9129 • 6½" • TJ
Issued: 1994 • Retired: 1997
Original: $12 • Value: $31

1016.
Elijah Bearringer
#912073 • 14" • TJ
Issued: 2000 • Retired: 2002
Original: $27 • Value: $30

1017.
Elise Frostbeary [QVC]
#93425V (C21218) • 10"
Issued: 2003 • Retired: 2003
Original: $21 • Value: $25

1018.
Elisia P. Bearypoppin with Ross & Darrell [QVC]
#(C45646) • 17"
LE of 2400 • Issued: 1997 • Retired: 1997
Original: $94 • Value: $151

BEARS	PRICE PAID	VALUE
1007.		
1008.		
1009.		
1010.		
1011.		
1012.		
1013.		
1014.		
1015.		
1016.		
1017.		
1018.		
TOTALS		

NOTES

Bears

1019.
Ella [Dillards]
#94724DL • 8"
Issued: 1997 • Retired: 1997
Original: $18 • Value: $36

1020.
Elliot (old face)
#5108 • 14" • JB
Issued: 1989 • Retired: 1990
Original: $20 • Value: $97

1021.
Elliot (new face)
#5108 • 14" • JB
Issued: 1991 • Retired: 1998
Original: $20 • Value: $39

1022.
Elliot [Harry & David]
#unknown • 14" • JB
Issued: 1996 • Retired: 1996
Original: $30 • Value: $50

1023.
Ellsworth [Little Debbie]
#94491LD • 10"
Issued: 2002 • Retired: 2002
Original: $12 • Value: $23

1024.
Elly Mae
#5850-10 • 9" • BB
Issued: 1994 • Retired: 1997
Original: $13 • Value: $50

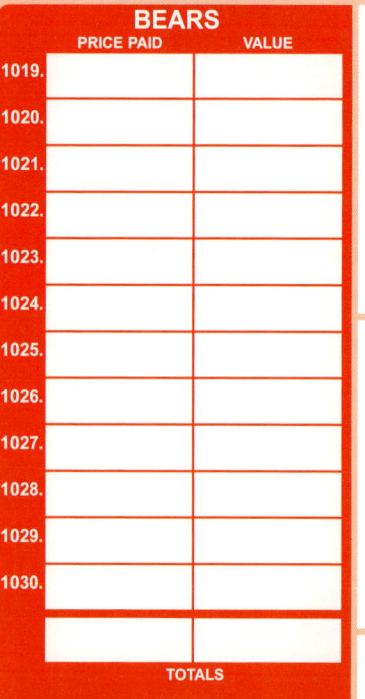

BEARS		
	PRICE PAID	VALUE
1019.		
1020.		
1021.		
1022.		
1023.		
1024.		
1025.		
1026.		
1027.		
1028.		
1029.		
1030.		
	TOTALS	

NOTES

1025.
Elmer O. Bearroad
#911531 • 12" • TJ
Issued: 2000 • Retired: 2001
Original: $24 • Value: $29

1026.
Elmo Q. Elfbeary LE Set [QVC]
#unknown • 10"
LE of 4000 • Issued: 2001 • Retired: 2001
Original: $40 • Value: $65
Sold with rocking horse.

1027.
Elmore Elf Bear [QVC]
#unknown • 10"
Issued: 1996 • Retired: 1996
Original: $21 • Value: $32
Same as Elton Elfberg and Edwin R.
Elfstein [Lord & Taylor].

1028.
Elmore Flatski
#5680-08 • 8" • FL
Issued: 1995 • Retired: 1997
Original: $13 • Value: $36

1029.
Eloise Willoughby
#918402 • 6" • TJ
Issued: 1999 • Retired: 2000
Original: $12 • Value: $14

1030.
Elsbeth [Dillards]
#94704DL • 10"
Issued: 1996 • Retired: 1996
Original: $16 • Value: $46

Bears

1031.
Elsworth
#1107-05 • 12" • CC
Issued: 1997 • Retired: 1999
Original: $12 • Value: $23

1032.
Elton [QVC]
#(C18404) • 12"
Issued: 1996 • Retired: 1996
Original: $35 • Value: $64

1033.
Elton Elfberg
#917306 • 10" • TJ
Issued: 1997 • Retired: 1998
Original: $21 • Value: $32

1034.
Elvin Q. Elfberg
#917301 • 10" • TJ
Issued: 1997 • Retired: 1999
Original: $25 • Value: $30

1035.
Emily Claire [Welcome Home]
#unknown • 12"
Issued: 1998 • Retired: 1998
Original: $N/E • Value: $51

1036.
Emily Daisydew [Kirlins]
#94535KR • 10"
Issued: 2003 • Retired: 2003
Original: $25 • Value: $35

1037.
Emily E. Dobbsey
[Coach House Gifts]
#unknown • 10"
Issued: 1999 • Retired: 1999
Original: $16 • Value: $45

1038.
Emily Starbright [Hello Shops]
#94185HL • 8"
Issued: 2003 • Retired: 2003
Original: $15 • Value: $30

1039.
Emma
#9101 • 14" • TJ
Issued: 1995 • Retired: 1997
Original: $27 • Value: $59

1040.
Emma [Frederick Atkins]
#unknown • 10"
Issued: 1998 • Retired: 1998
Original: $N/E • Value: $64

1041.
Emma Jane Mintly [Kirlins]
#94537KR • 10"
Issued: 2003 • Retired: 2003
Original: $29 • Value: $35

1042.
Emma Jean Bearsworth & Lil'
Pusskins [QVC]
#93468V (C3084) • 16"
Issued: 2003 • Retired: 2003
Original: $55 • Value: $66

BEARS	PRICE PAID	VALUE
1031.		
1032.		
1033.		
1034.		
1035.		
1036.		
1037.		
1038.		
1039.		
1040.		
1041.		
1042.		
TOTALS		

NOTES

Bears

1043.
Emma M. Sweetstuff [Hallmark]
#9698HM • 8"
Issued: 2003 • Retired: 2003
Original: $16 • Value: $19

1044.
Emmet Elfberg
#917305 • 10" • TJ
Issued: 1993 • Retired: 1999
Original: $21 • Value: $27

1045.
Emmie Bramblebeary
#912628 • 14" • TJ
Issued: 2000 • Retired: 2000
Original: $32 • Value: $45

1046.
Emmie Bramblebeary [SFMB]
#912628SF • 14"
Issued: 2002 • Retired: 2002
Original: $42 • Value: $55
♪ Für Elise ♪

1047.
Emmy Lou
#91001 • 10" • TJ
Issued: 1996 • Retired: 1999
Original: $24 • Value: $33

1048.
Endora Spellbound
#81004 • 10" • TJ
Issued: 2000 • Retired: 2000
Original: $20 • Value: $45

1049.
Engelbert Q. Elfberg [GCC]
#94857GCC • 10"
Issued: 1998 • Retired: 1998
Original: $N/E • Value: $34

1050.
Eric Burrbruin
#904023 • 10" • TJ
Issued: 2002 • Retired: 2004
Original: $18 • Value: $18

1051.
Erica Cherrybeary
#904091 • 13"
Issued: 2003 • Current
Original: $28 • Value: $R/E

1052.
Erin [Lord & Taylor]
#unknown • 7"
Issued: 1997 • Retired: 1997
Original: $15 • Value: $28

1053.
Erin K. Bear
#91562 • 7" • TJ
Issued: 1996 • Retired: 1999
Original: $11 • Value: $27

1054.
Erin Plumbeary
#913970 • 6" • TJ
Issued: 2001 • Retired: 2001
Original: $13 • Value: $21

BEARS	PRICE PAID	VALUE
1043.		
1044.		
1045.		
1046.		
1047.		
1048.		
1049.		
1050.		
1051.		
1052.		
1053.		
1054.		
TOTALS		

NOTES

Bears

1055.
Ernie Elfbeary
#918358 • 8" • TJ
Issued: 2001 • Retired: 2002
Original: $12 • Value: $18

1056.
Ervin Autumnfest
#904151 • 14" • TJ
Issued: 2003 • Current
Original: $33 • Value: $R/E

1057.
Esmeralda
#904200 • 10" • TJ
Issued: 2003 • Current
Original: $23 • Value: $R/E

1058.
Essex
#5701-10 • 12" • AS
Issued: 1994 • Retired: 1996
Original: $20 • Value: $38

1059.
Ethan
#917322 • 9" • TJ
Issued: 1998 • Retired: 1999
Original: $21 • Value: $42

1060.
Ethan B. Boyds [Macy's East]
#94165MA • 12"
Issued: 2002 • Retired: 2002
Original: $12 • Value: $26

1061.
Ethel B. Bruin
#912051 • 12" • TJ
Issued: 1997 • Retired: 1998
Original: $25 • Value: $44

1062.
Eubie Lovedalot [QVC]
#(C107573) • 8"
Issued: 2002 • Retired: 2002
Original: $12 • Value: $17

BEARS		
	PRICE PAID	VALUE
1055.		
1056.		
1057.		
1058.		
1059.		
1060.		
1061.		
1062.		
1063.		
1064.		
1065.		
1066.		
TOTALS		

NOTES

1063.
Eudemia Q. Quignapple
#91006 • 9" • TJ
Issued: 1997 • Retired: 1999
Original: $16 • Value: $27

1064.
Eugenia
#9120 • 16" • TJ
Issued: 1994 • Retired: 1996
Original: $45 • Value: $82

1065.
Eugenia (apple seller)
#9120-01 • 16" • AS
Issued: 1994 • Retired: 1995
Original: $50 • Value: $160
TOBY Award Winner

1066.
Eugenia [Dillards]
#9120DL • 16" • TJ
Issued: 1997 • Retired: 1997
Original: $35 • Value: $90

Bears

1067.
Eugenia II [SFMB]
#41-66848 • 16"
Issued: 1995 • Retired: 1995
Original: $50 • Value: $85
♪ Can't Help Falling in Love ♪

1068.
Eunice P. Snowbeary
#9137-01 • 9" • TJ
Issued: 1997 • Retired: 1999
Original: $20 • Value: $30

1069.
Evan & Sheldon Bearchild [QVC]
#unknown • 5½"
Issued: 1998 • Retired: 1998
Original: $15 • Value: $25

1070.
Evelyn
#91614 • 10" • TJ
Issued: 1997 • Retired: 1998
Original: $24 • Value: $50

1071.
Everest
#5844-05 • 8½" • AS
Issued: 1996 • Retired: 1999
Original: $17 • Value: $28

1072.
Ewell
#9127 • 8" • TJ
Issued: 1994 • Retired: 1999
Original: $15 • Value: $32

1073.
Ewell Manitoba Mooselman [CAN]
#BC94275 • 11"
LE of 2400 • Issued: 1997 • Retired: 1997
Original: $32 • Value: $65

1074.
F.E.B.B. (First Ever Bean Bear)
#510001-08 • 10" • JB
LE • Issued: 2001 • Retired: 2002
Original: $13 • Value: $16

1075.
Fairbanks
#58070-10 • 6" • AS
Issued: 2000 • Retired: 2000
Original: $7 • Value: $14

1076.
Faith [Longaberger]
#94647LB • 9"
Issued: 2002 • Retired: 2002
Original: $16 • Value: $31

1077.
Faith 'N Dreams [Hallmark]
#9692HM • 8"
Issued: 2002 • Retired: 2002
Original: $16 • Value: $22

1078.
Fargo Grizwold
#571540 • 16" • AS
Issued: 2002 • Retired: 2002
Original: $25 • Value: $35

BEARS

	PRICE PAID	VALUE
1067.		
1068.		
1069.		
1070.		
1071.		
1072.		
1073.		
1074.		
1075.		
1076.		
1077.		
1078.		
TOTALS		

NOTES

1079. Father Christmas
#9200B • 14"
LE of 250 • Issued: 1992 • Retired: 1992
Original: $70 • Value: $350

1080. Father Christmas
#9200B • 14"
LE of 200 • Issued: 1992 • Retired: 1992
Original: $70 • Value: $383

1081. Father Chrisbear
#9200B • 14"
LE of 750 • Issued: 1994 • Retired: 1994
Original: $70 • Value: $268

1082. Father Kristmas
#917310-01 • 16" • TJ
Issued: 2000 • Retired: 2002
Original: $30 • Value: $52

1083. Father Kristmas Bear & Northwind P. Bear [QVC]
#(C95186) • 16"
Issued: 2000 • Retired: 2000
Original: $43 • Value: $65

1084. Fawn W. Fallsbeary [Show Specials]
#919806 • 10"
Issued: 2000 • Retired: 2000
Original: $16 • Value: $29

1085. Fawn Woodsbeary
#913967 • 6" • TJ
Issued: 2001 • Retired: 2001
Original: $10 • Value: $16

1086. Faye & Jennifer [Carlton Cards]
#229742CC • 10"
Issued: 2004 • Retired: 2004
Original: $14 • Value: $15

BEARS	PRICE PAID	VALUE
1079.		
1080.		
1081.		
1082.		
1083.		
1084.		
1085.		
1086.		
1087.		
1088.		
1089.		
1090.		
TOTALS		

NOTES

1087. Federico
#1100-08 • 11" • CC
Issued: 1993 • Retired: 1997
Original: $10 • Value: $29

1088. Federico (with sweater)
#98039 • 11" • TJ
Issued: 1996 • Retired: 1997
Original: $21 • Value: $43

1089. Felicity [Lord & Taylor]
#unknown • 5½"
Issued: 1997 • Retired: 1997
Original: $16 • Value: $31

1090. Felicity Merrybeary [QVC]
#(C98197) • 10"
Issued: 2001 • Retired: 2001
Original: $22 • Value: $36

Bears

1091.
Felicity N. Hugs
#510301-01 • 10" • JB
Issued: 2000 • Retired: 2002
Original: $11 • Value: $13

1092.
Felicity S. Elfberg
#917300 • 5½" • TJ
Issued: 1997 • Retired: 1998
Original: $13 • Value: $25

1093.
Ferguson Q. Fuzzface [QVC]
#(C80533) • 18"
Issued: 2000 • Retired: 2000
Original: $35 • Value: $60

1094.
Fern Woodsbeary, the Woodland Guardian with Resin [QVC]
#99792V (C83810) • 13"
LE • Issued: 2001 • Retired: 2001
Original: $85 • Value: $120

1095.
Fetchen P. Patch
#81005 • 12" • TJ
Issued: 2000 • Retired: 2000
Original: $20 • Value: $27

1096.
Fidelity B. Morgan IV
#5110-05 • 17" • JB
Issued: 1997 • Retired: 1999
Original: $29 • Value: $37

1097.
Fidelity B. Morgan IV [SFMB]
#41-72638 • 17" • JB
Issued: 1998 • Retired: 1998
Original: $35 • Value: $54
♪ Love Will Keep Us Together ♪

1098.
Fifi Farklefrost
#91361 • 9" • TJ
Issued: 2000 • Retired: 2000
Original: $15 • Value: $19

1099.
Fillmore [QVC]
#900200 • 16" • MB
LE • Issued: 1998 • Retired: 1998
Original: $101 • Value: $186

1100.
Fiona Fitzbruin
#91203 • 14" • TJ
Issued: 1997 • Retired: 1998
Original: $26 • Value: $40

1101.
Fitz Farklefrost
#91360 • 6" • TJ
Issued: 2000 • Retired: 2000
Original: $10 • Value: $12

1102.
Fitzgerald D. Bearington
#590040-03 • 12" • MB
Issued: 1997 • Retired: 1997
Original: $48 • Value: $70

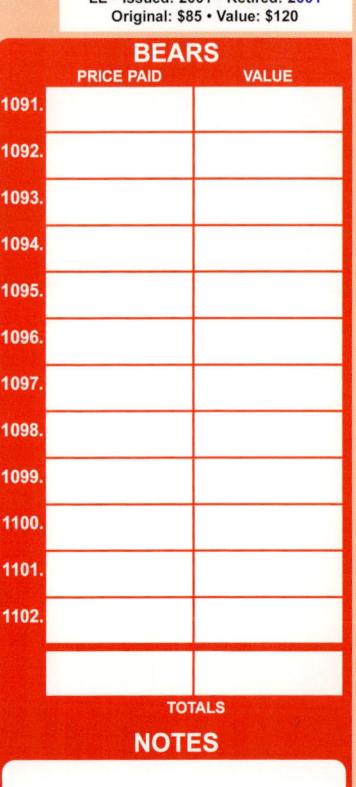

BEARS	PRICE PAID	VALUE
1091.		
1092.		
1093.		
1094.		
1095.		
1096.		
1097.		
1098.		
1099.		
1100.		
1101.		
1102.		
TOTALS		

NOTES

Bears

1103.
Fitzgerald O'Bruin
#91802 • 6" • TJ
Issued: 1995 • Retired: 1997
Original: $12 • Value: $32

1104.
Fitzroy
#5795 • 7½" • AS
Issued: 1992 • Retired: 1992
Original: $16 • Value: $85
Variation: royal blue sweater $72.

1105.
Flakey Bearifrost
#917380 • 10" • TJ
Issued: 2001 • Retired: 2002
Original: $20 • Value: $24

1106.
Fleurette
#6103B • 12"
LE of 6 • Issued: 1991 • Retired: 1991
Original: $25 • Value: $700

1107.
Flitter B. Bugsley
#918702 • 8"
Issued: 2003 • Retired: 2003
Original: $17 • Value: $17

1108.
Flora B. Flutterby
#917720 • 10" • TJ
Issued: 2001 • Retired: 2001
Original: $15 • Value: $18

1109.
Flora B. Lilac
[Lock, Stock & Barrel]
#unknown • 6"
Issued: 2000 • Retired: 2000
Original: $10 • Value: $22

1110.
Flora Mae Goodbear
[Country Clutter]
#unknown • 10"
Issued: 2001 • Retired: 2001
Original: $20 • Value: $29

1111.
Flora Thanksabunch
#903026 • 8" • ME
Issued: 2002 • Retired: 2002
Original: $10 • Value: $10

1112.
Florence B. Bearhugs [QVC]
#(C95121) • 12"
Issued: 1999 • Retired: 1999
Original: $26 • Value: $45

1113.
Florence Nightenbear
#912660 • 12" • ME
Issued: 2001 • Retired: 2001
Original: $23 • Value: $28

1114.
Florimae Bearley [QVC]
#(C100433) • 10"
Issued: 2001 • Retired: 2001
Original: $18 • Value: $27

BEARS

	PRICE PAID	VALUE
1103.		
1104.		
1105.		
1106.		
1107.		
1108.		
1109.		
1110.		
1111.		
1112.		
1113.		
1114.		
TOTALS		

NOTES

Bears

1115. Floyd
#917321 • 9" • TJ
Issued: 1998 • Retired: 1999
Original: $21 • Value: $32

1116. Flurry B. Bundleup
#913931 • 8" • TJ
Issued: 2001 • Retired: 2002
Original: $12 • Value: $19

1117. Forrest B. Bearsley
#91744 • 10" • TJ
Issued: 1999 • Retired: 2002
Original: $16 • Value: $26

1118. Francesca [Bon Ton]
#unknown • 14"
Issued: 1998 • Retired: 1998
Original: $N/E • Value: $36

1119. Francesca LaFlame
#912026 • 16" • TJ
Issued: 2000 • Retired: 2000
Original: $50 • Value: $65

1120. Francine deBearvoire [QVC]
#93299V (C107571) • 8"
Issued: 2002 • Retired: 2002
Original: $16 • Value: $29

1121. Frankie Bearberg [SLE]
#unknown • 12"
Issued: 1998 • Retired: 1998
Original: $N/E • Value: $39

1122. Franklin
#1050-06 • 8"
Issued: 1994 • Retired: 1996
Original: $11 • Value: $53

1123. Franz Farklefrost
#904027 • 10" • TJ
Issued: 2002 • Retired: 2004
Original: $24 • Value: $24

1124. Franz von Bruin
#5010-06 • 6" • WB
Issued: 1994 • Retired: 1995
Original: $16 • Value: $55

1125. Frazier
#913972 • 6" • TJ
Issued: 2001 • Retired: 2002
Original: $12 • Value: $25

1126. Frazier [BBC]
#918073SM • 10"
Issued: 2003 • Current
Original: $20 • Value: $R/E

BEARS	PRICE PAID	VALUE
1115.		
1116.		
1117.		
1118.		
1119.		
1120.		
1121.		
1122.		
1123.		
1124.		
1125.		
1126.		
TOTALS		

NOTES

Bears

1127.
Freddy Beanberger
#944904 • 10" • TJ
Issued: 1998 • Retired: 1998
Original: $27 • Value: $40

1128.
Frederick T. Bearsworth
#510902 • 6"
Issued: 2003 • Current
Original: $7 • Value: $R/E

1129.
Fredrica [Frederick Atkins]
#unknown • 17"
Issued: 1997 • Retired: 1997
Original: $46 • Value: $65

1130.
Freezy T. Frostman
#913962 • 6" • TJ
Issued: 2000 • Retired: 2002
Original: $13 • Value: $13

1131.
Friendship Bear Pair [EVENT]
#50009 • 6"
Issued: 2003 • Retired: 2003
Original: $10 • Value: $10
Available 10/18 & 10/19.

1132.
Fritter Appleton
#904304 • 6" • TJ
Issued: 2004 • Current
Original: $11 • Value: $R/E

1133.
Fritzle Farklefrost
#904028 • 8" • TJ
Issued: 2002 • Retired: 2002
Original: $19 • Value: $19

1134.
Fritzle Farklefrost with Frostley [QVC]
#(C20986) • 8"
Issued: 2002 • Retired: 2002
Original: $32 • Value: $42

BEARS		
	PRICE PAID	VALUE
1127.		
1128.		
1129.		
1130.		
1131.		
1132.		
1133.		
1134.		
1135.		
1136.		
1137.		
1138.		
TOTALS		

NOTES

1135.
Frostina with Kristy [QVC]
#(C6015) • 8"
LE of 4500 • Issued: 2003 • Retired: 2003
Original: $46 • Value: $55
Frostbeary Festival. Sold with a wooden fence.

1136.
Furley Bearsdale
#510404 • 16"
Issued: 2003 • Current
Original: $23 • Value: $R/E

1137.
Fuzzy Grizbear
#510502 • 12" • AS
Issued: 2004 • Current
Original: $17 • Value: $R/E

1138.
G.B. Gingerpeeker (6")
#913983 • 6" • TJ
Issued: 2002 • Retired: 2002
Original: $10 • Value: $13
Variations pictured together.

120

Bears

1139.
G.P. Hugabunch
#903000 • 8¼" • ME
Issued: 2001 • Retired: 2002
Original: $10 • Value: $12

1140.
G.P. Hugabunch [SFMB]
#92624SF • 10"
Issued: 2002 • Retired: 2002
Original: $15 • Value: $21
♪ You Are My Sunshine ♪

1141.
G.W. Bearyproud [QVC]
#99871V (C107568) • 10"
Issued: 2002 • Retired: 2002
Original: $30 • Value: $45
With rooster pull-toy.

1142.
Gabriel
#5825 • 9" • CB
Issued: 1991 • Retired: 1997
Original: $14 • Value: $55

1143.
Gabriella [POG]
#94579POG • 6"
Issued: 1998 • Retired: 1998
Original: $N/E • Value: $26

1144.
Gabriella [Boscovs]
#unknown • 10"
Issued: 1999 • Retired: 1999
Original: $N/E • Value: $35

1145.
Gabriella Angelfaith [QVC]
#(C95153) • 12"
Issued: 2000 • Retired: 2000
Original: $28 • Value: $40

1146.
Gala Applesmith
#917441 • 10" • TJ
Issued: 2001 • Retired: 2002
Original: $22 • Value: $26

1147.
Gannon Bear [GCC]
#94883GCC • 16"
Issued: 2000 • Retired: 2000
Original: $32 • Value: $45

1148.
Gardener B . Buzzoff [QVC]
#(C55509) • 10"
Issued: 1999 • Retired: 1999
Original: $15 • Value: $21

1149.
Have You Seen Me?
Gardner
#6162B • TJ
Issued: 1991 • Retired: 1991
Original: $63 • Value: $401

1150.
Gareth with Glynnis [QVC]
#unknown • 8"
Issued: 1998 • Retired: 1998
Original: $27 • Value: $49

BEARS	PRICE PAID	VALUE
1139.		
1140.		
1141.		
1142.		
1143.		
1144.		
1145.		
1146.		
1147.		
1148.		
1149.		
1150.		
TOTALS		

NOTES

1151.
Garnet & Sapphire [QVC]
#unknown • 10"
Issued: 2000 • Retired: 2000
Original: $21 • Value: $40

1152.
Garret T. Woodsbeary [QVC]
#unknown • 12"
Issued: 2001 • Retired: 2001
Original: $39 • Value: $50

1153.
Gary B. Bean [QVC]
#(C78136) • 10½"
Issued: 2000 • Retired: 2000
Original: $11 • Value: $28

1154.
Gary M. Bearenthal
#912500 • 16" • TJ
Issued: 1999 • Retired: 2001
Original: $47 • Value: $56

1155.
Gatsby [Bon Ton]
#unknown • 12"
Issued: 1998 • Retired: 1998
Original: $N/E • Value: $62

1156.
General P.D.Q. Pattington
#92001-05 • 14½" • MB
Issued: 2000 • Retired: 2002
Original: $40 • Value: $50

1157.
Geneva (nutmeg)
#9162 • 8"
Issued: 1993 • Retired: 1994
Original: $18 • Value: $82

1158.
Geneva [SLE]
#unknown • 8"
LE of 1200 • Issued: 1996 • Retired: 1996
Original: $15 • Value: $46

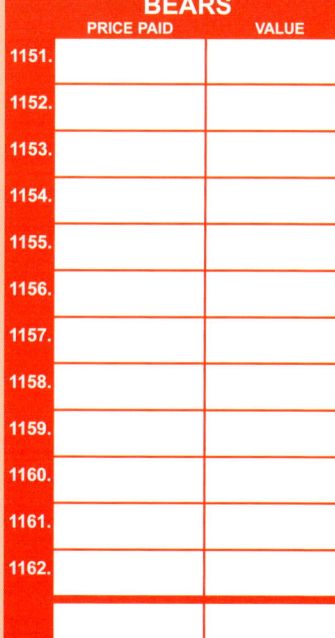

BEARS

	PRICE PAID	VALUE
1151.		
1152.		
1153.		
1154.		
1155.		
1156.		
1157.		
1158.		
1159.		
1160.		
1161.		
1162.		
	TOTALS	

NOTES

1159.
Genevieve Rose Frostbeary with
Blizz, Maddie, and Polaris [QVC]
#99950V (C21153) • 14"
LE of 40000 • Issued: 2003 • Retired: 2003
Original: $84 • Value: $101
Sold with matching Bearstone.

1160.
George [QVC]
#(C19471)
Issued: 1996 • Retired: 1996
Original: $N/E • Value: $45

1161.
George
#1100-03 • 11" • CC
Issued: 1996 • Retired: 1997
Original: $10 • Value: $32

1162.
George [May Company]
#unknown • 6"
Issued: 1998 • Retired: 1998
Original: $10 • Value: $21

Bears

1163.
George & Martha Jodibear [QVC]
#(C97875) • 5"
Issued: 2000 • Retired: 2000
Original: $23 • Value: $40

1164.
George & Thomas Bearington [QVC]
#(C99064) • 6" • MB
Issued: 2000 • Retired: 2000
Original: $27 • Value: $55

1165.
George Berriman [Show Specials]
#919803 • 10"
Issued: 2000 • Retired: 2000
Original: $19 • Value: $28

1166.
George W. Bearington [QVC]
#93279V (C39680) • 11" • MB
LE of 1500 • Issued: 2002 • Retired: 2002
Original: $35 • Value: $65

1167.
Georgie [POG]
#94583POG • 6"
Issued: 1999 • Retired: 1999
Original: $10 • Value: $25

1168.
Geraldine & Sylvester [QVC]
#(C47249) • 16"
Issued: 1998 • Retired: 1998
Original: $N/E • Value: $N/E

1169.
Geraldo
#912441 • 8" • TJ
Issued: 1996 • Retired: 1997
Original: $19 • Value: $34

1170.
Gerbie Daisydew
#904073 • 8"
Issued: 2003 • Current
Original: $14 • Value: $R/E

1171.
Gettie Mountberg [SLE]
#unknown • 6"
Issued: 1998 • Retired: 1998
Original: $10 • Value: $22

1172.
Gettysbear [BBC]
#918049SM • 30"
Issued: 2003 • Retired: 2003
Original: $57 • Value: $R/E
Chenille.

1173.
Ghoulia
#904345 • 6" • TJ
Issued: 2004 • Current
Original: $11 • Value: $R/E

1174.
Giddy-Up Ladybug
#904234 • 4½" • AS
Issued: 2004 • Current
Original: $10 • Value: $R/E

BEARS

	PRICE PAID	VALUE
1163.		
1164.		
1165.		
1166.		
1167.		
1168.		
1169.		
1170.		
1171.		
1172.		
1173.		
1174.		
TOTALS		

NOTES

Bears

1175.
Gideon [QVC]
#unknown • 10"
Issued: 1998 • Retired: 1998
Original: $N/E • Value: $24

1176.
Gimmie A. Hugster [QVC]
#(C107602) • 30"
Issued: 2002 • Retired: 2002
Original: $58 • Value: $75

1177.
Ginger McPunkin
#904325 • 6" • TJ
Issued: 2004 • Current
Original: $11 • Value: $R/E

1178.
Ginger Snap
#91523 • 8" • TJ
Issued: 2000 • Retired: 2000
Original: $15 • Value: $15

1179.
Ginnie Higgenthorpe
#918442 • 6" • TJ
Issued: 2000 • Retired: 2002
Original: $11 • Value: $13

1180.
Ginnie Witebred
#912074 • 14" • TJ
Issued: 2001 • Retired: 2002
Original: $30 • Value: $36

1181.
Girdwood & Juneau [QVC]
#(C80713) • 6½"
Issued: 2000 • Retired: 2000
Original: $14 • Value: $29

1182.
Glacier
#510817 • 14" • AS
Issued: 2004 • Current
Original: $22 • Value: $R/E

BEARS	PRICE PAID	VALUE
1175.		
1176.		
1177.		
1178.		
1179.		
1180.		
1181.		
1182.		
1183.		
1184.		
1185.		
1186.		
TOTALS		

NOTES

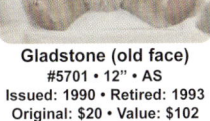

1183.
Gladstone (old face)
#5701 • 12" • AS
Issued: 1990 • Retired: 1993
Original: $20 • Value: $102

1184.
Gladstone (new face)
#5701 • 12" • AS
Issued: 1990 • Retired: 1993
Original: $N/E • Value: $74

1185.
Gladys Tidings [QVC]
#unknown • 8"
Issued: 2002 • Retired: 2002
Original: $12 • Value: $16

1186.
Glenda
#91891-04 • 12" • TJ
Issued: 1998 • Retired: 1999
Original: $21 • Value: $N/E

124

Bears

1187.
Glenda Z. Jodibear
#92000-17 • 6" • AR
Issued: 2001 • Retired: 2002
Original: $12 • Value: $14

1188.
Glenna [Dillards]
#94721DL • 17"
Issued: 1997 • Retired: 1997
Original: $N/E • Value: $55

1189.
Glimmer B. Snowflake
[Carson Pirie Scott]
#9300CP • TJ
Issued: 2002 • Retired: 2002
Original: $16 • Value: $24

1190.
Glinda the Good Witch
#904375 • 7" • TJ
Issued: 2004 • Current
Original: $16 • Value: $R/E

1191.
Gloria and Van [QVC]
#(C55538) • 14"
Issued: 1999 • Retired: 1999
Original: $36 • Value: $65

1192.
Gloria Bearsevelt
#912631 • 14" • TJ
Issued: 2001 • Retired: 2002
Original: $34 • Value: $65

1193.
Glory
#904194 • 6" • TJ
Issued: 2003 • Current
Original: $10 • Value: $R/E

1194.
Glory B. America [Country House]
#94390CH • 16"
Issued: 2002 • Retired: 2002
Original: $36 • Value: $45

1195.
Glory Steadsbeary [Longaberger]
#94646LB • 10"
Issued: 2002 • Retired: 2002
Original: $27 • Value: $53

1196.
Glory Steadsbeary (variation)
[Longaberger]
#94646LB • 10"
Issued: 2002 • Retired: 2002
Original: $27 • Value: $53

1197.
Glynnis
#918910-02 • 8" • TJ
Issued: 1998 • Retired: 1999
Original: $17 • Value: $24
Also with Gareth as QVC set.

1198.
Goldie McPunkin
#904322 • 10" • TJ
Issued: 2004 • Current
Original: $19 • Value: $R/E

BEARS

	PRICE PAID	VALUE
1187.		
1188.		
1189.		
1190.		
1191.		
1192.		
1193.		
1194.		
1195.		
1196.		
1197.		
1198.		

TOTALS

NOTES

1199.
Gomer P. Hugsley [QVC]
#93350V (C20909) • 30"
Issued: 2002 • Retired: 2002
Original: $58 • Value: $75

1200.
Gomer Q. Beanster
#510814 • 14"
Issued: 2003 • Current
Original: $15 • Value: $R/E

1201.
Gomez
#unknown • 10"
Issued: 1999 • Retired: 1999
Original: $18 • Value: $25

1202.
Goober Greenwood [QVC]
#(C02198) • 16"
Issued: 2004 • Retired: 2004
Original: $24 • Value: $32

1203.
Gorden B. Bean (original)
#5105 • 10" • JB
Issued: 1988 • Retired: 1989
Original: $14 • Value: $85

1204.
Gorden B. Bean (old face)
#5105 • 10" • JB
Issued: 1989 • Retired: 1990
Original: $14 • Value: $64

1205.
Gorden B. Bean (new face)
#5105 • 10" • JB
Issued: 1991 • Retired: 1998
Original: $14 • Value: $39

1206.
Gourdie Frightmare [SLE]
#unknown • 8"
Issued: 1999 • Retired: 1999
Original: $12 • Value: $21

1207.
Gourdon Punkinpeeker
#913982 • 6"
Issued: 2002 • Current
Original: $10 • Value: $R/E

1208.
GP Gold Bear [CAN]
#BC94280 • 10"
LE of 4380 • Issued: 1999 • Retired: 1999
Original: $22 • Value: $31

1209.
Grace
#91742 • 10" • TJ
Issued: 1991 • Retired: 1998
Original: $20 • Value: $33

1210.
Grace Bedlington
#912072 • 16" • TJ
Issued: 1999 • Retired: 2000
Original: $34 • Value: $41

BEARS	PRICE PAID	VALUE
1199.		
1200.		
1201.		
1202.		
1203.		
1204.		
1205.		
1206.		
1207.		
1208.		
1209.		
1210.		
TOTALS		

NOTES

Bears

1211.
Gracie [May Company]
#94153MC • 6"
Issued: 1998 • Retired: 1998
Original: $N/E • Value: $20

1212.
Gracie [Dillards]
#94739DL • 6"
Issued: 1999 • Retired: 1999
Original: $8 • Value: $26

1213.
Gracie Blossombeary [Longaberger]
#94628LB • 10"
Issued: 2003 • Retired: 2003
Original: $28 • Value: $34

1214.
Gracie C. Burrbruin [GCC]
#94925GCC • 10"
Issued: 2002 • Retired: 2002
Original: $24 • Value: $30

1215.
Graham Cocobeary
#904333 • 10" • TJ
Issued: 2004 • Current
Original: $19 • Value: $R/E

1216.
Gram
#5775 • 18" • HD
Issued: 1991 • Retired: 1991
Original: $39 • Value: $400

1217.
Grammy (heart pillow)
#903034 • 8"
Issued: 2003 • Current
Original: $10 • Value: $R/E

1218.
Grammy (square pillow)
#82535 • 8"
Issued: 2004 • Current
Original: $10 • Value: $R/E

1219.
Grammy Beariluv
#82516 • 8" • TJ
Issued: 2002 • Retired: 2002
Original: $11 • Value: $11

1220.
Grammy Quiltsbeary with Patches [Longaberger]
#94635LB • 10"
Issued: 2001 • Retired: 2001
Original: $38 • Value: $45

1221.
Gramps
#5770 • 18" • HD
Issued: 1991 • Retired: 1991
Original: $39 • Value: $420

1222.
Grandma Bearburg (taupe print)
#92038 • 14"
LE of 2500 • Issued: 1992 • Retired: 1992
Original: $70 • Value: $440

BEARS

	PRICE PAID	VALUE
1211.		
1212.		
1213.		
1214.		
1215.		
1216.		
1217.		
1218.		
1219.		
1220.		
1221.		
1222.		
	TOTALS	

NOTES

1223.

Grandma Bearburg
(burgundy print)
#92038 • 14"
LE of 2500 • Issued: 1992 • Retired: 1992
Original: $70 • Value: $440

1224.

Grandma Henrietta & Lizzie [QVC]
#(C45644) • 12"
LE of 1800 • Issued: 1997 • Retired: 1997
Original: $73 • Value: $124

1225.

Grandmother Beatrice B. Bearhugs,
Baileyanne Bearhugs & Tedley F.
Wuzzie [QVC]
#99718V (C66927) • 16"
LE of 37000 • Issued: 1999 • Retired: 1999
Original: $99 • Value: $130

1226.

Grannie Annie Wishkabibble
#90504 • 12" • TJ
Issued: 2001 • Retired: 2001
Original: $30 • Value: $36

1227.

Grannie Lovedalot [QVC]
#(C19893) • 8"
Issued: 2002 • Retired: 2002
Original: $12 • Value: $18

1228.

Granny Smith and Gala Bear
[QVC]
#(C40593) • 14"
LE of 2400 • Issued: 2001 • Retired: 2001
Original: $56 • Value: $95

1229.

Grant S. Bearington
[Norm Thompson]
#unknown • 10" • MB
Issued: 1997 • Retired: 1997
Original: $N/E • Value: $68

1230.

Gregory B. Elfbeary
#904051 • 10"
Issued: 2002 • Retired: 2002
Original: $20 • Value: $20

1231.

Gregory G. Bruin [QVC]
#(C100435) • 21"
Issued: 2001 • Retired: 2001
Original: $54 • Value: $75

1232.

Grenville
#5715 • 16" • AS
Issued: 1992 • Retired: 1999
Original: $32 • Value: $60

BEARS		
	PRICE PAID	VALUE
1223.		
1224.		
1225.		
1226.		
1227.		
1228.		
1229.		
1230.		
1231.		
1232.		
1233.		
1234.		
TOTALS		

NOTES

1233.

Gretchen Marie Pearsley
#904161 • 12" • TJ
Issued: 2003 • Current
Original: $30 • Value: $R/E

1234.

Griffin W. Bearsley
#572210-08 • 21" • AS
Issued: 2001 • Retired: 2002
Original: $53 • Value: $64

Bears

1235.
Grover
#91739 • 8" • TJ
Issued: 1997 • Retired: 1998
Original: $12 • Value: $22

1236.
Grovsnor S. Grizbear [QVC]
#(C97879) • 18"
Issued: 2000 • Retired: 2000
Original: $33 • Value: $50

1237.
Grumples Q. Beansley
#510401-10 • 16" • JB
Issued: 2002 • Retired: 2002
Original: $23 • Value: $31

1238.
Grumps
#5766 • 9" • HD
Issued: 1991 • Retired: 1994
Original: $14 • Value: $54

1239.
Guildford Q. Bearrister [QVC]
#(C76778) • 12"
Issued: 2000 • Retired: 2000
Original: $16 • Value: $25

1240.
Guilford [GCC]
#94852GCC • 6"
Issued: 1997 • Retired: 1997
Original: $15 • Value: $34

1241.
Guinella [Ideation]
#unknown • 11"
Issued: 1999 • Retired: 1999
Original: $19 • Value: $36

1242.
Guinevere
#91891-09 • 12" • TJ
Issued: 1996 • Retired: 1999
Original: $21 • Value: $31

1243.
Guinevere (with wings) [Lord & Taylor]
#unknown • 12"
Issued: 1996 • Retired: 1996
Original: $20 • Value: $40

1244.
Guinevere [SFMB]
#41-72139 • 12" • TJ
Issued: 1998 • Retired: 1998
Original: $25 • Value: $43
♫ La Vie En Rose ♫

1245.
Guinevieve [QVC]
#unknown • 12"
Issued: 1997 • Retired: 1997
Original: $20 • Value: $40

1246.
Gunnar [SLE]
#9123 • 8" • TJ
Issued: 1995 • Retired: 1995
Original: $24 • Value: $42

BEARS	PRICE PAID	VALUE
1235.		
1236.		
1237.		
1238.		
1239.		
1240.		
1241.		
1242.		
1243.		
1244.		
1245.		
1246.		
TOTALS		

NOTES

Bears

1247.
Gunter [Dillards]
#94722DL • 10"
Issued: 1997 • Retired: 1997
Original: $15 • Value: $32

1248.
Gunther Von Bruin
#5012 • 6" • WB
Issued: 1993 • Retired: 1994
Original: $13 • Value: $118

1249.
Gus Ghoulie
#919640 • 12" • TJ
Issued: 1999 • Retired: 1999
Original: $17 • Value: $50

1250.
Gustav von Bruin
#5011 • 10" • WB
Issued: 1993 • Retired: 1994
Original: $26 • Value: $57

1251.
Guthrie P. Mussy [QVC]
#(C39084) • 14"
Issued: 1997 • Retired: 1997
Original: $29 • Value: $55

1252.
Gwain
#91891-06 • 12" • TJ
Issued: 1997 • Retired: 1999
Original: $21 • Value: $23

1253.
Gwen Marie Bear
#912055 • 12" • TJ
Issued: 2000 • Retired: 2000
Original: $22 • Value: $22

1254.
Gwendina
#91891-12 • 11" • TJ
Issued: 1999 • Retired: 1999
Original: $21 • Value: $27

BEARS		
	PRICE PAID	VALUE
1247.		
1248.		
1249.		
1250.		
1251.		
1252.		
1253.		
1254.		
1255.		
1256.		
1257.		
1258.		
TOTALS		

NOTES

1255.
Gwendolyn
#91891-02 • 12" • TJ
Issued: 1997 • Retired: 1999
Original: $21 • Value: $25

1256.
Gwennora [QVC]
#(C57636) • 11"
Issued: 1999 • Retired: 1999
Original: $18 • Value: $31

1257.
Gwinton
#918910-06 • 8" • TJ
Issued: 1998 • Retired: 1999
Original: $17 • Value: $30

1258.
Gwynda
#918910-09 • 8" • TJ
Issued: 1998 • Retired: 1999
Original: $17 • Value: $27

Bears

1259.
H.B. Bearwish
#903003 • 8" • ME
Issued: 2001 • Retired: 2001
Original: $10 • Value: $12

1260.
H.B. Bearwish [SFMB]
#94263SF • 10"
Issued: 2001 • Retired: 2001
Original: $25 • Value: $35
♪ Happy Birthday ♪

1261.
H.C. Beezley
#904117 • 6"
Issued: 2003 • Current
Original: $10 • Value: $R/E

1262.
Hadley Flatski
#5680-05 • 8" • FL
Issued: 1994 • Retired: 1997
Original: $12 • Value: $23

1263.
Haley Angelfrost
#917379 • 10" • TJ
Issued: 2001 • Retired: 2001
Original: $15 • Value: $24

1264.
Hampton T. Bearington
#590052-08 • 10" • MB
Issued: 2000 • Retired: 2000
Original: $35 • Value: $60

1265.
Hancock
#1050-11 • 8"
Issued: 1995 • Retired: 1996
Original: $11 • Value: $41

1266.
Hannah [Elder Beerman]
#8242437EB • 8"
Issued: 1999 • Retired: 1999
Original: $24 • Value: $35

1267.
Hannah B. Punkinbeary [Kirlins]
#94533KR • 10"
LE of 3600 • Issued: 2002 • Retired: 2002
Original: $24 • Value: $41

1268.
Hannah H. Woodsbeary [Carlton Cards]
#919839CA • 10"
Issued: 2001 • Retired: 2001
Original: $24 • Value: $30

1269.
Hannah, Henry & Herbie [QVC]
#(C99313) • 6"
Issued: 2001 • Retired: 2001
Original: $20 • Value: $28

1270.
Hannah, Ursula, Greta, & Sarabeth [QVC]
#99334V (C98053) • 14"
LE • Issued: 2000 • Retired: 2000
Original: $75 • Value: $100

BEARS

	PRICE PAID	VALUE
1259.		
1260.		
1261.		
1262.		
1263.		
1264.		
1265.		
1266.		
1267.		
1268.		
1269.		
1270.		
TOTALS		

NOTES

1271.

Hans Q. Berriman
#91392 • 6" • TJ
Issued: 1997 • Retired: 1999
Original: $13 • Value: $N/E

1272.
Harding
#1051-06 • 8"
Issued: 1996 • Retired: 1998
Original: $11 • Value: $32

1273.

Harding G. Bearington
#590051-01 • 10" • MB
Issued: 1999 • Retired: 1999
Original: $28 • Value: $46

1274.

Harlan
#500081 • 30" • AS
Issued: 2004 • Current
Original: $57 • Value: $R/E

1275.

Harrison
#9176 • 10" • TJ
Issued: 1993 • Retired: 1997
Original: $20 • Value: $38

1276.

Harry Harvest [Hershey]
#95203HE • 6"
LE of 3600 • Issued: 2003 • Retired: 2003
Original: $8 • Value: $10
Free with $60.00 purchase.

1277.

Harry S. Pattington
#92001-01 • 16" • MB
Issued: 1999 • Retired: 1999
Original: $43 • Value: $65

1278.

Hartley [Lord & Taylor]
#unknown • 8"
Issued: 1996 • Retired: 1996
Original: $22 • Value: $48

1279.

Hartley B. Mine
#91521 • 8½" • TJ
Issued: 1999 • Retired: 2000
Original: $14 • Value: $22

1280.
Hastings P. Bearsford
#57250-11 • 6" • AS
Issued: 2000 • Retired: 2002
Original: $7 • Value: $5

1281.

Hattie & Annie
#9210 • 16"
Issued: 1993 • Retired: 1993
Original: $100 • Value: $320

1282.

Hawley Flatski
#56801-03 • 8" • FL
Issued: 1998 • Retired: 1999
Original: $13 • Value: $17

BEARS	PRICE PAID	VALUE
1271.		
1272.		
1273.		
1274.		
1275.		
1276.		
1277.		
1278.		
1279.		
1280.		
1281.		
1282.		
TOTALS		

NOTES

Bears

1283.
Hayden T. Bearsford
#57250-10 • 6" • AS
Issued: 2000 • Retired: 2002
Original: $7 • Value: $8

1284.
Hayes R Bearrington [SFMB]
#41-72766 • 15" • MB
LE of 2000 • Issued: 1999 • Retired: 1999
Original: $125 • Value: $188
♪ What A Feeling ♪
1st musical mohair.

1285.
Hayley and Austin with Stretch
#919828 • 10" • TJ
Issued: 2004 • Current
Original: $55 • Value: $R/E

1286.
Hazel
#1000-03 • 8" • CC
Issued: 1993 • Retired: 1996
Original: $6 • Value: $36

1287.
Hazel Q. Punkinbeary
#904012 • 12" • TJ
Issued: 2002 • Retired: 2002
Original: $30 • Value: $30

1288.
Hazelnut B. Bean
#500100-05 • 8¼" • JB
Issued: 2000 • Retired: 2001
Original: $9 • Value: $11

1289.
Heath
#5703 • 10" • AS
Issued: 1990 • Retired: 1992
Original: $18 • Value: $72

1290.
Heath II
#5703N • 10" • AS
Issued: 1992 • Retired: 1997
Original: $18 • Value: $30

1291.
Heathcliff [QVC]
#(C36214) • 8"
Issued: 1997 • Retired: 1997
Original: $16 • Value: $32

1292.
Heather and Heathcliffe Plumbeary
[Welcome Home]
#94536WH • 8"
LE of 4800 • Issued: 2001 • Retired: 2001
Original: $20 • Value: $35

1293.
Heather Goodbear [Country Clutter]
#unknown
Issued: 2004 • Retired: 2004
Original: $N/E • Value: $N/E

1294.
Heather Steadsbeary
[Longaberger]
#94632LB • 10"
Issued: 2001 • Retired: 2001
Original: $28 • Value: $60

BEARS	PRICE PAID	VALUE
1283.		
1284.		
1285.		
1286.		
1287.		
1288.		
1289.		
1290.		
1291.		
1292.		
1293.		
1294.		
TOTALS		

NOTES

Bears

1295.
Hector Hugsley
#500053 • 30"
Issued: 2003 • Current
Original: $57 • Value: $R/E

1296.
Hedda [QVC]
#(C18398) • 12"
LE of 2400 • Issued: 1996 • Retired: 1996
Original: $45 • Value: $65

1297.
Hefty B. Bear [QVC]
#93298V (C107593) • 10"
Issued: 2002 • Retired: 2002
Original: $18 • Value: $23

1298.
Heidi May Patchbeary [GoCollect]
#94919COL • 10"
LE of 3600 • Issued: 2002 • Retired: 2002
Original: $22 • Value: $35

1299.
Heidi Thistlebeary with Bethany Thistlebeary [QVC]
#(C55517) • 9"
Issued: 1999 • Retired: 1999
Original: $19 • Value: $28

1300.
Heidi Woodsbeary
#918335 • 10" • TJ
Issued: 2001 • Retired: 2001
Original: $23 • Value: $28

1301.
Helena Marie Boydsley [Coach House Gifts]
#unknown • 10"
Issued: 2001 • Retired: 2001
Original: $21 • Value: $60

1302.
Hemingway K. Grizzman
#91263 • 14" • TJ
Issued: 1999 • Retired: 2001
Original: $34 • Value: $39

1303.
Henley Fitzhampton
#912034 • 6" • TJ
Issued: 1999 • Retired: 2001
Original: $10 • Value: $12

1304.
Henrietta MacDonald
#917444 • 10" • TJ
Issued: 2002 • Current
Original: $18 • Value: $R/E

1305.
Henry
#1000-05 • 8" • CC
Issued: 1993 • Retired: 1995
Original: $6 • Value: $41

1306.
Henry [Dillards]
#94726DL • 14"
Issued: 1997 • Retired: 1997
Original: $25 • Value: $53

BEARS

	PRICE PAID	VALUE
1295.		
1296.		
1297.		
1298.		
1299.		
1300.		
1301.		
1302.		
1303.		
1304.		
1305.		
1306.		
TOTALS		

NOTES

Bears

1307.
Henry Bearyman [May Company]
#94159MC • 14"
Issued: 2000 • Retired: 2000
Original: $30 • Value: $55

1308.
Henry Bearymore [May Company]
#94156MC • 14"
Issued: 1999 • Retired: 1999
Original: $30 • Value: $45

1309.
Henson
#58011-05 • 10" • AS
Issued: 1998 • Retired: 2000
Original: $16 • Value: $41

1310.
Herbert Harrison McBearsley [QVC]
#(C21166) • 40"
LE of 500 • Issued: 2003 • Retired: 2003
Original: $203 • Value: $244

1311.
Herbert Henry Jodibear
#92000-05 • 9" • AR
Issued: 1999 • Retired: 2001
Original: $17 • Value: $20

1312.
Herbie Bearlove
#82001 • 6" • TJ
Issued: 2000 • Retired: 2000
Original: $10 • Value: $12

1313.
Herman B. Bearsdale [QVC]
#93283V (C60268) • 16"
Issued: 2002 • Retired: 2002
Original: $24 • Value: $33

1314.
Hermine Grisslin
#91206 • 16" • TJ
Issued: 1995 • Retired: 1997
Original: $45 • Value: $66

1315.
Hersh E. Kiss [Hershey]
#95201HE • 6"
LE of 3800 • Issued: 2003 • Retired: 2003
Original: $8 • Value: $10
Free with $40.00 purchase.

1316.
Hershal
#5125 • 16" • JB
Issued: 1991 • Retired: 1992
Original: $25 • Value: $149

1317.
Heywood Bearlanski [Bon Ton]
#unknown • 14"
Issued: 1999 • Retired: 1999
Original: $35 • Value: $54

1318.
Hilby Jamm
#917750 • 10" • TJ
Issued: 2002 • Retired: 2002
Original: $17 • Value: $17

BEARS

	PRICE PAID	VALUE
1307.		
1308.		
1309.		
1310.		
1311.		
1312.		
1313.		
1314.		
1315.		
1316.		
1317.		
1318.		
TOTALS		

NOTES

1319.
Hillary B. Bean
#5123-10 • 14" • CC
Issued: 1993 • Retired: 1998
Original: $19 • Value: $38

1320.
Hiram Q. Hamhock [QVC]
#93455V (C22639) • 8"
Issued: 2003 • Retired: 2003
Original: $14 • Value: $17

1321.
Hobson Q. Hugmeister [QVC]
#93234V (C98170) • 10"
LE of 804 • Issued: 2001 • Retired: 2001
Original: $131 • Value: $165

1322.
Hockley
#5640 • 16" • BA
Issued: 1992 • Retired: 1996
Original: $21 • Value: $54

1323.
Holden T. Punkinbeary
#904015 • 8" • TJ
Issued: 2002 • Retired: 2004
Original: $10 • Value: $10

1324.
Holiday [Hallmark]
#9702HM • 8"
Issued: 2003 • Retired: 2003
Original: $11 • Value: $13

1325.
Hollie and Ivy [QVC]
#99936V (C20908) • 6"
Issued: 2002 • Retired: 2002
Original: $21 • Value: $27

1326.
Holly [Lord & Taylor]
#unknown • 8"
Issued: 1999 • Retired: 1999
Original: $15 • Value: $35

1327.
Holly
#590064 • 10" • MB
Issued: 2003 • Current
Original: $30 • Value: $R/E

1328.
Holly B. Bearsley [QVC]
#unknown • 14"
Issued: 2001 • Retired: 2001
Original: $19 • Value: $25

1329.
Holly B. Kringlebeary [Kirlins]
#94534KR • 10"
Issued: 2002 • Retired: 2002
Original: $22 • Value: $34

1330.
Holly Bearberry [QVC]
#unknown • 10"
Issued: 1996 • Retired: 1996
Original: $N/E • Value: $45

BEARS

	PRICE PAID	VALUE
1319.		
1320.		
1321.		
1322.		
1323.		
1324.		
1325.		
1326.		
1327.		
1328.		
1329.		
1330.		
TOTALS		

NOTES

Bears

1331.
Holly Jolly Peeker [Longaberger]
#94664LB • 6"
Issued: 2003 • Retired: 2003
Original: $14 • Value: $19

1332.
Homer (10" baseball)
#6166B • 10"
LE • Issued: 1991 • Retired: 1991
Original: $70 • Value: $354

1333.
Homer (Himalayan)
#5760 • 14" • HD
Issued: 1991 • Retired: 1993
Original: $25 • Value: $210

1334.
Homer (8" baseball)
#9177 • 8" • TJ
Issued: 1993 • Retired: 1996
Original: $26 • Value: $51

1335.
Honey B. Bean [POG]
#94576POG • 15"
Issued: 1998 • Retired: 1998
Original: $16 • Value: $30

1336.
Honey B. Bear [Spiegel]
#unknown • 10"
Issued: 1994 • Retired: 1994
Original: $23 • Value: $37

1337.
Honey B. Beary [Longaberger]
#94637LB • 10"
Issued: 2001 • Retired: 2001
Original: $34 • Value: $75

1338.
Honey B. Elfberg [POG]
#94578POG • 14"
Issued: 1998 • Retired: 1998
Original: $24 • Value: $47

1339.
Honey B. Growin [POG]
#unknown • 14"
Issued: 1999 • Retired: 1999
Original: $23 • Value: $34

1340.
Honey Bee Bear [Faith Mountain]
#unknown • 14"
Issued: 1995 • Retired: 1995
Original: $N/E • Value: $48

1341.
Honey Buns
#903301 • 14" • ME
Issued: 2002 • Current
Original: $29 • Value: $R/E

1342.
Honey P. Snicklefritz
#51760-08 • 8" • BA
Issued: 1999 • Retired: 1999
Original: $12 • Value: $19

BEARS	PRICE PAID	VALUE
1331.		
1332.		
1333.		
1334.		
1335.		
1336.		
1337.		
1338.		
1339.		
1340.		
1341.		
1342.		
TOTALS		

NOTES

1343.
Honeycombe Mine
#unknown • 14"
Issued: 1998 • Retired: 1998
Original: $N/E • Value: $N/E

1344.
Honeypot
#5761 • 14" • HD
Issued: 1991 • Retired: 1994
Original: $27 • Value: $217

1345.
Hooper Q. Hugster
#500070-05 • 30" • JB
Issued: 2001 • Retired: 2002
Original: $57 • Value: $68

1346.
Hope
#903021 • 10" • ME
Issued: 2002 • Current
Original: $10 • Value: $R/E

1347.
Hope & A. Future [Hunter's Hope]
#900220HH • 10"
Issued: 2003 • Retired: 2003
Original: $20 • Value: $24

1348.
Hope L. Bearywell [Longaberger]
#94636LB • 9"
Issued: 2001 • Retired: 2001
Original: $15 • Value: $30

1349.
Horace B. Hugsworthy [QVC]
#(C80597) • 30"
Issued: 2000 • Retired: 2000
Original: $57 • Value: $80

1350.
Hoskins Q. Hugmeister [QVC]
#(C78127) • 30"
Issued: 2000 • Retired: 2000
Original: $57 • Value: $75

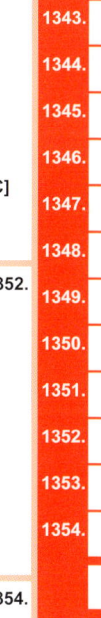

1351.
Howard McBeansley [QVC]
#(C6021) • 19"
Issued: 2003 • Retired: 2003
Original: $32 • Value: $39

1352.
Howard P. Potter [QVC]
#(C76774) • 12"
Issued: 2000 • Retired: 2000
Original: $16 • Value: $26

1353.
Hubbard [QVC]
#(C35945) • 12"
Issued: 1996 • Retired: 1996
Original: $N/E • Value: $26

1354.
Hubbard Q. Bearsley [QVC]
#93253V (C100312) • 16"
Issued: 2001 • Retired: 2001
Original: $29 • Value: $50

BEARS

	PRICE PAID	VALUE
1343.		
1344.		
1345.		
1346.		
1347.		
1348.		
1349.		
1350.		
1351.		
1352.		
1353.		
1354.		
	TOTALS	

NOTES

Bears

1355.
Hubbard W. Growler
#5721-01 • 12" • AS
Issued: 1997 • Retired: 1998
Original: $21 • Value: $38

1356.
Huck
#918051 • 6" • TJ
Issued: 1996 • Retired: 1998
Original: $10 • Value: $19

1357.
Huck, Mandy, & Zack [Show Specials]
#919811 • 11"
Issued: 2002 • Retired: 2002
Original: $51 • Value: $59

1358.
Hucklebeary B. Bear
#500100-06 • 8¼" • JB
Issued: 2001 • Retired: 2002
Original: $9 • Value: $11

1359.
Huett & Huntley [QVC]
#99524V (C37281) • 10"
Issued: 1997 • Retired: 1997
Original: $30 • Value: $55

1360.
Huff P. Wolf with Bacon, Porkchop & Hamlette
#91779 • 10" • TJ
Issued: 2002 • Current
Original: $25 • Value: $R/E

1361.
Huggabee
#903025 • 10" • ME
Issued: 2002 • Retired: 2002
Original: $14 • Value: $14

1362.
Huggleby B. Bearikind
#82003 • 8" • JB
Issued: 2000 • Retired: 2000
Original: $9 • Value: $11

1363.
Hugo P. Bearhugs [QVC]
#(C80564) • 40"
LE of 500 • Issued: 2000 • Retired: 2000
Original: $200 • Value: $260

1364.
Hugs N. Kisses (pair of bears)
#903010 • 6" • ME
Issued: 2002 • Retired: 2004
Original: $15 • Value: $15

1365.
Hugs N. Kisses (red heart peeker)
#82064 • 5"
Issued: 2004 • Current
Original: $11 • Value: $R/E

1366.
Humboldt
#5840-05 • 6" • AS
Issued: 1996 • Retired: 2002
Original: $9 • Value: $N/E
Also with Caledonia, Shasta as QVC set.
Award of Excellence Winner

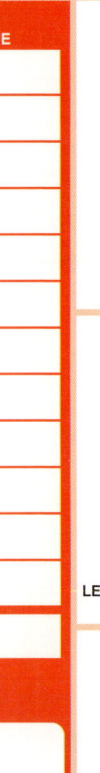

BEARS	PRICE PAID	VALUE
1355.		
1356.		
1357.		
1358.		
1359.		
1360.		
1361.		
1362.		
1363.		
1364.		
1365.		
1366.		
TOTALS		

NOTES

Bears

1367.
Hume
#unknown • 7"
Issued: 1994 • Retired: 1994
Original: $N/E • Value: $78

1368.
Humphrey P. Bearhugs [QVC]
#unknown • 40"
LE of 252 • Issued: 2001 • Retired: 2001
Original: $200 • Value: $265

1369.
Humphrey T. Bigfoot
#51110-05 • 18" • JB
Issued: 2001 • Retired: 2001
Original: $37 • Value: $44

1370.
Humpy Dumpy
#91781 • 10" • TJ
Issued: 2003 • Current
Original: $25 • Value: $R/E

1371.
Huney B. Keeper
#91774 • 9" • TJ
Issued: 2000 • Retired: 2001
Original: $20 • Value: $23

1372.
Hunnie Z. Beezley
#904114 • 10"
Issued: 2003 • Current
Original: $24 • Value: $R/E

1373.
Hunter [Hunter's Hope]
#900219HH • 10"
Issued: 2002 • Retired: 2002
Original: $20 • Value: $26

1374.
Hunter Bearsdale with Greenspan
#912625 • 14" • TJ
Issued: 2000 • Retired: 2000
Original: $27 • Value: $32

1375.
Hurshel
#5639-05 • 12" • BA
Issued: 1996 • Retired: 1999
Original: $16 • Value: $26

1376.
I Bea Lovinya & Lots [QVC]
#99854V (C52521) • 14"
LE of 7800 • Issued: 2002 • Retired: 2002
Original: $75 • Value: $100

1377.
I.B. Bearyproud
#913975 • 6"
Issued: 2002 • Retired: 2002
Original: $9 • Value: $9

1378.
I.C. Crystalfrost
#904185 • 5" • TJ
Issued: 2003 • Retired: 2003
Original: $14 • Value: $14

BEARS		
	PRICE PAID	VALUE
1367.		
1368.		
1369.		
1370.		
1371.		
1372.		
1373.		
1374.		
1375.		
1376.		
1377.		
1378.		
TOTALS		

NOTES

Bears

1379.
Icabod Scaredbear and Midnight [QVC]
#(C64861) • 19"
LE of 1800 • Issued: 2001 • Retired: 2001
Original: $63 • Value: $95

1380.
Ido Loveya
#903004 • 8" • ME
Issued: 2001 • Retired: 2002
Original: $10 • Value: $12

1381.
Iggy & Loo Frostbite
#568012 • 3½" • NO
Issued: 2002 • Current
Original: $10 • Value: $R/E

1382.
Ike D. Bearington [QVC]
#93084V (C34996) • 14" • MB
LE of 1800 • Issued: 1998 • Retired: 1998
Original: $86 • Value: $130

1383.
Ike Glorybear
#904192 • 10" • TJ
Issued: 2003 • Current
Original: $20 • Value: $R/E

1384.
Ima Bestfriend [Longaberger]
#993646LB • 8½"
Issued: 2004 • Retired: 2004
Original: $12 • Value: $R/E

1385.
Ima Hugginya [QVC]
#unknown • 8"
Issued: 2002 • Retired: 2002
Original: $12 • Value: $18

1386.
Ima Scholar
#917369-01 • 10" • ME
Issued: 2002 • Retired: 2004
Original: $22 • Value: $22

1387.
Ima Softheart
#82045 • 6"
Issued: 2003 • Current
Original: $10 • Value: $R/E

1388.
Indigo Jones [QVC]
#(C41091) • 12"
Issued: 1997 • Retired: 1997
Original: $31 • Value: $78

1389.
Inga B. Burrbruin
#904025 • 6" • TJ
Issued: 2002 • Retired: 2004
Original: $10 • Value: $10

1390.
Ingred S. Witebred [GCC]
#94871GCC • 8"
Issued: 1999 • Retired: 1999
Original: $16 • Value: $30

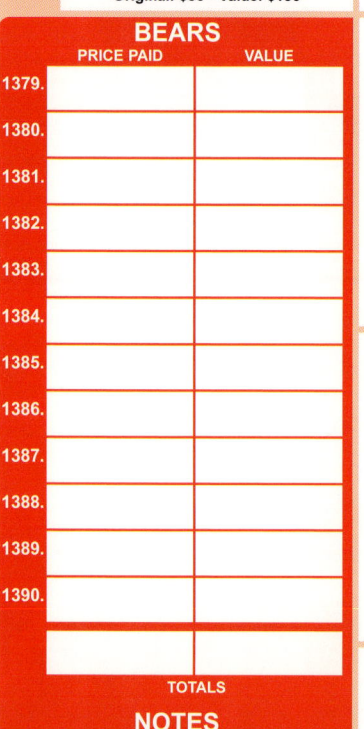

BEARS	PRICE PAID	VALUE
1379.		
1380.		
1381.		
1382.		
1383.		
1384.		
1385.		
1386.		
1387.		
1388.		
1389.		
1390.		
TOTALS		

NOTES

Bears

1391.
Ingrid & Heidi Svenbeary [QVC]
#99830V (C98195) • 14"
Issued: 2001 • Retired: 2001
Original: $40 • Value: $58

1392.
Ingrid & Tasha Norbruin with Toggle [QVC]
#(C98374) • 16"
LE of 2400 • Issued: 1999 • Retired: 1999
Original: $69 • Value: $95

1393.
Isabel Grizbearg [GCC]
#94892GCC • 12"
Issued: 2001 • Retired: 2001
Original: $30 • Value: $65

1394.
Isabella [Bon Ton]
#945608BT • 16"
Issued: 1999 • Retired: 1999
Original: $38 • Value: $56

1395.
Isabelle Dickens
#904224 • 8" • TJ
Issued: 2003 • Retired: 2003
Original: $15 • Value: $15

1396.
Isaiah
#917304 • 10" • TJ
Issued: 1996 • Retired: 1998
Original: $19 • Value: $40

1397.
Isaiah Q. Woodsley [QVC]
#93555V (C06208) • 12"
Issued: 2004 • Retired: 2004
Original: $17 • Value: $29

1398.
Ivanna Hugsley [QVC]
#93473V (C0423) • 30"
Issued: 2003 • Retired: 2003
Original: $58 • Value: $70

1399.
Ivanna Spendalot
#903401 • 8" • ME
Issued: 2002 • Retired: 2002
Original: $10 • Value: $16

1400.
Iza Basketcase [QVC]
#99875V (C107578) • 6"
Issued: 2002 • Retired: 2002
Original: $16 • Value: $35
With basket and quilt.

1401.
J.B. Bean (smooth fur)
#5106 • 10" • JB
Issued: 1990 • Retired: 1990
Original: $14 • Value: $155

1402.
J.B. Bean (old face)
#5106 • 10" • JB
Issued: 1991 • Retired: 1994
Original: $14 • Value: $52

BEARS	PRICE PAID	VALUE
1391.		
1392.		
1393.		
1394.		
1395.		
1396.		
1397.		
1398.		
1399.		
1400.		
1401.		
1402.		
TOTALS		

NOTES

Bears

1403. J.B. Bean (new face)
#5106 • 10" • JB
Issued: 1994 • Retired: 1997
Original: $14 • Value: $37

1404. J.B. Bigheart
#903307 • 8"
Issued: 2003 • Current
Original: $10 • Value: $R/E

1405. J.B. Pinesley [QVC]
#unknown • 16"
Issued: 2002 • Retired: 2002
Original: $45 • Value: $58
Sold as set with metal Tannebaum box.

1406. J.C. Von Fuzzner [J.C.Penney]
#unknown • 14"
Issued: 1999 • Retired: 1999
Original: $35 • Value: $52

1407. J.J. Honeypot [QVC]
#unknown • 40"
Issued: 2001 • Retired: 2001
Original: $200 • Value: $230

1408. J.J. Rugsley
#500100 • 40" • AS
Issued: 2001 • Retired: 2001
Original: $91 • Value: $109

1409. J.P. Huttin III
#5110-08 • 17" • JB
Issued: 1995 • Retired: 1998
Original: $29 • Value: $43

1410. J.P. Locksley
#57002-08 • 12" • AS
Issued: 1999 • Retired: 2000
Original: $16 • Value: $19

1411. J.T. Jordan III [Welcome Home]
#unknown • 14"
Issued: 1997 • Retired: 1997
Original: $33 • Value: $50

1412. J.W. VanWinkle & Snuggies
#912633 • 14" • TJ
Issued: 2001 • Retired: 2001
Original: $30 • Value: $36

1413. Jack B. Frostbeary [QVC]
#93263V (C98196) • 10"
Issued: 2001 • Retired: 2001
Original: $20 • Value: $25

1414. Jack B. Twinkletune [EVENT]
#50008 • 8"
Issued: 2002 • Retired: 2002
Original: $20 • Value: $26

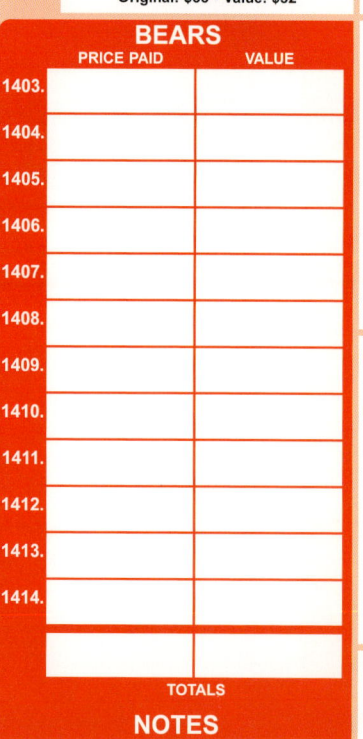

BEARS

	PRICE PAID	VALUE
1403.		
1404.		
1405.		
1406.		
1407.		
1408.		
1409.		
1410.		
1411.		
1412.		
1413.		
1414.		
TOTALS		

NOTES

Bears

1415.
Jack O. Lantern
#919631 • 13" • TJ
Issued: 2001 • Retired: 2002
Original: $18 • Value: $22

1416.
Jackie B. Beariproud [QVC]
#99012V (C06201) • 14"
LE of 1500 • Issued: 2004 • Retired: 2004
Original: $49 • Value: $60
With utensil holder.

1417.
Jackson [May Company]
#unknown • 8"
Issued: 1998 • Retired: 1998
Original: $12 • Value: $23

1418.
Jackson B. Beanster [QVC]
#93276V (C52790) • 16"
Issued: 2002 • Retired: 2002
Original: $22 • Value: $29

1419.
Jackson R. Bearington
#590021-05 • 16" • MB
Issued: 1998 • Retired: 1999
Original: $100 • Value: $156

1420.
Jacob Wishkabibble
#90505 • 14" • TJ
Issued: 2001 • Retired: 2001
Original: $33 • Value: $40

1421.
Jacqueline K. Bearington [QVC]
#(C53110) • 16" • MB
LE of 1200 • Issued: 1998 • Retired: 1998
Original: $80 • Value: $175

1422.
Jae Lynn Jackson [Bear Heaven]
#94183PP • 12"
Issued: 2003 • Retired: 2003
Original: $20 • Value: $33

1423.
Jaime Lisa [Dillards]
#94729DL • 16"
Issued: 1998 • Retired: 1998
Original: $40 • Value: $67

1424.
Jake [Dillards]
#94732DL • 8"
Issued: 1998 • Retired: 1998
Original: $18 • Value: $30

1425.
James & Malachi [QVC]
#(C47256) • 14"
Issued: 1998 • Retired: 1998
Original: $28 • Value: $65

1426.
James C. Penneybeary [J.C.Penney]
#94382JCP • 16"
Issued: 2002 • Retired: 2002
Original: $28 • Value: $35

BEARS

	PRICE PAID	VALUE
1415.		
1416.		
1417.		
1418.		
1419.		
1420.		
1421.		
1422.		
1423.		
1424.		
1425.		
1426.		
TOTALS		

NOTES

Bears

1427.
James Jodibear
#92000-22 • 9" • AR
Issued: 2003 • Current
Original: $15 • Value: $R/E

1428.
Jameson J. Bearsford
#57251-10 • 6" • AS
Issued: 1999 • Retired: 2002
Original: $8 • Value: $10
Sold with Deacon, Cameron as QVC set.

1429.
Jamie [CAN]
#BC94286PO • 6"
LE of 4800 • Issued: 2000 • Retired: 2000
Original: $13 • Value: $25

1430.
Jamison Ann Dickens [Elder Beerman]
#94619EB • 10"
Issued: 2003 • Retired: 2003
Original: $25 • Value: $30

1431.
Jan B. Bearberg [SLE]
#unknown • 14"
Issued: 1998 • Retired: 1998
Original: $18 • Value: $39

1432.
Janet C. Daisydew [Paw Dealer]
#919822 • 10"
Issued: 2003 • Retired: 2003
Original: $20 • Value: $24

1433.
Janie Icebeary [Macy's East]
#94171MA • 12"
Issued: 2004 • Retired: 2004
Original: $27 • Value: $R/E

1434.
Jarvis Boydsenberry [QVC]
#unknown • 16"
Issued: 1998 • Retired: 1998
Original: $53 • Value: $70

1435.
Jasper McBobble
#510305-05 • 10" • JB
Issued: 2001 • Retired: 2002
Original: $13 • Value: $16

1436.
Jasper T. Fisher with Paddle [QVC]
#(C22622) • 8"
LE of 1800 • Issued: 2003 • Retired: 2003
Original: $45 • Value: $54

1437.
Jaxton D. Bear
#510300-10 • 10" • JB
Issued: 2000 • Retired: 2001
Original: $11 • Value: $13

1438.
Jean [CAN]
#BC100905 • 14" • PM
Issued: 1997 • Retired: 1997
Original: $21 • Value: $36

BEARS	PRICE PAID	VALUE
1427.		
1428.		
1429.		
1430.		
1431.		
1432.		
1433.		
1434.		
1435.		
1436.		
1437.		
1438.		
TOTALS		

NOTES

Bears

1439.
Jeanine Jodibear
#92000-16 • 8" • AR
Issued: 2001 • Retired: 2002
Original: $17 • Value: $20

1440.
Jeannie S. Berriman
[Platinum Paw]
#919809 • 16"
Issued: 2001 • Retired: 2001
Original: $44 • Value: $59

1441.
Jeannine De Bearvoire
#904226 • 10" • TJ
Issued: 2003 • Current
Original: $18 • Value: $R/E

1442.
Jeb MacDonald
#912662 • 12" • TJ
Issued: 2002 • Current
Original: $20 • Value: $R/E

1443.
Jed Bruin (a.k.a. Snowball)
#5123W • 14" • JB
Issued: 1992 • Retired: 1993
Original: $20 • Value: $175

1444.
Jefferson
#1050-02 • 8"
Issued: 1995 • Retired: 1996
Original: $11 • Value: $54

1445.
Jefferson B. Beanster [QVC]
#(C22102) • 16"
Issued: 2003 • Retired: 2003
Original: $36 • Value: $43

1446.
Jeffrey T. Treetoes
#917376 • 10" • TJ
Issued: 2001 • Retired: 2002
Original: $13 • Value: $16

1447.
Jenna [Profitts]
#unknown • 16"
Issued: 1998 • Retired: 1998
Original: $68 • Value: $95

1448.
Jenna Rae [Cracker Barrel]
#94995CB • 10"
Issued: 2002 • Retired: 2002
Original: $21 • Value: $27

1449.
Jennie Glorybear
#904191 • 14" • TJ
Issued: 2003 • Current
Original: $25 • Value: $R/E

1450.
Jennie Lynn & Fussypuss [QVC]
#(C0544) • 10"
Issued: 2002 • Retired: 2002
Original: $22 • Value: $30

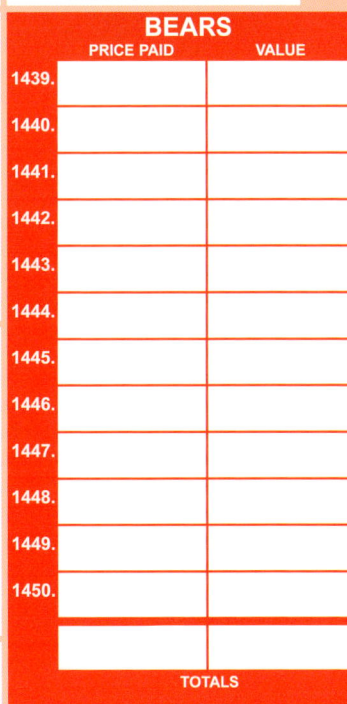

BEARS	PRICE PAID	VALUE
1439.		
1440.		
1441.		
1442.		
1443.		
1444.		
1445.		
1446.		
1447.		
1448.		
1449.		
1450.		
TOTALS		

NOTES

Bears

1451.
Jennie Marie Warmheart with Happy [QVC]
#99976V (C3129) • 14"
LE of 8500 • Issued: 2003 • Retired: 2003
Original: $49 • Value: $59
Sold with resin house pull toy.

1452.
Jennifer B. Bearheart [QVC]
#(C21157) • 16"
Issued: 2003 • Retired: 2003
Original: $45 • Value: $54

1453.
Jennifer Bearringer
#82532 • 16"
Issued: 2004 • Current
Original: $25 • Value: $R/E

1454.
Jenny McBruin [QVC]
#(C76782) • 16"
Issued: 2000 • Retired: 2000
Original: $36 • Value: $65

1455.
Jeremiah [Country Living]
#(C39372) • 16"
Issued: 1997 • Retired: 1997
Original: $30 • Value: $49

1456.
Jeremiah J. Woodsley
#92002-03 • 15" • AR
Issued: 2001 • Retired: 2001
Original: $18 • Value: $30

1457.
Jeremy [Dillards]
#94712DL • 14"
Issued: 1997 • Retired: 1997
Original: $25 • Value: $48

1458.
Jesse
#1100-05 • 11" • CC
Issued: 1993 • Retired: 1995
Original: $10 • Value: $57

1459.
Jesse [Lord & Taylor]
#unknown • 8"
Issued: 1999 • Retired: 1999
Original: $15 • Value: $31

1460.
Jesselyn R. Angel [Starlight]
#51114 • 12" • AS
Issued: 2003 • Retired: 2003
Original: $15 • Value: $18

1461.
Jessie Lu Goodbear [Country Clutter]
#94975CC • 10"
Issued: 2002 • Retired: 2002
Original: $19 • Value: $35

1462.
Jethro
#5630 • 9" • BA
Issued: 1995 • Retired: 1997
Original: $10 • Value: $37

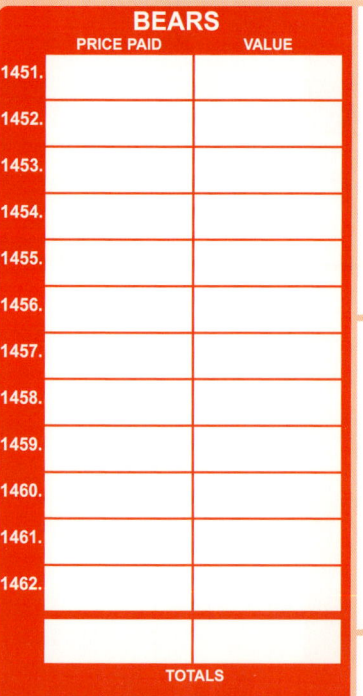

BEARS

	PRICE PAID	VALUE
1451.		
1452.		
1453.		
1454.		
1455.		
1456.		
1457.		
1458.		
1459.		
1460.		
1461.		
1462.		
TOTALS		

NOTES

1463.
Jethro T. Woodsley
#92002-05 • 10" • AR
Issued: 2002 • Retired: 2002
Original: $13 • Value: $25

1464.
Jilian G. Gingerbeary
#904031 • 14" • TJ
Issued: 2002 • Retired: 2004
Original: $28 • Value: $28

1465.
Jillian [Dillards]
#94734DL • 14"
Issued: 1998 • Retired: 1998
Original: $35 • Value: $58

1466.
Jimmy T. Bearheart
#904083 • 6"
Issued: 2003 • Current
Original: $10 • Value: $R/E

1467.
Joanne Pearl [Bon Ton]
#94561BT • 10"
Issued: 2000 • Retired: 2000
Original: $24 • Value: $55

1468.
Jobie & Kibby Bearington [QVC]
#(C49907) • 6" • MB
Issued: 1998 • Retired: 1998
Original: $20 • Value: $31

1469.
Jocelyn Bloomengrows
#912012 • 16" • TJ
Issued: 2001 • Retired: 2002
Original: $51 • Value: $61

1470.
Jocelyn Thistlebeary & Carson T. Bibbly [QVC]
#(C56965) • 16"
Issued: 1999 • Retired: 1999
Original: $42 • Value: $75

1471.
Jody
#5641-09 • 16" • BA
Issued: 1995 • Retired: 1996
Original: $24 • Value: $44

1472.
Joe [CAN]
#BC100508 • 10"
Issued: 1997 • Retired: 1997
Original: $15 • Value: $36

1473.
John
#5828 • 13" • CB
Issued: 1992 • Retired: 1997
Original: $20 • Value: $50

1474.
John [CAN]
#BC100508 • 10" • PM
Issued: 1997 • Retired: 1997
Original: $15 • Value: $35

BEARS

	PRICE PAID	VALUE
1463.		
1464.		
1465.		
1466.		
1467.		
1468.		
1469.		
1470.		
1471.		
1472.		
1473.		
1474.		
TOTALS		

NOTES

Bears

1475.
John B. Leadbottoms
#51021 • 9" • JB
Issued: 2002 • Retired: 2004
Original: $17 • Value: $17

1476.
John Henry
#572210-07 • 21" • AS
Issued: 2001 • Retired: 2002
Original: $53 • Value: $64

1477.
John William [QVC]
#(C41110) • 13"
Issued: 1997 • Retired: 1997
Original: $25 • Value: $43

1478.
JoJo DeBearvoire
#904076 • 6"
Issued: 2003 • Current
Original: $10 • Value: $R/E

1479.
Jolee [May Company]
#unknown • 8"
Issued: 1998 • Retired: 1998
Original: $N/E • Value: $29

1480.
Jolly B. Nick [QVC]
#(C21037) • 12"
Issued: 2002 • Retired: 2002
Original: $18 • Value: $23

1481.
Jolly Ol' St. Nick
#904350 • 17" • TJ
Issued: 2004 • Current
Original: $50 • Value: $R/E

1482.
Jolly T. Jodibear
#92000-24 • 8" • AR
Issued: 2004 • Current
Original: $15 • Value: $R/E

1483.
Jonathan Applesmith
#913969 • 6" • TJ
Issued: 2001 • Retired: 2002
Original: $9 • Value: $11

1484.
Jonathan Macbear [QVC]
#(C80714) • 16"
Issued: 2000 • Retired: 2000
Original: $23 • Value: $34

1485.
Jordan T. Fallsbeary [Show Specials]
#919805 • 8"
Issued: 2000 • Retired: 2000
Original: $14 • Value: $21

1486.
Joshua
#5826 • 9" • CB
Issued: 1992 • Retired: 1997
Original: $14 • Value: $39

BEARS

	PRICE PAID	VALUE
1475.		
1476.		
1477.		
1478.		
1479.		
1480.		
1481.		
1482.		
1483.		
1484.		
1485.		
1486.		
TOTALS		

NOTES

Bears

1487.
Josie K. Bearsmark [Hallmark]
#9689HM • 8"
Issued: 2001 • Retired: 2001
Original: $15 • Value: $26

1488.
JoyAnn Hugsbeary
#82505 • 14" • JB
Issued: 2001 • Retired: 2002
Original: $20 • Value: $24

1489.
Joyce M. Berriman
#82519 • 16" • TJ
Issued: 2003 • Retired: 2003
Original: $25 • Value: $25

1490.
Joyelle [Ideation]
#unknown • 16"
Issued: 1998 • Retired: 1998
Original: $35 • Value: $55

1491.
Jr. Mintly
#904215 • 10" • TJ
Issued: 2003 • Current
Original: $20 • Value: $R/E

1492.
Juilian and Justin Jodibear [QVC]
#99923V (C20186) • 6"
Issued: 2002 • Retired: 2002
Original: $27 • Value: $35

1493.
Julia [Dillards]
#94719DL • 14"
Issued: 1997 • Retired: 1997
Original: $25 • Value: $58

1494.
Julia Angelbrite
#91776 • 10" • TJ
Issued: 2000 • Retired: 2002
Original: $16 • Value: $21

1495.
Juliana de Bearvoire [QVC]
#(C100450) • 12"
Issued: 2001 • Retired: 2001
Original: $24 • Value: $40

1496.
Julianna Hugsley [QVC]
#(C99310) • 16"
Issued: 2001 • Retired: 2001
Original: $34 • Value: $50

1497.
Julie Ann Gingerbeary and Cookie [QVC]
#9992V (C20985) • 14"
LE of 4000 • Issued: 2002 • Retired: 2002
Original: $50 • Value: $64
Sold with Gingerbread House tug-a-long.

1498.
Juliella T. Frostfire
#83002 • 8" • TJ
Issued: 2000 • Retired: 2000
Original: $15 • Value: $24

BEARS	PRICE PAID	VALUE
1487.		
1488.		
1489.		
1490.		
1491.		
1492.		
1493.		
1494.		
1495.		
1496.		
1497.		
1498.		
TOTALS		

NOTES

Bears

1499.
Juliet S. Bearlove
#912651 • 12" • TJ
Issued: 2000 • Retired: 2002
Original: $23 • Value: $28

1500.
Juno Whatt Bearington
#590054 • 10" • MB
Issued: 2001 • Retired: 2002
Original: $33 • Value: $40

1501.
Justin [Dillards]
#510611DL • 10"
Issued: 1997 • Retired: 1997
Original: $12 • Value: $26

1502.
Justina & Matthew [QVC]
#(C43581) • 14"
LE of 1800 • Issued: 1997 • Retired: 1997
Original: $73 • Value: $160

1503.
Kacy Mae Sugarcone
& Lil' Scoop [QVC]
#93443V (C22637) • 12"
Issued: 2003 • Retired: 2003
Original: $33 • Value: $40

1504.
Kaitlyn Bearlove [Kirlins]
#94259KR • 11"
LE of 10000 • Issued: 2000 • Retired: 2000
Original: $24 • Value: $40

1505.
Karen A. Mulberry
#917364 • 10" • TJ
Issued: 2000 • Retired: 2002
Original: $20 • Value: $20

1506.
Karen B. Bearsdale [QVC]
#(C97881) • 13"
Issued: 2000 • Retired: 2000
Original: $26 • Value: $45

1507.
Karina Burrbruin
#904021 • 16" • TJ
Issued: 2002 • Retired: 2004
Original: $50 • Value: $51

1508.
Karissa Lynn Bearsdale [QVC]
#93468V (C19891) • 16"
Issued: 2002 • Retired: 2002
Original: $50 • Value: $75

1509.
Karl Von Fuzzner [QVC]
#unknown • 10"
Issued: 1998 • Retired: 1998
Original: $27 • Value: $35

1510.
Karla Mulbeary
#915500 • 8" • TJ
Issued: 1999 • Retired: 2000
Original: $18 • Value: $22
Variations pictured together.

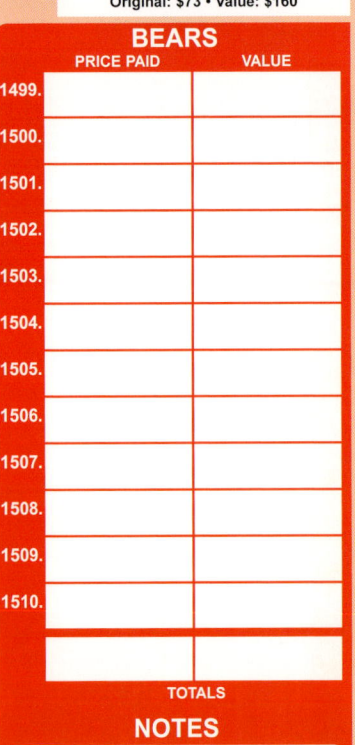

BEARS

	PRICE PAID	VALUE
1499.		
1500.		
1501.		
1502.		
1503.		
1504.		
1505.		
1506.		
1507.		
1508.		
1509.		
1510.		
TOTALS		

NOTES

Bears

1511.
Karley & Melanie Bearibug [QVC]
#99749V (C76932) • 6"
Issued: 2000 • Retired: 2000
Original: $18 • Value: $30

1512.
Karmen [Frederick Atkins]
#94767FA • 10"
Issued: 2000 • Retired: 2000
Original: $20 • Value: $38

1513.
Karyn Scarvesdale
#918456 • 6"
Issued: 2002 • Retired: 2002
Original: $8 • Value: $8

1514.
Kassandra P. Berriwinkle [QVC]
#(C45089) • 12"
Issued: 1997 • Retired: 1997
Original: $45 • Value: $80

1515.
Kassie Gingerbeary
#904032 • 10" • TJ
Issued: 2002 • Retired: 2004
Original: $20 • Value: $20

1516.
Katerina Winterbeary [QVC]
#93347V (C20943) • 10"
Issued: 2002 • Retired: 2002
Original: $27 • Value: $35

1517.
Kathy B. Bearsley [QVC]
#(C06197) • 8"
Issued: 2004 • Retired: 2004
Original: $12 • Value: $13

1518.
Katie B. Bearyproud
#918341 • 10"
Issued: 2002 • Retired: 2002
Original: $23 • Value: $23

1519.
Katie B. Berrijam
#910062 • 10" • TJ
Issued: 1999 • Retired: 2001
Original: $19 • Value: $22

1520.
Katrinka Berriman with Thor [QVC]
#unknown • 7"
Issued: 1998 • Retired: 1998
Original: $34 • Value: $61

1521.
Have You Seen Me?

Katy Bear
#5071 • 10" • WB
Issued: 1987 • Retired: 1988
Original: $N/E • Value: $308

1522.
Kay Cherrybeary
#904095 • 6"
Issued: 2003 • Current
Original: $10 • Value: $R/E

BEARS	PRICE PAID	VALUE
1511.		
1512.		
1513.		
1514.		
1515.		
1516.		
1517.		
1518.		
1519.		
1520.		
1521.		
1522.		
TOTALS		

NOTES

Bears

1523.
Kayla Bearimore [QVC]
#(C55532) • 10"
Issued: 1999 • Retired: 1999
Original: $17 • Value: $25

1524.
Kayla Mulbeary
#913941 • 6" • TJ
Issued: 1999 • Retired: 2001
Original: $12 • Value: $14
Also with Krista Blubeary as QVC set.

1525.
Kaylie Angelfrost & Kringle's Village St. Nicholas Chapel [QVC]
#99933V (C20340) • 10"
LE of 15000 • Issued: 2002 • Retired: 2002
Original: $56 • Value: $73

1526.
Kaytie & Mattie with R.J. [Show Specials]
#919820
Issued: 2002 • Retired: 2002
Original: $50 • Value: $65

1527.
Keifer B. Elfington
#590055 • 10" • MB
Issued: 2001 • Retired: 2001
Original: $38 • Value: $46

1528.
Kelby [Elder Beerman]
#unknown • 15"
Issued: 1998 • Retired: 1998
Original: $35 • Value: $55

1529.
Kelly O. Beary
#57252-08 • 6½" • AS
Issued: 2000 • Retired: 2002
Original: $8 • Value: $10

1530.
Kelly Sue Bearican [QVC]
#(C01905) • 16" • TJ
Issued: 2004 • Retired: 2004
Original: $50 • Value: $54

1531.
Kelsey [Dillards]
#94747DL • 11"
Issued: 1999 • Retired: 1999
Original: $35 • Value: $44

1532.
Kelsey M. Jodibear with Arby T. Tugalog
#900209 • 7½" • UB
LE of 12998 • Issued: 1999 • Retired: 2000
Original: $61 • Value: $73

1533.
Kemper Forbes
#51102-03 • 16" • JB
Issued: 2000 • Retired: 2002
Original: $25 • Value: $30

1534.
Kendall B. Learnin
#912661 • 12" • ME
Issued: 2001 • Retired: 2002
Original: $35 • Value: $42

BEARS	PRICE PAID	VALUE
1523.		
1524.		
1525.		
1526.		
1527.		
1528.		
1529.		
1530.		
1531.		
1532.		
1533.		
1534.		
TOTALS		

NOTES

Bears

1535.
Kendallyn H. Sugarcone
#904120 • 16"
Issued: 2003 • Current
Original: $46 • Value: $R/E

1536.
Kensington K. Braveheart [QVC]
#(C57650) • 21"
Issued: 1999 • Retired: 1999
Original: $53 • Value: $77

1537.
Kevin G. Bearsley
#917362 • 10" • TJ
Issued: 2000 • Retired: 2000
Original: $19 • Value: $28

1538.
Kevin Kringlebeary [J.C.Penney]
#unknown • 12"
Issued: 2003 • Retired: 2003
Original: $20 • Value: $24

1539.
Kibby T. Beansley
#510812 • 14"
Issued: 2003 • Current
Original: $20 • Value: $R/E

1540.
Kimberly Punkinbeary
#904014 • 10" • TJ
Issued: 2002 • Retired: 2004
Original: $19 • Value: $19

1541.
Kimmy
#917382 • 10" • TJ
Issued: 2002 • Retired: 2002
Original: $13 • Value: $13

1542.
Kinsey Snoopstein [QVC]
#(C56961) • 6"
Issued: 1999 • Retired: 1999
Original: $17 • Value: $46
Set of two.

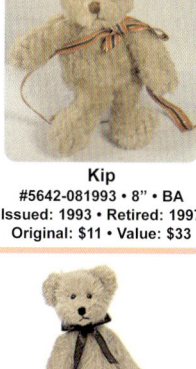
1543.
Kip
#5642-081993 • 8" • BA
Issued: 1993 • Retired: 1997
Original: $11 • Value: $33

1544.
Kirby Elfbeary
#904053 • 8"
Issued: 2002 • Retired: 2002
Original: $18 • Value: $23

1545.
Kirby Scruffles
#510701 • 8"
Issued: 2003 • Retired: 2003
Original: $9 • Value: $9

1546.
Kirsten DeBearvoire with Mimi DeBearvoire [QVC]
#99951V (C21445) • 6"
Issued: 2003 • Retired: 2003
Original: $21 • Value: $25

BEARS

	PRICE PAID	VALUE
1535.		
1536.		
1537.		
1538.		
1539.		
1540.		
1541.		
1542.		
1543.		
1544.		
1545.		
1546.		
TOTALS		

NOTES

Bears

1547.
Kirsten T. Oakley
#904003 • 10" • TJ
Issued: 2002 • Retired: 2004
Original: $25 • Value: $25

1548.
Kisslebeary
#590057 • 10" • MB
Issued: 2002 • Retired: 2002
Original: $30 • Value: $30

1549.
Kit, Bang & Kaboodle [QVC]
#99873V (C107576) • 6"
Issued: 2002 • Retired: 2002
Original: $20 • Value: $35

1550.
Klaus Von Fuzzner
#91262 • 14" • TJ
Issued: 1998 • Retired: 2001
Original: $34 • Value: $42

1551.
Klaus Von Fuzzner [SFMB]
#41-72564
Issued: 1999 • Retired: 1999
Original: $50 • Value: $75
♪ Let It Snow ♪

1552.
Klondike
#912820 • 14" • TJ
Issued: 2000 • Retired: 2000
Original: $26 • Value: $35

1553.
Knut C. Berriman [QVC]
#unknown • 8" • TJ
Issued: 1998 • Retired: 1998
Original: $24 • Value: $38

1554.
Knut V. Berriman
#91231 • 8" • TJ
Issued: 1997 • Retired: 1999
Original: $24 • Value: $33

1555.
Kortney Kringlebeary [GCC]
#94922GCC • 10"
Issued: 2002 • Retired: 2002
Original: $33 • Value: $51

1556.
Kringle Bear (10")
#9163 • 10" • TJ
Issued: 1993 • Retired: 1996
Original: $19 • Value: $48

1557.
Kringle Bear (14")
#9191 • 14" • TJ
Issued: 1993 • Retired: 1996
Original: $27 • Value: $67

1558.
Kringle's Retreat Set [QVC]
#99755V (C78176)
LE • Issued: 2000 • Retired: 2000
Original: $55 • Value: $90
Sold with resin cottage.

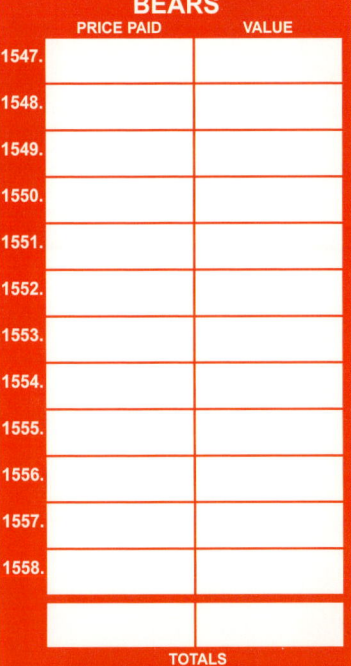

BEARS	PRICE PAID	VALUE
1547.		
1548.		
1549.		
1550.		
1551.		
1552.		
1553.		
1554.		
1555.		
1556.		
1557.		
1558.		
TOTALS		

NOTES

Bears

1559.
Krista Blubeary with Kayla Mulbeary [QVC]
#(C74398) • 6"
Issued: 1999 • Retired: 1999
Original: $23 • Value: $34

1560.
Krista Fuzzyfrost
#913974 • 6" • TJ
Issued: 2001 • Retired: 2002
Original: $9 • Value: $11

1561.
Kristen T. Beansley [Paw Dealer]
#919812 • 14"
Issued: 2002 • Retired: 2002
Original: $25 • Value: $41

1562.
Kristi & Kaylie Marie [SYN]
#94595SYN • 8"
Issued: 2002 • Retired: 2002
Original: $18 • Value: $31

1563.
Kristi Ann Bearibrook [QVC]
#(C107614) • 12"
Issued: 2002 • Retired: 2002
Original: $24 • Value: $40

1564.
Kristoff [QVC]
#unknown • 12"
Issued: 1998 • Retired: 1998
Original: $21 • Value: $30

1565.
Krystal Penneybeary [J.C.Penney]
#94381JCP
Issued: 2002 • Retired: 2002
Original: $31 • Value: $36

1566.
Krystle B. Bearbright with Joelle & Paz
#900102
LE • Issued: 2002 • Retired: 2002
Original: $66 • Value: $80
Golden Teddy Award Winner

1567.
Kudos Attabear
#903017 • 8" • ME
Issued: 2002 • Retired: 2002
Original: $10 • Value: $10

1568.
Kyle [SLE]
#unknown • 5½"
Issued: 1998 • Retired: 1998
Original: $10 • Value: $19

1569.
Kyle L. Berriman
#917401 • 10" • TJ
Issued: 2000 • Retired: 2001
Original: $16 • Value: $19

1570.
Kylie & Baabs [QVC]
#99829V (C100361) • 8"
Issued: 2001 • Retired: 2001
Original: $18 • Value: $30

BEARS

	PRICE PAID	VALUE
1559.		
1560.		
1561.		
1562.		
1563.		
1564.		
1565.		
1566.		
1567.		
1568.		
1569.		
1570.		
	TOTALS	

NOTES

Bears

1571.
LaBelle [Ideation]
#unknown • 8"
Issued: 1997 • Retired: 1997
Original: $12 • Value: $25

1572.
Lacy (10")
#6100B • 10" • TJ
Issued: 1989 • Retired: 1993
Original: $15 • Value: $125
Also in tan.

1573.
Lacy (14")
#6101B • 14" • TJ
Issued: 1989 • Retired: 1992
Original: $21 • Value: $166

1574.
LaDonna & Darlene DuBeary [QVC]
#99757V (C78115) • 10"
Issued: 2000 • Retired: 2000
Original: $32 • Value: $48

1575.
Lady B. Bug
#91775 • 10" • TJ
Issued: 2000 • Retired: 2002
Original: $17 • Value: $20

1576.
Lady B. Bugsley
#918701 • 8"
Issued: 2003 • Retired: 2003
Original: $17 • Value: $17

1577.
Lady Flora Monarch [GCC]
#94891GCC • 14"
Issued: 2001 • Retired: 2001
Original: $28 • Value: $45

1578.
Lancaster
#57051-08 • 8" • AS
Issued: 1998 • Retired: 2000
Original: $13 • Value: $19

1579.
Lancelot
#5722-11 • 21" • AS
Issued: 1996 • Retired: 1999
Original: $52 • Value: $80

1580.
Lankey S. Woodsley
#92002-06 • 12" • AR
Issued: 2002 • Current
Original: $10 • Value: $R/E

1581.
Lara [QVC]
#(C45642) • 16"
LE of 2400 • Issued: 1997 • Retired: 1997
Original: $78 • Value: $150

1582.
Lars
#91735 • 8" • AS
Issued: 1996 • Retired: 1997
Original: $18 • Value: $36

BEARS	PRICE PAID	VALUE
1571.		
1572.		
1573.		
1574.		
1575.		
1576.		
1577.		
1578.		
1579.		
1580.		
1581.		
1582.		
TOTALS		

NOTES

Bears

1583.
Latte O. Bear
#500100-01 • 8¼" • JB
Issued: 2000 • Retired: 2002
Original: $9 • Value: $11

1584.
Laura Ann [Dillards]
#94733DL • 14"
Issued: 1998 • Retired: 1998
Original: $25 • Value: $46

1585.
Laura B. Bearyproud [QVC]
#93301V (C107575) • 16"
Issued: 2002 • Retired: 2002
Original: $41 • Value: $65

1586.
Laura E. Bearburn [J.T. Webb]
#94285JTW • 8"
LE of 5000 • Issued: 1997 • Retired: 1997
Original: $20 • Value: $47

1587.
Laura Elizabeth Yachtley
[My Gift Cottage]
#94210MGC • 8"
Issued: 2002 • Retired: 2002
Original: $15 • Value: $30

1588.
Laura P. Bradbeary [QVC]
#(C57855) • 12"
Issued: 2001 • Retired: 2001
Original: $28 • Value: $52

1589.
Lauralee Pearsley
#904160 • 16" • TJ
Issued: 2003 • Current
Original: $53 • Value: $R/E

1590.
Laurel S. Berrijam
#913954 • 6" • TJ
Issued: 1999 • Retired: 2000
Original: $10 • Value: $17

1591.
Lauren
#904265 • 6" • TJ
Issued: 2004 • Current
Original: $10 • Value: $R/E

1592.
Lauren B. Ladybug with Spot [QVC]
#(C05172) • 14"
Issued: 2004 • Retired: 2004
Original: $32 • Value: $41

1593.
Lauren Ladybug [Kirlins]
#94260KR
Issued: 2004 • Retired: 2004
Original: $19 • Value: $19

1594.
Lauren Nicole [Country Clutter]
#94981CC • 10"
Issued: 2004 • Retired: 2004
Original: $22 • Value: $22

BEARS

	PRICE PAID	VALUE
1583.		
1584.		
1585.		
1586.		
1587.		
1588.		
1589.		
1590.		
1591.		
1592.		
1593.		
1594.		
	TOTALS	

NOTES

Bears

1595.
Layona Rugsley
#500100-08 • 40" • AS
Issued: 2002 • Current
Original: $90 • Value: $R/E

1596.
Lead B. Bottoms
#51020 • 10" • AR
Issued: 2001 • Retired: 2002
Original: $17 • Value: $28

1597.
Leanne Bearsdale [Gold Paw]
#919821 • 14"
Issued: 2003 • Retired: 2003
Original: $26 • Value: $31

1598.
LeGrand Ol' Bear [Lock, Stock & Barrel]
#unknown • 7"
LE • Issued: 2003 • Retired: 2003
Original: $20 • Value: $24

1599.
Leigh Ann Beansford [QVC]
#(C99067) • 10"
Issued: 2000 • Retired: 2000
Original: $16 • Value: $35

1600.
Leisel L. Burrbruin
#904024 • 8" • TJ
Issued: 2002 • Retired: 2004
Original: $15 • Value: $15

1601.
Leiselle Bloomengrows
#915502 • 8" • TJ
Issued: 2001 • Retired: 2002
Original: $15 • Value: $18

1602.
Lem Bruin
#5123 • 14" • JB
Issued: 1989 • Retired: 1993
Original: $20 • Value: $84

1603.
Leo Bruinski
#918320 • 10" • TJ
Issued: 1998 • Retired: 2000
Original: $27 • Value: $35

1604.
Leon
#1001-08 • 8" • CC
Issued: 1993 • Retired: 1999
Original: $8 • Value: $22

1605.
Leonardo B. Hartbreak [QVC]
#(C55511) • 12"
Issued: 1999 • Retired: 1999
Original: $26 • Value: $57

1606.
Leopold Q. Pouncely
#918668 • 10" • TJ
Issued: 2004 • Current
Original: $16 • Value: $R/E

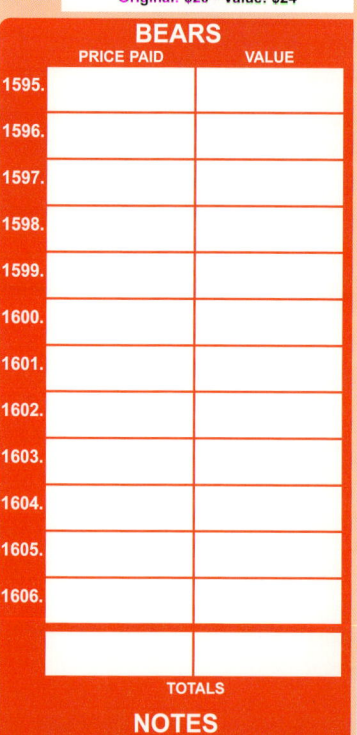

BEARS	PRICE PAID	VALUE
1595.		
1596.		
1597.		
1598.		
1599.		
1600.		
1601.		
1602.		
1603.		
1604.		
1605.		
1606.		
TOTALS		

NOTES

Bears

1607.
Leslie (with red heart)
#903029 • 8" • ME
Issued: 2003 • Current
Original: $10 • Value: $R/E

1608.
Leslie (nekkid)
#510903 • 6" • AS
Issued: 2004 • Current
Original: $7 • Value: $R/E

1609.
Leslie B. Ladybug
#904230 • 16" • TJ
Issued: 2004 • Current
Original: $47 • Value: $R/E

1610.
Lester [CAN]
#BC100705 • 12" • PM
Issued: 1997 • Retired: 1997
Original: $17 • Value: $40

1611.
Letitia T. Bearington [GCC]
#94879GCC • 10" • MB
Issued: 1999 • Retired: 1999
Original: $32 • Value: $50

1612.
Letti McVeggie [Paw Dealer]
#919829 • 10" • TJ
Issued: 2004 • Current
Original: $20 • Value: $R/E

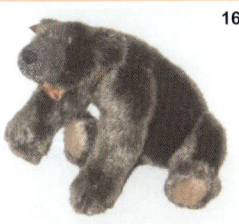

1613.
Lewis [QVC]
#(C34959) • 13"
Issued: 1998 • Retired: 1998
Original: $28 • Value: $56

1614.
Lexi Burrbruin [BtoB Website]
#919818 • 12"
Issued: 2002 • Retired: 2002
Original: $31 • Value: $35

1615.
Liam
#903030 • 8" • ME
Issued: 2003 • Current
Original: $10 • Value: $R/E

1616.
Libbee Bearamerica [Longaberger]
#94649LB • 10"
Issued: 2002 • Retired: 2002
Original: $32 • Value: $65
2002 Bee Bear

	BEARS	
	PRICE PAID	VALUE
1607.		
1608.		
1609.		
1610.		
1611.		
1612.		
1613.		
1614.		
1615.		
1616.		
1617.		
1618.		
	TOTALS	

NOTES

1617.
Libby B. Bunster
#916502 • 10" • TJ
Issued: 2000 • Retired: 2000
Original: $16 • Value: $19

1618.
Libby B. Ladybug
#904231 • 14" • TJ
Issued: 2004 • Current
Original: $25 • Value: $R/E

Bears

1619.
Libby Bearyproud [GCC]
#94903GCC • 12"
Issued: 2002 • Retired: 2002
Original: $32 • Value: $55

1620.
Libearty C. Star [Rocking Horse]
#94750RH • 10"
Issued: 2000 • Retired: 2000
Original: $20 • Value: $38

1621.
Licorice
#904341 • 10" • TJ
Issued: 2004 • Current
Original: $16 • Value: $R/E

1622.
Lil' Love [Longaberger]
#94629LB • 8"
Issued: 2003 • Retired: 2003
Original: $15 • Value: $25

1623.
Lil' Mischief [QVC]
#(C06207) • 6"
Issued: 2004 • Retired: 2004
Original: $11 • Value: $12

1624.
Lil' Missy Muffet
#91778 • 10" • TJ
Issued: 2002 • Retired: 2002
Original: $25 • Value: $25

1625.
Lil' Nicky Jodibear
#904354 • 6" • TJ
Issued: 2004 • Current
Original: $11 • Value: $R/E

1626.
Lil' Theodore [QVC]
#93560V (C06203) • 10"
LE of 5000 • Issued: 2004 • Retired: 2004
Original: $18 • Value: $25

1627.
Lillian K. Bearsley
#91743 • 10" • TJ
Issued: 1998 • Retired: 2001
Original: $16 • Value: $N/E

1628.
Lily Flutterby
#913934 • 8" • TJ
Issued: 2002 • Retired: 2002
Original: $15 • Value: $15

1629.
Lincoln B. Bearington
#590022-08 • 16" • MB
Issued: 1999 • Retired: 1999
Original: $100 • Value: $121

1630.
Lindsey [Belks]
#unknown • 10" • JB
Issued: 1997 • Retired: 1997
Original: $15 • Value: $38

BEARS	PRICE PAID	VALUE
1619.		
1620.		
1621.		
1622.		
1623.		
1624.		
1625.		
1626.		
1627.		
1628.		
1629.		
1630.		
TOTALS		

NOTES

Bears

1631.
Lindsey Ladybug
#904235 • 6" • TJ
Issued: 2004 • Current
Original: $10 • Value: $R/E

1632.
Lindsey Lou with Pee-Wee [QVC]
#99003V (C01904) • 12" • TJ
Issued: 2004 • Retired: 2004
Original: $30 • Value: $33

1633.
Lindsey Marie Goodbear [Country Clutter]
#94976CC • 10"
Issued: 2002 • Retired: 2002
Original: $22 • Value: $29

1634.
Lindsley Ladybug [Paw Dealer]
#919830 • 12" • TJ
Issued: 2004 • Current
Original: $23 • Value: $R/E

1635.
Lindy & Nell Bradbeary [QVC]
#(C55535) • 14"
Issued: 1999 • Retired: 1999
Original: $41 • Value: $65

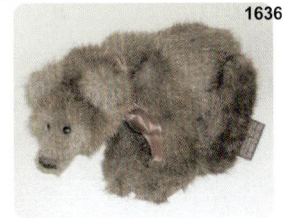

1636.
Linkin
#5811 • 6" • SB
Issued: 1992 • Retired: 1995
Original: $7 • Value: $50

1637.
Linsey McKenzie [QVC]
#(C39090) • 14"
Issued: 1997 • Retired: 1997
Original: $18 • Value: $49

1638.
Linus P. Fuzzfrost [QVC]
#(C80534) • 8"
Issued: 2000 • Retired: 2000
Original: $15 • Value: $25

1639.
Lion
#904371 • 8" • TJ
Issued: 2004 • Current
Original: $16 • Value: $R/E

1640.
Lisa T. Bearringer
#911950 • 16" • TJ
Issued: 1998 • Retired: 2001
Original: $51 • Value: $75

1641.
Lissa Angelwish
#904042 • 10" • TJ
Issued: 2002 • Retired: 2002
Original: $25 • Value: $25

1642.
Little Bangles [QVC]
#99957V (C22625) • 5"
Issued: 2003 • Retired: 2003
Original: $13 • Value: $22

BEARS	PRICE PAID	VALUE
1631.		
1632.		
1633.		
1634.		
1635.		
1636.		
1637.		
1638.		
1639.		
1640.		
1641.		
1642.		
TOTALS		

NOTES

Bears

1643.
Little Bearpeep and Friends
#912056 • 12" • TJ
Issued: 2001 • Retired: 2001
Original: $29 • Value: $48

1644.
Little Celeste [Gottschalks]
#unknown • 8"
Issued: 2000 • Retired: 2000
Original: $N/E • Value: $38

1645.
Little Larson [Ideation]
#94326I • 12"
Issued: 1997 • Retired: 1997
Original: $16 • Value: $32

1646.
Little Orchard Annie [POG]
#94605POG • 8"
Issued: 2003 • Retired: 2003
Original: $16 • Value: $19

1647.
Little Twink [BBC]
#918072SM • 10"
Issued: 2003 • Retired: 2003
Original: $20 • Value: $N/E

1648.
Liza Glorybear
#904190 • 16" • TJ
Issued: 2003 • Current
Original: $45 • Value: $R/E

1649.
Liza J. Berrijam
#910061 • 10" • TJ
Issued: 1999 • Retired: 2001
Original: $14 • Value: $17

1650.
Liza Mae & Alex [QVC]
#(C47247) • 12"
LE of 2400 • Issued: 1998 • Retired: 1998
Original: $66 • Value: $95

1651.
Lizzie McBee
#91005 • 8" • TJ
Issued: 1996 • Retired: 1997
Original: $20 • Value: $40

1652.
Lizzie McBee (red plaid dress) [QVC]
#(C47275) • 8"
Issued: 1998 • Retired: 1998
Original: $16 • Value: $N/E

1653.
Lizzie Wishkabibble [EVENT]
#50002 • 10" • TJ
Issued: 2000 • Retired: 2000
Original: $21 • Value: $31

1654.
Lloyd
#5714 • 10" • AS
Issued: 1990 • Retired: 1993
Original: $N/E • Value: $145

BEARS

	PRICE PAID	VALUE
1643.		
1644.		
1645.		
1646.		
1647.		
1648.		
1649.		
1650.		
1651.		
1652.		
1653.		
1654.		
TOTALS		

NOTES

Bears

1655.
Logan [QVC]
#(C45210) • 13"
Issued: 1997 • Retired: 1997
Original: $32 • Value: $50

1656.
Logan Fremont
#919611 • 8" • TJ
Issued: 1999 • Retired: 2000
Original: $11 • Value: $13
Variations pictured together.

1657.
Lois B. Bearlove
#913956 • 6" • TJ
Issued: 2000 • Retired: 2000
Original: $10 • Value: $12

1658.
Lone Star [Dillards]
#94707DL • 14"
Issued: 1997 • Retired: 1997
Original: $25 • Value: $65

1659.
Lorraine P. Bearsley [QVC]
#(C76777) • 15"
Issued: 2000 • Retired: 2000
Original: $26 • Value: $45

1660.
Lou Bearig
#91771-06 • 6" • TJ
Issued: 1998 • Retired: 2000
Original: $11 • Value: $23

1661.
Louella
#91242 • 10" • TJ
Issued: 1996 • Retired: 1998
Original: $24 • Value: $50

1662.
Louie B. Bear
#5114-11 • 16" • JB
Issued: 1995 • Retired: 1997
Original: $25 • Value: $50

1663.
Louisa Catherine Bearington [QVC]
#93314V (C19892) • 6" • MB
Issued: 2002 • Retired: 2002
Original: $17 • Value: $28

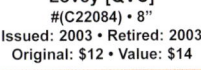
1664.
Lovey [QVC]
#(C22084) • 8"
Issued: 2003 • Retired: 2003
Original: $12 • Value: $14

1665.
Lovie
#82043 • 8"
Issued: 2003 • Current
Original: $10 • Value: $R/E

1666.
Luci T. Jodibear
#92000-18 • 9" • AR
Issued: 2002 • Retired: 2002
Original: $20 • Value: $20

BEARS		
	PRICE PAID	VALUE
1655.		
1656.		
1657.		
1658.		
1659.		
1660.		
1661.		
1662.		
1663.		
1664.		
1665.		
1666.		
TOTALS		

NOTES

Bears

1667.
Lucinda D. Bearsley [QVC]
#(C53072) • 10"
Issued: 1998 • Retired: 1998
Original: $16 • Value: $35

1668.
Lucky B. Ladybug
#904232 • 10" • TJ
Issued: 2004 • Current
Original: $18 • Value: $R/E

1669.
Lucky O'Beary [Longaberger]
#94640LB • 10"
Issued: 2002 • Retired: 2002
Original: $15 • Value: $33

1670.
Lucy [Gottschalks]
#unknown • 12"
Issued: 1999 • Retired: 1999
Original: $26 • Value: $39

1671.
Lucy Bea LeBruin [QVC]
#93037V (C39093) • 16"
Issued: 1997 • Retired: 1997
Original: $30 • Value: $65

1672.
Lucy Lynn Beansley [QVC]
#93466V (C3002) • 10"
Issued: 2003 • Retired: 2003
Original: $20 • Value: $29

1673.
Lucy McLemon
#904280 • 14" • TJ
Issued: 2004 • Current
Original: $34 • Value: $R/E

1674.
Ludmilla Berriman & Ludwig Von Fuzzner [QVC]
#unknown • 14"
LE of 2400 • Issued: 1998 • Retired: 1998
Original: $58 • Value: $119

1675.
Ludwigg V. Burrbruin
#904022 • 14" • TJ
Issued: 2002 • Retired: 2004
Original: $30 • Value: $30

1676.
Luke P. Jodibear
#92000-19 • 9" • AR
Issued: 2002 • Retired: 2002
Original: $20 • Value: $20

1677.
Lula B. Lightfoot [QVC]
#(C99066) • 12"
Issued: 2000 • Retired: 2000
Original: $23 • Value: $28

1678.
Lulu Mae Ladybug [QVC]
#93545V (C06192) • 8"
Issued: 2004 • Retired: 2004
Original: $13 • Value: $14

BEARS	PRICE PAID	VALUE
1667.		
1668.		
1669.		
1670.		
1671.		
1672.		
1673.		
1674.		
1675.		
1676.		
1677.		
1678.		
TOTALS		

NOTES

Bears

1679.
Luvey Heartstrings [Longaberger]
#993645LB • 8½"
Issued: 2004 • Retired: 2004
Original: $15 • Value: $15

1680.
Lydia Fitzbruin
#9180 • 14" • TJ
Issued: 1993 • Retired: 1996
Original: $27 • Value: $165

1681.
Lynette Bearlove
#918433 • 6" • TJ
Issued: 2000 • Retired: 2000
Original: $10 • Value: $12

1682.
M.B. Hugsley [QVC]
#unknown • 30"
Issued: 2002 • Retired: 2002
Original: $58 • Value: $75

1683.
M.T. FuzzieFriend [QVC]
#93514V (C02228) • 8"
Issued: 2004 • Retired: 2004
Original: $12 • Value: $13

1684.
Mac the Golfer
#unknown • 13"
LE • Issued: 1995 • Retired: 1995
Original: $N/E • Value: $177

1685.
Macho Z. Heartthrob
#82017 • 6" • JB
Issued: 2001 • Retired: 2001
Original: $10 • Value: $17

1686.
Maci E. Kringlebeary [Macy's East]
#unknown • 12"
Issued: 2000 • Retired: 2000
Original: $30 • Value: $41

1687.
Mackenzie Alexandra [Elder Beerman]
#94618EB • 8"
Issued: 2003 • Retired: 2003
Original: $20 • Value: $24

1688.
MacMillan
#5707-10 • 8" • AS
Issued: 1995 • Retired: 1997
Original: $12 • Value: $27

1689.
Macy Sunbeary
#911952 • 16" • TJ
Issued: 2001 • Retired: 2002
Original: $36 • Value: $43

1690.
Maddison Bearyproud [Cracker Barrel]
#94994CB • 10"
Issued: 2002 • Retired: 2002
Original: $22 • Value: $45

BEARS	PRICE PAID	VALUE
1679.		
1680.		
1681.		
1682.		
1683.		
1684.		
1685.		
1686.		
1687.		
1688.		
1689.		
1690.		
TOTALS		

NOTES

Bears

1691.
Madeline [Elder Beerman]
#94681EB • 8"
Issued: 1998 • Retired: 1998
Original: $15 • Value: $26

1692.
Madeline Ann Woodsbeary [Kirlins]
#94531KR • 10"
Issued: 2001 • Retired: 2001
Original: $21 • Value: $34

1693.
Madeline Willoughby
#918333 • 10" • TJ
Issued: 1999 • Retired: 2001
Original: $26 • Value: $31

1694.
Madison [SLE]
#unknown • 8"
Issued: 1996 • Retired: 1996
Original: $11 • Value: $34

1695.
Madison Glorybear [Kirlins]
#94536KR • 10"
Issued: 2003 • Retired: 2003
Original: $20 • Value: $28

1696.
Madison L. Bearington
#590080-08 • 6" • MB
Issued: 1997 • Retired: 1997
Original: $18 • Value: $40

BEARS	PRICE PAID	VALUE
1691.		
1692.		
1693.		
1694.		
1695.		
1696.		
1697.		
1698.		
1699.		
1700.		
1701.		
1702.		
	TOTALS	

NOTES

1697.
Mae B. Bearlove
#82002 • 6" • TJ
Issued: 2000 • Retired: 2000
Original: $11 • Value: $13

1698.
Mae I. Loveya [POG]
#94594POG • 6"
Issued: 2002 • Retired: 2002
Original: $12 • Value: $20

1699.
Magdalena [Frederick Atkins]
#unknown • 6"
Issued: 1998 • Retired: 1998
Original: $16 • Value: $26

1700.
Maggie B. Bearheart
#904082 • 10"
Issued: 2003 • Current
Original: $22 • Value: $R/E

1701.
Major
#5717 • 10" • AS
Issued: 1991 • Retired: 1992
Original: $18 • Value: $135

1702.
Major II
#5703B • 10" • AS
Issued: 1992 • Retired: 1996
Original: $18 • Value: $52

Bears

1703.
Malcolm
#5711 • 16" • AS
Issued: 1992 • Retired: 1999
Original: $30 • Value: $52

1704.
Malinda T. Bloomberg [QVC]
#93451V (C22626) • 16"
Issued: 2003 • Retired: 2003
Original: $49 • Value: $59

1705.
Mallory Witebruin [GCC]
#94866GCC • 14"
Issued: 1999 • Retired: 1999
Original: $25 • Value: $41

1706.
Mallow Cocobeary
#904332 • 14" • TJ
Issued: 2004 • Current
Original: $31 • Value: $R/E

1707.
Mamie E. Bearington [QVC]
#93074V (C49888) • 15" • MB
LE • Issued: 1998 • Retired: 1998
Original: $126 • Value: $160

1708.
Mamie Glorybear
#904195 • 6" • TJ
Issued: 2003 • Current
Original: $10 • Value: $R/E

1709.
Manchester S. Bearrister [QVC]
#(C63340) • 21"
Issued: 1999 • Retired: 1999
Original: $53 • Value: $72

1710.
Mandy Jo and Suzie [QVC]
#99896V (C20944) • 14"
Issued: 2003 • Retired: 2003
Original: $38 • Value: $46

BEARS		
	PRICE PAID	VALUE
1703.		
1704.		
1705.		
1706.		
1707.		
1708.		
1709.		
1710.		
1711.		
1712.		
1713.		
1714.		
	TOTALS	

NOTES

1711.
Maple T. Leafowitz [QVC]
#93225v (C64865) • 10"
Issued: 2001 • Retired: 2001
Original: $27 • Value: $35

1712.
Margaret Hollybeary [POG]
#94587POG • 14"
Issued: 2000 • Retired: 2000
Original: $26 • Value: $39

1713.
Margaret T. Pattington
#92001-03 • 12" • MB
Issued: 1999 • Retired: 1999
Original: $31 • Value: $55

1714.
Margarita
#911062 • 14" • AR
Issued: 1998 • Retired: 2001
Original: $16 • Value: $26
Also with Vermooth as QVC set.

Bears

1715.
Margo De Bearvoire
#904227 • 6" • TJ
Issued: 2003 • Current
Original: $10 • Value: $R/E

1716.
Margo DeBearvoire
#918340 • 10"
Issued: 2002 • Retired: 2002
Original: $19 • Value: $19

1717.
Margo duBeary
#904126 • 6"
Issued: 2003 • Retired: 2003
Original: $10 • Value: $10

1718.
Mariah Crystalfrost
#904180 • 16" • TJ
Issued: 2003 • Current
Original: $47 • Value: $R/E

1719.
Marian [Kirlins]
#unknown • 10"
Issued: 1998 • Retired: 1998
Original: $24 • Value: $37

1720.
Marie B. Bearlove
#912626 • 14" • TJ
Issued: 2000 • Retired: 2000
Original: $30 • Value: $36

1721.
Marilyn [SLE]
#unknown • 8"
LE of 1200 • Issued: 1996 • Retired: 1996
Original: $20 • Value: $48

1722.
Marina [Lord & Taylor]
#unknown • 10"
Issued: 1998 • Retired: 1998
Original: $20 • Value: $32

1723.
Marina Yachtley
#918343 • 10" • TJ
Issued: 2002 • Retired: 2002
Original: $20 • Value: $20

1724.
Marion T. Bestlove
#82514 • 10" • JB
Issued: 2002 • Retired: 2002
Original: $12 • Value: $12

1725.
Maris G. Pattington
#92001-04 • 12" • MB
Issued: 2000 • Retired: 2000
Original: $47 • Value: $62

1726.
Maris Q. Yachtley
#912018 • 16" • TJ
Issued: 2002 • Retired: 2002
Original: $45 • Value: $51

BEARS

	PRICE PAID	VALUE
1715.		
1716.		
1717.		
1718.		
1719.		
1720.		
1721.		
1722.		
1723.		
1724.		
1725.		
1726.		
TOTALS		

NOTES

Bears

1727.
Marissa duBeary [QVC]
#(C98198) • 14"
Issued: 2001 • Retired: 2001
Original: $45 • Value: $65

1728.
Marjorie Ellen Bearsley [GCC]
#94880GCC • 14"
Issued: 2000 • Retired: 2000
Original: $30 • Value: $45

1729.
Marla Dubeary
#918200 • 10"
Issued: 2002 • Retired: 2002
Original: $15 • Value: $21

1730.
Marla Mae Beary [Welcome Home]
#94531WH • 8"
Issued: 2000 • Retired: 2000
Original: $15 • Value: $32

1731.
Marla Sprucebeary
#915501 • 8" • TJ
Issued: 2000 • Retired: 2002
Original: $18 • Value: $31

1732.
Marlena Beargeaux and Deitrich
#900103 • 16" • TJ
Issued: 2003 • Retired: 2003
Original: $55 • Value: $65

1733.
Marley Dickens
#904221 • 14" • TJ
Issued: 2003 • Retired: 2003
Original: $30 • Value: $30

1734.
Marlowe Snoopstein
#91871 • 11" • TJ
Issued: 1999 • Retired: 2000
Original: $23 • Value: $35

1735.
Marnie [Elder Beerman]
#94685 • 10"
Issued: 1999 • Retired: 1999
Original: $28 • Value: $43

1736.
Marsha Cocobeary
#904331 • 14" • TJ
Issued: 2004 • Current
Original: $34 • Value: $R/E

1737.
Marshmallow Cocobeary
#904335 • 5½" • TJ
Issued: 2004 • Current
Original: $11 • Value: $R/E

1738.
Marshmallow Q. Furryfoot [QVC]
#(C59862) • 20"
Issued: 2001 • Retired: 2001
Original: $54 • Value: $65

BEARS		
	PRICE PAID	VALUE
1727.		
1728.		
1729.		
1730.		
1731.		
1732.		
1733.		
1734.		
1735.		
1736.		
1737.		
1738.		
TOTALS		

NOTES

Bears

1739.
Martha S. McBruin
#910063 • 10" • ME
Issued: 2001 • Retired: 2002
Original: $25 • Value: $30

1740.
Martha T. Bearyproud with Yankee Doodle [QVC]
#(C02190) • 14"
LE of 3000 • Issued: 2004 • Retired: 2004
Original: $54 • Value: $60
Sold with wooden rocking chair.

1741.
Marvin P. Snowbeary
#9136-01 • 6" • TJ
Issued: 1997 • Retired: 2000
Original: $12 • Value: $20

1742.
Mary Alice Weedsalot [GCC]
#94849GCC • 10"
Issued: 2003 • Retired: 2003
Original: $22 • Value: $27

1743.
Mary Ann Bearican
#904254 • 8" • TJ
Issued: 2004 • Current
Original: $13 • Value: $R/E

1744.
Mary B. Mistletoe [CAN]
#BC94297PO • 12"
LE of 1200 • Issued: 2003 • Retired: 2003
Original: $40 • Value: $46

1745.
Mary Beary
#904351 • 14" • TJ
Issued: 2004 • Current
Original: $34 • Value: $R/E

1746.
Mary Elizabeth, Becca & Ruth [QVC]
#99128V (C20978) • 14"
LE • Issued: 2000 • Retired: 2000
Original: $75 • Value: $100

1747.
Mary Ellen Patchbeary
#912643 • 14" • TJ
Issued: 2002 • Retired: 2002
Original: $25 • Value: $25

1748.
Mary Kate Gingerbeary
#904033 • 8" • TJ
Issued: 2002 • Retired: 2004
Original: $14 • Value: $14

1749.
Mary Louise Bearington (10" gold mohair) [QVC]
#(C78106) • 10" • MB
LE of 7500 • Issued: 2000 • Retired: 2000
Original: $38 • Value: $50

1750.
Mary Louise Bearington (6" white moahir) [QVC]
#93423V (C21446) • 6" • MB
LE of 2800 • Issued: 2003 • Retired: 2003
Original: $17 • Value: $20

BEARS

	PRICE PAID	VALUE
1739.		
1740.		
1741.		
1742.		
1743.		
1744.		
1745.		
1746.		
1747.		
1748.		
1749.		
1750.		
TOTALS		

NOTES

Bears

1751.
Mary Lucinda & Marjorie Mayberry [QVC]
#(C63338) • 10"
Issued: 1999 • Retired: 1999
Original: $37 • Value: $55

1752.
Maryanne McBeansley [QVC]
#93552V (C06189) • 16"
Issued: 2004 • Retired: 2004
Original: $40 • Value: $43

1753.
Mason [BBC]
#918014SM • 14"
Issued: 2002 • Current
Original: $35 • Value: $R/E

Have You Seen Me?

1754.
Matilda
#6161B • TJ
Issued: 1991 • Retired: 1991
Original: $63 • Value: $194

1755.
Matthew (Fall 1996)
#91756 • 8" • BF
Issued: 1996 • Retired: 1996
Original: $26 • Value: $41

1756.
Matthew (Fall 1997)
#91756-08 • 8" • BF
Issued: 1997 • Retired: 1997
Original: $26 • Value: $37

1757.
Matthew (Fall 1998)
#91756-10 • 8" • BF
Issued: 1998 • Retired: 1998
Original: $27 • Value: $34

1758.
Matthew (Fall 1999)
#91756-12 • 8" • BF
Issued: 1999 • Retired: 1999
Original: $21 • Value: $30

1759.
Matthew (Fall 2000)
#91756-15 • 8" • BF
Issued: 2001 • Retired: 2001
Original: $22 • Value: $26

1760.
Matthew (Fall 2001)
#91756-17 • 8" • BF
Issued: 2002 • Retired: 2002
Original: $17 • Value: $20

1761.
Matthew (Fall 2002)
#91756-19 • 8" • BF
Issued: 2002 • Retired: 2002
Original: $19 • Value: $22

1762.
Matthew (Fall 2003)
#91756-21 • 8" • BF
Issued: 2003 • Retired: 2003
Original: $15 • Value: $15

BEARS	
PRICE PAID	VALUE
1751.	
1752.	
1753.	
1754.	
1755.	
1756.	
1757.	
1758.	
1759.	
1760.	
1761.	
1762.	
TOTALS	

NOTES

Bears

1763. Matthew (Fall 2004)
#91756-23 • 8" • BF
Issued: 2004 • To Be Retired: 2004
Original: $15 • Value: $R/E

1764. Matthew Bear
#5070 • 10" • WB
Issued: 1985 • Retired: 1986
Original: $12 • Value: $387

1765. Matthew Bear (Anniversary Edition)
#912615 • 11" • WB
Issued: 1999 • Retired: 1999
Original: $14 • Value: $29

1766. Matthew H. Growler
#5721 • 12" • AS
Issued: 1996 • Retired: 1999
Original: $21 • Value: $41

1767. Mattie C. Bearsley [GCC]
#94882GCC • 6"
Issued: 2000 • Retired: 2000
Original: $12 • Value: $31

1768. Maximillian
#572210-05 • 21" • AS
Issued: 2000 • Retired: 2002
Original: $53 • Value: $64

1769. Maximillian, Thornton, & Elford [QVC]
#unknown • 14"
LE of 1800 • Issued: 1998 • Retired: 1998
Original: $60 • Value: $80

1770. Maxine T. Bearsley [GCC]
#94881GCC • 8"
Issued: 2000 • Retired: 2000
Original: $14 • Value: $35

1771. Maxton P. Bean with Craxton and Paxton [QVC]
#unknown • 10"
Issued: 1998 • Retired: 1998
Original: $21 • Value: $45

1772. Maya Berriman
#91394 • 6" • TJ
Issued: 1999 • Retired: 2001
Original: $12 • Value: $19

1773. McKenzie
#5840-03 • 6" • AS
Issued: 1997 • Retired: 2001
Original: $9 • Value: $16

1774. McKinley
#5848-05 • 12"
Issued: 1996 • Retired: 1999
Original: $21 • Value: $26

BEARS

	PRICE PAID	VALUE
1763.		
1764.		
1765.		
1766.		
1767.		
1768.		
1769.		
1770.		
1771.		
1772.		
1773.		
1774.		
TOTALS		

NOTES

1775.
McKinley Bearington
#590043-01 • 12" • MB
Issued: 2001 • Retired: 2002
Original: $50 • Value: $60

1776.
McMullen
#5702 • 12" • AS
Issued: 1990 • Retired: 1991
Original: $20 • Value: $126

1777.
McShamus O'Growler
#91732 • 9" • TJ
Issued: 1997 • Retired: 1998
Original: $21 • Value: $33

1778.
Meg [Dillards]
#94770DL • 14"
Issued: 2000 • Retired: 2000
Original: $35 • Value: $55

1779.
Meg
#919834 • 10" • TJ
Issued: 2004 • Current
Original: $20 • Value: $R/E

1780.
Meg Autumnfest
#904152 • 10" • TJ
Issued: 2003 • Current
Original: $25 • Value: $R/E

1781.
Megan [Kirlins]
#unknown • 10"
Issued: 1999 • Retired: 1999
Original: $20 • Value: $29

1782.
Megan Berriman
#912623 • 14" • TJ
Issued: 2000 • Retired: 2002
Original: $13 • Value: $31

1783.
Melanie Lockley & Sam [QVC]
#(C95152) • 13"
Issued: 1999 • Retired: 1999
Original: $32 • Value: $48

1784.
Melanie McRind
#912658 • 12" • TJ
Issued: 2001 • Retired: 2002
Original: $24 • Value: $29

1785.
Melbourne
#5719 • 12" • AS
Issued: 1992 • Retired: 1994
Original: $20 • Value: $99

1786.
Melinda M. Milestone [QVC]
#(C76934) • 10"
Issued: 2000 • Retired: 2000
Original: $11 • Value: $20

BEARS

	PRICE PAID	VALUE
1775.		
1776.		
1777.		
1778.		
1779.		
1780.		
1781.		
1782.		
1783.		
1784.		
1785.		
1786.		
TOTALS		

NOTES

Bears

1787.
Melinda McRind & Dixie LE Set [QVC]
#(C59819) • 14"
LE • Issued: 2001 • Retired: 2001
Original: $65 • Value: $121

1788.
Melinda S. Willoughby
#913961 • 6" • TJ
Issued: 2000 • Retired: 2000
Original: $10 • Value: $17

1789.
Memsy
#unknown • 12"
LE of 400 • Issued: 1993 • Retired: 1993
Original: $70 • Value: $375

1790.
Mercedes Fitzbruin
#91204 • 8" • TJ
Issued: 1998 • Retired: 2002
Original: $19 • Value: $27

1791.
Merci Bearcoo
#903001 • 8" • TJ
Issued: 2001 • Retired: 2001
Original: $10 • Value: $16

1792.
Meredith K. Pattington with Benjamin
#900204 • 14" • MB
LE of 10467 • Issued: 1999 • Retired: 1999
Original: $111 • Value: $133

BEARS		
	PRICE PAID	VALUE
1787.		
1788.		
1789.		
1790.		
1791.		
1792.		
1793.		
1794.		
1795.		
1796.		
1797.		
1798.		
	TOTALS	

NOTES

1793.
Meridian Wishkabibble
#90500 • 12" • TJ
Issued: 2001 • Retired: 2002
Original: $30 • Value: $36

Have You Seen Me?

1794.
Merlin
#6167B • TJ
Issued: 1991 • Retired: 1991
Original: $63 • Value: $382

1795.
Merry Beary [Platinum Paw]
#919825 • 12" • TJ
Issued: 2003 • Retired: 2003
Original: $23 • Value: $29

1796.
Merrybeary Beanster [QVC]
#(C20910) • 10"
Issued: 2002 • Retired: 2002
Original: $14 • Value: $24

1797.
Mia Goodfriends
#903027 • 8" • ME
Issued: 2003 • Current
Original: $10 • Value: $R/E

1798.
Michael [Dillards]
#94717DL • 14"
Issued: 1997 • Retired: 1997
Original: $26 • Value: $40

Bears

1799.
Michael David Bearsley
#510401-11 • 16" • JB
Issued: 2001 • Retired: 2002
Original: $23 • Value: $28

1800.
Michaela [Dillards]
#94718DL • 10"
Issued: 1997 • Retired: 1997
Original: $25 • Value: $45

1801.
Michelle B. Bearsley [QVC]
#(C78137) • 9"
Issued: 2000 • Retired: 2000
Original: $18 • Value: $30

1802.
Mickey
#9157-01 • 8" • TJ
Issued: 1993 • Retired: 1994
Original: $14 • Value: $64

1803.
Mikayla Springbeary
#912624 • 14" • TJ
Issued: 2000 • Retired: 2002
Original: $27 • Value: $32

1804.
Mikie O'Burr [Hallmark]
#9694HM • 8"
Issued: 2002 • Retired: 2002
Original: $17 • Value: $22

1805.
Millicent Sugarcone
#904121 • 10"
Issued: 2003 • Retired: 2003
Original: $18 • Value: $20

1806.
**Millie Marie Goodbear
[Country Clutter]**
#94974CC • 10"
Issued: 2001 • Retired: 2001
Original: $20 • Value: $35

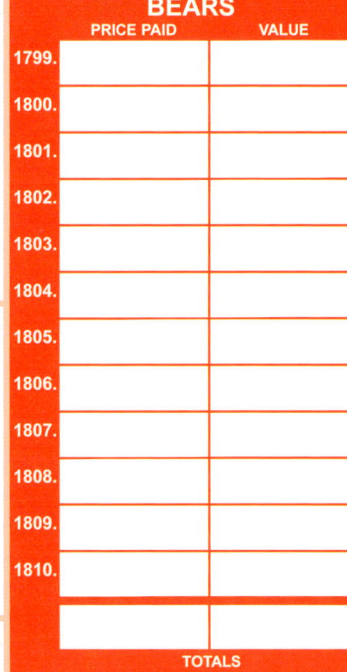

BEARS	PRICE PAID	VALUE
1799.		
1800.		
1801.		
1802.		
1803.		
1804.		
1805.		
1806.		
1807.		
1808.		
1809.		
1810.		

TOTALS

NOTES

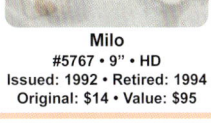

1807.
Milo
#5767 • 9" • HD
Issued: 1992 • Retired: 1994
Original: $14 • Value: $95

1808.
Mimi & Arlene [GCC]
#94904GCC • 6"
Issued: 2002 • Retired: 2002
Original: $32 • Value: $45
Sold with wagon.

1809.
Mimi Chapeau
#918449 • 6"
Issued: 2002 • Retired: 2002
Original: $10 • Value: $16

1810.
Mindy D. Beartucket [QVC]
#93548V (C06199) • 14"
Issued: 2004 • Retired: 2004
Original: $29 • Value: $32

Bears

1811. Mindy P. Elfbeary
#904052 • 9"
Issued: 2002 • Retired: 2004
Original: $20 • Value: $20

1812. Mindy S. Basketcase [QVC]
#(C40592) • 8"
Issued: 2001 • Retired: 2001
Original: $19 • Value: $35

1813. Mindy Witebruin [GCC]
#94867GCC • 6"
Issued: 1999 • Retired: 1999
Original: $12 • Value: $21

1814. Minkles D. Bearsdale
#510810-03 • 14" • JB
Issued: 2002 • Retired: 2002
Original: $15 • Value: $21

1815. Minnie Higgenthorpe
#918441 • 6" • TJ
Issued: 1999 • Retired: 1999
Original: $10 • Value: $22

1816. Miranda Cherrybeary and Bing
#904090 • 16"
Issued: 2003 • Current
Original: $45 • Value: $R/E

1817. Miranda Hollybeary [SYN]
#94588POG • 6"
Issued: 2000 • Retired: 2000
Original: $12 • Value: $21

1818. Miss Amirella & Ripley [QVC]
#(C98068) • 14"
LE of 3000 • Issued: 2000 • Retired: 2000
Original: $55 • Value: $80

Have You Seen Me?

1819. Miss Ashley
#unknown • 14" • TJ
Issued: 1992 • Retired: 1992
Original: $70 • Value: $450

1820. Miss Graduate
#903033 • 8"
Issued: 2003 • Current
Original: $10 • Value: $R/E

1821. Miss Hathabeary
#903018 • 8" • ME
Issued: 2002 • Current
Original: $10 • Value: $R/E

1822. Miss Hedda Bearimore
#918453 • 10" • TJ
Issued: 2000 • Retired: 2000
Original: $19 • Value: $27

BEARS

	PRICE PAID	VALUE
1811.		
1812.		
1813.		
1814.		
1815.		
1816.		
1817.		
1818.		
1819.		
1820.		
1821.		
1822.		
TOTALS		

NOTES

Bears

1823.
Miss Isabelle Q. Bearsworthy
[QVC]
#93095V (C53111) • 10"
Issued: 1998 • Retired: 1998
Original: $20 • Value: $32

1824.
Miss Lorriane & Abby Mae [QVC]
#99848V (C100848) • 10"
Issued: 2002 • Retired: 2002
Original: $30 • Value: $40

1825.
Miss Mabel & Mr. Miles
Bearister [QVC]
#(C57651) • 8"
Issued: 1999 • Retired: 1999
Original: $30 • Value: $56

1826.
Miss MacIntosh
#912652 • 12" • ME
Issued: 2001 • Retired: 2002
Original: $30 • Value: $36

1827.
Miss MacIntosh & Sarahbeth
with Topsey [QVC]
#99720V(C96372) • 16"
LE of 3000 • Issued: 1999 • Retired: 1999
Original: $63 • Value: $90

1828.
Miss Maggie & Theo
[Welcome Home]
#unknown • 10"
Issued: 1998 • Retired: 1998
Original: $N/E • Value: $50

1829.
Miss Niblers [QVC]
#93289V • 8"
Issued: 2002 • Retired: 2002
Original: $14 • Value: $22

1830.
Miss Nicole Plumbeary [GCC]
#94895GCC • 14"
LE of 1850 • Issued: 2001 • Retired: 2001
Original: $31 • Value: $58

BEARS		
	PRICE PAID	VALUE
1823.		
1824.		
1825.		
1826.		
1827.		
1828.		
1829.		
1830.		
1831.		
1832.		
1833.		
1834.		
	TOTALS	

NOTES

1831.
Miss Poinsley [QVC]
#(C20970) • 12"
Issued: 2002 • Retired: 2002
Original: $17 • Value: $22

1833.
Missy
#5642-10 • 8" • BA
Issued: 1995 • Retired: 1996
Original: $11 • Value: $41

1832.
Miss Winsalot [QVC]
#(C60266) • 14"
Issued: 2002 • Retired: 2002
Original: $35 • Value: $42

1834.
Missy Lou & Gilbert [QVC]
#(C0545) • 12"
Issued: 2002 • Retired: 2002
Original: $31 • Value: $40

178

Bears

1835.
Mistle
#5151-04 • 8"
Issued: 1994 • Retired: 1997
Original: $12 • Value: $25

1836.
Mistle & Taux [QVC]
#(C98259) • 6"
Issued: 2001 • Retired: 2001
Original: $14 • Value: $25

1837.
Mitchell Bearsdale
#912615 • 14" • TJ
Issued: 1999 • Retired: 2002
Original: $40 • Value: $55

1838.
Mizz Buzzley & Mrs. McFlutter [QVC]
#99879V (C19888) • 5½"
Issued: 2002 • Retired: 2002
Original: $19 • Value: $35

1839.
Mohley
#5771 • 9" • HD
Issued: 1992 • Retired: 1993
Original: $13 • Value: $185

1840.
Molly Maybeary [Welcome Home]
#unknown • 8"
Issued: 2001 • Retired: 2001
Original: $15 • Value: $30

1841.
Molly R. Berriman & Nathan
#900253 • UB
Issued: 1999 • Retired: 1999
Original: $65 • Value: $95

1842.
Molly R. Mistletoe [CAN]
#BC94296PO • 8½"
LE of 1200 • Issued: 2003 • Retired: 2003
Original: $17 • Value: $20

1843.
Mom & Baby Hugs [QVC]
#(C08501)
Issued: 2004 • Retired: 2004
Original: $17 • Value: $23

1844.
Momma Beansford & Sweet Cheeks [QVC]
#93311V (C19881) • 10"
Issued: 2002 • Retired: 2002
Original: $22 • Value: $35

1845.
Momma Bear, Alouetta, & Victor [QVC]
#(C39580) • 14"
LE of 1800 • Issued: 1997 • Retired: 1997
Original: $78 • Value: $147

1846.
Momma Bearhugs and Tory
#82507 • 10" • TJ
Issued: 2001 • Retired: 2002
Original: $30 • Value: $36

BEARS

	PRICE PAID	VALUE
1835.		
1836.		
1837.		
1838.		
1839.		
1840.		
1841.		
1842.		
1843.		
1844.		
1845.		
1846.		
	TOTALS	

NOTES

Bears

1847.
Momma Bearlove and Baby
#82533 • 10"
Issued: 2004 • Current
Original: $24 • Value: $R/E

1848.
Momma Bearsley & Baby Jack
#903203 • 10" • ME
Issued: 2002 • Retired: 2002
Original: $20 • Value: $20

1849.
Momma Bearsley with Baby Bundles
#919816 • 14"
Issued: 2003 • Current
Original: $57 • Value: $R/E

1850.
Momma Bearsworth with Mary-Margaret, Stuart & Frame [QVC]
#99811V (C61437) • 14"
LE of 27500 • Issued: 2001 • Retired: 2001
Original: $75 • Value: $90

1851.
Momma Bearybake [QVC]
#(C5098) • 13"
LE of 4500 • Issued: 2003 • Retired: 2003
Original: $49 • Value: $59
Sold as set with rolling pin, pie, wooden table.

1852.
Momma Berrywinkle & Woodrow [QVC]
#(C46472) • 12"
LE of 2400 • Issued: 1998 • Retired: 1998
Original: $76 • Value: $110

1853.
Momma Hollybeary with Baby Jingles [QVC]
#(C20885) • 10"
Issued: 2002 • Retired: 2002
Original: $22 • Value: $28

1854.
Momma MacBeansley & Toots [QVC]
#99864V (C60293) • 10"
Issued: 2002 • Retired: 2002
Original: $22 • Value: $35

1855.
Momma MacBearsley with Baby
#82515 • 10" • TJ
Issued: 2002 • Retired: 2002
Original: $24 • Value: $24

1856.
Momma McBear & Cedric [QVC]
#(C35536) • 10"
Issued: 1997 • Retired: 1997
Original: $N/E • Value: $N/E

1857.
Momma McBear & Delmar
#91007 • 10" • TJ
Issued: 1997 • Retired: 2000
Original: $N/E • Value: $N/E

1858.
Momma McBear & Delmar [SFMB]
#41-72585 • 10"
Issued: 1998 • Retired: 1998
Original: $30 • Value: $50
♪ You're Nobody Til Somebody Loves You ♪

BEARS	PRICE PAID	VALUE
1847.		
1848.		
1849.		
1850.		
1851.		
1852.		
1853.		
1854.		
1855.		
1856.		
1857.		
1858.		
TOTALS		

NOTES

Bears

1859.
Momma McBearlove & Baby
#82520 • 10" • TJ
Issued: 2003 • Retired: 2003
Original: $24 • Value: $24

1860.
Momma McBearsley with Jessica [Carlton Cards]
#919840CA • 10"
LE of 5000 • Issued: 2002 • Retired: 2002
Original: $28 • Value: $35

1861.
Momma McGoldberg & Cissy [GCC]
#94856GCC • 10"
Issued: 1998 • Retired: 1998
Original: $N/E • Value: $N/E

1862.
Momma McNew and Hugsley
#910021 • 10" • ME
Issued: 2001 • Retired: 2002
Original: $24 • Value: $29

1863.
Momma McNew with Hugsley [SFMB]
#910021SF • 10"
Issued: 2002 • Retired: 2002
Original: $35 • Value: $46
♪ Wind Beneath My Wings ♪

1864.
Momma McVeggie & The Sweetpeas
#904241 • 14" • TJ
Issued: 2004 • Current
Original: $30 • Value: $R/E

1865.
Mommie and Me [Harry & David]
#94204HD • 8"
Issued: 2003 • Retired: 2003
Original: $20 • Value: $24

1866.
Monica [Frederick Atkins]
#unknown • 10"
Issued: 1998 • Retired: 1998
Original: $N/E • Value: $35

1867.
Monique LaBearsley
#918447 • 6"
Issued: 2001 • Retired: N/E
Original: $10 • Value: $18

1868.
Monroe J. Bearington
#590023-11 • 16" • MB
Issued: 1999 • Retired: 2000
Original: $96 • Value: $115

1869.
Mookins
#91862 • 10"
Issued: 2002 • Retired: 2002
Original: $15 • Value: $15

1870.
Mooselkins
#91864 • 10"
Issued: 2002 • Current
Original: $15 • Value: $R/E

BEARS

	PRICE PAID	VALUE
1859.		
1860.		
1861.		
1862.		
1863.		
1864.		
1865.		
1866.		
1867.		
1868.		
1869.		
1870.		
TOTALS		

NOTES

Bears

1871.
Morgan B. Thumblover [SYN]
#94596SYN • 8"
Issued: 2002 • Retired: 2002
Original: $10 • Value: $14

1872.
Morgan T. Yachtley with Bill
#912644 • 14" • TJ
Issued: 2002 • Retired: 2002
Original: $30 • Value: $30

1873.
Moriarity (bean filled)
#9171 • 11" • TJ
Issued: 1993 • Retired: 1994
Original: $21 • Value: $105

1874.
Moriarity (polyfill)
#9171 • 11" • TJ
Issued: 1993 • Retired: 1995
Original: $21 • Value: $95

1875.
Morley
#510904 • 6" • AS
Issued: 2004 • Current
Original: $7 • Value: $R/E

1876.
Morris
#1003-05 • 8" • CC
Issued: 1997 • Retired: 1999
Original: $7 • Value: $20

1877.
Mother Bearston & Bluebell [QVC]
#(C49883) • 10"
Issued: 1998 • Retired: 1998
Original: $30 • Value: $N/E

1878.
Moxley Mooselkins [QVC]
#933380V (C20967) • 12"
Issued: 2002 • Retired: 2002
Original: $18 • Value: $23

1879.
Mr. & Mrs. Dooright
#903101 • 6½" • ME
Issued: 2002 • Retired: 2002
Original: $15 • Value: $15

1880.
Mr. & Mrs. Forevermore [QVC]
#(C39922) • 8"
Issued: 2002 • Retired: 2002
Original: $40 • Value: $55

1881.
Mr. Barnum [GCC]
#94872GCC • 14"
Issued: 1999 • Retired: 1999
Original: $18 • Value: $48

1882.
Mr. Baxter [QVC]
#(C5992) • 29"
LE of 800 • Issued: 2003 • Retired: 2003
Original: $113 • Value: $135

BEARS		
	PRICE PAID	VALUE
1871.		
1872.		
1873.		
1874.		
1875.		
1876.		
1877.		
1878.		
1879.		
1880.		
1881.		
1882.		
TOTALS		

NOTES

Bears

1883.
Mr. Baybeary
#917314 • 10" • TJ
Issued: 2000 • Retired: 2000
Original: $23 • Value: $35

1884.
Mr. Bojangles [QVC]
#(C57652) • 13"
Issued: 1999 • Retired: 1999
Original: $18 • Value: $50

1885.
Mr. BoJingles [SLE]
#unknown • 10"
Issued: 1997 • Retired: 1997
Original: $25 • Value: $43

1886.
Mr. Bojingles
#91264 • 14" • TJ
Issued: 2000 • Retired: 2000
Original: $18 • Value: $27

1887.
Mr. Chucklebeary [QVC]
#(C97880) • 12"
Issued: 2000 • Retired: 2000
Original: $19 • Value: $59

1888.
Mr. Everlove
#912655 • 12" • ME
Issued: 2001 • Current
Original: $29 • Value: $R/E

1889.
Mr. Graduate
#903032 • 8"
Issued: 2003 • Current
Original: $10 • Value: $R/E

1890.
Mr. Jones
#5869-08 • 16" • AR
Issued: 1997 • Retired: 1998
Original: $37 • Value: $69

1891.
Mr. Kringle
#904211 • 16" • TJ
Issued: 2003 • Current
Original: $43 • Value: $R/E

1892.
Mr. McFarkle
#912640 • 14" • TJ
Issued: 2000 • Retired: 2002
Original: $25 • Value: $30

1893.
Mr. McSnickers
#912641 • 14" • TJ
Issued: 2001 • Retired: 2002
Original: $26 • Value: $31

1894.
Mr. Nicholsby [QVC]
#unknown • 38"
LE of 750 • Issued: 2001 • Retired: 2001
Original: $155 • Value: $183

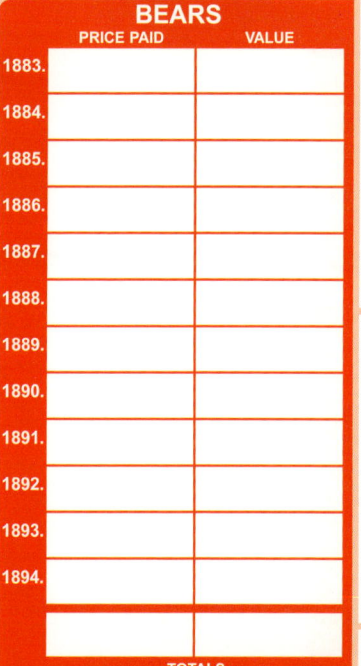

BEARS	PRICE PAID	VALUE
1883.		
1884.		
1885.		
1886.		
1887.		
1888.		
1889.		
1890.		
1891.		
1892.		
1893.		
1894.		
TOTALS		

NOTES

Bears

1895.
Mr. Noah and Friends
#900100 • 14" • TJ
LE • Issued: 2000 • Retired: 2001
Original: $61 • Value: $120
NALED Award Winner

1896.
Mr. Peepers [QVC]
#(C57638) • 10"
Issued: 1999 • Retired: 1999
Original: $24 • Value: $35

1897.
Mr. Smythe
#58691-05 • 12" • AR
Issued: 1998 • Retired: 1998
Original: $27 • Value: $53

1898.
Mr. Stuffle [QVC]
#93293V (C60251) • 10"
Issued: 2002 • Retired: 2002
Original: $14 • Value: $25

1899.
Mr. T. B. Shutterbear
#92003-02 • 12" • AR
Issued: 2004 • Current
Original: $21 • Value: $R/E

1900.
Mr. Tannebaum [QVC]
#93495V (C6039) • 20"
Issued: 2003 • Retired: 2003
Original: $70 • Value: $84

1901.
Mr. Trumbull
#918330 • 10" • TJ
Issued: 1998 • Retired: 2002
Original: $24 • Value: $45

1902.
Mr. Tweeter
#510407 • 16" • AS
Issued: 2004 • Current
Original: $23 • Value: $R/E

1903.
Mr. Webster [QVC]
#(C20968) • 30"
LE of 800 • Issued: 2002 • Retired: 2002
Original: $113 • Value: $147

1904.
Mrs. Baybeary
#917312 • 10" • TJ
Issued: 2000 • Retired: 2000
Original: $26 • Value: $35

1905.
Mrs. Bearberry
#unknown • 14"
LE • Issued: 1991 • Retired: 1991
Original: $70 • Value: $368

1906.
Mrs. Bearburg
#6161B • 14"
LE • Issued: 1991 • Retired: 1991
Original: $70 • Value: $358

BEARS

	PRICE PAID	VALUE
1895.		
1896.		
1897.		
1898.		
1899.		
1900.		
1901.		
1902.		
1903.		
1904.		
1905.		
1906.		
TOTALS		

NOTES

Bears

1907.
Mrs. Bearhugs [QVC]
#(C22624) • 16"
Issued: 2003 • Retired: 2003
Original: $29 • Value: $35

1908.
Mrs. Beariwell [GCC]
#94877GCC • 10"
Issued: 1999 • Retired: 1999
Original: $24 • Value: $45

1909.
Mrs. Beezley
#904110 • 16"
Issued: 2003 • Current
Original: $43 • Value: $R/E

1910.
Mrs. Bradley [Linda Anderson]
#94900CD • 10"
Issued: 1998 • Retired: 1998
Original: $25 • Value: $46

1911.
Mrs. Everlove
#912654 • 12" • ME
Issued: 2001 • Current
Original: $35 • Value: $R/E

1912.
Mrs. Fezziwig JodiBear
#92000-10 • 9" • AR
Issued: 2000 • Retired: 2000
Original: $20 • Value: $29

1913.
Mrs. Fiedler the Music Teacher
#9218B • 14"
LE of 500 • Issued: 1994 • Retired: 1994
Original: $70 • Value: $353

1914.
Mrs. Figgy Pudding
#917442 • 10" • TJ
Issued: 2001 • Retired: 2002
Original: $25 • Value: $35

1915.
Mrs. Kringlebeary
#904060 • 14" • TJ
Issued: 2002 • Retired: 2002
Original: $30 • Value: $47

1916.
Mrs. Kringles [QVC]
#(C6020) • 14"
Issued: 2003 • Retired: 2003
Original: $37 • Value: $53

1917.
Mrs. Mertz
#918331 • 10" • TJ
Issued: 1998 • Retired: 1998
Original: $28 • Value: $35

1918.
Mrs. Mother May I [SLE]
#unknown • 12"
Issued: 1999 • Retired: 1999
Original: $N/E • Value: $N/E

BEARS

	PRICE PAID	VALUE
1907.		
1908.		
1909.		
1910.		
1911.		
1912.		
1913.		
1914.		
1915.		
1916.		
1917.		
1918.		
	TOTALS	

NOTES

Bears

1919.
Mrs. Noah
#568008 • 7" • NO
Issued: 2002 • Current
Original: $13 • Value: $R/E

1920.
Mrs. Northstar
#917303-03 • 13" • TJ
Issued: 1999 • Retired: 1999
Original: $30 • Value: $51

1921.
Mrs. Northstar [SFMB]
#41-40001 • 13"
Issued: 2000 • Retired: 2000
Original: $40 • Value: $65
♪ Moonlight Serenade ♪

1922.
Mrs. Plumbles [QVC]
#93282V (C60289) • 10"
Issued: 2002 • Retired: 2002
Original: $13 • Value: $25

1923.
Mrs. Potter & Her Lil' Sprouts [QVC]
#99876V (C107172) • 14"
LE of 25008 • Issued: 2002 • Retired: 2002
Original: $71 • Value: $80

1924.
Mrs. Trumbull (no bow)
#91833 • 10" • TJ
Issued: 1998 • Retired: 1998
Original: $25 • Value: $42

1925.
Mrs. Trumbull (red plaid bow)
#91833 • 10" • TJ
Issued: 1998 • Retired: 1998
Original: $25 • Value: $42

1926.
Mrs. Trumbull [SFMB]
#41-72769 • 10"
Issued: 1999 • Retired: 1999
Original: $40 • Value: $60
♪ Puttin' on the Ritz ♪

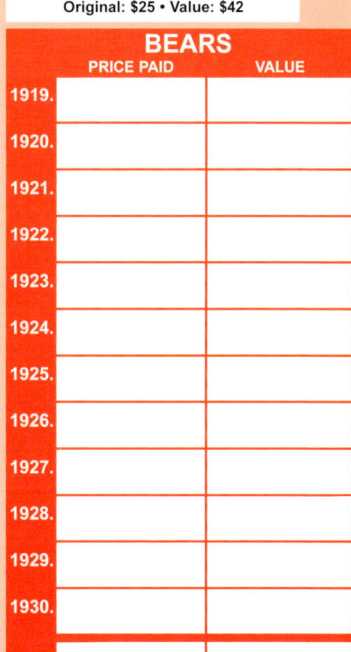

BEARS		
	PRICE PAID	VALUE
1919.		
1920.		
1921.		
1922.		
1923.		
1924.		
1925.		
1926.		
1927.		
1928.		
1929.		
1930.		
	TOTALS	

NOTES

1927.
Mrs. Tuttle [QVC]
#93233V (C64903) • 10"
Issued: 2001 • Retired: 2001
Original: $29 • Value: $45

1928.
Mrs. Tweeter and Purrsley [QVC]
#99015V (C05177) • 14"
LE of 1000 • Issued: 2004 • Retired: 2004
Original: $44 • Value: $65

1929.
Ms. Appleby & Olivia [QVC]
#(C20888) • 10"
LE of 2400 • Issued: 2003 • Retired: 2003
Original: $42 • Value: $60
Sold with blackboard.

1930.
Ms. Bee Beezley [CAN]
#BC94299PO • 10"
Issued: 2003 • Retired: 2003
Original: $20 • Value: $24

Bears

1931.
Ms. Odetta & Neville [QVC]
#(C34517) • 14"
LE of 1200 • Issued: 1996 • Retired: 1996
Original: $73 • Value: $149

1932.
Ms. Potter & Amadeus [QVC]
#(C45643) • 14"
LE of 1200 • Issued: 1997 • Retired: 1997
Original: $84 • Value: $139

1933.
Ms. Rouge Chapeau
#904197 • 10" • TJ
Issued: 2003 • Current
Original: $25 • Value: $R/E
Variation: no logo on paw.

1934.
Muffin
#56421-03 • 8" • BF
Issued: 1998 • Retired: 2002
Original: $9 • Value: $15

1935.
Muffin B. Bluebeary
[Yankee Candle]
#94693YC • 14"
LE • Issued: 2002 • Retired: 2002
Original: $27 • Value: $35
Sold with 22 oz candle and candle topper.

1936.
Mulligan T. Duffer
#918338 • 10" • ME
Issued: 2001 • Retired: 2001
Original: $23 • Value: $28

BEARS

	PRICE PAID	VALUE
1931.		
1932.		
1933.		
1934.		
1935.		
1936.		
1937.		
1938.		
1939.		
1940.		
1941.		
1942.		
TOTALS		

NOTES

1937.
Mumbley B. Bean
#515214 • 12" • JB
Issued: 2002 • Retired: 2002
Original: $17 • Value: $25

1938.
Mumsie
#590058 • 10" • MB
Issued: 2002 • Retired: 2002
Original: $30 • Value: $45

1939.
Nadia [Kirlins]
#unknown • 10" • TJ
Issued: 1998 • Retired: 1998
Original: $34 • Value: $50

1940.
Nadia Berriman [QVC]
#(C34957) • 10" • TJ
Issued: 1998 • Retired: 1998
Original: $28 • Value: $38

1941.
Nadia Berriman
#917420 • 10" • TJ
Issued: 1999 • Retired: 2001
Original: $26 • Value: $31

1942.
Nana
#82523 • 8" • TJ
Issued: 2003 • Retired: 2003
Original: $10 • Value: $10

Bears

1943.
Nana Bearhugs
#500050-08 • 40" • JB
Issued: 2001 • Retired: 2001
Original: $200 • Value: $215

1944.
Nana Bearhugs [SFMB]
#500050-08SF • 40"
LE of 50 • Issued: 2002 • Retired: 2002
Original: $225 • Value: $260
♪ Für Elise ♪

1945.
Nancy D. Bearington [QVC]
#93126V (C63244) • 16" • MB
LE of 5000 • Issued: 1999 • Retired: 1999
Original: $121 • Value: $175

1946.
Nancy Jo Warmheart [QVC]
#93524V (C01903) • 10" • TJ
Issued: 2004 • Retired: 2004
Original: $18 • Value: $39

1947.
Nandykins [QVC]
#C3091 • 8"
Issued: 2003 • Retired: 2003
Original: $12 • Value: $14

1948.
Nanette Dubeary
#918432 • 6" • TJ
Issued: 2000 • Retired: 2002
Original: $11 • Value: $18

1949.
Nanny Bear
#6172 • 14"
LE • Issued: 1991 • Retired: 1991
Original: $70 • Value: $440

1950.
Nantucket P. Bearington
#590102 • 4½" • MB
Issued: 2000 • Retired: 2000
Original: $11 • Value: $22

1951.
Naomi Bearlove
#913957 • 6" • ME
Issued: 2000 • Retired: 2002
Original: $12 • Value: $14

1952.
Natalie Plumbeary [GCC]
#94894GCC • 6"
LE of 2550 • Issued: 2001 • Retired: 2001
Original: $10 • Value: $32

1953.
Natasha Berriman
#918050 • 6" • TJ
Issued: 1998 • Retired: 2002
Original: $9 • Value: $16

1954.
Natasha Crystalfrost
#904183 • 8" • TJ
Issued: 2003 • Retired: 2003
Original: $18 • Value: $25

BEARS	PRICE PAID	VALUE
1943.		
1944.		
1945.		
1946.		
1947.		
1948.		
1949.		
1950.		
1951.		
1952.		
1953.		
1954.		
TOTALS		

NOTES

Bears

Nellie
#91105 • 14" • TJ
Issued: 1995 • Retired: 1997
Original: $20 • Value: $47

Nellie T. Bearypatch [Paw Dealer]
#919814 • 10"
Issued: 2002 • Retired: 2002
Original: $20 • Value: $28

Nelson
#91261 • 16" • TJ
Issued: 1997 • Retired: 1999
Original: $45 • Value: $66

Nettie [QVC]
#unknown • 14"
LE of 300 • Issued: 1994 • Retired: 1994
Original: $70 • Value: $295

Nettie Fisher
#904132 • 10"
Issued: 2003 • Current
Original: $20 • Value: $R/E

Neville (old face)
#5707 • 5½" • AS
Issued: 1990 • Retired: 1993
Original: $7 • Value: $34

Neville (new face)
#5707 • 5½" • AS
Issued: 1991 • Retired: 1999
Original: $7 • Value: $23

Newton
#9133 • 8" • TJ
Issued: 1994 • Retired: 1994
Original: $25 • Value: $41

Niagra [Centre Gift Shoppe]
#94282PO • 8"
LE of 3600 • Issued: 1999 • Retired: 1999
Original: $25 • Value: $32

Nibblekins
#91861 • 10"
Issued: 2002 • Retired: 2002
Original: $15 • Value: $23

Nichley [Dillards]
#94728DL • 8" • TJ
Issued: 1998 • Retired: 1998
Original: $16 • Value: $43

Nicholas
#9173 • 8" • TJ
Issued: 1993 • Retired: 1997
Original: $15 • Value: $35

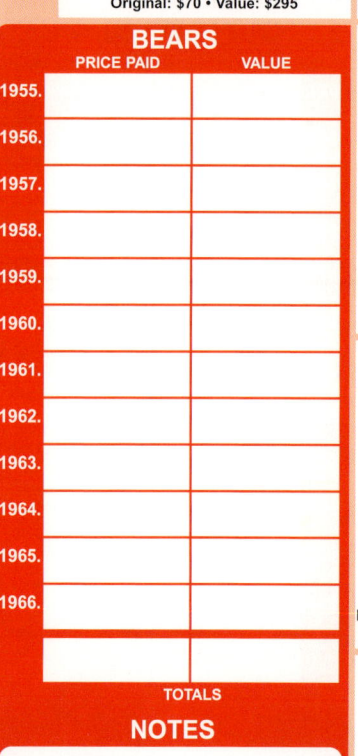

BEARS	PRICE PAID	VALUE
1955.		
1956.		
1957.		
1958.		
1959.		
1960.		
1961.		
1962.		
1963.		
1964.		
1965.		
1966.		
TOTALS		

NOTES

Bears

1967.
Nicholas [SLE]
#unknown • 11" • TJ
Issued: 1998 • Retired: 1998
Original: $20 • Value: $45

1968.
Nicholas with Ansel & Fitzgerald [QVC]
#(C35944) • 14"
LE of 1200 • Issued: 1996 • Retired: 1996
Original: $N/E • Value: $150

1969.
Nicklas T. Jodibear
#92000-12 • 9" • AR
Issued: 2000 • Retired: 2002
Original: $20 • Value: $23

1970.
Nickleby S. Claus
#83005 • 16" • TJ
Issued: 2000 • Retired: 2000
Original: $29 • Value: $29

1971.
Nickolas S. Hugsley
#500072 • 30" • TJ
Issued: 2002 • Retired: 2002
Original: $57 • Value: $58

1972.
Nicolas Bearington
#590107 • 4½" • MB
Issued: 2000 • Retired: 2000
Original: $11 • Value: $25

1973.
Nicolas Bearington & Tinker [QVC]
#(C95118) • 4½" • MB
Issued: 1999 • Retired: 1999
Original: $16 • Value: $32

1974.
Nicole [QVC]
#unknown • 10"
Issued: 2001 • Retired: 2001
Original: $27 • Value: $38

1975.
Nicole & Amy Berriman with Tassel [QVC]
#(C96371) • 16"
LE of 3000 • Issued: 1999 • Retired: 1999
Original: $66 • Value: $90

1976.
Nicole de la El-bee [Elder Beerman]
#unknown • 15"
LE of 1200 • Issued: 1997 • Retired: 1997
Original: $35 • Value: $54

1977.
Niki
#91730 • 6" • TJ
Issued: 1996 • Retired: 1997
Original: $13 • Value: $33

1978.
Niki II
#91730-1 • 7"
Issued: 1998 • Retired: 1998
Original: $13 • Value: $20

BEARS	PRICE PAID	VALUE
1967.		
1968.		
1969.		
1970.		
1971.		
1972.		
1973.		
1974.		
1975.		
1976.		
1977.		
1978.		
TOTALS		

NOTES

Bears

1979.
Niklas, Matilda & Trevor [QVC]
#(C45645) • 16"
LE of 1800 • Issued: 1997 • Retired: 1997
Original: $60 • Value: $110

1980.
Noah
#568001 • 8" • NO
Issued: 2002 • Current
Original: $14 • Value: $R/E

1981.
Noah with Puddles
#918434 • 14"
Issued: 1999 • Retired: 2002
Original: $37 • Value: $44

1982.
Noble Nutcracker
#904353 • 10" • TJ
Issued: 2004 • Current
Original: $21 • Value: $R/E

1983.
Nod (stark white)
#5810 • 6" • SB
Issued: 1991 • Retired: 1992
Original: $7 • Value: $60

1984.
Nod II (off-white)
#5810 • 6" • SB
Issued: 1992 • Retired: 1992
Original: $7 • Value: $34

1985.
Noella deBearvoire
with Holly [QVC]
#99988V (C6086) • 8"
Issued: 2003 • Retired: 2003
Original: $22 • Value: $35

1986.
Noelle [Ethel M. Chocolates]
#unknown • 6"
Issued: 1998 • Retired: 1998
Original: $N/E • Value: $25

1987.
Norbert D. Beariman
#510816 • 14" • AS
Issued: 2004 • Current
Original: $16 • Value: $R/E

1988.
Have You Seen Me?
North Pole Bear
#9201P • 14"
LE of 500 • Issued: 1992 • Retired: 1992
Original: $70 • Value: $360

1989.
Nurse Carin
#903303 • 8"
Issued: 2003 • Current
Original: $10 • Value: $R/E

1990.
O. Howie Luvsya
#82005 • 12" • JB
Issued: 2000 • Retired: 2000
Original: $17 • Value: $20

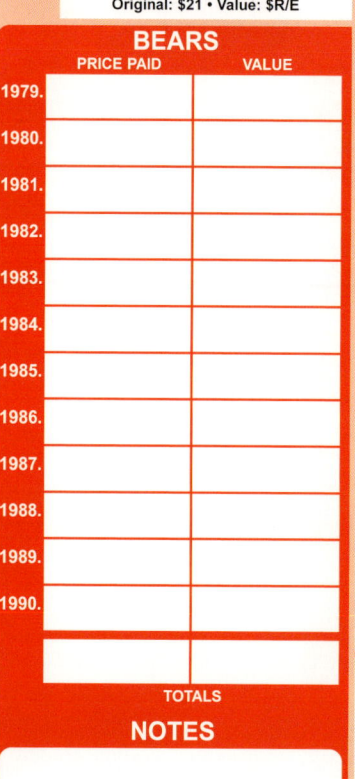

BEARS	PRICE PAID	VALUE
1979.		
1980.		
1981.		
1982.		
1983.		
1984.		
1985.		
1986.		
1987.		
1988.		
1989.		
1990.		
TOTALS		

NOTES

Bears

1991.
Oinkins
#918661 • 10" • TJ
Issued: 2003 • Current
Original: $15 • Value: $R/E

1992.
Ol' MacBruin...Down on the Farm [QVC]
#99927V (C22674)
Issued: 2003 • Retired: 2003
Original: $132 • Value: $150

1993.
Olaf
#9138 • 12" • TJ
Issued: 1994 • Retired: 1996
Original: $27 • Value: $46

1994.
Olive T. Leafowitz
#912014 • 16" • TJ
Issued: 2001 • Retired: 2001
Original: $50 • Value: $60

1995.
Oliver [Dillards]
#94701DL • 17"
Issued: 1996 • Retired: 1996
Original: $29 • Value: $50

1996.
Oliver [GCC]
#94850GCC • 12"
Issued: 1997 • Retired: 1997
Original: $25 • Value: $40

1997.
Olivia Beariluved [GCC]
#94923GCC • 12"
Issued: 2002 • Retired: 2002
Original: $26 • Value: $34

1998.
Olivia Q. Witebred [QVC]
#(C41101) • 15"
Issued: 1997 • Retired: 1997
Original: $26 • Value: $45

1999.
Olivia R. Thornbeary
#900252 • 16" • UB
LE of 12000 • Issued: 1999 • Retired: 1999
Original: $60 • Value: $72

2000.
Olivia T. Bearington [QVC]
#93440V (C22638) • 6" • MB
LE of 1500 • Issued: 2003 • Retired: 2003
Original: $17 • Value: $20

2001.
Omega T. Legacy & Alpha
#900099 • 16" • UB
Issued: 1999 • Retired: 1999
Original: $67 • Value: $100
Limited to 12 pieces per retailer.
NALED Award Winner

2002.
Ophelia
#91207-01 • 16" • TJ
Issued: 1997 • Retired: 1997
Original: $40 • Value: $65

BEARS	PRICE PAID	VALUE
1991.		
1992.		
1993.		
1994.		
1995.		
1996.		
1997.		
1998.		
1999.		
2000.		
2001.		
2002.		
TOTALS		

NOTES

Bears

2003.
Ophelia W. Witebred
#91207 • 16" • TJ
Issued: 1996 • Retired: 1998
Original: $29 • Value: $55

2004.
Ophelia W. Witebred [QVC]
#(C35625) • 16"
Issued: 1997 • Retired: 1997
Original: $35 • Value: $60

2005.
Opie Fishalot
#903310 • 8"
Issued: 2003 • Current
Original: $13 • Value: $R/E

2006.
Opie Paddypasture & T. Ferdinand Wuzzie [QVC]
#(C76935) • 11½"
Issued: 2000 • Retired: 2000
Original: $22 • Value: $35

2007.
Opie V. Beanster [QVC]
#(C06190) • 17"
Issued: 2004 • Retired: 2004
Original: $34 • Value: $38

2008.
Orabella Fitzbruin [QVC]
#93040V (C39080) • 14"
Issued: 1997 • Retired: 1997
Original: $26 • Value: $48

2009.
Orella Berrywinkle [QVC]
#93021V (C39086) • 8"
Issued: 1997 • Retired: 1997
Original: $14 • Value: $37

2010.
Orianna [Welcome Home]
#unknown • 16"
Issued: 1997 • Retired: 1997
Original: $33 • Value: $45

2011.
Orville Bearington
#590085-03 • 4½" • MB
Issued: 1998 • Retired: 1999
Original: $10 • Value: $23

2012.
Orvis T. Fisher with Tad
#904131 • 12"
Issued: 2003 • Current
Original: $27 • Value: $R/E

2013.
Oswald P. Beanster
#510408 • 16" • JB
Issued: 2004 • Current
Original: $23 • Value: $R/E

2014.
Otis B. Bean (open mouth)
#5108 • 14" • JB
Issued: 1989 • Retired: 1989
Original: $20 • Value: $276

BEARS	PRICE PAID	VALUE
2003.		
2004.		
2005.		
2006.		
2007.		
2008.		
2009.		
2010.		
2011.		
2012.		
2013.		
2014.		
TOTALS		

NOTES

2015.
Otis B. Bean (old face - smooth fur)
#5107 • 14" • JB
Issued: 1990 • Retired: 1990
Original: $20 • Value: $215

2016.
Otis B. Bean (old face)
#5107 • 14" • JB
Issued: 1990 • Retired: 1992
Original: $20 • Value: $91

2017.
Otis B. Bean (new face)
#5107 • 14" • JB
Issued: 1993 • Retired: 1997
Original: $20 • Value: $59

2018.
Ottie Wilhelmina [GCC]
#94860GCC • 12"
Issued: 1998 • Retired: 1998
Original: $30 • Value: $48

2019.
Otto Von Bruin
#5010 • 6" • WB
Issued: 1992 • Retired: 1994
Original: $10 • Value: $25

2020.
Oxford T. Bearrister
#57001-05 • 12" • AS
Issued: 1999 • Retired: 1999
Original: $20 • Value: $25

2021.
P.B. Punkinpaw [QVC]
#93338V (C20178) • 8"
Issued: 2002 • Retired: 2002
Original: $10 • Value: $14

2022.
P.J. [Lord & Taylor]
#unknown • 8"
Issued: 1998 • Retired: 1998
Original: $15 • Value: $26

BEARS		
	PRICE PAID	VALUE
2015.		
2016.		
2017.		
2018.		
2019.		
2020.		
2021.		
2022.		
2023.		
2024.		
2025.		
2026.		
	TOTALS	

NOTES

2023.
P.J. Bearsdale & Tink [QVC]
#(C95017) • 7"
Issued: 1999 • Retired: 1999
Original: $27 • Value: $35

2024.
P.J. McBeansley [QVC]
#93306V (C107582) • 8"
Issued: 2002 • Retired: 2002
Original: $15 • Value: $30

2025.
Paddikins
#918665 • 10" • TJ
Issued: 2004 • Current
Original: $15 • Value: $R/E

2026.
Paddy O'Beara
#903305 • 8"
Issued: 2003 • Current
Original: $17 • Value: $R/E

Bears

2027.
Paige Bearylove
#82534 • 8"
Issued: 2004 • Current
Original: $10 • Value: $R/E

2028.
Paige Willoughby
#918351 • 8" • TJ
Issued: 2000 • Retired: 2000
Original: $16 • Value: $23

2029.
Paigley B. Plumbeary [QVC]
#93346V (C20878) • 10"
Issued: 2002 • Retired: 2002
Original: $27 • Value: $45

2030.
Pamela P. Patchbeary
#912017 • 16" • TJ
Issued: 2002 • Retired: 2002
Original: $47 • Value: $47

2031.
Pamela Penneybeary [J.C.Penney]
#JP773-0401 • 8"
Issued: 2003 • Retired: 2003
Original: $20 • Value: $30

2032.
Pansey
#590060 • 10" • MB
LE of 5000 • Issued: 2003 • Retired: 2003
Original: $30 • Value: $30

BEARS

	PRICE PAID	VALUE
2027.		
2028.		
2029.		
2030.		
2031.		
2032.		
2033.		
2034.		
2035.		
2036.		
2037.		
2038.		
TOTALS		

NOTES

2033.
Pansie P. Potter [QVC]
#93310V (C65041) • 8"
Issued: 2002 • Retired: 2002
Original: $12 • Value: $25

2034.
Pansley B. Bean [QVC]
#93429V (C22077) • 10"
Issued: 2003 • Retired: 2003
Original: $13 • Value: $20

2035.
Pansy [QVC]
#unknown • 14"
LE of 1200 • Issued: 1995 • Retired: 1995
Original: $70 • Value: $258

2036.
Pat T. Spiker
#903502 • 10" • ME
Issued: 2002 • Current
Original: $20 • Value: $R/E

2037.
Patches B. Beariluved
#51000 • 10" • JB
Issued: 2000 • Retired: 2002
Original: $15 • Value: $23
Also with Tatters as QVC set.
TOBY Award Winner

2038.
Patricia L. Cooksbeary [Longaberger]
#94630LB • 10"
Issued: 2000 • Retired: 2000
Original: $28 • Value: $49

Bears

2039.
Patricia P. Bearheart
#904081 • 12"
Issued: 2003 • Current
Original: $22 • Value: $R/E

2040.
Patrick
#9901 • 8" • TJ
Issued: 1995 • Retired: 1996
Original: $16 • Value: $45

2041.
Patrick B. Beanster [QVC]
#(C05173) • 18"
Issued: 2004 • Retired: 2004
Original: $32 • Value: $45

2042.
Patrick Bearsevelt
#913966 • 6" • TJ
Issued: 2001 • Retired: 2002
Original: $11 • Value: $20

2043.
Patrick Henry [QVC]
#93550V (C06194) • 6"
Issued: 2004 • Retired: 2004
Original: $12 • Value: $25
In basket.

2044.
Patriotic Bailey [EVENT]
#50010 • 20"
LE • Issued: 2003 • Retired: 2003
Original: $N/E • Value: $150
Only available as a raffle prize.

2045.
Patsie Punkley
#919634 • 10"
Issued: 2002 • Retired: 2002
Original: $17 • Value: $17

2046.
Patsy
#9100 • 10" • TJ
Issued: 1995 • Retired: 1996
Original: $20 • Value: $55

BEARS	PRICE PAID	VALUE
2039.		
2040.		
2041.		
2042.		
2043.		
2044.		
2045.		
2046.		
2047.		
2048.		
2049.		
2050.		
TOTALS		

NOTES

2047.
Patton Q. Jodibear
#92000-20 • 9" • AR
Issued: 2002 • Retired: 2004
Original: $15 • Value: $15

2048.
Paula Cherrybeary with Tart [QVC]
#93405V (C21150) • 12"
Issued: 2003 • Retired: 2003
Original: $31 • Value: $37

2049.
Paulina P. Punkinbeary & Tisket [QVC]
#(C20229) • 16"
LE of 2400 • Issued: 2002 • Retired: 2002
Original: $60 • Value: $78
Sold with wooden pumpkin basket.

2050.
Pauly Punkley
#919637 • 6"
Issued: 2002 • Retired: 2002
Original: $9 • Value: $9

Bears

2051.
Paxton P. Bean
#510300-05 • 10" • JB
Issued: 1998 • Retired: 2001
Original: $11 • Value: $18
Also with Maxton, Craxton as QVC set.

2052.
Peary
#5807-10 • 16" • AS
Issued: 1998 • Retired: 2000
Original: $28 • Value: $35

2053.
Pee Wee & Yogi [QVC]
#99533V (C39077) • 6"
Issued: 1997 • Retired: 1997
Original: $23 • Value: $40

2054.
Peeker of the Month [QVC]
#99999V (C06925)
Issued: 2004 • Retired: 2004
Original: $43 • Value: $86

2055.
Peeker P. Heartlove [QVC]
#93421V (C21168) • 6"
Issued: 2003 • Retired: 2003
Original: $12 • Value: $14

2056.
Peepers P. MacDonald
#913937 • 8" • TJ
Issued: 2002 • Current
Original: $12 • Value: $R/E

2057.
Pelmon Thomas McBear [Welcome Home]
#unknown • 11"
Issued: 1999 • Retired: 1999
Original: $23 • Value: $35

2058.
Pendleton J. Bruin
#510400-11 • 16" • JB
Issued: 1998 • Retired: 2000
Original: $23 • Value: $35

2059.
Pendleton [SFMB]
#41-72934 • 16"
Issued: 2000 • Retired: 2000
Original: $35 • Value: $50
♪ Whistle a Happy Tune ♪

2060.
Penelope P. Punkinbeary
#904011 • 14" • TJ
Issued: 2002 • Retired: 2004
Original: $29 • Value: $29

2061.
Penelope Pearsley Gift Set [Country Clutter]
#94980CC • 14"
LE of 4200 • Issued: 2003 • Retired: 2003
Original: $50 • Value: $60

2062.
Penny Bearsley [J.C. Penney]
#(JP045-1010A) • 10"
Issued: 2000 • Retired: 2000
Original: $30 • Value: $41

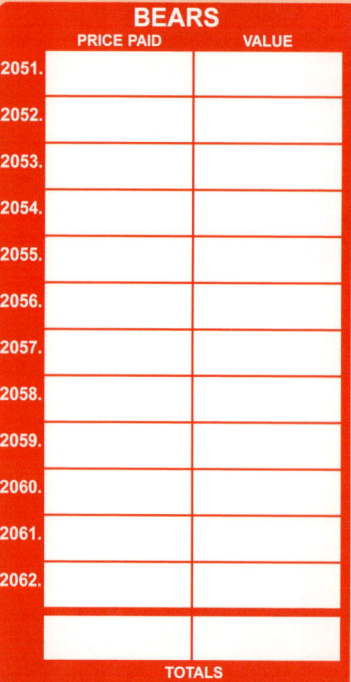

BEARS	PRICE PAID	VALUE
2051.		
2052.		
2053.		
2054.		
2055.		
2056.		
2057.		
2058.		
2059.		
2060.		
2061.		
2062.		
TOTALS		

NOTES

2063.
Penny Whistleby
#900251 • 8" • UB
Issued: 1999 • Retired: 1999
Original: $52 • Value: $75

2064.
Pepper Mintly
#904217 • 10" • TJ
Issued: 2003 • Retired: 2003
Original: $10 • Value: $16

2065.
Peppermint P. Bear
#510305-01 • 10" • JB
Issued: 2000 • Retired: 2000
Original: $11 • Value: $13

2066.
Perceval
#5703-08 • 10" • AS
Issued: 1992 • Retired: 1999
Original: $18 • Value: $34

2067.
Percy
#5725-11 • 5½" • AS
Issued: 1994 • Retired: 2001
Original: $7 • Value: $15

2068.
Percy P. Pawsley [QVC]
#93475V (C0437) • 16"
Issued: 2003 • Retired: 2003
Original: $24 • Value: $29

2069.
Perriwinkle P. Snicklefritz
#51760-06 • 8" • BA
Issued: 1999 • Retired: 1999
Original: $12 • Value: $15

2070.
Perry
#1000-11 • 8" • CC
Issued: 1994 • Retired: 1997
Original: $6 • Value: $36

BEARS

	PRICE PAID	VALUE
2063.		
2064.		
2065.		
2066.		
2067.		
2068.		
2069.		
2070.		
2071.		
2072.		
2073.		
2074.		
TOTALS		

NOTES

2071.
Petals Daisydew
#904077 • 6"
Issued: 2003 • Current
Original: $10 • Value: $R/E

2072.
Petals P. Peeker [QVC]
#93453V (C22628) • 6"
Issued: 2003 • Retired: 2003
Original: $15 • Value: $18

2073.
Peter Potter
#515211-10 • 12" • JB
Issued: 2001 • Retired: 2002
Original: $17 • Value: $20

2074.
Petula P. Fallsbeary
[Show Specials]
#919804 • 6"
Issued: 2000 • Retired: 2000
Original: $15 • Value: $22

Bears

2075.
Peyton [Frederick Atkins]
#unknown • 14"
Issued: 1999 • Retired: 1999
Original: $N/E • Value: $42

2076.
Phillip Bearhop
#5820 • 11"
LE of 5000 • Issued: 1991 • Retired: 1992
Original: $27 • Value: $327

2077.
Philomena
#91106 • 14" • TJ
Issued: 1995 • Retired: 1997
Original: $20 • Value: $41

2078.
Phoebe B. [QVC]
#(C64872) • 11"
Issued: 2001 • Retired: 2001
Original: $26 • Value: $45

2079.
Pierre [CAN]
#BC100908 • 14" • PM
Issued: 1997 • Retired: 1997
Original: $21 • Value: $38

2080.
Piper P. Plumbottom [QVC]
#(C99072) • 14"
Issued: 2000 • Retired: 2000
Original: $33 • Value: $50

2081.
Pipley McRind
#913965 • 6" • TJ
Issued: 2001 • Retired: 2001
Original: $10 • Value: $12

2082.
Pohley
#5768 • 9" • HD
Issued: 1991 • Retired: 1993
Original: $14 • Value: $131

2083.
Pokie
#918662 • 10" • TJ
Issued: 2003 • Current
Original: $15 • Value: $R/E

2084.
Polly Peapod
#904245 • 5½" • TJ
Issued: 2004 • Current
Original: $10 • Value: $R/E

2085.
Polly Quignapple
#910020 • 10" • TJ
Issued: 1999 • Retired: 2002
Original: $23 • Value: $27

2086.
Poof Pufflebeary
#51780-03 • 15" • BA
Issued: 2000 • Retired: 2000
Original: $23 • Value: $28

BEARS

	PRICE PAID	VALUE
2075.		
2076.		
2077.		
2078.		
2079.		
2080.		
2081.		
2082.		
2083.		
2084.		
2085.		
2086.		
	TOTALS	

NOTES

Bears

2087.
Poof Pufflebeary [SFMB]
#41-72981 • 15" • BA
Issued: 2000 • Retired: 2000
Original: $30 • Value: $45
♪ Rock-A-Bye Baby ♪

2088.
Pooh (Mohair Classic) [Disney]
#unknown • 16" • MB
LE of 600 • Issued: 1999 • Retired: 1999
Original: $95 • Value: $200

2089.
Pooh (Mohair Santa) [Disney]
#94959DS • 16" • MB
LE of 600 • Issued: 1999 • Retired: 1999
Original: $95 • Value: $200

2090.
Pooh (Santa with Ornament) [Disney]
#94965DS • 10"
Issued: 1999 • Retired: 1999
Original: $45 • Value: $80

2091.
Pooh (Mohair Winter Holiday) [Disney]
#unknown • 13" • MB
LE of 600 • Issued: 2000 • Retired: 2000
Original: $85 • Value: $113

2092.
Pooh (Winter Holiday) [Disney]
#959709DSP • 10"
Issued: 2000 • Retired: 2000
Original: $45 • Value: $68

2093.
Pooh (plaid coat) [Disney]
#95979DSP • 10"
Issued: 2001 • Retired: 2001
Original: $30 • Value: $42

2094.
Pooh (Mohair red pajamas) [Disney]
#95983DSP • 12" • MB
Issued: 2001 • Retired: 2001
Original: $86 • Value: $111

2095.
Pooh (Costume Party) [Disney]
#95902DSP • 10"
Issued: 2002 • Retired: 2002
Original: $30 • Value: $39

2096.
Pooh (Mohair Cozy Holiday) [Disney]
#95998DSP • 16" • MB
Issued: 2002 • Retired: 2002
Original: $85 • Value: $105

2097.
Pooh (Cozy Holiday) [Disney]
#95994DSP • 10"
Issued: 2002 • Retired: 2002
Original: $30 • Value: $45

2098.
Pooh (Winter Caroling) [Disney]
#95911DSP • 10"
Issued: 2003 • Retired: 2003
Original: $30 • Value: $35

BEARS	PRICE PAID	VALUE
2087.		
2088.		
2089.		
2090.		
2091.		
2092.		
2093.		
2094.		
2095.		
2096.		
2097.		
2098.		
TOTALS		

NOTES

Bears

2099.
Poor Ol' Bear
#903007 • 8" • BA
Issued: 2001 • Retired: 2002
Original: $10 • Value: $12

2100.
Poor Ol' Bear [SFMB]
#94536SF • 10"
LE of 651 • Issued: 2002 • Retired: 2002
Original: $25 • Value: $32
♪ Für Elise ♪

2101.
Pop Bruin
#5124 • 16" • JB
Issued: 1989 • Retired: 1995
Original: $25 • Value: $88

2102.
Poppa Bear & Noelle
#917302 • 10" • JB
Issued: 1997 • Retired: 1999
Original: $27 • Value: $52

Have You Seen Me?

2103.
Poppa Ted Truckingham [SLE]
#unknown • 14"
Issued: 1999 • Retired: 1999
Original: $25 • Value: $65
With cast-iron truck.

2104.
Pops
#903201 • 8" • ME
Issued: 2002 • Retired: 2002
Original: $10 • Value: $10

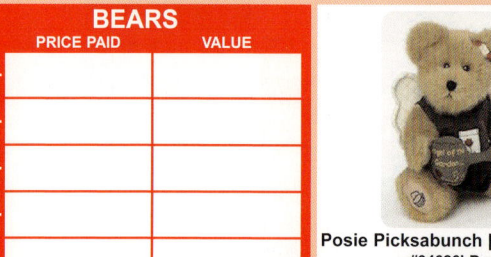

2105.
Posie Picksabunch [Longaberger]
#94626LB • 10"
Issued: 2003 • Retired: 2003
Original: $25 • Value: $35

2106.
Potsie Daisydew
#904078 • 4"
Issued: 2003 • Current
Original: $12 • Value: $R/E
TOBY Award Winner

2107.
Precious Plumbeary
[Welcome Home]
#94540WH • 8"
Issued: 2002 • Retired: 2002
Original: $24 • Value: $37

2108.
Prince Harry B. Nutcracker [POG]
#94598POG • 10"
Issued: 2002 • Retired: 2002
Original: $24 • Value: $35

2109.
Princess Nicole Bearyspoiled
[GCC]
#94653GCC • 8"
Issued: 2003 • Retired: 2003
Original: $18 • Value: $25

2110.
Proudly P. Peeker [QVC]
#93456V (C22854) • 6"
Issued: 2003 • Retired: 2003
Original: $12 • Value: $23

BEARS

	PRICE PAID	VALUE
2099.		
2100.		
2101.		
2102.		
2103.		
2104.		
2105.		
2106.		
2107.		
2108.		
2109.		
2110.		
TOTALS		

NOTES

Bears

2111.
Prudence Bearimore
#912053 • 12" • TJ
Issued: 1999 • Retired: 2002
Original: $30 • Value: $36

2112.
Prudence Berrimore [SFMB]
#41-72765 • 12"
Issued: 1999 • Retired: 1999
Original: $45 • Value: $68
♪ Oh, What A Beautiful Morning ♪

2113.
Puck
#9172 • 8" • TJ
Issued: 1993 • Retired: 1997
Original: $14 • Value: $42

2114.
Pucker McLemon
#904284 • 6" • TJ
Issued: 2004 • Current
Original: $10 • Value: $R/E

2115.
Pudgy Q. Honeypott [QVC]
#93273V (C52830) • 30"
LE of 600 • Issued: 2002 • Retired: 2002
Original: $100 • Value: $130

2116.
Puff & Poof Fuzzibutt [QVC]
#(C95788) • 10"
Issued: 1999 • Retired: 1999
Original: $25 • Value: $38

2117.
Pumpkin
#590065 • 10" • MB
Issued: 2003 • Current
Original: $30 • Value: $R/E

2118.
Punkie BooBear
#919630 • 10" • TJ
Issued: 1999 • Retired: 2002
Original: $20 • Value: $24

2119.
Punkin B. Beary
#904153 • 8" • TJ
Issued: 2003 • Current
Original: $14 • Value: $R/E

2120.
Punkley
#904202 • 8" • TJ
Issued: 2003 • Retired: 2003
Original: $9 • Value: $9

2121.
Putnam & Kent [QVC]
#(C41090) • 17"
Issued: 1997 • Retired: 1997
Original: $27 • Value: $45

2122.
Putnam P. Bearsley
#57250-08 • 6" • AS
Issued: 2001 • Retired: 2002
Original: $7 • Value: $8

BEARS	PRICE PAID	VALUE
2111.		
2112.		
2113.		
2114.		
2115.		
2116.		
2117.		
2118.		
2119.		
2120.		
2121.		
2122.		
TOTALS		

NOTES

Bears

2123.
Putter T. Parfore
#918339 • 10" • ME
Issued: 2001 • Retired: 2001
Original: $25 • Value: $30

2124.
Q.P. Peeker [QVC]
#93526V (C01906) • 10" • TJ
Issued: 2004 • Retired: 2004
Original: $12 • Value: $18

2125.
Quaker O. Brimley
#57150-10 • 16" • AS
Issued: 2000 • Retired: 2002
Original: $26 • Value: $36

2126.
Quincy & Corliss [QVC]
#unknown • 8"
Issued: 1998 • Retired: 1998
Original: $19 • Value: $29

2127.
Quincy B. Bibbly
#915611 • 8½" • TJ
Issued: 1999 • Retired: 1999
Original: $12 • Value: $14
Also with Corliss as QVC set.

2128.
Quinn [Frederick Atkins]
#unknown • 16"
Issued: 1999 • Retired: 1999
Original: $50 • Value: $85

2129.
Rachael & Phoebe Truefriends [QVC]
#99870V (C60292) • 6"
Issued: 2002 • Retired: 2002
Original: $17 • Value: $28

2130.
Rachel and B. Bearilove
#910070 • 10" • TJ
Issued: 2000 • Retired: 2000
Original: $19 • Value: $32

2131.
Radcliff McVeggie
#904243 • 10" • TJ
Issued: 2004 • Current
Original: $19 • Value: $R/E

2132.
Radcliffe Fitzbruin
#912020 • 16" • TJ
Issued: 2000 • Retired: 2002
Original: $35 • Value: $45

2133.
Ragna [SLE]
#unknown • 8"
Issued: 1998 • Retired: 1998
Original: $20 • Value: $36

2134.
Rainey Bloomengrows [Hallmark]
#9700HM • 8"
Issued: 2003 • Retired: 2003
Original: $25 • Value: $30
Sold with candle and candle topper.

BEARS

	PRICE PAID	VALUE
2123.		
2124.		
2125.		
2126.		
2127.		
2128.		
2129.		
2130.		
2131.		
2132.		
2133.		
2134.		
TOTALS		

NOTES

2135.
Raleigh
#5703M • 10" • AS
Issued: 1994 • Retired: 1997
Original: $18 • Value: $41

2136.
Ralph McFarmin [BBC]
#918057SM • 30"
Issued: 2003 • Retired: 2003
Original: $90 • Value: $108

2137.
Raylee [Dillards]
#94731DL • 11"
Issued: 1998 • Retired: 1998
Original: $24 • Value: $37

2138.
Reagan V. Bearington
#590070-05 • 8" • MB
Issued: 1997 • Retired: 1997
Original: $24 • Value: $49

2139.
Rebecca Bearimore
#912028 • 16" • TJ
Issued: 2000 • Retired: 2002
Original: $51 • Value: $59

2140.
Rebecca S. Duckworthy [QVC]
#(C40599) • 10"
Issued: 2001 • Retired: 2001
Original: $25 • Value: $40

2141.
Redford T. Woodsbeary
#912501 • 16" • TJ
Issued: 2001 • Retired: 2001
Original: $50 • Value: $60

2142.
Regan [Dillards]
#94772DL • 10"
Issued: 2000 • Retired: 2000
Original: $22 • Value: $33

2143.
Reginald [Lord & Taylor]
#94110-26 • 16"
Issued: 1996 • Retired: 1996
Original: $30 • Value: $85

2144.
Remington B. Bean [QVC]
#(C39087) • 17"
Issued: 1997 • Retired: 1997
Original: $25 • Value: $45

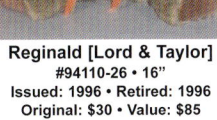

2145.
Remington Braveheart
#57210-05 • 18" • AS
Issued: 1999 • Retired: 1999
Original: $41 • Value: $41

2146.
Remus Q. Tweeter with Zip
#904467 • 8" • TJ
Issued: 2004 • Current
Original: $12 • Value: $R/E

BEARS

	PRICE PAID	VALUE
2135.		
2136.		
2137.		
2138.		
2139.		
2140.		
2141.		
2142.		
2143.		
2144.		
2145.		
2146.		
	TOTALS	

NOTES

Bears

2147.
Reva
#5630-02 • 9" • BA
Issued: 1995 • Retired: 1997
Original: $10 • Value: $32

2148.
Rex
#912440 • 8" • TJ
Issued: 1996 • Retired: 1998
Original: $18 • Value: $29

2149.
Rhoda [GCC]
#94854GCC • 8"
Issued: 1997 • Retired: 1997
Original: $15 • Value: $30

2150.
**Richard Tee Dobbsey
[Coach House Gifts]**
#unknown • 14"
Issued: 2000 • Retired: 2000
Original: $40 • Value: $50

2151.
Riesling Beardeaux
#904312 • 10" • TJ
Issued: 2004 • Current
Original: $19 • Value: $R/E

2152.
Riley B. Bean
#515212-10 • 12" • JB
Issued: 2002 • Retired: 2002
Original: $17 • Value: $17

2153.
Roberta
#912665 • 12" • TJ
Issued: 2002 • Retired: 2002
Original: $25 • Value: $25

2154.
Roberto [Ideation]
#900216IDE • 14"
Issued: 2000 • Retired: 2000
Original: $27 • Value: $40

2155.
Robin T. Tweeter with Goldie
#904260 • 16" • TJ
Issued: 2004 • Current
Original: $36 • Value: $R/E

2156.
Robyn [CAN]
#BC94287PO • 7"
LE of 4800 • Issued: 2000 • Retired: 2000
Original: $17 • Value: $40

2157.
Rochelle & Dessa [QVC]
#(C48175) • 10"
Issued: 1998 • Retired: 1998
Original: $22 • Value: $40

2158.
Rockie Mountberg [SLE]
#unknown • 6"
Issued: 1998 • Retired: 1998
Original: $10 • Value: $23

BEARS	PRICE PAID	VALUE
2147.		
2148.		
2149.		
2150.		
2151.		
2152.		
2153.		
2154.		
2155.		
2156.		
2157.		
2158.		
TOTALS		

NOTES

Bears 76

2159.
Rockwell B. Bruin
#57211-05 • 18" • AS
Issued: 2000 • Retired: 2000
Original: $40 • Value: $65

2160.
Rodney [SLE]
#unknown • 8½" • TJ
Issued: 1998 • Retired: 1998
Original: $14 • Value: $31

2161.
Rohley
#5769 • 9" • JB
Issued: 1991 • Retired: 1991
Original: $14 • Value: $172

2162.
Roland [Dillards]
#unknown • 11"
Issued: 1997 • Retired: 1997
Original: $22 • Value: $45

2163.
Roma Applesmith [BBC]
#918050SM • 16"
Issued: 2003 • Retired: 2003
Original: $49 • Value: $65

2164.
Ronald [May Company]
#unknown • 8"
Issued: 1997 • Retired: 1997
Original: $N/E • Value: $27

2165.

Have You Seen Me?

Roosevelt (14" mohair)
#6108B • 14" • MB
Issued: 1991 • Retired: 1992
Original: $27 • Value: $325

2166.
Roosevelt (8")
#9902 • 8" • AS
Issued: 1995 • Retired: 1996
Original: $18 • Value: $47

2167.
Roosevelt P. Bearington
#590020-08 • 16" • MB
Issued: 1997 • Retired: 1997
Original: $100 • Value: $151

2168.
Rootie T. McRooster [QVC]
#93519V (C02197) • 8"
Issued: 2004 • Retired: 2004
Original: $16 • Value: $23

2169.
Rosalie & Celina Dubeary [QVC]
#99867V • 6"
Issued: 2002 • Retired: 2002
Original: $19 • Value: $35

2170.
Rosalind [SFMB]
#41-72125 • 14"
Issued: 1997 • Retired: 1997
Original: $40 • Value: $60
♪ Mr. Sandman ♪

BEARS

	PRICE PAID	VALUE
2159.		
2160.		
2161.		
2162.		
2163.		
2164.		
2165.		
2166.		
2167.		
2168.		
2169.		
2170.		
TOTALS		

NOTES

206

Bears

2171.
Rosalind II [SFMB]
#41-72583 • 14"
Issued: 1998 • Retired: 1998
Original: $40 • Value: $55
♪ Mr. Sandman ♪

2172.
Rosanna duBeary
#904125 • 10"
Issued: 2003 • Retired: 2003
Original: $18 • Value: $18

2173.
Rosemont Bear [Rosemont]
#unknown • 10"
Issued: 2002 • Retired: 2002
Original: $N/A • Value: $25
Rosemont Town Chat gift.

2174.
Rosie [Yankee Candle]
#94695YC • 8"
Issued: 2004 • Retired: 2004
Original: $15 • Value: $16
Sold with candle.

2175.
Rosie B. Goodbear [Country Clutter]
#94971CC • 10"
Issued: 2000 • Retired: 2000
Original: $22 • Value: $45

2176.
Ross G. Jodibear
#92000-08 • 9" • AR
Issued: 2000 • Retired: 2001
Original: $18 • Value: $21

BEARS

	PRICE PAID	VALUE
2171.		
2172.		
2173.		
2174.		
2175.		
2176.		
2177.		
2178.		
2179.		
2180.		
2181.		
2182.		
TOTALS		

NOTES

2177.
Rowen Yachtley
#918342 • 10" • TJ
Issued: 2002 • Retired: 2002
Original: $23 • Value: $23

2178.
Roxanne K. Bear
#91741 • 10" • TJ
Issued: 1996 • Retired: 1998
Original: $20 • Value: $36

2179.
Roxie and Reba DuBeary [QVC]
#(C55534) • 6"
Issued: 1999 • Retired: 1999
Original: $18 • Value: $33

2180. 78
Royce
#6107B • 14" • JB
Issued: 1990 • Retired: 1991
Original: $32 • Value: $338

2181. 78
Royce Bear
#6107 • 12" • TJ
Issued: 1991 • Retired: 1992
Original: $32 • Value: $321

2182. 79
Rudolf
#58078 • 18" • SB
Issued: 1992 • Retired: 1993
Original: $30 • Value: $511

Bears

2183. **Rudolph [SLE]**
#unknown • 7½"
Issued: 1996 • Retired: 1996
Original: $12 • Value: $29

2184. **Rudy McRind**
#912630 • 14" • TJ
Issued: 2001 • Retired: 2002
Original: $25 • Value: $30

2185. **Rudy Pitoody**
#91880 • 11" • TJ
Issued: 2000 • Retired: 2002
Original: $18 • Value: $29

Have You Seen Me?

2186. **Rudy Valentino [Harry & David]**
#unknown • 11"
Issued: 2003 • Retired: 2003
Original: $30 • Value: $36

2187. **Rudy Z. Mooseburg [GCC]**
#94875GCC • 17"
Issued: 1999 • Retired: 1999
Original: $17 • Value: $35

2188. **Rufus (new face)**
#5111 • 16" • JB
Issued: 1990 • Retired: 1998
Original: $27 • Value: $52
Brown nose variation $100.

2189. **Rumsford Q. Bearsworth [QVC]**
#93353V (C21163) • 21"
Issued: 2003 • Retired: 2003
Original: $54 • Value: $65

2190. **Rupert**
#9142 • 8" • AS
Issued: 1994 • Retired: 1994
Original: $18 • Value: $42

2191. **Rupert B. Shutterbear**
#92003-01 • 15" • AR
Issued: 2003 • Current
Original: $25 • Value: $R/E

2192. **Rupert B. Shutterbear [QVC]**
#(C02195) • 12"
Issued: 2004 • Retired: 2004
Original: $22 • Value: $30

2193. **Ruskin K. Woodruff**
#57052-07 • 8" • AS
Issued: 2001 • Retired: 2002
Original: $11 • Value: $13

2194. **Russ Q. Goodfriends [QVC]**
#(C05181) • 8"
Issued: 2004 • Retired: 2004
Original: $20 • Value: $27
Sold as set.

BEARS	PRICE PAID	VALUE
2183.		
2184.		
2185.		
2186.		
2187.		
2188.		
2189.		
2190.		
2191.		
2192.		
2193.		
2194.		
TOTALS		

NOTES

Bears

2195.
Russet [Frederick Atkins]
#94762FA • 10"
Issued: 1999 • Retired: 1999
Original: $20 • Value: $45

2196.
Rustley Leadbottoms
#51020-11 • 10" • AR
Issued: 2002 • Retired: 2002
Original: $17 • Value: $29

2197.
Rusty & Scardycrow
#912642 • 14" • TJ
Issued: 2001 • Retired: 2004
Original: $20 • Value: $24

2198.
Rusty B. Autumnfest [BoydsBiz.com]
#919826 • 12" • TJ
Issued: 2003 • Retired: 2003
Original: $27 • Value: $27

2199.
Rusty McPunkin
#904324 • 6" • TJ
Issued: 2004 • Current
Original: $11 • Value: $R/E

2200.
Rusty Scaredybear [Longaberger]
#94667LB • 10"
Issued: 2003 • Retired: 2003
Original: $24 • Value: $33

2201.
Rutherford
#912610 • 16" • TJ
Issued: 1998 • Retired: 2000
Original: $58 • Value: $84

2202.
Ruthie
#82524 • 6" • TJ
Issued: 2003 • Retired: 2003
Original: $10 • Value: $10

2203.
Ruthy Appleton [Cracker Barrel]
#94993CB • 10"
Issued: 2001 • Retired: 2001
Original: $24 • Value: $58

2204.
Rutledge [QVC]
#(C49885) • 16"
Issued: 1998 • Retired: 1998
Original: $36 • Value: $75

2205.
Ryan [Dillards]
#94771DL • 14"
Issued: 2000 • Retired: 2000
Original: $25 • Value: $45

2206.
S.B. Twinklebeary [QVC]
#(C22822) • 10"
Issued: 2003 • Retired: 2003
Original: $10 • Value: $12

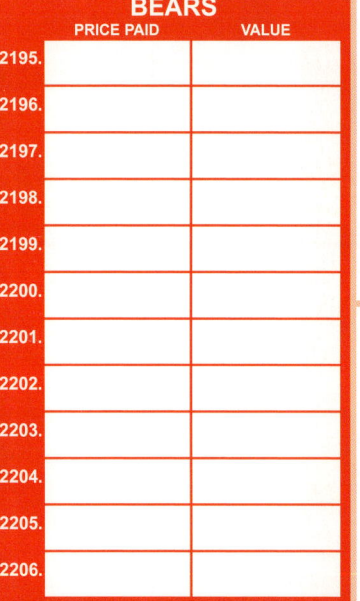

BEARS

	PRICE PAID	VALUE
2195.		
2196.		
2197.		
2198.		
2199.		
2200.		
2201.		
2202.		
2203.		
2204.		
2205.		
2206.		
TOTALS		

NOTES

Bears

2207.
S.C. Northstar
#917303 • 14" • TJ
Issued: 1997 • Retired: 1999
Original: $27 • Value: $56

2208.
S.K. [CAN]
#BC94290PO • 8"
LE of 4800 • Issued: 2001 • Retired: 2001
Original: $28 • Value: $38

2209.
Sable B. Bearsdale
#510810-05 • 14" • JB
Issued: 2001 • Retired: 2002
Original: $15 • Value: $18

2210.
Sadie [Kirlins]
#unknown • 10"
LE of 6000 • Issued: 1999 • Retired: 1999
Original: $26 • Value: $35

2211.
Sadie B. Bearcountry [QVC]
#92372V (C0696) • 14"
LE of 1500 • Issued: 2003 • Retired: 2003
Original: $32 • Value: $38

2212.
Sadie Bearyman [May Company]
#94160MC • 8"
Issued: 2000 • Retired: 2000
Original: $20 • Value: $30

2213.
Sadie Bearymore [May Company]
#94157MC • 8"
Issued: 1999 • Retired: 1999
Original: $15 • Value: $32

2214.
Sage Leafowitz
#918353 • 8" • TJ
Issued: 2001 • Retired: 2002
Original: $14 • Value: $17

2215.
Sage Steadsbeary [Longaberger]
#993644LB • 10"
Issued: 2004 • Retired: 2004
Original: $24 • Value: $26

BEARS		
	PRICE PAID	VALUE
2207.		
2208.		
2209.		
2210.		
2211.		
2212.		
2213.		
2214.		
2215.		
2216.		
2217.		
2218.		
	TOTALS	

NOTES

2216.
Sakary Millenia [Profitts]
#unknown • 10"
Issued: 1999 • Retired: 1999
Original: $24 • Value: $36

2217.
Sally and Harry [Lord & Taylor]
#unknown • 8"
Issued: 1996 • Retired: 1996
Original: $N/E • Value: $30
Sold separately.

2218.
Sally Quignapple and Annie
#91009 • 10" • TJ
Issued: 2000 • Retired: 2002
Original: $21 • Value: $25

Bears

2219.
Sally Quignapple and Annie
[SFMB]
#41-72978 • 10"
Issued: 2000 • Retired: 2000
Original: $30 • Value: $45

2220.
Sam Yule [Hallmark]
#9701HM • 10"
Issued: 2003 • Retired: 2003
Original: $17 • Value: $20

2221.
Samantha [Kirlins]
#unknown • 12"
Issued: 1997 • Retired: 1997
Original: $22 • Value: $44

2222.
Samantha Marie & Brady [SYN]
#94591SYN • 10"
Issued: 2001 • Retired: 2001
Original: $25 • Value: $34

2223.
Sammi B. Thumblover
[Linda Anderson]
#90021CD • 8"
Issued: 2002 • Retired: 2002
Original: $15 • Value: $21

2224.
Sammy Slugger
#903308 • 8"
Issued: 2003 • Current
Original: $15 • Value: $R/E

2225.
Samuel
#918052 • 6" • TJ
Issued: 1998 • Retired: 2000
Original: $10 • Value: $21

2226.
Samuel Adams
#915210 • 8½" • TJ
Issued: 2000 • Retired: 2002
Original: $12 • Value: $14

2227.
Samuel T. Kringlebear with George
#919832 • 16" • TJ
Issued: 2004 • Current
Original: $55 • Value: $R/E

2228.
Sandy Claus
#91731 • 16" • TJ
Issued: 1995 • Retired: 1998
Original: $29 • Value: $58

2229.
Sandy Claus II
#917310 • 16" • TJ
Issued: 1998 • Retired: 2000
Original: $29 • Value: $34

2230.
Sandy Sanditoes
#917443 • 10" • TJ
Issued: 2002 • Retired: 2002
Original: $20 • Value: $26

BEARS	PRICE PAID	VALUE
2219.		
2220.		
2221.		
2222.		
2223.		
2224.		
2225.		
2226.		
2227.		
2228.		
2229.		
2230.		
TOTALS		

NOTES

Bears

2231.

Have You Seen Me?

Santa Bear
#6164 • 14"
LE • Issued: 1990 • Retired: 1990
Original: $70 • Value: $330

2232.

Sapphire S. Bearington [QVC]
#93439V (C22079) • 6" • MB
LE of 2400 • Issued: 2003 • Retired: 2003
Original: $17 • Value: $28

2233.

Sara Beth [POG]
#94584POG • 14"
Issued: 2000 • Retired: 2000
Original: $26 • Value: $51

2234.

Sarabeth Crystalfrost
#904181 • 12" • TJ
Issued: 2003 • Retired: 2003
Original: $29 • Value: $35

2235.

Sarah [CAN]
#BC94288PO • 8"
LE of 4800 • Issued: 2000 • Retired: 2000
Original: $23 • Value: $32

2236.

Sarah Anne Bearsly & T. Foster Wuzzie [QVC]
#99701V (C95071) • 10"
Issued: 1999 • Retired: 1999
Original: $34 • Value: $48

2237.

Sarah Beth Jodibear
#92000-04 • 9" • AR
Issued: 1999 • Retired: 2002
Original: $17 • Value: $20

2238.

Sarah Jane [CAN]
#BC94292PO • 8"
Issued: 2001 • Retired: 2001
Original: $23 • Value: $30

2239.

Sarah Patchbeary [Kirlins]
#94532KR • 11"
LE of 5000 • Issued: 2002 • Retired: 2002
Original: $22 • Value: $30

2240.

Sasha
#9174 • 10" • TJ
Issued: 1995 • Retired: 1998
Original: $20 • Value: $34

2241.

Sasha Dubeary
#918100 • 6"
Issued: 2002 • Retired: 2002
Original: $10 • Value: $17

2242.

Savannah Berrywinkle & Bentley [QVC]
#93017V (C39085) • 13"
Issued: 1997 • Retired: 1997
Original: $32 • Value: $68

BEARS

	PRICE PAID	VALUE
2231.		
2232.		
2233.		
2234.		
2235.		
2236.		
2237.		
2238.		
2239.		
2240.		
2241.		
2242.		
TOTALS		

NOTES

Bears

2243. Scarecrow
#904373 • 8" • TJ
Issued: 2004 • Current
Original: $16 • Value: $R/E

2244. Scarlett Bearington
#590043-02 • 12" • MB
Issued: 2001 • Retired: 2002
Original: $45 • Value: $55

2245. Scoop
#904124 • 6"
Issued: 2003 • Current
Original: $10 • Value: $R/E

2246. Scooter
#5642-03 • 8" • BA
Issued: 1993 • Retired: 1995
Original: $11 • Value: $45

2247. Scotch [SLE]
#unknown • 10"
Issued: 1996 • Retired: 1996
Original: $20 • Value: $42

2248. Scruffy S. Beariluved
#51000-05 • 10" • JB
Issued: 2000 • Current
Original: $15 • Value: $R/E

2249. Sebastian
#5827 • 13" • CB
Issued: 1991 • Retired: 1997
Original: $20 • Value: $50

2250. Sedgewick T Bruin [QVC]
#(C53041) • 16"
Issued: 1998 • Retired: 1998
Original: $21 • Value: $35

2251. Serendipity Wishkabibble
#90501 • 10" • TJ
Issued: 2001 • Retired: 2001
Original: $20 • Value: $24

2252. Sergei Bearskov
#912619 • 14" • TJ
Issued: 2000 • Retired: 2002
Original: $39 • Value: $46

2253. Settia
#590059 • 10" • MB
Issued: 2002 • Retired: 2002
Original: $30 • Value: $30

2254. Seymour P. Snowbeary
#9138-01 • 12" • TJ
Issued: 1997 • Retired: 1999
Original: $27 • Value: $33

BEARS	PRICE PAID	VALUE
2243.		
2244.		
2245.		
2246.		
2247.		
2248.		
2249.		
2250.		
2251.		
2252.		
2253.		
2254.		
TOTALS		

NOTES

2255.
Shane B. Bearsford [QVC]
#unknown • 16"
Issued: 2001 • Retired: 2001
Original: $27 • Value: $45

2256.
Shane B. Bearsworth
#57153-03 • 16" • AS
Issued: 2002 • Retired: 2002
Original: $25 • Value: $25

2257.
Shannon Oakley & Mr. Hoots [QVC]
#99888V (C20179) • 14"
Issued: 2002 • Retired: 2002
Original: $37 • Value: $48

2258.
Shara Sugarcone [BtoB Website]
#919823 • 10" • TJ
Issued: 2003 • Retired: 2003
Original: $20 • Value: $24

2259.
Shari Beabeary [Longaberger]
#94665LB • 10"
Issued: 2003 • Retired: 2003
Original: $32 • Value: $60
Only available at 2003 Bee.

2260.
Shasta with Caledonia and Humbolt [QVC]
#unknown • 6"
Issued: 1998 • Retired: 1998
Original: $25 • Value: $42

2261.
Shasta Daisydew [POG]
#94603POG • 10"
Issued: 2003 • Retired: 2003
Original: $19 • Value: $26

2262.
Shawnee Fisher
#904130 • 16"
Issued: 2003 • Retired: 2003
Original: $36 • Value: $40

2263.
Shay Ann McLemon
#904282 • 8" • TJ
Issued: 2004 • Current
Original: $14 • Value: $R/E

2264.
Shelby McRind [Cracker Barrel]
#94992CB • 10"
Issued: 2001 • Retired: 2001
Original: $24 • Value: $60

2265.
Shelby T. Sanditoes
#913981 • 6" • TJ
Issued: 2002 • Retired: 2002
Original: $10 • Value: $17

2266.
Sheldon Bearchild
#918061 • 6" • TJ
Issued: 1998 • Retired: 2002
Original: $8 • Value: $16

214

Bears

2267.
Sherie B. Bearican & Cliff
#904250 • 16" • TJ
Issued: 2004 • Current
Original: $47 • Value: $R/E

2268.
Sherlock (pink paws)
#5821 • 11" • TJ
Issued: 1992 • Retired: 1992
Original: $20 • Value: $180

2269.
Sherlock (gray paws)
#9188 • 11" • TJ
Issued: 1993 • Retired: 1997
Original: $21 • Value: $53

2270.
Shivers Snowbeary
#918360 • 8" • TJ
Issued: 2001 • Retired: 2002
Original: $10 • Value: $12

2271.
Sidney [Dillards]
#94730DL • 10"
Issued: 1998 • Retired: 1998
Original: $25 • Value: $30

2272.
Sierra Woodsbeary
#912632 • 14" • TJ
Issued: 2001 • Retired: 2002
Original: $30 • Value: $36

2273.
Sigmund Von Bruin
#5010-08 • 6" • WB
Issued: 1994 • Retired: 1995
Original: $10 • Value: $55

2274.
Silvia Jubilee [BBC]
#918084SM • 12"
LE of 5000 • Issued: 2004 • Retired: 2004
Original: $10 • Value: $22

2275.
Simon Beanster and Andy
#910090 • 10" • TJ
Issued: 2000 • Retired: 2002
Original: $21 • Value: $25

2276.
Simone de Bearvoire
#9180 • 6" • AS
Issued: 1993 • Retired: 1996
Original: $9 • Value: $34

2277.
Sinclair Bearsford
#57150-03 • 16" • AS
Issued: 2000 • Retired: 2002
Original: $25 • Value: $31

2278.
Sinkin (stark white)
#5808 • 18" • SB
Issued: 1991 • Retired: 1992
Original: $32 • Value: $148

BEARS		
	PRICE PAID	VALUE
2267.		
2268.		
2269.		
2270.		
2271.		
2272.		
2273.		
2274.		
2275.		
2276.		
2277.		
2278.		
	TOTALS	

NOTES

2279.
Sinkin II (off-white)
#5808 • 18" • SB
Issued: 1992 • Retired: 1997
Original: $32 • Value: $50

2280.
Sippy McLemon
#904283 • 6" • AS
Issued: 2004 • Current
Original: $10 • Value: $R/E

2281.
Sir Henry
#5720 • 12" • AS
Issued: 1991 • Retired: 1992
Original: $20 • Value: $122

2282.
Sir Hugsalot
#82041 • 16"
Issued: 2003 • Current
Original: $20 • Value: $R/E

2283.
Have You Seen Me?
Sir Lotslove [Hershey]
#unknown • 10"
Issued: 2003 • Retired: 2003
Original: $35 • Value: $42

2284.
Sissy B. Bear
#903006 • 8" • ME
Issued: 2001 • Retired: 2001
Original: $10 • Value: $12

2285.
Sissy Bearyfriend [SYN]
#94604SYN • 8"
Issued: 2003 • Retired: 2003
Original: $16 • Value: $20

2286.
Skidoo
#9193 • 11" • TJ
Issued: 1992 • Retired: 1998
Original: $24 • Value: $37

BEARS

	PRICE PAID	VALUE
2279.		
2280.		
2281.		
2282.		
2283.		
2284.		
2285.		
2286.		
2287.		
2288.		
2289.		
2290.		
	TOTALS	

NOTES

2287.
Skip
#5638 • 12" • BA
Issued: 1992 • Retired: 1996
Original: $16 • Value: $39

2288.
Skip B. Yachtley
#913976 • 6" • BA
Issued: 2002 • Retired: 2002
Original: $10 • Value: $10

2289.
Skipper T. Pattington [QVC]
#93340V (C20215) • 10" • MB
LE of 700 • Issued: 2002 • Retired: 2002
Original: $44 • Value: $70

2290.
Skylar & Starlynn [QVC]
#unknown • 8"
Issued: 1997 • Retired: 1997
Original: $27 • Value: $38

Bears

2291.
Skylar Thistlebeary
#911951 • 16" • TJ
Issued: 1999 • Retired: 2002
Original: $36 • Value: $45

2292.
Skylar Thistlebeary [SFMB]
#41-72940 • 16"
Issued: 2000 • Retired: 2000
Original: $50 • Value: $65
♪ A Dream is a Wish Your Heart Makes ♪

2293.
Slim B. Woodsley
#92002-02 • 12" • AR
Issued: 2001 • Retired: 2001
Original: $13 • Value: $27
2002 TOBY Award Winner

2294.
Slugger
#9177-01 • 8" • TJ
Issued: 1996 • Retired: 1999
Original: $26 • Value: $46

2295.
Smith Applewish
#918357 • 8" • TJ
Issued: 2001 • Current
Original: $10 • Value: $R/E

2296.
Smith Witter 25th Anniversary [QVC]
#93539V (C05174) • 10"
LE of 9000 • Issued: 2004 • Retired: 2004
Original: $15 • Value: $25

2297.
Smith Witter II
#5110 • 17" • JB
Issued: 1994 • Retired: 1998
Original: $29 • Value: $45

2298.
Smith Witter II [SFMB]
#41-66846 • 17"
Issued: 1997 • Retired: 1997
Original: $35 • Value: $60
♪ You've Got a Friend ♪

2299.
Smokie Mountberg [SLE]
#unknown • 6"
Issued: 1998 • Retired: 1998
Original: $10 • Value: $25

2300.
Sneaky
#904203 • 8" • TJ
Issued: 2003 • Current
Original: $13 • Value: $R/E

2301.
Snickersnoodle
#91770 • 8" • TJ
Issued: 2001 • Retired: 2001
Original: $16 • Value: $19

2302.
Sniffles
#5773 • 9" • HD
Issued: 1991 • Retired: 1993
Original: $14 • Value: $141

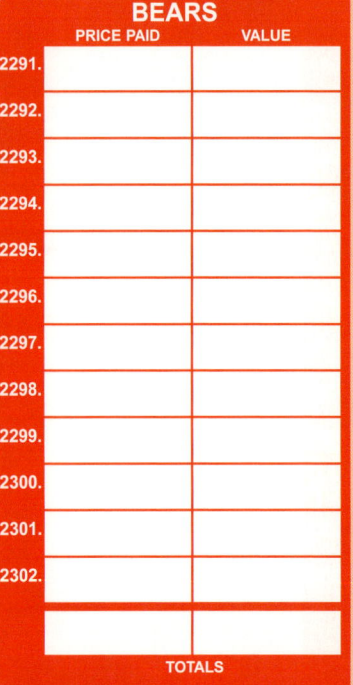

BEARS

	PRICE PAID	VALUE
2291.		
2292.		
2293.		
2294.		
2295.		
2296.		
2297.		
2298.		
2299.		
2300.		
2301.		
2302.		
TOTALS		

NOTES

Bears

2303.

Sniffles T. Woodsley
#92002-01 • 10" • AR
Issued: 2001 • Retired: 2002
Original: $13 • Value: $26

2304.

Snookie Snickelfritz
#51770-09 • 10" • BA
Issued: 2000 • Retired: 2001
Original: $11 • Value: $13

2305.

Snowy Crystalfrost
#904184 • 6" • TJ
Issued: 2003 • Retired: 2003
Original: $18 • Value: $18

2306.

Snuggems B. Joy [GCC]
#94884GCC • 12"
Issued: 2000 • Retired: 2000
Original: $20 • Value: $26

2307.

Sonja Frostbeary
#912058 • 12" • TJ
Issued: 2001 • Retired: 2002
Original: $25 • Value: $30

2308.

Sonny
#903023 • 10"
Issued: 2002 • Current
Original: $10 • Value: $R/E

2309.

Sonya B. Burrbruin [QVC]
#(C20975) • 16"
Issued: 2002 • Retired: 2002
Original: $51 • Value: $66

2310.

Sophie B. Goodbear [Country Clutter]
#94972CC • 10"
Issued: 2000 • Retired: 2000
Original: $22 • Value: $41

2311.

Sophie Jane Gingerbeary [GCC]
#94921GCC • 10"
Issued: 2002 • Retired: 2002
Original: $21 • Value: $35

2312.

Sparklefrost
#904355 • 5" • TJ
Issued: 2004 • Current
Original: $11 • Value: $R/E

2313.

Speara Mintly
#904212 • 14" • TJ
Issued: 2003 • Current
Original: $30 • Value: $R/E

2314.

Spearmint and Peppermint Hollibeary [QVC]
#(C95119) • 8"
LE of 3100 • Issued: 1999 • Retired: 1999
Original: $29 • Value: $45

BEARS		
	PRICE PAID	VALUE
2303.		
2304.		
2305.		
2306.		
2307.		
2308.		
2309.		
2310.		
2311.		
2312.		
2313.		
2314.		
TOTALS		

NOTES

Bears

2315.
Spencer
#5725 • 5½" • AS
Issued: 1992 • Retired: 2000
Original: $7 • Value: $16

2316.
Springley T. Hopplebear
#904143 • 8"
Issued: 2003 • Retired: 2003
Original: $13 • Value: $13

2317.
Spunky Boobear
#81003 • 8" • TJ
Issued: 2000 • Retired: 2000
Original: $10 • Value: $20

2318.
Squeekie (nutmeg)
#5615 • 8"
Issued: 1991 • Retired: 1991
Original: $10 • Value: $110

2319.
Squeekie (british tan)
#5616 • 8"
Issued: 1992 • Retired: 1993
Original: $10 • Value: $98

2320.
St. Niklas
#917311 • 10" • TJ
Issued: 1998 • Retired: 2002
Original: $18 • Value: $28

2321.
Stacey B. Beansley [QVC]
#93454V (C22636) • 12"
Issued: 2003 • Retired: 2003
Original: $20 • Value: $45

2322.
Stacey Daisydew
#904072 • 10"
Issued: 2003 • Current
Original: $18 • Value: $R/E

2323.
Stafford [GCC]
#94859GCC • 8"
Issued: 1998 • Retired: 1998
Original: $25 • Value: $39
Sold as a set with Devon.

2324.
Star S. Bangles [QVC]
#93424V (C21162) • 8"
Issued: 2003 • Retired: 2003
Original: $12 • Value: $25

2325.
Starlight B. Bearsworth [QVC]
#93151V • 17"
Issued: 2000 • Retired: 2000
Original: $23 • Value: $35

2326.
Starr B. Bearyproud with Sparkle
#912016 • 16"
Issued: 2002 • Retired: 2002
Original: $56 • Value: $68

BEARS

	PRICE PAID	VALUE
2315.		
2316.		
2317.		
2318.		
2319.		
2320.		
2321.		
2322.		
2323.		
2324.		
2325.		
2326.		
TOTALS		

NOTES

Bears

2327.
Starr E. Night [Hallmark]
#9695HM • 5"
Issued: 2002 • Retired: 2002
Original: $10 • Value: $19

2328.
Starry [Art House]
#unknown • 8"
LE of 3600 • Issued: 1999 • Retired: 1999
Original: $20 • Value: $35

2329.
Stella
#913973 • 6" • TJ
Issued: 2001 • Retired: 2002
Original: $13 • Value: $23

2330.
Stella and Baby Mae [QVC]
#(C76931) • 10"
Issued: 2000 • Retired: 2000
Original: $21 • Value: $55

2331.
Stella Seamstress
#6168B
LE • Issued: 1991 • Retired: 1991
Original: $70 • Value: $470

2332.
Stella Starbear [SFMB]
#41-72572
Issued: 2002 • Retired: 2002
Original: $20 • Value: $35
♪ Twinkle Twinkle Little Star ♪

2333.
Stephanie B. Bearyproud
[BtoB Website]
#919819 • 12" • TJ
Issued: 2002 • Retired: 2002
Original: $16 • Value: $27

2334.
Stephanie B. Learnin [QVC]
#93220V (C59854) • 10"
Issued: 2001 • Retired: 2001
Original: $28 • Value: $40

BEARS		
	PRICE PAID	VALUE
2327.		
2328.		
2329.		
2330.		
2331.		
2332.		
2333.		
2334.		
2335.		
2336.		
2337.		
2338.		
	TOTALS	

NOTES

2335.
Sterling (30") [EVENT]
#500201 • 30" • AS
Issued: 2004 • Retired: 2004
Original: $N/A • Value: $150
Raffle gift.

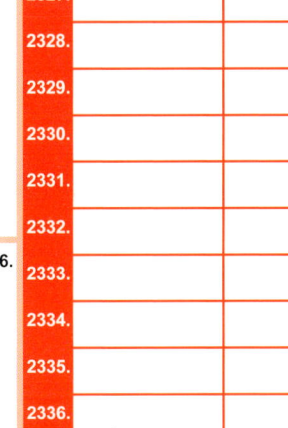

2336.
Sterling (16")
#500200 • 16" • AS
Issued: 2004 • Current
Original: $25 • Value: $R/E

2337.
Sterner [Frederick Atkins]
#unknown • 10"
Issued: 1998 • Retired: 1998
Original: $29 • Value: $45

2338.
Stevenson Q. Bearitage
#91736 • 10" • TJ
Issued: 1999 • Retired: 2002
Original: $20 • Value: $34

Bears

2339.

Have You Seen Me?

Stonewall Bear
#6108B
Issued: 1991 • Retired: 1991
Original: $25 • Value: $369

2340.

Strawberry [Smuckers]
#(C6500001) • 12"
Issued: 1999 • Retired: 1999
Original: $48 • Value: $125

2341.

Stretch
#918663 • 12" • TJ
Issued: 2003 • Current
Original: $15 • Value: $R/E

2342.

Stryker Scoresalot
#917372 • 10" • ME
Issued: 2001 • Retired: 2001
Original: $20 • Value: $24

2343.

Stuart McSnoozle
#904061 • 10"
Issued: 2002 • Retired: 2002
Original: $20 • Value: $26

2344.

Stubby McBobble
#510307 • 10" • JB
Issued: 2002 • Retired: 2002
Original: $10 • Value: $13

2345.

Stumper A. Potter
#515211-11 • 12" • JB
Issued: 2000 • Retired: 2000
Original: $17 • Value: $27

2346.

Sturbridge Q. Patriot
#91524 • 8" • TJ
Issued: 2001 • Retired: 2002
Original: $13 • Value: $25

2347.

Sue B. Bearkins
#917440 • 10" • TJ
Issued: 2001 • Retired: 2001
Original: $15 • Value: $22

2348.

Sugar McRind
#91746 • 10" • TJ
Issued: 2001 • Retired: 2002
Original: $20 • Value: $27

2349.

Sugar Plum Beary [POG]
#94597POG • 8"
Issued: 2002 • Retired: 2002
Original: $18 • Value: $25

2350.

Summer Sanditoes
#913933 • 8" • TJ
Issued: 2002 • Retired: 2002
Original: $14 • Value: $19

BEARS

	PRICE PAID	VALUE
2339.		
2340.		
2341.		
2342.		
2343.		
2344.		
2345.		
2346.		
2347.		
2348.		
2349.		
2350.		
	TOTALS	

NOTES

Bears

2351.
Sunnie Dae [Longaberger]
#993656LB • 10"
Issued: 2004 • Retired: 2004
Original: $16 • Value: $35

2352.
Sunnie Rae Daisydew
with Sprinkle [QVC]
#99947V (C21154) • 14"
LE of 3400 • Issued: 2003 • Retired: 2003
Original: $39 • Value: $65
Sold with watering can.

2353.
Sunny B. Goodcheer [POG]
#94593POG • 8"
Issued: 2002 • Retired: 2002
Original: $13 • Value: $19

2354.
Sunny B. Hugsworth [QVC]
#(C56960) • 14"
Issued: 1999 • Retired: 1999
Original: $16 • Value: $28

2355.
Sunny Buzzbee [J.T.Webb]
#94287JTW • 10"
LE of 3600 • Issued: 1999 • Retired: 1999
Original: $25 • Value: $45

2356.
Susie [Lord & Taylor]
#unknown • 8"
Issued: 1999 • Retired: 1999
Original: $25 • Value: $45

2357.
Susie B. Bearlove
#82521 • 8" • TJ
Issued: 2003 • Retired: 2003
Original: $10 • Value: $10

2358.
Susie Deerfriend [GCC]
#9487GCC • 14"
Issued: 2003 • Retired: 2003
Original: $23 • Value: $28

2359.
Susie Runsitall
#903304 • 8"
Issued: 2003 • Current
Original: $10 • Value: $R/E

2360.
Sutton
#57051 • 8" • AS
Issued: 2000 • Retired: 2002
Original: $10 • Value: $16

2361.
Suzella K. Bearington [QVC]
#93218V (C59858) • 6" • MB
LE • Issued: 2001 • Retired: 2001
Original: $17 • Value: $29

2362.
Suzie B. Spicebeary
Gift Set [Country Clutter]
#94692YC • 14"
Issued: 2002 • Retired: 2002
Original: $48 • Value: $52

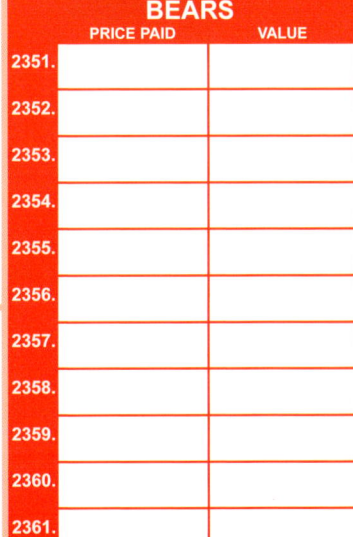

BEARS		
	PRICE PAID	VALUE
2351.		
2352.		
2353.		
2354.		
2355.		
2356.		
2357.		
2358.		
2359.		
2360.		
2361.		
2362.		
TOTALS		

NOTES

Bears

2363.
Suzie Q. Scootenpedal, Lil' Louis & Poochkins [QVC]
#(C19885) • 10"
LE • Issued: 2002 • Retired: 2002
Original: $43 • Value: $56
Tricycle.

2364.
Sven
#9122 • 8" • AS
Issued: 1994 • Retired: 1996
Original: $18 • Value: $35

2365.
Sven B. Frostman [QVC]
#(C95073) • 14"
Issued: 1999 • Retired: 1999
Original: $30 • Value: $45

2366.
Sweetie McLemon
#904281 • 12" • TJ
Issued: 2004 • Current
Original: $25 • Value: $R/E

2367.
Sydney [CAN]
#BC94276 • 8"
LE of 2400 • Issued: 1997 • Retired: 1997
Original: $25 • Value: $33

2368.
Sydney G. Bearsmark [Hallmark]
#9696HM • 10"
Issued: 2002 • Retired: 2002
Original: $18 • Value: $27

2369.
Sylvia G. Bearimore
#918538 • 6" • TJ
Issued: 2000 • Retired: 2002
Original: $11 • Value: $18

2370.
T. Dean Newberger III [GCC]
#948656GCC • 10"
Issued: 1998 • Retired: 1998
Original: $N/E • Value: $38

2371.
T. Farley Wuzzie
#595100-11 • 5" • TF
Issued: 1998 • Retired: 1999
Original: $9 • Value: $18

2372.
T. Frampton Wuzzie
#595100-05 • 5" • TF
Issued: 1999 • Retired: 2000
Original: $9 • Value: $14

2373.
T. Frasier Wuzzie
#595100-08 • 5" • TF
Issued: 1998 • Retired: 2000
Original: $9 • Value: $18

2374.
T. Fulton Wuzzie
#595100-06 • 3" • TF
Issued: 1998 • Retired: 2000
Original: $9 • Value: $18

BEARS

	PRICE PAID	VALUE
2363.		
2364.		
2365.		
2366.		
2367.		
2368.		
2369.		
2370.		
2371.		
2372.		
2373.		
2374.		
TOTALS		

NOTES

2375.
T. Lynne Bearyproud
#913932 • 8"
Issued: 2002 • Retired: 2002
Original: $13 • Value: $19

2376.
T.D. Gridiron
#917374 • 10" • ME
Issued: 2001 • Current
Original: $23 • Value: $R/E

2377.
T.G. Trickster
#919635 • 8"
Issued: 2002 • Retired: 2002
Original: $10 • Value: $10

2378.
T.J. Bearheart [QVC]
#93403V (C21155) • 10"
Issued: 2003 • Retired: 2003
Original: $20 • Value: $24

2379.
T.K. Bear [CAN]
#BC94289PO • 8"
LE of 4800 • Issued: 2001 • Retired: 2001
Original: $28 • Value: $39

2380.
T.L.C. Sparkleheart
#82016 • 5" • AS
Issued: 2001 • Retired: 2001
Original: $9 • Value: $11

2381.
Tabitha J. Spellbinder with Midnight Sneakypuss
#900201 • 16" • UB
LE of 12998 • Issued: 1999 • Retired: 1999
Original: $66 • Value: $97

2382.
Taddley
#918660 • 10" • TJ
Issued: 2003 • Current
Original: $15 • Value: $R/E

2383.
Tami P. Rally
#917367 • 10" • ME
Issued: 2000 • Retired: 2001
Original: $29 • Value: $35

2384.
Tammy [QVC]
#unknown • 12"
Issued: 1996 • Retired: 1996
Original: $25 • Value: $54

2385.
Tara & Tia F. Wuzzie with Tilly [QVC]
#(C56966) • 3½"
Issued: 1999 • Retired: 1999
Original: $21 • Value: $32

2386.
Tartan Tess [Country Peddler]
#91104CP • 12" • AR
Issued: 1996 • Retired: 1996
Original: $15 • Value: $34

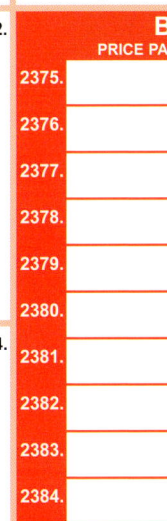

BEARS

	PRICE PAID	VALUE
2375.		
2376.		
2377.		
2378.		
2379.		
2380.		
2381.		
2382.		
2383.		
2384.		
2385.		
2386.		
TOTALS		

NOTES

Bears

2387.
Tasha B. Frostbeary
#900205 • 14" • UB
LE of 12998 • Issued: 1999 • Retired: 2000
Original: $66 • Value: $95

Have You Seen Me?

2388.
Tasha F. Wuzzie with Tami and Tatum [QVC]
#(C55518) • 3"
Issued: 1999 • Retired: 1999
Original: $22 • Value: $35

2389.
Tassel F. Wuzzie
#596004 • 3" • TF
Issued: 1999 • Retired: 1999
Original: $8 • Value: $17

Have You Seen Me?

2390.
Tatters Beariluved with Patches [QVC]
#(C97878) • 10"
Issued: 2000 • Retired: 2000
Original: $26 • Value: $35

2391.
Tatum F. Wuzzie
#596001 • 3" • TF
Issued: 1999 • Retired: 1999
Original: $8 • Value: $18
Also with Tami, Tasha as QVC set.

2392.
Tawny Tweeter with Scarlet
#904261 • 14" • TJ
Issued: 2004 • Current
Original: $30 • Value: $R/E

BEARS

	PRICE PAID	VALUE
2387.		
2388.		
2389.		
2390.		
2391.		
2392.		
2393.		
2394.		
2395.		
2396.		
2397.		
2398.		
	TOTALS	

NOTES

2393.
Taylor [Dillards]
#94705DL • 16"
Issued: 1996 • Retired: 1996
Original: $45 • Value: $75

2394.
Taylor Rene [Cracker Barrel]
#94996CB • 10"
Issued: 2003 • Retired: 2003
Original: $24 • Value: $35

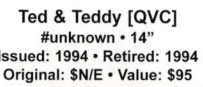
Have You Seen Me?

2395.
Ted & Teddy [QVC]
#unknown • 14"
Issued: 1994 • Retired: 1994
Original: $N/E • Value: $95

2396.
Ted Bear
#9156 • 8"
Issued: 1993 • Retired: 1996
Original: $16 • Value: $45

2397.
Teddie Collectibear [Longaberger]
#94627LB • 14"
Issued: 2003 • Retired: 2003
Original: $31 • Value: $37

2398.
Teddy B. Bear [EVENT]
#5004 • 10" • MB
Issued: 2001 • Retired: 2001
Original: $10 • Value: $20

2399.
Teddy Bauer [QVC]
#unknown • 16"
Issued: 1995 • Retired: 1995
Original: $55 • Value: $83

2400.
Teddy Beanberger
#9118 • 16" • TJ
Issued: 1995 • Retired: 1997
Original: $53 • Value: $73

2401.
Teresa D. Bestlove
#82512 • 12" • TJ
Issued: 2002 • Retired: 2002
Original: $25 • Value: $25

2402.
Tess Autumnbeary [Welcome Home]
#unknown • 8"
Issued: 2000 • Retired: 2000
Original: $15 • Value: $32

2403.
Tilden, Tori & Tessa F. Wuzzie [QVC]
#(C95123) • 3½"
Issued: 1999 • Retired: 1999
Original: $22 • Value: $33

2404.
Texanne [Dillards]
#94708DL • 14"
Issued: 1997 • Retired: 1997
Original: $25 • Value: $63

2405.
Thaddeus Von Bruin
#571541 • 16" • AS
Issued: 2002 • Retired: 2002
Original: $25 • Value: $25

2406.
Thatcher
#5706 • 5½" • AS
Issued: 1990 • Retired: 1997
Original: $7 • Value: $32

BEARS		
	PRICE PAID	VALUE
2399.		
2400.		
2401.		
2402.		
2403.		
2404.		
2405.		
2406.		
2407.		
2408.		
2409.		
2410.		
	TOTALS	

NOTES

2407.

2408.
Thea St. Griz & Everett Elfston [QVC]
#unknown • 17"
LE of 1800 • Issued: 1998 • Retired: 1998
Original: $64 • Value: $120

Thayer
#91570 • 8½" • TJ
Issued: 1997 • Retired: 2001
Original: $15 • Value: $17

2409.

2410.

Theodora Maria [QVC]
#(C46247) • 16"
Issued: 1998 • Retired: 1998
Original: $51 • Value: $85

Theodore
#9196 • 7½" • AS
Issued: 1992 • Retired: 1994
Original: $16 • Value: $56

Bears

2411. Theodore Jr.
#900300 • 16" • AS
Issued: 2002 • Retired: 2002
Original: $30 • Value: $57

2412. Theodore Jr. [SFMB]
#900300SF • 16"
LE of 1008 • Issued: 2002 • Retired: 2002
Original: $35 • Value: $90
♪ Pachalbel's Canon in D ♪

2413. Theodore M. Bear [QVC]
#99878V (C107732) • 16" • MB
LE of 35000 • Issued: 2002 • Retired: 2002
Original: $118 • Value: $153
Sold with matching Bearstone.

2414. Theodore Sr. [EVENT]
#50006 • 30"
Issued: 2002 • Retired: 2002
Original: $N/E • Value: $220
Raffle Gift

2415. Theresa Marie [Elder Beerman]
#94930MGC • 10" • TJ
Issued: 2002 • Retired: 2002
Original: $20 • Value: $35

2416. Thinkin
#5809 • 6" • SB
Issued: 1991 • Retired: 1994
Original: $7 • Value: $51

2417. Thisbey F. Wuzzie
#595160-02 • 2½" • TF
Issued: 1999 • Retired: 2000
Original: $7 • Value: $8

2418. Thomas T. Rugsley [QVC]
#unknown • 40"
Issued: 2001 • Retired: 2001
Original: $92 • Value: $110

2419. Thor M. Berriman
#91734 • 12" • TJ
Issued: 1998 • Retired: 1998
Original: $30 • Value: $42
Also with Katrinka as QVC set.

2420. Thurston [Clarion Bear Festival]
#99097CL • 10"
LE of 3600 • Issued: 2002 • Retired: 2002
Original: $20 • Value: $30

2421. Tia Cherrybeary
#904093 • 8"
Issued: 2003 • Current
Original: $14 • Value: $R/E

2422. Tiana [Frederick Atkins]
#94765FA • 6"
Issued: 2000 • Retired: 2000
Original: $12 • Value: $25

BEARS	PRICE PAID	VALUE
2411.		
2412.		
2413.		
2414.		
2415.		
2416.		
2417.		
2418.		
2419.		
2420.		
2421.		
2422.		

TOTALS

NOTES

Bears

2423.
Tibbs
#510308 • 10"
Issued: 2003 • Current
Original: $12 • Value: $R/E

2424.
Tillie
#unknown • 11"
Issued: 1998 • Retired: 1998
Original: $18 • Value: $40

2425.
Tilly F. Wuzzie
#596000 • 3" • TF
Issued: 1999 • Retired: 2001
Original: $8 • Value: $8
Also with Tara, Tia as QVC set.

2426.
Tilly Weedsalot
#903020 • 8" • ME
Issued: 2002 • Retired: 2002
Original: $10 • Value: $16

2427.
Timothy & Tiny Jodibear
#92000-14 • 5" • AR
Issued: 2001 • Retired: 2002
Original: $15 • Value: $18

2428.
Timothy F. Wuzzie
#595140 • 3½" • TF
Issued: 1998 • Retired: 2000
Original: $8 • Value: $14

2429.
Timothy T. Beansley
#510301-05 • 10" • JB
Issued: 2001 • Current
Original: $10 • Value: $R/E

2430.
Tina Autumnfest
#904154 • 6" • TJ
Issued: 2003 • Current
Original: $10 • Value: $R/E

2431. 86
Tinkin (stark white)
#5801 • 10" • SB
Issued: 1991 • Retired: 1992
Original: $20 • Value: $97

2432. 86
Tinkin II (off-white)
#5801 • 10" • SB
Issued: 1992 • Retired: 1997
Original: $20 • Value: $50

2433.
Tinman
#904372 • 8" • TJ
Issued: 2004 • Current
Original: $16 • Value: $R/E

2434.
Tiny T. JodiBear
#92000-11 • 5" • AR
Issued: 2000 • Retired: 2000
Original: $10 • Value: $17

BEARS		
	PRICE PAID	VALUE
2423.		
2424.		
2425.		
2426.		
2427.		
2428.		
2429.		
2430.		
2431.		
2432.		
2433.		
2434.		
TOTALS		

NOTES

Bears

2435.
Tippy Beartoes
#903400 • 8" • ME
Issued: 2002 • Current
Original: $14 • Value: $R/E

2436.
Tipton F. Wuzzie
#595160-07 • 2½" • TF
Issued: 1999 • Retired: 2001
Original: $7 • Value: $12

2437.
Toe
#5151-02 • 8½" • JB
Issued: 1994 • Retired: 1997
Original: $12 • Value: $49

2438.
Tomba Bearski
#912620 • 14" • TJ
Issued: 1999 • Retired: 2001
Original: $37 • Value: $47

2439.
Tommy Leafowitz
#918361 • 8" • TJ
Issued: 2001 • Retired: 2001
Original: $15 • Value: $22

2440.
Tommy Tomato
#904247 • 5½" • TJ
Issued: 2004 • Current
Original: $10 • Value: $R/E

2441.
Toof Beary
#903016 • 8" • BA
Issued: 2002 • Retired: 2002
Original: $14 • Value: $19

2442.
Tootie F. Wuzzie
#595160-01 • 2½" • TF
Issued: 1999 • Retired: 2000
Original: $7 • Value: $13

2443.
Townsend Q. Bearrister
#57001-03 • 12" • AS
Issued: 1999 • Retired: 2000
Original: $16 • Value: $22

2444.
Have You Seen Me?

Travis (early dressed)
#6108B
Issued: 1991 • Retired: 1991
Original: $25 • Value: $400

2445.
Travis (black and gold sweater)
[Banana Republic]
#unknown • 16"
Issued: 1996 • Retired: 1996
Original: $40 • Value: $75

2446.
Travis (dark blue sweater)
[Banana Republic]
#unknown • 16"
Issued: 1996 • Retired: 1996
Original: $40 • Value: $75

BEARS

	PRICE PAID	VALUE
2435.		
2436.		
2437.		
2438.		
2439.		
2440.		
2441.		
2442.		
2443.		
2444.		
2445.		
2446.		
TOTALS		

NOTES

2447.
Travis (red sweater with tree)
[Banana Republic]
#unknown • 16"
Issued: 1996 • Retired: 1996
Original: $40 • Value: $75

2448.
Travis B. Bean
#5114-05 • 16" • JB
Issued: 1993 • Retired: 1998
Original: $27 • Value: $47

2449.
Travis B. Bean (variation)
#5114-05 • 16"
Issued: 1994 • Retired: 1994
Original: $27 • Value: $150

2450.
Treat F. Wuzzie
#596002 • 3" • TF
Issued: 1999 • Retired: 1999
Original: $8 • Value: $16

2451.
Tremont
#56411-08 • 16" • BA
Issued: 1997 • Retired: 2000
Original: $23 • Value: $28

2452.
Trevor F. Wuzzie
#595160-08 • 2½" • TF
Issued: 1997 • Retired: 1999
Original: $7 • Value: $14

2453.
Trevor T. Elfbeary
#904050 • 12"
Issued: 2002 • Retired: 2004
Original: $30 • Value: $30
TOBY Award Winner

2454.
Trillium [CAN]
#94300GC • 8"
LE of 4800 • Issued: 2003 • Retired: 2003
Original: $15 • Value: $22

2455.
Trish Boombah
#903500 • 8"
Issued: 2002 • Current
Original: $14 • Value: $R/E

2456.
Trissy Teabeary [Longaberger]
#94643LB • 10"
Issued: 2002 • Retired: 2002
Original: $34 • Value: $49

2457.
Tristan [Frederick Atkins]
#94764FA • 16"
Issued: 1999 • Retired: 1999
Original: $30 • Value: $45

2458.
Trixsley [QVC]
#93485V (C0382) • 8"
Issued: 2003 • Retired: 2003
Original: $17 • Value: $28

BEARS

	PRICE PAID	VALUE
2447.		
2448.		
2449.		
2450.		
2451.		
2452.		
2453.		
2454.		
2455.		
2456.		
2457.		
2458.		
TOTALS		

NOTES

Bears

2459.
Trudie Ann Hugsalot [QVC]
#(C100101) • 8"
Issued: 2001 • Retired: 2001
Original: $12 • Value: $20

2460.
True Luv B. Mine
#57004-01 • 12" • AS
Issued: 2001 • Retired: 2001
Original: $15 • Value: $18

2461.
Truly B. Mine
#82018 • 10" • JB
Issued: 2001 • Retired: 2001
Original: $13 • Value: $16

2462.
Truly D. Bestmom
#82506 • 8" • TJ
Issued: 2001 • Retired: 2001
Original: $10 • Value: $12

2463.
Truman S. Bearington
#590010-05 • 18" • MB
Issued: 1998 • Retired: 1998
Original: $126 • Value: $161

2464.
Trundle B. Bear
#56391-10 • 12" • BA
Issued: 2000 • Retired: 2000
Original: $19 • Value: $23

2465.
Tucker Applesmith [GCC]
#94896GCC • 10"
LE of 1800 • Issued: 2001 • Retired: 2001
Original: $20 • Value: $65
Name tag misspelled Tucqer.

2466.
Tulla B. Bearfoot [Hallmark]
#9699HM • 8"
Issued: 2003 • Retired: 2003
Original: $15 • Value: $18

2467.
Tumble F. Wuzzie
#596005 • 3" • TF
Issued: 2000 • Retired: 2000
Original: $8 • Value: $10
Also with Theo, Topper as QVC set.

2468.
Tundra Northpole
#912810 • 12" • TJ
Issued: 1999 • Retired: 2000
Original: $20 • Value: $25

2469.
Turner with Kris [GCC]
#94888GCC • 10"
Issued: 2000 • Retired: 2000
Original: $16 • Value: $22

2470.
Tutti F. Sugarcone
#904123 • 8"
Issued: 2003 • Retired: 2003
Original: $14 • Value: $14

BEARS	PRICE PAID	VALUE
2459.		
2460.		
2461.		
2462.		
2463.		
2464.		
2465.		
2466.		
2467.		
2468.		
2469.		
2470.		
TOTALS		

NOTES

Bears

2471.

Have You Seen Me?
Tutu
#6169B • 16" • TJ
Issued: 1991 • Retired: 1991
Original: $63 • Value: $449

2472.

Twas F. Wuzzie
#596003 • 3" • TF
Issued: 1999 • Retired: 1999
Original: $8 • Value: $15

2473.

Twila Higgenthorpe
#91843 • 6" • TJ
Issued: 1997 • Retired: 2000
Original: $10 • Value: $21
Also with Delilah as QVC set.

2474.

Twilight F. Wuzzie
#595160-06 • 2½" • TF
Issued: 1999 • Retired: 2000
Original: $7 • Value: $12

2475.

Twink L. Starbeary
#918356 • 8" • TJ
Issued: 2001 • Retired: 2002
Original: $13 • Value: $16

2476.

Twinkle B. Beansley [QVC]
#(C20874) • 10"
Issued: 2002 • Retired: 2002
Original: $14 • Value: $22

2477.

Twinkle Bear [Macy's East]
#94164MA
Issued: 2001 • Retired: 2001
Original: $20 • Value: $35

2478.

Twinkles Starbeary [Longaberger]
#25777LB • 8"
Issued: 2001 • Retired: 2001
Original: $16 • Value: $26

2479.

Twizzle F. Wuzzie
#595141 • 3½" • TF
Issued: 1998 • Retired: 1999
Original: $8 • Value: $12

2480.

Tylar F. Wuzzie
#595160-11 • 2½" • TF
Issued: 1997 • Retired: 1999
Original: $7 • Value: $13

2481.

Tyler [Dillards]
#99473DL • 11"
Issued: 1998 • Retired: 1998
Original: $20 • Value: $52

2482.

Tyler Glorybear
#904193 • 8" • TJ
Issued: 2003 • Current
Original: $10 • Value: $R/E

BEARS		
	PRICE PAID	VALUE
2471.		
2472.		
2473.		
2474.		
2475.		
2476.		
2477.		
2478.		
2479.		
2480.		
2481.		
2482.		
TOTALS		

NOTES

Bears

2483.
Tyler Summerfield
#7124 • 12" • TJ
Issued: 1996 • Retired: 1997
Original: $37 • Value: $61

2484.
Tyler T. Bear
#57253-03 • 6" • AS
Issued: 2002 • Retired: 2002
Original: $7 • Value: $10

2485.
Tyrone F. Wuzzie
#595160-05 • 2½" • TF
Issued: 1997 • Retired: 2000
Original: $7 • Value: $11

2486.
U.B. Mine with Heart [QVC]
#(C21167) • 8"
Issued: 2003 • Retired: 2003
Original: $12 • Value: $18

2487.
Uncle Ben Bearington
#590103 • 4½" • MB
Issued: 2000 • Retired: 2000
Original: $11 • Value: $21

2488.
Uncle Edward O'Beary [GCC]
#94889GCC • 14"
Issued: 2000 • Retired: 2000
Original: $42 • Value: $68

2489.
Uncle Gus & Honeybunch [QVC]
#99526V (C37630) • 12" • MB
LE of 40000 • Issued: 1997 • Retired: 1997
Original: $106 • Value: $173
Sold with resin.

2490.
Uncle Sam
#51100-01 • 16" • JB
Issued: 2001 • Retired: 2002
Original: $25 • Value: $36

2491.
Uncle Zeb & Cousin Minnow [QVC]
#unknown • 16"
LE of 2400 • Issued: 1998 • Retired: 1998
Original: $70 • Value: $150

2492.
Union T. Jack Bear [United Kingdom]
#94660 • 10"
Issued: 2002 • Retired: 2002
Original: $25 • Value: $41

2493.
Ursa
#5720-07 • 14" • AS
Issued: 1995 • Retired: 1998
Original: $24 • Value: $49

2494.
Ursula Berriman [QVC]
#(C53093) • 12"
Issued: 1998 • Retired: 1998
Original: $27 • Value: $70

BEARS

	PRICE PAID	VALUE
2483.		
2484.		
2485.		
2486.		
2487.		
2488.		
2489.		
2490.		
2491.		
2492.		
2493.		
2494.		
TOTALS		

NOTES

Bears

2495.
Valentina B. Bearhugs [SFMB]
#94261SF (41-40215) • 10"
Issued: 2001 • Retired: 2001
Original: $25 • Value: $32
♪ Let Me Be Your Teddy Bear ♪

2496.
Valentina with Evalina, Caterina, & Michelina [QVC]
#(C46252) • 16"
LE • Issued: 1998 • Retired: 1998
Original: $57 • Value: $90

2497.
Valentino
#82042 • 10"
Issued: 2003 • Retired: 2003
Original: $12 • Value: $12

2498.
Valerie [Ideation]
#943281IDE • 6"
Issued: 1999 • Retired: 1999
Original: $12 • Value: $25

2499.
Valerie B. Bearhugs
#510301 • 10"
Issued: 2000 • Retired: 2000
Original: $11 • Value: $13

2500.
Vance Bearsworth
#570521 • 8" • AS
Issued: 2002 • Retired: 2002
Original: $10 • Value: $18

2501.
Vanessa R. Angel [Starlight]
#51111 • 14"
Issued: 2001 • Retired: 2001
Original: $15 • Value: $22

2502.
Varsity Bear (16")
#9198 • 16" • JB
Issued: 1992 • Retired: 1992
Original: $25 • Value: $226

2503.
Varsity Bear (8")
#9194 • 8" • AS
Issued: 1992 • Retired: 1992
Original: $15 • Value: $125

2504.
Vera W. Bearsworth
#572211-08 • 21" • AS
Issued: 2002 • Retired: 2004
Original: $50 • Value: $51

2505.
Verdeia [Frederick Atkins]
#unknown • 16"
Issued: 1998 • Retired: 1998
Original: $N/E • Value: $85

2506.
Vernette [Frederick Atkins]
#94764FA • 8"
Issued: 1999 • Retired: 1999
Original: $15 • Value: $28

BEARS

	PRICE PAID	VALUE
2495.		
2496.		
2497.		
2498.		
2499.		
2500.		
2501.		
2502.		
2503.		
2504.		
2505.		
2506.		
TOTALS		

NOTES

Bears

2507.
Veronica Bearskov [Platinum Paw]
#9198078 • 16"
Issued: 2000 • Retired: 2000
Original: $56 • Value: $75

2508.
Veronica Laflame [QVC]
#(C87024) • 16"
Issued: 2000 • Retired: 2000
Original: $51 • Value: $79

2509.
Veronica Marie Bearington [QVC]
#93525V (C01902) • 6" • MB
LE of 2400 • Issued: 2004 • Retired: 2004
Original: $17 • Value: $28

2510.
Victoria Bearybright
[Yankee Candle]
#94696YC • 12"
Issued: 2003 • Retired: 2003
Original: $40 • Value: $65

2511.
Victoria L. Plumbeary
#912015 • 16" • TJ
Issued: 2001 • Retired: 2001
Original: $50 • Value: $60

2512.
Victoria Lynn Primsley
#918344 • 10"
Issued: 2002 • Retired: 2002
Original: $25 • Value: $34

2513.
Vincent
#1100-11 • 11" • CC
Issued: 1995 • Retired: 1997
Original: $10 • Value: $39

2514.
Viola Flutterby [QVC]
#93285V • 10"
Issued: 2002 • Retired: 2002
Original: $17 • Value: $25

2515.
Virginia Dobbsey
[Coach House Gifts]
#unknown • 12"
Issued: 1999 • Retired: 1999
Original: $28 • Value: $45

2516.
Virginia Thistlebeary
[Show Specials]
#919802 • 8"
Issued: 2000 • Retired: 2000
Original: $18 • Value: $27

2517.
Vivian Q. Dickens
#904220 • 16" • TJ
Issued: 2003 • Current
Original: $47 • Value: $R/E

2518.
Waddlekins
#91865 • 10"
Issued: 2002 • Current
Original: $19 • Value: $R/E

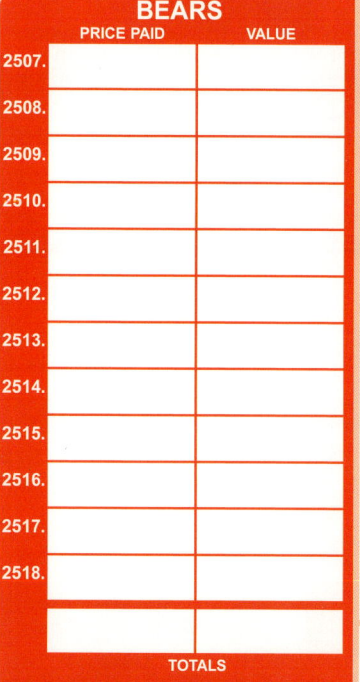

BEARS	PRICE PAID	VALUE
2507.		
2508.		
2509.		
2510.		
2511.		
2512.		
2513.		
2514.		
2515.		
2516.		
2517.		
2518.		
	TOTALS	

NOTES

Bears

2519.
Wade N. Sanditoes with Buster the Crab
#913938 • 8" • TJ
Issued: 2002 • Retired: 2002
Original: $13 • Value: $18

2520.
Waitsfield [GCC]
#94853GCC • 11"
Issued: 1997 • Retired: 1997
Original: $28 • Value: $48

2521.
Waldo Bearsworth
#912045 • 11" • TJ
Issued: 1999 • Retired: 2002
Original: $23 • Value: $35

2522.
Wally B. Beartoes
#510310 • 10" • AS
Issued: 2003 • Current
Original: $14 • Value: $R/E

2523.
Walpole (old face)
#5705M • 8" • AS
Issued: 1993 • Retired: 1997
Original: $13 • Value: $41

2524.
Walpole (new face)
#5705M • 8" • AS
Issued: 1993 • Retired: 1997
Original: $13 • Value: $30

2525.
Walter, Wayne and Wilbert Tinkerbeary [QVC]
#(C20938) • 6"
LE of 4000 • Issued: 2002 • Retired: 2002
Original: $42 • Value: $55
Comes with wooden ladder.

2526.
Walton
#9128 • 11" • TJ
Issued: 1994 • Retired: 1997
Original: $21 • Value: $49

2527.
Wanna B. Ladybug
#904233 • 8" • TJ
Issued: 2004 • Current
Original: $13 • Value: $R/E

2529.
Warren
#1002-01 • 8" • CC
Issued: 1993 • Retired: 1997
Original: $6 • Value: $30

2530.
Watson
#9187 • 8" • TJ
Issued: 1993 • Retired: 1999
Original: $17 • Value: $27

2528.
Warner Von Bruin
#57151-05 • 16" • AS
Issued: 2001 • Retired: 2001
Original: $25 • Value: $36

BEARS

	PRICE PAID	VALUE
2519.		
2520.		
2521.		
2522.		
2523.		
2524.		
2525.		
2526.		
2527.		
2528.		
2529.		
2530.		
	TOTALS	

NOTES

Bears

2531.
Wayfer North
#917360 • 10" • TJ
Issued: 1999 • Retired: 2000
Original: $22 • Value: $32

2532.
Wayne B. Bear [CAN]
#94295PO • 10"
LE of 4800 • Issued: 2002 • Retired: 2002
Original: $30 • Value: $38

2533.
Weaver Bearyproud [Longaberger]
#993654LB • 10"
Issued: 2004 • Retired: 2004
Original: $24 • Value: $R/E

2534.
Weaver Berrybrook
#911930 • 12" • TJ
Issued: 1999 • Retired: 1999
Original: $17 • Value: $30

2535.
Webber Vanguard
#51100-07 • 16" • JB
Issued: 2000 • Retired: 2001
Original: $25 • Value: $35

2536.
Webster T. Bearsworth
#57253-11 • 6" • AS
Issued: 2001 • Retired: 2002
Original: $7 • Value: $11

2537.
Wellington
#5722 • 21" • AS
Issued: 1992 • Retired: 1997
Original: $53 • Value: $90

2538.
Wendy S. Appleby & Anna Mae [SLE]
#99806V • 12"
Issued: 2002 • Retired: 2002
Original: $27 • Value: $35
Originally intended for QVC.

2539.
Wendy Weaver (a.k.a. Weaver Girl) [Longaberger]
#94662LB • 8"
Issued: 2003 • Retired: 2003
Original: $15 • Value: $24

2540.
Werner Von Bruin
#5010-11 • 6" • WB
Issued: 1993 • Retired: 1995
Original: $10 • Value: $42

2541.
Wesley Bearimore
#912027 • 16" • TJ
Issued: 2000 • Retired: 2000
Original: $45 • Value: $63

2542.
Wesley, Willoughby & Woodward [QVC]
#(C46239) • 6"
Issued: 1998 • Retired: 1998
Original: $19 • Value: $35

BEARS

	PRICE PAID	VALUE
2531.		
2532.		
2533.		
2534.		
2535.		
2536.		
2537.		
2538.		
2539.		
2540.		
2541.		
2542.		
TOTALS		

NOTES

Bears

2543.
Westin Woodsley [QVC]
#93364V (C20883) • 12" • MB
Issued: 2003 • Retired: 2003
Original: $14 • Value: $37

2544.
Wheaton Flatski
#5680-10 • 8" • FL
Issued: 1996 • Retired: 1996
Original: $13 • Value: $45

2545.
Whihley with Winkle & Pip [QVC]
#99722V (C96376) • 16"
LE of 3000 • Issued: 2000 • Retired: 2000
Original: $53 • Value: $83

2546.
Whilley Frostifeet
#918359 • 8" • TJ
Issued: 2001 • Retired: 2002
Original: $9 • Value: $11

2547.
Whimsie T. Faeriebear [QVC]
#93302V (C107581) • 10"
Issued: 2002 • Retired: 2002
Original: $28 • Value: $35

2548.
Whitaker A. Bruin
#91806 • 5½" • TJ
Issued: 1996 • Retired: 1998
Original: $11 • Value: $27

2549.

Have You Seen Me?

White Bean Bear
#5103 • 13" • JB
Issued: 1987 • Retired: 1988
Original: $N/E • Value: $325

2550.
Whitley B. Beariluved [QVC]
#(C78119) • 10"
Issued: 2000 • Retired: 2000
Original: $15 • Value: $34

2551.
Whittington P. Bearsford
#57152-08 • 16" • AS
Issued: 2001 • Retired: 2002
Original: $13 • Value: $16

2552.
Wicked Witch of the West
#904374 • 8" • TJ
Issued: 2004 • Current
Original: $16 • Value: $R/E

2553.
Wilbur Bearington
#590085-10 • 4½" • MB
Issued: 1998 • Retired: 1999
Original: $10 • Value: $17

2554.
Wilby Beardeaux
#904315 • 5" • TJ
Issued: 2004 • Current
Original: $11 • Value: $R/E

BEARS

	PRICE PAID	VALUE
2543.		
2544.		
2545.		
2546.		
2547.		
2548.		
2549.		
2550.		
2551.		
2552.		
2553.		
2554.		

TOTALS

NOTES

Bears

2555.
Wilcox J. Beansford
#51081-05 • 14" • JB
Issued: 1999 • Retired: 2001
Original: $16 • Value: $34

2556.
Wilhelmina Q. Bearsworth [QVC]
#(C6046) • 16"
Issued: 2003 • Retired: 2003
Original: $54 • Value: $65

2557.
Will [Dillards]
#94736DL • 6"
Issued: 1998 • Retired: 1998
Original: $12 • Value: $24

2558.
Willa Bruin
#91205 • 11" • TJ
Issued: 1995 • Retired: 1997
Original: $30 • Value: $55

2559.
William [CAN]
#BC94291PO • 8"
LE of 1200 • Issued: 2001 • Retired: 2001
Original: $23 • Value: $32

2560.
William Henry Bearington [QVC]
#93527V (C01900) • 12" • MB
LE of 1800 • Issued: 2004 • Retired: 2004
Original: $43 • Value: $65

2561.
William P.
#1107-03 • 12" • CC
Issued: 1998 • Retired: 1999
Original: $12 • Value: $24

2562.
Wilma & Gracey Bearfriends [QVC]
#93332V (C20182) • 6"
Issued: 2002 • Retired: 2002
Original: $17 • Value: $22

2563.
Willmar Flatski
#56801-05 • 8" • FL
Issued: 1998 • Retired: 1999
Original: $13 • Value: $22

2564.
Wilson (old face)
#5705 • 8" • AS
Issued: 1990 • Retired: 1992
Original: $12 • Value: $50

2565.
Wilson (new face)
#5705 • 8" • AS
Issued: 1993 • Retired: 1997
Original: $12 • Value: $37

2566.
Wilson with Boat [QVC]
#unknown • 8"
Issued: 1995 • Retired: 1995
Original: $N/E • Value: $45

BEARS

	PRICE PAID	VALUE
2555.		
2556.		
2557.		
2558.		
2559.		
2560.		
2561.		
2562.		
2563.		
2564.		
2565.		
2566.		
TOTALS		

NOTES

Bears

2567.
Wilson with Pie [QVC]
#unknown • 8"
Issued: 1994 • Retired: 1994
Original: $N/E • Value: $60

2568.
Windsor & Sarasota [QVC]
#(C49881) • 14"
Issued: 1998 • Retired: 1998
Original: $27 • Value: $55

2569.
Winifred [SLE]
#unknown • 8"
Issued: 1997 • Retired: 1997
Original: $N/E • Value: $39

2570.
Winifred Witebred
#912071 • 14" • TJ
Issued: 1998 • Retired: 1998
Original: $34 • Value: $49

2571.
Winkie II
#5639-08 • 12" • BA
Issued: 1992 • Retired: 1998
Original: $16 • Value: $31

2572.
Winkin
#5800 • 10" • SB
Issued: 1991 • Retired: 1993
Original: $20 • Value: $93

2573.
Winnie II
#912071-01 • 14" • TJ
Issued: 1998 • Retired: 2001
Original: $34 • Value: $48

2574.
Winnie II [SFMB]
#41-726426 • 14" • TJ
Issued: 1999 • Retired: 1999
Original: $35 • Value: $52
♪ Love is Blue ♪

2575.
Winnie Stillwithus
#912071-03 • 14" • TJ
Issued: 2000 • Retired: 2000
Original: $30 • Value: $41

2576.
Winnie Stillwithus [SFMB]
#41-402113 • 14"
Issued: 2001 • Retired: 2001
Original: $38 • Value: $50
♪ Oh, What a Beautiful Morning ♪

2577.
Winnie Wuzzwhite
#912071-02 • 14" • TJ
Issued: 1999 • Retired: 1999
Original: $34 • Value: $47

2578.
Winnie Wuzzwhite [SFMB]
#41-72939 • 14"
Issued: 2000 • Retired: 2000
Original: $35 • Value: $52
♪ You Are The Sunshine of My Life ♪

BEARS

	PRICE PAID	VALUE
2567.		
2568.		
2569.		
2570.		
2571.		
2572.		
2573.		
2574.		
2575.		
2576.		
2577.		
2578.		

TOTALS

NOTES

Bears

2579.
Winny Wimbleton
#903309 • 8"
Issued: 2003 • Current
Original: $13 • Value: $R/E

2580.
Winstead & Pensacola [QVC]
#(C52973) • 15"
Issued: 1998 • Retired: 1998
Original: $27 • Value: $40

2581.
Winstead P. Bear
#515210-03 • 15" • JB
Issued: 1998 • Retired: 2000
Original: $19 • Value: $29

2582.
Winston B. Bean (early smooth fur)
#5104 • 10" • JB
Issued: 1988 • Retired: 1989
Original: $14 • Value: $125

2583.
Winston B. Bean (old face)
#5104 • 10" • JB
Issued: 1989 • Retired: 1990
Original: $14 • Value: $80

2584.
Winston B. Bean (new face)
#5104 • 10" • JB
Issued: 1991 • Retired: 1996
Original: $14 • Value: $39

2585.
Winter Mintly
#904210 • 16" • TJ
Issued: 2003 • Retired: 2003
Original: $24 • Value: $24

2586.
Wishley B. Bunnybear [QVC]
#(C60262) • 36"
LE of 1008 • Issued: 2002 • Retired: 2002
Original: $155 • Value: $180

2587.
Witch-A-Ma-Call-It
#9214 • 14"
LE of 500 • Issued: 1993 • Retired: 1993
Original: $70 • Value: $320

2588.
Witchy-Boo
#904340 • 14" • TJ
Issued: 2004 • Current
Original: $26 • Value: $R/E

2589.
Wixie Lee Hackett
#918444 • 6" • TJ
Issued: 2001 • Retired: 2001
Original: $10 • Value: $22

2590.
Woodrow T. Bearington
#590041-03 • 12" • MB
Issued: 1999 • Retired: 1999
Original: $48 • Value: $65

BEARS

	PRICE PAID	VALUE
2579.		
2580.		
2581.		
2582.		
2583.		
2584.		
2585.		
2586.		
2587.		
2588.		
2589.		
2590.		
TOTALS		

NOTES

Bears

2591.
Woodruff K. Bearsford
#57251-05 • 6" • AS
Issued: 1999 • Retired: 2001
Original: $8 • Value: $8

2592.
Woody Puttsalot [Longaberger]
#94644LB • 10"
Issued: 2002 • Retired: 2002
Original: $28 • Value: $41

2593.
Wookie Snickelfritz
#51770-06 • 10" • BA
Issued: 2000 • Retired: 2001
Original: $11 • Value: $13

2594.
Worthington Fitzbruin
#912032 • 8½" • TJ
Issued: 1997 • Retired: 2000
Original: $14 • Value: $23

2595.
Wuvey B. Bear
#82062 • 10"
Issued: 2004 • Current
Original: $14 • Value: $R/E

2596.
Yankee & Doodle McBear [QVC]
#(C95163) • 6"
Issued: 1999 • Retired: 1999
Original: $19 • Value: $28

2597.
Yardley Fitzhampton
#912030 • 14" • TJ
Issued: 1999 • Retired: 2000
Original: $26 • Value: $36

2598.
Yeager Bearington
#590085-05 • 4½" • MB
Issued: 1999 • Retired: 2000
Original: $10 • Value: $14

2599.
Yeti A. Bominable
#904020 • 18" • TJ
Issued: 2002 • Retired: 2004
Original: $45 • Value: $45

2600.
Yippeeyo Beanster [QVC]
#(C3016) • 14"
Issued: 2003 • Retired: 2003
Original: $31 • Value: $55

2601.
Yogi
#91771-02 • 6" • AR
Issued: 1997 • Retired: 2000
Original: $11 • Value: $21
Also as set with Pee Wee.

2602.
York
#57051-05 • 8" • AS
Issued: 1998 • Retired: 2000
Original: $13 • Value: $21

BEARS

	PRICE PAID	VALUE
2591.		
2592.		
2593.		
2594.		
2595.		
2596.		
2597.		
2598.		
2599.		
2600.		
2601.		
2602.		
TOTALS		

NOTES

Bears

2603.
You and Me [QVC]
#93398V (C21165) • 6"
Issued: 2003 • Retired: 2003
Original: $16 • Value: $22

2604.
Yu'Kon B. Bear [CAN]
#BC94278 • 10"
LE of 10000 • Issued: 1998 • Retired: 1998
Original: $22 • Value: $35

2605.
Yvette Dubeary
#918431 • 6" • TJ
Issued: 1999 • Retired: 2002
Original: $11 • Value: $14

2606.
Yvonne & Yvette [QVC]
#unknown • 10"
Issued: 1998 • Retired: 1998
Original: $N/E • Value: $36

2607.
Zazu
#5641-05 • 16" • BA
Issued: 1996 • Retired: 2000
Original: $23 • Value: $32

2608.
Have You Seen Me?
Ziggy Bear
#5060 • 12" • WB
Issued: 1985 • Retired: 1989
Original: $17 • Value: $450

2609.
Zinny Beardeaux
#919833 • 12" • TJ
Issued: 2004 • Current
Original: $27 • Value: $R/E

2610.
Zwick [Dillards]
#94748DL • 10"
Issued: 1999 • Retired: 1999
Original: $25 • Value: $34

BEARS

	PRICE PAID	VALUE
2603.		
2604.		
2605.		
2606.		
2607.		
2608.		
2609.		
2610.		
	TOTALS	

NOTES

Critters

Alligators

2611.
Irwin S. Crockpot
#55228 • 10" • JB
Issued: 2002 • Retired: 2002
Original: $15 • Value: $23

Beavers

2612.
Bucky Beaverdam
#55216 • 10" • JB
Issued: 2001 • Retired: 2001
Original: $14 • Value: $17

Camels

2613.
Abdul Duneworthy [QVC]
#93124V (C78125) • 9"
Issued: 2000 • Retired: 2000
Original: $14 • Value: $21

2614.
Lawrence and Sheherazade O'Sand
#568004 • 3½" • NO
Issued: 2002 • Current
Original: $10 • Value: $R/E

2615.
Sir Humpsley
#57850 • 8½" • AS
Issued: 2001 • Retired: 2001
Original: $15 • Value: $18

ALLIGATORS	
PRICE PAID	VALUE
2611.	

BEAVERS	
PRICE PAID	VALUE
2612.	

CAMELS	
PRICE PAID	VALUE
2613.	
2614.	
2615.	
TOTALS	

NOTES

Critters (Cats)

Cats

2616.
Alley McCat [QVC]
#93344V (C20913) • 12"
Issued: 2002 • Retired: 2002
Original: $24 • Value: $40

2617.
Allie Oppsey
#530310 • 8"
Issued: 2003 • Retired: 2003
Original: $10 • Value: $10

2618.
Amy Z. Sassycat
#590250-10 • 11" • MB
Issued: 2001 • Retired: 2001
Original: $40 • Value: $55

2619.
Armstrong Cattington
#590087-07 • 4½" • MB
Issued: 1999 • Retired: 2000
Original: $10 • Value: $14

2620.
Aspen P. Ninelives [GCC]
#94870GCC • 12"
Issued: 1999 • Retired: 1999
Original: $27 • Value: $49

2621.
Auden S. Penworthy
#57410-11 • 8" • AS
Issued: 2001 • Retired: 2002
Original: $11 • Value: $13

Have You Seen Me?

2622.
Baby
#6105C • 11" • TJ
Issued: 1990 • Retired: 1990
Original: $18 • Value: $314

2623.
Blake & Ogden Wordsworth with Dickens [QVC]
#(C99063) • 6"
Issued: 2000 • Retired: 2000
Original: $21 • Value: $29

2624.
Blake B. Wordsworth
#5745-06 • 5½" • AS
Issued: 2000 • Retired: 2000
Original: $7 • Value: $11

2625.
Bobbi Kat
#530400 • 5½" • AS
Issued: 2004 • Current
Original: $8 • Value: $R/E

2626.
Boots Alleyruckus
#5308-07 • 14" • JB
Issued: 1999 • Retired: 2002
Original: $18 • Value: $27

CATS

	PRICE PAID	VALUE
2616.		
2617.		
2618.		
2619.		
2620.		
2621.		
2622.		
2623.		
2624.		
2625.		
2626.		
TOTALS		

NOTES

Critters (Cats)

Bronte
#5742-10 • 5½" • AS
Issued: 1994 • Retired: 1996
Original: $8 • Value: $50

Browning
#5741 • 8" • AS
Issued: 1992 • Retired: 1999
Original: $12 • Value: $25

Byron
#5940 • 8" • AS
Issued: 1992 • Retired: 1999
Original: $12 • Value: $25

Cabin Cat
#9010C • 12" • TJ
Issued: 1992 • Retired: 1993
Original: $N/E • Value: $305

Caleigh [Dillards]
#94735DL • 11"
Issued: 1998 • Retired: 1998
Original: $18 • Value: $48

Callaway Flatcat
#56951-06 • 8" • FL
Issued: 1998 • Retired: 1999
Original: $13 • Value: $22

Callie P. Snugglepuss
#918081SM • 14" • JB
Issued: 2004 • Current
Original: $18 • Value: $R/E

Candy Corn Cat
#91971 • 8" • TJ
Issued: 1995 • Retired: 1997
Original: $18 • Value: $57

Carlyle Wordsworth
#57440-01 • 5½" • AS
Issued: 2000 • Retired: 2000
Original: $7 • Value: $11

Casper Cat O'Lantern [SLE]
#unknown • 11"
Issued: 1999 • Retired: 1999
Original: $19 • Value: $39

Cassandra Purrsley [QVC]
#(C97883) • 14"
Issued: 2000 • Retired: 2000
Original: $21 • Value: $35

Catherine Q. Fuzzberg
#5303-08 • 8" • JB
Issued: 1997 • Retired: 2001
Original: $10 • Value: $17

CATS	PRICE PAID	VALUE
2627.		
2628.		
2629.		
2630.		
2631.		
2632.		
2633.		
2634.		
2635.		
2636.		
2637.		
2638.		
TOTALS		

NOTES

Critters (Cats)

2639.
Catia Clawford
#91712 • 8" • TJ
Issued: 2000 • Retired: 2002
Original: $15 • Value: $22

2640.
Catterina Cuddlepuss
#53110-03 • 16" • JB
Issued: 2002 • Retired: 2002
Original: $25 • Value: $31

2641.
Chaucer (mauve)
#9135 • 8" • TJ
Issued: 1995 • Retired: 1995
Original: $20 • Value: $59

2642.
Chaucer (red)
#9135-01 • 8" • TJ
Issued: 1995 • Retired: 1995
Original: $20 • Value: $46

2643.
Cher Fussberg [SLE]
#unknown • 8"
Issued: 1998 • Retired: 1998
Original: $13 • Value: $24

2644.
Chester L. Snicklepuss
#530803 • 14" • AS
Issued: 2004 • Current
Original: $18 • Value: $R/E

2645.
Chris B. Trickpuss [QVC]
#93520V (C01901) • 11"
Issued: 2004 • Retired: 2004
Original: $18 • Value: $35

2646.
Cinnamon P. Pussytoes [QVC]
#93490V (C6087) • 11"
Issued: 2003 • Retired: 2003
Original: $15 • Value: $30

2647.
Claude Q. Catberg [QVC]
#(C57653) • 14"
Issued: 1999 • Retired: 1999
Original: $16 • Value: $33

2648.
Claudette Prissypuss
#912091-08 • 12" • TJ
Issued: 2001 • Retired: 2001
Original: $23 • Value: $37

2649.
Claudette Tatterpuss [QVC]
#93237V (C98179) • 10"
Issued: 2001 • Retired: 2001
Original: $17 • Value: $34

2650.
Claudia & Rowena P. Pussytoes [QVC]
#(C41095) • 8"
Issued: 1997 • Retired: 1997
Original: $23 • Value: $55

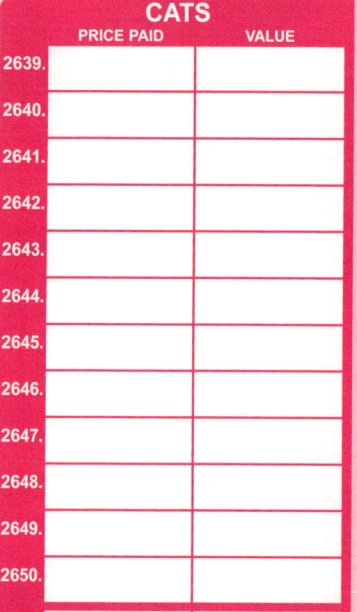

CATS

	PRICE PAID	VALUE
2639.		
2640.		
2641.		
2642.		
2643.		
2644.		
2645.		
2646.		
2647.		
2648.		
2649.		
2650.		
TOTALS		

NOTES

Critters (Cats)

2651.
Claudine de la Plumtete
#91710 • 6" • TJ
Issued: 1999 • Retired: 1999
Original: $9 • Value: $22

2652.
Claudine P. Pussyfoot [QVC]
#93462V (C3014) • 12"
Issued: 2003 • Retired: 2003
Original: $26 • Value: $45

2653.
Cleo P. Pussytoes [QVC]
#unknown • 16"
Issued: 1997 • Retired: 1997
Original: $N/E • Value: $75

2654.
Cleo P. Pussytoes
#91209 • 16" • TJ
Issued: 1997 • Retired: 1999
Original: $40 • Value: $48

2655.
Cleo P. Pussytoes [SFMB]
#41-72140 • 16" • TJ
Issued: 1998 • Retired: 1998
Original: $40 • Value: $55
♪ What's New Pussycat ♪

2656.
Coalcracker Ninelives
#53040-07 • 11" • JB
Issued: 2000 • Retired: 2000
Original: $14 • Value: $19

2657.
Cookie Grimilkin (old face)
#5306 • 11" • JB
Issued: 1991 • Retired: 1993
Original: $14 • Value: $65

2658.
Cookie Grimilkin (new face)
#5306 • 11" • JB
Issued: 1993 • Retired: 2001
Original: $14 • Value: $30

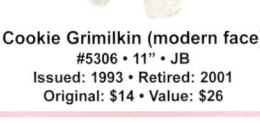

2659.
Cookie Grimilkin (modern face)
#5306 • 11" • JB
Issued: 1993 • Retired: 2001
Original: $14 • Value: $26

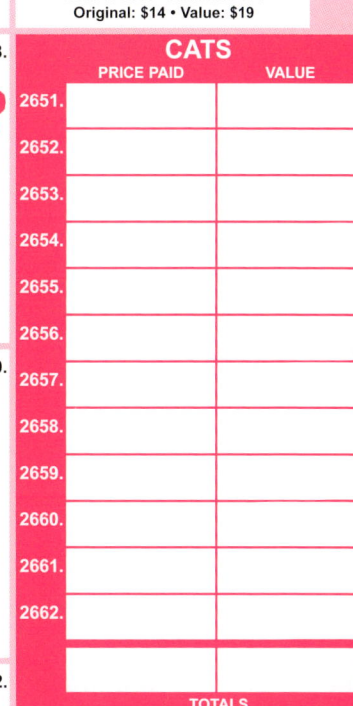

2660.
Crackers & Roquefort [QVC]
#(C46241) • 11"
Issued: 1998 • Retired: 1998
Original: $28 • Value: $55

2661.
Cuthbert Catberg
#5314 • 16" • JB
Issued: 1992 • Retired: 1993
Original: $27 • Value: $165

2662.
Dewey Q. Grimilkin
#5302 • 11" • JB
Issued: 1989 • Retired: 1990
Original: $16 • Value: $165

CATS	PRICE PAID	VALUE
2651.		
2652.		
2653.		
2654.		
2655.		
2656.		
2657.		
2658.		
2659.		
2660.		
2661.		
2662.		
TOTALS		

NOTES

Critters (Cats)

2663.
Dewey R. Cat
#5302T • 11" • JB
Issued: 1990 • Retired: 1990
Original: $13 • Value: $166

2664.
Dickens Q. Wordsworth
#5745-03 • 5½" • AS
Issued: 2000 • Retired: 2000
Original: $7 • Value: $13
Also with Blake, Ogden as QVC set.

2665.
Dorchester Catsworth with Artie
#919760 • 10" • TJ
Issued: 2000 • Retired: 2001
Original: $26 • Value: $41

2666.
Dreyfus Q. Wordsworth
#5745-07 • 5½" • AS
Issued: 2001 • Retired: N/E
Original: $7 • Value: $12

2667.
Eleanor
#6012C • TJ
Issued: 1989 • Retired: 1990
Original: $70 • Value: $306

2668.
Ellsworth Flatcat II
#5695-08 • 8" • FL
Issued: 1994 • Retired: 1999
Original: $12 • Value: $24

CATS

	PRICE PAID	VALUE
2663.		
2664.		
2665.		
2666.		
2667.		
2668.		
2669.		
2670.		
2671.		
2672.		
2673.		
2674.		
TOTALS		

NOTES

2669.
Emerson T. Penworthy
#57410-03 • 8" • AS
Issued: 2000 • Retired: 2002
Original: $11 • Value: $16

2670.
Ernest Q. Grimilkin (smooth fur)
#5304 • JB
Issued: 1989 • Retired: 1990
Original: $14 • Value: $95

2671.
Ernest Q. Grimilkin (white on chin)
#5304 • JB
Issued: 1989 • Retired: 1989
Original: $14 • Value: $165

2672.
Ernest Q. Grimilkin (blaze face)
#5304 • 11" • JB
Issued: 1989 • Retired: 1992
Original: $14 • Value: $76

2673.
Ernest Q. Grimilkin (new face)
#5304 • JB
Issued: 1993 • Retired: 2000
Original: $14 • Value: $24

2674.
Ernest Q. Grimilkin (modern face)
#5304 • 11" • JB
Issued: 1993 • Retired: 2000
Original: $14 • Value: $24

Critters (Cats)

2675.
Felicia Fuzzbuns
#912090 • 12" • TJ
Issued: 2000 • Retired: 2000
Original: $25 • Value: $35

2676.
Felina B. Catterwall (in black)
#919701 • 8" • TJ
Issued: 1998 • Retired: 1999
Original: $10 • Value: $31

2677.
Felina B. Catterwall (in brown)
#919701-01 • 8" • TJ
Issued: 1999 • Retired: 2000
Original: $12 • Value: $25

2678.
Finicky Snottykat
#53030-10 • 8" • JB
Issued: 2001 • Retired: 2002
Original: $9 • Value: $14

2679.
Fraid E. Cat
#9198 • 5½" • TJ
Issued: 1994 • Retired: 1997
Original: $12 • Value: $41

2680.
Fuzzy Jake Cattington [QVC]
#(C95194) • 10" • MB
LE of 2400 • Issued: 1999 • Retired: 1999
Original: $28 • Value: $55

2681.

Gae A. Grimilkin (smooth fur)
#5324 • 14" • JB
Issued: 1989 • Retired: 1992
Original: $20 • Value: $185

2682.
Gae A. Grimilkin (white on chin)
#5324 • 14" • JB
Issued: 1989 • Retired: 1989
Original: $20 • Value: $210

2683.

Gae A. Grimilkin (regular plush)
#5324 • 14" • JB
Issued: 1989 • Retired: 1992
Original: $20 • Value: $155

2684.

Have You Seen Me?

Gardner
#6162C
Issued: 1991 • Retired: 1991
Original: $63 • Value: $350

2685.
Garner J. Cattington
#59050-11 • 10" • MB
Issued: 1998 • Retired: 1998
Original: $31 • Value: $53

2686.
Ginger P. Purrski [QVC]
#(C99327) • 10"
Issued: 2001 • Retired: 2001
Original: $21 • Value: $45

CATS

	PRICE PAID	VALUE
2675.		
2676.		
2677.		
2678.		
2679.		
2680.		
2681.		
2682.		
2683.		
2684.		
2685.		
2686.		
	TOTALS	

NOTES

Critters (Cats)

2687.
Glenwood Flatcat
#56951-08 • 8" • FL
Issued: 1998 • Retired: 1999
Original: $13 • Value: $23

2688.
Golda Meow
#53030-08 • 8" • JB
Issued: 2001 • Current
Original: $9 • Value: $R/E

2689.
Have You Seen Me?
Grace
#6163C • TJ
Issued: 1991 • Retired: 1991
Original: $63 • Value: $325

2690.
Greybeard
#5312 • 16" • JB
Issued: 1991 • Retired: 1993
Original: $29 • Value: $189

2691.
Grosvenor Catberg [QVC]
#93083V (C39094) • 14"
Issued: 1997 • Retired: 1997
Original: $18 • Value: $77

2692.
Hattie
#9105 • 6" • TJ
Issued: 1995 • Retired: 1997
Original: $12 • Value: $42

2693.
Heranamous
#5911-07 • 16" • JB
Issued: 1996 • Retired: 1999
Original: $29 • Value: $51

2694.
Heranamous [SFMB]
#41-72639 • 16" • JB
Issued: 1998 • Retired: 1998
Original: $35 • Value: $55
♪ Ebony and Ivory ♪

2695.
Holloway Flatcat
#5695-09 • 8" • FL
Issued: 1994 • Retired: 1999
Original: $12 • Value: $25

2696.
Holly [Elder Beerman]
#unknown • 8"
Issued: 1999 • Retired: 1999
Original: $13 • Value: $70

2697.
Huxley W. Penworthy
#57411-08 • 8" • AS
Issued: 2000 • Retired: 2000
Original: $10 • Value: $15

2698.
Inkley Boocat
#919636 • 5½"
Issued: 2002 • Retired: 2002
Original: $10 • Value: $14

CATS

	PRICE PAID	VALUE
2687.		
2688.		
2689.		
2690.		
2691.		
2692.		
2693.		
2694.		
2695.		
2696.		
2697.		
2698.		
TOTALS		

NOTES

Critters (Cats)

2699.
Inky Catterwall
#91972 • 9" • TJ
Issued: 1998 • Retired: 1999
Original: $15 • Value: $24

2700.
Ivana Purrkins [QVC]
#(C53108) • 11" • TJ
Issued: 1998 • Retired: 1998
Original: $16 • Value: $56

2701.
Java B. Bean
#500102-07 • 8¼" • JB
Issued: 2000 • Retired: 2000
Original: $9 • Value: $14

2702.
Jenna Kathleen [Dillards]
#94740DL • 11" • TJ
Issued: 1999 • Retired: 1999
Original: $18 • Value: $51

2703.
Katie Kat [Lord & Taylor]
#unknown • 16" • TJ
Issued: 1998 • Retired: 1998
Original: $35 • Value: $55

2704.
Katie Kat II [Lord & Taylor]
#unknown • 16" • TJ
Issued: 1999 • Retired: 1999
Original: $35 • Value: $70

2705.
Kattelina Purrsley
#91978 • 11" • TJ
Issued: 1999 • Retired: 2001
Original: $20 • Value: $28

2706.
Keats
#5743 • 5½" • AS
Issued: 1992 • Retired: 2000
Original: $8 • Value: $20

CATS		
	PRICE PAID	VALUE
2699.		
2700.		
2701.		
2702.		
2703.		
2704.		
2705.		
2706.		
2707.		
2708.		
2709.		
2710.		
	TOTALS	

NOTES

2707.
Kimberlyn Woodsbeary [GCC]
#94898GCC • 8"
Issued: 2001 • Retired: 2001
Original: $14 • Value: $35

2708.
Kitt Purrsley
#91711 • 8" • TJ
Issued: 1999 • Retired: 2000
Original: $15 • Value: $18

2710. (95)
Lacy (11")
#6101C • 11" • TJ
Issued: 1990 • Retired: 1991
Original: $21 • Value: $250

2709. (96)
Lacy (14")
#6100C • 14" • TJ
Issued: 1990 • Retired: 1992
Original: $16 • Value: $225

Critters (Cats)

2711.
Lavender Q. Prissyfoot [QVC]
#93305V (C107583) • 14"
Issued: 2002 • Retired: 2002
Original: $28 • Value: $50

2712.
Leslie G Catberg [SLE]
#unknown • 14"
Issued: 1998 • Retired: 1998
Original: $25 • Value: $41

2713.
Lindbergh Cattington
#590087-03 • 4½" • MB
Issued: 1999 • Retired: 2000
Original: $10 • Value: $16

2714.
Lindsey II & Tucker F Wuzzie [QVC]
#(C34989) • 13"
Issued: 1998 • Retired: 1998
Original: $33 • Value: $50

2715.
Lindsey P. Pussytoes
#912091 • 12" • TJ
Issued: 1998 • Retired: 2000
Original: $31 • Value: $37

2716.
Lola Ninelives
#919751 • 9" • TJ
Issued: 1999 • Retired: 2001
Original: $20 • Value: $31

2717.
Lyndon & Mondale Cattington [QVC]
#unknown • 7½"
Issued: 1998 • Retired: 1998
Original: $47 • Value: $65

2718.
Margaux P. Pussyfoot [QVC]
#(C63341) • 14" • TJ
Issued: 1999 • Retired: 1999
Original: $32 • Value: $48

2719.
Marissa P. Pussyfoot
#912093 • 14" • TJ
Issued: 1999 • Retired: 2001
Original: $32 • Value: $41

2720.
Marissa P. Pussytoes [SFMB]
#41-72979 • 14"
Issued: 2000 • Retired: 2000
Original: $40 • Value: $60
♪ Mr. Sandman ♪

2721.
Marmalade Sneakypuss
#530800-08 • 14" • JB
Issued: 2000 • Retired: 2002
Original: $18 • Value: $18

2722.
Merrimew McPurrsley [QVC]
#93501V (C5165) • 11"
Issued: 2003 • Retired: 2003
Original: $18 • Value: $27

CATS

	PRICE PAID	VALUE
2711.		
2712.		
2713.		
2714.		
2715.		
2716.		
2717.		
2718.		
2719.		
2720.		
2721.		
2722.		
TOTALS		

NOTES

Critters (Cats)

2723.
Midge Meowsworth
#5745-11 • 5½" • AS
Issued: 2001 • Retired: 2001
Original: $7 • Value: $13

2724.
Midnight Sneakypuss
#81002 • 6" • TJ
Issued: 2000 • Retired: 2000
Original: $11 • Value: $18

2725.
Millicent P. Pussytoes
#91976 • 11" • TJ
Issued: 1997 • Retired: 1998
Original: $20 • Value: $45

2726.
Milton R. Penworthy
#57410-07 • 8" • AS
Issued: 2000 • Retired: 2000
Original: $11 • Value: $17

2727.
Miss Annie Fuzzybuns [QVC]
#93127V (C63339) • 14"
Issued: 1999 • Retired: 1999
Original: $20 • Value: $45

2728.
Miss Flufficat [QVC]
#(C100353) • 11"
Issued: 2001 • Retired: 2001
Original: $25 • Value: $56

2729.
Miss Prissy Fussybuns
#912094 • 14" • TJ
Issued: 2000 • Retired: 2000
Original: $25 • Value: $29

2730.
**Miss Pussyfoot
& Mr. McScurry [QVC]**
#93337V (C20184) • 11"
Issued: 2002 • Retired: 2002
Original: $16 • Value: $35

2731.
Miss Sourpuss with McLemon [QVC]
#(C06195) • 8"
Issued: 2004 • Retired: 2004
Original: $20 • Value: $26
With resin sign.

2732.
Missie Meowsworth
#57411-06 • 8" • AS
Issued: 2001 • Retired: 2001
Original: $10 • Value: $18

2733.
**Missy P. Pusskins
and Squeekers [QVC]**
#99939V (C21160) • 9"
Issued: 2003 • Retired: 2003
Original: $25 • Value: $45

2734.
Momma McFuzz and Missy
#910080 • 12" • TJ
Issued: 2000 • Retired: 2001
Original: $25 • Value: $34

CATS	PRICE PAID	VALUE
2723.		
2724.		
2725.		
2726.		
2727.		
2728.		
2729.		
2730.		
2731.		
2732.		
2733.		
2734.		
TOTALS		

NOTES

Critters (Cats)

2735.
Momma McFuzz and Missy [SFMB]
#41-72977 • 12"
Issued: 2000 • Retired: 2000
Original: $35 • Value: $52
♪ You & Me Against The World ♪

2736.
Momma Purrsalot & Pusskins [QVC]
#93224V (C19889) • 14"
Issued: 2002 • Retired: 2002
Original: $26 • Value: $41

2737.
Mondale W. Cattington
#590250-05 • 10" • MB
Issued: 1999 • Retired: 1999
Original: $28 • Value: $39

2738.
Mrs. Partridge
#919750 • 9" • TJ
Issued: 1998 • Retired: 1999
Original: $26 • Value: $35

2739.
Mrs. Petrie
#919752 • 9" • TJ
Issued: 1999 • Retired: 2000
Original: $26 • Value: $35

2740.
Mrs. Petrie [SFMB]
#919752SF • 9" • TJ
Issued: 2000 • Retired: 2000
Original: $35 • Value: $55
♪ Unforgettable ♪

2741.
Muffles T. Toastytoes [QVC]
#(C95130) • 11"
LE of 1300 • Issued: 1999 • Retired: 1999
Original: $25 • Value: $51

2742.
Nana Purrington & Gouda [SLE]
#unknown • 14"
Issued: 1999 • Retired: 1999
Original: $N/E • Value: $56

2743.
Ned
#5656-03 • 12" • BA
Issued: 1993 • Retired: 1995
Original: $16 • Value: $67

2744.
Opel Catberg (satin bow)
#5324-10
Issued: 1995 • Retired: 1999
Original: $20 • Value: $35

2745.
Opel Catberg (blue fabric bow)
#5324-10
Issued: 1995 • Retired: 1999
Original: $20 • Value: $35

2746.
Ophilia Q. Grimilkin
#5323 • 14" • JB
Issued: 1989 • Retired: 1991
Original: $20 • Value: $183

CATS

	PRICE PAID	VALUE
2735.		
2736.		
2737.		
2738.		
2739.		
2740.		
2741.		
2742.		
2743.		
2744.		
2745.		
2746.		
TOTALS		

NOTES

Critters (Cats)

2747.
Oscar P. Alleyruckus [QVC]
#(C100436) • 14"
Issued: 2001 • Retired: 2001
Original: $19 • Value: $35

2748.
Ozzie N. Harrycat
#53060-11 • 11" • JB
Issued: 2001 • Retired: 2002
Original: $14 • Value: $20

2749.
Pamela P. Prissypuss with Nibley [QVC]
#(C40635) • 14"
Issued: 2001 • Retired: 2001
Original: $32 • Value: $48

2750.
Pauline & Penelope [QVC]
#(C40598) • 8"
Issued: 2001 • Retired: 2001
Original: $17 • Value: $28

2751.
Peachie P. Pussyfoot [QVC]
#93445V (C22627) • 14" • TJ
Issued: 2003 • Retired: 2003
Original: $26 • Value: $40

2752.
Pearl Catberg
#5324-01 • 14" • JB
Issued: 1994 • Retired: 1995
Original: $20 • Value: $91

2753.
Penny P. Copperpuss
#53080-06 • 14" • JB
Issued: 2001 • Retired: 2001
Original: $18 • Value: $32

2754.
Pepper [Dillards]
#94746DL • 11" • TJ
Issued: 1999 • Retired: 1999
Original: $20 • Value: $53

2755.
Pepper B. Scaredycat
#919700-02 • 8" • TJ
Issued: 2001 • Retired: 2002
Original: $10 • Value: $16

2756.
Phoebe Purrsmore
#917101 • 5½" • TJ
Issued: 2000 • Retired: 2000
Original: $10 • Value: $22

2757.
Pitty Pat Pussytoes [QVC]
#93537V (C05178) • 11"
Issued: 2004 • Retired: 2004
Original: $15 • Value: $30

2758.
Pittypat Pussyfoot [QVC]
#93223V (C59860) • 11"
Issued: 2001 • Retired: 2001
Original: $15 • Value: $30

CATS	PRICE PAID	VALUE
2747.		
2748.		
2749.		
2750.		
2751.		
2752.		
2753.		
2754.		
2755.		
2756.		
2757.		
2758.		
TOTALS		

NOTES

Critters (Cats)

2759.
Poe
#5742-07 • 5½" • AS
Issued: 1993 • Retired: 1999
Original: $8 • Value: $20

2760.
Pookie W. Penworthy & Midnight Sneakypuss [QVC]
#99753V (C78112) • 8"
Issued: 2000 • Retired: 2000
Original: $17 • Value: $26

2761.
Princess Pussytoes [QVC]
#93427V (C22075) • 11"
Issued: 2003 • Retired: 2003
Original: $15 • Value: $23

2762.
Princess P. Pussytoes
#531101 • 16"
Issued: 2003 • Current
Original: $24 • Value: $R/E

2763.
Punkin Puss
#9197 • 8" • TJ
Issued: 1992 • Retired: 1997
Original: $18 • Value: $46

2764.
Purrcilla P. Pussytoes
#53040-01 • 11" • JB
Issued: 2001 • Retired: 2002
Original: $14 • Value: $21

2765.
Purrcilla P. Sugarcone
#904122 • 11"
Issued: 2003 • Retired: 2003
Original: $18 • Value: $23

2766.
Purrcilla Pusskins [QVC]
#(C76779) • 14"
Issued: 2000 • Retired: 2000
Original: $16 • Value: $30

2767.
Purrkins P. Pussytoes
#530501 • 11" • AS
Issued: 2003 • Current
Original: $14 • Value: $R/E

2768.
Purrsnicitty Snotty-Kat
#53050-10 • 11" • JB
Issued: 2000 • Retired: 2002
Original: $14 • Value: $23

2769.
Puss N. Boo
#9164 • 8" • TJ
Issued: 1993 • Retired: 1995
Original: $18 • Value: $51

2770.
Pussy Broomski
#unknown • 5½"
Issued: 1999 • Retired: 1999
Original: $13 • Value: $30

CATS

	PRICE PAID	VALUE
2759.		
2760.		
2761.		
2762.		
2763.		
2764.		
2765.		
2766.		
2767.		
2768.		
2769.		
2770.		
TOTALS		

NOTES

Critters (Cats)

2771.
Quayle D. Cattington
#590270-07 • 6" • MB
Issued: 1999 • Retired: 1999
Original: $16 • Value: $45

2772.
Robyn Purrsmore
#915600 • 8" • TJ
Issued: 2000 • Retired: 2001
Original: $10 • Value: $12

2773.
Rowena Prissypuss
#915601 • 8" • TJ
Issued: 2001 • Retired: 2002
Original: $13 • Value: $32

Have You Seen Me?

2774.
Royce
#6101
LE • Issued: 1990 • Retired: 1991
Original: $32 • Value: $265

2775.
Sabrina P. Catterwall
#919700 • 8" • TJ
Issued: 1998 • Retired: 1999
Original: $12 • Value: $28

2776.
Sabrina P. Catterwall
#919700-01 • 8" • TJ
Issued: 1999 • Retired: 2000
Original: $14 • Value: $23

2777.
Salem Thumpkin
#unknown • 16" • TJ
Issued: 1999 • Retired: 1999
Original: $35 • Value: $55

2778.
Samantha Sneakypuss
#91979 • 11" • TJ
Issued: 1999 • Retired: 2000
Original: $17 • Value: $33

2779.
Sammy Snicklepuss
#530801 • 14" • JB
Issued: 2002 • Retired: 2002
Original: $18 • Value: $26

2780.
Samuel Catberg
#5306 • 12" • JB
Issued: 1989 • Retired: 1990
Original: $11 • Value: $215

2781.
Scratches P. Whiskerpuss
#53000 • 11" • JB
Issued: 2001 • Retired: 2001
Original: $15 • Value: $24

2782.
Shelly
#5742 • 5½" • AS
Issued: 1992 • Retired: 2000
Original: $8 • Value: $14

CATS

	PRICE PAID	VALUE
2771.		
2772.		
2773.		
2774.		
2775.		
2776.		
2777.		
2778.		
2779.		
2780.		
2781.		
2782.		
	TOTALS	

NOTES

Critters (Cats)

2783.
Sly Alleyruckus
#53041-07 • 11" • JB
Issued: 2001 • Retired: 2002
Original: $14 • Value: $17

2784.
Smokey B. Pusskins
#530311 • 8" • AS
Issued: 2004 • Current
Original: $11 • Value: $R/E

2785.
Smokey Ninelives
#53030-06 • 8" • JB
Issued: 2001 • Retired: 2002
Original: $9 • Value: $11

2786.
Snackers Sneakypuss [QVC]
#(C99284) • 11"
Issued: 2001 • Retired: 2001
Original: $15 • Value: $25

2787.
Sneaky P. Snottypuss [QVC]
#(C64871) • 12"
Issued: 2001 • Retired: 2001
Original: $15 • Value: $24

2788.
Snooker T. Sootyfoot [QVC]
#93177V (C78108) • 14" • JB
Issued: 2000 • Retired: 2000
Original: $16 • Value: $30

2789.
Snottie Snicklepuss
#530802 • 14"
Issued: 2003 • Retired: 2003
Original: $18 • Value: $18

2790.
Socks Grimilkin
#5324-07 • 14" • JB
Issued: 1993 • Retired: 1998
Original: $20 • Value: $47

2791.
Sooty
#904204 • 6" • TJ
Issued: 2003 • Retired: 2003
Original: $8 • Value: $8

2792.
Sooty P. Pussyfoot
#574200 • 7"
Issued: 2002 • Retired: 2002
Original: $12 • Value: $18

2793.
Spiro T. Cattington
#59040-07 • 12" • MB
Issued: 1998 • Retired: 1998
Original: $51 • Value: $75

2794.
Spooky Tangaween
#91975 • 11" • TJ
Issued: 1996 • Retired: 1998
Original: $20 • Value: $32

CATS

	PRICE PAID	VALUE
2783.		
2784.		
2785.		
2786.		
2787.		
2788.		
2789.		
2790.		
2791.		
2792.		
2793.		
2794.		
TOTALS		

NOTES

Critters (Cats)

2795.
Star Steadsbeary [Longaberger]
#94645LB • 11"
Issued: 2002 • Retired: 2002
Original: $23 • Value: $48

2796.
Suzie Purrkins
#91977 • 11" • TJ
Issued: 1998 • Retired: 1998
Original: $20 • Value: $31
Also with Thomasina as QVC set.

2797.
Suzy Snugglepuss
#530804 • 14" • AS
Issued: 2004 • Current
Original: $18 • Value: $R/E

2798.
Sweetpea Catberg (old face)
#5305 • 11" • JB
Issued: 1989 • Retired: 1992
Original: $14 • Value: $108

2799.
Sweetpea Catberg (new face)
#5407 • 11" • JB
Issued: 1992 • Retired: 1998
Original: $14 • Value: $28

2800.
T. Frankel Wuzzie
#595103 • 5" • TF
Issued: 1999 • Retired: 2000
Original: $9 • Value: $12

2801.
Tabby F. Wuzzie
#595240-07 • 3" • TF
Issued: 1999 • Retired: 2000
Original: $7 • Value: $13

2802.
Taylor Purrski
#912095 • 14" • TJ
Issued: 2000 • Retired: 2001
Original: $32 • Value: $42

2803.
Tennyson
#5744 • 5½" • AS
Issued: 1992 • Retired: 1999
Original: $8 • Value: $22

2804.
Tessa Fluffypaws
#5309-01 • 14" • JB
Issued: 2000 • Retired: 2002
Original: $19 • Value: $23

2805.
Thom
#5656-07 • 12" • BA
Issued: 1993 • Retired: 1995
Original: $16 • Value: $65

2806.
Thomasina Purrkins with Suzie [QVC]
#unknown • 6"
Issued: 1998 • Retired: 1998
Original: $10 • Value: $65

CATS	PRICE PAID	VALUE
2795.		
2796.		
2797.		
2798.		
2799.		
2800.		
2801.		
2802.		
2803.		
2804.		
2805.		
2806.		
TOTALS		

NOTES

Critters (Cats)

2807. Thoreau
#5740-08 • 8" • AS
Issued: 1995 • Retired: 1999
Original: $12 • Value: $26

2808. Tibsley Purrsalot [QVC]
#93226V (C0546) • 11"
Issued: 2002 • Retired: 2002
Original: $15 • Value: $25

2809. Tigerlily (old face)
#5311 • 16" • JB
Issued: 1989 • Retired: 1992
Original: $29 • Value: $190

2810. Tigerlily (new face)
#5311 • 16" • JB
Issued: 1992 • Retired: 1995
Original: $29 • Value: $79

2811. Tom, Dick & Harry [QVC]
#(C41102) • 6"
Issued: 1997 • Retired: 1997
Original: $19 • Value: $60

2812. Tommy Kat
#530401 • 5½" • AS
Issued: 2004 • Current
Original: $8 • Value: $R/E

CATS

	PRICE PAID	VALUE
2807.		
2808.		
2809.		
2810.		
2811.		
2812.		
2813.		
2814.		
2815.		
2816.		
2817.		
2818.		
TOTALS		

NOTES

2813. Turner F. Wuzzie
#595240-06 • 3" • TF
Issued: 1998 • Retired: 2000
Original: $7 • Value: $10

2814. Vanessa V. Fluffypaws
#53110-01 • 16" • JB
Issued: 2001 • Retired: 2002
Original: $25 • Value: $30

2815. Vanessa Fluffypaws [SFMB]
#53110-01SF • 16"
Issued: 2002 • Retired: 2002
Original: $35 • Value: $46
♪ Lara's Theme ♪

2816. Walter Q. Fuzzberg
#5303-07 • 8" • JB
Issued: 1997 • Retired: 2001
Original: $10 • Value: $18

2817. Whiskers P. Tweeter with B.B.
#904262 • 10" • TJ
Issued: 2004 • Current
Original: $18 • Value: $R/E

2818. Whitefurd Felinsky
#93096V (C53112) • 12"
Issued: 1999 • Retired: 1999
Original: $20 • Value: $35

Critters (Cats)

2819.
Yowley Alleyruckus
#53110-06 • 16" • JB
Issued: 2001 • Retired: N/E
Original: $25 • Value: $41

2820.
Zachariah Alleyruckus
#5308-06 • 14" • JB
Issued: 1999 • Retired: 2001
Original: $18 • Value: $32

2821.
Zap Catberg
#5325 • 14" • JB
Issued: 1992 • Retired: 1992
Original: $20 • Value: $265

 100

2822.
Zelda Catberg
#5324-06 • 14" • JB
Issued: 1993 • Retired: 1993
Original: $20 • Value: $270
Very rare.

2823.
Zelda Z. Witchypuss
#919790 • 11" • TJ
Issued: 2001 • Retired: 2002
Original: $20 • Value: $24

2824.
Zenus W. Grimilkin (smooth fur)
#5303 • 11" • JB
Issued: 1989 • Retired: 1991
Original: $14 • Value: $169

101

2825.
Zenus W. Grimilkin (regular plush)
#5303 • 11" • JB
Issued: 1989 • Retired: 1991
Original: $14 • Value: $150

101

2826.
Zip Catberg
#5325 • 14" • JB
Issued: 1989 • Retired: 1992
Original: $20 • Value: $262
Very rare.

2827.
Zoe R. Grimilkin
#5304-07 • 11" • JB
Issued: 1994 • Retired: 1999
Original: $14 • Value: $25

2828.
Zoe R. Grimilkin [QVC]
#(C35266) • 11"
Issued: 1997 • Retired: 1997
Original: $20 • Value: $65

2829.
Zoom Catberg
#5326 • 14" • JB
Issued: 1992 • Retired: 1993
Original: $20 • Value: $240

CATS

	PRICE PAID	VALUE
2819.		
2820.		
2821.		
2822.		
2823.		
2824.		
2825.		
2826.		
2827.		
2828.		
2829.		
TOTALS		

NOTES

Cloth Dolls

2830.
Abigail (blue print dress)
#7430 • 7" • CD
Issued: 1993 • Retired: 1993
Original: $10 • Value: $98

2831.
Abigail (tan dress)
#7430 • 7" • CD
Issued: 1993 • Retired: 1993
Original: $10 • Value: $107

2832.
Abigail (red & white print dress)
#7430 • 7" • CD
Issued: 1993 • Retired: 1994
Original: $10 • Value: $106

2833.
Dolly
#7434 • 17" • CD
Issued: 1993 • Retired: 1993
Original: $30 • Value: $202

2834.
Frannie
#7436 • 11" • CD
Issued: 1993 • Retired: 1993
Original: $18 • Value: $169

2835.
Priscilla (brown print)
#7432 • 11" • CD
Issued: 1993 • Retired: 1993
Original: $18 • Value: $191

2836.
Priscilla (tan print)
#7432 • 11" • CD
Issued: 1993 • Retired: 1993
Original: $18 • Value: $179

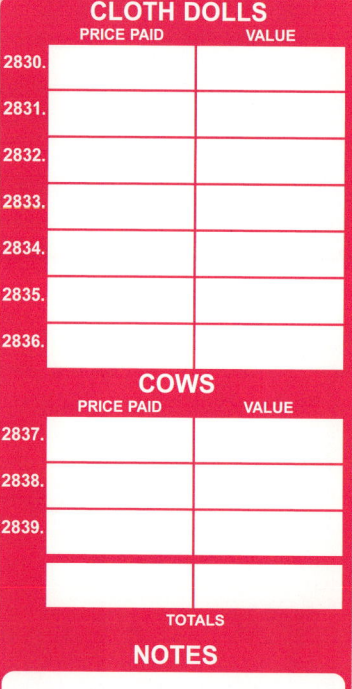

CLOTH DOLLS		
	PRICE PAID	VALUE
2830.		
2831.		
2832.		
2833.		
2834.		
2835.		
2836.		

COWS		
	PRICE PAID	VALUE
2837.		
2838.		
2839.		
	TOTALS	

NOTES

Cows

2837.
Adelaide & Aggie [QVC]
#(C47273 • 9"
Issued: 1998 • Retired: 1998
Original: $N/E • Value: $N/E

2838.
Angus MacMoo
#91341 • 11" • TJ
Issued: 1999 • Retired: 2000
Original: $20 • Value: $30

2839.
Bertha Utterberg
#5758 • 8" • AS
Issued: 1996 • Retired: 1996
Original: $13 • Value: $53

Critters (Cows)

2840.
Bessie and Chuck Moosley
#568014 • 3½" • NO
Issued: 2003 • Current
Original: $10 • Value: $R/E

2841.
Bessie Moostein (old face)
#5532 • 11" • AM
Issued: 1991 • Retired: 1992
Original: $14 • Value: $45

2842.
Bessie Moostein (new face)
#5532 • 11" • AM
Issued: 1992 • Retired: 2000
Original: $14 • Value: $27

2843.
Betsey B. Hoofenudder [QVC]
#93553V (C06196) • 14"
Issued: 2004 • Retired: 2004
Original: $28 • Value: $36

2844.
Butch Hoofenutter
#55330-07 • 14" • AM
Issued: 2001 • Retired: 2001
Original: $20 • Value: $30

2845.
Chocolate [Hershey]
#95204HE • TJ
Issued: 2003 • Retired: 2003
Original: $17 • Value: $35

2846.
Clarabelle Moo
#553155 • 16"
Issued: 2003 • Current
Original: $25 • Value: $R/E

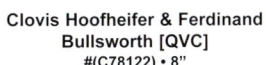

2847.
Have You Seen Me?
Clovis Hoofheifer & Ferdinand Bullsworth [QVC]
#(C78122) • 8"
Issued: 2000 • Retired: 2000
Original: $16 • Value: $28

2848.
Clovis Moosdale
#553150 • 8"
Issued: 2003 • Current
Original: $10 • Value: $R/E

2849.
Corabelle Hoofenutter
#55320-11 • 11" • AM
Issued: 2001 • Retired: N/E
Original: $10 • Value: $16

2850.
Elford Bullsworth
#55330-05 • 14" • AM
Issued: 2000 • Retired: 2000
Original: $20 • Value: $23

2851.
Elmer Beefcake
#5535-11 • 14" • AM
Issued: 1995 • Retired: 1996
Original: $20 • Value: $33

COWS		
	PRICE PAID	VALUE
2840.		
2841.		
2842.		
2843.		
2844.		
2845.		
2846.		
2847.		
2848.		
2849.		
2850.		
2851.		
	TOTALS	

NOTES

Critters (Cows)

2852.
Elmo Beefcake (old face)
#5532-03 • 11" • AM
Issued: 1993 • Retired: 1994
Original: $14 • Value: $73

2853.
Elmo Beefcake (new face)
#5532 • 11" • AM
Issued: 1994 • Retired: 2000
Original: $14 • Value: $32

2854.
Ernestine Vanderhoof
#55312-05 • 8" • AM
Issued: 1999 • Retired: 2000
Original: $9 • Value: $16

2855.
Fernando Uttermost
#55314-05 • 8" • AM
Issued: 2001 • Retired: 2002
Original: $11 • Value: $13

2856.
Florabelle Uttermost
#55314-07 • 8" • AM
Issued: 2001 • Retired: 2001
Original: $10 • Value: $12

2857.
Herman Beefcake
#5534 • 16" • AM
Issued: 1992 • Retired: 1994
Original: $27 • Value: $177
Also available in new face.

2858.
Hester
#5660-10 • 12" • BA
Issued: 1996 • Retired: 1997
Original: $16 • Value: $65

2859.
Hortense Moostein
#5533 • 16" • AM
Issued: 1994 • Retired: 1995
Original: $29 • Value: $116
Also available in new face.

2860.
Ida Moostein
#5535-10 • 14" • AM
Issued: 1994 • Retired: 1996
Original: $20 • Value: $75

2861.
Kisses [Hershey]
#94210HE • 10" • TJ
Issued: 2004 • Retired: 2004
Original: $16 • Value: $18

2862.
Mildred Q. Moostein [QVC]
#(C64873) • 10½" • TJ
Issued: 2001 • Retired: 2001
Original: $18 • Value: $45

2863.
Moocha Latte
#553310 • 12" • AM
Issued: 2004 • Current
Original: $15 • Value: $R/E

COWS

	PRICE PAID	VALUE
2852.		
2853.		
2854.		
2855.		
2856.		
2857.		
2858.		
2859.		
2860.		
2861.		
2862.		
2863.		
TOTALS		

NOTES

Critters (Cows, Crows, Dogs)

2864.
Mooshell Patchbeary
#912096 • 14" • TJ
Issued: 2002 • Retired: 2002
Original: $25 • Value: $25

2865.
Mooshell Patchbeary [SFMB]
#912096SF • 14" • TJ
Issued: 2002 • Retired: 2002
Original: $34 • Value: $44
♪ Old MacDonald Had A Farm ♪

2866.
Myrtle MacMoo [QVC]
#93110V (C56962) • 11" • TJ
Issued: 1999 • Retired: 1999
Original: $19 • Value: $65

2867.
Sadie Utterburg
#5533-10 • 16" • AM
Issued: 1996 • Retired: 1999
Original: $29 • Value: $41

2868.
Silo Q. Vanderhoof
#55312-07 • 8" • AM
Issued: 1999 • Retired: 2000
Original: $9 • Value: $19

2869.
T. Fodder Wuzzie
#595105-01 • 5" • AM
Issued: 2000 • Retired: 2000
Original: $9 • Value: $24

Crows

2870.
Edgar
#5864-07 • 6" • AR
Issued: 1996 • Retired: 1997
Original: $9 • Value: $69

2871.
Hank Krow Jr.
#5865-07 • 11" • AR
Issued: 1995 • Retired: 1997
Original: $14 • Value: $44

Dogs

2872.
Ambrose P. Hydrant III [QVC]
#(C39082) • 17"
Issued: 1997 • Retired: 1997
Original: $25 • Value: $40

2873.
Have You Seen Me?
Ambrose Q. Hydrant [Lord & Taylor]
#unknown • 16" • AM
Issued: 1998 • Retired: 1998
Original: $23 • Value: $48

COWS	PRICE PAID	VALUE
2864.		
2865.		
2866.		
2867.		
2868.		
2869.		

CROWS	PRICE PAID	VALUE
2870.		
2871.		

DOGS	PRICE PAID	VALUE
2872.		
2873.		

TOTALS

NOTES

Critters (Dogs)

2874.
Arno-w-ld
#5655-07 • 12" • BA
Issued: 1996 • Retired: 1997
Original: $16 • Value: $47

2875.
B.W. Poochley [QVC]
#(C99634) • 10"
Issued: 2001 • Retired: 2001
Original: $13 • Value: $25

2876.
Bagley Flatberg
#5690-03 • 8" • FL
Issued: 1996 • Retired: 1999
Original: $13 • Value: $26

2877.
Bart Barkenfarkle
#540303 • 14" • AS
Issued: 2004 • Current
Original: $18 • Value: $R/E

2878.
Bartley & Wilbur [QVC]
#(C97887) • 10"
Issued: 2000 • Retired: 2000
Original: $24 • Value: $33

2879.
Bath & Body Works Dog [Bath & Body Works]
#unknown • 16"
Issued: 1996 • Retired: 1996
Original: $30 • Value: $66

2880.
Betty Biscuit (a.k.a. Betty Cocker)
#5402-08 • 10" • JB
Issued: 1994 • Retired: 1997
Original: $14 • Value: $36

2881.
Eddie Bauer Betty [Eddie Bauer]
#unknown • 10"
Issued: 1995 • Retired: 1995
Original: $20 • Value: $65

2882.
Beulah Canine
#5403 • 11" • JB
Issued: 1989 • Retired: 1991
Original: $14 • Value: $136

2883.
Bowser Barksalot
#54000 • 10" • JB
Issued: 2002 • Retired: 2002
Original: $18 • Value: $18

2884.
Buzz [Lord & Taylor]
#unknown • 10"
Issued: 1997 • Retired: 1997
Original: $16 • Value: $55

2885.
Caesar Q. & Cosmo Hydrant [QVC]
#unknown • 10"
Issued: 1998 • Retired: 1998
Original: $24 • Value: $30

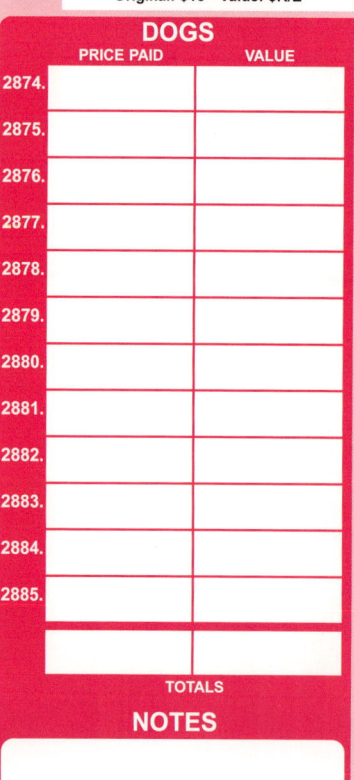

DOGS

	PRICE PAID	VALUE
2874.		
2875.		
2876.		
2877.		
2878.		
2879.		
2880.		
2881.		
2882.		
2883.		
2884.		
2885.		
TOTALS		

NOTES

Critters (Dogs)

2886.
Carson B. Barker
#540300-05 • 16" • JB
Issued: 2000 • Retired: 2000
Original: $25 • Value: $33

2887.
Charles
#904225 • 6" • TJ
Issued: 2003 • Current
Original: $10 • Value: $R/E

2888.
Checkers P. Hydrant
#54051-07 • 10" • JB
Issued: 2000 • Retired: 2001
Original: $13 • Value: $15

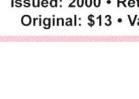
2889.
Clancy G. Hydrant, Jr.
#5404 • 10" • JB
Issued: 1998 • Retired: 2000
Original: $14 • Value: $33
Also with Corky as QVC set.

2890.
Collier P. Hydrant II
#5403 • 16" • JB
Issued: 1997 • Retired: 1999
Original: $29 • Value: $32

Have You Seen Me?
2891.
Corky with Clancy G. Hydrant, Jr. [QVC]
#unknown • 8"
Issued: 1998 • Retired: 1998
Original: $12 • Value: $14

2892.
Duffy P. Hydrant
#540301-07 • 16" • JB
Issued: 2001 • Retired: 2002
Original: $25 • Value: $30

2893.
Duncan Doodledog
#54040-11 • 12" • JB
Issued: 2001 • Retired: 2001
Original: $15 • Value: $18

2894.
Duncan Doodledog [SFMB]
#41-398036 • 12"
Issued: 2002 • Retired: 2002
Original: $30 • Value: $39
♪ Where Oh Where Has My Little Dog Gone ♪

2895.
Fearless Fido
#918056 • 5" • TJ
Issued: 2001 • Retired: 2001
Original: $10 • Value: $12

2896.
Fred Farfle [QVC]
#(C76780) • 10"
Issued: 2000 • Retired: 2000
Original: $12 • Value: $22

2897.
Fritz Von Bruin
#5014 • 6" • WB
Issued: 1992 • Retired: 1992
Original: $10 • Value: $120

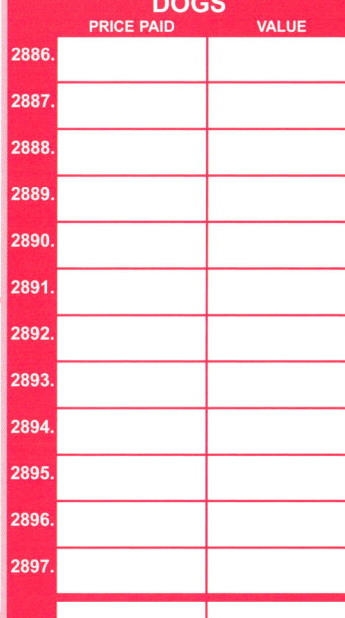

DOGS	PRICE PAID	VALUE
2886.		
2887.		
2888.		
2889.		
2890.		
2891.		
2892.		
2893.		
2894.		
2895.		
2896.		
2897.		
TOTALS		

NOTES

Critters (Dogs)

2898.
Guthrie and Gibbley [QVC]
#unknown • 11"
Issued: 2001 • Retired: 2001
Original: $21 • Value: $30

2899.
Hector Flatberg
#5690-07 • 8" • FL
Issued: 1995 • Retired: 1996
Original: $13 • Value: $32

2900.
Hercules von Mutt
#5014-01 • 6" • WB
Issued: 1993 • Retired: 1994
Original: $10 • Value: $110

2901.
Indy (Fall 1997)
#91757 • 5½" • BF
Issued: 1997 • Retired: 1998
Original: $12 • Value: $22

2902.
Indy (Fall 1998)
#91757-10 • 5½" • BF
Issued: 1998 • Retired: 1999
Original: $12 • Value: $21

2903.
Indy (Fall 1999)
#91757-12 • 5" • BF
Issued: 1999 • Retired: 1999
Original: $10 • Value: $22

2904.
Indy (Spring 2000)
#91757-14 • 5" • BF
Issued: 2000 • Retired: 2000
Original: $10 • Value: $19

2905.
Indy (Fall 2000)
#91757-15 • 5" • BF
Issued: 2000 • Retired: 2001
Original: $10 • Value: $12

2906. 53
Irving Poochberg
#5420 • 14" • JB
Issued: 1989 • Retired: 1992
Original: $16 • Value: $167

2907.
Martin Muttsky (smooth fur)
#5400 • 11" • JB
Issued: 1989 • Retired: 1992
Original: $14 • Value: $130

2908.
Martin Muttsky (regular plush)
#5400 • 11" • JB
Issued: 1989 • Retired: 1992
Original: $14 • Value: $105

2909.
Martin Muttsky (dark brown)
#5400 • 11" • JB
Issued: 1989 • Retired: 1992
Original: $14 • Value: $110

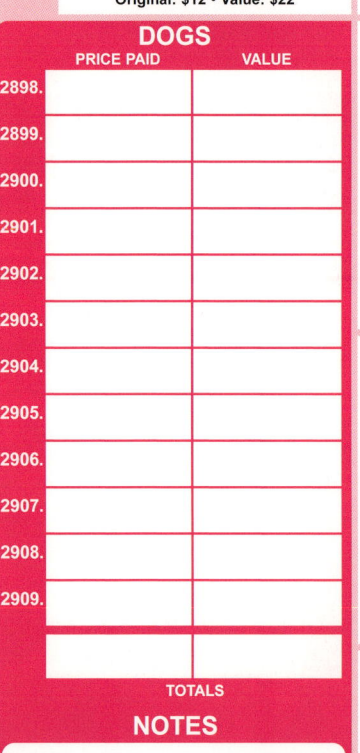

DOGS

	PRICE PAID	VALUE
2898.		
2899.		
2900.		
2901.		
2902.		
2903.		
2904.		
2905.		
2906.		
2907.		
2908.		
2909.		
TOTALS		

NOTES

Critters (Dogs)

2910.
Merritt M. Muttsky
#5401 • 11" • JB
Issued: 1989 • Retired: 1991
Original: $14 • Value: $134

2911.
Merton Flatberg
#5690-08 • 8" • FL
Issued: 1994 • Retired: 1997
Original: $12 • Value: $30

2912.
Mozart B. Barken
#540302 • 16" • JB
Issued: 2002 • Retired: 2002
Original: $29 • Value: $29

2913.
Mystery Dawg
#unknown • 10"
Issued: 1990 • Retired: 1990
Original: $15 • Value: $159

2914.
Northrop Flatberg
#5690-01 • 8" • FL
Issued: 1994 • Retired: 1999
Original: $12 • Value: $27

2915.
Parker B. Pooch
#54050-08 • 10" • JB
Issued: 2000 • Retired: 2002
Original: $13 • Value: $15

2916.
Pat McPunkin
#904323 • 8" • TJ
Issued: 2004 • Current
Original: $12 • Value: $R/E

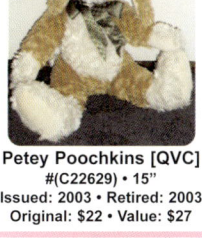
2917.
Petey Poochkins [QVC]
#(C22629) • 15"
Issued: 2003 • Retired: 2003
Original: $22 • Value: $27

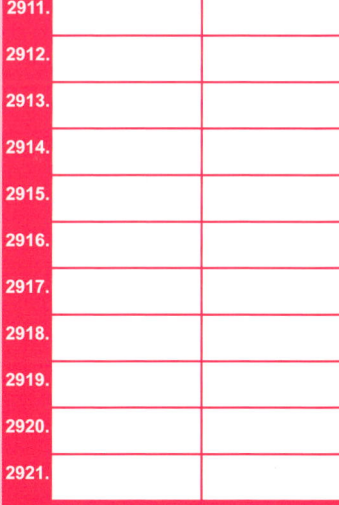

DOGS	PRICE PAID	VALUE
2910.		
2911.		
2912.		
2913.		
2914.		
2915.		
2916.		
2917.		
2918.		
2919.		
2920.		
2921.		
TOTALS		

NOTES

2918.
Petey von Pupp [GCC]
#94887GCC • 6"
Issued: 2000 • Retired: 2000
Original: $12 • Value: $20

2919.
Philo Puddlemaker
#56551-07 • 12" • BA
Issued: 1999 • Retired: 2002
Original: $14 • Value: $16

2920.
Have You Seen Me?
Preston Flatberg
#56961-01 • 12" • FL
Issued: 1996 • Retired: 1996
Original: $N/E • Value: $28

2921.
Ralph Poochstein
#5400-10 • 10" • JB
Issued: 1995 • Retired: 1997
Original: $14 • Value: $34

Critters (Dogs)

2922.
Rocky B. Barken
#541204 • 10" • AS
Issued: 2004 • Current
Original: $13 • Value: $R/E

2923. 53
Roosevelt
#6108D • 15" • TJ
Issued: 1989 • Retired: 1991
Original: $27 • Value: $218
Comes with flag.

2924.
Salty [Casual Living]
#unknown • 10"
Issued: 1995 • Retired: 1995
Original: $25 • Value: $80

2925.
Scout P. Poochley
#540402 • 12" • JB
Issued: 2002 • Retired: 2002
Original: $15 • Value: $15

2926.
Shiloh P. Poochdale
#541201 • 10"
Issued: 2003 • Retired: 2003
Original: $14 • Value: $14

2927.
Simon T. Poochley
#54052-08 • 10" • JB
Issued: 2001 • Retired: 2002
Original: $13 • Value: $16

2928.
Snoozer Bedoozer [QVC]
#(C40594) • 12"
Issued: 2001 • Retired: 2001
Original: $17 • Value: $25

2929.
Snuffy B. Barker
#5405 • 10" • JB
Issued: 2000 • Retired: 2001
Original: $13 • Value: $13

2930. 83
Speed Poochberg (smooth fur)
#5402 • 11" • JB
Issued: 1989 • Retired: 1992
Original: $14 • Value: $133

2931. 83
Speed Poochberg (regular plush)
#5402 • 11" • JB
Issued: 1989 • Retired: 1992
Original: $14 • Value: $110

2932.
Stewart MacGregor
#91400 • 10" • TJ
Issued: 2000 • Retired: 2002
Original: $15 • Value: $15

2933.
T. Foley Wuzzie
#595104-05 • 5" • TF
Issued: 2000 • Retired: 2000
Original: $9 • Value: $13

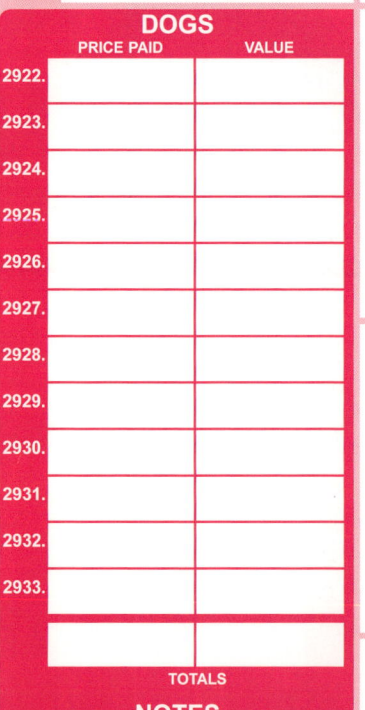

DOGS

	PRICE PAID	VALUE
2922.		
2923.		
2924.		
2925.		
2926.		
2927.		
2928.		
2929.		
2930.		
2931.		
2932.		
2933.		
	TOTALS	

NOTES

Critters (Dogs, Donkeys)

2934.
Toby F. Wuzzie
#595500-08 • 3" • TF
Issued: 1999 • Retired: 2000
Original: $7 • Value: $16

2935.
Trixie B. Barken
#904343 • 8" • TJ
Issued: 2004 • Current
Original: $12 • Value: $R/E

2936.
Tucker P. Woofensniff
#541202 • 10" • AS
Issued: 2003 • Current
Original: $14 • Value: $R/E

2937.
Walker
#5655-08 • 12"
Issued: 1994 • Retired: 1997
Original: $16 • Value: $38

2938.
Wheatley B. Barker
#541203 • 12" • AS
Issued: 2004 • Current
Original: $18 • Value: $R/E

2939.
Woolfie P. Poorpooch [QVC]
#932064 (C59852) • 10"
Issued: 2001 • Retired: 2001
Original: $17 • Value: $24

2940.
Zsa-Zsa Yippsalot
#54052-01 • 10" • JB
Issued: 2002 • Retired: 2002
Original: $14 • Value: $20

Donkeys

2941.
Brayburn
#5670 • 8" • FL
Issued: 1996 • Retired: 1997
Original: $13 • Value: $29

2942.
Eeyore [Disney]
#unknown • 10"
Issued: 1999 • Retired: 1999
Original: $30 • Value: $45

2943.
Eeyore (Winter Holiday) [Disney]
#unknown • 12"
Issued: 2000 • Retired: 2000
Original: $45 • Value: $68

2944.
Eeyore (plaid vest) [Disney]
#95981DSP • 11"
Issued: 2001 • Retired: 2001
Original: $30 • Value: $42

DOGS	PRICE PAID	VALUE
2934.		
2935.		
2936.		
2937.		
2938.		
2939.		
2940.		

DONKEYS	PRICE PAID	VALUE
2941.		
2942.		
2943.		
2944.		
TOTALS		

NOTES

Critters (Donkeys, Doves, Ducks, Elephants)

2945.
Eeyore (Costume Party) [Disney]
#unknown • 8"
Issued: 2002 • Retired: 2002
Original: $30 • Value: $39

2946.
Eeyore (Cozy Holiday) [Disney]
#9599DSP • 8"
Issued: 2002 • Retired: 2002
Original: $30 • Value: $39

2947.
Eeyore (Holiday Caroling) [Disney]
#95912DSP • 10"
Issued: 2003 • Retired: 2003
Original: $30 • Value: $35

Doves

2948.
Coo and Lou
#568017 • 2½" • NO
Issued: 2003 • Current
Original: $6 • Value: $R/E

Ducks

2949.
Donna Duck
#590068 • 8" • MB
LE of 5000 • Issued: 2004 • Retired: 2004
Original: $20 • Value: $45

2950.
Ducklebuns
#825320 • 4½"
Issued: 2004 • Current
Original: $5 • Value: $R/E

2951.
Monsieur Jodibear
#92000-21 • 6" • AR
Issued: 2003 • Retired: 2003
Original: $12 • Value: $12

2952.
Webb Q. Yachtley
#91603 • 8" • TJ
Issued: 2002 • Retired: 2004
Original: $13 • Value: $13

Elephants

2953.
Hannibel Trunkster
#55223 • 16" • AM
Issued: 2001 • Retired: 2001
Original: $40 • Value: $48

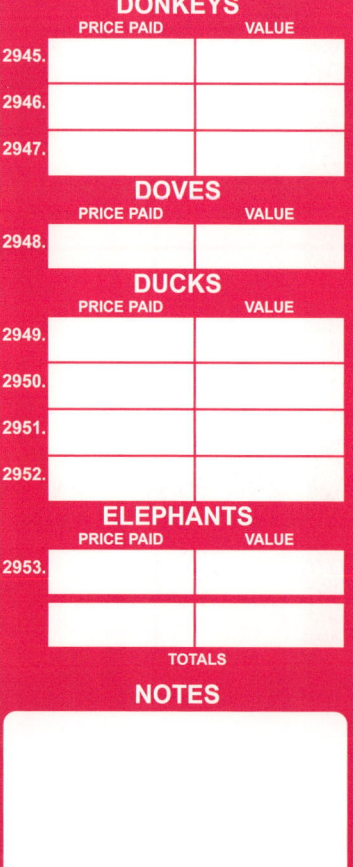

DONKEYS	PRICE PAID	VALUE
2945.		
2946.		
2947.		

DOVES	PRICE PAID	VALUE
2948.		

DUCKS	PRICE PAID	VALUE
2949.		
2950.		
2951.		
2952.		

ELEPHANTS	PRICE PAID	VALUE
2953.		

TOTALS

NOTES

Critters (Elephants, Foxes)

2954.
Isadora T. Lightfoot
#913201 • 8" • TJ
Issued: 2001 • Retired: 2002
Original: $18 • Value: $22

2955.
Newton
#5665 • 8" • FL
Issued: 1996 • Retired: 1997
Original: $13 • Value: $40

2956.
Nicholai A. Pachydermsky
#5528-06 • 16" • AM
Issued: 1993 • Retired: 1994
Original: $28 • Value: $243

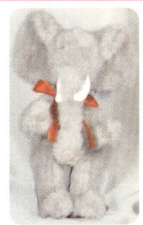
2957.
Olivia A. Pachydermsky
#5527-06 • 10" • AM
Issued: 1993 • Retired: 1994
Original: $14 • Value: $138

2958.
Omar A. Pachydermsky
#5526-06 • 7½" • AM
Issued: 1993 • Retired: 1994
Original: $8 • Value: $90

2959.
P. Gallery Trunkster
#55250 • 10" • AM
Issued: 2000 • Retired: 2002
Original: $15 • Value: $17

2960.
P. Gallery Trunkster [SFMB]
#55250SF • 10"
Issued: 2002 • Retired: 2002
Original: $25 • Value: $32
♪ Entry of the Gladiator ♪

2961.
Packy and Dermah Trunkspace
#568005 • 3½" • NO
Issued: 2002 • Current
Original: $10 • Value: $R/E

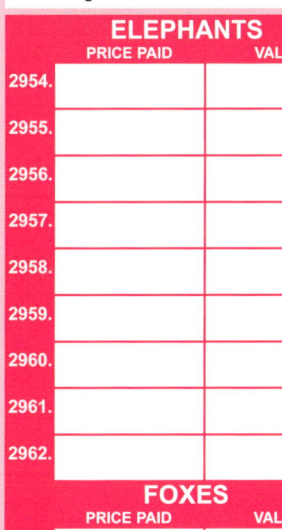

2962.
Tutu F. Wuzzie
#596011 • 3" • TF
Issued: 2001 • Retired: 2002
Original: $8 • Value: $10

Foxes

2963.
Ernie Z. Foxworthy
#913968 • 6" • TJ
Issued: 2001 • Retired: 2001
Original: $10 • Value: $12

2964.
Redmond Foxworthy [QVC]
#(C63342) • 10"
Issued: 1999 • Retired: 1999
Original: $13 • Value: $24

ELEPHANTS

	PRICE PAID	VALUE
2954.		
2955.		
2956.		
2957.		
2958.		
2959.		
2960.		
2961.		
2962.		

FOXES

	PRICE PAID	VALUE
2963.		
2964.		

TOTALS

NOTES

Critters (Foxes, Frogs)

2965. Reggie Foxworthy
#55210 • 8" • AM
Issued: 1999 • Retired: 2002
Original: $9 • Value: $12

Frogs

2966. Bobber
#904133 • 6"
Issued: 2003 • Retired: 2003
Original: $10 • Value: $10

2967. Ezra R. Ribbit
#566470 • 6" • BA
Issued: 1998 • Retired: 2002
Original: $5 • Value: $9

2968. G. Kelly Ribbit
#91320 • 9" • BA
Issued: 1999 • Retired: 2001
Original: $20 • Value: $24
♪ Singin' in the Rain ♪

2969. Jacque Le Grenouille
#5018 • 8" • WB
Issued: 1993 • Retired: 1995
Original: $10 • Value: $82

2970. Jeremiah B. Ribbit
#566450 • 9½" • BA
Issued: 1997 • Retired: 1999
Original: $12 • Value: $20

2971. Nikali Q. Ribbit [QVC]
#unknown • 9½"
Issued: 1997 • Retired: 1997
Original: $16 • Value: $21

2972. Rachael Q. Ribbit
#566340 • 12" • BA
Issued: 1997 • Retired: 2000
Original: $21 • Value: $28

2973. Ripple
#904134 • 4" • JB
Issued: 2003 • Retired: 2003
Original: $5 • Value: $5

2974. S.C. Ribbit
#917309 • 12" • BA
Issued: 1998 • Retired: 1999
Original: $25 • Value: $36

2975. Taddy
#561942 • 6" • JB
Issued: 2004 • Current
Original: $7 • Value: $R/E

FOXES	PRICE PAID	VALUE
2965.		

FROGS	PRICE PAID	VALUE
2966.		
2967.		
2968.		
2969.		
2970.		
2971.		
2972.		
2973.		
2974.		
2975.		
TOTALS		

NOTES

Geese

2976.
Mother Goosebeary
#91780 • 10"
Issued: 2003 • Current
Original: $30 • Value: $R/E

Giraffes

2977.
Milton Q. Stiltwalker [QVC]
#(C107594) • 10"
Issued: 2002 • Retired: 2002
Original: $15 • Value: $20

2978.
Stretch and Skye Longnecker
#568003 • 4½" • NO
Issued: 2002 • Current
Original: $10 • Value: $R/E

2979.
Wilt Stiltwalker
#55221 • 14" • AM
Issued: 2001 • Retired: 2002
Original: $19 • Value: $23

Gorillas

2980.
Jake, Jay & Jette Magilla [QVC]
#(C46238) • 6"
Issued: 1998 • Retired: 1998
Original: $22 • Value: $45

2981.
Joe Magilla
#5525 • 11" • AM
Issued: 1995 • Retired: 1998
Original: $14 • Value: $30

2982.
Kirby Lovebug
#82044 • 6"
Issued: 2003 • Current
Original: $10 • Value: $R/E

2983.
Mike Magilla
#55251 • 8" • AM
Issued: 1998 • Retired: 1999
Original: $12 • Value: $23

2984.
Viola Magillacuddy
#91351 • 8" • TJ
Issued: 1999 • Retired: 1999
Original: $14 • Value: $28

Critters (Guinea Pigs, Hares)

Guinea Pigs

Hares

2985. George
#55215 • 6" • JB
Issued: 2001 • Retired: 2002
Original: $9 • Value: $15

2986. Alexandra (short ears - small feet)
#5730 • 14" without ears • AS
Issued: 1991 • Retired: 1991
Original: $20 • Value: $149

2987. Alexandra (big ears - small feet)
#5730 • 14" without ears • AS
Issued: 1992 • Retired: 1993
Original: $20 • Value: $98

2988. Alexandra (big ears - big feet)
#5730 • 14" without ears • AS
Issued: 1993 • Retired: 1995
Original: $20 • Value: $71

2989. Alice (old face)
#5750 • 7½" without ears • AS
Issued: 1992 • Retired: 1999
Original: $7 • Value: $28

2990. Alice (new face)
#1101-08 • 11" without ears • AS
Issued: 1993 • Retired: 1999
Original: $7 • Value: $21

2991. Alice Hopplebeary [Boscovs]
#94542BV • 9" without ears
Issued: 2000 • Retired: 2000
Original: $18 • Value: $33

2992. Allison Babbit
#9166 • 14" with ears • TJ
Issued: 1994 • Retired: 1998
Original: $20 • Value: $29

2993. Alison Babbit [SFMB]
#41-72141 • 9" without ears
Issued: 1998 • Retired: 1998
Original: $25 • Value: $46
♪ I Only Have Eyes For You ♪

2994. Alpine [SLE]
#unknown • 6" without ears
Issued: 1998 • Retired: 1998
Original: $10 • Value: $19

GUINEA PIGS	PRICE PAID	VALUE
2985.		

HARES	PRICE PAID	VALUE
2986.		
2987.		
2988.		
2989.		
2990.		
2991.		
2992.		
2993.		
2994.		
TOTALS		

NOTES

Critters (Hares)

2995.
Alvin Q. Hopster
#522001 • 12" without ears • AS
Issued: 2004 • Current
Original: $18 • Value: $R/E

2996.
Amarretto
#9110 • 17" with ears • TJ
Issued: 1995 • Retired: 1997
Original: $19 • Value: $45

2997.
Amelia R. Hare
(original old face - smooth fur)
#5203 • 9" without ears • JB
Issued: 1988 • Retired: 1989
Original: $14 • Value: $67

2998.
Amelia R. Hare (old face)
#5203 • 12" without ears • JB
Issued: 1989 • Retired: 1990
Original: $14 • Value: $52

2999.
Amelia R. Hare (new face)
#5203 • 10" without ears • JB
Issued: 1991 • Retired: 1998
Original: $14 • Value: $29

3000.
Amelia R. Hare (modern face)
#5203 • 10" without ears • JB
Issued: 1991 • Retired: 1998
Original: $14 • Value: $25

3001.
Anastasia (nekkid)
#5876 • 14" without ears • HT
Issued: 1992 • Retired: 1992
Original: $32 • Value: $235

3002.
Anastasia (dressed)
#912081 • 12" without ears • TJ
Issued: 1998 • Retired: 2001
Original: $26 • Value: $45

3003.
Anisette
#9109-07 • 12" without ears • TJ
Issued: 1996 • Retired: 1996
Original: $12 • Value: $38

3004.
Anissa [SLE]
#unknown • 9" without ears
Issued: 1998 • Retired: 1998
Original: $13 • Value: $39

3005.
Anna
#5870 • 6" without ears • HT
Issued: 1992 • Retired: 1993
Original: $9 • Value: $90

3006.
Anne (old face)
#5734 • 7½" without ears • AS
Issued: 1991 • Retired: 1993
Original: $7 • Value: $32

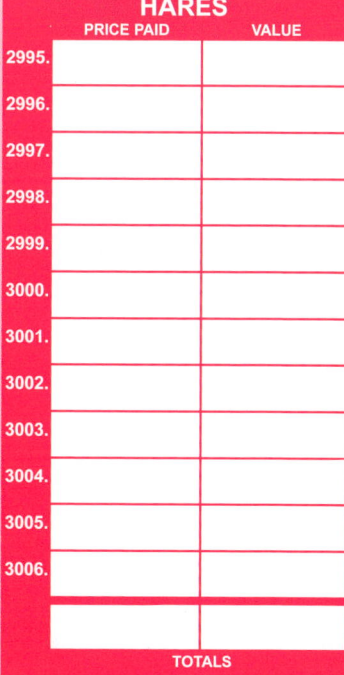

HARES	PRICE PAID	VALUE
2995.		
2996.		
2997.		
2998.		
2999.		
3000.		
3001.		
3002.		
3003.		
3004.		
3005.		
3006.		
TOTALS		

NOTES

Critters (Hares)

3007.
Anne (new face)
#5734 • 7½" without ears • AS
Issued: 1993 • Retired: 1997
Original: $7 • Value: $30

3008.
Annie & Jennifer Hopkins [QVC]
#(C56957) • 8" without ears
Issued: 1999 • Retired: 1999
Original: $24 • Value: $36

3009.
Archer
#91544 • 10" without ears • TJ
Issued: 1996 • Retired: 1998
Original: $24 • Value: $40

3010.
Ashley
#9132 • 12" without ears • TJ
Issued: 1995 • Retired: 1998
Original: $20 • Value: $29

3011.
Ashley [SFMB]
#41-66847 • 14" without ears
Issued: 1997 • Retired: 1997
Original: $25 • Value: $40
♪ Love Me Tender ♪
2 versions.

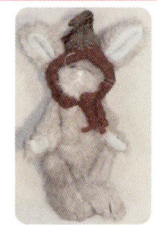

3012.
Aubergine
#9107 • 7½" without ears • TJ
Issued: 1995 • Retired: 1998
Original: $12 • Value: $22

3013.
Auntie Adina
#9218H • 14" without ears • TJ
LE of 500 • Issued: 1994 • Retired: 1994
Original: $70 • Value: $276

3014.
Auntie Babbit
#91660 • 12" without ears • TJ
Issued: 1996 • Retired: 1998
Original: $30 • Value: $46

3015.
Auntie Harestein (burgundy print)
#unknown • 14" without ears
LE of 350 • Issued: 1993 • Retired: 1993
Original: $70 • Value: $348

3016.
Auntie Harestein (tan print)
#unknown • 14" without ears
LE of 350 • Issued: 1993 • Retired: 1993
Original: $70 • Value: $343

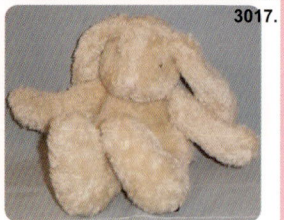

3017.
Babs
#5650-09 • 12" without ears • BA
Issued: 1994 • Retired: 1998
Original: $16 • Value: $33

3018.
Have You Seen Me?
Baby
#6105H • 14" with ears • TJ
Issued: 1990 • Retired: 1991
Original: $20 • Value: $256

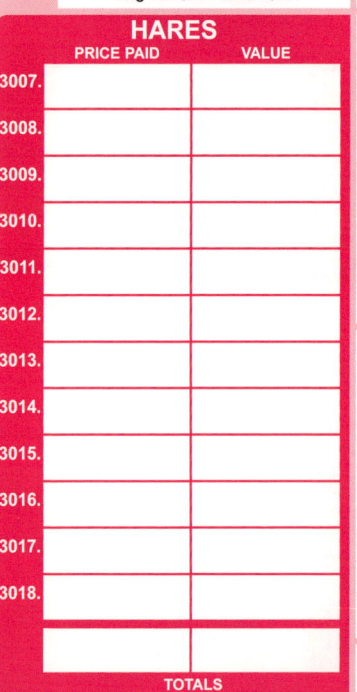

HARES

	PRICE PAID	VALUE
3007.		
3008.		
3009.		
3010.		
3011.		
3012.		
3013.		
3014.		
3015.		
3016.		
3017.		
3018.		
	TOTALS	

NOTES

Critters (Hares)

3019.

Have You Seen Me?

Beatrice
#6168H • 14" without ears • TJ
Issued: 1991 • Retired: 1991
Original: $63 • Value: $305

3020.

Bedford Boneah
#58091-05 • 17" without ears
Issued: 1998 • Retired: 1999
Original: $23 • Value: $27

3021.

Bedford Boneah II
#582910-05 • 14" without ears
Issued: 2000 • Retired: 2000
Original: $20 • Value: $24

3022.

Beecher B. Bunny
#5250-10 • 10" without ears • JB
Issued: 1996 • Retired: 1998
Original: $16 • Value: $35

3023.

Have You Seen Me?

Belle [Harry & David]
#945634 • 8" without ears
Issued: 1998 • Retired: 1998
Original: $20 • Value: $35

3024.

Benson T. Hopabout
#916503 • 10" without ears • TJ
Issued: 2002 • Retired: 2002
Original: $19 • Value: $22

3025.

Bixie
#56501-10 • 12" without ears • BA
Issued: 1998 • Retired: 2000
Original: $14 • Value: $20

3026.

Bopper
#5748 • 14" without ears • HD
Issued: 1991 • Retired: 1992
Original: $27 • Value: $175

3027.

Bramble B. Thumperton
#58340-03 • 12" without ears • AS
Issued: 2002 • Retired: 2002
Original: $19 • Value: $27

3028.

Brigette Delapain
#91691 • 10" without ears • TJ
Issued: 1996 • Retired: 1998
Original: $21 • Value: $27

3029.

Brigham Boneah
#58291 • 15" without ears
Issued: 1997 • Retired: 1999
Original: $23 • Value: $28

3030.

Brigham Boneah II
#582910 • 14" without ears
Issued: 2000 • Retired: 2000
Original: $20 • Value: $29

HARES	PRICE PAID	VALUE
3019.		
3020.		
3021.		
3022.		
3023.		
3024.		
3025.		
3026.		
3027.		
3028.		
3029.		
3030.		
TOTALS		

NOTES

Critters (Hares)

3031.
Briton R. Hare (smooth fur)
#5204 • 15" without ears • JB
Issued: 1989 • Retired: 1991
Original: $20 • Value: $173

3032.
Briton R. Hare (regular plush)
#5204 • 15" without ears • JB
Issued: 1989 • Retired: 1991
Original: $20 • Value: $141

3033.
Brittany [Dillards]
#94711DL • 8" without ears
Issued: 1997 • Retired: 1997
Original: $12 • Value: $28

3034.
Brittney Q. Hopplebuns
#916633 • 8" without ears • TJ
Issued: 2002 • Retired: 2002
Original: $15 • Value: $15

3035.
Buffie Bunnyhop
#522700-03 • 8" without ears • JB
Issued: 2000 • Retired: 2000
Original: $9 • Value: $11

3036.
Bumpus
#5746 • 9" without ears • HD
Issued: 1991 • Retired: 1992
Original: $14 • Value: $119

3037.
Bunnie B. Springbeary [Longaberger]
#94625LB • 8" without ears
Issued: 2003 • Retired: 2003
Original: $20 • Value: $24

3038.
Bunnylove Rarebit
#91314 • 9" without ears • TJ
Issued: 1996 • Retired: 1998
Original: $20 • Value: $38

3039.
Camilla
#5732 • 7½" without ears • AS
Issued: 1993 • Retired: 1998
Original: $7 • Value: $19

3040.
Cara Z. Bunnyhugs
#91649 • 9" without ears • TJ
Issued: 2000 • Retired: 2000
Original: $12 • Value: $24

3041.
Carlin Wabbit
#9115 • 8" without ears • TJ
Issued: 1995 • Retired: 1998
Original: $13 • Value: $32

3042.
Carly Crystalfrost
#904186 • 10" without ears • TJ
Issued: 2003 • Retired: 2003
Original: $20 • Value: $20

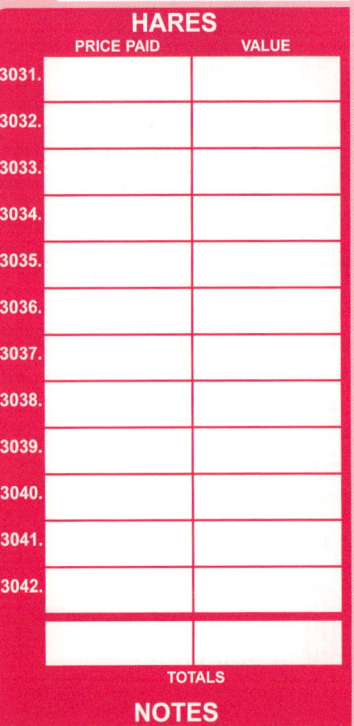

HARES

	PRICE PAID	VALUE
3031.		
3032.		
3033.		
3034.		
3035.		
3036.		
3037.		
3038.		
3039.		
3040.		
3041.		
3042.		
TOTALS		

NOTES

Critters (Hares)

3043.
Cassie B. Nibbles
#58290-01 • 14" without ears • AS
Issued: 2002 • Retired: 2002
Original: $20 • Value: $20

3044.
Cathy J. Hiphop
#917030 • 6" without ears • TJ
Issued: 2000 • Retired: 2000
Original: $10 • Value: $22

3045.
Cecilia
#5648-01 • 8" without ears • BA
Issued: 1993 • Retired: 1998
Original: $11 • Value: $22

3046.
Chantanay [SLE]
#unknown • 12" without ears
Issued: 1998 • Retired: 1998
Original: $19 • Value: $33

3047.
Chardonnay
#9106 • 7½" without ears • TJ
Issued: 1995 • Retired: 1998
Original: $12 • Value: $29

3048.
Charlotte R. Hare (old face)
#5224 • 14" without ears • JB
Issued: 1992 • Retired: 1993
Original: $20 • Value: $54

3049.
Charlotte R. Hare (new face)
#5224 • 14" without ears • JB
Issued: 1993 • Retired: 1998
Original: $20 • Value: $43

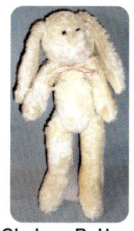

3050.
Chelsea R. Hare
#5217-01 • 14" without ears • JB
Issued: 1993 • Retired: 1998
Original: $20 • Value: $30

HARES		
	PRICE PAID	VALUE
3043.		
3044.		
3045.		
3046.		
3047.		
3048.		
3049.		
3050.		
3051.		
3052.		
3053.		
3054.		
	TOTALS	

NOTES

3051.
Chesterfield Q. Burpee
#91546 • 8" without ears • TJ
Issued: 1996 • Retired: 1998
Original: $21 • Value: $35

3052.
Chloe [Elder Beerman]
#94691EL • 11" without ears
Issued: 2000 • Retired: 2000
Original: $22 • Value: $40

3053.
Chloe Fitzhare
#5240-03 • 17" without ears • JB
Issued: 1996 • Retired: 1998
Original: $19 • Value: $38

3054.
Clara R. Hare
#5227-08 • 8" without ears • JB
Issued: 1994 • Retired: 1998
Original: $10 • Value: $24

Critters (Hares)

3055.
Clarrisse
#91208 • 16" without ears • TJ
Issued: 1997 • Retired: 1998
Original: $40 • Value: $52

3056.
Columbine Dubois
#91402 • 6" without ears • TJ
Issued: 1996 • Retired: 1998
Original: $12 • Value: $24

3057.
Cora B. Bunny (old face)
#5212 • 20" with ears • JB
Issued: 1989 • Retired: 1990
Original: $29 • Value: $159

3058.
Cora B. Bunny (new face)
#5212 • 20" with ears • JB
Issued: 1991 • Retired: 1994
Original: $29 • Value: $145

3059.
Cordilia R. Hare
#5205 • 15" without ears • JB
Issued: 1989 • Retired: 1992
Original: $20 • Value: $115

3060.
Cossette D. Lapine
#916601 • 10" without ears • TJ
Issued: 1997 • Retired: 1999
Original: $27 • Value: $32

HARES

	PRICE PAID	VALUE
3055.		
3056.		
3057.		
3058.		
3059.		
3060.		
3061.		
3062.		
3063.		
3064.		
3065.		
3066.		
TOTALS		

NOTES

3061.
Cotton Bunnytoes
#522801-08 • 8" without ears • JB
Issued: 2002 • Retired: 2002
Original: $10 • Value: $10

3062.
Cousin Rose Anjanette
#91112-01 • 7½" without ears • TJ
Issued: 1998 • Retired: 2000
Original: $12 • Value: $20

3063.
Curley Lapin (old face)
#5207 • 14" with ears • JB
Issued: 1989 • Retired: 1990
Original: $14 • Value: $82

3064.
Curly Lapin (new face)
#5207 • 14" with ears • JB
Issued: 1991 • Retired: 1995
Original: $14 • Value: $71

3065.
Dabney P. Powderfoot
#58290-10 • 14" without ears • JB
Issued: 2001 • Retired: 2001
Original: $20 • Value: $24

3066.
Daisey
#9109 • 12" without ears • TJ
Issued: 1995 • Retired: 1998
Original: $12 • Value: $22

Critters (Hares)

3067.

Daphne R. Hare
#5225 • 14" without ears • JB
Issued: 1992 • Retired: 1998
Original: $20 • Value: $38

3068.

Darcy Babbit
#9178 • 14" with ears • TJ
Issued: 1993 • Retired: 1995
Original: $18 • Value: $107

3069.

Darcy Babbit II
#9178-01 • 14" with ears
Issued: 1994 • Retired: 1994
Original: $N/E • Value: $125

3070.

Darcy Babbit II (variation)
#9178-01 • 14" with ears
Issued: 1994 • Retired: 1994
Original: $N/E • Value: $155

3071.

Delanie D. Hopplebuns
#912078 • 16" without ears • TJ
Issued: 2001 • Retired: 2001
Original: $36 • Value: $43

3072.

Delia R. Hare
#5202 • 12" without ears • JB
Issued: 1992 • Retired: 1992
Original: $14 • Value: $142

3073.

Demi (chenille)
#9112 • 10½" without ears • TJ
Issued: 1994 • Retired: 1997
Original: $20 • Value: $30

3074.

Demi II (regular plush)
#9112-00 • 12" without ears • TJ
Issued: 1995 • Retired: 1997
Original: $21 • Value: $38

3075.

Diana (nekkid)
#5738 • 10½" with ears • AS
Issued: 1991 • Retired: 1993
Original: $14 • Value: $43

3076.

Diana (red sweater and hat)
#9181-01 • 8" without ears • TJ
Issued: 1996 • Retired: 1997
Original: $21 • Value: $36

3077.

Diana (a.k.a. Elizabeth)
#98041 • 7½" without ears • TJ
Issued: 1996 • Retired: 1996
Original: $12 • Value: $26

3078.

Dippletoes
#825316 • 10" without ears
Issued: 2004 • Current
Original: $15 • Value: $R/E

HARES	PRICE PAID	VALUE
3067.		
3068.		
3069.		
3070.		
3071.		
3072.		
3073.		
3074.		
3075.		
3076.		
3077.		
3078.		
TOTALS		

NOTES

284

Critters (Hares)

3079.
Dippy D. Hopplebuns
#904142 • 10" without ears
Issued: 2003 • Retired: 2003
Original: $15 • Value: $15

3080.
Dixie
#56541-08 • 16" without ears • BA
Issued: 1996 • Retired: 1998
Original: $24 • Value: $32

3081.
Dolly Q. Bunnycombe
#590150-01 • 10" without ears • MB
Issued: 1998 • Retired: 1998
Original: $24 • Value: $43

3082.
Donna
#1200-01 • 8" without ears • CC
Issued: 1994 • Retired: 1998
Original: $7 • Value: $20

3083.
Doppity
#825305 • 6" without ears
Issued: 2003 • Retired: 2003
Original: $10 • Value: $10

3084.
Dora B. Bunny
#5211 • 20" with ears • JB
Issued: 1989 • Retired: 1994
Original: $29 • Value: $147

3085.
Dottie Q. Hopples
#825301 • 12" without ears
Issued: 2003 • Retired: 2003
Original: $19 • Value: $19

3086.
Dudley Hopson
#91663 • 8" without ears • TJ
Issued: 1999 • Retired: 2000
Original: $12 • Value: $16

3087.
Dutch [SLE]
#unknown • 12" without ears
Issued: 1998 • Retired: 1998
Original: $20 • Value: $42

3088.
Earhart Harington
#590086-01 • 4½" without ears • MB
Issued: 1999 • Retired: 2000
Original: $10 • Value: $18

3089.
Edina Flatstein
#5685-05 • 8" without ears • FL
Issued: 1996 • Retired: 2000
Original: $13 • Value: $26

3090.
Edith Q. Harington
#590160-03 • 9" without ears • MB
Issued: 1999 • Retired: 1999
Original: $26 • Value: $35

HARES

	PRICE PAID	VALUE
3079.		
3080.		
3081.		
3082.		
3083.		
3084.		
3085.		
3086.		
3087.		
3088.		
3089.		
3090.		
TOTALS		

NOTES

Critters (Hares)

3091.
Edith Q. Harington II
#5901600-03 • 9" without ears • MB
Issued: 2000 • Retired: 2001
Original: $30 • Value: $30

3092.
Egglebert
#825302 • 10" without ears
Issued: 2003 • Retired: 2003
Original: $14 • Value: $14

3093.
Eleanor
#5737-01 • 10½" with ears • AS
Issued: 1995 • Retired: 1997
Original: $14 • Value: $35

3094.
Elizabeth
#5733 • 7½" without ears • AS
Issued: 1991 • Retired: 1999
Original: $7 • Value: $21

3095.
Elli Bean [Longaberger]
#94634LB • 10" without ears • TJ
Issued: 2001 • Retired: 2001
Original: $19 • Value: $75

3096.
Ellie [SLE]
#unknown • 7½" without ears • TJ
Issued: 1998 • Retired: 1998
Original: $11 • Value: $23

3097.
Ellie Hopplebuns
#904145 • 6" without ears
Issued: 2003 • Retired: 2003
Original: $10 • Value: $10

3098.
Eloise R. Hare
#5230-10 • 8½" without ears • JB
Issued: 1994 • Retired: 1999
Original: $12 • Value: $21

3099.
Elsinore
#5732-05 • 7½" without ears • AS
Issued: 1996 • Retired: 1999
Original: $7 • Value: $15

3100. **41**
Emily Babbit (Spring 1993)
#9185 • 8" without ears • BF
Issued: 1993 • Retired: 1994
Original: $20 • Value: $260

3101.
Emily Babbit (Fall 1993)
#9158 • 8" without ears • BF
Issued: 1993 • Retired: 1994
Original: $24 • Value: $244

3102. **42**
Emily Babbit
(Spring 1994 - white sweater)
#9150 • 8" without ears • BF
Issued: 1994 • Retired: 1995
Original: $27 • Value: $75

HARES		
	PRICE PAID	VALUE
3091.		
3092.		
3093.		
3094.		
3095.		
3096.		
3097.		
3098.		
3099.		
3100.		
3101.		
3102.		
TOTALS		

NOTES

Critters (Hares)

3103.
Emily Babbit
(Spring 1994 - blue sweater)
#9150 • 8" without ears • BF
Issued: 1994 • Retired: 1994
Original: $20 • Value: $81

3104.
Emily Babbit (Spring 1995)
#9150-01 • 8" without ears • BF
Issued: 1995 • Retired: 1996
Original: $20 • Value: $59

3105.
Emily Babbit (Fall 1995)
#9150-04 • 8" without ears • BF
Issued: 1995 • Retired: 1996
Original: $20 • Value: $51

3106.
Emily Babbit (Spring 1996)
#9150-05 • 8" without ears • BF
Issued: 1996 • Retired: 1997
Original: $24 • Value: $44

3107.
Emily Babbit (Fall 1996)
#9150-06 • 8" without ears • BF
Issued: 1996 • Retired: 1998
Original: $25 • Value: $38

3108.
Emily Babbit (Spring 1997)
#9150-07 • 8" without ears • BF
Issued: 1997 • Retired: 1998
Original: $24 • Value: $36

3109.
Emily Babbit (Fall 1997)
#9150-08 • 8" without ears • BF
Issued: 1997 • Retired: 1998
Original: $25 • Value: $34

3110.
Emily Babbit (Spring 1998)
#9150-09 • 8" without ears • BF
Issued: 1998 • Retired: 1999
Original: $27 • Value: $32

3111.
Emily Babbit (Spring 1998 squiggles on hat) [QVC]
#9150-09 • 8" without ears • BF
Issued: 1998 • Retired: 1998
Original: $27 • Value: $37

3112.
Emily Babbit (Fall 1998)
#9150-10 • 8" without ears • BF
Issued: 1998 • Retired: 1999
Original: $27 • Value: $32

3113.
Emily Babbit (Spring 1999)
#9150-11 • 8" without ears • BF
Issued: 1999 • Retired: 1999
Original: $27 • Value: $34

3114.
Emily Babbit (Fall 1999)
#9150-12 • 8" without ears • BF
Issued: 1999 • Retired: 1999
Original: $18 • Value: $33

HARES

	PRICE PAID	VALUE
3103.		
3104.		
3105.		
3106.		
3107.		
3108.		
3109.		
3110.		
3111.		
3112.		
3113.		
3114.		
TOTALS		

NOTES

Critters (Hares)

3115.
Emily Babbit (Spring 2000)
#9150-14 • 8" without ears • BF
Issued: 2000 • Retired: 2000
Original: $23 • Value: $32

3116.
Emily Babbit (Fall 2000)
#9150-15 • 8" without ears • BF
Issued: 2000 • Retired: 2001
Original: $24 • Value: $25

3117.
Emily Babbit (Spring 2001)
#9150-16 • 8" without ears • BF
Issued: 2001 • Retired: 2001
Original: $23 • Value: $28

3118.
Emily Babbit (Fall 2001)
#9150-17 • 8" without ears • BF
Issued: 2001 • Retired: 2002
Original: $19 • Value: $23

3119.
Emily Babbit (Spring 2002)
#9150-18 • 8" without ears • BF
Issued: 2002 • Retired: 2002
Original: $19 • Value: $25

3120.
Emily Babbit (Spring 2003)
#9150-20 • 8" without ears • BF
LE • Issued: 2003 • Retired: 2003
Original: $18 • Value: $18

3121.
Emily Babbit (Spring 2004)
#9150-22 • 8" without ears • BF
Issued: 2004 • To Be Retired: N/E
Original: $15 • Value: $15

3122.
Emily R. Hare
#5226 • 14" without ears • JB
Issued: 1992 • Retired: 1993
Original: $20 • Value: $111

3123.
Emma R. Hare
#5225-08 • 14" without ears • JB
Issued: 1994 • Retired: 1996
Original: $20 • Value: $62

3124.
Emma Rose [QVC]
#(C100432) • 10" without ears
Issued: 2001 • Retired: 2001
Original: $27 • Value: $39

3125.
Estelle [SLE]
#unknown • 9" without ears
Issued: 1998 • Retired: 1998
Original: $15 • Value: $32

3126.
Esther Bunny
#825315 • 12" without ears
Issued: 2004 • Current
Original: $20 • Value: $R/E

HARES		
	PRICE PAID	VALUE
3115.		
3116.		
3117.		
3118.		
3119.		
3120.		
3121.		
3122.		
3123.		
3124.		
3125.		
3126.		
	TOTALS	

NOTES

Critters (Hares)

3127.
Farnsworth Jr.
#5870-08 • 9½" without ears • AR
Issued: 1995 • Retired: 1998
Original: $8 • Value: $24

3128.
Farnsworth Sr.
#5875-08 • 15" without ears • AR
Issued: 1995 • Retired: 1998
Original: $20 • Value: $29

3129.
Fergie
#5735 • 7½" without ears • AS
Issued: 1991 • Retired: 1992
Original: $7 • Value: $123

3130.
Fern Blumenshine
#91692 • 6" without ears • TJ
Issued: 1999 • Retired: 2000
Original: $10 • Value: $20

3131.
Have You Seen Me?
Fletcher [SLE]
#unknown • 9" without ears
Issued: 1999 • Retired: 1999
Original: $N/E • Value: $28

3132.
Fleurette Hare
#6103H • 14" without ears
Issued: 1991 • Retired: 1991
Original: $25 • Value: $352

HARES

	PRICE PAID	VALUE
3127.		
3128.		
3129.		
3130.		
3131.		
3132.		
3133.		
3134.		
3135.		
3136.		
3137.		
3138.		
TOTALS		

NOTES

3133.
Flopsie Bunnyears [Longaberger]
#94671LB • 8" without ears
Issued: 2004 • Retired: 2004
Original: $18 • Value: $20

3134.
Flora B. Bunny (old face)
#5210 • 20" with ears • JB
Issued: 1990 • Retired: 1991
Original: $29 • Value: $181

3135.
Flora B. Bunny (new face)
#5210 • 20" with ears • JB
Issued: 1991 • Retired: 1994
Original: $29 • Value: $143

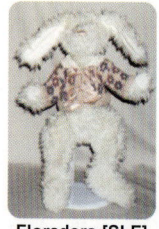
3136.
Floradora [SLE]
#unknown • 15" without ears
Issued: 1998 • Retired: 1998
Original: $N/E • Value: $35

3137.
Flossie B. Hopplebuns
#56481-10 • 8" without ears • BA
Issued: 1999 • Retired: 1999
Original: $11 • Value: $17

3138.
Fluffie Bunnyhop
#522700-01 • 8" without ears • JB
Issued: 2000 • Retired: 2002
Original: $9 • Value: $11

Critters (Hares)

3139.
Frangelica
#9109-10 • 12" without ears • TJ
Issued: 1996 • Retired: 1998
Original: $12 • Value: $26

3140.
G.G. Willikers
#91162 • 8" without ears • TJ
Issued: 1996 • Retired: 1998
Original: $20 • Value: $35

3141.
Gabby Bunnyhop
#522700-09 • 8" without ears • JB
Issued: 2000 • Retired: 2000
Original: $8 • Value: $15

3142.
Have You Seen Me?
Gardner
#6162H • TJ
Issued: 1991 • Retired: 1991
Original: $69 • Value: $279

3143.
Giselle de la Fleur
#91703 • 6" without ears • TJ
Issued: 1998 • Retired: 1999
Original: $10 • Value: $22
Also with Monique as QVC set.

3144.
Golda
#9146 • 10½" with ears • TJ
Issued: 1994 • Retired: 1995
Original: $20 • Value: $41

3145.
Have You Seen Me?
Grace
#6163H • TJ
Issued: 1991 • Retired: 1991
Original: $63 • Value: $274

3146.
Grace Agnes
#5830-01 • 11" without ears • CB
Issued: 1994 • Retired: 1995
Original: $21 • Value: $82

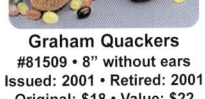

3147.
Graham Quackers
#81509 • 8" without ears
Issued: 2001 • Retired: 2001
Original: $18 • Value: $22

3148.
Grandma Babbit [QVC]
#(C19276) • 14" without ears
LE of 1200 • Issued: 1996 • Retired: 1996
Original: $73 • Value: $176

3149.
Grayling [SLE]
#unknown • 9" without ears
Issued: 1998 • Retired: 1998
Original: $13 • Value: $24

3150.
Grayson R. Hare (pewter)
#5230-06 • 9" without ears • JB
Issued: 1997 • Retired: 1999
Original: $12 • Value: $25

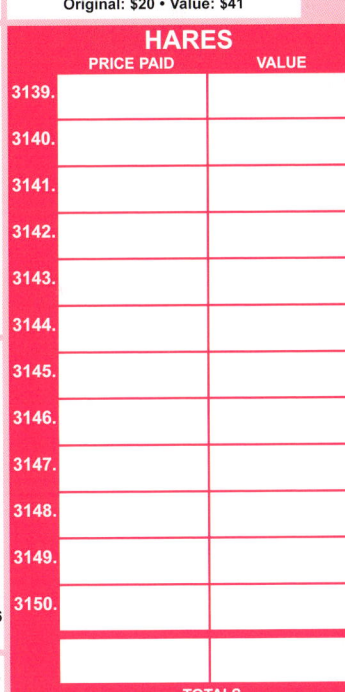

HARES	
PRICE PAID	VALUE
3139.	
3140.	
3141.	
3142.	
3143.	
3144.	
3145.	
3146.	
3147.	
3148.	
3149.	
3150.	
TOTALS	

NOTES

Critters (Hares)

3151.
Grayson R. Hare (blue-gray)
#5230-06 • 9" without ears • JB
Issued: 1997 • Retired: 1999
Original: $29 • Value: $35

3152.
Greta de la Fleur
#91704 • 6" without ears • TJ
Issued: 1999 • Retired: 1999
Original: $9 • Value: $18

3153.
Gretchen
#911210 • 10" without ears • TJ
Issued: 1998 • Retired: 1999
Original: $17 • Value: $25

3154.
Gretchen [Elder Beerman]
#unknown • 10" without ears
Issued: 1998 • Retired: 1998
Original: $20 • Value: $35

3155.
Hailey
#9168 • 8" without ears • TJ
Issued: 1995 • Retired: 1998
Original: $11 • Value: $28

3156.
Hannah
#91111 • 7½" without ears • TJ
Issued: 1997 • Retired: 1999
Original: $12 • Value: $19

3157.
Harriet R. Hare
#5200-08 • 12" without ears • JB
Issued: 1994 • Retired: 1996
Original: $14 • Value: $43

3158.
Harry Lapin II
#5217 • 17" with ears • JB
Issued: 1992 • Retired: 1993
Original: $20 • Value: $199

3159.
Harry R. Hare
#5217-03 • 17" with ears • JB
Issued: 1993 • Retired: 1994
Original: $20 • Value: $118

3160.
Harvey [QVC]
#(C18403) • 10" without ears
Issued: 1995 • Retired: 1995
Original: $24 • Value: $51

3161.
Hattie Hopsalot
#52401-01 • 16" without ears • JB
Issued: 2001 • Retired: 2001
Original: $28 • Value: $34

3162.
Heather [Dillards]
#94709DL • 8" without ears
Issued: 1997 • Retired: 1997
Original: $12 • Value: $28

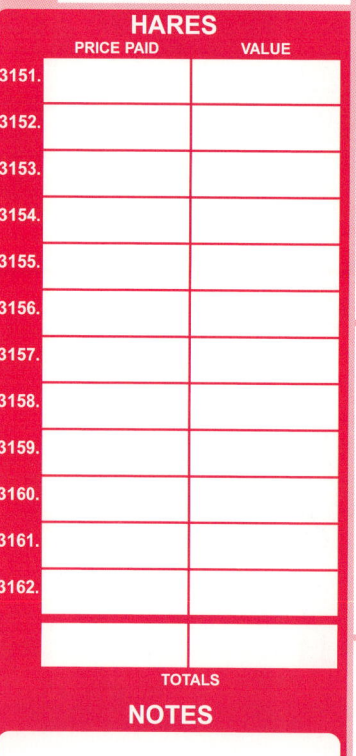

HARES

	PRICE PAID	VALUE
3151.		
3152.		
3153.		
3154.		
3155.		
3156.		
3157.		
3158.		
3159.		
3160.		
3161.		
3162.		
TOTALS		

NOTES

Critters (Hares)

3163.

Hedy Hare
#9186-01 • 10½" with ears • TJ
Issued: 1994 • Retired: 1998
Original: $20 • Value: $34

3164.

Heloise Haresworth
#533180 • 12" without ears
Issued: 2003 • Current
Original: $17 • Value: $R/E

3165.

Higgins
#5877-06 • 10" without ears • AR
Issued: 1995 • Retired: 1997
Original: $21 • Value: $45

3166.

Higgins D. Nibbleby
#58330 • 8" without ears • AS
Issued: 2001 • Retired: 2002
Original: $10 • Value: $18

3167.

Higgy
#5876-03 • 7" without ears • AR
Issued: 1996 • Retired: 1997
Original: $20 • Value: $37

3168.

Hippity & Hoppity Thumpster [QVC]
#unknown • 8" without ears
Issued: 2002 • Retired: 2002
Original: $20 • Value: $28

3169.

Have You Seen Me?
Homer
#6166H • TJ
Issued: 1991 • Retired: 1991
Original: $63 • Value: $325

3170.
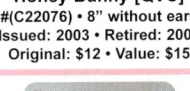
Have You Seen Me?
Honey Bunny [QVC]
#(C22076) • 8" without ears
Issued: 2003 • Retired: 2003
Original: $12 • Value: $15

3171.

Honeybee Cottontail [SLE]
#unknown • 6" without ears
Issued: 1998 • Retired: 1998
Original: $10 • Value: $18

3172.

Hopkins
#91121 • 10½" without ears • TJ
Issued: 1998 • Retired: 1999
Original: $18 • Value: $27

HARES	PRICE PAID	VALUE
3163.		
3164.		
3165.		
3166.		
3167.		
3168.		
3169.		
3170.		
3171.		
3172.		
3173.		
3174.		
TOTALS		

NOTES

3173.

Hopper Q. Bunsley
#533181 • 10" without ears
Issued: 2003 • Current
Original: $14 • Value: $R/E

3174.

Hoppity
#825304 • 6" without ears
Issued: 2003 • Retired: 2003
Original: $10 • Value: $10

Critters (Hares)

3175.
Hoppy E. Star [Hershey]
#95202HE • 5½" without ears
Issued: 2003 • Retired: 2003
Original: $8 • Value: $10

3176.
Hopson Q. Woodsley [QVC]
#93532V (C05176) • 10" without ears • AR
Issued: 2004 • Retired: 2004
Original: $16 • Value: $28

3177.
Iris Rosenbunny
#91651 • 10" without ears • TJ
Issued: 1999 • Retired: 2000
Original: $20 • Value: $28

3178.
Jack
#5215 • 20" with ears • JB
Issued: 1991 • Retired: 1992
Original: $29 • Value: $261

3179.
Jack R. Woodsley
#92002-04 • 12" without ears • AR
Issued: 2002 • Retired: 2002
Original: $16 • Value: $35

3180.
Jane (14")
#5732 • 14" without ears • AS
Issued: 1992 • Retired: 1992
Original: $20 • Value: $293

3181.
Jane (two-tone)
#5737-05 • 10½" with ears • AS
Issued: 1994 • Retired: 1999
Original: $14 • Value: $25

3182.
Janet
#1200-03 • 8" without ears • CC
Issued: 1994 • Retired: 1997
Original: $7 • Value: $30

3183.
Jebel Cottontail [SLE]
#unknown • 9" without ears
Issued: 1999 • Retired: 1999
Original: $15 • Value: $28

3184.
Jellie B. Bunny
#825318 • 6" without ears
Issued: 2004 • Current
Original: $8 • Value: $R/E

3185.
Jenna D. Lapinne
#916630 • 8½" without ears • TJ
Issued: 2000 • Retired: 2002
Original: $14 • Value: $21

3186.
Jessica
#9168-02 • 8" without ears • TJ
Issued: 1997 • Retired: 2000
Original: $12 • Value: $25

HARES

	PRICE PAID	VALUE
3175.		
3176.		
3177.		
3178.		
3179.		
3180.		
3181.		
3182.		
3183.		
3184.		
3185.		
3186.		
TOTALS		

NOTES

Critters (Hares)

3187.
Jill
#5216 • 20" with ears • JB
Issued: 1991 • Retired: 1992
Original: $29 • Value: $256

3188.
Josephine
#91701 • 6" without ears • TJ
Issued: 1996 • Retired: 1998
Original: $9 • Value: $21

3189.
Juliana Hopkins
#91122 • 8" without ears • TJ
Issued: 1999 • Retired: 1999
Original: $17 • Value: $21

3190.
Juliana Hopkins II
#911220 • 8" without ears • TJ
Issued: 2000 • Retired: 2000
Original: $15 • Value: $28

3191.
Julip O'Harea
#91664 • 12" with ears • TJ
Issued: 1996 • Retired: 1998
Original: $23 • Value: $34

3192.
Juniper Bunnyhugs
#916501 • 10" without ears
Issued: 2000 • Retired: 2000
Original: $16 • Value: $32

3193.
Kandi B. Bunny
#825319 • 6" without ears
Issued: 2004 • Current
Original: $8 • Value: $R/E

3194.
Kandy B. Hopensit [QVC]
#(C60244) • 11" without ears
Issued: 2002 • Retired: 2002
Original: $37 • Value: $45

3195.
Katerina
#5874 • 10" without ears • HT
Issued: 1992 • Retired: 1993
Original: $20 • Value: $95

3196.
Kathryn
#5732-01 • 7½" without ears • AS
Issued: 1994 • Retired: 1998
Original: $7 • Value: $20

3197.
Keefer P. Lightfoot
#52200-06 • 12" without ears • JB
Issued: 2001 • Retired: 2001
Original: $18 • Value: $22

3198.
Kellie Hopplebuns
#904144 • 6" without ears
Issued: 2003 • Retired: 2003
Original: $10 • Value: $10

HARES	PRICE PAID	VALUE
3187.		
3188.		
3189.		
3190.		
3191.		
3192.		
3193.		
3194.		
3195.		
3196.		
3197.		
3198.		
TOTALS		

NOTES

Critters (Hares)

3199.
Kerry Q. Hopgood
#52401-03 • 17" without ears • JB
Issued: 1999 • Retired: 2001
Original: $23 • Value: $25

3200.
Key Lime Thumpster
#52010-08 • 10" without ears • JB
Issued: 2001 • Retired: 2002
Original: $14 • Value: $17

3201.
Lacey V. Hare [QVC]
#unknown • 10" without ears
Issued: 1998 • Retired: 1998
Original: $17 • Value: $30

3202.
Lacy Hare (tan)
#6101H • 17" with ears • TJ
Issued: 1990 • Retired: 1992
Original: $21 • Value: $162

3203.
Lacy Hare (taupe curly)
#6101H • 17" with ears
Issued: 1990 • Retired: 1992
Original: $21 • Value: $162

3204.
Lacy Hare (white curly)
#6100H • 14" with ears • TJ
Issued: 1990 • Retired: 1994
Original: $16 • Value: $146
Also in white plush.

3205.
Lady Harrington [QVC]
#(C37299) • 9" without ears
Issued: 1997 • Retired: 1997
Original: $20 • Value: $38

3206.
Lady Harriwell
#91892-14 • 11" without ears • TJ
Issued: 1998 • Retired: 1998
Original: $21 • Value: $25

3207.
Lady Pembroke
#91892-09 • 15" without ears • TJ
Issued: 1997 • Retired: 1999
Original: $21 • Value: $27

3208.
Lady Pembroke [SFMB]
#41-72647 • 15" without ears
Issued: 1999 • Retired: 1999
Original: $25 • Value: $38
♪ Music Box Dancer ♪

3209.
Lady Peyton
#918921-09 • 10½" without ears • TJ
Issued: 1998 • Retired: 1999
Original: $17 • Value: $28

3210.
Lana Hare
#9186 • 10½" with ears • TJ
Issued: 1993 • Retired: 1994
Original: $20 • Value: $55

HARES

	PRICE PAID	VALUE
3199.		
3200.		
3201.		
3202.		
3203.		
3204.		
3205.		
3206.		
3207.		
3208.		
3209.		
3210.		
TOTALS		

NOTES

Critters (Hares)

3211.
Larry Lapin
#5209 • 17" with ears • JB
Issued: 1989 • Retired: 1991
Original: $20 • Value: $145

3212.
Have You Seen Me?
Larry Too
#5217 • 17" with ears • JB
Issued: 1991 • Retired: 1992
Original: $20 • Value: $95

3213.
Lauralee Hopplebuns
#904291 • 10" without ears • TJ
Issued: 2004 • Current
Original: $15 • Value: $R/E

3214.
Lauren
#9168-01 • 8" without ears • TJ
Issued: 1996 • Retired: 1998
Original: $11 • Value: $24

3215.
Lavinia V. Hariweather
#91661 • 10" without ears • TJ
Issued: 1997 • Retired: 1999
Original: $20 • Value: $27

3216.
Lavinia V. Hariweather [SFMB]
#41-72644 • 10" without ears
Issued: 1998 • Retired: 1998
Original: $25 • Value: $N/E
♪ You Are My Sunshine ♪

3217.
Leisel
#904292 • 6" without ears • TJ
Issued: 2004 • Retired: 2004
Original: $10 • Value: $10

3218.
Lenora Flatstein
#5685-08 • 8" without ears • FL
Issued: 1994 • Retired: 1998
Original: $12 • Value: $30

3219.
Leona B. Bunny
#5214 • 20" without ears • JB
Issued: 1989 • Retired: 1992
Original: $29 • Value: $245

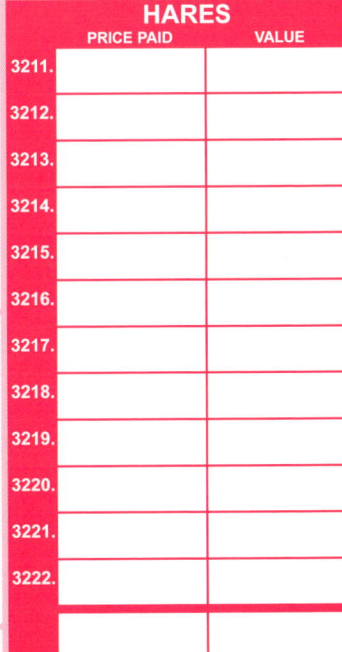

3220.
Libby Lapinette
#91681 • 6" without ears • TJ
Issued: 1999 • Retired: 1999
Original: $11 • Value: $14

3221.
Lila Hopkins
#91124 • 8" without ears • TJ
Issued: 2000 • Retired: 2000
Original: $15 • Value: $18

3222.
Lily R. Hare
#5227-01 • 8" without ears • JB
Issued: 1994 • Retired: 2000
Original: $10 • Value: $19

HARES	PRICE PAID	VALUE
3211.		
3212.		
3213.		
3214.		
3215.		
3216.		
3217.		
3218.		
3219.		
3220.		
3221.		
3222.		
TOTALS		

NOTES

Critters (Hares)

3223.
Lindsey [Dillards]
#94710DL • 8" without ears
Issued: 1997 • Retired: 1997
Original: $12 • Value: $35

3224.
Lindy [Elder Beerman]
#unknown • 13" without ears
Issued: 1999 • Retired: 1999
Original: $15 • Value: $29

3225.
Livingston R. Hare (early smooth fur)
#5200 • 10" without ears • JB
Issued: 1988 • Retired: 1989
Original: $14 • Value: $75

3226.
Livingston R. Hare (old face)
#5200 • 12" without ears • JB
Issued: 1990 • Retired: 1992
Original: $14 • Value: $59

3227.
Livingston R. Hare (new face)
#5200 • 12" without ears • JB
Issued: 1993 • Retired: 1999
Original: $14 • Value: $30

3228.
Lottie de Lopear
#91648 • 9" without ears • TJ
Issued: 2000 • Retired: 2000
Original: $13 • Value: $26

3229.
Lucille
#91141 • 13½" without ears • TJ
Issued: 1997 • Retired: 1998
Original: $24 • Value: $37

3230.
Lucinda de La Fleur
#91705 • 6" without ears • TJ
Issued: 1999 • Retired: 2000
Original: $9 • Value: $14

3231.
Lucy P. Blumenshine
#91702 • 6" without ears • TJ
Issued: 1997 • Retired: 1998
Original: $10 • Value: $25

3232.
Lula Mae Loppenhop
#573304-08 • 6" without ears • AS
Issued: 2001 • Retired: 2001
Original: $7 • Value: $8

3233.
Lynn
#904293 • 6" without ears • TJ
Issued: 2004 • Retired: 2004
Original: $10 • Value: $10

3234.
Magnolia O'Harea
#91667 • 17" without ears • TJ
Issued: 1996 • Retired: 1998
Original: $31 • Value: $40

HARES

	PRICE PAID	VALUE
3223.		
3224.		
3225.		
3226.		
3227.		
3228.		
3229.		
3230.		
3231.		
3232.		
3233.		
3234.		
TOTALS		

NOTES

Critters (Hares)

3235.
Mallory [SLE]
#unknown • 8" without ears
LE • Issued: 1997 • Retired: 1997
Original: $11 • Value: $25

3236.
Margaret Mary
#5830 • 11" without ears • CB
Issued: 1992 • Retired: 1995
Original: $21 • Value: $74

3237.
Margaret Q. Harington [QVC]
#93531V (C05183) • 6" without ears • MB
LE of 2400 • Issued: 2004 • Retired: 2004
Original: $17 • Value: $25

3238.
Maribel Gardenglow [SFMB]
#41-40214 • 10" without ears
Issued: 2001 • Retired: 2001
Original: $38 • Value: $49
♪ Food Glorious Food ♪

3239.
Marigold McHare
#52270-08 • 8" without ears • JB
Issued: 1999 • Retired: 2000
Original: $10 • Value: $12

3240.
Marlena
#9154 • 10½" with ears • TJ
Issued: 1994 • Retired: 1997
Original: $20 • Value: $35

3241.
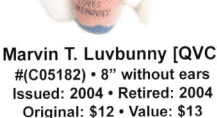
Marta M. Hare
#5206 • 12" without ears • JB
Issued: 1989 • Retired: 1992
Original: $14 • Value: $95

3242.
Martha T. Bunnycombe
#590140-03 • 15½" without ears • MB
Issued: 1998 • Retired: 1998
Original: $51 • Value: $67

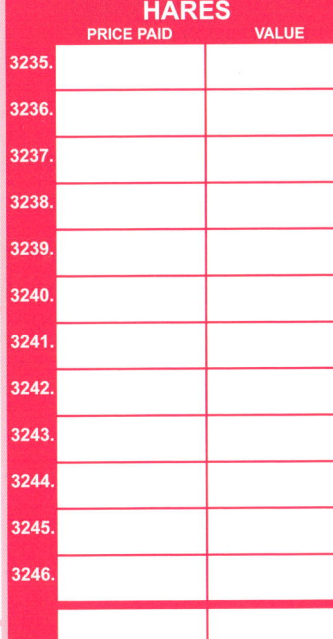

HARES		
	PRICE PAID	VALUE
3235.		
3236.		
3237.		
3238.		
3239.		
3240.		
3241.		
3242.		
3243.		
3244.		
3245.		
3246.		
TOTALS		

NOTES

3243.
Marvin T. Luvbunny [QVC]
#(C05182) • 8" without ears
Issued: 2004 • Retired: 2004
Original: $12 • Value: $13

3244.
Mary (old face)
#5737 • 10½" with ears • AS
Issued: 1991 • Retired: 1993
Original: $14 • Value: $42

3245.
Mary (new face)
#5737 • 10½" with ears • AS
Issued: 1993 • Retired: 1997
Original: $14 • Value: $32

3246.
Mary Catherine
#5829 • 9" without ears • CB
Issued: 1992 • Retired: 1995
Original: $16 • Value: $67

Critters (Hares)

3247. Mary Regina
#5829-01 • 9" without ears • CB
Issued: 1994 • Retired: 1995
Original: $16 • Value: $66

3248. Matilda
#6161H • TJ
Issued: 1991 • Retired: 1991
Original: $63 • Value: $275

3249. Maureen O'Hare
#52200-08 • 12" without ears • JB
Issued: 2002 • Retired: 2002
Original: $18 • Value: $18

3250. Mazie Q. Lightfoot
#58300-05 • 9" without ears • AS
Issued: 2001 • Retired: 2001
Original: $12 • Value: $14

3251. Meredith [Frederick Atkins]
#unknown • 10" without ears
Issued: 1999 • Retired: 1999
Original: $18 • Value: $35
Variation: Dark Yellow Jumper.

3252. Merlin
#6167H • TJ
Issued: 1991 • Retired: 1991
Original: $63 • Value: $295

3253. Michele S. Hopplebuns
#916629 • 9" without ears • TJ
Issued: 2002 • Retired: 2002
Original: $15 • Value: $20

3254. Michelline
#91815 • 7½" with ears • TJ
Issued: 1996 • Retired: 1997
Original: $13 • Value: $27

3255. Mickey
#1200-08 • 8" without ears • CC
Issued: 1994 • Retired: 1995
Original: $7 • Value: $51

3256. Mickie (chenille)
#5654 • 16" without ears • BA
Issued: 1992 • Retired: 1998
Original: $21 • Value: $29

3257. Mickie (sherpa fur)
#5654 • 16" without ears • BA
Issued: 1992 • Retired: 1998
Original: $21 • Value: $29

3258. Millie Hopkins
#91123 • 8" without ears • TJ
Issued: 1999 • Retired: 2000
Original: $18 • Value: $22

HARES

	PRICE PAID	VALUE
3247.		
3248.		
3249.		
3250.		
3251.		
3252.		
3253.		
3254.		
3255.		
3256.		
3257.		
3258.		
TOTALS		

NOTES

Critters (Hares)

3259.
Mimi Delapain
#9169 • 8" without ears • JB
Issued: 1995 • Retired: 1998
Original: $9 • Value: $25

3260.
Mimosa
#9110-10 • 17" with ears • TJ
Issued: 1996 • Retired: 1998
Original: $19 • Value: $26

3261.
Mipsie Blumenshine
#917040 • 6" without ears • TJ
Issued: 2000 • Retired: 2000
Original: $10 • Value: $19

3262.
Miracle Gardenglow
#916632 • 8" without ears • TJ
Issued: 2001 • Retired: 2002
Original: $17 • Value: $25

3263.
Miranda Blumenshine
#91142 • 10" without ears • TJ
Issued: 1999 • Retired: 2000
Original: $19 • Value: $28

3264.
Miss Abby and Lexie Dowbunny [QVC]
#(C99070) • 8" without ears
Issued: 2000 • Retired: 2000
Original: $23 • Value: $34

3265.
Mitzie Mae [Kirlins]
#94258KR • 12" without ears
LE of 7000 • Issued: 2000 • Retired: 2000
Original: $24 • Value: $45

3266.
Moe Lapin (old face)
#5208 • 14" with ears • JB
Issued: 1990 • Retired: 1991
Original: $14 • Value: $78

3267.
Moe Lapin (new face)
#5208 • 14" without ears • JB
Issued: 1991 • Retired: 1995
Original: $14 • Value: $65

3268.
Molly
#unknown • 14" without ears
LE of 400 • Issued: 1993 • Retired: 1993
Original: $75 • Value: $321

3269.
Momma O'Harea & Bonnie Blue
#91008 • 12" without ears • TJ
Issued: 1998 • Retired: 1998
Original: $29 • Value: $45

3270.
Monique de la Fleur with Giselle [QVC]
#unknown • 6" without ears
Issued: 1998 • Retired: 1998
Original: $N/E • Value: $N/E

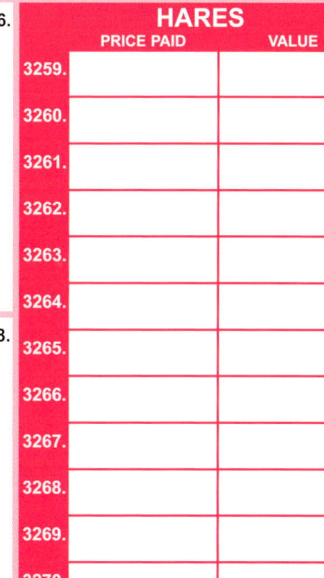

HARES

	PRICE PAID	VALUE
3259.		
3260.		
3261.		
3262.		
3263.		
3264.		
3265.		
3266.		
3267.		
3268.		
3269.		
3270.		
TOTALS		

NOTES

Critters (Hares)

3271.
Montgomery Flatstein
#5685-10 • 8" without ears • FL
Issued: 1994 • Retired: 2000
Original: $12 • Value: $21

3272.
Mrs. Harelwig
#unknown • 14" without ears
LE • Issued: 1991 • Retired: 1991
Original: $70 • Value: $318

3273.
Mrs. Harestein
#9204H • 14" without ears
LE • Issued: 1992 • Retired: 1992
Original: $70 • Value: $375

3274.
Ms. Magnolia [QVC]
#unknown • 17" with ears
LE of 1200 • Issued: 1997 • Retired: 1997
Original: $64 • Value: $139

3275.
Nanna O'Harea & Audrey [QVC]
#unknown • 11" without ears
Issued: 1998 • Retired: 1998
Original: $24 • Value: $42

3276.
Nanny II
#6172H • 13" without ears
LE • Issued: 1991 • Retired: 1991
Original: $70 • Value: $360

3277.
Natalie [Dillards]
#94716DL • 14" without ears
Issued: 1997 • Retired: 1997
Original: $16 • Value: $35

3278.
Natalie Nibblenose
#573300-01 • 6" without ears • AS
Issued: 2000 • Retired: 2000
Original: $7 • Value: $14

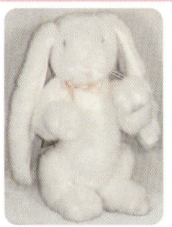

3279.
Natasha
#5873 • 10" without ears • HT
Issued: 1992 • Retired: 1994
Original: $20 • Value: $75

3280.
Nibbie Bunnyhop
#522700-06 • 8" without ears
Issued: 2000 • Retired: 2000
Original: $8 • Value: $13

3281.
Nibbley Sweetreats
#825303 • 8" without ears
Issued: 2003 • Retired: 2003
Original: $13 • Value: $13

3282.
Have You Seen Me?
Nickie
#5653 • 16" without ears • BA
Issued: 1992 • Retired: 1993
Original: $21 • Value: $39

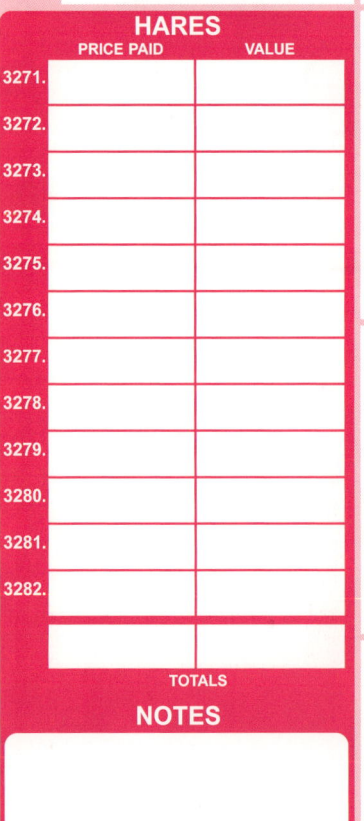

HARES

	PRICE PAID	VALUE
3271.		
3272.		
3273.		
3274.		
3275.		
3276.		
3277.		
3278.		
3279.		
3280.		
3281.		
3282.		
TOTALS		

NOTES

Critters (Hares)

3283.
Nickie Nibblenose
#573303-03 • 6" without ears • AS
Issued: 2000 • Retired: 2000
Original: $7 • Value: $16

3284.
Olga
#5871 • 6" without ears • HT
Issued: 1992 • Retired: 1992
Original: $9 • Value: $95

3285.
Oliver
#91110 • 6" without ears • TJ
Issued: 1998 • Retired: 2000
Original: $10 • Value: $17

3286.
Orchid de la Hoppsack
#91405 • 8" without ears • TJ
Issued: 1998 • Retired: 1999
Original: $13 • Value: $22

3287.
Pansey & Parsley Hopsalot [QVC]
#unknown • 8" without ears
Issued: 2001 • Retired: 2001
Original: $20 • Value: $26

3288.
Pansy Rosenbunny
#91652 • 10" without ears • TJ
Issued: 1999 • Retired: 1999
Original: $20 • Value: $21

3289.
Parker [SLE]
#unknown • 12" without ears
Issued: 1998 • Retired: 1998
Original: $15 • Value: $25

3290.
Paula Hoppleby
#91125 • 8" without ears • TJ
Issued: 2000 • Retired: 2000
Original: $15 • Value: $18

3291.
Pauline [Kirlins]
#unknown • 10" without ears
Issued: 1997 • Retired: 1997
Original: $24 • Value: $45

3292.
Peaches Thumpster
#52010-06 • 10" without ears • JB
Issued: 2002 • Retired: 2002
Original: $14 • Value: $14

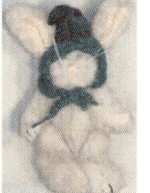
3293.
Peapod
#91071 • 6" without ears • TJ
Issued: 1996 • Retired: 1997
Original: $12 • Value: $33

3294.
Penelope
#5729 • 14" without ears • AS
Issued: 1992 • Retired: 1995
Original: $20 • Value: $73

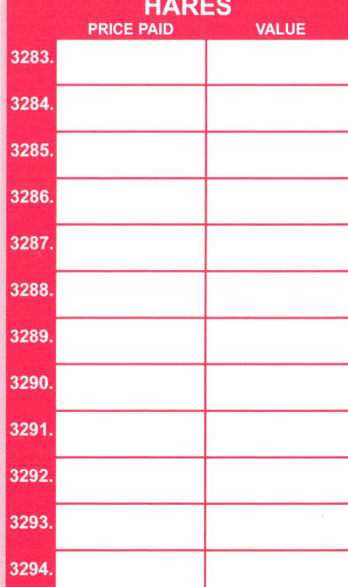

HARES	PRICE PAID	VALUE
3283.		
3284.		
3285.		
3286.		
3287.		
3288.		
3289.		
3290.		
3291.		
3292.		
3293.		
3294.		
TOTALS		

NOTES

Critters (Hares)

3295.
Penelope [SLE]
#unknown • 10" without ears
Issued: 1998 • Retired: 1998
Original: $20 • Value: $N/E

3296.
Pete E. Bunny
#825317 • 8" without ears
Issued: 2004 • Current
Original: $14 • Value: $R/E

3297.
Peter
#9111 • 6" without ears • TJ
Issued: 1995 • Retired: 1997
Original: $11 • Value: $25

3298.
Petey Thumpster
#52010-09 • 10" without ears • JB
Issued: 2002 • Retired: 2002
Original: $14 • Value: $14

3299.
Peyton C. Hopplebuns
#500071-01 • 30" without ears • JB
Issued: 2002 • Retired: 2004
Original: $57 • Value: $65

3300.
Piper
#590067 • 8" without ears • MB
LE of 5000 • Issued: 2004 • Current
Original: $25 • Value: $R/E

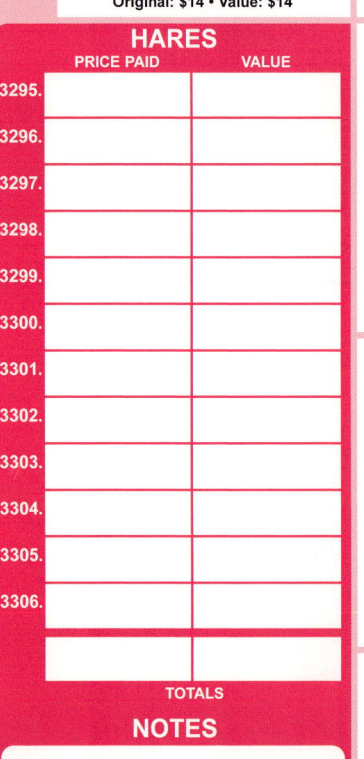

3301.
Piper Angelbuns [QVC]
#93437V (C22099) • 6" without ears
Issued: 2003 • Retired: 2003
Original: $10 • Value: $18

3302.
Piper Lapine
#918430 • 6" without ears
Issued: 2002 • Retired: 2002
Original: $10 • Value: $18

3303.
Pixie (taupe curly)
#5651 • 12" without ears • BA
Issued: 1992 • Retired: 1993
Original: $16 • Value: $53

3304.
Pixie (two-tone)
#56510-05 • 12" without ears • BA
Issued: 1998 • Retired: 2000
Original: $14 • Value: $20

3305.
Polly Bunnytoes
#522801-03 • 8" without ears • JB
Issued: 2002 • Retired: 2002
Original: $10 • Value: $10

3306.
Priscilla R. Hare (17")
#5217-12 • 17" without ears • JB
Issued: 1993 • Retired: 1994
Original: $20 • Value: $65

HARES

	PRICE PAID	VALUE
3295.		
3296.		
3297.		
3298.		
3299.		
3300.		
3301.		
3302.		
3303.		
3304.		
3305.		
3306.		
	TOTALS	

NOTES

Critters (Hares)

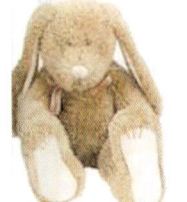
3307.
Priscilla R. Hare (14")
#5217-08 • 14" without ears • JB
Issued: 1995 • Retired: 1997
Original: $16 • Value: $33

3308.
Prissie Hopplebuns
#912082 • 12" without ears • TJ
Issued: 2002 • Retired: 2002
Original: $21 • Value: $28

3309.
Prissie Hopplebuns II
#904140 • 12" without ears • TJ
Issued: 2003 • Retired: 2003
Original: $20 • Value: $23

3310.
Prissie Hopplebuns III
#904290 • 12" without ears • TJ
Issued: 2004 • Current
Original: $20 • Value: $R/E

3311.
Regena Haresford
#916490 • 13" without ears • TJ
Issued: 2000 • Retired: 2002
Original: $26 • Value: $29

3312.
Regina (short ears - small feet)
#5731 • 14" without ears • AS
Issued: 1991 • Retired: 1991
Original: $20 • Value: $151

3313.
Have You Seen Me?
Regina (big ears - small feet)
#unknown • AS
Issued: 1991 • Retired: 1992
Original: $20 • Value: $125

3314.
Regina (big ears - big feet)
#5731 • 14" without ears • AS
Issued: 1992 • Retired: 1993
Original: $20 • Value: $90

3315.

Regina (two-tone)
#5737-08 • 10½" without ears • AS
Issued: 1998 • Retired: 1999
Original: $14 • Value: $20

3316.
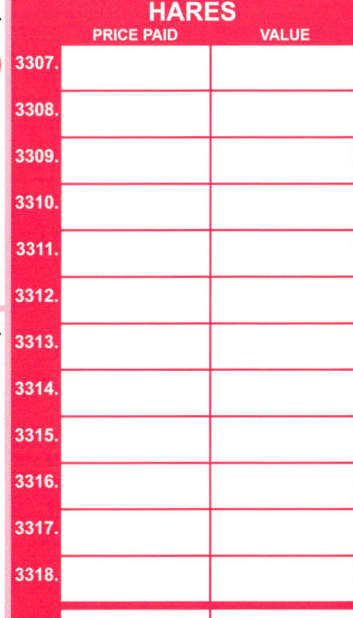
Rita
#1201-08 • 11" without ears • CC
Issued: 1994 • Retired: 1995
Original: $10 • Value: $60

3317.
Rosalie Bloomengrows
#916500 • 10" without ears • TJ
Issued: 2001 • Retired: 2002
Original: $23 • Value: $28

3318.
Rosalynn P. Harington
#590140-01 • 12" without ears • MB
Issued: 1999 • Retired: 1999
Original: $51 • Value: $58

HARES	PRICE PAID	VALUE
3307.		
3308.		
3309.		
3310.		
3311.		
3312.		
3313.		
3314.		
3315.		
3316.		
3317.		
3318.		
TOTALS		

NOTES

Critters (Hares)

3319.
Rosalynn P. Harington II
#5901400-01 • 12" without ears • MB
Issued: 2000 • Retired: 2000
Original: $54 • Value: $65

3320.
Rosanna P. Angelbuns [QVC]
#unknown • 6" without ears
Issued: 2002 • Retired: 2002
Original: $9 • Value: $15

3321.
Roscoe P. Bumpercrop
#912079 • 17" without ears • TJ
Issued: 1999 • Retired: 2001
Original: $34 • Value: $44
TOBY Award Winner

3322.
Rose
#91112 • 7½" with ears • TJ
Issued: 1997 • Retired: 1998
Original: $12 • Value: $20

3323.
Roslyn Hiphop
#912080 • 14" without ears • TJ
Issued: 2000 • Retired: 2001
Original: $27 • Value: $34

3324.
Roxbunny R. Hare
#5878-06 • 14" without ears • AR
Issued: 1997 • Retired: 1998
Original: $14 • Value: $33

3325.
Royce Hare
#6107H • 15" without ears • TJ
Issued: 1990 • Retired: 1992
Original: $32 • Value: $325

3326.
Rumpus
#5745 • 9" without ears • HD
Issued: 1991 • Retired: 1992
Original: $14 • Value: $141

3327.
Ruth
#1201-01 • 11" without ears • CC
Issued: 1994 • Retired: 1995
Original: $10 • Value: $70

3328.
Sangria
#9110-05 • 17" with ears • TJ
Issued: 1998 • Retired: 1999
Original: $20 • Value: $24

3329.
Sara
#9140 • 7½" without ears • TJ
Issued: 1994 • Retired: 1996
Original: $13 • Value: $42

3330.
Sara II
#91401 • 6" without ears • TJ
Issued: 1996 • Retired: 1998
Original: $13 • Value: $25

HARES

	PRICE PAID	VALUE
3319.		
3320.		
3321.		
3322.		
3323.		
3324.		
3325.		
3326.		
3327.		
3328.		
3329.		
3330.		
TOTALS		

NOTES

Critters (Hares)

3331.
Sarah
#5739 • 10½" with ears • AS
Issued: 1991 • Retired: 1993
Original: $14 • Value: $57

3332.
Sarina [Frederick Atkins]
#94766FA • 9" without ears
Issued: 2000 • Retired: 2000
Original: $22 • Value: $35

3333.
Savannah Buttercup
#91650 • 10" without ears • TJ
Issued: 2000 • Retired: 2000
Original: $23 • Value: $31

3334.
Sharona
#5737-10 • 10½" without ears • AS
Issued: 1998 • Retired: 1999
Original: $14 • Value: $25

3335.
Snowbunny [Bath & Body Works]
#unknown • 12" without ears
Issued: 1997 • Retired: 1997
Original: $29 • Value: $41

3336.
Sophie
#9114 • 12" without ears • TJ
Issued: 1995 • Retired: 1998
Original: $20 • Value: $39

3337.
Sophie B. Bunny
#5215 • 20" without ears • JB
Issued: 1993 • Retired: 1994
Original: $29 • Value: $194

3338.
Springsley Hopplebuns [QVC]
#(C22074) • 16" without ears
Issued: 2003 • Retired: 2003
Original: $29 • Value: $35

3339.
Squeekie (white)
#5620 • 8" without ears
Issued: 1991 • Retired: 1992
Original: $10 • Value: $289

3340.
Squeekie (british tan)
#5621 • 8" without ears
Issued: 1992 • Retired: 1992
Original: $10 • Value: $92

3341.
Stamford (a.k.a. Stanford) [QVC]
#(C37278) • 14" without ears
Issued: 1997 • Retired: 1997
Original: $20 • Value: $35

3342.
Stanley R. Hare (old face)
#5201 • 12" without ears • JB
Issued: 1991 • Retired: 1992
Original: $14 • Value: $77

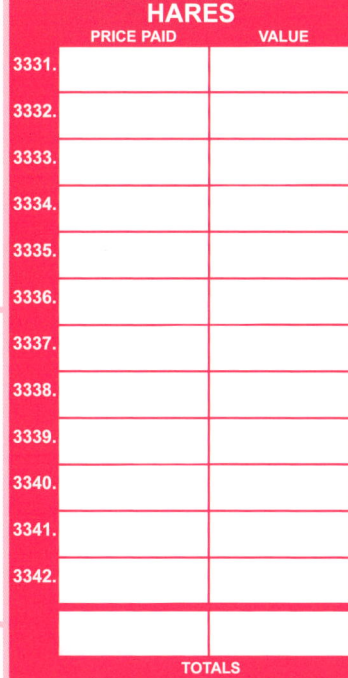

HARES	PRICE PAID	VALUE
3331.		
3332.		
3333.		
3334.		
3335.		
3336.		
3337.		
3338.		
3339.		
3340.		
3341.		
3342.		
TOTALS		

NOTES

Critters (Hares)

3343.
Stanley R. Hare (new face)
#5201 • 12" without ears • JB
Issued: 1992 • Retired: 1995
Original: $14 • Value: $31

3344.
Stanley R. Hare (modern face)
#5201 • 10" without ears • JB
Issued: 1995 • Retired: 2001
Original: $14 • Value: $25

3345.
Stellina Hopswell
#573700-01 • 8" without ears • AS
Issued: 2000 • Retired: 2001
Original: $11 • Value: $14

3346.
Sterling Hopswell
#573701-06 • 8" without ears • AS
Issued: 2000 • Retired: 2001
Original: $11 • Value: $17

3347.
Stewart Rarebit
#9116 • 8" without ears • TJ
Issued: 1995 • Retired: 1998
Original: $13 • Value: $30

3348.
T. Farrell Wuzzie
#595101-06 • 5" without ears • TF
Issued: 2000 • Retired: 2000
Original: $9 • Value: $11

3349.
T. Hopplewhite
#52200-01 • 12" without ears • JB
Issued: 2000 • Retired: 2000
Original: $15 • Value: $24

3350.
Taffy C. Hopplebuns
#56481-03 • 8" without ears • BA
Issued: 1999 • Retired: 1999
Original: $11 • Value: $16

3351.
Talia [SLE]
#unknown • 6" without ears
Issued: 1999 • Retired: 1999
Original: $11 • Value: $21

3352.
Tami F. Wuzzie
#596100 • 3" without ears • TF
Issued: 1999 • Retired: 2001
Original: $8 • Value: $10
Also with Tasha, Tatum as QVC set.

3353.
Tangerine Thumpster
#52031-01 • 10" without ears • JB
Issued: 2001 • Retired: 2002
Original: $14 • Value: $17

3354.
Tanner F. Wuzzie
#595300-08 • 3" without ears • TF
Issued: 1998 • Retired: 2000
Original: $7 • Value: $8

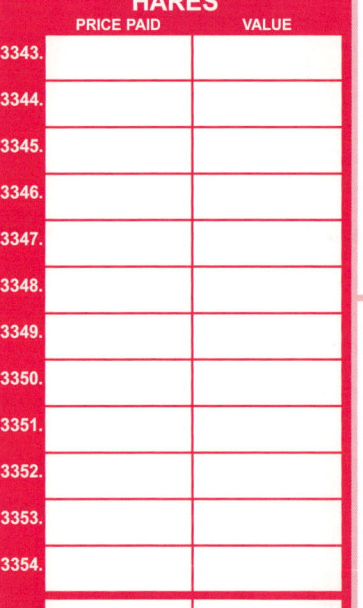

HARES

	PRICE PAID	VALUE
3343.		
3344.		
3345.		
3346.		
3347.		
3348.		
3349.		
3350.		
3351.		
3352.		
3353.		
3354.		
TOTALS		

NOTES

Critters (Hares)

3355.
Tapper F. Wuzzie
#595300-06 • 3" without ears • TF
Issued: 1999 • Retired: 2000
Original: $7 • Value: $9

3356.
Tarragon
#9110-07 • 17" with ears • TJ
Issued: 1996 • Retired: 1997
Original: $19 • Value: $44

3357.
Tatiana
#5877 • 14" without ears • HT
Issued: 1992 • Retired: 1992
Original: $32 • Value: $240

3358.
Tatters T. Hareloom
#52000 • 10" without ears • JB
Issued: 2001 • Retired: 2002
Original: $16 • Value: $19

3359.
Teddy Hare (golden tan)
#5082 • 12" without ears • WB
Issued: 1986 • Retired: 1990
Original: $15 • Value: $242

3360.
Teddy Hare (rust)
#5081 • 12" without ears • WB
Issued: 1986 • Retired: 1988
Original: $15 • Value: $275

3361.
Teddy Hare (tan)
#5080 • 10" without ears • WB
Issued: 1986 • Retired: 1991
Original: $13 • Value: $222

3362.
Teddy Hare (white)
#5083 • 10" without ears • WB
Issued: 1986 • Retired: 1990
Original: $13 • Value: $240

3363.
Tessie T. Nibblenose
#917050 • 6" without ears • TJ
Issued: 2001 • Retired: 2002
Original: $10 • Value: $12

3364.
Thump
#5747 • 14" without ears • HD
Issued: 1991 • Retired: 1992
Original: $27 • Value: $233

3365.
Tibbles Q. Woodsley
#92002-07 • 7½" without ears • AR
Issued: 2003 • Retired: 2003
Original: $12 • Value: $12

3366.
Tina Marie Hopgood
#81507 • 6" without ears • TJ
Issued: 2001 • Retired: 2001
Original: $12 • Value: $14

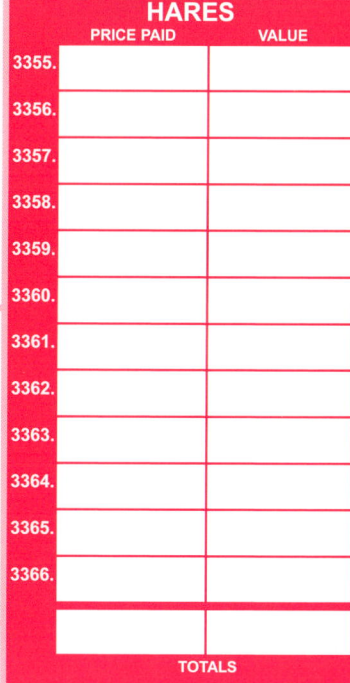

HARES

	PRICE PAID	VALUE
3355.		
3356.		
3357.		
3358.		
3359.		
3360.		
3361.		
3362.		
3363.		
3364.		
3365.		
3366.		
TOTALS		

NOTES

Critters (Hares)

3367.
Tipper
#5648-08 • 8" without ears • BA
Issued: 1993 • Retired: 1997
Original: $11 • Value: $38

3368.
Tippy F. Wuzzie
#595300-01 • 3" without ears • TF
Issued: 1998 • Retired: 2000
Original: $7 • Value: $8

3369.
Tippy P. Hopplebuns
#904141 • 10" without ears • TJ
Issued: 2003 • Retired: 2003
Original: $15 • Value: $15

3370.
Trixie
#5654-08 • 16" without ears • BA
Issued: 1993 • Retired: 1996
Original: $24 • Value: $55

3371.
Tulip [SLE]
#unknown • 6" without ears • TJ
Issued: 1999 • Retired: 1999
Original: $10 • Value: $19

3372.
Tutu
#6169H • 16" without ears • TJ
Issued: 1993 • Retired: 1991
Original: $63 • Value: $337

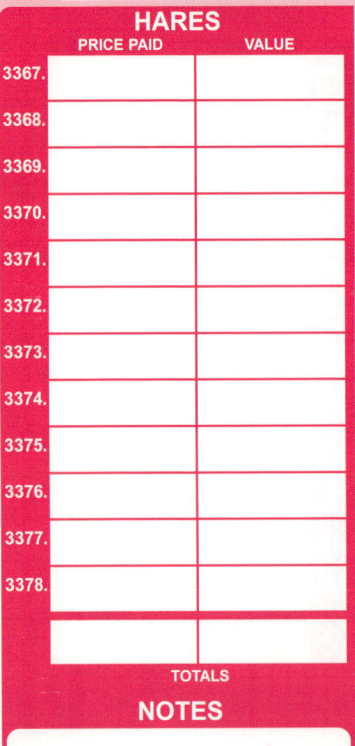

HARES		
	PRICE PAID	VALUE
3367.		
3368.		
3369.		
3370.		
3371.		
3372.		
3373.		
3374.		
3375.		
3376.		
3377.		
3378.		
	TOTALS	

NOTES

3373.
Twigley Hopsalot
#522701-08 • 8" without ears • JB
Issued: 2001 • Retired: 2002
Original: $9 • Value: $11

3374.
Vanessa D. LaPinne
#91662 • 10" without ears • TJ
Issued: 1999 • Retired: 2000
Original: $27 • Value: $33

3375.
Vanna Hopkins
#91113 • 6" without ears • TJ
Issued: 2001 • Retired: 2002
Original: $10 • Value: $17

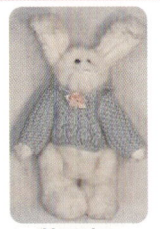

3376.
Veronica
#9181 • 10½" with ears • TJ
Issued: 1994 • Retired: 1997
Original: $20 • Value: $50

3377.
Victoria
#5736 • 7½" without ears • AS
Issued: 1991 • Retired: 1999
Original: $7 • Value: $19

3378.
Violet Dubois
#91403 • 6" without ears • TJ
Issued: 1996 • Retired: 1998
Original: $12 • Value: $25

Critters (Hares, Hens)

3379.
Virginia Bluebell [SFMB]
#41-72938 • 10" without ears
Issued: 2000 • Retired: 2000
Original: $25 • Value: $42
♪ April Love ♪

3380.
Wabbit McVeggie
#904242 • 11" without ears • TJ
Issued: 2004 • Current
Original: $20 • Value: $R/E

3381.
Webster Hopplebuns
#916631 • 8" without ears • TJ
Issued: 2001 • Retired: 2001
Original: $17 • Value: $20

3382.
Wedgewood J. Hopgood
#52401 • 17" without ears • JB
Issued: 1999 • Retired: 2000
Original: $29 • Value: $33

3383.
Whitney
#9130 • 14" with ears • TJ
Issued: 1995 • Retired: 1998
Original: $20 • Value: $33

3384.
Wilhelm van Bruin
#5015 • 12" without ears • WB
Issued: 1992 • Retired: 1995
Original: $9 • Value: $45

3385.
Wixie
#5650 • 12" without ears • BA
Issued: 1992 • Retired: 1998
Original: $16 • Value: $31

3386.
Zelda Fitzhare
#5241-10 • 17" without ears • JB
Issued: 1995 • Retired: 1998
Original: $29 • Value: $37

3387.
Zelda Fitzhare [SFMB]
#41-72643 • 17" without ears
Issued: 1999 • Retired: 1999
Original: $35 • Value: $52
♪ Feelin' Groovy ♪

Hens

3388.
Henita P. Cooper [BBC]
#918018SM • 12"
Issued: 2003 • Retired: 2003
Original: $28 • Value: $34

3389.
Henrietta Eggbert
#553170 • 9"
Issued: 2003 • Current
Original: $15 • Value: $R/E

HARES		
	PRICE PAID	VALUE
3379.		
3380.		
3381.		
3382.		
3383.		
3384.		
3385.		
3386.		
3387.		
HENS		
	PRICE PAID	VALUE
3388.		
3389.		
	TOTALS	

NOTES

Critters (Hens...)

3390.

Mrs. Nestor [QVC]
#(C01909) • 10"
Issued: 2004 • Retired: 2004
Original: $20 • Value: $22
With basket.

Hippos

3391.

Hilda P. Pottamus
#55229 • 12" • JB
Issued: 2002 • Current
Original: $18 • Value: $R/E

Horses

3392.

Clyde Clopsdale
#55224 • 15" • JB
Issued: 2002 • Current
Original: $24 • Value: $R/E

3393.

Shoeless P. Clopsdale [QVC]
#(C57732) • 9"
Issued: 2002 • Retired: 2002
Original: $14 • Value: $25

Kangaroos

3394.

Adelaide and Joey Downunder
#55222 • 12" • AM
Issued: 2001 • Retired: 2001
Original: $25 • Value: $30

3395.

Joey and Alice Outback
#568007 • 3½" • NO
Issued: 2002 • Current
Original: $10 • Value: $R/E

Lambs

3396.

Abbey Ewe
#91311-01 • 14" • TJ
Issued: 1996 • Retired: 1998
Original: $29 • Value: $40

3397.

Abbey Ewe [SFMB]
#41-72648 • 14"
Issued: 1999 • Retired: 1999
Original: $35 • Value: $48
♪ Mairzy Doats ♪

HENS
	PRICE PAID	VALUE
3390.		

HIPPOS
	PRICE PAID	VALUE
3391.		

HORSES
	PRICE PAID	VALUE
3392.		
3393.		

KANGAROOS
	PRICE PAID	VALUE
3394.		
3395.		

LAMBS
	PRICE PAID	VALUE
3396.		
3397.		

TOTALS

NOTES

Critters (Lambs)

3398.
Abbie Mae Woolsey
#552022 • 11"
Issued: 2003 • Retired: 2003
Original: $12 • Value: $12

3399.
Babs and Baab Woolsley
#568015 • 3½" • NO
Issued: 2003 • Current
Original: $10 • Value: $R/E

3400.
Brianne [SLE]
#unknown • 8"
Issued: 1997 • Retired: 1997
Original: $11 • Value: $32

3401.
Daisy Ewe
#5500 • 10" • AM
Issued: 1989 • Retired: 1994
Original: $14 • Value: $55

3402.
Dazey Ewe
#913122 • 10" • TJ
Issued: 2002 • Retired: 2002
Original: $22 • Value: $27

3403.
Dick Butkus
#9155 • 10" • TJ
Issued: 1994 • Retired: 1994
Original: $20 • Value: $144

3404.
Elspethe Ewe
#91312 • 8" • TJ
Issued: 1997 • Retired: 1998
Original: $11 • Value: $24

3405.
Embraceable Ewe
#913121 • 8" • TJ
Issued: 2000 • Retired: 2001
Original: $10 • Value: $12

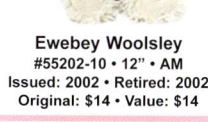

3406.
Ewebey Woolsley
#55202-10 • 12" • AM
Issued: 2002 • Retired: 2002
Original: $14 • Value: $14

3407.
Fleecie B. Ewe
#552032 • 14"
Issued: 2003 • Current
Original: $16 • Value: $R/E

3408.
Ivy M. Fuzzyfleece [QVC]
#(C57637) • 10"
Issued: 1999 • Retired: 1999
Original: $19 • Value: $33

3409.
Lambert Fuzzyfleece
#55201-06 • 10" • AM
Issued: 2002 • Retired: 2002
Original: $10 • Value: $13

LAMBS	PRICE PAID	VALUE
3398.		
3399.		
3400.		
3401.		
3402.		
3403.		
3404.		
3405.		
3406.		
3407.		
3408.		
3409.		
TOTALS		

NOTES

Critters (Lambs)

3410.
Lambsie Divy
#904074 • 7"
Issued: 2003 • Current
Original: $10 • Value: $R/E

3411.
Liza Fuzzyfleece
#55203-01 • 14" • AM
Issued: 2001 • Retired: 2001
Original: $18 • Value: $22

3412.
Lucibelle Fuzzyfleece
#55203-06 • 14" • AM
Issued: 2001 • Retired: 2002
Original: $18 • Value: $22

3413.
Lucy Belle Lambston [QVC]
#93111V (C56958) • 14"
Issued: 1999 • Retired: 1999
Original: $23 • Value: $54

3414.
Madabout Ewe
#91312-01 • 6" • TJ
Issued: 1998 • Retired: 2000
Original: $11 • Value: $20

3415.
Maisey Ewe
#5501 • 10" • AM
Issued: 1989 • Retired: 1994
Original: $14 • Value: $96

3416.
Matilda Baahead
#55200-01 • 10" • AM
Issued: 2000 • Retired: 2002
Original: $11 • Value: $14

3417.
Maude
#5510-07 • 7" • AM
Issued: 1994 • Retired: 1996
Original: $7 • Value: $45

3418.
McNeil Mutton
#91311-07 • 14" • TJ
Issued: 1996 • Retired: 1998
Original: $29 • Value: $37

3419.
Olivia [Dillards]
#94780DL • 10"
Issued: 2000 • Retired: 2000
Original: $20 • Value: $45

3420.
Pansy
#5501-01 • 10" • AM
Issued: 1994 • Retired: 1995
Original: $13 • Value: $80

3421.
Phoebe Ewe
#5510-01 • 7" • AM
Issued: 1994 • Retired: 1996
Original: $7 • Value: $47

LAMBS

	PRICE PAID	VALUE
3410.		
3411.		
3412.		
3413.		
3414.		
3415.		
3416.		
3417.		
3418.		
3419.		
3420.		
3421.		
TOTALS		

NOTES

Critters (Lambs, Lions)

3422.
Rose Mutton
#5520 • 15" • AM
Issued: 1989 • Retired: 1994
Original: $20 • Value: $55

3423.
Sadie Ewe
#5510-03 • 7" • AM
Issued: 1994 • Retired: 1994
Original: $7 • Value: $78

3424.
Squeeky
#5622 • 8"
Issued: 1992 • Retired: 1992
Original: $10 • Value: $73

3425.
Tallulah Baahead
#5520-01 • 14" • AM
Issued: 1995 • Retired: 2000
Original: $20 • Value: $47

3426.
Have You Seen Me?
Tutu
#6169L • 14" • TJ
Issued: 1991 • Retired: 1991
Original: $63 • Value: $275

3427.
U.B. Fuzzyfleece
#552033 • 14" • AM
Issued: 2004 • Current
Original: $18 • Value: $R/E

3428.
Violet Ewe
#5500-07 • 10" • AM
Issued: 1996 • Retired: 1998
Original: $14 • Value: $34

3429.
Wannabee Ewe Too
#91312-02 • 8" • TJ
Issued: 1999 • Retired: 1999
Original: $11 • Value: $20

Lions

3430.
Braden [SLE]
#unknown • 8"
Issued: 1997 • Retired: 1997
Original: $10 • Value: $24

3431.
Butch
#5861 • 8" • BB
Issued: 1994 • Retired: 1994
Original: $14 • Value: $96

3432.
Dickie The Lionheart
#51700 • 6" • BA
Issued: 1997 • Retired: 1999
Original: $5 • Value: $14

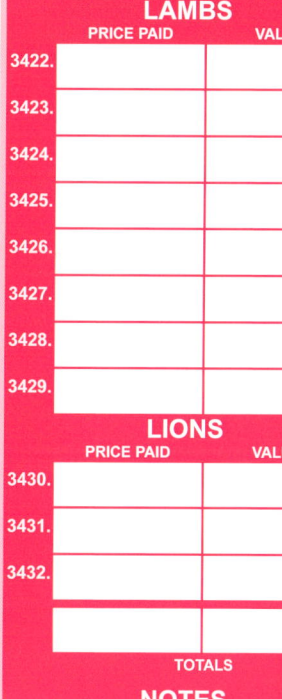

LAMBS		
	PRICE PAID	VALUE
3422.		
3423.		
3424.		
3425.		
3426.		
3427.		
3428.		
3429.		

LIONS		
	PRICE PAID	VALUE
3430.		
3431.		
3432.		
	TOTALS	

NOTES

Critters (Lions)

3433. Elvis
#5859 • 12" • AR
Issued: 1995 • Retired: 1996
Original: $20 • Value: $58

3434. I.M. Uproarius
#55220 • 11" • AM
Issued: 2000 • Current
Original: $13 • Value: $R/E

3435. Lance
#51900 • 8" • BA
Issued: 1997 • Retired: 1999
Original: $8 • Value: $13

3436. Leonard S. Uproarius [QVC]
#93145V (C99069) • 14"
Issued: 2000 • Retired: 2000
Original: $18 • Value: $35

3437. Leopold Q. Lion (old face)
#5530 • 10" • AM
Issued: 1989 • Retired: 1990
Original: $14 • Value: $146

3438. Leopold Q. Lion (new face)
#5530 • 10" • AM
Issued: 1991 • Retired: 1993
Original: $14 • Value: $131

3439. Leopold Q. Roarsmore [QVC]
#93229V (C64876) • 14"
Issued: 2001 • Retired: 2001
Original: $23 • Value: $35

3440. Merlin
#61671 • 14"
LE • Issued: 1991 • Retired: 1991
Original: $70 • Value: $275

3441. Sampson T. Lion
#5531 • 14" • AM
Issued: 1989 • Retired: 1992
Original: $29 • Value: $200

3442. Spike T. Lion
#5860 • 14" • BB
Issued: 1992 • Retired: 1994
Original: $20 • Value: $130

3443. Theo F. Wuzzie
#596007 • 3" • TF
Issued: 2000 • Retired: 2002
Original: $7 • Value: $8
Also with Topper, Tumble as QVC set.

3444. Zack [QVC]
#(C37283) • 8"
Issued: 1997 • Retired: 1997
Original: $11 • Value: $31

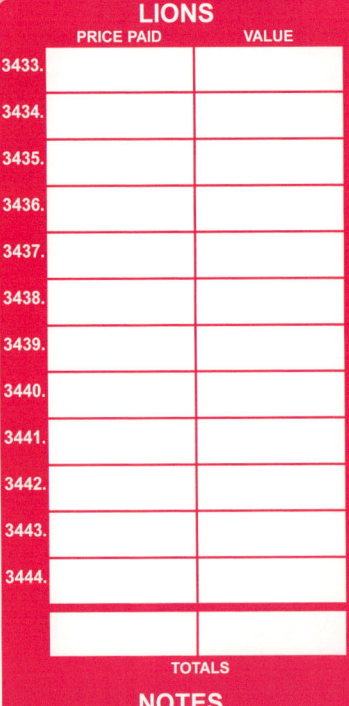

LIONS

	PRICE PAID	VALUE
3433.		
3434.		
3435.		
3436.		
3437.		
3438.		
3439.		
3440.		
3441.		
3442.		
3443.		
3444.		
TOTALS		

NOTES

Llamas

Mice

Critters (Llamas, Mice)

3445.
Dolly Llama
#57860 • 12" • AM
Issued: 2002 • Retired: 2002
Original: $18 • Value: $18

3446.
Chedda Mousaka (old face)
#5756-06 • 6" • AS
Issued: 1993 • Retired: 2000
Original: $8 • Value: $30

3447.
Chedda Mousaka (new face)
#5756-06 • 6" • AS
Issued: 1993 • Retired: 2000
Original: $8 • Value: $10

3448.
Brie Mouski (old face)
#5756 • 6" • AS
Issued: 1993 • Retired: 2002
Original: $8 • Value: $35

3449.
Brie Mouski (new face)
#5756 • 6" • AS
Issued: 1993 • Retired: 2002
Original: $8 • Value: $13

3450.
Bebe (pink sweater)
#9167 • 6" • TJ
Issued: 1994 • Retired: 1996
Original: $13 • Value: $41

LLAMAS		
	PRICE PAID	VALUE
3445.		

MICE		
	PRICE PAID	VALUE
3446.		
3447.		
3448.		
3449.		
3450.		
3451.		
3452.		
3453.		
3454.		
	TOTALS	

NOTES

3451.
Bebe (red sweater)
#9167-01 • 6" • TJ
Issued: 1994 • Retired: 1995
Original: $13 • Value: $45

3452.
Chutney Cheeseworthy
#916710 • 8" • TJ
Issued: 2000 • Retired: 2002
Original: $15 • Value: $18

3453.
Colby S. Mouski
#91672 • 6" • TJ
Issued: 1998 • Retired: 1999
Original: $12 • Value: $19
Also with Port as QVC set.

3454.
Cottage McNibble
#91673 • 6" • TJ
Issued: 1999 • Retired: 2000
Original: $10 • Value: $18

Critters (Mice)

3455.
Edam & Gouda [QVC]
#(C43991) • 6"
Issued: 1998 • Retired: 1998
Original: $19 • Value: $41

3456.
Felix Poppinsquash
#904017 • 3½" • TJ
Issued: 2002 • Retired: 2004
Original: $8 • Value: $8

3457.
Feta
#1075 • 6" • TJ
Issued: 1995 • Retired: 1996
Original: $12 • Value: $72

3458.
Gouda
#91671 • 6" • TJ
Issued: 1998 • Retired: 2000
Original: $10 • Value: $16

3459.
Havarti Chrismouse [GCC]
#94864GCC • 6"
Issued: 1998 • Retired: 1998
Original: $14 • Value: $21

3460.
Joy Chrismouse
#9165-06 • 6" • TJ
Issued: 1993 • Retired: 1996
Original: $12 • Value: $60
Also comes with burgundy scarf $70.

3461.
Kibbie
#525010 • 4" • AS
Issued: 2004 • Current
Original: $8 • Value: $R/E

3462.
Monterey Mouski
#91675 • 6" • TJ
Issued: 1999 • Retired: 2001
Original: $10 • Value: $11

3463.
Munster Q. Fondue
#5755-06 • 6" • AS
Issued: 2000 • Retired: 2000
Original: $7 • Value: $8

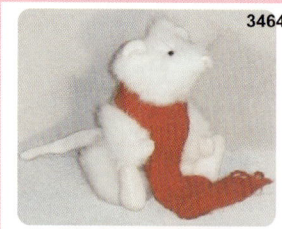

3464.
Noel Chrismouse (red scarf)
#9165-01 • 6" • TJ
Issued: 1993 • Retired: 1994
Original: $12 • Value: $70

3465.
Noel Chrismouse (striped scarf)
#9165-01 • 6" • TJ
Issued: 1993 • Retired: 1996
Original: $23 • Value: $55

3466.
Port S. Mouski with Colby [QVC]
#(C53094) • 6"
Issued: 1998 • Retired: 1998
Original: $19 • Value: $40

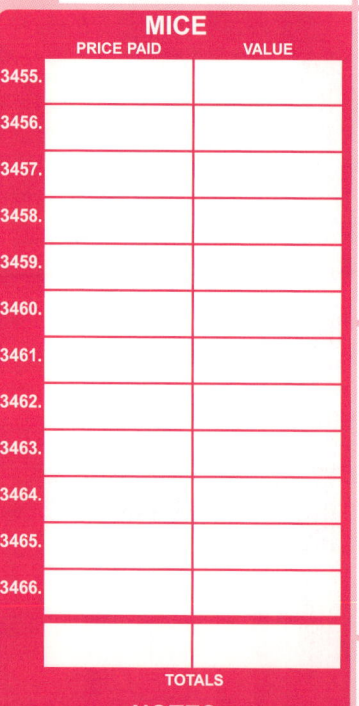

MICE

	PRICE PAID	VALUE
3455.		
3456.		
3457.		
3458.		
3459.		
3460.		
3461.		
3462.		
3463.		
3464.		
3465.		
3466.		
	TOTALS	

NOTES

Critters (Mice, Monkeys)

3467.
Romano B. Grated
#5755 • 6" • AS
Issued: 2000 • Retired: 2000
Original: $7 • Value: $15

3468.
Roq
#5757-01 • 8" • AS
Issued: 1994 • Retired: 1995
Original: $14 • Value: $65

3469.
Sharp McNibble
#91674 • 6" • TJ
Issued: 1999 • Retired: 2001
Original: $10 • Value: $15

3470.
Snackers McSnoozle
#904067 • 5"
Issued: 2002 • Retired: 2002
Original: $8 • Value: $16

3471.
Squeekers McPoppin [QVC]
#93335V (C20185) • 4"
Issued: 2002 • Retired: 2002
Original: $9 • Value: $17

3472.
Stilton Mouseberg
#5757 • 8" • AS
Issued: 1993 • Retired: 1995
Original: $14 • Value: $55

3473.
Swiss C. Mouski
#91670 • 6" • TJ
Issued: 2001 • Retired: 2002
Original: $10 • Value: $16

3474.
Tidbit F. Wuzzie
#595170 • 2½" • TF
Issued: 1999 • Retired: 2000
Original: $7 • Value: $13

3475.
Willie B. Mouseking [POG]
#94599POG • 6"
Issued: 2002 • Retired: 2002
Original: $12 • Value: $24

Monkeys

3476.
Ace Swingster [QVC]
#unknown • 10"
Issued: 2002 • Retired: 2002
Original: $12 • Value: $21

3477.
Bertha S. Simianski
#5524-11 • 10" • AM
Issued: 1993 • Retired: 1996
Original: $14 • Value: $40

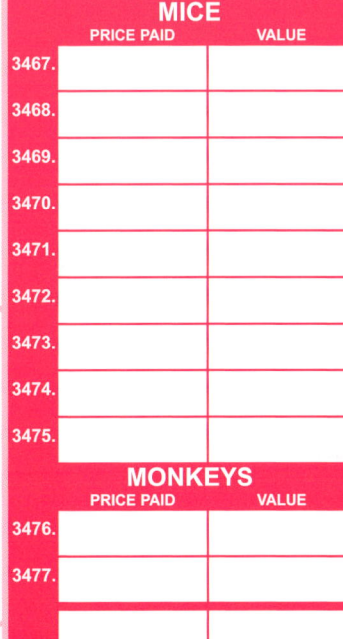

MICE		
	PRICE PAID	VALUE
3467.		
3468.		
3469.		
3470.		
3471.		
3472.		
3473.		
3474.		
3475.		

MONKEYS		
	PRICE PAID	VALUE
3476.		
3477.		
TOTALS		

NOTES

Critters (Monkeys)

3478.
Chuck Darwin
#55225 • 10" • JB
Issued: 2002 • Current
Original: $14 • Value: $R/E

3479.
Dalton Monkbury
#55242-08 • 8" • AM
Issued: 1998 • Retired: 2001
Original: $9 • Value: $12

3480.
Darwin Monkbury
#55242-05 • 8" • AM
Issued: 1998 • Retired: 2001
Original: $9 • Value: $12

3481.
Finster R. Tsuris
#55241-05 • 10" • AM
Issued: 1997 • Retired: 1999
Original: $14 • Value: $35

3482.
Giseppi Renaldi [QVC]
#(C78113) • 8" • AR
Issued: 2000 • Retired: 2000
Original: $18 • Value: $28

3483.
Imogene R. Tsursis
#55241-11 • 10" • AM
Issued: 1997 • Retired: 1999
Original: $14 • Value: $34

3484.
Jim I. Swingster
#55241-08 • 10" • AM
Issued: 2000 • Retired: 2000
Original: $14 • Value: $16

3485.
Monkey See & Monkey Do
#568009 • 3½" • NO
Issued: 2002 • Current
Original: $10 • Value: $R/E

3486.
Simianne Z. Jodibear
#92000-15 • 7" • AR
Issued: 2001 • Retired: 2002
Original: $16 • Value: $19

3487.
Simon S. Simianski
#5524-10 • 10" • AM
Issued: 1993 • Retired: 1996
Original: $14 • Value: $55

3488.
Toodles F. Wuzzie
#596006 • 3" • TF
Issued: 2000 • Retired: 2000
Original: $8 • Value: $10

Have You Seen Me?

3489.
Topper F. Wuzzie with Theo and Tumble [QVC]
#unknown • 3"
Issued: 2000 • Retired: 2000
Original: $7 • Value: $10

MONKEYS

	PRICE PAID	VALUE
3478.		
3479.		
3480.		
3481.		
3482.		
3483.		
3484.		
3485.		
3486.		
3487.		
3488.		
3489.		
TOTALS		

NOTES

Moose

3490.
Beatrice Von Hindenmoose (beige)
#5542 • 17" with antlers • NL
Issued: 1991 • Retired: 1993
Original: $16 • Value: $247

3491.
Beatrice Von Hiddenmoose (mocha)
#5542 • 17" with antlers • NL
Issued: 1993 • Retired: 1997
Original: $19 • Value: $73

3492.
Bismark Von Hindenmoose
#5545-05 • 20" with antlers • NL
Issued: 1995 • Retired: 1996
Original: $18 • Value: $77

3493.
Cocoa Mousse [Sarah's Bears]
#unknown • 8" without antlers
LE of 1000 • Issued: 2003 • Retired: 2003
Original: $20 • Value: $N/E

3494.
Corny Mooseltreat
#904342 • 8" without antlers • TJ
Issued: 2004 • Current
Original: $12 • Value: $R/E

3495.
Cousin Murray (burgundy hat) [Alps]
#unknown • 14" without antlers
Issued: 1998 • Retired: 1998
Original: $20 • Value: $60

3496.
Cousin Murray [Alps]
#unknown • 14" without antlers
Issued: 2001 • Retired: 2001
Original: $23 • Value: $50

MOOSE		
	PRICE PAID	VALUE
3490.		
3491.		
3492.		
3493.		
3494.		
3495.		
3496.		
3497.		
3498.		
3499.		
3500.		
	TOTALS	

NOTES

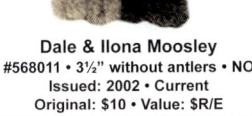

3497.
Dale & Ilona Moosley
#568011 • 3½" without antlers • NO
Issued: 2002 • Current
Original: $10 • Value: $R/E

3498.
Eddie Bauer Moose [Eddie Bauer]
#unknown • 17" with antlers
Issued: 1994 • Retired: 1994
Original: $N/E • Value: $95

3499.
Edwina
#9144 • 14" with antlers • TJ
Issued: 1994 • Retired: 1997
Original: $20 • Value: $38

3500.
Egon Von HindenMoose
#5546 • 6" without antlers • NL
Issued: 1993 • Retired: 1997
Original: $8 • Value: $40

Critters (Moose)

3501.
Emily Ann [Lord & Taylor]
#unknown • 14" without antlers
Issued: 1997 • Retired: 1997
Original: $24 • Value: $165

3502.
Euphoria
#91446 • 8" without antlers • TJ
Issued: 1995 • Retired: 1998
Original: $14 • Value: $24

3503.
Father Kissmoose
#917280 • 14" without antlers • TJ
Issued: 2001 • Retired: 2002
Original: $21 • Value: $25

3504.
Father Krismoose
#9192M • 17" with antlers
LE of 400 • Issued: 1992 • Retired: 1992
Original: $70 • Value: $450

3505.
Father Moose Moss
#9211 • 17" with antlers
LE of 500 • Issued: 1993 • Retired: 1993
Original: $70 • Value: $448

Have You Seen Me?
3506.
Father Moosemas
#9200M • 17" with antlers
LE of 500 • Issued: 1993 • Retired: 1993
Original: $70 • Value: $423

3507.
Festus
#91444 • 14" with antlers • TJ
Issued: 1995 • Retired: 1996
Original: $21 • Value: $55

3508.
Gertrude
#6108 • 17" with antlers • TJ
Issued: 1993 • Retired: 1993
Original: $25 • Value: $292

3509.
Gustaf Mooseltoff
#904026 • 12" without antlers • TJ
Issued: 2002 • Retired: 2004
Original: $27 • Value: $27

3510.
Helmut (green sweater)
#9145 • 14" with antlers • TJ
Issued: 1994 • Retired: 1995
Original: $27 • Value: $139

3511.
Helmut (red or burgundy sweater)
#9145 • 14" with antlers • TJ
Issued: 1994 • Retired: 1995
Original: $27 • Value: $150

3512.
Ilona B. Mooseltoes [QVC]
#93303V (C107579) • 12" without antlers
Issued: 2002 • Retired: 2002
Original: $29 • Value: $60

MOOSE

	PRICE PAID	VALUE
3501.		
3502.		
3503.		
3504.		
3505.		
3506.		
3507.		
3508.		
3509.		
3510.		
3511.		
3512.		
TOTALS		

NOTES

Critters (Moose)

3513.
Irwin Mooseltoe
#917296 • 12" without antlers • TJ
Issued: 2000 • Retired: 2000
Original: $24 • Value: $40

3514.
Izzy [Dillards]
#94745DL • 10" without antlers
Issued: 1999 • Retired: 1999
Original: $20 • Value: $45

3515.
Justina (formerly Philomena)
#91443 • 14" without antlers • TJ
Issued: 1995 • Retired: 1997
Original: $27 • Value: $59

3516.
Kris Moose
#9192 • 14" without antlers • JB
Issued: 1992 • Retired: 1996
Original: $27 • Value: $94

3517.
Krismoose
#6167M • 17" with antlers
LE of 500 • Issued: 1992 • Retired: 1992
Original: $70 • Value: $450

3518.
Lester Mintly
#904214 • 12" without antlers • TJ
Issued: 2003 • Current
Original: $25 • Value: $R/E

3519.
Macadoo McSnoozle with Ernie [QVC]
#93368V (C20915) • 14" without antlers
Issued: 2002 • Retired: 2002
Original: $32 • Value: $55

3520.
Macy M. Mooselmuff [QVC]
#93235V • 11" without antlers
Issued: 2001 • Retired: 2001
Original: $21 • Value: $75

3521.
Magillacuddy
#554310 • 18" without antlers • AS
Issued: 2004 • Current
Original: $26 • Value: $R/E

3522.
Magnus P. Moosefield [QVC]
#(C53089) • 17" without antlers
Issued: 1998 • Retired: 1998
Original: $21 • Value: $167

3523.
Mahoney S. Mooseltoof
#554211 • 14" without antlers • AS
Issued: 2003 • Current
Original: $18 • Value: $R/E

3524.
Malcolm Mooselfluff [QVC]
#unknown • 10" without antlers
Issued: 2000 • Retired: 2000
Original: $20 • Value: $65

MOOSE	PRICE PAID	VALUE
3513.		
3514.		
3515.		
3516.		
3517.		
3518.		
3519.		
3520.		
3521.		
3522.		
3523.		
3524.		
TOTALS		

NOTES

Critters (Moose)

3525.
Malley Q. Mooselfluff
#554111 • 10" without antlers • AM
Issued: 2002 • Current
Original: $12 • Value: $R/E

3526.
Malone E. Moosetrax
#554110-05 • 10" without antlers • NL
Issued: 2000 • Retired: 2000
Original: $12 • Value: $14

3527.
Manfred von Merrymoose [GCC]
#94581GCC • 13" without antlers
Issued: 1997 • Retired: 1997
Original: $23 • Value: $53

3528.
Manheim Von Hindenmoose
#5545 • 20" with antlers • NL
Issued: 1992 • Retired: 1996
Original: $29 • Value: $120

3529.
Markle
#590070 • 8" without antlers • MB
Issued: 2004 • Current
Original: $26 • Value: $R/E

3530.
Martin V. Moosington
#590301-05 • 10" without antlers • MB
Issued: 2000 • Retired: 2001
Original: $31 • Value: $60

3531.
Martini
#91109 • 12" without antlers • TJ
Issued: 1998 • Retired: 1999
Original: $12 • Value: $25

3532.
Marwood
#917298 • 36" without antlers • TJ
Issued: 2001 • Retired: 2001
Original: $40 • Value: $85

3533.
Mattie Frostbuns [QVC]
#unknown • 10" without antlers
Issued: 2001 • Retired: 2001
Original: $21 • Value: $85

3534.
Maurice Von Hindenmoose
#5540-05 • 14" with antlers • NL
Issued: 1996 • Retired: 1999
Original: $14 • Value: $18

3535.
Maury McSnoozle
#904065 • 8" without antlers
Issued: 2002 • Retired: 2002
Original: $15 • Value: $25

3536.
Maxine von HindenMoose [QVC]
#unknown • 14" without antlers
Issued: 1997 • Retired: 1997
Original: $23 • Value: $185

MOOSE

	PRICE PAID	VALUE
3525.		
3526.		
3527.		
3528.		
3529.		
3530.		
3531.		
3532.		
3533.		
3534.		
3535.		
3536.		
TOTALS		

NOTES

Critters (Moose)

3537.
Maynard Von Hindenmoose [Spiegel]
#unknown • 14" with antlers
Issued: N/E • Retired: N/E
Original: $N/E • Value: $75

3538.
Maynard Von HindenMoose
#5541 • 14" with antlers • NL
Issued: 1992 • Retired: 1997
Original: $14 • Value: $43

3539.
McCormic T. Moosleton [GCC]
#94873Gcc • 10" without antlers
Issued: 1999 • Retired: 1999
Original: $18 • Value: $29

3540.
McKinley [QVC]
#(C95009) • 10" without antlers • MB
LE of 1800 • Issued: 1999 • Retired: 1999
Original: $33 • Value: $71

3541.
Meeka (green sweater) [Alps]
#unknown • 14" without antlers
Issued: 1995 • Retired: 1995
Original: $28 • Value: $125

3542.
Meeka (green plaid pajamas) [Alps]
#unknown • 14" without antlers
Issued: 1996 • Retired: 1996
Original: $28 • Value: $78

3543.
Meeka (red sweater) [Alps]
#unknown • 14" without antlers
Issued: 1998 • Retired: 1998
Original: $28 • Value: $70

3544.
Meeka (purple sweater) [Alps]
#326 • 14" without antlers
Issued: 1999 • Retired: 1999
Original: $28 • Value: $67

3545.
**Meeka
(green sweater with flowers) [Alps]**
#unknown • 14" without antlers
Issued: 2000 • Retired: 2000
Original: $30 • Value: $55

3546.
Meeka (mint green sweater) [Alps]
#unknown • 14" without antlers
Issued: 2001 • Retired: 2001
Original: $30 • Value: $43

3547.
Menachem
#91212 • 8½" without antlers • TJ
Issued: 1996 • Retired: 1998
Original: $20 • Value: $34

3548.
Mendel Von HindenMoose
#5547 • 6" without antlers • NL
Issued: 1996 • Retired: 2000
Original: $8 • Value: $18

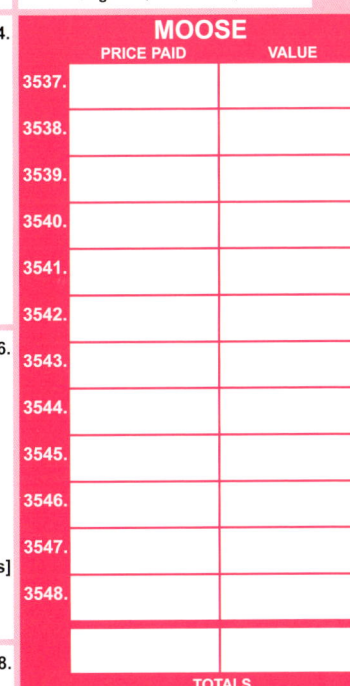

MOOSE		
	PRICE PAID	VALUE
3537.		
3538.		
3539.		
3540.		
3541.		
3542.		
3543.		
3544.		
3545.		
3546.		
3547.		
3548.		
	TOTALS	

NOTES

Critters (Moose)

3549.
Mervin Q. Rugsley [QVC]
#93359V • 36" without antlers
Issued: 2002 • Retired: 2002
Original: $95 • Value: $123

3550.
Milhous N. Moosington
#590300 • 14" without antlers • MB
Issued: 1999 • Retired: 1999
Original: $81 • Value: $112

3551.
Miliken von Hiddenmoose
(closed mouth)
#55421-05 • 17" without antlers • NL
Issued: 1997 • Retired: 1999
Original: $20 • Value: $35

3552.
Miliken von Hindenmoose
(nibble mouth)
#55421-05 • 17" without antlers • NL
Issued: 1997 • Retired: 1999
Original: $20 • Value: $45

3553.
Miller G. Mooselhuggs [QVC]
#93246V • 30" without antlers
Issued: 2001 • Retired: 2001
Original: $58 • Value: $85

3554.
Minney Moose
#91108 • 14" with antlers • TJ
Issued: 1998 • Retired: 1998
Original: $20 • Value: $33

3555.
Moe Munchencrunch [GCC]
#94899GCC • 14" without antlers
LE of 3375 • Issued: 2001 • Retired: 2001
Original: $22 • Value: $65

3556.
Montague
#9121 • 8" without antlers • TJ
Issued: 1994 • Retired: 1996
Original: $20 • Value: $47

3557.
Montana Mooski
#917295 • 12" without antlers • TJ
Issued: 1999 • Retired: 2001
Original: $26 • Value: $35

3558.
Monte Mooselton
#917290 • 12" without antlers • TJ
Issued: 1998 • Retired: 1999
Original: $21 • Value: $44

3559.
Mookie (cream sweater) [Alps]
#8697 • 11" without antlers
Issued: 1995 • Retired: 1995
Original: $20 • Value: $68

3560.
Mookie (navy sweater with red and white stripe) [Alps]
#327 • 11" without antlers
Issued: 1998 • Retired: 1998
Original: $20 • Value: $55

MOOSE

	PRICE PAID	VALUE
3549.		
3550.		
3551.		
3552.		
3553.		
3554.		
3555.		
3556.		
3557.		
3558.		
3559.		
3560.		
TOTALS		

NOTES

Critters (Moose)

3561. Mookie (beige sweater with aztec trim) [Alps]
#unknown • 11" without antlers
Issued: 2000 • Retired: 2000
Original: $20 • Value: $52

3562. Morley P. Moosetrax
#554112 • 14" without antlers • AM
Issued: 2002 • Retired: 2002
Original: $17 • Value: $17

3563. Mortimer [Lord & Taylor]
#94107-26 • 14" without antlers
Issued: 1996 • Retired: 1996
Original: $30 • Value: $175
Very rare.

3564. Mortimer Von Hindenmoose
#55411-05 • 14" without antlers • NL
Issued: 1997 • Retired: 1999
Original: $14 • Value: $35

3565. Morton Elfbeary [QVC]
#(C20886) • 10" without antlers
Issued: 2002 • Retired: 2002
Original: $31 • Value: $40

3566. Mother Moosemas
#unknown • 17" with antlers • JB
Issued: 1992 • Retired: 1992
Original: $70 • Value: $400

3567. Mountie Moosletoe [GCC]
#94926GCC • 15" without antlers
Issued: 2002 • Retired: 2002
Original: $30 • Value: $45

3568. Moxley Von Mooseltoes
#904054 • 8" without antlers
Issued: 2002 • Retired: 2004
Original: $14 • Value: $14

3569. Mr. Mufflemoose [QVC]
#93494V (C6277) • 14" without antlers
Issued: 2003 • Retired: 2003
Original: $22 • Value: $26

3570. Muddles T. Moxley [BBC]
#918034SM • 40" without antlers
Issued: 2003 • Retired: 2003
Original: $150 • Value: $180

3571. Muffles P. Mooseltoof
#554114 • 10" without antlers • AS
Issued: 2003 • Current
Original: $12 • Value: $R/E

3572. Mukluk (blue sweater) [Alps]
#8631 • 14" without antlers
Issued: 1995 • Retired: 1995
Original: $30 • Value: $95

MOOSE

	PRICE PAID	VALUE
3561.		
3562.		
3563.		
3564.		
3565.		
3566.		
3567.		
3568.		
3569.		
3570.		
3571.		
3572.		
TOTALS		

NOTES

Critters (Moose)

3573.
Mukluk (red plaid pajamas) [Alps]
#unknown • 14" without antlers
Issued: 1996 • Retired: 1996
Original: $28 • Value: $60

3574.
Mukluk (blue/green sweater) [Alps]
#unknown • 14" without antlers
Issued: 1997 • Retired: 1997
Original: $30 • Value: $75

3575.
Mukluk (2000) [Alps]
#unknown • 14" without antlers
Issued: 2000 • Retired: 2000
Original: $25 • Value: $30

3576.
Mukluk (blue sweater with ribbon trim) [Alps]
#unknown • 14" without antlers
Issued: 2000 • Retired: 2000
Original: $30 • Value: $65

3577.
Mukluk (Weekender) [Alps]
#unknown • 14" without antlers
Issued: 2001 • Retired: 2001
Original: $30 • Value: $36

3578.
Mukluk (Super Mukluk) [Alps]
#unknown • 14" without antlers
Issued: 2001 • Retired: 2001
Original: $30 • Value: $39

3579.
Mukluk (American Mukluk) [Alps]
#unknown • 14" without antlers
Issued: 2002 • Retired: 2002
Original: $30 • Value: $39

3580.
Mukluk (Varsity Mukluk) [Alps]
#unknown • 14" without antlers
Issued: 2002 • Retired: 2002
Original: $30 • Value: $39

3581.
Mukluk (Super Mukluk III) [Alps]
#unknown • 14" without antlers
Issued: 2002 • Retired: 2002
Original: $30 • Value: $35

3582.
Mukluk (Cold Springs) [Alps]
#unknown • 14" without antlers
Issued: 2003 • Retired: 2003
Original: $30 • Value: $35

3583.
Mukluk (Holiday) [Alps]
#unknown • 14" without antlers
Issued: 2003 • Retired: 2003
Original: $30 • Value: $35

3584.
Mukluk (Outdoorsman) [Alps]
#unknown • 14" without antlers
Issued: 2003 • Retired: 2003
Original: $30 • Value: $35

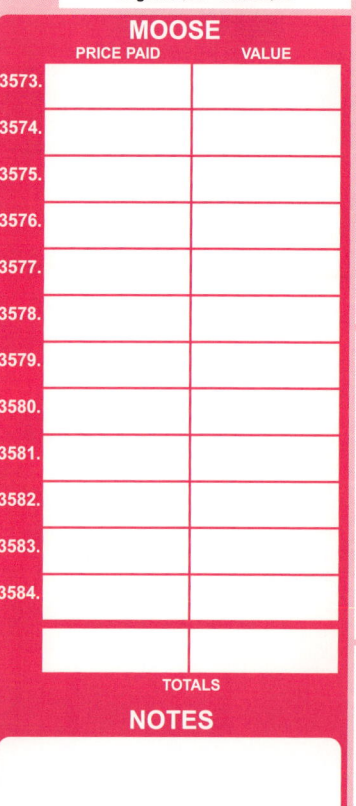

MOOSE	PRICE PAID	VALUE
3573.		
3574.		
3575.		
3576.		
3577.		
3578.		
3579.		
3580.		
3581.		
3582.		
3583.		
3584.		
TOTALS		

NOTES

Critters (Moose)

3585.
Mukluk (Weekender Mukluk II) [Alps]
#unknown • 14" without antlers
Issued: 2003 • Retired: 2003
Original: $30 • Value: $35

3586.
Mukluk (Tobacco Weekender) [Alps]
#unknown • 14" without antlers
Issued: 2004 • Retired: 2004
Original: $30 • Value: $30

3587.
Mungo Mooselwood [QVC]
#93506V (C5079) • 14" without antlers
Issued: 2003 • Retired: 2003
Original: $29 • Value: $35

3588.
Murdock Q. Moosley
#554115 • 10" without antlers • AS
Issued: 2004 • Current
Original: $11 • Value: $R/E

3589.
Murgatroyd (cream tree sweater)
#5540 • 14" with antlers
Issued: 1991 • Retired: 1994
Original: $14 • Value: $64

3590.
Murgatroyd (taupe tree sweater)
#5540 • 14" with antlers
Issued: 1991 • Retired: 1994
Original: $14 • Value: $60

3591.
Murgatroyd Von Hindenmoose
#5540 • 14" with antlers • NL
Issued: 1991 • Retired: 1993
Original: $14 • Value: $60

3592.
Murgatroyd Von HindenMoose II
#5540 • 14" with antlers • NL
Issued: 1993 • Retired: 1997
Original: $14 • Value: $47

3593.
Murphy Mooselfluff
#917291 • 10" without antlers • TJ
Issued: 1999 • Retired: 2002
Original: $20 • Value: $24

3594.
Murray Moosehoofer
#554210-05 • 14" without antlers • NL
Issued: 2000 • Retired: 2000
Original: $15 • Value: $20

3595.
Murtaugh Moosetrax
#917297 • 12" without antlers • TJ
Issued: 2001 • Retired: 2001
Original: $18 • Value: $22

3596.
Murtaugh Moosetrax [SFMB]
#917297SF • 12" without antlers • TJ
Issued: 2002 • Retired: 2002
Original: $20 • Value: $26
♪ Home On The Range ♪

MOOSE

	PRICE PAID	VALUE
3585.		
3586.		
3587.		
3588.		
3589.		
3590.		
3591.		
3592.		
3593.		
3594.		
3595.		
3596.		
TOTALS		

NOTES

Critters (Moose, Owls)

3597.
Myles VonHinden Moose
#55470-05 • 6" without antlers • NL
Issued: 2000 • Retired: 2000
Original: $9 • Value: $11

3598.
Myron Von Hindenmoose
#912121 • 10" without antlers • TJ
Issued: 1997 • Retired: 1998
Original: $21 • Value: $34
Hat may or may not have bells.

3599.
Nadia Von Hindenmoose
#5542-01 • 17" with antlers • NL
Issued: 1994 • Retired: 1996
Original: $20 • Value: $120

3600.
Siegfried Von Hindenmoose
#5544 • 20" with antlers • NL
Issued: 1991 • Retired: 1995
Original: $29 • Value: $222

3601.
Spruce McMoose
#904352 • 10" without antlers • TJ
Issued: 2004 • Current
Original: $20 • Value: $R/E

3602.
T. Fargo Wuzzie
#595102 • 5" without antlers • TF
Issued: 1999 • Retired: 2000
Original: $9 • Value: $14
Also sold with T. Fuzzball,
T. Foster as QVC set.

3603.

Have You Seen Me?

T. Fargo, T. Foster & T. Fuzzball Wuzzie [QVC]
#unknown • 5" without antlers
Issued: 1999 • Retired: 1999
Original: $24 • Value: $36

3604.
Talbot F. Wuzzie
#595440 • 3½" without antlers • TF
Issued: 1998 • Retired: 1999
Original: $7 • Value: $14

3605.
Vermooth with Margarita [QVC]
#unknown • 12" without antlers
Issued: 1998 • Retired: 1998
Original: $26 • Value: $48

3606.
Windberg
#5675-05 • 8" without antlers • FL
Issued: 1995 • Retired: 1999
Original: $13 • Value: $21

Owls

3607.
Lester McHootle
#904006 • 4" • TJ
Issued: 2002 • Retired: 2002
Original: $10 • Value: $10

MOOSE

	PRICE PAID	VALUE
3597.		
3598.		
3599.		
3600.		
3601.		
3602.		
3603.		
3604.		
3605.		
3606.		

OWLS

	PRICE PAID	VALUE
3607.		

TOTALS

NOTES

Critters (Owls, Pandas)

3608.
Mr. Hooter
#55227 • 7" • JB
Issued: 2002 • Current
Original: $14 • Value: $R/E

3609.
Mr. McHootle [QVC]
#(C98543) • 8"
Issued: 2001 • Retired: 2001
Original: $14 • Value: $20

Pandas

3610.
Bamboo Bearington
#590030 • 14" • MB
Issued: 2000 • Retired: 2001
Original: $50 • Value: $75

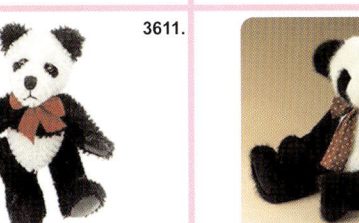

3611.
C. Carryout Bearington
#590106 • 4½" • MB
Issued: 2000 • Retired: 2002
Original: $10 • Value: $12

3612.
Checkers
#501001 • 18" • AS
Issued: 2004 • Current
Original: $26 • Value: $R/E

3613.
Chopsticks
#51200-07 • 13" • JB
Issued: 2001 • Retired: 2001
Original: $15 • Value: $18

3614.
Dewey P. Wongvruin
#5154 • 16" • JB
Issued: 1997 • Retired: 1999
Original: $29 • Value: $34

3615.
Domino
#57004-07 • 12" • AS
Issued: 2001 • Retired: 2001
Original: $16 • Value: $19

3616.
Hsing Hsing and Ling Ling Wongbruin
#568002 • 3½" • NO
Issued: 2002 • Current
Original: $10 • Value: $R/E

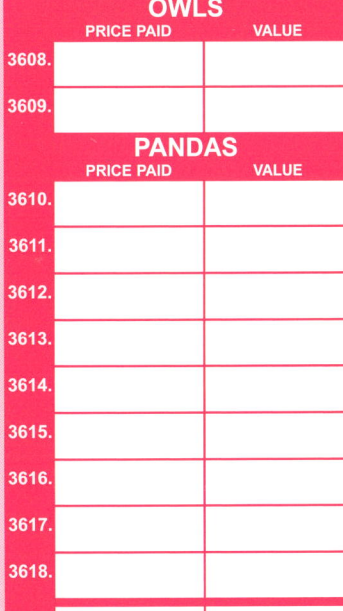

3617.
Hsing-Hsing Wongbruin
#51540-07 • 14" • JB
Issued: 1999 • Retired: 2001
Original: $16 • Value: $25

3618.
Ma Shen San [QVC]
#93211V (C59859) • 16"
Issued: 2001 • Retired: 2001
Original: $26 • Value: $35

OWLS

	PRICE PAID	VALUE
3608.		
3609.		

PANDAS

	PRICE PAID	VALUE
3610.		
3611.		
3612.		
3613.		
3614.		
3615.		
3616.		
3617.		
3618.		
TOTALS		

NOTES

Critters (Pandas)

3619.
Ming-Ming Woodsley
#92002-09 • 16" • AR
Issued: 2003 • Current
Original: $20 • Value: $R/E

3620.
Nana Panda
#5765 • 14" • HD
Issued: 1991 • Retired: 1992
Original: $19 • Value: $575

3621.
Ogden B. Bean (small version)
#5153 • 8" • JB
Issued: 1994 • Retired: 1994
Original: $12 • Value: $45

3622.
Ogden B. Bean (large version)
#5153 • 10" • JB
Issued: 1994 • Retired: 1999
Original: $12 • Value: $27

3623.
Olas & Omar [QVC]
#unknown • 6"
Issued: 1997 • Retired: 1997
Original: $14 • Value: $32

3624.
P.B. Woodsley [QVC]
#93458V (C3136) • 16"
Issued: 2003 • Retired: 2003
Original: $19 • Value: $23

3625.
Panda-Boo Woodsley
#92002-12 • 14" • MB
Issued: 2004 • Current
Original: $25 • Value: $R/E

3626.
Pandemonium [QVC]
#93551V (C06202) • 14"
Issued: 2004 • Retired: 2004
Original: $24 • Value: $35

3627.
Pandora
#500052 • 40" • AS
Issued: 2002 • Retired: 2002
Original: $200 • Value: $204

3628.
Shao Pan Yo [QVC]
#93254V (C100423) • 30"
LE of 504 • Issued: 2001 • Retired: 2001
Original: $100 • Value: $130

3629.
Shao Pan Yo
#500080 • 30" • JB
Issued: 2002 • Retired: 2002
Original: $99 • Value: $101

3630.
Shi Wong [QVC]
#(C95180) • 12" • MB
LE of 2508 • Issued: 2000 • Retired: 2000
Original: $36 • Value: $75

PANDAS	PRICE PAID	VALUE
3619.		
3620.		
3621.		
3622.		
3623.		
3624.		
3625.		
3626.		
3627.		
3628.		
3629.		
3630.		
	TOTALS	

NOTES

Critters (Pandas, Penguins, Pigs)

3631.
Ting F. Wuzzie
#595161 • 2½" • TF
Issued: 1999 • Retired: 2000
Original: $7 • Value: $16

3632.
Xin Fu Wongbruin [QVC]
#(C99065) • 12"
Issued: 2000 • Retired: 2000
Original: $11 • Value: $20

3633.
Yolanda Panda [QVC]
#(C46248) • 12" • BA
Issued: 1998 • Retired: 1998
Original: $25 • Value: $40

3634.
Yolanda Panda
#57701 • 6" • AS
Issued: 1998 • Retired: 2001
Original: $9 • Value: $15

Penguins

3635.
Pennsley
#590071 • 8" • MB
Issued: 2004 • Current
Original: $26 • Value: $R/E

3636.
Sillie Waddlewalk
#555002 • 6" • AM
Issued: 2001 • Retired: 2001
Original: $9 • Value: $11

3637.
Tuxie Waddlewalk
#55500 • 8" • NL
Issued: 1999 • Retired: 2001
Original: $11 • Value: $12
Also with Opie, Tweedle as QVC set.

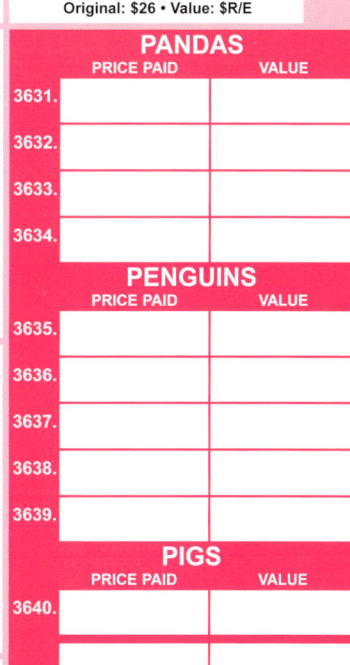

3638.
Tweedle & Opie with Tuxie Waddlewalk [QVC]
#(C95074) • 6"
Issued: 1999 • Retired: 1999
Original: $25 • Value: $35

3639.
Willie Waddlewalk
#555001 • 6" • NL
Issued: 2000 • Retired: 2002
Original: $9 • Value: $11

Pigs

3640.
Aphrodite (without heart)
#5539 • 7" • AM
Issued: 1994 • Retired: 1995
Original: $12 • Value: $55

PANDAS		
	PRICE PAID	VALUE
3631.		
3632.		
3633.		
3634.		

PENGUINS		
	PRICE PAID	VALUE
3635.		
3636.		
3637.		
3638.		
3639.		

PIGS		
	PRICE PAID	VALUE
3640.		

TOTALS

NOTES

Critters (Pigs)

3641.
Aphrodite (with heart)
#5539 • 7" • AM
Issued: 1995 • Retired: 1996
Original: $12 • Value: $44

3642.
Baby Rosebud [Harry & David]
#473E • 8"
Issued: 1996 • Retired: 1996
Original: $20 • Value: $35

3643.
Betty Jane [SLE]
#unknown • 11"
Issued: 1999 • Retired: 1999
Original: $26 • Value: $45
Comes with quilt.

3644.
Big Pig, Little Pig [CAN]
#BC94279 • 12"
LE of 10000 • Issued: 1998 • Retired: 1998
Original: $29 • Value: $50

3645.
Charlotte and Wilbur Hamstein
#568016 • 3½" • NO
Issued: 2003 • Current
Original: $10 • Value: $R/E

3646.
Erin O'Pigg
#5536-09 • 11" • AM
Issued: 1996 • Retired: 1997
Original: $14 • Value: $38

3647.
Erin Shaughnessy [Dillards]
#94738DL • 8"
Issued: 1998 • Retired: 1998
Original: $16 • Value: $33

3648.
Farland O'Pigg
#5538 • 16" • AM
Issued: 1992 • Retired: 1997
Original: $29 • Value: $72
Sold as "Buddy" at Harry and David stores.

3649.
Farley O'Pigg
#55392-07 • 8" • AM
Issued: 2001 • Retired: 2002
Original: $11 • Value: $13

3650.
G. Wilbur McSwine [QVC]
#(C41096) • 8"
Issued: 1997 • Retired: 1997
Original: $16 • Value: $49

3651.
Hamilton [Cracker Barrel]
#unknown • 11"
Issued: 1999 • Retired: 1999
Original: $25 • Value: $42

3652.
Hamlet
#55360 • 8" • AM
Issued: 2001 • Retired: 2002
Original: $11 • Value: $13

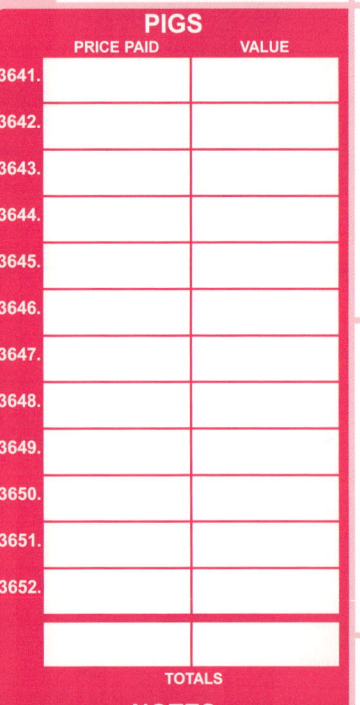

PIGS	PRICE PAID	VALUE
3641.		
3642.		
3643.		
3644.		
3645.		
3646.		
3647.		
3648.		
3649.		
3650.		
3651.		
3652.		
TOTALS		

NOTES

Critters (Pigs)

3653.
Ivy Bloomengrows
#91602 • 8" • TJ
Issued: 2001 • Retired: 2001
Original: $16 • Value: $26

3654.
Jubilation P. Hambone [QVC]
#(C60294) • 9"
Issued: 2002 • Retired: 2002
Original: $20 • Value: $45

3655.
Kaitlin & Kendall McSwine [QVC]
#unknown • 8"
Issued: 1998 • Retired: 1998
Original: $N/E • Value: $45
This Kendall is different plaid than regular line.

3656.
Kaitlin K. Trufflesnout
#91601-03 • 8" • TJ
Issued: 1999 • Retired: 1999
Original: $12 • Value: $25

3657.
Kaitlin McSwine
#91601 • 8" • TJ
Issued: 1997 • Retired: 1999
Original: $12 • Value: $30

3658.
Kaitlin McSwine II
#91601-01 • 8" • TJ
Issued: 1997 • Retired: 1999
Original: $14 • Value: $26

3659.
Kaitlin McSwine III
#91601-02 • 8"
Issued: 1998 • Retired: 2001
Original: $13 • Value: $25

3660.
Katie [SLE]
#unknown • 5"
Issued: 1998 • Retired: 1998
Original: $13 • Value: $35

3661.
Katie O'Pigg [Dillards]
#unknown • 6"
Issued: 1997 • Retired: 1997
Original: $N/E • Value: $38

3662.
Lena O'Pigg [Dillards]
#94706DL • 11"
Issued: 1996 • Retired: 1996
Original: $15 • Value: $45

3663.
Lofton Q. McSwine
#55391-09 • 8" • AM
Issued: 1997 • Retired: 2000
Original: $11 • Value: $16

3664.
Maggie O'Pigg
#5536-07 • 11" • AM
Issued: 1993 • Retired: 1999
Original: $14 • Value: $32
Found both bean filled and poly-fil.

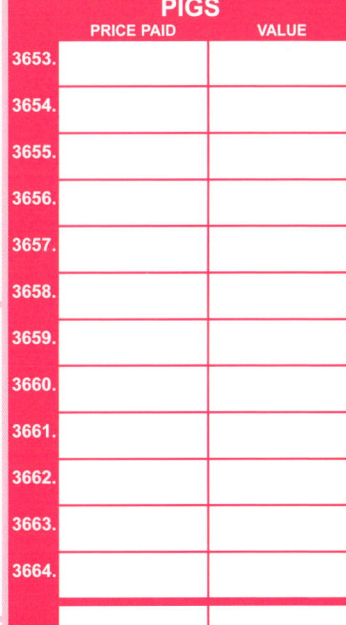

PIGS	PRICE PAID	VALUE
3653.		
3654.		
3655.		
3656.		
3657.		
3658.		
3659.		
3660.		
3661.		
3662.		
3663.		
3664.		

TOTALS

NOTES

Critters (Pigs)

3665.
Merentha [Dillards]
#94727DL • 11"
Issued: 1997 • Retired: 1997
Original: $24 • Value: $60

3666.
Muddles Q. Piggytoes
#553931 • 15" • AS
Issued: 2004 • Current
Original: $25 • Value: $R/E

3667.
Olympia [QVC]
#unknown • 7"
Issued: 1997 • Retired: 1997
Original: $12 • Value: $30

3668.
Petunia Steadsbeary [Longaberger]
#94633LB • 11"
Issued: 2001 • Retired: 2001
Original: $22 • Value: $38

3669.
Piglet (Santa's Helper) [Disney]
#23718-F51 • 10"
Issued: 1999 • Retired: 1999
Original: $30 • Value: $45

3670.
Piglet (Winter Holiday) [Disney]
#unknown • 9"
Issued: 2000 • Retired: 2000
Original: $45 • Value: $60

3671.
Piglet (cardigan and hat) [Disney]
#95982DSP • 9"
Issued: 2001 • Retired: 2001
Original: $30 • Value: $40

3672.
Piglet (Costume Party) [Disney]
#unknown • 10"
Issued: 2002 • Retired: 2002
Original: $30 • Value: $39

3673.
Piglet (Cozy Holiday) [Disney]
#95997DSP • 10"
Issued: 2002 • Retired: 2002
Original: $30 • Value: $36

3674.
Piglet (Holiday Caroling) [Disney]
#95914DSP • 8"
Issued: 2003 • Retired: 2003
Original: $30 • Value: $35

3675.
Porker P. Piggytoes
#553160 • 8"
Issued: 2003 • Current
Original: $10 • Value: $R/E

3676.
Primrose
#9160 • 11" • TJ
Issued: 1993 • Retired: 1996
Original: $20 • Value: $54

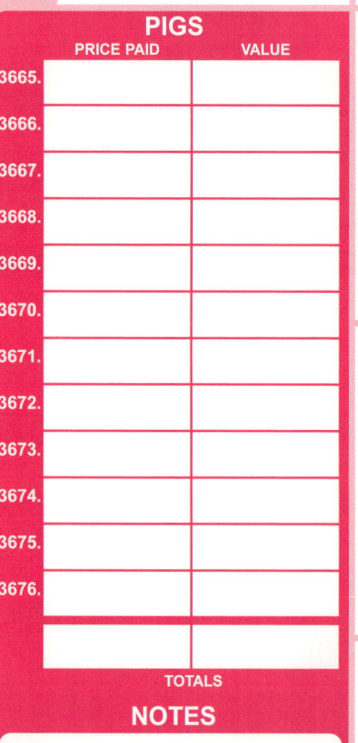

PIGS

	PRICE PAID	VALUE
3665.		
3666.		
3667.		
3668.		
3669.		
3670.		
3671.		
3672.		
3673.		
3674.		
3675.		
3676.		
	TOTALS	

NOTES

Critters (Pigs)

3677.
Primrose [QVC]
#(C56956) • 11"
Issued: 1999 • Retired: 1999
Original: $17 • Value: $31

3678.
Primrose II
#9160-01 • 11" • TJ
Issued: 1997 • Retired: 1997
Original: $20 • Value: $50

3679.
Primrose III
#9160-02 • 11" • TJ
Issued: 1998 • Retired: 2002
Original: $21 • Value: $28

3680.
Primrose IV
#9160-04 • 11" • TJ
Issued: 2000 • Retired: 2002
Original: $19 • Value: $35

3681.
Primrose P. Trufflesnout
#9160-03 • 11" • TJ
Issued: 1999 • Retired: 1999
Original: $23 • Value: $37

3682.
Reilly O'Pigg
#5538-07 • 16" • AM
Issued: 1993 • Retired: 1995
Original: $29 • Value: $80

3683.
Rose Bud [Harry & David]
#94203HD • 8"
LE of 9000 • Issued: 2001 • Retired: 2001
Original: $25 • Value: $35

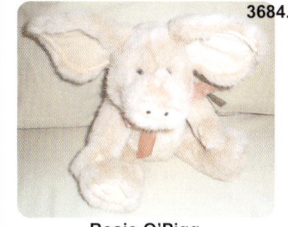
3684.
Rosie O'Pigg
#5536 • 11" • AM
Issued: 1992 • Retired: 1998
Original: $14 • Value: $33

3685.
Rosie O'Pigg [SFMB]
#5536SF • 11" • AM
Issued: 2001 • Retired: 2001
Original: $26 • Value: $35
♪ Second Hand Rose ♪

3686.
Sheffield O'Swine
#55391-07 • 8" • AM
Issued: 1997 • Retired: 2000
Original: $11 • Value: $15

3687.
Sue E. Appleton
#904303 • 8" • TJ
Issued: 2004 • Current
Original: $13 • Value: $R/E

3688.
Truffleina & Twila [QVC]
#(C99071) • 6"
Issued: 2000 • Retired: 2000
Original: $19 • Value: $28

PIGS	PRICE PAID	VALUE
3677.		
3678.		
3679.		
3680.		
3681.		
3682.		
3683.		
3684.		
3685.		
3686.		
3687.		
3688.		
TOTALS		

NOTES

Critters (Pigs, Raccoons, Roosters)

Truffles O'Pigg
#916010-01 • 9" • TJ
Issued: 2000 • Retired: 2002
Original: $14 • Value: $24

3689.

Willie B. Bacon
#55393-09 • 16" • AM
Issued: 2002 • Current
Original: $25 • Value: $R/E

3690.

Willie B. Porkroast [BBC]
#918016SM • 30"
Issued: 2003 • Retired: 2003
Original: $120 • Value: $144

3691.

Raccoons

Bandit Bushytail
#55211 • 6" • AM
Issued: 2000 • Retired: 2002
Original: $10 • Value: $12

3692.

Burwell Busheytail with Bud [QVC]
#99727V (C76927) • 10"
Issued: 2000 • Retired: 2000
Original: $20 • Value: $28

3693.

Ricky & Lucy Bandito
#568010 • 3½" • NO
Issued: 2002 • Current
Original: $10 • Value: $R/E

3694.

Roosters

Archie Strutencrow
#55316-05 • 9" • AM
Issued: 2002 • Current
Original: $13 • Value: $R/E
TOBY Award Winner

3695.

Manley Strutencrow [BBC]
#918017SM • 24"
Issued: 2003 • Retired: 2003
Original: $75 • Value: $90

3696.

Yankee Doodle Doo [QVC]
#93543V (C06191) • 9"
Issued: 2004 • Retired: 2004
Original: $14 • Value: $15

3697.

Skunks

PIGS

	PRICE PAID	VALUE
3689.		
3690.		
3691.		

RACCOONS

	PRICE PAID	VALUE
3692.		
3693.		
3694.		

ROOSTERS

	PRICE PAID	VALUE
3695.		
3696.		
3697.		

TOTALS

NOTES

3698.

Oda Parfume
#55212 • 10" • AM
Issued: 2001 • Retired: 2002
Original: $16 • Value: $19

Squirrels

3699.

Grabby Nutcruncher
#904005 • 5" • TJ
Issued: 2002 • Retired: 2002
Original: $10 • Value: $14

3700.

Merle B. Squirrel
#55214 • 7" • AM
Issued: 2001 • Retired: 2002
Original: $13 • Value: $16

Tigers

3701.

Taj Tigertail
#55217 • 12" • JB
Issued: 2001 • Retired: N/E
Original: $15 • Value: $18

Critters (Skunks, Squirrels, Tigers)

3702.

Tigger (Winter Holiday) [Disney]
#unknown • 12"
Issued: 2000 • Retired: 2000
Original: $45 • Value: $68

3703.

Tigger (plaid hat) [Disney]
#95980DSP • 11"
Issued: 2001 • Retired: 2001
Original: $30 • Value: $42

3704.

Tigger (Costume Party) [Disney]
#unknown • 10"
Issued: 2002 • Retired: 2002
Original: $30 • Value: $39

3705.

Tigger (Cozy Holiday) [Disney]
#95996DSP • 10"
Issued: 2002 • Retired: 2002
Original: $30 • Value: $39

3706.

Tigger (Holiday Caroling) [Disney]
#95913DSP • 10"
Issued: 2003 • Retired: 2003
Original: $30 • Value: $35

3707.

Tigger Resin and Plush Set (Elf) [Disney]
#20213MM • 12"
LE of 10000 • Issued: 1999 • Retired: 1999
Original: $30 • Value: $45

SKUNKS	PRICE PAID	VALUE
3698.		

SQUIRRELS	PRICE PAID	VALUE
3699.		
3700.		

TIGERS	PRICE PAID	VALUE
3701.		
3702.		
3703.		
3704.		
3705.		
3706.		
3707.		

TOTALS

NOTES

Critters (Tigers, Turtles, Walruses)

3708.
Zeiggy and Roary Tigertooth
#568006 • 3½" • NO
Issued: 2002 • Current
Original: $10 • Value: $R/E

Turtles

3709.
Flash
#55226 • 9" • JB
Issued: 2002 • Retired: 2002
Original: $13 • Value: $17

Walruses

3710.
Wally Fishbreath
#55218 • 8" • JB
Issued: 2001 • Retired: 2001
Original: $13 • Value: $18

TIGERS
	PRICE PAID	VALUE
3708.		

TURTLES
	PRICE PAID	VALUE
3709.		

WALRUSES
	PRICE PAID	VALUE
3710.		
TOTALS		

NOTES

339

Others

Ornaments

Adriana Angelwish
#562330 • 5½" • OR
Issued: 2001 • Retired: 2002
Original: $7 • Value: $10

Adrienne Berrifrost
#56202-06 • 5½" • OR
Issued: 1999 • Retired: 2000
Original: $9 • Value: $12

Aimee Berrifrost
#56202-04 • 5½" • OR
Issued: 1999 • Retired: 2000
Original: $9 • Value: $10

Alvin D. Elf [QVC]
#93376V • 5"
Issued: 2002 • Retired: 2002
Original: $10 • Value: $13

Alyssa Berrifrost
#56202-02 • 5½" • OR
Issued: 1999 • Retired: 2000
Original: $9 • Value: $13

Ambrosia Angelwish [QVC]
#unknown • 6"
Issued: 2002 • Retired: 2002
Original: $9 • Value: $15

Amie & Pam Goodfriends
#562418 • 3½" • OR
Issued: 2002 • Retired: 2002
Original: $10 • Value: $10

Anarose
#562501 • 5½" • OR
Issued: 2003 • Retired: 2003
Original: $8 • Value: $8

ORNAMENTS	PRICE PAID	VALUE
3711.		
3712.		
3713.		
3714.		
3715.		
3716.		
3717.		
3718.		
TOTALS		

NOTES

Others (Ornaments)

3719. Angela [QVC]
#93261V (C99319) • 6"
Issued: 2001 • Retired: 2001
Original: $11 • Value: $19

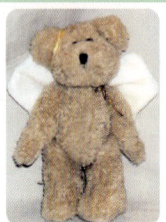

3720. Angelica
#5611-08 • 7" • OR
Issued: 1993 • Retired: 1997
Original: $12 • Value: $23

3721. Angelina
#5615-07 • 5½" • OR
Issued: 1995 • Retired: 1997
Original: $7 • Value: $18

3722. Angelina [SFMB]
#41-72768 • 5½"
Issued: 2000 • Retired: 2000
Original: $10 • Value: $15
♪ Love Me Tender ♪

3723. Angelina II
#56151-07 • 5" • OR
Issued: 1998 • Retired: 2001
Original: $7 • Value: $7
Sold with blue or green eyes.

3724. Annette Bearberg [SLE]
#unknown • 5½"
Issued: 1998 • Retired: 1998
Original: $10 • Value: $18

3725. Arcturus with Aurora Goodnight [QVC]
#unknown • 5½"
Issued: 1998 • Retired: 1998
Original: $13 • Value: $25
This Aurora is slightly different than regular line.

3726. Ardyth [GCC]
#94861GCC • 5½"
Issued: 1998 • Retired: 1998
Original: $8 • Value: $15

3727. Aria & Astra Angelwish [QVC]
#unknown • 6"
Issued: 2001 • Retired: 2001
Original: $20 • Value: $22

3728. Ariel
#5620-08 • 5" • OR
Issued: 1995 • Retired: 1999
Original: $7 • Value: $17

3729. Ariel [QVC]
#unknown • 8"
Issued: 1996 • Retired: 1996
Original: $8 • Value: $13

3730. Ariel [SFMB]
#41-66894 • 5"
Issued: 1997 • Retired: 1997
Original: $9 • Value: $16
♪ Jingle Bells ♪

ORNAMENTS

	PRICE PAID	VALUE
3719.		
3720.		
3721.		
3722.		
3723.		
3724.		
3725.		
3726.		
3727.		
3728.		
3729.		
3730.		
TOTALS		

NOTES

Others (Ornaments)

3731.
Arinna Goodnight
#56231-04 • 5½" • OR
Issued: 1997 • Retired: 1999
Original: $7 • Value: $11

3732.
Astoria Angelwish
#562331 • 5½" • OR
Issued: 2001 • Retired: 2002
Original: $7 • Value: $8

3733.
Athena
#5617-01 • 5½" • OR
Issued: 1995 • Retired: 1996
Original: $7 • Value: $25

3734.
Athena with Holly Berries [Lord & Taylor]
#94100-26 • 5½"
Issued: 1994 • Retired: 1994
Original: $8 • Value: $18

3735.
Aunt Carole Beary [Macy's East]
#94169MA • 5½"
Issued: 2003 • Retired: 2003
Original: $10 • Value: $16

3736.
Aunt Elaine Wilbear [Macy's East]
#94170MA • 5½"
Issued: 2003 • Retired: 2003
Original: $10 • Value: $16

3737.
Aurora Goodnight
#56232-12 • 5½"
Issued: 1999 • Retired: 1999
Original: $7 • Value: $17

3738.
Ava Marie
#562430 • 5" • OR
Issued: 2002 • Retired: 2002
Original: $8 • Value: $8

3739.
B. Angelboy
#562401 • 5" • OR
Issued: 2001 • Retired: 2001
Original: $7 • Value: $8

3740.
B. Angelgirl
#562400 • 5" • OR
Issued: 2001 • Retired: 2002
Original: $7 • Value: $8

3741.
B.B. Starcatcher
#562408 • 5" • OR
Issued: 2002 • Current
Original: $9 • Value: $R/E

3742.
Baby Baakins
#562433 • 3½" • OR
Issued: 2003 • Current
Original: $5 • Value: $R/E

ORNAMENTS

	PRICE PAID	VALUE
3731.		
3732.		
3733.		
3734.		
3735.		
3736.		
3737.		
3738.		
3739.		
3740.		
3741.		
3742.		
TOTALS		

NOTES

Others (Ornaments)

3743.
Baby Bailey 1999 & 2000 [QVC]
#(C95172) • 6"
Issued: 2000 • Retired: 2000
Original: $18 • Value: $25

3744.
Baby C. Corn
#562426 • 3½" • OR
Issued: 2002 • Retired: 2004
Original: $7 • Value: $7

3745.
Babykins 2002
#562427 • 5" • OR
Issued: 2002 • Retired: 2002
Original: $7 • Value: $7

Have You Seen Me?

3746.
Barret, Belinda & Berg Blizzard [QVC]
#unknown • 4½"
Issued: 1999 • Retired: 1999
Original: $18 • Value: $27

3747.
Becca & Bethany Angelwish [QVC]
#unknown • 6"
Issued: 2002 • Retired: 2002
Original: $16 • Value: $30

3748.
Becky Sue, Bobbi Jo & Mary Lou [QVC]
#unknown • 7"
Issued: 2001 • Retired: 2001
Original: $20 • Value: $27

ORNAMENTS

	PRICE PAID	VALUE
3743.		
3744.		
3745.		
3746.		
3747.		
3748.		
3749.		
3750.		
3751.		
3752.		
3753.		
3754.		
TOTALS		

NOTES

3749.
Benson Bushytail
#562651 • 3½" • OR
Issued: 2001 • Retired: 2002
Original: $6 • Value: $7

3750.
Bernice Blizzard
#56193 • 3½" • OR
Issued: 1999 • Retired: 2002
Original: $7 • Value: $7

3751.
Bert Blizzard
#56192 • 3½" • OR
Issued: 1999 • Retired: 2002
Original: $7 • Value: $7

3752.
Bess
#562504 • 5½" • OR
Issued: 2003 • Current
Original: $8 • Value: $R/E

3753.
Betsie Angelstar
#562403 • 5½" • OR
Issued: 2002 • Current
Original: $8 • Value: $R/E

3754.
Bibi Buzzby
#56220-12 • 5½" • OR
Issued: 1999 • Retired: 2002
Original: $7 • Value: $8

Others (Ornaments)

3755.
Billy Bob
#56201-06 • 5" • OR
Issued: 1997 • Retired: 1999
Original: $7 • Value: $15

3756.
Biscuit B. Beggar
#56250 • 5½" • OR
Issued: 2000 • Retired: 2000
Original: $9 • Value: $11

3757.
Bitsey Nibblekins
#562434 • 3½" • OR
Issued: 2003 • Current
Original: $5 • Value: $R/E

3758.
Bizz
#562435 • 3½" • OR
Issued: 2003 • Current
Original: $5 • Value: $R/E

3759.
Brady Swingenamiss
#56301 • 5" • OR
Issued: 2001 • Retired: 2001
Original: $10 • Value: $12

3760.
Brendalynn Blizzard
#56193-06 • 3½" • OR
Issued: 2000 • Retired: 2000
Original: $7 • Value: $8

3761.
Bud Buzzby
#56220-08 • 5½" • OR
Issued: 1999 • Retired: 1999
Original: $7 • Value: $8

3762.
Bud Buzzby [SFMB]
#41-72937 • 5½"
Issued: 2000 • Retired: 2000
Original: $10 • Value: $15
♪ My Favorite Things ♪

3763.
Buzz
#562436 • 3½" • OR
Issued: 2003 • Current
Original: $5 • Value: $R/E

3764.
C.C. Peeker [BBC]
#918070SM • 10"
Issued: 2003 • Current
Original: $20 • Value: $R/E

3765.
Candy [QVC]
#93260V • 6"
Issued: 2001 • Retired: 2001
Original: $11 • Value: $17

3766.
Cappuccino Frenzy
#56271 • 5½" • OR
Issued: 1999 • Retired: 2001
Original: $7 • Value: $7

ORNAMENTS		
	PRICE PAID	VALUE
3755.		
3756.		
3757.		
3758.		
3759.		
3760.		
3761.		
3762.		
3763.		
3764.		
3765.		
3766.		
TOTALS		

NOTES

344

Others (Ornaments)

 3767.
Carlie Icebeary [Macy's East]
#94172MA • 5½"
Issued: 2004 • Current
Original: $9 • Value: $R/E

 3768.
Carly Anna   [GCC]
#94927GCC • 5"
Issued: 2002 • Retired: 2002
Original: $8 • Value: $15

 3769.
Cassandra C. Angelflight
#83001 • 5½" • OR
Issued: 2000 • Retired: 2000
Original: $10 • Value: $12

 3770.
Cassie Goodnight
#56232-01 • 5½" • OR
Issued: 1998 • Retired: 1999
Original: $7 • Value: $12

 3771.
Celeste
#5609-01 • 5" • OR
Issued: 1994 • Retired: 1999
Original: $7 • Value: $20

 3772.
Celestina Goodnight
#56231-02 • 5½" • OR
Issued: 1997 • Retired: 1999
Original: $7 • Value: $15

 3773.
Charity Angelbeary
#56240-04 • 5½" • OR
Issued: 2000 • Retired: 2000
Original: $9 • Value: $14

 3774.
Chilly Frostbite
#56260 • 3½" • OR
Issued: 1999 • Retired: 2000
Original: $7 • Value: $9

 3775.
Cindy Lou Stuffins
#562414 • 8" • OR
Issued: 2002 • Retired: 2002
Original: $7 • Value: $7

 3776.
Clarence
#5608-08 • 4½" • OR
Issued: 1993 • Retired: 1996
Original: $6 • Value: $28

 3777.
Comet
#5622 • 5½" • OR
Issued: 1996 • Retired: 1999
Original: $7 • Value: $16

 3778.
Comet [Lord & Taylor]
#unknown • 5½"
Issued: 1996 • Retired: 1996
Original: $8 • Value: $20

ORNAMENTS

	PRICE PAID	VALUE
3767.		
3768.		
3769.		
3770.		
3771.		
3772.		
3773.		
3774.		
3775.		
3776.		
3777.		
3778.		
TOTALS		

NOTES

Others (Ornaments)

3779.

Corona Goodspeed
#5624-09 • 5½" • OR
Issued: 1998 • Retired: 2000
Original: $7 • Value: $16

3780.

Cosmos [Elder Beerman]
#unknown • 5½"
Issued: 1998 • Retired: 1998
Original: $9 • Value: $16

3781.

Have You Seen Me?

Country Angel
#7401 • 4½" • OR
Issued: 1993 • Retired: 1993
Original: $N/E • Value: $39

3782.

Cowsies
#5607 • 5" • OR
Issued: 1993 • Retired: 1994
Original: $5 • Value: $45

3783.

Cupid Braveheart
#82028 • 5½"
Issued: 2003 • Retired: 2003
Original: $9 • Value: $9

3784.

D.B. Chillymitts
#562653 • 3½" • OR
Issued: 2001 • Retired: 2002
Original: $6 • Value: $7

3785.

Darby & Drew Polartrek with Douglas [QVC]
#(C80440) • 3¼"
Issued: 2000 • Retired: 2000
Original: $19 • Value: $25

3786.

Dawn Angelstar
#562406 • 5½" • OR
Issued: 2002 • Retired: 2002
Original: $9 • Value: $9

3787.

Deitrich
#5608-06 • 5½" • OR
Issued: 1996 • Retired: 1997
Original: $6 • Value: $22

3788.

Dinkle B. Bumbles
#56221-12 • 5½" • OR
Issued: 2000 • Retired: 2002
Original: $8 • Value: $10

3789.

Dipper
#5611-09 • 7" • OR
Issued: 1996 • Retired: 1998
Original: $12 • Value: $22

3790.

Dolly & Jed [QVC]
#(C41097) • 5"
Issued: 1997 • Retired: 1997
Original: $12 • Value: $35

ORNAMENTS

	PRICE PAID	VALUE
3779.		
3780.		
3781.		
3782.		
3783.		
3784.		
3785.		
3786.		
3787.		
3788.		
3789.		
3790.		
TOTALS		

NOTES

Others (Ornaments)

3791.
Douglas Polartrek
#561919 • 3½" • OR
Issued: 2000 • Retired: 2002
Original: $7 • Value: $8
Also with Darby and Drew as QVC set.

3792.
Echo Goodnight
#56232-14 • 5½" • OR
Issued: 1999 • Retired: 1999
Original: $7 • Value: $11

3793.
Edna May
#56201-02 • 5" • OR
Issued: 1997 • Retired: 1999
Original: $7 • Value: $19

3794.
Eeyore 1999 [Disney]
#unknown • 8"
Issued: 1999 • Retired: 1999
Original: $13 • Value: $18

3795.
Eeyore 2000 [Disney]
#unknown • 6"
Issued: 2000 • Retired: 2000
Original: $15 • Value: $22

3796.
Eeyore, Piglet, Pooh & Tiger [Disney]
#unknown • 6"
Issued: 1998 • Retired: 1998
Original: $45 • Value: $65

3797.
Eldon Elfberg
#562416 • 5" • OR
Issued: 2002 • Current
Original: $8 • Value: $R/E

3798.
Espresso Frisky
#56272 • 5½" • OR
Issued: 1999 • Retired: 2001
Original: $7 • Value: $7

3799.
Have You Seen Me?
Evan E. Elfbear [Macy's East]
#94166MA • 5½"
Issued: 2002 • Retired: 2002
Original: $12 • Value: $21

3800.
Evangeline [QVC]
#93270V (C57731) • 6"
Issued: 2002 • Retired: 2002
Original: $12 • Value: $22

3801.
Evergreen Elfston [GCC]
#94876GCC • 5½"
Issued: 1999 • Retired: 1999
Original: $6 • Value: $15

3802.
Faith Angelbeary
#56240-02 • 5½" • OR
Issued: 2000 • Retired: 2000
Original: $9 • Value: $13

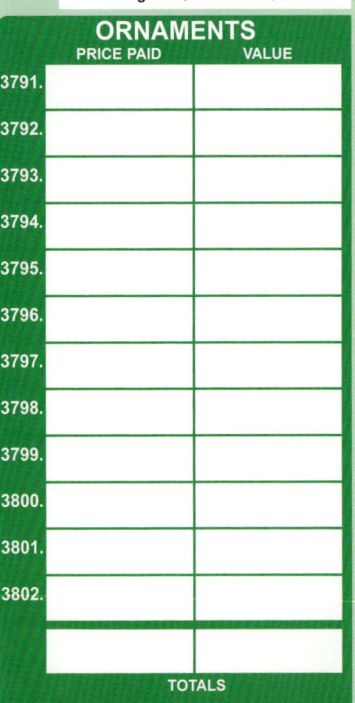

ORNAMENTS

	PRICE PAID	VALUE
3791.		
3792.		
3793.		
3794.		
3795.		
3796.		
3797.		
3798.		
3799.		
3800.		
3801.		
3802.		
TOTALS		

NOTES

Others (Ornaments)

3803.

Have You Seen Me?

Fannie, Farrah & Flora [QVC]
#unknown • 5½"
Issued: 2000 • Retired: 2000
Original: $19 • Value: $28

3804.

Farkle R. Snowmose
#562411 • 4" • OR
Issued: 2002 • Retired: 2002
Original: $7 • Value: $7

3805.

Fenton & Forrest with Silverton [QVC]
#unknown • 5"
Issued: 1998 • Retired: 1998
Original: $19 • Value: $27

3806.

Flip Hopsey
#81505 • 3½" • OR
Issued: 2001 • Retired: 2001
Original: $7 • Value: $8

3807.

Flit Angelwish
#56265-01 • 3½" • OR
Issued: 2000 • Retired: 2002
Original: $7 • Value: $8

3808.

Flopsie, Mopsie & Moxie Angelbuns [QVC]
#(C99062) • 5½"
Issued: 2000 • Retired: 2000
Original: $19 • Value: $28

3809.

Florabun
#562659 • 3½" • OR
Issued: 2002 • Retired: 2002
Original: $6 • Value: $6

3810.

Flutter Flowerflit
#562200 • 5½" • OR
Issued: 2001 • Retired: 2002
Original: $10 • Value: $12

3811.

G.B. Gingerpeeker (10") [BBC]
#918069SM • 10"
Issued: 2003 • Current
Original: $20 • Value: $R/E

3812.

Gabriella (red skirt)
#7408 • 8" • OR
Issued: 1994 • Retired: 1995
Original: $8 • Value: $30

3813.

Gabriella (plaid skirt)
#7408-08 • 8" • OR
Issued: 1996 • Retired: 1997
Original: $8 • Value: $30

3814.

Galaxy
#56111-01 • 7" • OR
Issued: 1998 • Retired: 1999
Original: $12 • Value: $17

ORNAMENTS	PRICE PAID	VALUE
3803.		
3804.		
3805.		
3806.		
3807.		
3808.		
3809.		
3810.		
3811.		
3812.		
3813.		
3814.		
TOTALS		

NOTES

Others (Ornaments)

3815.
Galaxy [SFMB]
#41-72767 • 7"
Issued: 1999 • Retired: 1999
Original: $15 • Value: $22
♪ Twinkle Twinkle Little Star ♪

3816.
Gonna Luvya
#56200-01 • 5" • OR
Issued: 2000 • Retired: 2002
Original: $7 • Value: $8

3817.
Gweneth
#56031 • 5" • OR
Issued: 1997 • Retired: 1999
Original: $6 • Value: $18

3818.
H.B. Starcatcher
#562407 • 5" • OR
Issued: 2002 • Current
Original: $9 • Value: $R/E

3819.
H.K. Bearlove
#82054 • 5½"
Issued: 2003 • Current
Original: $7 • Value: $R/E

3820.
Homer & Yukon [QVC]
#(C80725) • 7"
Issued: 2000 • Retired: 2000
Original: $15 • Value: $60

3821.
Iddy Biddy Ladybug
#562201 • 5" • OR
Issued: 2001 • Retired: 2001
Original: $9 • Value: $11

3822.
Immanuella
#5609-09 • 5" • OR
Issued: 1996 • Retired: 1999
Original: $7 • Value: $15

3823.
Jangle S. Stuffins
#562031 • 8" • OR
Issued: 2001 • Retired: 2001
Original: $7 • Value: $8

3824.
Jenessa T. Angelbear [QVC]
#93329V (C20177) • 6"
Issued: 2002 • Retired: 2002
Original: $9 • Value: $19

3825.
Jeri Hopkins
#56241-06 • 5" • OR
Issued: 2000 • Retired: 2000
Original: $7 • Value: $8

3826.
Jewell & Rainbow Flowerflit [QVC]
#99872V (C107569) • 5"
Issued: 2002 • Retired: 2002
Original: $18 • Value: $35

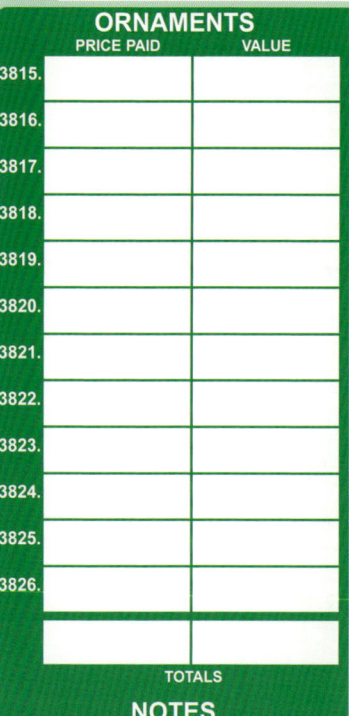

ORNAMENTS

	PRICE PAID	VALUE
3815.		
3816.		
3817.		
3818.		
3819.		
3820.		
3821.		
3822.		
3823.		
3824.		
3825.		
3826.		
TOTALS		

NOTES

Others (Ornaments)

3827.
Jill Hopkins
#56241-12 • 5" • OR
Issued: 2000 • Retired: 2000
Original: $7 • Value: $8

3828.
Jingle Bear
#562428 • 3½" • OR
Issued: 2002 • Retired: 2002
Original: $7 • Value: $7

3829.
Jingle S. Stuffins
#562030 • 8" • OR
Issued: 2001 • Retired: 2001
Original: $7 • Value: $8

3830.
Jolly S. Stuffins
#562032 • 8" • OR
Issued: 2001 • Retired: 2002
Original: $7 • Value: $8

3831.
Josanna Java
#56273 • 5½" • OR
Issued: 2000 • Retired: 2002
Original: $7 • Value: $8
Also with Katalina Kafinata, Latte Lapine as QVC set.

3832.
Josie Hopkins
#56241-09 • 5" • OR
Issued: 2000 • Retired: 2000
Original: $7 • Value: $8

3833.
Juliette
#5612-01 • 4½" • OR
Issued: 1994 • Retired: 1999
Original: $7 • Value: $15

3834.
Juliette [SFMB]
#41-72646 • 5½"
Issued: 1999 • Retired: 1999
Original: $10 • Value: $18
♪ Love Me Tender ♪

3835.
Jupiter [QVC]
#unknown • 6"
Issued: 1996 • Retired: 1996
Original: $10 • Value: $18

3836.
Jupiter Goodspeed
#5624-06 • 5½" • OR
Issued: 1998 • Retired: 1999
Original: $7 • Value: $17

3837.
Katalina Kafinata
#56274 • 5½" • OR
Issued: 2000 • Retired: 2000
Original: $7 • Value: $8
Also with Josanna Java, Latte Lapine as QVC set.

3838.
Lady B. Lovebug
#595104 • 5" • TF
Issued: 2000 • Retired: 2000
Original: $9 • Value: $16

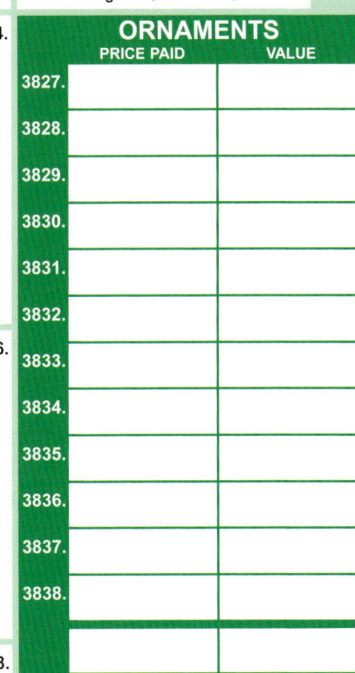

ORNAMENTS		
	PRICE PAID	VALUE
3827.		
3828.		
3829.		
3830.		
3831.		
3832.		
3833.		
3834.		
3835.		
3836.		
3837.		
3838.		
TOTALS		

NOTES

Others (Ornaments)

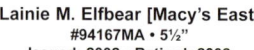

3839. Lambsies
#5603 • 4½" • OR
Issued: 1991 • Retired: 1995
Original: $5 • Value: $23

3840. Lainie M. Elfbear [Macy's East]
#94167MA • 5½"
Issued: 2002 • Retired: 2002
Original: $12 • Value: $15

3841. Lana Hoppennibble
#561932 • 3½" • OR
Issued: 2001 • Retired: 2002
Original: $7 • Value: $8

3842. Lapis [QVC]
#unknown • 7"
Issued: 1996 • Retired: 1996
Original: $12 • Value: $38

3843. Latte Lapine with Josanna Java and Katalina Kafinata [QVC]
#(C97581) • 5½" • OR
Issued: 2000 • Retired: 2000
Original: $19 • Value: $35

3844. Lil' Einstein
#562425 • 3½" • OR
Issued: 2002 • Retired: 2004
Original: $7 • Value: $7

3845. Lil' Einstein, Baby C. Corn & Gourdy [QVC]
#562425 (C20220) • 3½"
Issued: 2002 • Retired: 2002
Original: $20 • Value: $26

3846. Lil' Frazier
#562417 • 3½" • OR
Issued: 2002 • Retired: 2002
Original: $7 • Value: $7

3847. Lil' Peach
#562404 • 5½" • OR
Issued: 2002 • Retired: 2002
Original: $8 • Value: $8

3848. Lil' Petey
#562405 • 5½" • OR
Issued: 2002 • Retired: 2002
Original: $8 • Value: $8

3849. Lil' Quackenwaddle
#562431 • 3½" • OR
Issued: 2003 • Current
Original: $5 • Value: $R/E

3850. Lil' Stella with Lil' Frazier [QVC]
#unknown • 3½"
Issued: 2002 • Retired: 2002
Original: $16 • Value: $21

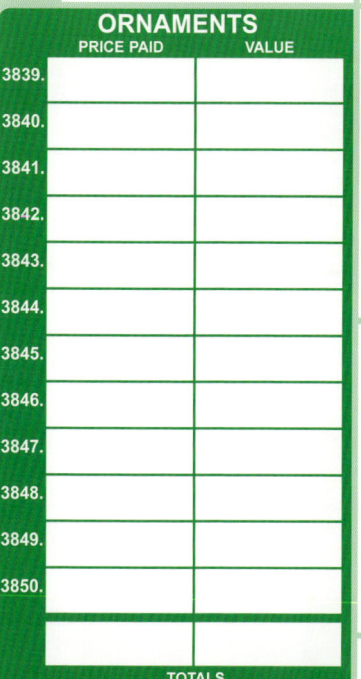

ORNAMENTS

	PRICE PAID	VALUE
3839.		
3840.		
3841.		
3842.		
3843.		
3844.		
3845.		
3846.		
3847.		
3848.		
3849.		
3850.		
TOTALS		

NOTES

Others (Ornaments)

3851.
Lilith Angel Ewe
#56030-01 • 5" • OR
Issued: 2000 • Retired: 2000
Original: $7 • Value: $8

3852.
Lilly R. Ribbit
#56194 • 4"
Issued: 2000 • Retired: 2001
Original: $7 • Value: $8
Also with Tilly, Toots as QVC set.

3853.
Linnea
#5610-01 • 7" • OR
Issued: 1994 • Retired: 1997
Original: $12 • Value: $22

3854.
Lionsies (old face)
#5604 • 4½" • OR
Issued: 1991 • Retired: 1994
Original: $5 • Value: $55

3855.
Lionsies (new face)
#5604 • 4½" • OR
Issued: 1991 • Retired: 1994
Original: $5 • Value: $23

3856.
Little Ted [QVC]
#93339V (C19772) • 4½" • OR
Issued: 2002 • Retired: 2002
Original: $12 • Value: $16

3857.
Lorelei
#56141 • 5½" • OR
Issued: 1997 • Retired: 2000
Original: $7 • Value: $15

3858.
Lula Quackenwaddle
#561930 • 3" • OR
Issued: 2001 • Retired: 2001
Original: $7 • Value: $8

3859.
Lulu
#562502 • 5½" • OR
Issued: 2003 • Retired: 2003
Original: $8 • Value: $8

3860.
Luna
#5621-10 • 5" • OR
Issued: 1996 • Retired: 1997
Original: $6 • Value: $18

3861.
Lyla Quackenwaddle
#561931 • 3" • OR
Issued: 2001 • Retired: 2002
Original: $7 • Value: $8

3862.
M.C. Twinklemoose
#562429 • 5" • OR
Issued: 2002 • Retired: 2002
Original: $9 • Value: $9

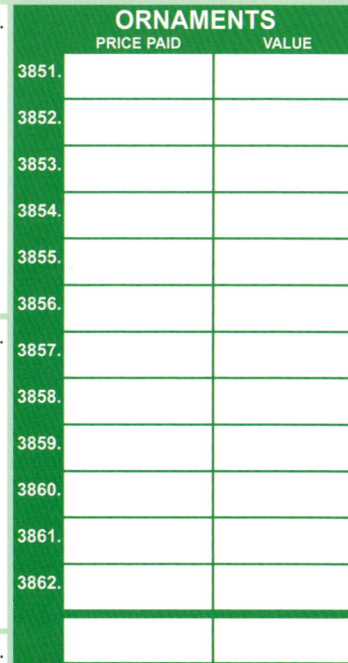

ORNAMENTS

	PRICE PAID	VALUE
3851.		
3852.		
3853.		
3854.		
3855.		
3856.		
3857.		
3858.		
3859.		
3860.		
3861.		
3862.		
	TOTALS	

NOTES

Others (Ornaments)

3863.
Mabel Witmoose
#56172 • 5" • OR
Issued: 1999 • Retired: 2000
Original: $8 • Value: $8

3864.
Marigold
#562658 • 3½" • OR
Issued: 2002 • Retired: 2002
Original: $6 • Value: $6

3865.
Matilda
#5617-05 • 5½" • OR
Issued: 1995 • Retired: 1999
Original: $7 • Value: $15

3866.
Matilda with Holly Berries
[Lord & Taylor]
#unknown • 5½"
Issued: 1994 • Retired: 1994
Original: $8 • Value: $19

3867.
Max [Lord & Taylor]
#unknown • 8"
Issued: 1999 • Retired: 1999
Original: $15 • Value: $35

3868.
Melba, Mimsie & Myrtle
Bahsworth [QVC]
#(C57656) • 5"
Issued: 1999 • Retired: 1999
Original: $18 • Value: $30

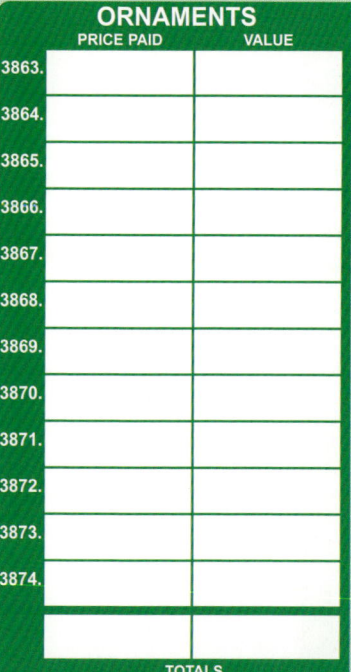

ORNAMENTS		
	PRICE PAID	VALUE
3863.		
3864.		
3865.		
3866.		
3867.		
3868.		
3869.		
3870.		
3871.		
3872.		
3873.		
3874.		
	TOTALS	

NOTES

3869.
Mercer
#56171-03 • 5" • OR
Issued: 1998 • Retired: 2000
Original: $7 • Value: $9

3870.
Mercury
#5610-09 • 7" • OR
Issued: 1996 • Retired: 1998
Original: $12 • Value: $18

3871.
Mini Mookins
#562432 • 3½" • OR
Issued: 2003 • Current
Original: $5 • Value: $R/E

3872.
Mintley [QVC]
#93372V (C20939) • 6"
Issued: 2002 • Retired: 2002
Original: $12 • Value: $21

3873.
Mitt, Muff & Puff [QVC]
#999897V • 7"
Issued: 2002 • Retired: 2002
Original: $22 • Value: $28

3874.
Mo Mooseltoes
#562650 • 3½" • OR
Issued: 2001 • Retired: 2002
Original: $6 • Value: $7

Others (Ornaments)

3875.
Mocha Mooseby
#56270 • 5½" • OR
Issued: 1999 • Retired: 2001
Original: $7 • Value: $7

3876.
Moondust Goodspeed
#5624-08 • 5½" • OR
Issued: 1999 • Retired: 1999
Original: $7 • Value: $14

3877.
Moosies
#5605 • 6" • OR
Issued: 1993 • Retired: 1996
Original: $5 • Value: $32

3878.
Morley Moose [QVC]
#unknown • 5½"
Issued: 1998 • Retired: 1998
Original: $7 • Value: $59
Originally sold as set of three.

3879.
Morty [Elder Beerman]
#unknown • 5"
Issued: 1999 • Retired: 1999
Original: $10 • Value: $119

3880.
Ms. Teachbeary
#562506 • 5½" • OR
Issued: 2003 • Current
Original: $8 • Value: $R/E

3881.
Narcissus
#5621-08 • 5" • OR
Issued: 1996 • Retired: 1997
Original: $6 • Value: $16

3882.
Ollie B. Elf [QVC]
#93373V • 5"
Issued: 2002 • Retired: 2002
Original: $10 • Value: $13

ORNAMENTS

	PRICE PAID	VALUE
3875.		
3876.		
3877.		
3878.		
3879.		
3880.		
3881.		
3882.		
3883.		
3884.		
3885.		
3886.		

TOTALS

NOTES

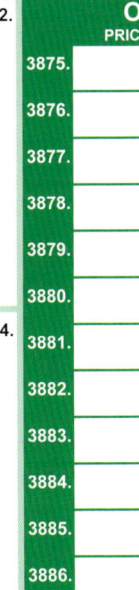

3883.
Orion
#5612-09 • 5" • OR
Issued: 1996 • Retired: 2000
Original: $7 • Value: $14

3884.
Otis T. Elf [QVC]
#93374V • 5"
Issued: 2002 • Retired: 2002
Original: $10 • Value: $13

3885.
Otto Z. Elf [QVC]
#93375V • 5"
Issued: 2002 • Retired: 2002
Original: $10 • Value: $13

3886.
Ovid
#5614 • 4½" • OR
Issued: 1994 • Retired: 1996
Original: $7 • Value: $38

354

Others (Ornaments)

3887.
P.B. Starcatcher
#562409 • 5" • OR
Issued: 2002 • Current
Original: $9 • Value: $R/E

3888.
Pair O'Bears (old face)
#5601 • 4½" • OR
Issued: 1989 • Retired: 1992
Original: $5 • Value: $52

3889.
Pair O'Bears (new face)
#5604 • 4½" • OR
Issued: 1993 • Retired: 1996
Original: $5 • Value: $42

3890.
Pair O'Hares (old face)
#5600 • 6" • OR
Issued: 1990 • Retired: 1991
Original: $5 • Value: $59

3891.
Pair O'Hares (new face)
#5602 • 6" • OR
Issued: 1992 • Retired: 1992
Original: $5 • Value: $38

3892.
Pair O'Highland Plaid Bears
#5618-02 • 5" • OR
Issued: 1996 • Retired: 1998
Original: $4 • Value: $14

3893.
Pair O'Homespun Bears
#5618 • 5" • OR
Issued: 1995 • Retired: 1996
Original: $4 • Value: $35

3894.
Pair O'Piggs
#5606 • 6" • OR
Issued: 1993 • Retired: 1996
Original: $5 • Value: $50

3895.
Pansey
#562657 • 3½" • OR
Issued: 2002 • Retired: 2002
Original: $6 • Value: $6

3896.
Patience
#562505 • 5½" • OR
Issued: 2003 • Current
Original: $8 • Value: $R/E

3897.
Peggy Sue Stuffins
#562415 • 8" • OR
Issued: 2002 • Retired: 2002
Original: $7 • Value: $7

3898.
Perky P. Rally
#56300 • 5" • OR
Issued: 2001 • Retired: 2002
Original: $10 • Value: $12

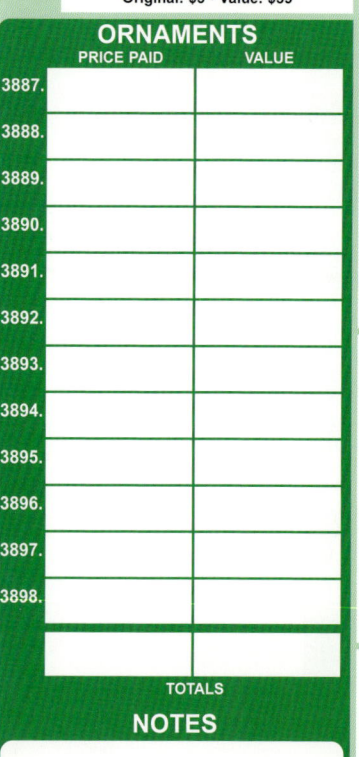

ORNAMENTS	PRICE PAID	VALUE
3887.		
3888.		
3889.		
3890.		
3891.		
3892.		
3893.		
3894.		
3895.		
3896.		
3897.		
3898.		
TOTALS		

NOTES

Others (Ornaments)

3899.
Philip A. Stocking [Longaberger]
#94661LB • 5½"
Issued: 2003 • Retired: 2003
Original: $12 • Value: $18

3900.
Piglet 1999 [Disney]
#unknown • 8"
Issued: 1999 • Retired: 1999
Original: $13 • Value: $18

3901.
Piglet 2000 [Disney]
#unknown • 6"
Issued: 2000 • Retired: 2000
Original: $15 • Value: $22

3902.
Pinkle B. Bumbles
#56221-09 • 5½" • OR
Issued: 2000 • Retired: 2002
Original: $8 • Value: $10

3903.
Pooh 1999 [Disney]
#94958DS • 6"
Issued: 1999 • Retired: 1999
Original: $13 • Value: $22

3904.
Pooh 1999 (stocking) [Disney]
#unknown • 8"
Issued: 1999 • Retired: 1999
Original: $13 • Value: $19

3905.
Pooh 2000 [Disney]
#94957DS • 6"
Issued: 2000 • Retired: 2000
Original: $15 • Value: $25

3906.
Pooh 2000 (sweater) [Disney]
#unknown • 6"
Issued: 2000 • Retired: 2000
Original: $15 • Value: $22

3907.
Pooh (santa hat) [Disney]
#95984DSP • 5½" • MB
Issued: 2001 • Retired: 2001
Original: $26 • Value: $38

3908.
Pooh 2002 (mohair) [Disney]
#95999DSP • 5" • MB
Issued: 2002 • Retired: 2002
Original: $26 • Value: $35

3909.
Raggedy Twins
#7400 • 4½" • OR
Issued: 1993 • Retired: 1995
Original: $6 • Value: $80

3910.
Regulus P. Roar
#56041 • 5" • OR
Issued: 1997 • Retired: 1999
Original: $6 • Value: $15

ORNAMENTS

	PRICE PAID	VALUE
3899.		
3900.		
3901.		
3902.		
3903.		
3904.		
3905.		
3906.		
3907.		
3908.		
3909.		
3910.		
TOTALS		

NOTES

356

Others (Ornaments)

3911.
Roary Maneford
#56032 • 5" • OR
Issued: 2000 • Retired: 2002
Original: $7 • Value: $8

3912.
Ross Angelstar
#562402 • 5½" • OR
Issued: 2002 • Retired: 2002
Original: $8 • Value: $8

3913.
Sammy Sue [GCC]
#94928GCC • 5"
Issued: 2002 • Retired: 2002
Original: $7 • Value: $12

3914.
Sassafrass
#56280-01 • 5½" • OR
Issued: 2000 • Retired: 2001
Original: $7 • Value: $8

3915.
Serafina [QVC]
#unknown • 6"
Issued: 2001 • Retired: 2001
Original: $11 • Value: $20

3916.
Seraphina
#5615 • 5" • OR
Issued: 1994 • Retired: 1999
Original: $7 • Value: $18

3917.
Serena Goodnight
#56232-08 • 5½" • OR
Issued: 1998 • Retired: 2000
Original: $7 • Value: $14

3918.
Sheila [Lord & Taylor]
#unknown • 5"
Issued: 1999 • Retired: 1999
Original: $8 • Value: $15

3919.
Silverton Snowbeary
#56191 • 5" • OR
Issued: 1998 • Retired: 2002
Original: $7 • Value: $7
Also with Fenton, Forrest as QVC set.

3920.
Skip Hopsey
#81506 • 3½" • OR
Issued: 2001 • Retired: 2001
Original: $7 • Value: $8

3921.
Sly Foxworthy
#562652 • 3½" • OR
Issued: 2001 • Retired: 2002
Original: $6 • Value: $7

3922.
Smooch & Snuggle
#562422 • 3½" • OR
Issued: 2002 • Retired: 2002
Original: $10 • Value: $10

ORNAMENTS

	PRICE PAID	VALUE
3911.		
3912.		
3913.		
3914.		
3915.		
3916.		
3917.		
3918.		
3919.		
3920.		
3921.		
3922.		
TOTALS		

NOTES

Others (Ornaments)

3923.
Snowbeary
#5619 • 5" • OR
Issued: 1995 • Retired: 1996
Original: $6 • Value: $29

3924.
Socksley [QVC]
#93369V (C20920) • 6"
Issued: 2002 • Retired: 2002
Original: $12 • Value: $19

3925.
Sparkle Q. Snowbeary
#562410 • 4" • OR
Issued: 2002 • Retired: 2002
Original: $7 • Value: $7

3926.
Squeek McSnoozle
#56180-02 • 5½" • OR
Issued: 2000 • Retired: 2000
Original: $11 • Value: $13
Also with Squirt as QVC set.

3927.
Squirt McSnoozle with Squeek [QVC]
#unknown • 5½"
Issued: 2000 • Retired: 2000
Original: $20 • Value: $55

3928.
Stardust Goodspeed
#5624-01 • 5½" • OR
Issued: 1999 • Retired: 2000
Original: $7 • Value: $12

3929.
Stella [BBC]
#918071SM • 10"
Issued: 2003 • Retired: 2003
Original: $20 • Value: $24

3930.
Stella Goodnight
#5623-09 • 5½" • OR
Issued: 1997 • Retired: 1999
Original: $7 • Value: $8

3931.
T. F. Wuzziewitch
#81001 • 3" • TF
Issued: 2000 • Retired: 2000
Original: $8 • Value: $10
Also with Tabble, Tricky as QVC set.

3932.
T.F. Buzzie Wuzzie
#595180 • 2½" • TF
Issued: 2000 • Retired: 2000
Original: $7 • Value: $8

3933.
Have You Seen Me?
Tabbie F. Wuzzie with T. F. Wuzziewitch and Tricky [QVC]
#(C78129) • 3"
Issued: 2000 • Retired: 2000
Original: $22 • Value: $32

3934.
Tad Northpole
#561940 • 4" • OR
Issued: 2000 • Retired: 2000
Original: $7 • Value: $8

ORNAMENTS

	PRICE PAID	VALUE
3923.		
3924.		
3925.		
3926.		
3927.		
3928.		
3929.		
3930.		
3931.		
3932.		
3933.		
3934.		
TOTALS		

NOTES

Others (Ornaments)

3935.
Taira [QVC]
#93262V • 6"
Issued: 2001 • Retired: 2001
Original: $11 • Value: $20

3936.
Tess
#562503 • 5½" • OR
Issued: 2003 • Current
Original: $8 • Value: $R/E

3937.
Tessa [Lord & Taylor]
#unknown • 8"
Issued: 1999 • Retired: 1999
Original: $15 • Value: $40

3938.
Thomasina F. Wuzzie
#596009 • 3" • TF
Issued: 2000 • Retired: 2000
Original: $8 • Value: $10

3939.
Tigger 1999 [Disney]
#unknown • 8"
Issued: 1999 • Retired: 1999
Original: $13 • Value: $24

3940.
Tigger 2000 [Disney]
#unknown • 6"
Issued: 2000 • Retired: 2000
Original: $15 • Value: $22

3941.
Have You Seen Me?
Tilly & Toots Ribbit with Lilly [QVC]
#unknown • 4"
Issued: 2000 • Retired: 2000
Original: $18 • Value: $25

3942.
Timmy [Lord & Taylor]
#unknown • 5"
Issued: 1999 • Retired: 1999
Original: $8 • Value: $15

3943.
Tootall F. Wuzzie
#596012 • 3" • TF
Issued: 2001 • Retired: 2002
Original: $8 • Value: $10

3944.
Tricky F. Wuzzie
#596008 • 3" • TF
Issued: 2000 • Retired: 2000
Original: $8 • Value: $10
Also with T.F. Wuzziewitch, Tabbie as QVC set.

3945.
Trudy F. Wuzzie
#595184 • 2½" • TF
Issued: 2001 • Retired: 2002
Original: $8 • Value: $10

3946.
Truelove F. Wuzzie
#82000 • 3" • TF
Issued: 2000 • Retired: 2001
Original: $6 • Value: $7

ORNAMENTS

	PRICE PAID	VALUE
3935.		
3936.		
3937.		
3938.		
3939.		
3940.		
3941.		
3942.		
3943.		
3944.		
3945.		
3946.		
TOTALS		

NOTES

Others (Ornaments)

3947.

Tuttle F. Wuzzie
#596010 • 2½" • TF
Issued: 2001 • Retired: 2001
Original: $8 • Value: $10

3948.

Twaddle F. Wuzzie
#595186 • 2½" • TF
Issued: 2001 • Retired: 2002
Original: $8 • Value: $10

3949.

Tweedle F. Wuzzie
#595181 • 2½" • TF
Issued: 2000 • Retired: 2000
Original: $7 • Value: $8

3950.

Tweek McSnoozle
#83000 • 5½" • OR
Issued: 2000 • Retired: 2000
Original: $11 • Value: $13

3951.

Twickenham F. Wuzzie
#595183 • 2½" • TF
Issued: 2001 • Retired: 2001
Original: $8 • Value: $10

3952.

Twiddle F. Wuzzie
#595182 • 2½" • TF
Issued: 2000 • Retired: 2000
Original: $7 • Value: $8

3953.

Twila Twinkletoes
#56302 • 5" • OR
Issued: 2001 • Retired: 2001
Original: $10 • Value: $12

3954.

**Twinkle Crystalfrost
[Country Clutter]**
#94979CC • 5½"
Issued: 2003 • Retired: 2003
Original: $10 • Value: $12

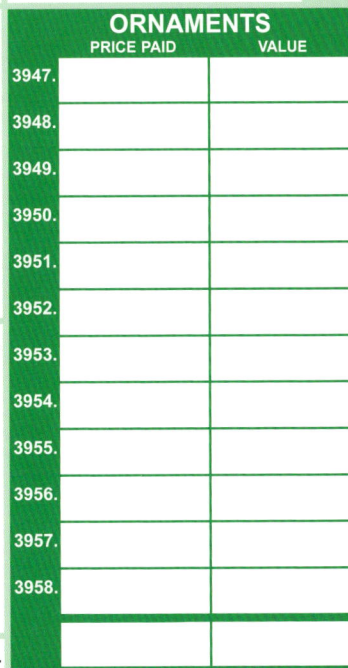

ORNAMENTS

	PRICE PAID	VALUE
3947.		
3948.		
3949.		
3950.		
3951.		
3952.		
3953.		
3954.		
3955.		
3956.		
3957.		
3958.		
	TOTALS	

NOTES

3955.

Twinksley [QVC]
#93371V (C20879) • 6"
Issued: 2002 • Retired: 2002
Original: $12 • Value: $21

3956.

Venus
#5616 • 4½" • OR
Issued: 1994 • Retired: 1996
Original: $7 • Value: $32

3957.

Venus [Elder Beerman]
#unknown • 5½"
Issued: 1998 • Retired: 1998
Original: $10 • Value: $18

3958.

Violet Flowerflit
#562202 • 5" • OR
Issued: 2002 • Retired: 2002
Original: $8 • Value: $8

360

Others (Ornaments, Pins)

3959.
Weezie Flitenfly
#561941 • 4" • OR
Issued: 2001 • Retired: 2001
Original: $8 • Value: $10

3960.
Willie B. Chillymitts
#562654 • 3½" • OR
Issued: 2001 • Retired: 2002
Original: $6 • Value: $7

3961.
Willie S. Hydrant IV
#5625 • 5½" • OR
Issued: 1998 • Retired: 2000
Original: $7 • Value: $10

3962.
Winkle B. Bumbles
#56221-06 • 5½" • OR
Issued: 2000 • Retired: 2002
Original: $8 • Value: $10

3963.
Ying & Yang Bearington [QVC]
#unknown • 4¼" • MB
Issued: 2000 • Retired: 2000
Original: $17 • Value: $35

3964.
Zephyr Goodnight
#5623-06 • 5½" • OR
Issued: 1997 • Retired: 1999
Original: $7 • Value: $14

3965.
Zinnia
#562656 • 3½" • OR
Issued: 2002 • Retired: 2002
Original: $6 • Value: $6

3966.
Zipp Angelwish
#56265-03 • 3½" • OR
Issued: 2000 • Retired: 2002
Original: $7 • Value: $8

Pins

3967.
B. Burt Bundleup
#599914 • 2" • WW
Issued: 2000 • Retired: 2000
Original: $6 • Value: $7

3968.
Hopley F. Wuzzie
#599919 • 2" • WW
Issued: 2001 • Retired: 2001
Original: $6 • Value: $7

3969.
Juggles F. Wuzzie
#599918 • 2" • WW
Issued: 2001 • Retired: 2001
Original: $6 • Value: $7

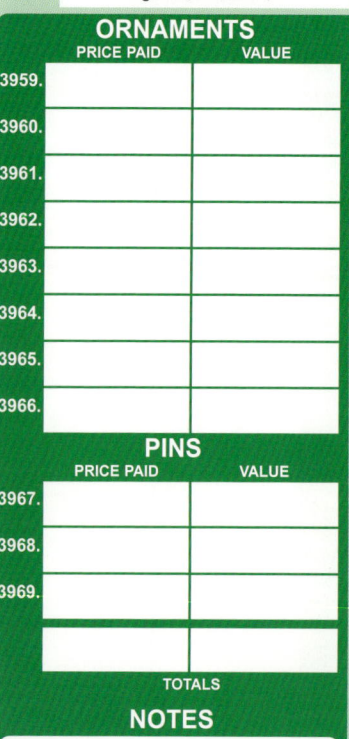

ORNAMENTS	PRICE PAID	VALUE
3959.		
3960.		
3961.		
3962.		
3963.		
3964.		
3965.		
3966.		

PINS	PRICE PAID	VALUE
3967.		
3968.		
3969.		
TOTALS		

NOTES

Others (Pins)

3970.
Lizzie [EVENT]
#50003 • 2" • WW
Issued: 2000 • Retired: 2000
Original: $6 • Value: $9

3971.
Miss Minnie Partridge
#81000 • 2" • WW
Issued: 2000 • Retired: 2000
Original: $6 • Value: $7

3972.
Riblet F. Wuzzie
#599917 • 2" • WW
Issued: 2001 • Retired: 2001
Original: $6 • Value: $7

3973.
St. Moosekins
#599916 • 2" • WW
Issued: 2000 • Retired: 2000
Original: $6 • Value: $7

3974.
Tina F. Wuzzie [EVENT]
#50001 • 2" • WW
Issued: 1999 • Retired: 1999
Original: $4 • Value: $6

3975.
Teedle F. Wuzzie
#599911-02 • 2" • WW
Issued: 2000 • Retired: 2000
Original: $6 • Value: $7
Also with Tiffany, Tinger as QVC set.

3976.
Tess F. Wuzzie
#599901-06 • 2" • WW
Issued: 1999 • Retired: 2000
Original: $5 • Value: $8

3977.
Thistle F. Wuzzie
#599912-07 • 2" • WW
Issued: 2000 • Retired: 2000
Original: $6 • Value: $7

3978.
Thomas F. Wuzzie
#599903-07 • 2" • WW
Issued: 1999 • Retired: 2000
Original: $5 • Value: $8

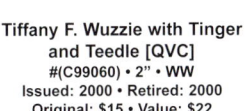

Have You Seen Me?

3979.
Tiffany F. Wuzzie with Tinger and Teedle [QVC]
#(C99060) • 2" • WW
Issued: 2000 • Retired: 2000
Original: $15 • Value: $22

3980.
Tinger F. Wuzzie
#599910-08 • 2" • WW
Issued: 2000 • Retired: 2000
Original: $6 • Value: $7
Also with Teedle, Tiffany as QVC set.

3981.
Tinker F. Wuzzie
#599900-02 • 2" • WW
Issued: 1999 • Retired: 2000
Original: $6 • Value: $8

PINS

	PRICE PAID	VALUE
3970.		
3971.		
3972.		
3973.		
3974.		
3975.		
3976.		
3977.		
3978.		
3979.		
3980.		
3981.		
TOTALS		

NOTES

Others (Pins, Puppets)

3982.
Tinsel F. Wuzzie
#599900-08 • 2" • WW
Issued: 1999 • Retired: 2000
Original: $6 • Value: $8

3983.
Tiny Tux Waddlewalk
#599915 • 2" • WW
Issued: 2000 • Retired: 2000
Original: $6 • Value: $7

3984.
Tucker F. Wuzzie
#599902-08 • 2" • WW
Issued: 1999 • Retired: 2000
Original: $5 • Value: $8

3985.
Twinkle F. Wuzzie
#599900-01 • 2" • WW
Issued: 1999 • Retired: 2000
Original: $6 • Value: $8

Puppets

3986.
Benny P. Chatsworth
#585010-10 • 16" • IF
Issued: 2000 • Retired: 2000
Original: $30 • Value: $31

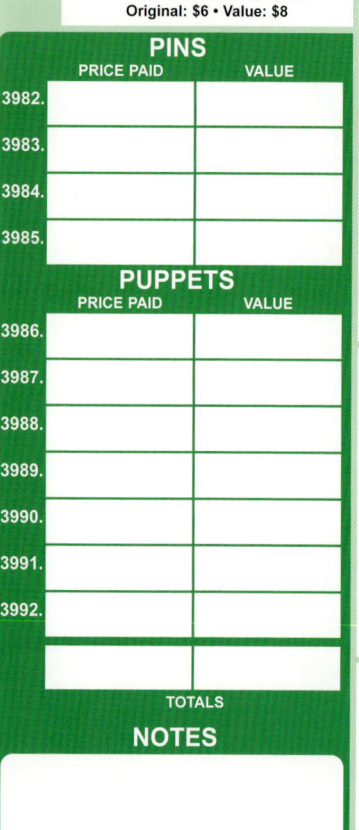

PINS

	PRICE PAID	VALUE
3982.		
3983.		
3984.		
3985.		

PUPPETS

	PRICE PAID	VALUE
3986.		
3987.		
3988.		
3989.		
3990.		
3991.		
3992.		
	TOTALS	

NOTES

3987.
Charlie P. Chatsworth
#585000-08 • 18" • IF
Issued: 1999 • Retired: 2000
Original: $35 • Value: $38

3988.
Fillabuster P. Chatsworth
#585001-03 • 18" • IF
Issued: 1999 • Retired: 2000
Original: $35 • Value: $44

3989.
Howlin P. Chatsworth
#585101-05 • 18" • IF
Issued: 2000 • Retired: 2000
Original: $35 • Value: $40

3990.
Katawalin P. Chatsworth
#585200-07 • 18" • IF
Issued: 2000 • Retired: 2000
Original: $35 • Value: $41

3991.
Maxwell (Max) Mittbruin [QVC]
#(C57649) • 16" • IF
Issued: 1999 • Retired: 1999
Original: $35 • Value: $50

3992.
Montell P. Chatsworth
#585310-05 • 16" • IF
Issued: 2000 • Retired: 2000
Original: $30 • Value: $45

Others (Puppets, String Alongs, Tree Toppers)

3993.
Peekers
#58600-05 • 10" • IF
Issued: 2001 • Retired: 2001
Original: $13 • Value: $16

3994.
Sneekers
#58601-07 • 10" • IF
Issued: 2001 • Retired: 2002
Original: $13 • Value: $16

3995.
Wiley P. Chatsworth
#585000-05 • 18" • IF
Issued: 1999 • Retired: 2000
Original: $35 • Value: $42

3996.
Wink
#58600-08 • 10" • IF
Issued: 2001 • Retired: 2002
Original: $13 • Value: $16

String Alongs

3997.
Giddyup Stringalong
#596200 • 3" • TF
Issued: 2000 • Retired: 2000
Original: $8 • Value: $13

3998.
Petey B. Stringalong
#596201 • 3" • TF
Issued: 2000 • Retired: 2000
Original: $8 • Value: $13

3999.
Squirt M. Stringalong
#596202 • 3" • TF
Issued: 2000 • Retired: 2000
Original: $8 • Value: $13

Tree Toppers

4000.
Alina
#744120 • 8" • TJ
Issued: 2004 • Current
Original: $21 • Value: $R/E

4001.
Anais Angelwish [QVC]
#(C100426) • 12" • TJ
Issued: 2001 • Retired: 2001
Original: $20 • Value: $30

4002.
Angeline Angelfrost
#744115-06 • 12" • TJ
Issued: 2001 • Retired: 2002
Original: $20 • Value: $24

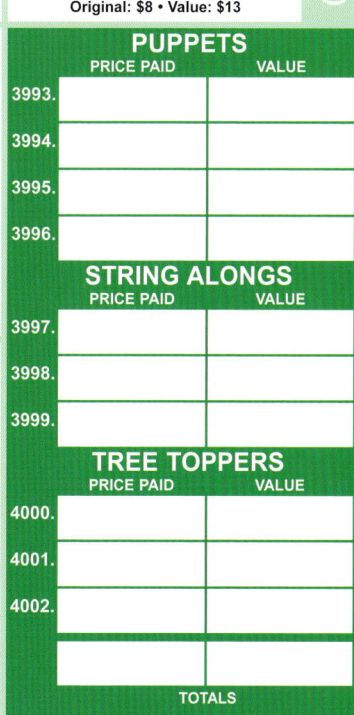

PUPPETS		
	PRICE PAID	VALUE
3993.		
3994.		
3995.		
3996.		

STRING ALONGS		
	PRICE PAID	VALUE
3997.		
3998.		
3999.		

TREE TOPPERS		
	PRICE PAID	VALUE
4000.		
4001.		
4002.		

TOTALS

NOTES

Others (Tree Toppers)

4003.
Angelique Angelfrost
#744110-06 • 10" • TJ
Issued: 2000 • Retired: 2000
Original: $15 • Value: $31

4004.
Annalee Angelberry
#744117 • 12" • TJ
Issued: 2002 • Retired: 2002
Original: $25 • Value: $25

4005.
Ariella Angelfrost
#744110 • 10" • TJ
Issued: 1999 • Retired: 2000
Original: $15 • Value: $32

4006.
Auriela Angelfrost [QVC]
#(C74399) • 10" • TJ
Issued: 1999 • Retired: 1999
Original: $15 • Value: $30

4007.
Azania Sparklefrost [QVC]
#(C5123) • 15" • TJ
Issued: 2003 • Retired: 2003
Original: $26 • Value: $31

4008.
Gloranna Angelstar
#744116 • 12" • TJ
Issued: 2002 • Current
Original: $25 • Value: $R/E

4009.
Glorianna Angelbear [QVC]
#(C6083) • 15" • TJ
Issued: 2003 • Retired: 2003
Original: $26 • Value: $31

4010.
Holly Beary
#744115-02 • 12" • TJ
Issued: 2000 • Retired: 2000
Original: $20 • Value: $34

4011.
Holly Beary [Longaberger]
#94648LB • 13" • TJ
Issued: 2002 • Retired: 2002
Original: $24 • Value: $31

4012.
Jenessa
#744121 • 8" • TJ
Issued: 2004 • Current
Original: $21 • Value: $R/E

4013.
Joella Angelstar
#744118 • 12" • TJ
Issued: 2003 • Current
Original: $25 • Value: $R/E

4014.
Joy N. Goodcheer [QVC]
#(C80701) • 12" • TJ
Issued: 2000 • Retired: 2000
Original: $20 • Value: $35

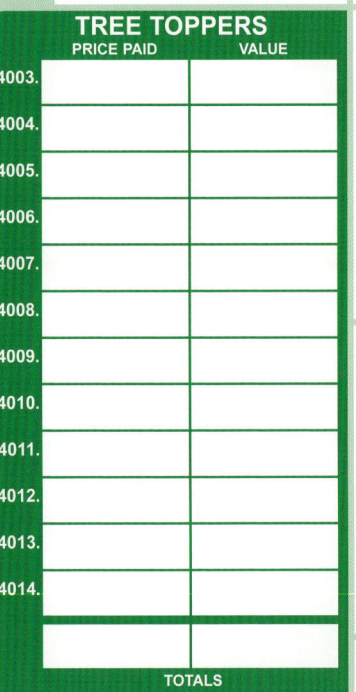

TREE TOPPERS

	PRICE PAID	VALUE
4003.		
4004.		
4005.		
4006.		
4007.		
4008.		
4009.		
4010.		
4011.		
4012.		
4013.		
4014.		
	TOTALS	

NOTES

Others (Tree Toppers)

4015.
Mary Angelwish [QVC]
#unknown • 12" • TJ
Issued: 2001 • Retired: 2001
Original: $21 • Value: $35

4016.
Merry Beth Angelwish
#744110-04 • 10" • TJ
Issued: 2001 • Retired: 2002
Original: $15 • Value: $18

4017.
Veronica Angelbright
#744119 • 12" • TJ
Issued: 2003 • Current
Original: $25 • Value: $R/E

TREE TOPPERS

	PRICE PAID	VALUE
4015.		
4016.		
4017.		
TOTALS		

NOTES

Notes

Here's some space so you can jot down any notes or comments you might have about your collection or wishlist.

Notes

Here's some space so you can jot down any notes or comments you might have about your collection or wishlist.

Future Releases

Who knows what new bears and critters are coming down the pike. Here's plenty of space so you can record 'em as they are released!

BoydsTracker Plush	Original Price	Price Paid	Value
Total:		Price Paid	Value

Future Releases

Who knows what new bears and critters are coming down the pike. Here's plenty of space so you can record 'em as they are released!.

BoydsTracker Plush	Original Price	Price Paid	Value
	Total:	Price Paid	Value

VALUE OF MY COLLECTION
PAGE TOTALS

What's your collection worth? Add the totals from the bottom of each page. Add your subtotals and place them on page 378 to obtain the GRAND TOTAL!

(A) Pages 21 - 47			(B) Pages 48 - 74		
Page Number	Price Paid	Value	Page Number	Price Paid	Value
Page 21			Page 48		
Page 22			Page 49		
Page 23			Page 50		
Page 24			Page 51		
Page 25			Page 52		
Page 26			Page 53		
Page 27			Page 54		
Page 28			Page 55		
Page 29			Page 56		
Page 30			Page 57		
Page 31			Page 58		
Page 32			Page 59		
Page 33			Page 60		
Page 34			Page 61		
Page 35			Page 62		
Page 36			Page 63		
Page 37			Page 64		
Page 38			Page 65		
Page 39			Page 66		
Page 40			Page 67		
Page 41			Page 68		
Page 42			Page 69		
Page 43			Page 70		
Page 44			Page 71		
Page 45			Page 72		
Page 46			Page 73		
Page 47			Page 74		
Subtotal:			Subtotal:		

VALUE OF MY COLLECTION
PAGE TOTALS

What's your collection worth? Add the totals from the bottom of each page. Add your subtotals and place them on page 378 to obtain the GRAND TOTAL!

(C) Pages 75 - 101			(D) Pages 102 - 128		
Page Number	Price Paid	Value	Page Number	Price Paid	Value
Page 75			Page 102		
Page 76			Page 103		
Page 77			Page 104		
Page 78			Page 105		
Page 79			Page 106		
Page 80			Page 107		
Page 81			Page 108		
Page 82			Page 109		
Page 83			Page 110		
Page 84			Page 111		
Page 85			Page 112		
Page 86			Page 113		
Page 87			Page 114		
Page 88			Page 115		
Page 89			Page 116		
Page 90			Page 117		
Page 91			Page 118		
Page 92			Page 119		
Page 93			Page 120		
Page 94			Page 121		
Page 95			Page 122		
Page 96			Page 123		
Page 97			Page 124		
Page 98			Page 125		
Page 99			Page 126		
Page 100			Page 127		
Page 101			Page 128		
Subtotal:			**Subtotal:**		

VALUE OF MY COLLECTION
PAGE TOTALS

What's your collection worth? Add the totals from the bottom of each page. Add your subtotals and place them on page 378 to obtain the GRAND TOTAL!

(E) Pages 129-155			(F) Pages 156-182		
Page Number	Price Paid	Value	Page Number	Price Paid	Value
Page 129			Page 156		
Page 130			Page 157		
Page 131			Page 158		
Page 132			Page 159		
Page 133			Page 160		
Page 134			Page 161		
Page 135			Page 162		
Page 136			Page 163		
Page 137			Page 164		
Page 138			Page 165		
Page 139			Page 166		
Page 140			Page 167		
Page 141			Page 168		
Page 142			Page 169		
Page 143			Page 170		
Page 144			Page 171		
Page 145			Page 172		
Page 146			Page 173		
Page 147			Page 174		
Page 148			Page 175		
Page 149			Page 176		
Page 150			Page 177		
Page 151			Page 178		
Page 152			Page 179		
Page 153			Page 180		
Page 154			Page 181		
Page 155			Page 182		
Subtotal:			**Subtotal:**		

VALUE OF MY COLLECTION
PAGE TOTALS

What's your collection worth? Add the totals from the bottom of each page. Add your subtotals and place them on page 378 to obtain the GRAND TOTAL!

(G) Pages 183-209

Page Number	Price Paid	Value
Page 183		
Page 184		
Page 185		
Page 186		
Page 187		
Page 188		
Page 189		
Page 190		
Page 191		
Page 192		
Page 193		
Page 194		
Page 195		
Page 196		
Page 197		
Page 198		
Page 199		
Page 200		
Page 201		
Page 202		
Page 203		
Page 204		
Page 205		
Page 206		
Page 207		
Page 208		
Page 209		
Subtotal:		

(H) Pages 210-236

Page Number	Price Paid	Value
Page 210		
Page 211		
Page 212		
Page 213		
Page 214		
Page 215		
Page 216		
Page 217		
Page 218		
Page 219		
Page 220		
Page 221		
Page 222		
Page 223		
Page 224		
Page 225		
Page 226		
Page 227		
Page 228		
Page 229		
Page 230		
Page 231		
Page 232		
Page 233		
Page 234		
Page 235		
Page 236		
Subtotal:		

VALUE OF MY COLLECTION
PAGE TOTALS

What's your collection worth? Add the totals from the bottom of each page. Add your subtotals and place them on page 378 to obtain the GRAND TOTAL!

(I) Pages 237-263			(J) Pages 264-290		
Page Number	Price Paid	Value	Page Number	Price Paid	Value
Page 237			Page 264		
Page 238			Page 265		
Page 239			Page 266		
Page 240			Page 267		
Page 241			Page 268		
Page 242			Page 269		
Page 243			Page 270		
Page 244			Page 271		
Page 245			Page 272		
Page 246			Page 273		
Page 247			Page 274		
Page 248			Page 275		
Page 249			Page 276		
Page 250			Page 277		
Page 251			Page 278		
Page 252			Page 279		
Page 253			Page 280		
Page 254			Page 281		
Page 255			Page 282		
Page 256			Page 283		
Page 257			Page 284		
Page 258			Page 285		
Page 259			Page 286		
Page 260			Page 287		
Page 261			Page 288		
Page 262			Page 289		
Page 263			Page 290		
Subtotal:			Subtotal:		

VALUE OF MY COLLECTION
PAGE TOTALS

What's your collection worth? Add the totals from the bottom of each page. Add your subtotals and place them on page 378 to obtain the GRAND TOTAL!

(K) Pages 291-317			(L) Pages 318-344		
Page Number	Price Paid	Value	Page Number	Price Paid	Value
Page 291			Page 318		
Page 292			Page 319		
Page 293			Page 320		
Page 294			Page 321		
Page 295			Page 322		
Page 296			Page 323		
Page 297			Page 324		
Page 298			Page 325		
Page 299			Page 326		
Page 300			Page 327		
Page 301			Page 328		
Page 302			Page 329		
Page 303			Page 330		
Page 304			Page 331		
Page 305			Page 332		
Page 306			Page 333		
Page 307			Page 334		
Page 308			Page 335		
Page 309			Page 336		
Page 310			Page 337		
Page 311			Page 338		
Page 312			Page 339		
Page 313			Page 340		
Page 314			Page 341		
Page 315			Page 342		
Page 316			Page 343		
Page 317			Page 344		
Subtotal:			**Subtotal:**		

VALUE OF MY COLLECTION
PAGE TOTALS

What's your collection worth? Add the totals from the bottom of each page. Add your subtotals and place them on page 378 to obtain the GRAND TOTAL!

(M) Pages 345-355			(N) Pages 356-366		
Page Number	Price Paid	Value	Page Number	Price Paid	Value
Page 345			Page 356		
Page 346			Page 357		
Page 347			Page 358		
Page 348			Page 359		
Page 349			Page 360		
Page 350			Page 361		
Page 351			Page 362		
Page 352			Page 363		
Page 353			Page 364		
Page 354			Page 365		
Page 355			Page 366		
Subtotal:			**Subtotal:**		

VALUE OF MY COLLECTION
GRAND TOTAL

What's your collection worth? Get your subtotals from pages 371-377 and place them below to obtain the GRAND TOTAL!

	SUBTOTALS		
	Subtotals	Price Paid	Value
(A)	Pages 21-47		
(B)	Pages 48-74		
(C)	Pages 75-101		
(D)	Pages 102-128		
(E)	Pages 129-155		
(F)	Pages 156-182		
(G)	Pages 183-209		
(H)	Pages 210-236		
(I)	Pages 237-263		
(J)	Pages 264-290		
(K)	Pages 291-317		
(L)	Pages 318-344		
(M)	Pages 345-355		
(N)	Pages 356-366		
	GRAND TOTAL:		

PAWNOTES

PAWNOTE #1
Alice, the little bunny wabbit, is a classic example of what the Archive hares went through before perfecting their great looks. Almost all of the early Archive hares evolved over the years and can be found in 'old face' & 'new face' styles. Note the difference in the size, the ears and the shape of the face.

- Alice (old face) - Page:277 TID:2989
- Alice (new face) - Page:277 TID:2990

PAWNOTE #2
Alexandra is a unique white hare, who underwent three different body style changes. The original version had a smaller snout, shorter ears and smaller feet. The second version was given longer ears. The third version was given even bigger ears, bigger feet, and a more well defined face. These evolutionary pieces are a rare find indeed!
- Alexandra (short ears - small feet) - Page:277 TID:2986
- Alexandra (big ears - small feet) - Page:277 TID:2987
- Alexandra (big ears - big feet) - Page:277 TID:2988

PAWNOTE #3
Amelia R. Hare underwent face-lifts and a fur change. The original is 9" tall and has smooth fur. Her second look added 3" to her height and changed her fur to plush white. The third version was released with a restyled face.

- Amelia R. Hare (original old face - smooth fur) - Page:278 TID:2997
- Amelia R. Hare (old face) - Page:278 TID:2998
- Amelia R. Hare (new face) - Page:278 TID:2999
- Amelia R. Hare (modern face) - Page:278 TID:3000

PAWNOTE #4
Amos is one of the most unique bears in the entire Boyds line, with a 'one of a kind' fur, style and look. His coat was made of the softest gold plush fur. He feels lighter than other bears of the same size. He was only sold for one year, which makes him very rare. He was also sold under the name of MacKenzie. Talk about an identity crisis!
- Amos (a.k.a. MacKenzie) - Page:56 TID:364

PAWNOTE #5
At 14" Anastasia is the biggest of the Toyland series. She was produced in 1992 with white fur. Because of her age and light color of her coat, it is rare to find her in mint condition. Though the Toyland Hare series is long retired, you can see a hint of the old style in the current Regena Haresford.
• Anastasia (nekkid) - Page:278 TID:3001
• Regena Haresford - Page:304 TID:3311

PAWNOTE #6
Auntie Adina was a Limited Edition hare of 500. She is dressed as a music teacher and was sold with a miniature replica of a violin. It is rumored that a working violin was sent to China to use as a model for this scaled-down accessory.
• Auntie Adina - Page:279 TID:3013

PAWNOTE #7
Arthur, Chamberlain and Clement are classics in the old style teddy bear look. They are characterized by long arms that are curved at the end, ears on the side of their heads, and noses that come to a point. White bears of this age are a rare treat to find!

• Arthur - Page:59 TID:406
• Chamberlain - Page:90 TID:770
• Clement - Page:95 TID:830

PAWNOTE #8
Attlee is the little Archive guy that went on to become Green Cord Bailey in the Fall of 1992. Because of this he was retired soon after his release.
• Attlee - Page:60 TID:417

PAWNOTE #9
A truly unique limited piece, Auntie Harestein is said to have been designed by Tina Lowenthal. Tina created the Early Limiteds with help from several women in the Gettysburg area. The skirts, sweaters, and accessories were all hand made. A unique feature on Auntie Harestein is the purple material used for her skirt, which was said to have been recycled from the Lowethals' kitchen curtains.

• Auntie Harestein (burgundy print) - Page:279 TID:3015
• Auntie Harestein (tan print) - Page:279 TID:3016

PAW NOTES

PAWNOTE #10
The first Avery B. Bean was made in 1985 and was simply known as the Dark Brown Bean Bear. He also has the honors of being the first JBB to be produced. Take a look at his evolution! The second version was made in 1988 and had smooth chocolate fur with an 'old style' face. In 1989 he was produced with an open mouth. Because the open mouth was hard to reproduce, this variation was only produced for a short time. Just a few hundred of this version was produced, with no two alike! In 1990, his fur was changed from smooth to plush just before he retired. All Avery's have a place in Boyds history!
- Avery B. Bean (open mouth) - Page:63 TID:453
- Avery B. Bean (smooth fur) - Page:63 TID:454
- Avery B. Bean (regular plush) - Page:64 TID:455
- Dark Brown Bean Bear - Page:100 TID:888

PAWNOTE #11
Fall 1992 marked the debut of Bailey Ann (named after Gary & Tina's daughter). This also marked the birth of the 'Bailey & Friends' series that includes her best friend Emily (hare) & boyfriend Edmund. Matthew & his dog Indy were added to the series 1996. What makes this Bailey very rare is that she is the first in the series. A variation exists with no collar.
- Bailey (Fall 1992) - Page:65 TID:474

PAWNOTE #12
Spring 1993 marked a change for Bailey. Her fur color was changed to the gold we know today.
- Bailey (Spring 1993) - Page:65 TID:475

PAWNOTE #13
There are two variations for Bailey this season. She was first dressed in a navy & cream checked outfit. However, it was quickly changed to black & white checked to better match Edmund.
- Bailey (Spring 1994 - black) - Page:65 TID:477
- Bailey (Spring 1994 - navy) - Page:65 TID:478

PAWNOTE #14
Bailey made her debut on QVC, wearing a shiny purple dress. This was changed to a softer fabric, which was sold in the regular line. This Bailey with the shiny dress was available on QVC only.
- Bailey (Spring 1996) - Page:66 TID:482
- Bailey (QVC, shiny purple dress) - Page:66 TID:483

PAWNOTE #15
Bailey had two variations for Spring 1997. She appeared on QVC wearing a lilac dress and matching hat; for the regular line she wore a purple dress with a lilac hat.
• Bailey (QVC, lilac dress) - Page:66 TID:486
• Bailey (Spring 1997) - Page:66 TID:487

PAWNOTE #16
Bear-Among-Bears is in the Merino Wool series and was the first Boyds Bear ever sold. What sets these bears apart is that they were purchased pre-manufactured. Look for the Boyds hangtag and a striped silk ribbon. The hangtags are commonly referred to as the 'storybook' tags, because they tell the story of the company and the history of the bear. The Boyds hangtag is very important in determining if a bear is an authentic Boyds.

• Bear-Among-Bears (brown) - Page:70 TID:529 (not pictured)
• Bear-Among-Bears (tan) - Page:70 TID:530

PAWNOTE #17
The Bears' Bear is also of the Merino Wool series. At 12" he was produced in brown, golden tan, and rust wool. However, the most rare are the rust colored bears with as few as 100 out there. Rust can also be found in 16", though I have never seen one! As with all the Merino Wool Bears & Hares, they have Boyds' 'storybook' hangtag & ribbon to authenticate them.

• Bears' Bear (brown) - Page:70 TID:537
• Bears' Bear (rust) - Page:70 TID:538
• Bears' Bear (tan) - Page:71 TID:539

PAWNOTE #18
These 10" Bearly-a-Bears came from the Merino Wool series, and were produced in both brown and golden tan wool. As with all the Merino Wool Bears & Hares, they have the Boyds 'storybook' hangtag & ribbon to authenticate them.
• Bearly-a-Bear (brown) - Page:70 TID:535 (not pictured)
• Bearly-a-Bear (tan) - Page:70 TID:536

PAWNOTE #19
8" Bear-let comes from the Merino Wool series. I have heard that Gary discovered these little guys at a Bear show in 1984. He reportedly liked the Classic look and style of these bears. Bear-let was sold with two different fur colors, brown and golden tan. Each of these bears was accompanied by the Boyds 'storybook' hangtag and ribbon. Bears in the Merino Wool Series do not have Boyds body tags.

• Bear-let (brown) - Page:70 TID:531
• Bear-let (tan) - Page:70 TID:532

PAWNOTE #20
It is said that Beatrice was the first of the Limited Editions to be named after Gary's mother.
• Beatrice - Page:71 TID:542

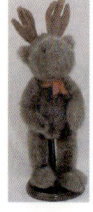

PAWNOTE #21
Beatrice Von Hindenmoose changed fur colors from light beige to mocha in 1993.
• Beatrice Von Hindenmoose (beige) - Page:320 TID:3490
• Beatrice Von Hiddenmoose (mocha) - Page:320 TID:3491

PAWNOTE #22
Bubba, Betty Lou and Beauregard are from the very popular Bubba Bears Series. These bears have unmistakable charm! It is my understanding that Beauregard was the last Bubba in the series to be sold before they were retired. The most popular and valuable of the Bubbas is Betty Lou, who sold out on QVC in an instant.
• Beauregard (QVC) - Page:71 TID:547
• Betty Lou (QVC) - Page:74 TID:585
• Bubba - Page:82 TID:679

PAWNOTE #23
Berrybear is the most rare of the Himalayan Dancing Bears! He is set apart from Homer & Honeypot by his size and type of filling (beans rather than poly-fill). He has smooth (velvet like), rust colored fur. A rare beauty for sure!
• Berrybear - Page:73 TID:570
• Honeypot - Page:138 TID:1344

PAWNOTE #24
Bill was the first of his kind to sell on QVC. Sold as a limited but not a numbered series, I have heard that as few as 600 of these were manufactured.
• Bill (QVC) - Page:75 TID:593

PAWNOTE #25
Binkie B. Bean is my favorite white JBB! What sets him apart from all Binkie II's is his gray nose and white fur. Some later Binkies can be found with a black nose.
• Binkie B. Bean (original) - Page:76 TID:600
• Binkie B. Bean (black nose) - Page:76 TID:601

PAWNOTE #26
Binkie B. Bean was the first bear that was named second generation after being restyled. Binkie's coat was changed to a cream fur with dark gold paws pads and was renamed Binkie B. Bean II.
• Binkie B. Bean II - Page:76 TID:602

PAWNOTE #27
Brewin was released with two style numbers, 5806 & 5802. There is no difference between the two; both Brewins are very popular.
• Brewin - Page:80 TID:649

PAWNOTE #28
Briton R. Hare is another critter that changed his fur color; he can be found in both smooth nutmeg and British tan plush. Any style is a rare find.
• Briton R. Hare (smooth fur) - Page:281 TID:3031
• Briton R. Hare (regular plush) - Page:281 TID:3032

PAWNOTE #29
Burke Derr was a wonderful young man who was absolutely crazy about Boyds Bears. Burke had Cystic Fibrosis. His life touched everyone he met. Burke Derr was the inspiration and namesake behind Burke P. Bear. Burke passed away, but a portion of the proceeds from sale of Burke P. Bear were donated to Cystic Fibrosis Research. Burke's Father, Bob Derr, established a foundation for CF and continues his charitable work in the hope of a cure. Burke P. Bear was named the Ambassador of Love and traveled the U.S. to raise money for Cystic Fibrosis.
• Burke P. Bear - Page:84 TID:699

PAWNOTE #30
Buzz B. Bean is another rare JBB critter. Like the Merino Wool bears, Buzz has a golden tan coat. The thing that makes his fur unique is that it is also smooth to the touch.
• Buzz B. Bean - Page:85 TID:707

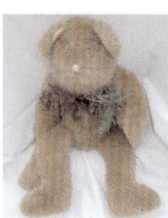

PAWNOTE #31
Cabin Bear is a very early JBB who was accessorized with pinecones and pine fur needles. It has been said that as few as fifty were produced. Cabin Cat was produced around the same time.
• Cabin Cat - Page:246 TID:2630
• Cabin Bear - Page:86 TID:721 (not pictured)

PAWNOTE #32
Churchill is a classic example of an 'evolutionary' piece. The original was characterized by a pointed nose, ears on the sides of his head and long arms that are curved at the end. Then in '91 his face was redefined to make his cheeks rounder with ears still on the side of the head. The third version, released in '93 had the ears moved up on top of the head, resulting in the classic look that Boyds continues to use to this day.
• Churchill (old face) - Page:93 TID:803
• Churchill (2nd version) - Page:93 TID:804
• Churchhill (new face) - Page:93 TID:805

PAWNOTE #33
Abigail, Frannie, and Priscilla are proving to be quite collectable country dolls. Several different fabrics were used to produce these gals and the faces were all hand painted.

• Abigail (blue print dress) - Page:263 TID:2830
• Frannie - Page:263 TID:2834
• Priscilla (brown print) - Page:263 TID:2835
• Priscilla (tan print) - Page:263 TID:2836

PAWNOTE #34

Cora B. Bunny is another evolutionary piece. The stout nose in the new face version is more 'bunny' like than the original Cora, who had a flatter nose.
• Cora B. Bunny (old face) - Page:283 TID:3057
• Cora B. Bunny (new face) - Page:283 TID:3058

PAWNOTE #35

Diana is another example of an early piece dressed by Tina. This piece was sold with either a boy cub or a girl cub. As with some other early pieces, Diana was produced in small quantities, but was not numbered as a limited edition. It is said that as few as one hundred were produced.
• Diana (with boy cub) - Page:102 TID:919 (not pictured)
• Diana (with girl cub) - Page:102 TID:920

PAWNOTE #36

Edgar's rare because he is an odd duck... and for a crow that's something! He was not a big seller, but his release was big in the minds of collectors. Edgar is viewed by many collectors as Boyds first step out of the realm of the ordinary. He and Hank Crow Jr. were the only crows ever made.

• Edgar - Page:266 TID:2870
• Hank Krow Jr. - Page:266 TID:2871

PAWNOTE #37

Fall 1993 Edmund was another first in the 'Bailey & Friends' series to be produced every 6 months along with Bailey.
• Edmund (Fall 1993) - Page:107 TID:978

PAWNOTE #38

There are two variations to the Spring 1994 Edmund... not to confuse you! His pants were done in both navy & black wool. The navy Edmund is the harder to find of the two variations. Edmund wears a black and white checked shirt in both versions.
• Edmund (Spring 1994 - black) - Page:107 TID:980
• Edmund (Spring 1994 - navy) - Page:107 TID:981

PAWNOTE #39
The Eddie Bauer Edmund is the only piece in the 'Bailey & Friends' series to be sold as a store exclusive. He wears a snowflake sweater and was only available through Eddie Bauer.
• Edmund (Eddie Bauer) - Page:107 TID:979

PAWNOTE #40
Elmo Beefcake is a perfect example of an evolutionary cow! The unmistakable pink flat nose is a very noticeable feature on the first release (old face). Boyds restyled Elmo's nose for the "new face" version. You can also find early Bessie Moostein and Herman Beefcake sporting this snout!
• Bessie Moostein (old face) - Page:264 TID:2841
• Bessie Moostein (new face) - Page:264 TID:2842
• Elmo Beefcake (old face) - Page:265 TID:2852
• Elmo Beefcake (new face) - Page:265 TID:2853

PAWNOTE #41
Bailey's best friend, Emily Babbit, made her debut in '93 sporting a blue floral romper to match Bailey. The Bailey & Friends series was released every 6 months but, since 2002, they are now produced only once a year.
• Emily Babbit (Spring 1993) - Page:286 TID:3100

PAWNOTE #42
Emily Babbit has two variations for the Spring 1999 season. Normally manufactured with chenille fur, Emily was produced briefly with plush fur. Wearing a dark blue anchor sweater, Emily with the plush fur is quite rare. The chenille furred Emily is wearing a cream anchor sweater with a boat accessory.
• Emily Babbit (Spring 1994 - white sweater) - Page:286 TID:3102
• Emily Babbit (Spring 1994 - blue sweater) - Page:287 TID:3103

PAWNOTE #43
Emily Babbit was beefed up for her Fall 1999 release. She underwent a face-lift to give her a huskier look.
• Emily Babbit (Fall 1999) - Page:287 TID:3114

PAWNOTE #44
Eugenia the Apple Seller won Boyds the Toby award in 1995. The apple basket accessory was quickly retired, but Eugenia the bear was not retired until 1996. Complete sets are a rare find indeed! There are subtle ways to tell the difference in the later versions, such as varying dye lots in the fabric and different colored buttons on her dress.

- Eugenia - Page:114 TID:1064
- Eugenia (apple seller) - Page:114 TID:1065

PAWNOTE #45
Along with getting her name from a member of the royal family… Fergie is unique because of her fur color, a rare bluish / gray. She was retired after only 2 years of production.
- Fergie - Page:289 TID:3129

PAWNOTE #46
Fitzroy is another of the rare classics. He can be found in two different blue sweaters, with two style numbers assigned to him, 5795 or 9195. Almost every Fitzroy I have ever seen seems to have two left feet… a feature only a mother could love!
- Fitzroy - Page:118 TID:1104

PAWNOTE #47
Fleurette is the most rare piece ever made because of her history and quantity! It is said that it was Tina's desire to dress the "nekkid" bears and give them more character. Capt*n Ron and I have heard that Tina designed this bear sitting at the kitchen table. She fashioned a silk headdress with dried flowers and added a doily around her neck. She named this bear Fleurette. There were only a half dozen of these ever made since the flowers proved to be extremely fragile. A Fleurette hare was produced later in larger quantities with a necklace of faux pearls instead of the flowers.
- Fleurette Hare - Page:289 TID:3132
- Fleurette - Page:118 TID:1106

PAWNOTE #48
Flora B. Bunny's earlier style is very rare because of her floral ribbon. It is said that Tina went out on a shopping spree and came back with floral patterned silk ribbon, which was 10 times more expensive than the ribbon used previously. These 'old face' bunnies with the floral silk ribbon are a real treasure!

- Flora B. Bunny (old face) - Page:289 TID:3134
- Flora B. Bunny (new face) - Page:289 TID:3135

PAWNOTE #49

Gorden B. Bean was one of the earliest JBB's to be produced in 1988. In 1988 he started out 8" tall with smooth cinnamon fur. By 1989 he had grown to 10", and his fur was changed to the British tan plush. In 1990 he got a new look that was used until he retired.

- Gorden B. Bean (original) - Page:126 TID:1203
- Gorden B. Bean (old face) - Page:126 TID:1204
- Gorden B. Bean (new face) - Page:126 TID:1205

PAWNOTE #50

Gram and Gramps are the largest of the HDB series at 18" tall. They were only out for one year, in 1991, making them a very hot commodity and highly sought after.
- Gram - Page:127 TID:1216
- Gramps - Page:127 TID:1221

PAWNOTE #51

5000 Gunther VonBruin's were manufactured. His red nose and red collar give him that clown appeal.
- Gunther Von Bruin - Page:130 TID:1248

PAWNOTE #52

Sporting a baseball uniform designed by Tina, Homer is extremely rare because of the limited quantity made.
- Homer (10" baseball) - Page:137 TID:1332

PAWNOTE #53

Irving Poochberg was the largest of the early dogs. Complete with a red tongue, he has smooth fur. Boyds added a bandana, a hat, and an American flag, then renamed him Roosevelt.
- Irving Poochberg - Page:269 TID:2906
- Roosevelt - Page:271 TID:2923

PAWNOTE #54
It is rumored that the JB stands for the 'Jelly Bean,' describing the body shape that these bean filled bears have. The first J.B. Bean is very rare, standing only 8" with a smooth lemon yellow fur. He too underwent the classic evolutionary change. In 1989 his fur was changed to the butter color plush you see today. He can be found in an 'old face' and 'new face' variation.
• J.B. Bean (smooth fur) - Page:142 TID:1401
• J.B. Bean (old face) - Page:142 TID:1402
• J.B. Bean (new face) - Page:143 TID:1403

PAWNOTE #55
Jacque Le Grenouille is unique because he is wool and filled with beans. This frog appealed to collectors, to kids, and non-Boyds collectors. He was quickly sold out, making him the most elusive in the series!
• Jacque Le Grenouille - Page:275 TID:2969

PAWNOTE #56
14" Jane has a blend of four different colors in her fur and a blue stiched nose. Retired after just one year, no other piece has this type of fur.
• Jane (14") - Page:293 TID:3180

PAWNOTE #57
Jed Bruin is the only JBB bear to be done with a white curly sherpa coat. He was sold as Jed or Snowball. White bears in good condition are a rare find.
• Jed Bruin (a.k.a. Snowball) - Page:146 TID:1443

PAWNOTE #58
Along the same lines as Amelia, Livingston Hare has gone through change too. The first version was done in smooth cinnamon fur and was around 8-9" in height. The second version came when he switched fur to British Tan. Then came the final face-lift to 'new face' and the finished product.
• Livingston R. Hare (early smooth fur) - Page:297 TID:3225
• Livingston R. Hare (old face) - Page:297 TID:3226
• Livingston R. Hare (new face) - Page:297 TID:3227

PAW NOTES

PAWNOTE #59
Matthew Bear was named after the Lowenthals first born, Matthew Harrison. Matthew Bear first debuted in 1985 in the Merino Wool bear series. He joined the Bailey & Friends series in 1996, and is currently produced every fall.
• Matthew (Fall 1996) - Page:172 TID:1755
• Matthew Bear - Page:173 TID:1764

PAWNOTE #60
Marta M. Hare is another member of the 'one of a kind fur' family, with her distinguished bluish-gray plush fur.
• Marta M. Hare - Page:298 TID:3241

PAWNOTE #61
McMullen has a unique coat. I was told that Gary was experimenting with a new fur type to give the bear a velvety feel.
• McMullen - Page:174 TID:1776

PAWNOTE #62
Retiring Nadia Von Hindenmoose left a void in the hearts of moose lovers. Then Boyds introduced Meeka Moose as an Exclusive for the Alps Company. Her popularity soared and she was released in several other sporty sweaters, making all moose collectors very happy! Check out her friends Mukluk, Mookie and Cousin Murray!
• Cousin Murray (Alps) - Page:320 TID:3496
• Meeka (Alps, green sweater) - Page:324 TID:3541
• Mookie (Alps, cream sweater) - Page:325 TID:3559
• Mukluk (Alps, blue sweater) - Page:326 TID:3572
• Nadia Von Hindenmoose - Page:329 TID:3599

PAWNOTE #63
Melbourne is another classic in the old Archive Series and can be found in the 'old face' and 'new face' variations.
• Melbourne - Page:174 TID:1785

PAWNOTE #64
Merlin is said to be another of Tina's early dressed. Sold as a Bear or a Lion, a purple velvet cape gives him a magical look!
- Merlin - Page:315 TID:3440
- Merlin - Page:175 TID:1794 (not pictured)

PAWNOTE #65
Mohley is one of my favorite HDB. He is also the most elusive in the series. The smallest HDB at 9", this bear is bean filled and has rich, smooth cream fur.
- Mohley - Page:179 TID:1839

PAWNOTE #66
Another great Master of Disguise! What you may not have known is that you can find him in bean filled or polyfill.
- Moriarity (bean filled) - Page:182 TID:1873
- Moriarity (polyfill) - Page:182 TID:1874

PAWNOTE #67
As one of the early limited editions of 500, Mrs. Fiedler is dressed as a Music teacher accessorized with miniature Bass Fiddle. A later version of this piece was done in the same outfit and appeared on QVC as a limited edition named Nettie.
- Mrs. Fiedler the Music Teacher - Page:185 TID:1913
- Nettie (QVC) - Page:189 TID:1958

PAWNOTE #68
On the road to perfecting pooches, Mystery Dawg was retired so quickly that he was never given a style number.
- Mystery Dawg - Page:270 TID:2913

PAW NOTES

PAWNOTE #69
Perfect from her creation, Nana Panda is one of the most valuable HDB's. Part of the appeal to the Himalayan series is the classic 'humped' back and curved arms. Pandas are very popular in any line, and this one's a classic!
• Nana Panda - Page:331 TID:3620

 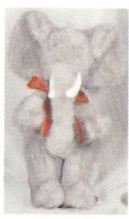 

PAWNOTE #70
It is rumored that because Nicholai, Omar, and Olivia were released during an election year, Republicans bought them in droves. These elephants were wildly popular! Nicholai, the largest, is the hardest to find.

• Nicholai A. Pachydermsky - Page:274 TID:2956
• Olivia A. Pachydermsky - Page:274 TID:2957
• Omar A. Pachydermsky - Page:274 TID:2958

PAWNOTE #71
Nod and Nod II are not always easy to distinguish from one another. Nod is stark white, and Nod II is off-white. Dates on the body tag can help identify the generation.
• Nod (stark white) - Page:191 TID:1983
• Nod II ((off-white)) - Page:191 TID:1984

PAWNOTE #72
Ogden can be found as small as 7", but in later versions this panda was made 10" tall and much chubbier.
• Ogden B. Bean (small version) - Page:331 TID:3621
• Ogden B. Bean (large version) - Page:331 TID:3622

PAWNOTE #73
Otis is the second oldest in the Boyds line of JBB's. He has an evolutionary history like Avery B. Bean. The original Otis debuted in 1989 with smooth cinnamon fur. Later that year he was released open-mouthed. In 1990 he was changed to plush British tan fur with an 'old face.' In 1992 he received a face-lift to the 'new face' style, and kept that look until his retirement in '97.
• Otis B. Bean (open mouth) - Page:193 TID:2014
• Otis B. Bean (old face - smooth fur) - Page:194 TID:2015
• Otis B. Bean (old face) - Page:194 TID:2016
• Otis B. Bean (new face) - Page:194 TID:2017

PAWNOTE #74

Pansy was the first QVC Limited Edition. Originally only 600 were manufactured, but because they proved to be so popular, the quantity was doubled in the following batch. The first release was numbered "___ of 600", and the second, "___ of 1200".
• Pansy (QVC) - Page:195 TID:2035

PAWNOTE #75

Phillip Bearhop is a rather adorable little bellhop. He was a number limited edition of 5000. All Phillips have hand numbered hangtags!
• Phillip Bearhop - Page:199 TID:2076

PAWNOTE #76

9" bean filled Pohley has a unique smooth rust colored fur. Except for color, he is identical to Rohley.
• Pohley - Page:199 TID:2082
• Rohley - Page:206 TID:2161

PAWNOTE #77

The original version of Regina had a smaller snout, shorter ears and smaller feet. The second version was given longer ears. The third version was given even bigger ears, bigger feet, and a more defined face. Alexandra hare can also be found with these variations.

• Regina (short ears - small feet) - Page:304 TID:3312
• Regina (big ears - small feet) - Page:304 TID:3313 (not pictured)
• Regina (big ears - big feet) - Page:304 TID:3314

PAWNOTE #78

Royce is another of Tina's early works. Did you every wonder why the sweaters look like argyle socks? It is my understanding that Tina used material from Gary's brother's sock factory to outfit the bears. She took apart a doll's sweater to use for a pattern, and used both poly-fill bears (such as 'old face' Heath) and JBB's (like Otis B. Bean) to make Royce Bear. Royce was also produced as a Hare, using either Cordilia or Briton hare. It is rumored that as few as 100 were produced.
• Royce Hare - Page:305 TID:3325
• Royce - Page:207 TID:2180
• Royce Bear - Page:207 TID:2181

PAWNOTE #79
Rudolf is the largest and most rare of the long retired, original SnowBears. He ranks high on my 'most wanted' list!
• Rudolf - Page:207 TID:2182

PAWNOTE #80
It is rumored that outside of his children's namesakes, Gary's favorite critter was Rufus. It is said that Rufus was a Boyds business milestone and that Gary particularly liked the mink color coat. Rufus as an early JBB was a bit smaller and had a flat face with a brown stitched nose. You can also find this 'old face' variation in Dufus Bear and Daryl Bear.
• Daryl Bear (old face) - Page:100 TID:890
• Dufus Bear (old face) - Page:105 TID:955
• Rufus (new face) - Page:208 TID:2188

PAWNOTE #81
Sherlock was the first of the now very popular 'Masters of Disguise' series. Dressed in a Rabbit suit (with removable hat), he debuted in 1992. This version was barely over 8" tall and came with pink paws pads. The later versions are much taller and have two different shades of gray paws pads.
• Sherlock (pink paws) - Page:215 TID:2268
• Sherlock (gray paws) - Page:215 TID:2269

PAWNOTE #82
Just as with Nods, the only difference between these two is their color. Sinkin is white and Sinkin II is off white.
• Sinkin (stark white) - Page:215 TID:2278
• Sinkin II (off-white) - Page:216 TID:2279

PAWNOTE #83
Speed Poochberg is an early dog that can be found with two fur types. The first is a smooth cinnamon fur, which then changed to British tan. He was retired early, making him a rarity.
• Speed Poochberg (smooth fur) - Page:271 TID:2930
• Speed Poochberg (regular plush) - Page:271 TID:2931

PAWNOTE #84
Teddy Hare is from the Merino Wool series. Teddy Hare was made in two styles with two colors in each style. A lop-eared version came in rust and tan, and a regular-eared version came in white, and golden tan. As with the rest of the Merino Wool series, the Boyds' hangtag and ribbon authenticates the piece.
- Teddy Hare (golden tan) - Page:308 TID:3359
- Teddy Hare (rust) - Page:308 TID:3360
- Teddy Hare (tan) - Page:308 TID:3361
- Teddy Hare (white) - Page:308 TID:3362

PAWNOTE #85
Made to mark the celebration of the 100th anniversary of the Teddy Bear, Theodore Sr. was an Exclusive to Paw Dealers only. Theodore Jr. is a smaller version, which was released first, and sold out in only 2 weeks. A mohair variation was made, and appeared on the QVC broadcast from the Boyds Bear Country Grand Opening.
- Theodore Jr. - Page:227 TID:2411
- Theodore Sr. (EVENT) - Page:227 TID:2414

PAWNOTE #86
The only difference between these two is that Tinkin is white and Tinkin II is off white.
- Tinkin (stark white) - Page:228 TID:2431
- Tinkin II (off-white) - Page:228 TID:2432

PAWNOTE #87
This bear's retirement was a classic 'oops'. It is rumored that Thor was accidentally retired instead of the bear next to him on a product list. Thor was the first white bear to come with blue eyes and was extremely popular.
- Thor M. Berriman - Page:227 TID:2419

PAWNOTE #88
Tutu is actually Pop Bruin dressed as a ballerina. She was an early Limited Edition, but was not numbered. Tutu was also made as a hare.
- Tutu - Page:309 TID:3372
- Pop Bruin - Page:201 TID:2101
- Tutu - Page:232 TID:2471 (not pictured)

PAWNOTE #89
Vanessa was first of the Starlight Foundations charity bears. She was named after a very special little 'Angel' who lost her battle to leukemia in August of 2001. The second in the series is Alisa R. Angel. Sales from these bears benefit children in hospitals.
• Alisa R. Angel (Starlight) - Page:54 TID:344
• Vanessa R. Angel (Starlight) - Page:234 TID:2501

PAWNOTE #90
Ziggy Bear was part of the Merino Wool series. He has a body style like that of Bea Bear except it is a golden tan color. As with all of the Merino's, the hangtag and silk ribbon authenticate it as a Boyds.
• Bea Bear - Page:69 TID:526
• Ziggy Bear - Page:243 TID:2608 (not pictured)

PAWNOTE #91
Cookie Grimilkin - Came in three face styles. Early version, white blaze goes up between the eyes to top of face. Second version, white under chin only (rare), and most recent, white from the cheeks down. Evolution of piece means some recent versions have stitched toes on paws.

• Cookie Grimilkin (old face) - Page:248 TID:2657
• Cookie Grimilkin (new face) - Page:248 TID:2658
• Cookie Grimilkin (modern face) - Page:248 TID:2659

PAWNOTE #92
Ernest Grimilkin - Came in all three face styles. Early version, white blaze goes up between the eyes to top of face. Second version, white under chin only (rare), and most recent, white from the cheeks down. Evolution of piece means some recent versions have stitched toes on paws. Very first version is slightly smaller with smooth shiny fur and a blazed face.
• Ernest Q. Grimilkin (smooth fur) - Page:249 TID:2670
• Ernest Q. Grimilkin (white on chin) - Page:249 TID:2671
• Ernest Q. Grimilkin (blaze face) - Page:249 TID:2672
• Ernest Q. Grimilkin (new face) - Page:249 TID:2673
• Ernest Q. Grimilkin (modern face) - Page:249 TID:2674

PAWNOTE #93
Gae Grimilkin - came in two versions; blazed face, and white on chin only. Also can be found in early smooth fur with blazed face. Named for designer Gae Sharp.

- Gae A. Grimilkin (smooth fur) - Page:250 TID:2681
- Gae A. Grimilkin (white on chin) - Page:250 TID:2682
- Gae A. Grimilkin (regular plush) - Page:250 TID:2683

PAWNOTE #94
Greybeard - came in two versions; blazed face, and with white from cheeks down.
- Greybeard - Page:251 TID:2690

PAWNOTE #95
Lacy - 11"; came in crème or tan.
- Lacy (11") - Page:252 TID:2710

PAWNOTE #96
Lacy - 14"; came in tan or cinnamon.
- Lacy (14") - Page:252 TID:2709

PAWNOTE #97
Ophilia - early versions were a smooth shiny cinnamon fur, changed to British tan in the regular plush. Eyes also changed from green to black.
- Ophilia Q. Grimilkin - Page:255 TID:2746

PAWNOTE #98
Sweetpea - early version is a blue/gray color with white on chin only, later versions pewter and crème.
- Sweetpea Catberg (old face) - Page:260 TID:2798
- Sweetpea Catberg (new face) - Page:260 TID:2799

PAWNOTE #99

Tigerlily - came in 3 styles; blazed face, white on chin only, and white from cheeks down.
- Tigerlily (old face) - Page:261 TID:2809
- Tigerlily (new face) - Page:261 TID:2810

PAWNOTE #100

Zap Catberg - rare mixture of gray and white plush, like Jane hare and Ashley the bear. Only cat in this color plush.
- Zap Catberg - Page:262 TID:2821

PAWNOTE #101

Zenus Grimilkin - early versions were a smooth shiny cinnamon fur, changed to British tan in the regular plush. Eyes also changed from green to black.
- Zenus W. Grimilkin (smooth fur) - Page:262 TID:2824
- Zenus W. Grimilkin (regular plush) - Page:262 TID:2825

PAWNOTE #102

Ol' MacBruin…Down on the Farm Auto-Delivery QVC Price $22.00 for each of 6 deliveries: Squiggley-Piggley 7" plush pig, Cabot the Rabbit 5" plush rabbit, C. Pattie Hoofenudder plush cow, Punsley P. Pussyfoot plush cat, Ol' Farmer MacBruin 12" plush bear, Ol' MacBruin's Rustic Hay Wagon Accessory, Bo Trotsalot plush horse, I.O. Ewe plush lamb, Rooster McStrutten plush rooster, Sunny Side-Up plush chicken, Jimmy Bob plush bear, and Sniffles plush dog.
- Ol' MacBruin…Down on the Farm (QVC) - Page:192 TID:1992

PAWNOTE #103

Peeker of the Month - JANUBEARY, FEBUBEARY, MARCHBEARY, APRILBEARY, MAYBEARY, JUNEBEARY, JULYBEARY, AUGUSTBEARY, SEPTEMBEARY, OCTOBEARY, NOVEMBEARY, AND DECEMBEARY AND 100% cotton display quilt.
- Peeker of the Month (QVC) - Page:197 TID:2054

BoydsTracker
Alphabetical Index and Checklist
Items are listed in alphabetical order followed by page number.

Name	Page
☐ 20th Anniversary Bear (QVC, bear)	50
☐ A. J. Blixen (bear)	50
☐ Abbey Ewe (lamb)	311
☐ Abbey Ewe (SFMB, lamb)	311
☐ Abbie Mae Woolsey (lamb)	312
☐ Abbott Q. Beanster (bear)	50
☐ Abby & Katie Forever Friends (Carlton Cards, bear)	50
☐ Abby Grace (POG, bear)	50
☐ Abdul Duneworthy (QVC, camel)	244
☐ Abercrombie B. Beanster (bear)	50
☐ Aberdeen (QVC, bear)	50
☐ Abigail (cloth doll, blue print dress))	263
☐ Abigail (cloth doll, tan dress)	263
☐ Abigail (cloth doll, red & white print dress)	263
☐ Abigail (Bon Ton, bear)	50
☐ Abigail (Elder Beerman, bear)	50
☐ Abigail A. Beanster (QVC, bear)	51
☐ Abigail and Beryl Bramblebeary (QVC, bear)	51
☐ Abigail Bramblebeary (bear)	51
☐ Abigail Rose Primsley (bear)	51
☐ Ace Bruin (bear)	51
☐ Ace Q. Dooright (bear)	51
☐ Ace Swingster (QVC, monkey)	318
☐ Adaline Bearett (bear)	51
☐ Adam Appleton (bear)	51
☐ Adam (York Fair, bear)	51
☐ Adams F. Bearington (bear)	51
☐ Addington (bear)	51
☐ Adelaide & Aggie (QVC, cow)	263
☐ Adelaide and Joey Downunder (kangaroo)	311
☐ Adeline B. Appleton (bear)	51
☐ Adeline LaBearsley (bear)	52
☐ Adkin (Frederick Atkins, bear)	52
☐ Adriana Angelwish (ornament)	340
☐ Adrienne Berrifrost (ornament)	340
☐ Agatha B. Bearington (QVC, bear)	52
☐ Agatha Snoopstein (bear)	52
☐ Agnes MacBear (CAN, bear)	52
☐ Aimee Berrifrost (ornament)	340
☐ Aimee Warmheart (bear)	52
☐ Aissa Witebred (bear)	52
☐ Alabaster B. Bigfoot (bear)	52
☐ Alastair (bear)	52
☐ Alastair & Camilla (bear)	52
☐ Albert B. Bean (bear)	52
☐ Albert Merrybeary (bear)	52
☐ Al'Berta B. Bear (CAN, bear)	53
☐ Albin and Tootie Whizzalong (QVC, bear)	53
☐ Aldina (Dillards, bear)	53
☐ Alec (bear, a.k.a. Alex)	53
☐ Aleesha Bearlet (QVC, bear)	53
☐ Aletha The Bearmaker (bear)	53
☐ Alex Berriman with Nikita (bear)	53
☐ Alex Nicole (Dillards, bear)	53
☐ Alexander M. Pattington (QVC, bear)	53
☐ Alexander P. Bearsworth (bear)	53
☐ Alexandra (hare, short ears - small feet)	277
☐ Alexandra (hare, big ears - small feet)	277
☐ Alexandra (hare, big ears - big feet)	277
☐ Alexandra & Jessica Bearyfriends (Carlton Cards, bear)	53
☐ Alexandra and Belle (QVC, bear)	53
☐ Alexis Bearinsky (GCC, bear)	54
☐ Alexis Berriman (bear)	54
☐ Alexis Berriman (SFMB, bear)	54
☐ Alfred Q. Rothsbury (bear)	54
☐ Ali Marie Beansley (Country Living, bear)	54
☐ Alice (hare, old face)	277
☐ Alice (hare, new face)	277
☐ Alice (bear)	54
☐ Alice B. Patchbeary (bear)	54
☐ Alice Hopplebeary (Boscovs, hare)	277
☐ Alice II (bear)	54
☐ Alicia Bearsley (Platinum Paw, bear)	54
☐ Alina (tree topper)	364
☐ Alisa R. Angel (Starlight, bear)	54
☐ Alison Babbit (SFMB, hare)	277
☐ Alissa Angelhope (bear)	54
☐ Alley McCat (QVC, cat)	245
☐ Allie Bearington (Welcome Home, bear)	54
☐ Allie Oppsey (cat)	245
☐ Allison B. Beansley (QVC, bear)	55
☐ Allison Babbit (hare)	277
☐ Allison Bearburg (QVC, bear)	55
☐ Allison Rose Berriweather (f.o.b 2003)	48
☐ Ally (Lord & Taylor, bear)	55
☐ Ally II (Lord & Taylor, bear)	55
☐ Alouetta de Grizetta (bear)	55
☐ Alouysius Quackenwaddle (bear)	55
☐ Alpine (SLE, hare)	277
☐ Alvin (bear)	55
☐ Alvin D. Elf (QVC, ornament)	340
☐ Alvin Q. Hopster (hare)	278
☐ Alvis Q. Bearnap with Snoozy T. Puddlemaker (bear)	55
☐ Alyssa Berrifrost (ornament)	340
☐ Alyssa M. Punkinbeary (GCC, bear)	55
☐ Amanda K. Huntington (bear)	55
☐ Amarretto (hare)	278
☐ Amber B. Oakley (bear)	55
☐ Amber Glorybear (QVC, bear)	55
☐ Amber McPunkin (bear)	56
☐ Amber Woodsbeary (Welcome Home, bear)	56
☐ Ambrose P. Hydrant III (QVC, dog)	266
☐ Ambrose Q. Hydrant (Lord & Taylor, dog)	266
☐ Ambrosia Angelwish (QVC, ornament)	340
☐ Amelia P. Quignapple (QVC, bear)	56
☐ Amelia R. Hare (hare, original old face - smooth fur)	278
☐ Amelia R. Hare (hare, old face)	278
☐ Amelia R. Hare (hare, new face)	278
☐ Amelia R. Hare (hare, modern face)	278
☐ Americana Angelbear (QVC, bear)	56
☐ Americus P. Bearsley (Clarion Bear Festival, bear)	56

Name	Page
☐ Amie & Pam Goodfriends (ornament)	340
☐ Amos (bear, a.k.a. MacKenzie)	56
☐ Amos T. Woodsley (QVC, bear)	56
☐ Amy Lynn Flutterfoot (QVC, bear)	56
☐ Amy Z. Sassycat (cat)	245
☐ Anais Angelwish (QVC, tree topper)	364
☐ Anarose (ornament)	340
☐ Anastasia (hare, nekkid)	278
☐ Anastasia (hare, dressed)	278
☐ Anastasia (QVC, bear)	56
☐ Anastasia Bearskoff (J.C.Penney, bear)	56
☐ Andrea DeBearvoire (bear)	56
☐ Andrea Jane (GCC, bear)	56
☐ Andrea Oakley (bear)	57
☐ Andrei Berriman (bear)	57
☐ Andrew (Dillards, bear)	57
☐ Andrew Huntington (bear)	57
☐ Andy B. Pattington (bear)	57
☐ Angel (GCC, bear)	57
☐ Angel Bear (ornament, red)	33
☐ Angel Bear (ornament, blue)	33
☐ Angela (QVC, ornament)	341
☐ Angela Keepsafe (bear)	57
☐ Angelica (ornament)	341
☐ Angelina (ornament)	341
☐ Angelina (SFMB, ornament)	341
☐ Angelina II (ornament)	341
☐ Angeline (QVC, bear)	57
☐ Angeline Angelfrost (tree topper)	364
☐ Angelique Angelfrost (tree topper)	365
☐ Angus MacMoo (cow)	263
☐ Anisette (hare)	278
☐ Anissa (SLE, hare)	278
☐ Anissa Whittlebear (bear)	57
☐ Anita Lotsalove with Basket (QVC, bear)	57
☐ Ann I. Bearsary (BBC, bear)	57
☐ Ann Marie (bear)	57
☐ Anna (hare)	278
☐ Anna Belle (POG, bear)	58
☐ Anna Eleanor Bearington (QVC, bear)	58
☐ Anna Mae Bakersbear with Li'l Snap (Miss Yvonne's, bear)	58
☐ Anna Manymore (bear)	58
☐ Annabella (GCC, bear)	58
☐ Annabelle Dickens (bear)	58
☐ Annabelle Z. Witebred (QVC, bear)	58
☐ Annalee Angelberry (tree topper)	365
☐ Anne (hare, old face)	278
☐ Anne (hare, new face)	279
☐ Annette Bearberg (SLE, ornament)	341
☐ Annie & Jennifer Hopkins (QVC, hare)	279
☐ Annie B. Appleton (bear)	58
☐ Ansel (bear)	58
☐ Anthony (bear)	58
☐ Antique Santa (ornament)	33
☐ Antoinette de Bearvoire (bear)	58
☐ Anya Frostfire (bear)	58
☐ AP Gold Bear (CAN, bear)	59
☐ Aphrodite (pig, without heart)	332
☐ Aphrodite (pig, with heart)	333
☐ (The) Apple Harvest Stand (fruit stand)	32
☐ April Mae (bear)	59
☐ April Mae McVeggie (bear)	59
☐ Archer (hare)	279
☐ Archibald McBearlie (bear)	59
☐ Archie Strutencrow (rooster)	337

Name	Page
☐ Arctic Bear (bear)	59
☐ Arcturus (QVC, ornament, with Aurora Goodnight)	341
☐ Ardyth (GCC, ornament)	341
☐ Aria & Astra Angelwish (QVC, ornament)	341
☐ Ariana Angelwish (bear)	59
☐ Ariel (ornament)	341
☐ Ariel (QVC, ornament)	341
☐ Ariel (SFMB, ornament)	341
☐ Ariella Angelfrost (tree topper)	365
☐ Arinna Goodnight (ornament)	342
☐ Arlington B. Beanster (bear)	59
☐ Arlo (bear, red vest)	59
☐ Arlo (bear, pumpkin sweater)	59
☐ Armstrong Cattington (cat)	245
☐ Arno-w-ld (dog)	267
☐ Artemus (bear)	59
☐ Artemus J. Bear (Country Living, bear, a.k.a John Michael)	59
☐ Arthur (bear)	59
☐ Arthur C. Bearington (bear)	60
☐ Ashlee R. Angel (Starlight, bear)	60
☐ Ashley (hare)	279
☐ Ashley (SFMB, hare)	279
☐ Ashley B. Bean (bear)	60
☐ Ashley Huntington (bear)	60
☐ Ashley Lynn (Elder Beerman, bear)	60
☐ Ashlyn Bloomengrows (bear)	60
☐ Ashlyn LaBearsley (bear)	60
☐ Aspen P. Ninelives (GCC, cat)	245
☐ Asquith (bear)	60
☐ Astoria Angelwish (ornament)	342
☐ Astrid (bear)	60
☐ Athena (ornament)	342
☐ Athena with Holly Berries (Lord & Taylor, ornament)	342
☐ Attie (Frederick Atkins, bear)	60
☐ Attlee (bear)	60
☐ Aubergine (hare)	279
☐ Aubrey (Dillards, bear)	60
☐ Aubrey (GCC, bear)	61
☐ Aubrey T. Autumnfest (bear)	61
☐ Aubrey T. Tippeetoes (SFMB, bear)	61
☐ Aubrey Tippeetoes (bear)	61
☐ Aubry T. Autumnfest with Buckeye (QVC, bear)	61
☐ Auden S. Penworthy (cat)	245
☐ Auggie Bruin (bear)	61
☐ Augusta (bear)	61
☐ Aunt Bea (bear)	61
☐ Aunt Becky Bearchild (bear)	61
☐ Aunt Becky Bearchild (SFMB, bear)	61
☐ Aunt Bessie Skidoo (bear)	61
☐ Aunt Birdie (f.o.b 2003, pin)	47
☐ Aunt Birdie Berriweather...A Sprinkle A Day (f.o.b 2003)	48
☐ Aunt Carole Beary (Macy's East, ornament)	342
☐ Aunt Elaine Wilbear (Macy's East, ornament)	342
☐ Aunt Fanny Fremont (bear)	61
☐ Aunt Jo Ann O'Beary (Macy's East, bear)	62
☐ Aunt Mable with Snowy (bear)	62
☐ Aunt Mamie Bearington (bear)	62
☐ Aunt Mattie MacDolittle (QVC, bear)	62
☐ Aunt Phiddy Bearburn (J.T.Webb, bear)	62
☐ Aunt Yvonne Dubeary (bear)	62
☐ Auntie Adeline (Carson Pirie Scott, bear)	62

Name	Page
☐ Auntie Adina (hare)	279
☐ Auntie Aleena de Bearvoire (bear)	62
☐ Auntie Alice (bear)	62
☐ Auntie Autumn and Lil' Harvey (Show Specials, bear)	62
☐ Auntie Babbit (hare)	279
☐ Auntie Bearburg (bear)	62
☐ Auntie Edna with Flora & Tillie (QVC, bear)	62
☐ Auntie Erma (bear)	63
☐ Auntie Esther and Theona J Doolittle (QVC, bear)	63
☐ Auntie Harestein (hare, burgundy print)	279
☐ Auntie Harestein (hare, tan print)	279
☐ Auntie Iola (bear)	63
☐ Auntie Lavonne Higgenthorpe (bear)	63
☐ Auntie Marguerite, Honeybruin, Beesley Honeybruin, and Topaz F. Wuzzie (QVC, bear)	63
☐ Auntie Sheila Bearisch (Peebles/Gottschalks, bear)	63
☐ Auriela Angelfrost (QVC, tree topper)	365
☐ Aurora Goodnight (ornament)	342
☐ Autumn & Fallston (QVC, bear)	63
☐ Autumn Fallsbeary (bear)	63
☐ Autumn Pumpkin Patch (Longaberger, bear)	63
☐ Ava Marie (ornament)	342
☐ Ava Marie (SYN, bear)	63
☐ Avery B. Bean (bear, open mouth)	63
☐ Avery B. Bean (bear, smooth fur)	63
☐ Avery B. Bean (bear, regular plush)	64
☐ Azalea & Jordan Rosebeary (QVC, bear)	64
☐ Azania Sparklefrost (QVC, tree topper)	365
☐ Azure Lee, Ginger. & Sunbeam P. Snickelfritz (QVC, bear)	64
☐ B. Angelboy (ornament)	342
☐ B. Angelgirl (ornament)	342
☐ B. Burt Bundleup (pin)	361
☐ B. Everluvin (bear)	64
☐ B. Jay Tweeter (bear)	64
☐ B.A. Bigfoot (QVC, bear)	64
☐ B.A. Blackbelt (bear)	64
☐ B.A. Scholar (bear)	64
☐ B.B. Bugsley with Lil' Lady Bugsley (QVC, bear)	64
☐ B.B. Country Bear (BBC, bear)	64
☐ B.B. Starcatcher (ornament)	342
☐ B.J. Bearricane (bear)	64
☐ B.W. Poochley (QVC, dog)	267
☐ B.Y. Lotsaluck (bear)	64
☐ Baah'b (bear, beige)	65
☐ Baah'b (bear, tan)	65
☐ Baakins (bear)	65
☐ Babs (hare)	279
☐ Babs and Baab Woolsley (lamb)	312
☐ Baby (cat)	245
☐ Baby (hare)	279
☐ Baby (bear)	65
☐ Baby Baakins (ornament)	342
☐ Baby Bailey 1999 & 2000 (QVC, ornament)	343
☐ Baby C. Corn (ornament)	343
☐ Baby Mae Wishkabibble (bear)	65
☐ Baby Mookins (bear)	65
☐ Baby Noel (bear)	65
☐ Baby Rosebud (Harry & David, pig)	333
☐ Babykins 2002 (ornament)	343
☐ Bagley Flatberg (dog)	267
☐ Bailey (bear, Fall 1992)	65

Name	Page
☐ Bailey (bear, Spring 1993)	65
☐ Bailey (bear, Fall 1993)	65
☐ Bailey (bear, Spring 1994 - black)	65
☐ Bailey (bear, Spring 1994 - navy)	65
☐ Bailey (bear, Fall 1994)	66
☐ Bailey (bear, Spring 1995)	66
☐ Bailey (bear, Fall 1995)	66
☐ Bailey (bear, Spring 1996)	66
☐ Bailey (QVC, bear, shiny purple dress)	66
☐ Bailey (bear, Fall 1996)	66
☐ Bailey (QVC, bear, lilac dress)	66
☐ Bailey (bear, Spring 1997)	66
☐ Bailey (bear, Fall 1997)	66
☐ Bailey (bear, Spring 1998)	66
☐ Bailey (bear, Fall 1998)	67
☐ Bailey (bear, Spring 1999)	67
☐ Bailey (bear, Spring 2000)	67
☐ Bailey (bear, Fall 2000)	67
☐ Bailey (bear, Spring 2001)	67
☐ Bailey (bear, Fall 2001)	67
☐ Bailey (bear, Spring 2002)	67
☐ Bailey (bear, Fall 2002)	68
☐ Bailey (bear, Spring 2003)	68
☐ Bailey (bear, Fall 2003)	68
☐ Bailey (bear, Spring 2004)	68
☐ Bailey (bear, Fall 2004)	68
☐ Bailey & Matthew with Resin Ornaments (bear, Fall 1996)	66
☐ Bailey & Matthew with Resin Ornaments (bear, Fall 1997)	66
☐ Bailey & Matthew with Resin Ornaments (bear, Fall 1998)	67
☐ Bailey & Matthew with Resin Ornaments (bear, Fall 1999)	67
☐ Bailey & Matthew with Resin Ornaments (bear, Fall 2000)	67
☐ Bailey with Dottie (bear, Fall 1999)	67
☐ Bailey with Squiggles (QVC, bear)	67
☐ Baldwin (bear, old face)	68
☐ Baldwin (bear, new face)	68
☐ Bamboo Bearington (panda)	330
☐ Bandit Bushytail (raccoon)	337
☐ Barbara Mary (Boscovs, bear)	68
☐ Barnaby B. Bean (bear)	68
☐ Barnegat Swan (white group)	30
☐ Barnegat Swan (white group, large)	30
☐ Barnegat Swan (white group, preener)	30
☐ Barney B. Keeper (Bon Ton, bear)	68
☐ Barney Bowlsalot (bear)	68
☐ Barret, Belinda & Berg Blizzard (QVC, ornament)	343
☐ Barrett (SLE, bear)	68
☐ Barston Q. Growler (QVC, bear)	69
☐ Bart Barkenfarkle (dog)	267
☐ Bartholemew B. Bean (bear)	69
☐ Bartholomew (Eddie Bauer, bear)	69
☐ Bartholomew (J.C.Penney, bear)	69
☐ Bartlett (bear)	69
☐ Bartley & Wilbur (QVC, dog)	267
☐ Barton (Alps, bear)	69
☐ Bashful T. Bearhugs (bear)	69
☐ Bath & Body Works Bear (Bath & Body Works, bear)	69
☐ Bath & Body Works Dog (Bath & Body Works, dog)	267
☐ Bauer B. Bear (Eddie Bauer, bear)	69

402

Name	Page
☐ Baxter B. Bean (bear)	69
☐ Baxter T. Birch (Hallmark, bear)	69
☐ Bea Bear (bear)	69
☐ Bea Beary (Longaberger, bear)	70
☐ Bear Gabriel (ornament, angel)	33
☐ Bear Gabriel (ornament, with horn)	33
☐ Bear Gabriel Plaque (ornament)	33
☐ Bear Hollow Honey Stand (fruit stand)	32
☐ Bear in Basket (ornament)	33
☐ Bear Lee Survivedit (Boyds Family Reunion, bear)	70
☐ Bear Skater (ornament)	33
☐ Bear Sweep (ornament)	33
☐ Bear with Bunny (ornament)	33
☐ Bear with Tree (ornament)	33
☐ Bear-Among-Bears (bear, brown)	70
☐ Bear-Among-Bears (bear, tan)	70
☐ Bearie (f.o.b 2004, pin)	48
☐ Bear-let (bear, brown)	70
☐ Bear-let (bear, tan)	70
☐ Bearlove (bear)	70
☐ Bearly A. Hare (Harry & David, bear)	70
☐ Bearly-a-Bear (bear, brown)	70
☐ Bearly-a-Bear (bear, tan)	70
☐ Bears' Bear (bear, brown)	70
☐ Bears' Bear (bear, rust)	70
☐ Bears' Bear (bear, tan)	71
☐ (The) Bearsleys (Show Specials, bear)	71
☐ Bearwinkle (Harry & David, bear)	71
☐ Beatrice (hare)	280
☐ Beatrice (bear)	71
☐ Beatrice (Frederick Atkins, bear)	71
☐ Beatrice Bearyman (May Company, bear)	71
☐ Beatrice Bearymore (May Company, bear)	71
☐ Beatrice Von Hiddenmoose (moose, mocha)	320
☐ Beatrice Von Hindenmoose (moose, beige)	320
☐ Beauregard (SLE, bear)	71
☐ Beauregard (QVC, bear)	71
☐ Bebe (mouse, pink sweater)	316
☐ Bebe (mouse, red sweater)	316
☐ Bebe Z. Beezley with Bizzybee (QVC, bear)	71
☐ Becca & Bethany Angelwish (QVC, ornament)	343
☐ Becca Bearheart (bear)	71
☐ Becky (bear, green plaid dress)	71
☐ Becky (bear, red plaid dress)	72
☐ Becky Sue, Bobbi Jo & Mary Lou (QVC, ornament)	343
☐ Bedford B. Bean (bear)	72
☐ Bedford Boneah (hare)	280
☐ Bedford Boneah II (hare)	280
☐ Bee Mihoney (POG, bear)	72
☐ Beecher B. Bunny (hare)	280
☐ Beesley Buzzoff (QVC, bear)	72
☐ Beezer B. Goodlebear (QVC, bear)	72
☐ Beggin' D. Bones (bear)	72
☐ Belle (Harry & David, hare)	280
☐ Ben Hardley Doinnuttin (bear)	72
☐ Benjamin (f.o.b 2004)	48
☐ Benjamin (bear)	72
☐ Benjamin (SFMB, bear)	72
☐ Benjamin Beanbeary (Belks, bear)	72
☐ Benjamin F. Almanac (QVC, bear, with Caroline Mayflower)	72
☐ Benjamin W. Bear (Barnes & Noble, bear)	72
☐ Bennington W. Bruin (bear)	73
☐ Benny P. Chatsworth (puppet)	363
☐ Benson Bushytail (ornament)	343
☐ Benson T. Hopabout (hare)	280
☐ Bentley B. Woodsley (bear)	73
☐ Bernadette B. Bearington (QVC, bear)	73
☐ Bernadette Bearbuck (QVC, bear)	73
☐ Bernadette de Bearvoire (bear)	73
☐ Bernard B. Bear (Barnes & Noble, bear)	73
☐ Bernice B. Bear (Barnes & Noble, bear)	73
☐ Bernice Blizzard (ornament)	343
☐ Berrybear (bear)	73
☐ Bert Blizzard (ornament)	343
☐ Bertha S. Simianski (monkey)	318
☐ Bertha Utterberg (cow)	263
☐ Bess (ornament)	343
☐ Bess Bearman (Welcome Home, bear)	73
☐ Bess W. Pattington (bear)	73
☐ Bessie and Chuck Moosley (cow)	264
☐ Bessie Moostein (cow, old face)	264
☐ Bessie Moostein (cow, new face)	264
☐ Bestest & Buddy Truefriends (bear)	73
☐ Bestest & Buddy Truefriends (SFMB, bear)	73
☐ Bethany Bearington (bear)	74
☐ Bethany Thistlebeary (bear)	74
☐ Betsey (bear)	74
☐ Betsey B. Hoofenudder (QVC, cow)	264
☐ Betsey Lou Bearyproud (QVC, bear)	74
☐ Betsie Angelstar (ornament)	343
☐ Betsie B. Jodibear (bear)	74
☐ Betsie L. Steadsbeary (Longaberger, bear)	74
☐ Betsy B. Bearyproud (QVC, bear)	74
☐ Betty B. Learnin (bear)	74
☐ Betty Biscuit (dog, a.k.a. Betty Cocker)	267
☐ Betty Fisher (CAN, bear)	74
☐ Betty Jane (SLE, pig)	333
☐ Betty Jane Maybeary (bear)	74
☐ Betty Lou (QVC, bear)	74
☐ Betty Lou, Clementine & Josie McCoy (Show Specials, bear)	74
☐ Beulah Canine (dog)	267
☐ Bianca T. Witebred (bear)	75
☐ Bibi Buzzby (ornament)	343
☐ Biddle Beezley (bear)	75
☐ Biff Grizzwood (bear)	75
☐ Big Ben Bearhugs (bear)	75
☐ Big Boy (bear)	75
☐ Big Harry (bear)	75
☐ Big Pig, Little Pig (CAN, pig)	333
☐ Bill (QVC, bear)	75
☐ Billy Bob (ornament)	344
☐ Billy Bob Bruin with Froggie (bear)	75
☐ Billy Ray (bear)	75
☐ Billy Ray Beanster with Petey Porker (bear)	75
☐ Bingham (QVC, bear)	75
☐ Bingle Beartoes (bear)	75
☐ Bingles (QVC, bear)	76
☐ Binkie B. Bean (bear, original)	76
☐ Binkie B. Bean (bear, black nose)	76
☐ Binkie B. Bean II (bear)	76
☐ Bird Bear (ornament)	34
☐ Biscuit B. Beggar (ornament)	344
☐ Bismark Von Hindenmoose (moose)	320
☐ Bitsey Nibblekins (ornament)	344
☐ Bixby B. Bear (QVC, bear)	76
☐ Bixby Trufflebeary (bear)	76
☐ Bixie (hare)	280
☐ Bizz (ornament)	344

Name	Page
☐ Black Swan (black hills, ¾ size)	21
☐ Blackstone (bear, small eyes)	76
☐ Blackstone (QVC, bear, big eyes)	76
☐ Blake & Ogden Wordsworth (QVC, cat, with Dickens)	245
☐ Blake B. Wordsworth (cat)	245
☐ Blanche de Bearvoire (bear)	76
☐ Blessed B. Babybear (bear)	76
☐ Blink, Hush & Shush (QVC, bear)	76
☐ Blinkin (bear)	76
☐ Bloomin' F.o.B. (f.o.b 1999, pin)	45
☐ Blossom B. Berriweather...Bloom With Joy! (f.o.b 1999)	45
☐ Blossom DuBearvoire (QVC, bear)	77
☐ Blossom Monarch (GCC, bear)	77
☐ Bluebeary (bear)	77
☐ Bluebeary (Smuckers, bear)	77
☐ Blueberry (bear)	77
☐ Bobber (frog)	275
☐ Bobbi Frostbeary (SYN, bear)	77
☐ Bobbi Jo Bearican (bear)	77
☐ Bobbi Kat (cat)	245
☐ Bobbi McBobble (bear)	77
☐ Bobbie Jo (bear)	77
☐ Bobbie Sue Maybeary (QVC, bear, with Betty Jane)	77
☐ Bobble B. Beansford (QVC, bear)	77
☐ Bobby Labonte #18 (bobby labonte, firesuit)	40
☐ Bobby Labonte #18 (bobby labonte, jacket)	40
☐ Bobby Labonte #18 (bobby labonte, plush ornament)	40
☐ Bobby Labonte #18 (bobby labonte, resin ornament)	40
☐ Bobby Labonte #18 (bobby labonte, sweatshirt)	40
☐ Bojingles (SFMB, bear)	77
☐ Bon-Bon Sweetbeary (f.o.b. 2005, pin)	49
☐ Bonnie (bear)	78
☐ Boo B. Bear (QVC, bear)	78
☐ Boo Bear (Marshall Field's, bear)	78
☐ Boo Boo Bear (bear)	78
☐ Boo-Boo (SLE, bear)	78
☐ Boots Alleyruckus (cat)	245
☐ Bopper (hare)	280
☐ Boris Berriman (bear)	78
☐ Bosc P. Pearsley (bear)	78
☐ Bosley (bear)	78
☐ Bowser Barksalot (dog)	267
☐ Braden (SLE, lion)	314
☐ Braden P. Oakley (bear)	78
☐ Bradford (bear)	78
☐ Bradie B. Bearsley (Clarion Bear Festival, bear)	78
☐ Bradley Boobear (bear)	78
☐ Bradshaw P. Beansford (bear)	79
☐ Brady Bearimore (bear)	79
☐ Brady Swingenamiss (ornament)	344
☐ Bramble B. Thumperton (hare)	280
☐ Brambley B. Bigfoot (QVC, bear)	79
☐ Brandie & Madeira (QVC, bear)	79
☐ Brandon (Dillards, bear)	79
☐ Brandon A. Bearski (GCC, bear)	79
☐ Brandon Michael (bear)	79
☐ Brantley B. Beansley (QVC, bear)	79
☐ Braxton B. Bear (bear)	79
☐ Braxton B. Bear (SFMB, bear)	79

Name	Page
☐ Brayburn (donkey)	272
☐ Breezy T. Frostman (bear)	79
☐ Brendalynn Blizzard (ornament)	344
☐ Brendon B. Beanster (QVC, bear)	79
☐ Brett B. Bearican (bear)	80
☐ Breven B. Bearski with Willie Waddlewalk (bear)	80
☐ Brewin (bear)	80
☐ Brewin' F.o.B Mini-Tea Set (f.o.b 2000)	46
☐ Brewster McRooster (QVC, bear)	80
☐ Brewster T. Bear (bear)	80
☐ Bria (Frederick Atkins, bear)	80
☐ Brian (CAN, bear)	80
☐ Briana Bearlov (POG, bear)	80
☐ Brianna (Elder Beerman, bear)	80
☐ Brianna Angelbless (QVC, bear)	80
☐ Brianna B. Bearican (bear)	80
☐ Brianna Q. Yachtley with Mr. Waddlesworth (QVC, bear)	80
☐ Brianna Tippeetoes (bear)	81
☐ Brianne (SLE, lamb)	312
☐ Bridgette & Suzanne Dubeary (QVC, bear)	81
☐ Bridgette Beardeaux (bear)	81
☐ Brie Mouski (mouse, old face)	316
☐ Brie Mouski (mouse, new face)	316
☐ Brigette Delapain (hare)	280
☐ Brigham Boneah (hare)	280
☐ Brigham Boneah II (hare)	280
☐ Brighton, Salisbury & Somerset (QVC, bear)	81
☐ Brinkley Bearsdale (bear)	81
☐ Brinsley Bruin (QVC, bear)	81
☐ Brinton S. Beansford (QVC, bear)	81
☐ Bristol B. Windsor (bear)	81
☐ Briton R. Hare (hare, smooth fur)	281
☐ Briton R. Hare (hare, regular plush)	281
☐ Brittany (Dillards, hare)	281
☐ Brittney (York Fair, bear)	81
☐ Brittney Q. Hopplebuns (hare)	281
☐ Bromley Q. Bear (bear)	81
☐ Bronson (SLE, bear)	81
☐ Bronte (cat)	246
☐ Brooke B. Bearsley (bear)	81
☐ Browning (cat)	246
☐ Bruce (bear, nekkid)	82
☐ Bruce (bear, heart sweater)	82
☐ Bruce (bear, Ted sweater)	82
☐ Bruce (bear, bat costume)	82
☐ Bruinhilda Von Bruin (bear)	82
☐ Brumley (QVC, bear)	82
☐ Bruno Bedlington (QVC, bear)	82
☐ Bryson Beansley (QVC, bear)	82
☐ Bubba (bear)	82
☐ Buchanan J Bearington (QVC, bear)	82
☐ Buckingham (bear)	82
☐ Buckles (Lord & Taylor, bear)	82
☐ Buckley (bear)	83
☐ Buckley (QVC, bear)	83
☐ Buckley the Fireman (bear)	83
☐ Buckley the Fireman (SFMB, bear)	83
☐ Bucky Beaverdam (beaver)	244
☐ Bud Buzzby (ornament)	344
☐ Bud Buzzby (SFMB, ornament)	344
☐ Buffie Bunnyhop (hare)	281
☐ Buffington Fitzbruin (bear)	83
☐ Buffy (bear)	83
☐ Buffy (Victoria's Secret, bear)	83

Name	Page
☐ Buford B. (QVC, bear)	83
☐ Buford B. Beezley (bear)	83
☐ Bumbershoot B. Jodibear (bear)	83
☐ Bumble B. Bugsley (bear)	83
☐ Bumble B. Buzzoff (bear)	83
☐ Bumbles S. Beezley (QVC, bear)	84
☐ Bumbley B. Bear (bear)	84
☐ Bumpkin…Country Bear (BBC, bear)	84
☐ Bumpus (hare)	281
☐ Bunker Bedlington (GCC, bear)	84
☐ Bunnie B. Springbeary (Longaberger, hare)	281
☐ Bunnylove Rarebit (hare)	281
☐ Burke P. Bear (bear)	84
☐ Burl (bear)	84
☐ Burlington P. Beanster (bear)	84
☐ Burwell Busheytail with Bud (QVC, raccoon)	337
☐ Buster McRind (bear)	84
☐ Butch (lion)	314
☐ Butch Hoofenutter (cow)	264
☐ Buttercup C. Snicklefritz (bear)	84
☐ Buttercup Pufflefluff (bear)	84
☐ Butterfly Kisses & Bear Hugs (POG, bear)	84
☐ Buxton B. Beansley (QVC, bear)	84
☐ Buzz (Lord & Taylor, dog)	267
☐ Buzz (ornament)	344
☐ Buzz B. Bean (bear)	85
☐ Buzzby (bear)	85
☐ Byron (cat)	246
☐ Byron (bear)	85
☐ C. Carryout Bearington (panda)	330
☐ C. Elbert (Dillards, bear)	85
☐ C. Fallin' Leafowitz (QVC, bear)	85
☐ C.B. (QVC, bear)	85
☐ C.C. Beansley (QVC, bear)	85
☐ C.C. Boobear (bear)	85
☐ C.C. Cocoa Bear (Carlton Cards, bear)	85
☐ C.C. Goodbear (Country Clutter, bear)	85
☐ C.C. Peeker (BBC, ornament)	344
☐ C.C. Peekers (bear)	85
☐ C.J. Cherrybeary (bear)	85
☐ C.Z. Comet (bear)	86
☐ C.Z. Sparklefrost Sparkling (QVC, bear)	86
☐ Cabin Bear (bear)	86
☐ Cabin Cat (cat)	246
☐ Caesar Q. & Cosmo Hydrant (QVC, dog)	267
☐ Cagney (bear)	86
☐ Caitlin Berriweather (f.o.b 2000, pin)	45
☐ Caitlin Berriweather (f.o.b 2000)	46
☐ Caitlin Cherry Berry (Elder Beerman, bear)	86
☐ Caitlynn P.J. Crystalfrost (Cracker Barrel, bear)	86
☐ Cal Doubleplay (bear)	86
☐ Caledonia (bear)	86
☐ Caleigh (Dillards, cat)	246
☐ Callaghan (bear, old face)	86
☐ Callaghan (bear, new face)	86
☐ Callaway Flatcat (cat)	246
☐ Callie P. Snugglepuss` (cat)	246
☐ Calvin Ellis (bear)	86
☐ Cambridge Q. Bearrister (bear)	86
☐ Cameron G. & Deacon T. Bearsford (QVC, bear, with Jameson)	87
☐ Cameron W. Bearsmark (Hallmark, bear)	87
☐ Camilla (hare)	281
☐ Camille du Bear (bear)	87
☐ Camryn B. Bear (bear)	87
☐ Camryn B. Pearsley (bear)	87
☐ Canada Goose (minnesota flats, swimmer)	25
☐ Canada Goose (traditional group)	28
☐ Canada Goose (wooden stained group)	30
☐ Canada Goose (minnesota flats, preener)	25
☐ Canada Goose (minnesota flats, sentinel)	25
☐ Candy (QVC, ornament)	344
☐ Candy B. Corn (bear)	87
☐ Candy Corn Cat (cat)	246
☐ Canute (bear)	87
☐ Canvasback (traditional group, drake)	28
☐ Canvasback (wooden stained group)	30
☐ Canvasback (traditional group, hen)	28
☐ Cappuccino Frenzy (ornament)	344
☐ Cara Sue (SLE, bear)	87
☐ Cara Z. Bunnyhugs (hare)	281
☐ Caramel, Meringue, Molasses Bearenburg (QVC, bear)	87
☐ Cari Carrot (bear)	87
☐ Carin Angelmom (bear)	87
☐ Carina T. McBeansley with Bah-Bah (QVC, bear)	87
☐ Carlie & Kristen (Profitts, bear)	88
☐ Carlie Icebeary (Macy's East, ornament)	345
☐ Carlin Wabbit (hare)	281
☐ Carly Anna (GCC, ornament)	345
☐ Carly Bearworth (Show Specials, bear)	88
☐ Carly Crystalfrost (hare)	281
☐ Carlyle Wordsworth (cat)	246
☐ Carmela Cocobeary (bear)	88
☐ Carmella de Bearvoire (bear)	88
☐ Carol Anne Primsley (bear)	88
☐ Caroline (QVC, bear)	88
☐ Caroline Mayflower (bear)	88
☐ Carrie B. Beansley (QVC, bear)	88
☐ Carrle N. Lotsalove (bear)	88
☐ (The) Carrot Stand (fruit stand)	32
☐ Carson B. Barker (dog)	268
☐ Carter M. Bearington (bear)	88
☐ Carvers Goose (traditional group)	28
☐ Carvers Mallard (traditional group)	28
☐ Carvers Pintail (traditional group)	28
☐ Casey Renee (SYN, bear)	88
☐ Casimir B. Bean (GCC, bear)	88
☐ Casper Cat O'Lantern (SLE, cat)	246
☐ Cass (SLE, bear)	89
☐ Cassandra C. Angelflight (ornament)	345
☐ Cassandra Purrsley (QVC, cat)	246
☐ Cassidy (QVC, bear)	89
☐ Cassidy L. Bearsmark (Hallmark, bear)	89
☐ Cassie B. Nibbles (hare)	282
☐ Cassie Goodnight (ornament)	345
☐ Catherine And Caitlin Berriweather With Little Scruff…Family Traditions (f.o.b 2000)	46
☐ Catherine And Caitlin Berriweather… Fine Cup of Tea (f.o.b 2000)	46
☐ Catherine Berriweather and Little Scruff (f.o.b 2000)	46
☐ Catherine Q. Fuzzberg (cat)	246
☐ Cathy J. Hiphop (hare)	282
☐ Catia Clawford (cat)	247
☐ Catterina Cuddlepuss (cat)	247
☐ Cavendish (bear)	89
☐ CB The Skater (Sparx, bear)	89
☐ Cecelia DeBearvoire (bear)	89
☐ Cecelia T. Bearington (bear)	89

Name	Page
☐ Cecil (bear)	89
☐ Cecile Bearnet (Carlton Cards, bear)	89
☐ Cecilia (hare)	282
☐ Cedar T. Woodsley (bear)	89
☐ Cela Bration (Carlton Cards, bear)	89
☐ Celana Cсleste Angelwish (bear)	89
☐ Celeste (ornament)	345
☐ Celeste Angeltrust with Hope (bear)	90
☐ Celestina Goodnight (ornament)	345
☐ Ceylon Pekoe (QVC, bear)	90
☐ Chadwick (QVC, bear, with Bosley)	90
☐ Chamberlain (bear)	90
☐ Chamomille Q. Quignapple (bear)	90
☐ Chamomille Quignapple (SFMB, bear)	90
☐ Chan (bear)	90
☐ Chance Furgold (Welcome Home, bear)	90
☐ Chanceford Q. Beansley (QVC, bear)	90
☐ Chandler (Younker's, bear)	90
☐ Chandler Crystalfrost (bear)	90
☐ Chanel de la Plumtete (bear)	90
☐ Chanelle Cocobeary (bear)	91
☐ Chantanay (SLE, hare)	282
☐ Chantelle Chapeau (bear)	91
☐ Chardonnay (hare)	282
☐ Chardonnay Beardeaux (bear)	91
☐ Charity Angelbeary (ornament)	345
☐ Charles (dog)	268
☐ Charlie P. Chatsworth (puppet)	363
☐ Charlotte and Wilbur Hamstein (pig)	333
☐ Charlotte B. Beezley (bear)	91
☐ Charlotte R. Hare (hare, old face)	282
☐ Charlotte R. Hare (hare, new face)	282
☐ Charlotte Tewksbeary with Hobbes (QVC, bear)	91
☐ Chase Bearimore (bear)	91
☐ Chaucer (cat, mauve)	247
☐ Chaucer (cat, red)	247
☐ Chauncey Fitzbruin (bear)	91
☐ Checkers (panda)	330
☐ Checkers P. Hydrant (dog)	268
☐ Chedda Mousaka (mouse, old face)	316
☐ Chedda Mousaka (mouse, new face)	316
☐ Cheese N. Crackers (bear)	91
☐ Chelci Robear (Ideation, bear)	91
☐ Chelsea & Cornwell (QVC, bear, with Bristol B. Windsor)	91
☐ Chelsea R. Hare (hare)	282
☐ Cher Fussberg (SLE, cat)	247
☐ Cher N. Hugs (bear)	91
☐ Cherry Blossom Bear (Smithsonian Institute, bear)	91
☐ Cherry Blossom Kimono Bear (Smithsonian Institute, bear)	92
☐ Cheryl S. Grammykins (bear)	92
☐ Chester B. Bearsworth (bear)	92
☐ Chester L. Snicklepuss (cat)	247
☐ Chesterfield Q. Burpee (hare)	282
☐ Chilly Frostbite (ornament)	345
☐ Chimney Santa (ornament)	34
☐ Chimney Santa (ornament, stand-up)	34
☐ Chipper (bear)	92
☐ Chloe (Elder Beerman, hare)	282
☐ Chloe Fitzhare (hare)	282
☐ Chocolate (Hershey, cow)	264
☐ Choir Boy (ornament)	34
☐ Choir Girl (ornament)	34

Name	Page
☐ Chopsticks (panda)	330
☐ Chris B. Trickpuss (QVC, cat)	247
☐ Christian (bear, with boat)	92
☐ Christian (Dillards, bear)	92
☐ Christiana LaBearsley (bear)	92
☐ Christine P. Plumbeary (bear)	92
☐ Christmas Bear (QVC, bear)	92
☐ Christmas Goose (ornament)	34
☐ Christopher (bear)	92
☐ Christopher T. Beansley (QVC, bear)	92
☐ Chuck Darwin (monkey)	319
☐ Chuck Woodbeary (bear)	92
☐ Churchhill (bear, new face)	93
☐ Churchill (bear, old face)	93
☐ Churchill (bear, 2nd version)	93
☐ Chutney Cheeseworthy (mouse)	316
☐ Cimmaron (QVC, bear)	93
☐ Cindy (CAN, bear)	93
☐ Cindy Lou Bearican (Cracker Barrel, bear)	93
☐ Cindy Lou Stuffins (ornament)	345
☐ Cindy McSnoozle (bear)	93
☐ Cindyrella (bear)	93
☐ Cinnamon P. Pussytoes (QVC, cat)	247
☐ Cinnebelle McPunkin (bear)	93
☐ Cissy (Lord & Taylor, bear)	93
☐ Claire (bear)	93
☐ Clancy G. Hydrant, Jr. (dog)	268
☐ Clara (bear)	93
☐ Clara (Kirlins, bear)	94
☐ Clara (Bon Ton, bear)	94
☐ Clara B. Bearcountry (QVC, bear)	94
☐ Clara R. Hare (hare)	282
☐ Clarabelle Moo (cow)	264
☐ Clarence (ornament)	345
☐ Clarissa (bear)	94
☐ Clarissa (SFMB, bear)	94
☐ Clark (QVC, bear)	94
☐ Clark II (Platinum Paw, bear)	94
☐ Clark S. Bearhugs (bear)	94
☐ Clarrisse (hare)	283
☐ Classic Blue Wing Teal (classic group, drake)	22
☐ Classic Bufflehead (classic group, drake)	22
☐ Classic Canvasback (classic group, drake)	22
☐ Classic Canvasback (classic group, hen)	22
☐ Classic Green Wing Teal (classic group, drake)	22
☐ Classic Green Wing Teal (classic group, hen)	22
☐ Classic Mallard (classic group, drake)	23
☐ Classic Mallard (classic group, hen)	23
☐ Classic Pintail (classic group, drake)	23
☐ Classic Puffin (classic group)	23
☐ Classic Puffin (classic group, standing)	23
☐ Classic Redhead (classic group, drake)	23
☐ Classic Redhead (classic group, hen)	23
☐ Classic Sleeper Goose (classic group)	23
☐ Classic Widegon (classic group, drake)	23
☐ Claude Q. Catberg (QVC, cat)	247
☐ Claudette Beardeaux (bear)	94
☐ Claudette Prissypuss (cat)	247
☐ Claudette Tatterpuss (QVC, cat)	247
☐ Claudia & Rowena P. Pussytoes (QVC, cat)	247
☐ Claudine de la Plumtete (cat)	248
☐ Claudine P. Pussyfoot (QVC, cat)	248
☐ Claudius B. Bean (QVC, bear)	94
☐ Claudius B. Bean (Lord & Taylor, bear)	94
☐ Claus Kringlebeary (bear)	94

Name	Page
☐ Claus Kringlebeary (SFMB, bear)	95
☐ Cleason (bear)	95
☐ Clem Cladiddlebear (bear)	95
☐ Clement (bear)	95
☐ Clementine (Frederick Atkins, bear)	95
☐ Clementine (bear)	95
☐ Cleo P. Pussytoes (QVC, cat)	248
☐ Cleo P. Pussytoes (cat)	248
☐ Cleo P. Pussytoes (SFMB, cat)	248
☐ Cleveland G. Bearington (bear)	95
☐ Clinton B. Bean (bear)	95
☐ Clover I. Buzzoff (bear)	95
☐ Clovis Hoofheifer & Ferdinand Bullsworth (QVC, cow)	264
☐ Clovis Moosdale (cow)	264
☐ Clyde Clopsdale (horse)	311
☐ Coach Hayden (bear)	95
☐ Coalcracker Ninelives (cat)	248
☐ Coco Bruin (brown nose, bear)	95
☐ Coco DeBearvoire (bear)	95
☐ Cocoa B. Sweetbeary (f.o.b. 2005)	49
☐ Cocoa Mousse (Sarah's Bears, moose)	320
☐ Coco's Candy Box w/Morsel McNibble (f.o.b. 2005, box)	49
☐ Colby S. Mouski (mouse)	316
☐ Colette Dubeary (bear)	96
☐ Colleen (QVC, bear)	96
☐ Colleen O'Bruin (bear)	96
☐ Collette (SLE, bear)	96
☐ Collier P. Hydrant II (dog)	268
☐ Collin Q. Bearsworth (QVC, bear)	96
☐ Columbine Dubois (hare)	283
☐ Comet (ornament)	345
☐ Comet (Lord & Taylor, ornament)	345
☐ Comfort Bird (wooden stained group, gift boxed)	30
☐ Comfy B. Bear (QVC, bear)	96
☐ Common Loon (black hills)	21
☐ Common Loon (black hills, superior)	21
☐ Conner D. Devilbear (bear)	96
☐ Constance (bear)	96
☐ Constance Bearyfine (GCC, bear)	96
☐ Coo and Lou (dove)	273
☐ Cookie Bearchild (bear)	96
☐ Cookie Grimilkin (cat, old face)	248
☐ Cookie Grimilkin (cat, new face)	248
☐ Cookie Grimilkin (cat, modern face)	248
☐ Cooper T. Wishkabibble (bear)	96
☐ Cora B. Applesmith (bear)	96
☐ Cora B. Bunny (hare, old face)	283
☐ Cora B. Bunny (hare, new face)	283
☐ Corabelle Hoofenutter (cow)	264
☐ Cordilia R. Hare (hare)	283
☐ Corey Allen Bearsmoore (bear)	97
☐ Cori Beariburg (bear)	97
☐ Corinna (bear)	97
☐ Corinna II (bear)	97
☐ Corky (QVC, dog, with Clancy G. Hydrant, Jr.)	268
☐ Cornelius McPunkin (bear)	97
☐ Cornwallis (bear, overalls)	97
☐ Cornwallis (bear, heart sweater)	97
☐ Corny Mooseltreat (moose)	320
☐ Corona Goodspeed (ornament)	346
☐ Corrine Patchbeary (GCC, bear)	97
☐ Cosmos (Elder Beerman, ornament)	346
☐ Cossette D. Lapine (hare)	283
☐ Cottage McNibble (mouse)	316
☐ Cotton Bunnytoes (hare)	283
☐ Country Angel (ornament)	346
☐ Courtney (bear)	97
☐ Courtney (QVC, bear, burgundy plaid)	97
☐ Cousin Marty with Rover (bear)	97
☐ Cousin Matilda with Ted (bear)	97
☐ Cousin Murray (Alps, moose, burgundy hat)	320
☐ Cousin Murray (Alps, moose)	320
☐ Cousin Rose Anjanette (hare)	283
☐ Cowsies (ornament)	346
☐ Crackers with Roquefort (QVC, cat)	248
☐ Cranbeary N. Bear (bear)	98
☐ Cranston (GCC, bear)	98
☐ Craxton B. Bean (bear)	98
☐ Creme Bearleigh (QVC, bear)	98
☐ Cromwell (QVC, bear)	98
☐ Crystal & Frosty Icebeary (Welcome Home, bear)	98
☐ Crystal B. Goodbear (Country Clutter, bear)	98
☐ Cubby T. Bearington (QVC, bear)	98
☐ Cupid Braveheart (ornament)	346
☐ Curley Lapin (hare, old face)	283
☐ Curly Lapin (hare, new face)	283
☐ Cuthbert Catberg (cat)	248
☐ Cybill Quackenwaddle (bear)	98
☐ Cynthia Berrijam (QVC, bear)	98
☐ D.B. Chillymitts (ornament)	346
☐ D.L. Merrill (bear)	98
☐ Dabney P. Powderfoot (hare)	283
☐ Dahlia (bear)	98
☐ Daisey (hare)	283
☐ Daisy Anna Goodbear (Country Clutter, bear)	99
☐ Daisy Bearylove (Kirlins, bear)	99
☐ Daisy Bloomengrows (bear)	99
☐ Daisy Ewe (lamb)	312
☐ Dale & Ilona Moosley (moose)	320
☐ Dale Earnhardt #3 (dale earnhardt, firesuit)	40
☐ Dale Earnhardt #3 (dale earnhardt, jacket)	40
☐ Dale Earnhardt #3 (dale earnhardt, plush ornament)	41
☐ Dale Earnhardt #3 (dale earnhardt, resin ornament)	41
☐ Dale Earnhardt #3 (dale earnhardt, sweatshirt)	41
☐ Dale Earnhardt, Jr. #8 (dale earnhardt, jr., firesuit)	41
☐ Dale Earnhardt, Jr. #8 (dale earnhardt, jr., jacket)	41
☐ Dale Earnhardt, Jr. #8 (dale earnhardt, jr., plush ornament)	41
☐ Dale Earnhardt, Jr. #8 (dale earnhardt, jr., resin ornament)	41
☐ Dale Earnhardt, Jr. #8 (dale earnhardt, jr., sweatshirt)	41
☐ Dalton Monkbury (monkey)	319
☐ Dana & Desiree DeBearvoire (QVC, bear)	99
☐ Dana Marie Bearsley (GCC, bear)	99
☐ Dandy B. Doodlebear (QVC, bear)	99
☐ Daniel (Sight & Sound Ministries, bear)	99
☐ Daniel & Darbey Bearimore (QVC, bear)	99
☐ Danielle & Elizabieta de Bearvoire (QVC, bear)	99
☐ Daphne (Elder Beerman, bear)	99
☐ Daphne R. Hare (hare)	284
☐ Darby (SLE, bear)	99
☐ Darby & Drew Polartrek (QVC, ornament, with Douglas)	346

Name	Page
☐ Darby Beariburg (bear)	99
☐ Darcy Babbit (hare)	284
☐ Darcy Babbit II (hare)	284
☐ Darcy Babbit II (hare, variation)	284
☐ Daria & Dickens Jodibear (QVC, bear)	100
☐ Dark Brown Bean Bear (bear)	100
☐ Darla May & Ann Marie (QVC, bear)	100
☐ Darwin Monkbury (monkey)	319
☐ Daryl Bear (bear, old face)	100
☐ Daryl Bear (bear, new face)	100
☐ Dawn Angelstar (ornament)	346
☐ Dawson B. Bearsworth (bear)	100
☐ Dazey Ewe (lamb)	312
☐ Dazie (bear)	100
☐ Dean B. Bearberg (SLE, bear)	100
☐ Dean S. Bearslot (bear)	100
☐ Debbie Claire (Dillards, bear)	100
☐ Debbie M. Dobbsey (Coach House Gifts, bear)	100
☐ Deborah Sue Bearington (QVC, bear)	100
☐ Deirdre Rose (Bon Ton, bear)	101
☐ Deitrich (ornament)	346
☐ Delaney and the Duffer (bear)	101
☐ Delanie B. Beansford (bear)	101
☐ Delanie B. Beansford (SFMB, bear)	101
☐ Delanie D. Hopplebuns (hare)	284
☐ Delbert Quignapple (bear)	101
☐ Delia R. Hare (hare)	284
☐ Delilah Higgenthorpe (QVC, bear, with Twila)	101
☐ Delmarva V. Crackenpot (bear)	101
☐ Delmarva V. Crackenpot (QVC, bear)	101
☐ Delta (QVC, bear)	101
☐ Demi (hare, chenille)	284
☐ Demi II (hare, regular plush)	284
☐ Denise N. Daisydew (bear)	101
☐ Denise Needsmoreshoes (GCC, bear)	101
☐ Denton P. Jodibear (bear)	101
☐ Derby Scruffles (bear)	102
☐ Derry O. Beary (bear)	102
☐ Desdomona T. Witebred (bear)	102
☐ Destiny Angelbear (GCC, bear)	102
☐ Devin (bear)	102
☐ Devin Fallsbeary (bear)	102
☐ Devon (GCC, bear)	102
☐ Dewey P. Wongvruin (panda)	330
☐ Dewey Q. Grimilkin (cat)	248
☐ Dewey R. Cat (cat)	249
☐ Dexter (bear)	102
☐ Diana (hare, nekkid)	284
☐ Diana (hare, red sweater and hat)	284
☐ Diana (hare, a.k.a. Elizabeth)	284
☐ Diana (bear, with boy cub)	102
☐ Diana (bear, with girl cub)	102
☐ Diane Bearyfriend (GCC, bear)	102
☐ Diane D. Beansford and Topsey F. Wuzzie (QVC, bear)	102
☐ Dick Butkus (lamb)	312
☐ Dickens (bear)	103
☐ Dickens Q. Wordsworth (cat)	249
☐ Dickie The Lionheart (lion)	314
☐ Dingle B. Bumbles (bear)	103
☐ Dingle Beartoes (bear)	103
☐ Dingles (QVC, bear)	103
☐ Dink (bear, first version)	103
☐ Dink (bear, chenille)	103
☐ Dinkle B. Bumbles (ornament)	346
☐ Dion Bearberg (SLE, bear)	103
☐ Dipper (ornament)	346
☐ Dippletoes (hare)	284
☐ Dippy D. Hopplebuns (hare)	285
☐ Disraeli (bear)	103
☐ Dixie (hare)	285
☐ Dixie Hackett (bear)	103
☐ Dixie Hackett (SFMB, bear)	103
☐ Dixon (BBC, bear)	103
☐ Doc Bearsley (bear)	103
☐ Dolley M. Jodibear (bear)	104
☐ Dolly (cloth doll)	263
☐ Dolly & Jed (QVC, ornament)	346
☐ Dolly Llama (llama)	316
☐ Dolly M. Bearington (QVC, bear)	104
☐ Dolly M. Bearsevelt (BBC, bear)	104
☐ Dolly Q. Bunnycombe (hare)	285
☐ Domino (panda)	330
☐ Donna (hare)	285
☐ Donna Duck (duck)	273
☐ Donna Scarvesdale (bear)	104
☐ Donovan B. Bear (bear)	104
☐ Doodle & Dandy (Longaberger, bear)	104
☐ Doodle B. Beanster (QVC, bear)	104
☐ Doolittle Buckshot (bear)	104
☐ Doomoore Buckshot (bear)	104
☐ Doonuttin Buckshot (QVC, bear)	104
☐ Doppity (hare)	285
☐ Dora B. Bunny (hare)	285
☐ Dorchester Catsworth with Artie (cat)	249
☐ Doreen Q. Daisydew (bear)	104
☐ Dorinda & Donna (Show Specials, bear)	104
☐ Dorothea Laceley (bear)	105
☐ Dorothy (bear)	105
☐ Dorothy B. Beansley (bear)	105
☐ Dottie B. Bug (bear)	105
☐ Dottie Q. Hopples (hare)	285
☐ Douglas (SLE, bear)	105
☐ Douglas Polartrek (ornament)	347
☐ Dover D. Windsor (bear)	105
☐ Drema Yawnsalot (GCC, bear)	105
☐ Dreyfus Q. Wordsworth (cat)	249
☐ Drummer Bear (ornament)	34
☐ Dubley (bear)	105
☐ Ducklebuns (duck)	273
☐ Dudley Hopson (hare)	285
☐ Duffer Bear (ornament, golfer)	34
☐ Duffy P. Hydrant (dog)	268
☐ Dufus Bear (bear, old face)	105
☐ Dufus Bear (bear, new face)	105
☐ Dugan B. Beansley (QVC, bear)	105
☐ Duncan (SLE, bear)	105
☐ Duncan Doodledog (dog)	268
☐ Duncan Doodledog (SFMB, dog)	268
☐ Dunkin' (bear)	106
☐ Dunston J. Bearsford (bear)	106
☐ Dustin D. Bearican (bear)	106
☐ Dutch (SLE, hare)	285
☐ Dutch P. Beansford (bear)	106
☐ Dwight D. Bearington (bear)	106
☐ Dylan T. Beansford (bear)	106
☐ Earhart Harington (hare)	285
☐ Eastwick Bearington (bear)	106
☐ Ebenezer S. JodiBear (bear)	106
☐ Ebony Angel (ornament)	34
☐ Echo Goodnight (ornament)	347
☐ Eco Bear (ornament)	34

Name	Page
☐ Eco Bear (ornament, stand-up large)	34
☐ Edam & Gouda (QVC, mouse)	317
☐ Eddie Bauer Betty (Eddie Bauer, dog)	267
☐ Eddie Bauer Diamond (Eddie Bauer, bear)	106
☐ Eddie Bauer Hunter (Eddie Bauer, bear)	106
☐ Eddie Bauer Moose (Eddie Bauer, moose)	320
☐ Eddie Beanberger (bear, red striped sweater with star)	106
☐ Eddie Beanberger (bear, blue and red sweater)	106
☐ Eden (bear, old face)	107
☐ Eden (bear, new face)	107
☐ Eden (bear, red sweater)	107
☐ Eden II (bear)	107
☐ Edgar (crow)	266
☐ Edgar Eggplant (bear)	107
☐ Edina Flatstein (hare)	285
☐ Edith & James Henry Maybeary (QVC, bear)	107
☐ Edith Glorybear (bear)	107
☐ Edith Q. Harington (hare)	285
☐ Edith Q. Harington II (hare)	286
☐ Edmund (bear, Fall 1993)	107
☐ Edmund (Eddie Bauer, bear)	107
☐ Edmund (bear, Spring 1994 - black)	107
☐ Edmund (bear, Spring 1994 - navy)	107
☐ Edmund (bear, Fall 1994)	107
☐ Edmund (bear, Spring 1995)	108
☐ Edmund (bear, Fall 1995)	108
☐ Edmund (bear, Spring 1996)	108
☐ Edmund (bear, Fall 1996)	108
☐ Edmund (bear, Spring 1997)	108
☐ Edmund (bear, Spring 1997- big heart)	108
☐ Edmund (bear, Fall 1997)	108
☐ Edmund (bear, Spring 1998)	108
☐ Edmund (bear, Fall 1998)	108
☐ Edmund (bear, Spring 1999)	108
☐ Edmund (bear, Fall 1999)	108
☐ Edmund (bear, Spring 2000)	108
☐ Edmund (bear, Fall 2000)	109
☐ Edmund (bear, Spring 2001)	109
☐ Edmund (bear, Fall 2001)	109
☐ Edmund (bear, Spring 2002)	109
☐ Edmund (bear, Fall 2002)	109
☐ Edmund (bear, Spring 2003)	109
☐ Edmund (bear, Fall 2003)	109
☐ Edmund (bear, Spring 2004)	109
☐ Edmund (bear, Fall 2004)	109
☐ Edna May (ornament)	347
☐ Edward & Binkie LE Set (QVC, bear)	109
☐ Edward Q. Bearston & Apopka (GCC, bear)	109
☐ Edwin R. Elfstein (Lord & Taylor, bear)	109
☐ Edwina (moose)	320
☐ Eeyore (Disney, donkey)	272
☐ Eeyore (Disney, donkey, Winter Holiday)	272
☐ Eeyore (Disney, donkey, plaid vest)	272
☐ Eeyore (Disney, donkey, Costume Party)	273
☐ Eeyore (Disney, donkey, Cozy Holiday)	273
☐ Eeyore (Disney, donkey, Holiday Caroling)	273
☐ Eeyore 1999 (Disney, ornament)	347
☐ Eeyore 2000 (Disney, ornament)	347
☐ Eeyore, Piglet, Pooh & Tiger [Disney] (Disney, ornament)	347
☐ Effie May (Bon Ton, bear)	110
☐ Egbert Q. Bearsford (bear)	110
☐ Egglebert (hare)	286
☐ Egon Von HindenMoose (moose)	320
☐ Einstein Q. Scaredybear (bear)	110

Name	Page
☐ Elder with Newton (EVENT, bear)	110
☐ Eldon Elfberg (ornament)	347
☐ Eldora (bear)	110
☐ Eleanor (f.o.b 1998)	45
☐ Eleanor (cat)	249
☐ Eleanor (hare)	286
☐ Eleanor Bear (bear)	110
☐ Eleanore Bearsvelt (bear)	110
☐ Elford Bullsworth (cow)	264
☐ Elfwood Bearington (bear)	110
☐ Elgin (bear, elf bear)	110
☐ Elijah Bearringer (bear)	110
☐ Elise Frostbeary (QVC, bear)	110
☐ Elisia P. Bearypoppin with Ross & Darrell (QVC, bear)	110
☐ Elizabeth (hare)	286
☐ Ella (Dillards, bear)	111
☐ Elli Bean (Longaberger, hare)	286
☐ Ellie (SLE, hare)	286
☐ Ellie Hopplebuns (hare)	286
☐ Elliot (bear, old face)	111
☐ Elliot (bear, new face)	111
☐ Elliot (Harry & David, bear)	111
☐ Ellsworth (Little Debbie, bear)	111
☐ Ellsworth Flatcat II (cat)	249
☐ Elly Mae (bear)	111
☐ Elmer Beefcake (cow)	264
☐ Elmer O. Bearroad (bear)	111
☐ Elmo Beefcake (cow, old face)	265
☐ Elmo Beefcake (cow, new face)	265
☐ Elmo Q. Elfbeary LE Set (QVC, bear)	111
☐ Elmore Elf Bear (QVC, bear)	111
☐ Elmore Flatski (bear)	111
☐ Eloise R. Hare (hare)	286
☐ Eloise Willoughby (bear)	111
☐ Elsbeth (Dillards, bear)	111
☐ Elsinore (hare)	286
☐ Elspethe Ewe (lamb)	312
☐ Elsworth (bear)	112
☐ Elton (QVC, bear)	112
☐ Elton Elfberg (bear)	112
☐ Elvin Q. Elfberg (bear)	112
☐ Elvis (lion)	315
☐ Embraceable Ewe (lamb)	312
☐ Emerson T. Penworthy (cat)	249
☐ Emily Ann (Lord & Taylor, moose)	321
☐ Emily Babbit (hare, Spring 1993)	286
☐ Emily Babbit (hare, Fall 1993)	286
☐ Emily Babbit (hare, Spring 1994 - white sweater)	286
☐ Emily Babbit (hare, Spring 1994 - blue sweater)	287
☐ Emily Babbit (hare, Spring 1995)	287
☐ Emily Babbit (hare, Fall 1995)	287
☐ Emily Babbit (hare, Spring 1996)	287
☐ Emily Babbit (hare, Fall 1996)	287
☐ Emily Babbit (hare, Spring 1997)	287
☐ Emily Babbit (hare, Fall 1997)	287
☐ Emily Babbit (hare, Spring 1998)	287
☐ Emily Babbit (QVC, hare, Spring 1998 squiggles on hat)	287
☐ Emily Babbit (hare, Fall 1998)	287
☐ Emily Babbit (hare, Spring 1999)	287
☐ Emily Babbit (hare, Fall 1999)	287
☐ Emily Babbit (hare, Spring 2000)	288
☐ Emily Babbit (hare, Fall 2000)	288

Name	Page
☐ Emily Babbit (hare, Spring 2001)	288
☐ Emily Babbit (hare, Fall 2001)	288
☐ Emily Babbit (hare, Spring 2002)	288
☐ Emily Babbit (hare, Spring 2003)	288
☐ Emily Babbit (hare, Spring 2004)	288
☐ Emily Claire (Welcome Home, bear)	112
☐ Emily Daisydew (Kirlins, bear)	112
☐ Emily E. Dobbsey (Coach House Gifts, bear)	112
☐ Emily R. Hare (hare)	288
☐ Emily Starbright (Hello Shops, bear)	112
☐ Emma (bear)	112
☐ Emma (Frederick Atkins, bear)	112
☐ Emma Jane Mintly (Kirlins, bear)	112
☐ Emma Jean Bearsworth & Lil' Pusskins (QVC, bear)	112
☐ Emma M. Sweetstuff (Hallmark, bear)	113
☐ Emma R. Hare (hare)	288
☐ Emma Rose (QVC, hare)	288
☐ Emmet Elfberg (bear)	113
☐ Emmie Bramblebeary (bear)	113
☐ Emmie Bramblebeary (SFMB, bear)	113
☐ Emmy Lou (bear)	113
☐ Endora Spellbound (bear)	113
☐ Engelbert Q. Elfberg (GCC, bear)	113
☐ Eric Burrbruin (bear)	113
☐ Erica Cherrybeary (bear)	113
☐ Erin (Lord & Taylor, bear)	113
☐ Erin K. Bear (bear)	113
☐ Erin O'Pigg (pig)	333
☐ Erin Plumbeary (bear)	113
☐ Erin Shaughnessy (Dillards, pig)	333
☐ Ernest Q. Grimilkin (cat, smooth fur)	249
☐ Ernest Q. Grimilkin (cat, white on chin)	249
☐ Ernest Q. Grimilkin (cat, blaze face)	249
☐ Ernest Q. Grimilkin (cat, new face)	249
☐ Ernest Q. Grimilkin (cat, nodern face)	249
☐ Ernestine Vanderhoof (cow)	265
☐ Ernie Elfbeary (bear)	114
☐ Ernie Z. Foxworthy (fox)	274
☐ Ervin Autumnfest (bear)	114
☐ Esmeralda (bear)	114
☐ Espresso Frisky (ornament)	347
☐ Essex (bear)	114
☐ Estelle (SLE, hare)	288
☐ Esther Bunny (hare)	288
☐ Ethan (bear)	114
☐ Ethan B. Boyds (Macy's East, bear)	114
☐ Ethel B. Bruin (bear)	114
☐ Eubie Lovedalot (QVC, bear)	114
☐ Eudemia Q. Quignapple (bear)	114
☐ Eugenia (bear)	114
☐ Eugenia (bear, apple seller)	114
☐ Eugenia (Dillards, bear)	114
☐ Eugenia II (SFMB, bear)	115
☐ Eunice P. Snowbeary (bear)	115
☐ Euphoria (moose)	321
☐ Evan & Sheldon Bearchild (QVC, bear)	115
☐ Evan E. Elfbear (Macy's East, ornament)	347
☐ Evangeline (QVC, ornament)	347
☐ Evelyn (bear)	115
☐ Everest (bear)	115
☐ Evergreen Elfston (GCC, ornament)	347
☐ Ewebey Woolsley (lamb)	312
☐ Ewell (bear)	115
☐ Ewell Manitoba Mooselman (CAN, bear)	115
☐ Ezra R. Ribbit (frog)	275

Name	Page
☐ F.E.B.B. (bear, First Ever Bean Bear)	115
☐ F.o.B. Exclusive Paw Print Charm (f.o.b 2004)	48
☐ Fairbanks (bear)	115
☐ Faith (Longaberger, bear)	115
☐ Faith Angelbeary (ornament)	347
☐ Faith 'N Dreams (Hallmark, bear)	115
☐ Fannie, Farrah & Flora (QVC, ornament)	348
☐ Fargo Grizwold (bear)	115
☐ Farkle R. Snowmose (ornament)	348
☐ Farland O'Pigg (pig)	333
☐ Farley O'Pigg (pig)	333
☐ Farmyard Duck (white group)	30
☐ Farmyard Duckling (white group)	30
☐ Farnsworth Jr. (hare)	289
☐ Farnsworth Sr. (hare)	289
☐ Father Chrisbear (bear)	116
☐ Father Christmas (ornament, small)	35
☐ Father Christmas (ornament, large)	35
☐ Father Christmas (bear)	116
☐ Father Christmas (bear)	116
☐ Father Christmas Ornament (ornament)	34
☐ Father Kissmoose (moose)	321
☐ Father Krismoose (moose)	321
☐ Father Kristmas (bear)	116
☐ Father Kristmas Bear & Northwind P. Bear (QVC, bear)	116
☐ Father Moose Moss (moose)	321
☐ Father Moosemas (moose)	321
☐ Fawn W. Fallsbeary (Show Specials, bear)	116
☐ Fawn Woodsbeary (bear)	116
☐ Faye & Jennifer (Carlton Cards, bear)	116
☐ Fearless Fido (dog)	268
☐ Federico (bear)	116
☐ Federico (bear, with sweater)	116
☐ Felicia Fuzzbuns (cat)	250
☐ Felicity (Lord & Taylor, bear)	116
☐ Felicity Merrybeary (QVC, bear)	116
☐ Felicity N. Hugs (bear)	117
☐ Felicity S. Elfberg (bear)	117
☐ Felina B. Catterwall (cat, in black)	250
☐ Felina B. Catterwall (cat, in brown)	250
☐ Felix Poppinsquash (mouse)	317
☐ Fenton & Forrest Snowbeary (QVC, ornament, with Silverton)	348
☐ Fergie (hare)	289
☐ Ferguson Q. Fuzzface (QVC, bear)	117
☐ Fern Blumenshine (hare)	289
☐ Fern Woodsbeary, the Woodland Guardian with Resin (QVC, bear)	117
☐ Fernando Uttermost (cow)	265
☐ Festus (moose)	321
☐ Feta (mouse)	317
☐ Fetchen P. Patch (bear)	117
☐ Fidelity B. Morgan IV (bear)	117
☐ Fidelity B. Morgan IV (SFMB, bear)	117
☐ Fifi Farklefrost (bear)	117
☐ Fillabuster P. Chatsworth (puppet)	363
☐ Fillmore (QVC, bear)	117
☐ Finicky Snottykat (cat)	250
☐ Finster R. Tsuris (monkey)	319
☐ Fiona Fitzbruin (bear)	117
☐ Fisher Loon Full Body (minnesota flats)	25
☐ Fitz Farklefrost (bear)	117
☐ Fitzgerald D. Bearington (bear)	117
☐ Fitzgerald O'Bruin (bear)	118
☐ Fitzroy (bear)	118

Name	Page
☐ Flakey Bearifrost (bear)	118
☐ Flash (turtle)	339
☐ Fleecie B. Ewe (lamb)	312
☐ Fletcher (SLE, hare)	289
☐ Fleurette (bear)	118
☐ Fleurette Hare (hare)	289
☐ Flip Hopsey (ornament)	348
☐ Flit Angelwish (ornament)	348
☐ Flitter B. Bugsley (bear)	118
☐ Flopsie Bunnyears (Longaberger, hare)	289
☐ Flopsie, Mopsie & Moxie Angelbuns (QVC, ornament)	348
☐ Flora B. Bunny (hare, old face)	289
☐ Flora B. Bunny (hare, new face)	289
☐ Flora B. Flutterby (bear)	118
☐ Flora B. Lilac (Lock, Stock & Barrel, bear)	118
☐ Flora Mae Berriweather (f.o.b 1999)	45
☐ Flora Mae Goodbear (Country Clutter, bear)	118
☐ Flora Thanksabunch (bear)	118
☐ Florabelle Uttermost (cow)	265
☐ Florabun (ornament)	348
☐ Floradora (SLE, hare)	289
☐ Florence B. Bearhugs (QVC, bear)	118
☐ Florence Nightenbear (bear)	118
☐ Florimae Bearley (QVC, bear)	118
☐ Flossie B. Hopplebuns (hare)	289
☐ Floyd (bear)	119
☐ Fluffie Bunnyhop (hare)	289
☐ Flurry B. Bundleup (bear)	119
☐ Flutter Flowerflit (ornament)	348
☐ Flying Santa (ornament)	35
☐ Folk Art Loon (black hills)	21
☐ Folk Art Santa (ornament)	35
☐ Forrest B. Bearsley (bear)	119
☐ Fox Hollow Honey Stand (fruit stand)	32
☐ Fraid E. Cat (cat)	250
☐ Francesca (Bon Ton, bear)	119
☐ Francesca LaFlame (bear)	119
☐ Francine deBearvoire (QVC, bear)	119
☐ Frangelica (hare)	290
☐ Frank, Oscar, Barney...& Stu (f.o.b 2004)	48
☐ Frankie Bearberg (SLE, bear)	119
☐ Franklin (bear)	119
☐ Frannie (cloth doll)	263
☐ Franz Farklefrost (bear)	119
☐ Franz von Bruin (bear)	119
☐ Frazier (bear)	119
☐ Frazier (BBC, bear)	119
☐ Fred Farfle (QVC, dog)	268
☐ Freddy Beanberger (bear)	120
☐ Frederick T. Bearsworth (bear)	120
☐ Fredrica (Frederick Atkins, bear)	120
☐ Freezy T. Frostman (bear)	120
☐ Friendship Bear Pair (EVENT, bear)	120
☐ Fritter Appleton (bear)	120
☐ Fritz Von Bruin (dog)	268
☐ Fritzle Farklefrost (bear)	120
☐ Fritzle Farklefrost with Frostley (QVC, bear)	120
☐ Frontier Santa (ornament)	35
☐ Frostina with Kristy (QVC, bear)	120
☐ Frosty (ornament)	35
☐ Furley Bearsdale (bear)	120
☐ Fuzzy Grizbear (bear)	120
☐ Fuzzy Jake Cattington (QVC, cat)	250
☐ G. Kelly Ribbit (frog)	275
☐ G. Wilbur McSwine (QVC, pig)	333

Name	Page
☐ G.B. Gingerpeeker (BBC, ornament, 10")	348
☐ G.B. Gingerpeeker (bear, 6")	120
☐ G.G. Willikers (hare)	290
☐ G.P. Hugabunch (bear)	121
☐ G.P. Hugabunch (SFMB, bear)	121
☐ G.W. Bearyproud (QVC, bear)	121
☐ Gabby Bunnyhop (hare)	290
☐ Gabriel (bear)	121
☐ Gabriella (ornament, red skirt)	348
☐ Gabriella (ornament, plaid skirt)	348
☐ Gabriella (POG, bear)	121
☐ Gabriella (Boscovs, bear)	121
☐ Gabriella Angelfaith (QVC, bear)	121
☐ Gadget (f.o.b 2001)	46
☐ Gae A. Grimilkin (cat, smooth fur)	250
☐ Gae A. Grimilkin (cat, white on chin)	250
☐ Gae A. Grimilkin (cat, regular plush)	250
☐ Gala Applesmith (bear)	121
☐ Galaxy (ornament)	348
☐ Galaxy (SFMB, ornament)	349
☐ Gannon Bear (GCC, bear)	121
☐ Gardener B . Buzzoff (QVC, bear)	121
☐ Gardner (cat)	250
☐ Gardner (hare)	290
☐ Gardner (bear)	121
☐ Gardner Bear (ornament)	35
☐ Gareth (QVC, bear, with Glynnis)	121
☐ Garner J. Cattington (cat)	250
☐ Garnet & Sapphire (QVC, bear)	122
☐ Garret T. Woodsbeary (QVC, bear)	122
☐ Gary B. Bean (QVC, bear)	122
☐ Gary M. Bearenthal (bear)	122
☐ Gatsby (Bon Ton, bear)	122
☐ General P.D.Q. Pattington (bear)	122
☐ Geneva (bear, nutmeg)	122
☐ Geneva (SLE, bear)	122
☐ Genevieve Rose Frostbeary with Blizz, Maddie, and Polaris (QVC, bear)	122
☐ George (guinea pig)	277
☐ George (QVC, bear)	122
☐ George (bear)	122
☐ George (May Company, bear)	122
☐ George & Martha Jodibear (QVC, bear)	123
☐ George & Thomas Bearington (QVC, bear)	123
☐ George Berriman (Show Specials, bear)	123
☐ George W. Bearington (QVC, bear)	123
☐ Georgie (POG, bear)	123
☐ Geraldine & Sylvester (QVC, bear)	123
☐ Geraldo (bear)	123
☐ Gerbie Daisydew (bear)	123
☐ Gertie Mae Berriweather...Take Time (f.o.b 2003)	48
☐ Gertrude (moose)	321
☐ Gettie Mountberg (SLE, bear)	123
☐ Gettysbear (BBC, bear)	123
☐ Ghoulia (bear)	123
☐ Giddy-Up Ladybug (bear)	123
☐ Giddyup Stringalong (string along)	364
☐ Gideon (QVC, bear)	124
☐ Gimmie A. Hugster (QVC, bear)	124
☐ Ginger McPunkin (bear)	124
☐ Ginger P. Purrski (QVC, cat)	250
☐ Ginger Snap (bear)	124
☐ Ginnie Higgenthorpe (bear)	124
☐ Ginnie Witebred (bear)	124
☐ Girdwood & Juneau (QVC, bear)	124

Name	Page
Giselle de la Fleur (hare)	290
Giseppi Renaldi (QVC, monkey)	319
Gizmoe...Life's A Juggle (f.o.b 2001)	46
Gizmoe's Big Top With Giggle McNibble (f.o.b 2001, box)	47
Glacier (bear)	124
Gladstone (bear, old face)	124
Gladstone (bear, new face)	124
Gladys Tidings (QVC, bear)	124
Glenda (bear)	124
Glenda Z. Jodibear (bear)	125
Glenna (Dillards, bear)	125
Glenwood Flatcat (cat)	251
Glimmer B. Snowflake (Carson Pirie Scott, bear)	125
Glinda the Good Witch (bear)	125
Gloranna Angelstar (tree topper)	365
Gloria and Van (QVC, bear)	125
Gloria Bearsevelt (bear)	125
Glorianna Angelbear (QVC, tree topper)	365
Glory (bear)	125
Glory B. America (Country House, bear)	125
Glory Steadsbeary (Longaberger, bear)	125
Glory Steadsbeary (Longaberger, variation, bear)	125
Glynnis (bear)	125
Golda (hare)	290
Golda Meow (cat)	251
Goldie McPunkin (bear)	125
Gomer P. Hugsley (QVC, bear)	126
Gomer Q. Beanster (bear)	126
Gomez (bear)	126
Gonna Luvya (ornament)	349
Goober Greenwood (QVC, bear)	126
Gorden B. Bean (bear, original)	126
Gorden B. Bean (bear, old face)	126
Gorden B. Bean (bear, new face)	126
Gouda (mouse)	317
Gourdie Frightmare (SLE, bear)	126
Gourdon Punkinpeeker (bear)	126
GP Gold Bear (CAN, bear)	126
Grabby Nutcruncher (squirrel)	338
Grace (cat)	251
Grace (hare)	290
Grace (bear)	126
Grace Agnes (hare)	290
Grace Bedlington (bear)	126
Gracie (May Company, bear)	127
Gracie (Dillards, bear)	127
Gracie Blossombeary (Longaberger, bear)	127
Gracie C. Burrbruin (GCC, bear)	127
Graham Cocobeary (bear)	127
Graham Quackers (hare)	290
Gram (bear)	127
Grammy (bear, heart pillow)	127
Grammy (bear, square pillow)	127
Grammy Beariluv (bear)	127
Grammy Quiltsbeary with Patches (Longaberger, bear)	127
Gramps (bear)	127
Grandma Babbit (QVC, hare)	290
Grandma Bearburg (bear, taupe print)	127
Grandma Bearburg (bear, burgundy print)	128
Grandma Henrietta & Lizzie (QVC, bear)	128
Grandmother Beatrice B. Bearhugs, Baileyanne Bearhugs & Tedley F. Wuzzie (QVC, bear)	128

Name	Page
Grannie Annie Wishkabibble (bear)	128
Grannie Lovedalot (QVC, bear)	128
Granny Smith and Gala Bear (QVC, bear)	128
Grant S. Bearington (Norm Thompson, bear)	128
Grayling (SLE, hare)	290
Grayson R. Hare (hare, pewter)	290
Grayson R. Hare (hare, blue-gray)	291
Greatest F.o.B On Earth (f.o.b 2001, pin)	46
Green Wing Teal (traditional group)	28
Green Wing Teal (traditional group, hen)	29
Gregory B. Elfbeary (bear)	128
Gregory G. Bruin (QVC, bear)	128
Grenville (bear)	128
Greta de la Fleur (hare)	291
Gretchen (hare)	291
Gretchen (Elder Beerman, hare)	291
Gretchen Marie Pearsley (bear)	128
Greybeard (cat)	251
Griffin W. Bearsley (bear)	128
Grosvenor Catberg (QVC, cat)	251
Grover (bear)	129
Grovsnor S. Grizbear (QVC, bear)	129
Grumples Q. Beansley (bear)	129
Grumps (bear)	129
Guildford Q. Bearrister (QVC, bear)	129
Guilford (GCC, bear)	129
Guinella (Ideation, bear)	129
Guinevere (bear)	129
Guinevere (Lord & Taylor, bear, with wings)	129
Guinevere (SFMB, bear)	129
Guinevieve (QVC, bear)	129
Gunnar (SLE, bear)	129
Gunter (Dillards, bear)	130
Gunther Von Bruin (bear)	130
Gus Ghoulie (bear)	130
Gussie...Life is a Balancing Act (f.o.b 2001)	46
Gustaf Mooseltoff (moose)	321
Gustav von Bruin (bear)	130
Guthrie and Gibbley (QVC, dog)	269
Guthrie P. Mussy (QVC, bear)	130
Gwain (bear)	130
Gwen Marie Bear (bear)	130
Gwendina (bear)	130
Gwendolyn (bear)	130
Gweneth (ornament)	349
Gwennora (QVC, bear)	130
Gwinton (bear)	130
Gwynda (bear)	130
H.B. Bearwish (bear)	131
H.B. Bearwish (SFMB, bear)	131
H.B. Starcatcher (ornament)	349
H.C. Beezley (bear)	131
H.K. Bearlove (ornament)	349
Hadley Flatski (bear)	131
Hailey (hare)	291
Haley Angelfrost (bear)	131
Hamilton (Cracker Barrel, pig)	333
Hamlet (pig)	333
Hampton T. Bearington (bear)	131
Hancock (bear)	131
Hank Krow Jr. (crow)	266
Hannah (hare)	291
Hannah (Elder Beerman, bear)	131
Hannah B. Punkinbeary (Kirlins, bear)	131
Hannah H. Woodsbeary (Carlton Cards, bear)	131
Hannah, Henry, Herbie (QVC, bear)	131

Name	Page
☐ Hannah, Ursula, Greta, & Sarabeth (QVC, bear)	131
☐ Hannibal Trunkster (elephant)	273
☐ Hans Q. Berriman (bear)	132
☐ Harding (bear)	132
☐ Harding G. Bearington (bear)	132
☐ Harlan (bear)	132
☐ Harp Angel (ornament)	35
☐ Harriet R. Hare (hare)	291
☐ Harrison (bear)	132
☐ Harry Harvest (Hershey, bear)	132
☐ Harry Lapin II (hare)	291
☐ Harry R. Hare (hare)	291
☐ Harry S. Pattington (bear)	132
☐ Hartley (Lord & Taylor, bear)	132
☐ Hartley B. Mine (bear)	132
☐ Harvey (QVC, hare)	291
☐ Hastings P. Bearsford (bear)	132
☐ Hattie (cat)	251
☐ Hattie & Annie (bear)	132
☐ Hattie Hopsalot (hare)	291
☐ Havarti Chrismouse (GCC, mouse)	317
☐ Hawley Flatski (bear)	132
☐ Hayden T. Bearsford (bear)	133
☐ Hayes R Bearrington (SFMB, bear)	133
☐ Hayley and Austin with Stretch (bear)	133
☐ Hazel (bear)	133
☐ Hazel Q. Punkinbeary (bear)	133
☐ Hazelnut B. Bean (bear)	133
☐ Heart Angel (ornament)	35
☐ Heath (bear)	133
☐ Heath II (bear)	133
☐ Heathcliff (QVC, bear)	133
☐ Heather (Dillards, hare)	291
☐ Heather and Heathcliffe Plumbeary (Welcome Home, bear)	133
☐ Heather Goodbear (Country Clutter, bear)	133
☐ Heather Steadsbeary (Longaberger, bear)	133
☐ Hector Flatberg (dog)	269
☐ Hector Hugsley (bear)	134
☐ Hedda (QVC, bear)	134
☐ Hedy Hare (hare)	292
☐ Hefty B. Bear (QVC, bear)	134
☐ Heidi May Patchbeary (GoCollect, bear)	134
☐ Heidi Thistlebeary (QVC, bear, with Bethany Thistlebeary)	134
☐ Heidi Woodsbeary (bear)	134
☐ Helena Marie Boydsley (Coach House Gifts, bear)	134
☐ Helmut (moose, green sweater)	321
☐ Helmut (moose, red or burgundy sweater)	321
☐ Heloise Haresworth (hare)	292
☐ Hemingway K. Grizzman (bear)	134
☐ Henita P. Cooper (BBC, hen)	310
☐ Henley Fitzhampton (bear)	134
☐ Henrietta Eggbert (hen)	310
☐ Henrietta MacDonald (bear)	134
☐ Henry (bear)	134
☐ Henry (Dillards, bear)	134
☐ Henry Bearyman (May Company, bear)	135
☐ Henry Bearymore (May Company, bear)	135
☐ Henson (bear)	135
☐ Heranamous (cat)	251
☐ Heranamous (SFMB, cat)	251
☐ Herbert Harrison McBearsley (QVC, bear)	135
☐ Herbert Henry Jodibear (bear)	135

Name	Page
☐ Herbie Bearlove (bear)	135
☐ Hercules von Mutt (dog)	269
☐ Herman B. Bearsdale (QVC, bear)	135
☐ Herman Beefcake (cow)	265
☐ Hermine Grisslin (bear)	135
☐ Hersh E. Kiss (Hershey, bear)	135
☐ Hershal (bear)	135
☐ Hester (cow)	265
☐ Heywood Bearlanski (Bon Ton, bear)	135
☐ Higgins (hare)	292
☐ Higgins D. Nibbleby (hare)	292
☐ Higgy (hare)	292
☐ Hiking Santa (ornament)	35
☐ Hilby Jamm (bear)	135
☐ Hilda P. Pottamus (hippo)	311
☐ Hillary B. Bean (bear)	136
☐ Hippity & Hoppity Thumpster (QVC, hare)	292
☐ Hiram Q. Hamhock (QVC, bear)	136
☐ Hobson Q. Hugmeister (QVC, bear)	136
☐ Hockley (bear)	136
☐ Holden T. Punkinbeary (bear)	136
☐ Holiday (Hallmark, bear)	136
☐ Hollie and Ivy (QVC, bear)	136
☐ Holloway Flatcat (cat)	251
☐ Holly (Elder Beerman, cat)	251
☐ Holly (Lord & Taylor, bear)	136
☐ Holly (bear)	136
☐ Holly B. Bearsley (QVC, bear)	136
☐ Holly B. Kringlebeary (Kirlins, bear)	136
☐ Holly Bearberry (QVC, bear)	136
☐ Holly Beary (tree topper)	365
☐ Holly Beary (Longaberger, tree topper)	365
☐ Holly Jolly Peeker (Longaberger, bear)	137
☐ Homer (hare)	292
☐ Homer (bear, 10" baseball)	137
☐ Hurner (bear, Himalayan)	137
☐ Homer (bear, 8" baseball)	137
☐ Homer & Yukon (QVC, ornament)	349
☐ Honey B. Bean (POG, bear)	137
☐ Honey B. Bear (Spiegel, bear)	137
☐ Honey B. Beary (Longaberger, bear)	137
☐ Honey B. Elfberg (POG, bear)	137
☐ Honey B. Growin (POG, bear)	137
☐ Honey Bee Bear (Faith Mountain, bear)	137
☐ Honey Bunny (QVC, hare)	292
☐ Honey Buns (bear)	137
☐ Honey P. Snicklefritz (bear)	137
☐ Honeybee Cottontail (SLE, hare)	292
☐ Honeycombe Mine (bear)	138
☐ Honeypot (bear)	138
☐ Hooper Q. Hugster (bear)	138
☐ Hope (bear)	138
☐ Hope & A. Future (Hunter's Hope, bear)	138
☐ Hope L. Bearywell (Longaberger, bear)	138
☐ Hopkins (hare)	292
☐ Hopley F. Wuzzie (pin)	361
☐ Hopper Q. Bunsley (hare)	292
☐ Hoppity (hare)	292
☐ Hoppy E. Star (Hershey, hare)	293
☐ Hopson Q. Woodsley (QVC, hare)	293
☐ Horace B. Hugsworthy (QVC, bear)	138
☐ Hortense Moostein (cow)	265
☐ Hoskins Q. Hugmeister (QVC, bear)	138
☐ Howard McBeansley (QVC, bear)	138
☐ Howard P. Potter (QVC, bear)	138
☐ Howlin P. Chatsworth (puppet)	363

Name	Page
☐ Hsing Hsing and Ling Ling Wongbruin (panda)	330
☐ Hsing-Hsing Wongbruin (panda)	330
☐ Hubbard (QVC, bear)	138
☐ Hubbard Q. Bearsley (QVC, bear)	138
☐ Hubbard W. Growler (bear)	139
☐ Huck (bear)	139
☐ Huck, Mandy, & Zack (Show Specials, bear)	139
☐ Hucklebeary B. Bear (bear)	139
☐ Huckleberry Tree Farm (fruit stand)	32
☐ Huett & Huntley (QVC, bear)	139
☐ Huff P. Wolf with Bacon, Porkchop & Hamlette (bear)	139
☐ Huggabee (bear)	139
☐ Huggleby B. Bearikind (bear)	139
☐ Hugo P. Bearhugs (QVC, bear)	139
☐ Hugs N. Kisses (bear, pair of bears)	139
☐ Hugs N. Kisses (bear, red heart peeker)	139
☐ Humboldt (bear)	139
☐ Hume (bear)	140
☐ Humphrey P. Bearhugs (QVC, bear)	140
☐ Humphrey T. Bigfoot (bear)	140
☐ Humpy Dumpy (bear)	140
☐ Huney B. Keeper (bear)	140
☐ Hunnie Z. Beezley (bear)	140
☐ Hunter (Hunter's Hope, bear)	140
☐ Hunter Bearsdale with Greenspan (bear)	140
☐ Hunter's Blue Wing Teal (hunter's group)	23
☐ Hunter's Canvasback (hunter's group)	23
☐ Hunter's Goose (hunter's group)	24
☐ Hunter's Green Wing Teal (hunter's group)	24
☐ Hunter's Loon (hunter's group)	24
☐ Hunter's Loon (hunter's group, open mouth)	24
☐ Hunter's Mallard (hunter's group)	24
☐ Hunter's Mallard (hunter's group, sleeper)	24
☐ Hunter's Pheasant (hunter's group)	24
☐ Hunter's Pintail (hunter's group)	24
☐ Hunter's Redhead (hunter's group)	24
☐ Hunter's Ruddy Duck (hunter's group)	24
☐ Hunter's Wood Duck (hunter's group)	24
☐ Hurshel (bear)	140
☐ Huxley W. Penworthy (cat)	251
☐ I Bea Lovinya & Lots (QVC, bear)	140
☐ I.B. Bearyproud (bear)	140
☐ I.C. Crystalfrost (bear)	140
☐ I.M. Uproarius (lion)	315
☐ Icabod Scaredbear and Midnight (QVC, bear)	141
☐ Ida Moostein (cow)	265
☐ Iddy Biddy Ladybug (ornament)	349
☐ Ido Loveya (bear)	141
☐ Iggy & Loo Frostbite (bear)	141
☐ Ike D. Bearington (QVC, bear)	141
☐ Ike Glorybear (bear)	141
☐ Ilona B. Mooseltoes (QVC, moose)	321
☐ Ima Bestfriend (Longaberger, bear)	141
☐ Ima Hugginya (QVC, bear)	141
☐ Ima Scholar (bear)	141
☐ Ima Softheart (bear)	141
☐ Immanuella (ornament)	349
☐ Imogene R. Tsursis (monkey)	319
☐ Indigo Jones (QVC, bear)	141
☐ Indy (dog, Fall 1997)	269
☐ Indy (dog, Fall 1998)	269
☐ Indy (dog, Fall 1999)	269
☐ Indy (dog, Spring 2000)	269
☐ Indy (dog, Fall 2000)	269

Name	Page
☐ Inga B. Burrbruin (bear)	141
☐ Ingred S. Witebred (GCC, bear)	141
☐ Ingrid & Heidi Svenbeary (QVC, bear)	142
☐ Ingrid & Tasha Norbruin with Toggle (QVC, bear)	142
☐ Inkley Boocat (cat)	251
☐ Inky Catterwall (cat)	252
☐ Iris Rosenbunny (hare)	293
☐ Irving Poochberg (dog)	269
☐ Irwin Mooseltoe (moose)	322
☐ Irwin S. Crockpot (alligator)	244
☐ Isabel Grizbearg (GCC, bear)	142
☐ Isabella (Bon Ton, bear)	142
☐ Isabelle Dickens (bear)	142
☐ Isadora T. Lightfoot (elephant)	274
☐ Isaiah (bear)	142
☐ Isaiah Q. Woodsley (QVC, bear)	142
☐ Ivana Purrkins (QVC, cat)	252
☐ Ivanna Hugsley (QVC, bear)	142
☐ Ivanna Spendalot (bear)	142
☐ Ivy Bloomengrows (pig)	334
☐ Ivy M. Fuzzyfleece (QVC, lamb)	312
☐ Iza Basketcase (QVC, bear)	142
☐ Izzy (Dillards, moose)	322
☐ J.B. Bean (bear, smooth fur)	142
☐ J.B. Bean (bear, old face)	142
☐ J.B. Bean (bear, new face)	143
☐ J.B. Bigheart (bear)	143
☐ J.B. Pinesley (QVC, bear)	143
☐ J.C. Von Fuzzner (J.C.Penney, bear)	143
☐ J.J. Honeypot (QVC, bear)	143
☐ J.J. Rugsley (bear)	143
☐ J.P. Huttin III (bear)	143
☐ J.P. Locksley (bear)	143
☐ J.T. Jordan III (Welcome Home, bear)	143
☐ J.W. VanWinkle & Snuggies (bear)	143
☐ Jack (hare)	293
☐ Jack B. Frostbeary (QVC, bear)	143
☐ Jack B. Twinkletune (EVENT, bear)	143
☐ Jack O. Lantern (bear)	144
☐ Jack R. Woodsley (hare)	293
☐ Jackie B. Beariproud (QVC, bear)	144
☐ Jackson (May Company, bear)	144
☐ Jackson B. Beanster (QVC, bear)	144
☐ Jackson R. Bearington (bear)	144
☐ Jacob Wishkabibble (bear)	144
☐ Jacqueline K. Bearington (QVC, bear)	144
☐ Jacque Le Grenouille (frog)	275
☐ Jae Lynn Jackson (Bear Heaven, bear)	144
☐ Jaime Lisa (Dillards, bear)	144
☐ Jake (Dillards, bear)	144
☐ Jake, Jay & Jette Magilla (QVC, gorilla)	276
☐ James & Malachi (QVC, bear)	144
☐ James C. Penneybeary (J.C.Penney, bear)	144
☐ James Jodibear (bear)	145
☐ Jameson J. Bearsford (bear)	145
☐ Jamie (CAN, bear)	145
☐ Jamison Ann Dickens (Elder Beerman, bear)	145
☐ Jan B. Bearberg (SLE, bear)	145
☐ Jane (hare, 14")	293
☐ Jane (hare, two-tone)	293
☐ Janet (hare)	293
☐ Janet C. Daisydew (Paw Dealer, bear)	145
☐ Jangle S. Stuffins (ornament)	349
☐ Janie Icebeary (Macy's East, bear)	145
☐ Jarvis Boydsenberry (QVC, bear)	145

BoydsTracker - Alphabetical Index

Name	Page
☐ Jasper McBobble (bear)	145
☐ Jasper T. Fisher with Paddle (QVC, bear)	145
☐ Java B. Bean (cat)	252
☐ Jaxton D. Bear (bear)	145
☐ Jean (CAN, bear)	145
☐ Jeanine Jodibear (bear)	146
☐ Jeannie S. Berriman (Platinum Paw, bear)	146
☐ Jeannine De Bearvoire (bear)	146
☐ Jeb MacDonald (bear)	146
☐ Jebel Cottontail (SLE, hare)	293
☐ Jed Bruin (bear, a.k.a. Snowball)	146
☐ Jeff Gordon #24 (jeff gordon, firesuit)	41
☐ Jeff Gordon #24 (jeff gordon, jacket)	41
☐ Jeff Gordon #24 (jeff gordon, plush ornament)	42
☐ Jeff Gordon #24 (jeff gordon, resin ornament)	42
☐ Jeff Gordon #24 (jeff gordon, sweatshirt)	42
☐ Jefferson (bear)	146
☐ Jefferson B. Beanster (QVC, bear)	146
☐ Jeffrey T. Treetoes (bear)	146
☐ Jellie B. Bunny (hare)	293
☐ Jenessa (tree topper)	365
☐ Jenessa T. Angelbear (QVC, ornament)	349
☐ Jenna (Profitts, bear)	146
☐ Jenna D. Lapinne (hare)	293
☐ Jenna Kathleen (Dillards, cat)	252
☐ Jenna Rae (Cracker Barrel, bear)	146
☐ Jennie Glorybear (bear)	146
☐ Jennie Lynn & Fussypuss (QVC, bear)	146
☐ Jennie Marie Warmheart with Happy (QVC, bear)	147
☐ Jennifer B. Bearheart (QVC, bear)	147
☐ Jennifer Bearringer (bear)	147
☐ Jenny McBruin (QVC, bear)	147
☐ Jenny Sweet-Tooth... It's Dairy To Me (f.o.b 2004)	48
☐ Jeremiah (Country Living, bear)	147
☐ Jeremiah B. Ribbit (frog)	275
☐ Jeremiah J. Woodsley (bear)	147
☐ Jeremy (Dillards, bear)	147
☐ Jeri Hopkins (ornament)	349
☐ Jesse (bear)	147
☐ Jesse (Lord & Taylor, bear)	147
☐ Jesselyn R. Angel (Starlight, bear)	147
☐ Jessica (hare)	293
☐ Jessie Lu Goodbear (Country Clutter, bear)	147
☐ Jethro (bear)	147
☐ Jethro T. Woodsley (bear)	148
☐ Jewell & Rainbow Flowerflit (QVC, ornament)	349
☐ Jilian G. Gingerbeary (bear)	148
☐ Jill (hare)	294
☐ Jill Hopkins (ornament)	350
☐ Jillian (Dillards, bear)	148
☐ Jim I. Swingster (monkey)	319
☐ Jimmy Johnson #48 (jimmy johnson, firesuit)	42
☐ Jimmy Johnson #48 (jimmy johnson, jacket)	42
☐ Jimmy Johnson #48 (jimmy johnson, plush ornament)	42
☐ Jimmy Johnson #48 (jimmy johnson, resin ornament)	42
☐ Jimmy Johnson #48 (jimmy johnson, sweatshirt)	42
☐ Jimmy T. Bearheart (bear)	148
☐ Jingle Bear (ornament)	350
☐ Jingle S. Stuffins (ornament)	350
☐ Joanne Pearl (Bon Ton, bear)	148
☐ Jobie & Kibby Bearington (QVC, bear)	148
☐ Jocelyn Bloomengrows (bear)	148
☐ Jocelyn Thistlebeary & Carson T. Bibbly (QVC, bear)	148
☐ Jody (bear)	148
☐ Joe (CAN, bear)	148
☐ Joe Magilla (gorilla)	276
☐ Joella Angelstar (tree topper)	365
☐ Joey and Alice Outback (kangaroo)	311
☐ John (bear)	148
☐ John (CAN, bear)	148
☐ John B. Leadbottoms (bear)	149
☐ John Henry (bear)	149
☐ John William (QVC, bear)	149
☐ JoJo DeBearvoire (bear)	149
☐ Jolee (May Company, bear)	149
☐ Jolly B. Nick (QVC, bear)	149
☐ Jolly Ol' St. Nick (bear)	149
☐ Jolly S. Stuffins (ornament)	350
☐ Jolly T. Jodibear (bear)	149
☐ Jonathan Applesmith (bear)	149
☐ Jonathan Macbear (QVC, bear)	149
☐ Jordan T. Fallsbeary (Show Specials, bear)	149
☐ Josanna Java (ornament)	350
☐ Josephine (hare)	294
☐ Joshua (bear)	149
☐ Joshua Bear (ornament)	35
☐ Josie Hopkins (ornament)	350
☐ Josie K. Bearsmark (Hallmark, bear)	150
☐ Joy Chrismouse (mouse)	317
☐ Joy N. Goodcheer (QVC, tree topper)	365
☐ JoyAnn Hugsbeary (bear)	150
☐ Joyce M. Berriman (bear)	150
☐ Joyelle (Ideation, bear)	150
☐ Jr. Mintly (bear)	150
☐ Jubilation P. Hambone (QVC, pig)	334
☐ Juggles F. Wuzzie (pin)	361
☐ Juilian and Justin Jodibear (QVC, bear)	150
☐ Julia (Dillards, bear)	150
☐ Julia Angelbrite (bear)	150
☐ Juliana de Bearvoire (QVC, bear)	150
☐ Juliana Hopkins (hare)	294
☐ Juliana Hopkins II (hare)	294
☐ Julianna Hugsley (QVC, bear)	150
☐ Julie Ann Gingerbeary and Cookie (QVC, bear)	150
☐ Juliella T. Frostfire (bear)	150
☐ Juliet S. Bearlove (bear)	151
☐ Juliette (ornament)	350
☐ Juliette (SFMB, ornament)	350
☐ Julip O'Harea (hare)	294
☐ Juniper Bunnyhugs (hare)	294
☐ Juno Whatt Bearington (bear)	151
☐ Jupiter (QVC, ornament)	350
☐ Jupiter Goodspeed (ornament)	350
☐ Justin (Dillards, bear)	151
☐ Justina (moose, formerly Philomena)	322
☐ Justina & Matthew (QVC, bear)	151
☐ Kacy Mae Sugarcone & Lil' Scoop (QVC, bear)	151
☐ Kaitlin & Kendall McSwine (QVC, pig)	334
☐ Kaitlin K. Trufflesnout (pig)	334
☐ Kaitlin McSwine (pig)	334
☐ Kaitlin McSwine II (pig)	334
☐ Kaitlin McSwine III (pig)	334
☐ Kaitlyn Bearlove (Kirlins, bear)	151
☐ Kandi B. Bunny (hare)	294
☐ Kandy B. Hopensit (QVC, hare)	294

Name	Page
☐ Karen A. Mulberry (bear)	151
☐ Karen B. Bearsdale (QVC, bear)	151
☐ Karina Burrbruin (bear)	151
☐ Karissa Lynn Bearsdale (QVC, bear)	151
☐ Karl Von Fuzzner (QVC, bear)	151
☐ Karla Mulbeary (bear)	151
☐ Karley & Melanie Bearibug (QVC, bear)	152
☐ Karmen (Frederick Atkins, bear)	152
☐ Karyn Scarvesdale (bear)	152
☐ Kassandra P. Berriwinkle (QVC, bear)	152
☐ Kassie Gingerbeary (bear)	152
☐ Katalina Kafinata (ornament)	350
☐ Katawalin P. Chatsworth (puppet)	363
☐ Katerina (hare)	294
☐ Katerina Winterbeary (QVC, bear)	152
☐ Kathryn (hare)	294
☐ Kathy B. Bearsley (QVC, bear)	152
☐ Katie (SLE, pig)	334
☐ Katie B. Bearyproud (bear)	152
☐ Katie B. Berrijam (bear)	152
☐ Katie Kat (Lord & Taylor, cat)	252
☐ Katie Kat II (Lord & Taylor, cat)	252
☐ Katie O'Pigg (Dillards, pig)	334
☐ Katrinka Berriman (QVC, bear, with Thor)	152
☐ Kattelina Purrsley (cat)	252
☐ Katy Bear (bear)	152
☐ Kay Cherrybeary (bear)	152
☐ Kayla Bearimore (QVC, bear)	153
☐ Kayla Mulbeary (bear)	153
☐ Kaylie Angelfrost & Kringle's Village St. Nicholas Chapel (QVC, bear)	153
☐ Kaytie & Mattie with R.J. (Show Specials, bear)	153
☐ Keats (cat)	252
☐ Keefer P. Lightfoot (hare)	294
☐ Keifer B. Elfington (bear)	153
☐ Kelby (Elder Beerman, bear)	153
☐ Kellie Hopplebuns (hare)	294
☐ Kelly O. Beary (bear)	153
☐ Kelly Sue Bearican (QVC, bear)	153
☐ Kelsey (Dillards, bear)	153
☐ Kelsey M. Jodibear with Arby T. Tugalog (bear)	153
☐ Kemper Forbes (bear)	153
☐ Kendall B. Learnin (bear)	153
☐ Kendallyn H. Sugarcone (bear)	154
☐ Kensington K. Braveheart (QVC, bear)	154
☐ Kerchief Bunny (ornament, stand-up)	35
☐ Kerry Q. Hopgood (hare)	295
☐ Kevin G. Bearsley (bear)	154
☐ Kevin Harvick #29 (kevin harvick, firesuit)	42
☐ Kevin Harvick #29 (kevin harvick, jacket)	42
☐ Kevin Harvick #29 (kevin harvick, plush ornament)	43
☐ Kevin Harvick #29 (kevin harvick, resin ornament)	43
☐ Kevin Harvick #29 (kevin harvick, sweatshirt)	43
☐ Kevin Kringlebeary (J.C.Penney, bear)	154
☐ Key Lime Thumpster (hare)	295
☐ Kibbie (mouse)	317
☐ Kibby T. Beansley (bear)	154
☐ Kimberly Punkinbeary (bear)	154
☐ Kimberlyn Woodsbeary (GCC, cat)	252
☐ Kimmy (bear)	154
☐ Kinsey Snoopstein (QVC, bear)	154
☐ Kip (bear)	154

Name	Page
☐ Kirby Elfbeary (bear)	154
☐ Kirby Lovebug (gorilla)	276
☐ Kirby Scruffles (bear)	154
☐ Kirsten DeBearvoire with Mimi DeBearvoire (QVC, bear)	154
☐ Kirsten T. Oakley (bear)	155
☐ Kisses (Hershey, cow)	265
☐ Kisslebeary (bear)	155
☐ Kit, Bang & Kaboodle (QVC, bear)	155
☐ Kitt Purrsley (cat)	252
☐ Klaus Von Fuzzner (bear)	155
☐ Klaus Von Fuzzner (SFMB, bear)	155
☐ Klondike (bear)	155
☐ Knut C. Berriman (QVC, bear)	155
☐ Knut V. Berriman (bear)	155
☐ Kortney Kringlebeary (GCC, bear)	155
☐ Kringle Bear (bear, 10")	155
☐ Kringle Bear (bear, 14")	155
☐ Kringle's Retreat Set (QVC, bear)	155
☐ Kris Moose (moose)	322
☐ Krismoose (moose)	322
☐ Krista Blubeary (QVC, bear, with Kayla Mulbeary)	156
☐ Krista Fuzzyfrost (bear)	156
☐ Kristen T. Beansley (Paw Dealer, bear)	156
☐ Kristi & Kaylie Marie (SYN, bear)	156
☐ Kristi Ann Bearibrook (QVC, bear)	156
☐ Kristoff (QVC, bear)	156
☐ Krystal Penneybeary (J.C.Penney, bear)	156
☐ Krystle B. Bearbright with Joelle & Paz (bear)	156
☐ Kudos Attabear (bear)	156
☐ Kyle (SLE, bear)	156
☐ Kyle L. Berriman (bear)	156
☐ Kylie & Baabs (QVC, bear)	156
☐ L.S. Black Swan (black hills)	21
☐ L.S. Canada Goose (black hills, drake)	21
☐ L.S. Canada Goose (black hills, hen)	21
☐ L.S. Preening Whistling Swan (black hills)	21
☐ L.S. Whistling Swan (black hills)	22
☐ LaBelle (Ideation, bear)	157
☐ Lacey V. Hare (QVC, hare)	295
☐ Lacy (cat, 14")	252
☐ Lacy (cat, 11")	252
☐ Lacy (bear, 10")	157
☐ Lacy (bear, 14")	157
☐ Lacy Hare (hare, tan)	295
☐ Lacy Hare (hare, taupe curly)	295
☐ Lacy Hare (hare, white curly)	295
☐ LaDonna & Darlene DuBeary (QVC, bear)	157
☐ Lady B. Bug (bear)	157
☐ Lady B. Bugsley (bear)	157
☐ Lady B. Lovebug (ornament)	350
☐ Lady Flora Monarch (GCC, bear)	157
☐ Lady Harrington (QVC, hare)	295
☐ Lady Harriwell (hare)	295
☐ Lady Libearty (f.o.b 1998, pin)	44
☐ Lady Libearty (f.o.b 1998)	44
☐ Lady Pembroke (hare)	295
☐ Lady Pembroke (SFMB, hare)	295
☐ Lady Peyton (hare)	295
☐ Lainie M. Elfbear (Macy's East, ornament)	351
☐ Lambert Fuzzyfleece (lamb)	312
☐ Lambsie Divy (lamb)	313
☐ Lambsies (ornament)	351
☐ Lana Hare (hare)	295
☐ Lana Hoppennibble (ornament)	351

Name	Page
Lancaster (bear)	157
Lance (lion)	315
Lancelot (bear)	157
Lankey S. Woodsley (bear)	157
Lapis (QVC, ornament)	351
Lara (QVC, bear)	157
Larry Lapin (hare)	296
Larry Too (hare)	296
Lars (bear)	157
Latte Lapine (QVC, ornament, with Josanna Java and Katalina Kafinata)	351
Latte O. Bear (bear)	158
Laura Ann (Dillards, bear)	158
Laura B. Bearyproud (QVC, bear)	158
Laura E. Bearburn (J.T. Webb, bear)	158
Laura Elizabeth Yachtley (My Gift Cottage, bear)	158
Laura P. Bradbeary (QVC, bear)	158
Lauralee Hopplebuns (hare)	296
Lauralee Pearsley (bear)	158
Laurel S. Berrijam (bear)	158
Lauren (hare)	296
Lauren (bear)	158
Lauren B. Ladybug with Spot (QVC, bear)	158
Lauren Ladybug (Kirlins, bear)	158
Lauren Nicole (Country Clutter, bear)	158
Lavender Q. Prissyfoot (QVC, cat)	253
Lavinia V. Hariweather (hare)	296
Lavinia V. Hariweather (SFMB, hare)	296
Lawrence and Sheherazade O'Sand (camel)	244
Layona Rugsley (bear)	159
Lead B. Bottoms (bear)	159
Leanne Bearsdale (Gold Paw, bear)	159
LeGrand Ol' Bear (Lock, Stock & Barrel, bear)	159
Leigh Ann Beansford (QVC, bear)	159
Leisel (hare)	296
Leisel L. Burrbruin (bear)	159
Leiselle Bloomengrows (bear)	159
Lem Bruin (bear)	159
(The) Lemonade Stand (fruit stand)	32
Lena O'Pigg (Dillards, pig)	334
Lenora Flatstein (hare)	296
Leo Bruinski (bear)	159
Leon (bear)	159
Leona B. Bunny (hare)	296
Leonard S. Uproarius (QVC, lion)	315
Leonardo B. Hartbreak (QVC, bear)	159
Leopold Q. Lion (lion, old face)	315
Leopold Q. Lion (lion, new face)	315
Leopold Q. Pouncely (bear)	159
Leopold Q. Roarsmore (QVC, lion)	315
Leslie (bear, with red heart)	160
Leslie (bear, nekkid)	160
Leslie B. Ladybug (bear)	160
Leslie G Catberg (SLE, cat)	253
Lester (CAN, bear)	160
Lester McHootle (owl)	329
Lester Mintly (moose)	322
Letitia T. Bearington (GCC, bear)	160
Letti McVeggie (Paw Dealer, bear)	160
Lewis (QVC, bear)	160
Lexi Burrbruin (BtoB Website, bear)	160
Liam (bear)	160
Libbee Bearamerica (Longaberger, bear)	160
Libby B. Bunster (bear)	160
Libby B. Ladybug (bear)	160
Libby Bearyproud (GCC, bear)	161
Libby Lapinette (hare)	296
Libearty C. Star (Rocking Horse, bear)	161
Licorice (bear)	161
Lil' Einstein (ornament)	351
Lil' Einstein, Baby C. Corn & Gourdy (QVC, ornament)	351
Lil' Frazier (ornament)	351
Lil' Love (Longaberger, bear)	161
Lil' Mischief (QVC, bear)	161
Lil' Missy Muffet (bear)	161
Lil' Nicky Jodibear (bear)	161
Lil' Peach (ornament)	351
Lil' Petey (ornament)	351
Lil' Quackenwaddle (ornament)	351
Lil' Stella with Lil' Frazier (QVC, ornament)	351
Lil' Theodore (QVC, bear)	161
Lila Hopkins (hare)	296
Lilith Angel Ewe (ornament)	352
Lillian K. Bearsley (bear)	161
Lilly R. Ribbit (ornament)	352
Lily Flutterby (bear)	161
Lily R. Hare (hare)	296
Lincoln B. Bearington (bear)	161
Lindbergh Cattington (cat)	253
Lindsey (Dillards, hare)	297
Lindsey (Belks, bear)	161
Lindsey II & Tucker F Wuzzie (QVC, cat)	253
Lindsey Ladybug (bear)	162
Lindsey Lou with Pee-Wee (QVC, bear)	162
Lindsey Marie Goodbear (Country Clutter, bear)	162
Lindsey P. Pussytoes (cat)	253
Lindsley Ladybug (Paw Dealer, bear)	162
Lindy (Elder Beerman, hare)	297
Lindy & Nell Bradbeary (QVC, bear)	162
Linkin (bear)	162
Linnea (ornament)	352
Linsey McKenzie (QVC, bear)	162
Linus P. Fuzzfrost (QVC, bear)	162
Lion (bear)	162
Lionsies (ornament, old face)	352
Lionsies (ornament, new face)	352
Lisa T. Bearringer (bear)	162
Lissa Angelwish (bear)	162
Listed Santa (ornament)	36
Little Bangles (QVC, bear)	162
Little Bear Blue (ornament)	36
Little Bearpeep and Friends (bear)	163
Little Celeste (Gottschalks, bear)	163
Little Larson (Ideation, bear)	163
Little Orchard Annie (POG, bear)	163
Little Ted 100th Anniversary Mohair Bear (QVC, ornament)	352
Little Twink (BBC, bear)	163
Livingston R. Hare (hare, early smooth fur)	297
Livingston R. Hare (hare, old face)	297
Livingston R. Hare (hare, new face)	297
Liza Fuzzyfleece (lamb)	313
Liza Glorybear (bear)	163
Liza J. Berrijam (bear)	163
Liza Mae & Alex (QVC, bear)	163
Lizzie [EVENT, pin]	362
Lizzie McBee (bear)	163
Lizzie McBee (QVC, bear, red plaid dress)	163
Lizzie Wishkabibble (EVENT, bear)	163

Name	Page
☐ Lloyd (bear)	163
☐ Lofton Q. McSwine (pig)	334
☐ Logan (QVC, bear)	164
☐ Logan Fremont (bear)	164
☐ Lois B. Bearlove (bear)	164
☐ Lola Ninelives (cat)	253
☐ Lone Star (Dillards, bear)	164
☐ Loon (wooden stained group)	30
☐ Loon (minnesota flats, feeder)	25
☐ Loon (minnesota flats, preener)	25
☐ Loon (minnesota flats, swimmer)	25
☐ Lorelei (ornament)	352
☐ Lorraine P. Bearsley (QVC, bear)	164
☐ Lottie de Lopear (hare)	297
☐ Lou Bearig (bear)	164
☐ Louella (bear)	164
☐ Louie B. Bear (bear)	164
☐ Louisa Catherine Bearington (QVC, bear)	164
☐ Love Conquers All Plaque (ornament)	36
☐ Lovey (QVC, bear)	164
☐ Lovie (bear)	164
☐ Luci T. Jodibear (bear)	164
☐ Lucibelle Fuzzyfleece (lamb)	313
☐ Lucille (hare)	297
☐ Lucinda D. Bearsley (QVC, bear)	165
☐ Lucinda de La Fleur (hare)	297
☐ Lucky B. Ladybug (bear)	165
☐ Lucky O'Beary (Longaberger, bear)	165
☐ Lucy (Gottschalks, bear)	165
☐ Lucy Bea LeBruin (QVC, bear)	165
☐ Lucy Belle Lambston (QVC, lamb)	313
☐ Lucy Lynn Beansley (QVC, bear)	165
☐ Lucy McLemon (bear)	165
☐ Lucy P. Blumenshine (hare)	297
☐ Ludmilla Berriman & Ludwig Von Fuzzner (QVC, bear)	165
☐ Ludwigg V. Burrbruin (bear)	165
☐ Luke P. Jodibear (bear)	165
☐ Lula B. Lightfoot (QVC, bear)	165
☐ Lula Mae Loppenhop (hare)	297
☐ Lula Quackenwaddle (ornament)	352
☐ Lulu (ornament)	352
☐ Lulu Mae Ladybug (QVC, bear)	165
☐ Luna (ornament)	352
☐ Luvey Heartstrings (Longaberger, bear)	166
☐ Lydia Fitzbruin (bear)	166
☐ Lyla Quackenwaddle (ornament)	352
☐ Lyndon & Mondale Cattington (QVC, cat)	253
☐ Lynette Bearlove (bear)	166
☐ Lynn (hare)	297
☐ M.B. Hugsley (QVC, bear)	166
☐ M.C. Twinklemoose (ornament)	352
☐ M.T. FuzzieFriend (QVC, bear)	166
☐ Ma Shen San (QVC, panda)	330
☐ Mabel Witmoose (ornament)	353
☐ Mac the Golfer (bear)	166
☐ Macadoo McSnoozle with Ernie (QVC, moose)	322
☐ Macho Z. Heartthrob (bear)	166
☐ Maci E. Kringlebeary (Macy's East, bear)	166
☐ Mackenzie Alexandra (Elder Beerman, bear)	166
☐ MacMillan (bear)	166
☐ Macy M. Mooselmuff (QVC, moose)	322
☐ Macy Sunbeary (bear)	166
☐ Madabout Ewe (lamb)	313
☐ Maddison Bearyproud (Cracker Barrel, bear)	166
☐ Madeline (Elder Beerman, bear)	167

Name	Page
☐ Madeline Ann Woodsbeary (Kirlins, bear)	167
☐ Madeline Willoughby (bear)	167
☐ Madison (SLE, bear)	167
☐ Madison Glorybear (Kirlins, bear)	167
☐ Madison L. Bearington (bear)	167
☐ Mae B. Bearlove (bear)	167
☐ Mae I. Loveya (POG, bear)	167
☐ Magdalena (Frederick Atkins, bear)	167
☐ Maggie B. Bearheart (bear)	167
☐ Maggie D. Berriweather and basket (f.o.b 2002)	47
☐ Maggie O'Pigg (pig)	334
☐ Magic Santa (ornament, green)	36
☐ Magic Santa (ornament, red)	36
☐ Magic Santa (ornament, blue)	36
☐ Magillacuddy (moose)	322
☐ Magnolia O'Harea (hare)	297
☐ Magnus P. Moosefield (QVC, moose)	322
☐ Mahoney S. Mooseltoof (moose)	322
☐ Maisey Ewe (lamb)	313
☐ Major (bear)	167
☐ Major II (bear)	167
☐ Malcolm (bear)	168
☐ Malcolm Mooselfluff (QVC, moose)	322
☐ Malinda T. Bloomberg (QVC, bear)	168
☐ Mallard (wooden stained group)	31
☐ Mallard (minnesota flats, preener)	25
☐ Mallard (minnesota flats, sentinel)	25
☐ Mallard (traditional group, drake)	29
☐ Mallard (minnesota flats, swimmer)	25
☐ Malley Q. Mooselfluff (moose)	323
☐ Mallory (SLE, hare)	298
☐ Mallory Witebruin (GCC, bear)	168
☐ Mallow Cocobeary (bear)	168
☐ Malone E. Moosetrax (moose)	323
☐ Mamie E. Bearington (QVC, bear)	168
☐ Mamie Glorybear (bear)	168
☐ Manchester S. Bearrrister (QVC, bear)	168
☐ Mandy Jo and Suzie (QVC, bear)	168
☐ Manfred von Merrymoose (GCC, moose)	323
☐ Manheim Von Hindenmoose (moose)	323
☐ Manley Strutencrow (BBC, rooster)	337
☐ Maple T. Leafowitz (QVC, bear)	168
☐ Margaret Hollybeary (POG, bear)	168
☐ Margaret Mary (hare)	298
☐ Margaret Q. Harington (QVC, hare)	298
☐ Margaret T. Pattington (bear)	168
☐ Margarita (bear)	168
☐ Margaux P. Pussyfoot (QVC, cat)	253
☐ Margo De Bearvoire (bear)	169
☐ Margo DeBearvoire (bear)	169
☐ Margo duBeary (bear)	169
☐ Mariah Crystalfrost (bear)	169
☐ Marian (Kirlins, bear)	169
☐ Maribel Gardenglow (SFMB, hare)	298
☐ Marie B. Bearlove (bear)	169
☐ Marigold (ornament)	353
☐ Marigold McHare (hare)	298
☐ Marilyn (SLE, bear)	169
☐ Marina (Lord & Taylor, bear)	169
☐ Marina Yachtley (bear)	169
☐ Marion T. Bestlove (bear)	169
☐ Maris G. Pattington (bear)	169
☐ Maris Q. Yachtley (bear)	169
☐ Marissa duBeary (QVC, bear)	170
☐ Marissa P. Pussyfoot (cat)	253

Name	Page
☐ Marissa P. Pussytoes (SFMB, cat)	253
☐ Marjorie Ellen Bearsley (GCC, bear)	170
☐ Markle (moose)	323
☐ Marla Dubeary (bear)	170
☐ Marla Mae Beary (Welcome Home, bear)	170
☐ Marla Sprucebeary (bear)	170
☐ Marlena (hare)	298
☐ Marlena Beargeaux and Deitrich (bear)	170
☐ Marley Dickens (bear)	170
☐ Marlowe Snoopstein (bear)	170
☐ Marmalade Sneakypuss (cat)	253
☐ Marnie (Elder Beerman, bear)	170
☐ Marsha Cocobeary (bear)	170
☐ Marshmallow Cocobeary (bear)	170
☐ Marshmallow Q. Furryfoot (QVC, bear)	170
☐ Marta M. Hare (hare)	298
☐ Martha S. McBruin (bear)	171
☐ Martha T. Bearyproud with Yankee Doodle (QVC, bear)	171
☐ Martha T. Bunnycombe (hare)	298
☐ Martin Muttsky (dog, smooth fur)	269
☐ Martin Muttsky (dog, regular plush)	269
☐ Martin Muttsky (dog, dark brown)	269
☐ Martin V. Moosington (moose)	323
☐ Martini (moose)	323
☐ Marvin P. Snowbeary (bear)	171
☐ Marvin T. Luvbunny (QVC, hare)	298
☐ Marwood (moose)	323
☐ Mary (hare, old face)	298
☐ Mary (hare, new face)	298
☐ Mary Alice Weedsalot (GCC, bear)	171
☐ Mary Angelwish (QVC, tree topper)	366
☐ Mary Ann Bearican (bear)	171
☐ Mary B. Mistletoe (CAN, bear)	171
☐ Mary Beary (bear)	171
☐ Mary Catherine (hare)	298
☐ Mary Elizabeth, Becca & Ruth (QVC, bear)	171
☐ Mary Ellen Patchbeary (bear)	171
☐ Mary Kate Gingerbeary (bear)	171
☐ Mary Louise Bearingto (QVC, bear, 10" gold mohair)	171
☐ Mary Louise Bearington (QVC, bear, 6" white mohair)	171
☐ Mary Lucinda & Marjorie Mayberry (QVC, bear)	172
☐ Mary Regina (hare)	299
☐ Maryanne McBeansley (QVC, bear)	172
☐ Mason (BBC, bear)	172
☐ Matilda (ornament)	353
☐ Matilda (hare)	299
☐ Matilda (bear)	172
☐ Matilda Baahead (lamb)	313
☐ Matilda with Holly Berries (Lord & Taylor, ornament)	353
☐ Matthew (bear, Fall 1996)	172
☐ Matthew (bear, Fall 1997)	172
☐ Matthew (bear, Fall 1998)	172
☐ Matthew (bear, Fall 1999)	172
☐ Matthew (bear, Fall 2000)	172
☐ Matthew (bear, Fall 2001)	172
☐ Matthew (bear, Fall 2002)	172
☐ Matthew (bear, Fall 2003)	172
☐ Matthew (bear, Fall 2004)	173
☐ Matthew Bear (bear)	173
☐ Matthew Bear (bear, Anniversary Edition)	173
☐ Matthew H. Growler (bear)	173
☐ Mattie C. Bearsley (GCC, bear)	173
☐ Mattie Frostbuns (QVC, moose)	323
☐ Maude (lamb)	313
☐ Maureen O'Hare (hare)	299
☐ Maurice Von Hindenmoose (moose)	323
☐ Maury McSnoozle (moose)	323
☐ Max (Lord & Taylor, ornament)	353
☐ Maximillian (bear)	173
☐ Maximillian, Thornton, & Elford (QVC, bear)	173
☐ Maxine T. Bearsley (GCC, bear)	173
☐ Maxine von HindenMoose (QVC, moose)	323
☐ Maxton P. Bean (QVC, bear, with Craxton and Paxton)	173
☐ Maxwell (Max) Mittbruin (QVC, puppet)	363
☐ Maya Berriman (bear)	173
☐ Maynard Von Hindenmoose (Spiegel, moose)	324
☐ Maynard Von HindenMoose (moose)	324
☐ Mazie Q. Lightfoot (hare)	299
☐ McCormic T. Moosleton (GCC, moose)	324
☐ McKenzie (bear)	173
☐ McKinley (QVC, moose)	324
☐ McKinley (bear)	173
☐ McKinley Bearington (bear)	174
☐ McMullen (bear)	174
☐ McNeil Mutton (lamb)	313
☐ McShamus O'Growler (bear)	174
☐ Meeka (Alps, moose, green sweater)	324
☐ Meeka (Alps, moose, green plaid pajamas)	324
☐ Meeka (Alps, moose, red sweater)	324
☐ Meeka (Alps, moose, purple sweater)	324
☐ Meeka (Alps, moose, green sweater with flowers)	324
☐ Meeka (Alps, moose, mint green sweater)	324
☐ Meg (Dillards, bear)	174
☐ Meg (bear)	174
☐ Meg Autumnfest (bear)	174
☐ Megan (Kirlins, bear)	174
☐ Megan Berriman (bear)	174
☐ Melanie Lockley & Sam (QVC, bear)	174
☐ Melanie McRind (bear)	174
☐ Melba, Mimsie & Myrtle Bahsworth (QVC, ornament)	353
☐ Melbourne (bear)	174
☐ Melinda M. Milestone (QVC, bear)	174
☐ Melinda McRind & Dixie LE Set (QVC, bear)	175
☐ Melinda S. Willoughby (bear)	175
☐ Melvin Sortalion (f.o.b 2001)	47
☐ Memsy (bear)	175
☐ Menachem (moose)	324
☐ Mendel Von HindenMoose (moose)	324
☐ Mercedes Fitzbruin (bear)	175
☐ Mercer (ornament)	353
☐ Merci Bearcoo (bear)	175
☐ Mercury (ornament)	353
☐ Meredith (Frederick Atkins, hare)	299
☐ Meredith K. Pattington with Benjamin (bear)	175
☐ Merentha (Dillards, pig)	335
☐ Merganser (traditional group, drake)	29
☐ Meridian Wishkabibble (bear)	175
☐ Merle B. Squirrel (squirrel)	338
☐ Merlin (lion)	315
☐ Merlin (hare)	299
☐ Merlin (bear)	175
☐ Merrimew McPurrsley (QVC, cat)	253
☐ Merritt M. Muttsky (dog)	270
☐ Merry Beary (Platinum Paw, bear)	175

Name	Page
☐ Merry Beth Angelwish (tree topper)	366
☐ Merrybeary Beanster (QVC, bear)	175
☐ Merton Flatberg (dog)	270
☐ Mervin Q. Rugsley (QVC, moose)	325
☐ Mia Goodfriends (bear)	175
☐ Michael (Dillards, bear)	175
☐ Michael David Bearsley (bear)	176
☐ Michaela (Dillards, bear)	176
☐ Michele S. Hopplebuns (hare)	299
☐ Michelle B. Bearsley (QVC, bear)	176
☐ Michelline (hare)	299
☐ Mickey (hare)	299
☐ Mickey (bear)	176
☐ Mickie (hare, chenille)	299
☐ Mickie (hare, sherpa fur)	299
☐ Midge Meowsworth (cat)	254
☐ Midnight Sneakypuss (cat)	254
☐ Mikayla Springbeary (bear)	176
☐ Mike Magilla (gorilla)	276
☐ Mikie O'Burr (Hallmark, bear)	176
☐ Mildred Q. Moostein (QVC, cow)	265
☐ Milhous N. Moosington (moose)	325
☐ Miliken von Hiddenmoose (moose, closed mouth)	325
☐ Miliken von Hindenmoose (moose, nibble mouth)	325
☐ Miller G. Mooselhuggs (QVC, moose)	325
☐ Millicent P. Pussytoes (cat)	254
☐ Millicent Sugarcone (bear)	176
☐ Millie Hopkins (hare)	299
☐ Millie Marie Goodbear (Country Clutter, bear)	176
☐ Milo (bear)	176
☐ Milton Q. Stiltwalker (QVC, giraffe)	276
☐ Milton R. Penworthy (cat)	254
☐ Mimi & Arlene (GCC, bear)	176
☐ Mimi Chapeau (bear)	176
☐ Mimi Delapain (hare)	300
☐ Mimosa (hare)	300
☐ Mindy D. Beartucket (QVC, bear)	176
☐ Mindy P. Elfbeary (bear)	177
☐ Mindy S. Basketcase (QVC, bear)	177
☐ Mindy Witebruin (GCC, bear)	177
☐ Ming-Ming Woodsley (panda)	331
☐ Mini Canada Goose (minnesota flats, set of 3)	25
☐ Mini Loons (minnesota flats, set of 3)	26
☐ Mini Mallards (minnesota flats, set of 3)	26
☐ Mini Minnesota Cats (minnesota flats, b/w - set of 3)	26
☐ Mini Minnesota Cats (minnesota flats, tiger - set of 3)	26
☐ Mini Mookins (ornament)	353
☐ Mini Pintail (minnesota flats, set of 3)	26
☐ Mini Swans (minnesota flats, set of 3)	26
☐ Mini Wood Duck Flats (minnesota flats, set of 3)	26
☐ Minkle B. Beansley (f.o.b 2004)	48
☐ Minkles D. Bearsdale (bear)	177
☐ Minnesota Cats (minnesota flats, b/w jumping)	26
☐ Minnesota Cats (minnesota flats, b/w lying)	26
☐ Minnesota Cats (minnesota flats, b/w sitting)	26
☐ Minnesota Cats (minnesota flats, tiger jumping)	26
☐ Minnesota Cats (minnesota flats, tiger sitting)	26
☐ Minnesota Cats (minnesota flats, tiger stretching)	27
☐ Minney Moose (moose)	325
☐ Minnie Higgenthorpe (bear)	177
☐ Mintley (QVC, ornament)	353
☐ Mipsie Blumenshine (hare)	300
☐ Miracle Gardenglow (hare)	300
☐ Miranda Blumenshine (hare)	300
☐ Miranda Cherrybeary and Bing (bear)	177
☐ Miranda Hollybeary (SYN, bear)	177
☐ Miss Abby and Lexie Dowbunny (QVC, hare)	300
☐ Miss Amirella & Ripley (QVC, bear)	177
☐ Miss Annie Fuzzybuns (QVC, cat)	254
☐ Miss Ashley (bear)	177
☐ Miss Flufficat (QVC, cat)	254
☐ Miss Graduate (bear)	177
☐ Miss Hathabeary (bear)	177
☐ Miss Hedda Bearimore (bear)	177
☐ Miss Isabelle Q. Bearsworthy (QVC, bear)	178
☐ Miss Lorriane & Abby Mae (QVC, bear)	178
☐ Miss Mabel & Mr. Miles Bearister (QVC, bear)	178
☐ Miss Macintosh (bear)	178
☐ Miss MacIntosh & Sarahbeth with Topsey (QVC, bear)	178
☐ Miss Maggie & Theo (Welcome Home, bear)	178
☐ Miss Minnie Partridge (pin)	362
☐ Miss Niblers (QVC, bear)	178
☐ Miss Nicole Plumbeary (GCC, bear)	178
☐ Miss Poinsley (QVC, bear)	178
☐ Miss Prissy Fussybuns (cat)	254
☐ Miss Pussyfoot & Mr. McScurry (QVC, cat)	254
☐ Miss Sourpuss with McLemon (QVC, cat)	254
☐ Miss Winsalot (QVC, bear)	178
☐ Missie Meowsworth (cat)	254
☐ Missy (bear)	178
☐ Missy Lou & Gilbert (QVC, bear)	178
☐ Missy P. Pusskins and Squeekers (QVC, cat)	254
☐ Mistle (bear)	179
☐ Mistle & Taux (QVC, bear)	179
☐ Mistletoe Santa (ornament)	36
☐ Mitchell Bearsdale (bear)	179
☐ Mitt, Muff & Puff (QVC, ornament)	353
☐ Mitzie Mae (Kirlins, hare)	300
☐ Mizz Buzzley & Mrs. McFlutter (QVC, bear)	179
☐ Mo Mooseltoes (ornament)	353
☐ Mocha Mooseby (ornament)	354
☐ Moe Lapin (hare, old face)	300
☐ Moe Lapin (hare, new face)	300
☐ Moe Munchencrunch (GCC, moose)	325
☐ Mohley (bear)	179
☐ Molly (hare)	300
☐ Molly B. Beariweather (f.o.b 2002, pin)	47
☐ Molly B. Beariweather... Teddy Bear's Picnic (f.o.b 2002)	47
☐ Molly Maybeary (Welcome Home, bear)	179
☐ Molly R. Berriman & Nathan (bear)	179
☐ Molly R. Mistletoe (CAN, bear)	179
☐ Mom & Baby Hugs (QVC, bear)	179
☐ Momma Beansford & Sweet Cheeks (QVC, bear)	179
☐ Momma Bear, Alouetta, & Victor (QVC, bear)	179
☐ Momma Bearhugs and Tory (bear)	179
☐ Momma Bearlove and Baby (bear)	180
☐ Momma Bearsley & Baby Jack (bear)	180
☐ Momma Bearsley with Baby Bundles (bear)	180
☐ Momma Bearsworth with Mary-Margaret, Stuart & Frame (QVC, bear)	180
☐ Momma Bearybake (QVC, bear)	180

Name	Page
☐ Momma Berrywinkle & Woodrow (QVC, bear)	180
☐ Momma Hollybeary with Baby Jingles (QVC, bear)	180
☐ Momma MacBeansley & Toots (QVC, bear)	180
☐ Momma MacBearsley with Baby (bear)	180
☐ Momma McBear & Cedric (QVC, bear)	180
☐ Momma McBear & Delmar (bear)	180
☐ Momma McBear & Delmar (SFMB, bear)	180
☐ Momma McBearlove & Baby (bear)	181
☐ Momma McBearsley with Jessica (Carlton Cards, bear)	181
☐ Momma McFuzz and Missy (cat)	254
☐ Momma McFuzz and Missy (SFMB, cat)	255
☐ Momma McGoldberg & Cissy (GCC, bear)	181
☐ Momma McNew with Hugsley (bear)	181
☐ Momma McNew with Hugsley (SFMB, bear)	181
☐ Momma McVeggie & The Sweetpeas (bear)	181
☐ Momma O'Harea & Bonnie Blue (hare)	300
☐ Momma Purrsalot & Pusskins (QVC, cat)	255
☐ Mommie and Me (Harry & David, bear)	181
☐ Mondale W. Cattington (cat)	255
☐ Monica (Frederick Atkins, bear)	181
☐ Monique de la Fleur (QVC, hare, with Giselle)	300
☐ Monique LaBearsley (bear)	181
☐ Monkey See & Monkey Do (monkey)	319
☐ Monroe J. Bearington (bear)	181
☐ Monsieur Jodibear (duck)	273
☐ Montague (moose)	325
☐ Montana Mooski (moose)	325
☐ Monte Mooselton (moose)	325
☐ Montell P. Chatsworth (puppet)	363
☐ Monterey Mouski (mouse)	317
☐ Montgomery Flatstein (hare)	301
☐ Moocha Latte (cow)	265
☐ Mookie (Alps, moose, cream sweaters)	325
☐ Mookie (Alps, moose, navy sweater with red and white stripe)	325
☐ Mookie (Alps, moose, beige sweater with aztec trim)	326
☐ Mookins (bear)	181
☐ Moon Santa (ornament, tree topper)	36
☐ Moondust Goodspeed (ornament)	354
☐ Mooselkins (bear)	181
☐ Mooshell Patchbeary (cow)	266
☐ Mooshell Patchbeary (SFMB, cow)	266
☐ Moosies (ornament)	354
☐ Morgan B. Berriweather (f.o.b 2002)	47
☐ Morgan B. Thumblover (SYN, bear)	182
☐ Morgan T. Yachtley with Bill (bear)	182
☐ Moriarity (bear, bean filled)	182
☐ Moriarity (bear, polyfill)	182
☐ Morley (bear)	182
☐ Morley Moose (QVC, ornament)	354
☐ Morley P. Moosetrax (moose)	326
☐ Morris (bear)	182
☐ Mortimer (Lord & Taylor, moose)	326
☐ Mortimer Von Hindenmoose (moose)	326
☐ Morton Elfbeary (QVC, moose)	326
☐ Morty (Elder Beerman, ornament)	354
☐ Mother Bearston & Bluebell (QVC, bear)	182
☐ Mother Goosebeary (goose)	276
☐ Mother Moosemas (moose)	326
☐ Mountie Moosletoe (GCC, moose)	326
☐ Moxley Mooselkins (QVC, bear)	182
☐ Moxley Von Mooseltoes (moose)	326
☐ Mozart B. Barken (dog)	270

Name	Page
☐ Mr. & Mrs. Dooright (bear)	182
☐ Mr. & Mrs. Forevermore (QVC, bear)	182
☐ Mr. Barnum (GCC, bear)	182
☐ Mr. Baxter (QVC, bear)	182
☐ Mr. Baybeary (bear)	183
☐ Mr. Bojangles (QVC, bear)	183
☐ Mr. BoJingles (SLE, bear)	183
☐ Mr. Bojingles (bear)	183
☐ Mr. Chucklebeary (QVC, bear)	183
☐ Mr. Everlove (bear)	183
☐ Mr. Graduate (bear)	183
☐ Mr. Hooter (owl)	330
☐ Mr. Jones (bear)	183
☐ Mr. Kringle (bear)	183
☐ Mr. McFarkle (bear)	183
☐ Mr. McHootle (QVC, owl)	330
☐ Mr. McSnickers (bear)	183
☐ Mr. Mufflemoose (QVC, moose)	326
☐ Mr. Nicholsby (QVC, bear)	183
☐ Mr. Noah and Friends (bear)	184
☐ Mr. Peepers (QVC, bear)	184
☐ Mr. Smythe (bear)	184
☐ Mr. Stuffle (QVC, bear)	184
☐ Mr. T. B. Shutterbear (bear)	184
☐ Mr. Tannebaum (QVC, bear)	184
☐ Mr. Trumbull (bear)	184
☐ Mr. Tweeter (bear)	184
☐ Mr. Webster (QVC, bear)	184
☐ Mrs. Baybeary (bear)	184
☐ Mrs. Bearberry (bear)	184
☐ Mrs. Bearburg (bear)	184
☐ Mrs. Bearhugs (QVC, bear)	185
☐ Mrs. Beariwell (GCC, bear)	185
☐ Mrs. Beezley (bear)	185
☐ Mrs. Bradley (Linda Anderson, bear)	185
☐ Mrs. Everlove (bear)	185
☐ Mrs. Fezziwig JodiBear (bear)	185
☐ Mrs. Fiedler the Music Teacher (bear)	185
☐ Mrs. Figgy Pudding (bear)	185
☐ Mrs. Harelwig (hare)	301
☐ Mrs. Harestein (hare)	301
☐ Mrs. Kringlebeary (bear)	185
☐ Mrs. Kringles (QVC, bear)	185
☐ Mrs. Mertz (bear)	185
☐ Mrs. Mother May I (SLE, bear)	185
☐ Mrs. Nestor (QVC, hen)	311
☐ Mrs. Noah (bear)	186
☐ Mrs. Northstar (bear)	186
☐ Mrs. Northstar (SFMB, bear)	186
☐ Mrs. Partridge (cat)	255
☐ Mrs. Petrie (cat)	255
☐ Mrs. Petrie (SFMB, cat)	255
☐ Mrs. Plumbles (QVC, bear)	186
☐ Mrs. Potter & Her Lil' Sprouts (QVC, bear)	186
☐ Mrs. Trumbull (bear, no bow)	186
☐ Mrs. Trumbull (bear, red plaid bow)	186
☐ Mrs. Trumbull (SFMB, bear)	186
☐ Mrs. Tuttle (QVC, bear)	186
☐ Mrs. Tweeter and Purrsley (QVC, bear)	186
☐ Ms. Appleby & Olivia (QVC, bear)	186
☐ Ms. Bee Beezley (CAN, bear)	186
☐ Ms. Berriweather's Cottage (f.o.b 1998)	45
☐ Ms. Magnolia (QVC, hare)	301
☐ Ms. Odetta & Neville (QVC, bear)	187
☐ Ms. Potter & Amadeus (QVC, bear)	187
☐ Ms. Rouge Chapeau (bear)	187

Name	Page
Ms. Teachbeary (ornament)	354
Muddles Q. Piggytoes (pig)	335
Muddles T. Moxley (BBC, moose)	326
Muffin (bear)	187
Muffin B. Bluebeary (Yankee Candle, bear)	187
Muffles P. Mooseltoof (moose)	326
Muffles T. Toastytoes (QVC, cat)	255
Mukluk (Alps, moose, blue sweater)	326
Mukluk (Alps, moose, red plaid pajamas)	327
Mukluk (Alps, moose, blue sweater)	327
Mukluk (Alps, moose, 2000)	327
Mukluk (Alps, moose, blue sweater with ribbon trim)	327
Mukluk (Alps, moose, Weekender)	327
Mukluk (Alps, moose, Super Mukluk)	327
Mukluk (Alps, moose, American Mukluk)	327
Mukluk (Alps, moose, Varsity Mukluk)	327
Mukluk (Alps, moose, Super Mukluk III)	327
Mukluk (Alps, moose, Cold Springs)	327
Mukluk (Alps, moose, Holiday)	327
Mukluk (Alps, moose, Outdoorsman)	327
Mukluk (Alps, moose, Weekender Mukluk II)	328
Mukluk (Alps, moose, Tobacco Weekender)	328
Mulligan T. Duffer (bear)	187
Mumbley B. Bean (bear)	187
Mumsie (bear)	187
Mungo Mooselwood (QVC, moose)	328
Munster Q. Fondue (mouse)	317
Murdock Q. Moosley (moose)	328
Murgatroyd (moose, cream tree sweater)	328
Murgatroyd (moose, taupe tree sweater)	328
Murgatroyd Von Hindenmoose (moose)	328
Murgatroyd Von Hindenmoose II (moose)	328
Murphy Mooselfluff (moose)	328
Murray Mooseshoofer (moose)	328
Murtaugh Moosetrax (moose)	328
Murtaugh Moosetrax (SFMB, moose)	328
Museum Bluebill (museum series)	27
Museum Bufflehead (museum series)	28
Museum Mallard (museum series)	28
Museum Pintail (museum series)	28
Museum Wood Duck (museum series)	28
Myles VonHinden Moose (moose)	329
Myron Von Hindenmoose (moose)	329
Myrtle MacMoo (QVC, cow)	266
Mystery Bunny (ornament, Bunny in a Basket)	36
Mystery Dawg (dog)	270
Nadia (Kirlins, bear)	187
Nadia Berriman (QVC, bear)	187
Nadia Berriman (bear)	187
Nadia Von Hindenmoose (moose)	329
Nana (bear)	187
Nana Bearhugs (bear)	188
Nana Bearhugs (SFMB, bear)	188
Nana Panda (panda)	331
Nana Purrington & Gouda (SLE, cat)	255
Nancy D. Bearington (QVC, bear)	188
Nancy Jo Warmheart (QVC, bear)	188
Nandykins (QVC, bear)	188
Nanette Dubeary (bear)	188
Nanna O'Harea and Audrey (QVC, hare)	301
Nanny Bear (bear)	188
Nanny II (hare)	301
Nantucket P. Bearington (bear)	188
Naomi Bearlove (bear)	188
Narcissus (ornament)	354

Name	Page
Natalie (Dillards, hare)	301
Natalie Nibblenose (hare)	301
Natalie Plumbeary (GCC, bear)	188
Natasha (hare)	301
Natasha Berriman (bear)	188
Natasha Crystalfrost (bear)	188
Ned (cat)	255
Nellie (bear)	189
Nellie T. Bearypatch (Paw Dealer, bear)	189
Nelson (bear)	189
Nettie (QVC, bear)	189
Nettie Fisher (bear)	189
Neville (bear, old face)	189
Neville (bear, new face)	189
Newton (elephant)	274
Newton (bear)	189
Niagra (Centre Gift Shoppe, bear)	189
Nibbie Bunnyhop (hare)	301
Nibblekins (bear)	189
Nibbley Sweetreats (hare)	301
Nichley (Dillards, bear)	189
Nicholai A. Pachydermsky (elephant)	274
Nicholas (bear)	189
Nicholas (SLE, bear)	190
Nicholas with Ansel & Fitzgerald (QVC, bear)	190
Nickie (hare)	301
Nickie Nibblenose (hare)	302
Nicklas T. Jodibear (bear)	190
Nickleby S. Claus (bear)	190
Nickolas S. Hugsley (bear)	190
Nicolas Bearington (bear)	190
Nicolas Bearington & Tinker (QVC, bear)	190
Nicole (QVC, bear)	190
Nicole & Amy Berriman with Tassel (QVC, bear)	190
Nicole de la El-bee (Elder Beerman, bear)	190
Nikali Q. Ribbit (QVC, frog)	275
Niki (bear)	190
Niki II (bear)	190
Niklas, Matilda & Trevor (QVC, bear)	191
Noah (bear)	191
Noah with Puddles (bear)	191
Noah's Bookshelf (f.o.b 2001)	47
Noah's Genius At Work Table (f.o.b 1999)	45
Noah's Life Boat (f.o.b 2002)	47
Noah's Toolbox (f.o.b 2000)	46
Noble Nutcracker (bear)	191
Nod (bear, stark white)	191
Nod II (bear, (off-white))	191
Noel Bear (ornament)	36
Noel Chrismouse (mouse, red scarf)	317
Noel Chrismouse (mouse, striped scarf)	317
Noella deBearvoire with Holly (QVC, bear)	191
Noelle (Ethel M. Chocolates, bear)	191
Norbert D. Beariman (bear)	191
North Pole Bear (bear)	191
Northrop Flatberg (dog)	270
Nurse Carin (bear)	191
O. Howie Luvsya (bear)	191
Oda Parfume (skunk)	338
Ogden B. Bean (panda, small version)	331
Ogden B. Bean (panda, large version)	331
Oinkins (bear)	192
Ol' MacBruin...Down on the Farm (QVC, bear)	192
Olaf (bear)	192

Name	Page
Olas & Omar (QVC, panda)	331
Olga (hare)	302
Olive T. Leafowitz (bear)	192
Oliver (hare)	302
Oliver (Dillards, bear)	192
Oliver (GCC, bear)	192
Olivia (Dillards, lamb)	313
Olivia A. Pachydermsky (elephant)	274
Olivia Beariluved (GCC, bear)	192
Olivia Q. Witebred (QVC, bear)	192
Olivia R. Thornbeary (bear)	192
Olivia T. Bearington (QVC, bear)	192
Ollie B. Elf (QVC, ornament)	354
Olympia (QVC, pig)	335
Omar A. Pachydermsky (elephant)	274
Omega T. Legacy & Alpha [Retailer Special Event] (bear)	192
Oops Bear (ornament)	36
Opel Catberg (cat, satin bow)	255
Opel Catberg (cat, blue fabric bow)	255
Ophelia (bear)	192
Ophelia W. Witebred (bear)	193
Ophelia W. Witebred (QVC, bear)	193
Ophilia Q. Grimilkin (cat)	255
Opie Fishalot (bear)	193
Opie Paddypasture & T. Ferdinand Wuzzie (QVC, bear)	193
Opie V. Beanster (QVC, bear)	193
Orabella Fitzbruin (QVC, bear)	193
Orchid de la Hoppsack (hare)	302
Orella Berrywinkle (QVC, bear)	193
Orianna (Welcome Home, bear)	193
Orion (ornament)	354
Orville Bearington (bear)	193
Orvis T. Fisher with Tad (bear)	193
Oscar P. Alleyruckus (QVC, cat)	256
Oswald P. Beanster (bear)	193
Otis B. Bean (bear, open mouth)	193
Otis B. Bean (bear, old face - smooth fur)	194
Otis B. Bean (bear, old face)	194
Otis B. Bean (bear, new face)	194
Otis T. Elf (QVC, ornament)	354
Ottie Wilhelmina (GCC, bear)	194
Otto Von Bruin (bear)	194
Otto Z. Elf (QVC, ornament)	354
Ovid (ornament)	354
Oxford T. Bearrister (bear)	194
Ozzie N. Harrycat (cat)	256
P. Gallery Trunkster (elephant)	274
P. Gallery Trunkster (SFMB, elephant)	274
P.B. Punkinpaw (QVC, bear)	194
P.B. Starcatcher (ornament)	355
P.B. Woodsley (QVC, panda)	331
P.J. (Lord & Taylor, bear)	194
P.J. Bearsdale & Tink (QVC, bear)	194
P.J. McBeansley (QVC, bear)	194
Packy and Dermah Trunkspace (elephant)	274
Paddikins (bear)	194
Paddy O'Beara (bear)	194
Paige Bearylove (bear)	195
Paige Willoughby (bear)	195
Paigley B. Blumbeary (QVC, bear)	195
Pair O'Bears (ornament, old face)	355
Pair O'Bears (ornament, new face)	355
Pair O'Hares (ornament, old face)	355
Pair O'Hares (ornament, new face)	355

Name	Page
Pair O'Highland Plaid Bears` (ornament)	355
Pair O'Homespun Bears (ornament)	355
Pair O'Piggs (ornament)	355
Pamela P. Patchbeary (bear)	195
Pamela P. Prissypuss with Nibley (QVC, cat)	256
Pamela Penneybeary (J.C.Penney, bear)	195
Panda-Boo Woodsley (panda)	331
Pandemonium (QVC, panda)	331
Pandora (panda)	331
Pansey (ornament)	355
Pansey (bear)	195
Pansey & Parsley Hopsalot (QVC, hare)	302
Pansie P. Potter (QVC, bear)	195
Pansley B. Bean (QVC, bear)	195
Pansy (lamb)	313
Pansy (QVC, bear)	195
Pansy Rosenbunny (hare)	302
Parker (SLE, hare)	302
Parker B. Pooch (dog)	270
Pat McPunkin (dog)	270
Pat T. Spiker (bear)	195
Patches B. Beariluved (bear)	195
Patchwork Bunny (ornament)	36
Patience (ornament)	355
Patricia L. Cooksbeary (Longaberger, bear)	195
Patricia P. Bearheart (bear)	196
Patrick (bear)	196
Patrick B. Beanster (QVC, bear)	196
Patrick Bearsevelt (bear)	196
Patrick Henry (QVC, bear)	196
Patriotic Bailey (EVENT, bear)	196
Patsie Punkley (bear)	196
Patsy (bear)	196
Patti and John Berriweather... Havin' A Wonderful Time (f.o.b 2002)	47
Patton Q. Jodibear (bear)	196
Paula Cherrybeary with Tart (QVC, bear)	196
Paula Hoppleby (hare)	302
Paulina P. Punkinbeary & Tisket (QVC, bear)	196
Pauline (Kirlins, hare)	302
Pauline & Penelope (QVC, cat)	256
Pauly Punkley (bear)	196
Paxton P. Bean (bear)	197
Peace Santa (ornament)	37
Peaches Thumpster (hare)	302
Peachie P. Pussyfoot (QVC, cat)	256
Peapod (hare)	302
Pearl Catberg (cat)	256
Peary (bear)	197
Pee Wee & Yogi (QVC, bear)	197
Peeker of the Month (QVC, bear)	197
Peeker P. Heartlove (QVC, bear)	197
Peekers (puppet)	364
Peepers P. MacDonald (bear)	197
Peggy Sue Stuffins (ornament)	355
Pelmon Thomas McBear (Welcome Home, bear)	197
Pendleton (SFMB, bear)	197
Pendleton J. Bruin (bear)	197
Penelope (hare)	302
Penelope (SLE, hare)	303
Penelope P. Punkinbeary (bear)	197
Penelope Pearsley Gift Set (Country Clutter, bear)	197
Pennsley (penguin)	332
Penny Bearsley (J.C. Penney, bear)	197

Name	Page
☐ Penny P. Copperpuss (cat)	256
☐ Penny Whistleby (bear)	198
☐ Pepper (Dillards, cat)	256
☐ Pepper B. Scaredycat (cat)	256
☐ Pepper Mintly (bear)	198
☐ Peppermint P. Bear (bear)	198
☐ Perceval (bear)	198
☐ Percy (bear)	198
☐ Percy P. Pawsley (QVC, bear)	198
☐ Perky P. Rally (ornament)	355
☐ Perriwinkle P. Snicklefritz (bear)	198
☐ Perry (bear)	198
☐ Petals Daisydew (bear)	198
☐ Petals P. Peeker (QVC, bear)	198
☐ Pete E. Bunny (hare)	303
☐ Peter (hare)	303
☐ Peter Potter (bear)	198
☐ Petey B. Stringalong (string along)	364
☐ Petey Poochkins (QVC, dog)	270
☐ Petey Thumpster (hare)	303
☐ Petey von Pupp (GCC, dog)	270
☐ Petula P. Fallsbeary (Show Specials, bear)	198
☐ Petunia P. Berriweather (f.o.b 2003)	48
☐ Petunia Steadsbeary (Longaberger, pig)	335
☐ Peyton (Frederick Atkins, bear)	199
☐ Peyton C. Hopplebuns (hare)	303
☐ Philip A. Stocking (Longaberger, ornament)	356
☐ Phillip Bearhop (bear)	199
☐ Philo Puddlemaker (dog)	270
☐ Philomena (bear)	199
☐ Phoebe B. (QVC, bear)	199
☐ Phoebe Ewe (lamb)	313
☐ Phoebe Purrsmore (cat)	256
☐ Pierre (CAN, bear)	199
☐ Piglet (Disney, pig, Santa's Helper)	335
☐ Piglet (Disney, pig, Winter Holiday)	335
☐ Piglet (Disney, pig, cardigan and hat)	335
☐ Piglet (Disney, pig, Costume Party)	335
☐ Piglet (Disney, pig, Cozy Holiday)	335
☐ Piglet (Disney, pig, Holiday Caroling)	335
☐ Piglet 1999 (Disney, ornament)	356
☐ Piglet 2000 (Disney, ornament)	356
☐ Pinkle B. Bumbles (ornament)	356
☐ Pintail (wooden stained group)	31
☐ Pintail (traditional group, drake)	29
☐ Pintail (minnesota flats, preener)	27
☐ Pintail (minnesota flats, sentinel)	27
☐ Pintail (minnesota flats, swimmer)	27
☐ Piper (hare)	303
☐ Piper Angelbuns (QVC, hare)	303
☐ Piper Lapine (hare)	303
☐ Piper P. Plumbottom (QVC, bear)	199
☐ Pipley McRind (bear)	199
☐ Pitty Pat Pussytoes (QVC, cat)	256
☐ Pittypat Pussyfoot (QVC, cat)	256
☐ Pixie (hare, taupe curly)	303
☐ Pixie (hare, two tone)	303
☐ Plant With Hope, Grow With Love, Bloom With Joy (f.o.b 1999)	45
☐ Poe (cat)	257
☐ Pohley (bear)	199
☐ Pokie (bear)	199
☐ Polly Bunnytoes (hare)	303
☐ Polly Peapod (bear)	199
☐ Polly Quignapple (bear)	199
☐ Poof Pufflebeary (bear)	199

Name	Page
☐ Poof Pufflebeary (SFMB, bear)	200
☐ Pooh (Disney, ornament, santa hat)	356
☐ Pooh (Disney, bear, Mohair Classic)	200
☐ Pooh (Disney, bear, Mohair Santa)	200
☐ Pooh (Disney, bear, Santa with Ornament)	200
☐ Pooh (Disney, bear, Mohair Winter Holiday)	200
☐ Pooh (Disney, bear, Winter Holiday)	200
☐ Pooh (Disney, bear, plaid coat)	200
☐ Pooh (Disney, bear, Mohair red pajamas)	200
☐ Pooh (Disney, bear, Costume Party)	200
☐ Pooh (Disney, bear, Mohair Cozy Holiday)	200
☐ Pooh (Disney, bear, Cozy Holiday)	200
☐ Pooh (Disney, bear, Winter Caroling)	200
☐ Pooh 1999 (Disney, ornament)	356
☐ Pooh (Disney, stocking, ornament)	356
☐ Pooh 2000 (Disney, ornament)	356
☐ Pooh (Disney, sweater, ornament)	356
☐ Pooh 2002 (Disney, ornament, mohair)	356
☐ Pookie W. Penworthy & Midnight Sneakypuss (QVC, cat)	257
☐ Poor Ol' Bear (bear)	201
☐ Poor Ol' Bear (SFMB, bear)	201
☐ Pop Bruin (bear)	201
☐ Poppa Bear & Noelle (bear)	201
☐ Poppa Ted Truckingham (SLE, bear)	201
☐ Pops (bear)	201
☐ Porker P. Piggytoes (pig)	335
☐ Port S. Mouski (QVC, mouse, with Colby)	317
☐ Posie Picksabunch (Longaberger, bear)	201
☐ Potsie Daisydew (bear)	201
☐ Precious Plumbeary (Welcome Home, bear)	201
☐ Preston Flatberg (dog)	270
☐ Primrose (pig)	335
☐ Primrose (QVC, pig)	336
☐ Primrose II (pig)	336
☐ Primrose III (pig)	336
☐ Primrose IV (pig)	336
☐ Primrose P. Trufflesnout (pig)	336
☐ Prince Harry B. Nutcracker (POG, bear)	201
☐ Princess Nicole Bearyspoiled (GCC, bear)	201
☐ Princess P. Pussytoes (cat)	257
☐ Princess Pussytoes [QVC] (QVC, cat)	257
☐ Priscilla (cloth doll, brown print)	263
☐ Priscilla (cloth doll, tan print)	263
☐ Priscilla R. Hare (hare, 17")	303
☐ Priscilla R. Hare (hare, 14")	304
☐ Prissie Hopplebuns (hare)	304
☐ Prissie Hopplebuns II (hare)	304
☐ Prissie Hopplebuns III (hare)	304
☐ Proudly P. Peeker (QVC, bear)	201
☐ Prudence Bearimore (bear)	202
☐ Prudence Berrimore (SFMB, bear)	202
☐ Puck (bear)	202
☐ Pucker McLemon (bear)	202
☐ Pudgy Q. Honeypott (QVC, bear)	202
☐ Puff & Poof Fuzzibutt (QVC, bear)	202
☐ Pumpkin (bear)	202
☐ Pumpkin Hollow Stand (fruit stand)	32
☐ Punkie BooBear (bear)	202
☐ Punkin B. Beary (bear)	202
☐ Punkin Puss (cat)	257
☐ Punkley (bear)	202
☐ Purrcilla P. Pussytoes (cat)	257
☐ Purrcilla P. Sugarcone (cat)	257
☐ Purrcilla Pusskins (QVC, cat)	257
☐ Purrkins P. Pussytoes (cat)	257

Name	Page
☐ Purrsnicitty Snotty-Kat (cat)	257
☐ Puss N. Boo (cat)	257
☐ Pussy Broomski (cat)	257
☐ Putnam & Kent (QVC, bear)	202
☐ Putnam P. Bearsley (bear)	202
☐ Putter T. Parfore (bear)	203
☐ Q.P. Peeker (QVC, bear)	203
☐ Quaker O. Brimley (bear)	203
☐ Quayle D. Cattington (cat)	258
☐ Quincy & Corliss (QVC, bear)	203
☐ Quincy B. Bibbly (bear)	203
☐ Quinn (Frederick Atkins, bear)	203
☐ R.B. Merganser (traditional group, drake - 16")	29
☐ R.B. Merganser (traditional group, drake - 18")	29
☐ Rabbit Gabriel (ornament)	37
☐ Rabbit Gabriel Plaque (ornament)	37
☐ Rachael & Phoebe Truefriends (QVC, bear)	203
☐ Rachael Q. Ribbit (frog)	275
☐ Rachel and B. Bearilove (bear)	203
☐ Radcliff McVeggie (bear)	203
☐ Radcliffe Fitzbruin (bear)	203
☐ Raeburn (f.o.b 1996)	44
☐ Rag Doll (ornament)	37
☐ Raggedy Twins (ornament)	356
☐ Ragna (SLE, bear)	203
☐ Rainey Bloomengrows (Hallmark, bear)	203
☐ Raleigh (bear)	204
☐ Ralph McFarmin (BBC, bear)	204
☐ Ralph Poochstein (dog)	270
☐ Raylee (Dillards, bear)	204
☐ Reagan V. Bearington (bear)	204
☐ Rebecca Bearimore (bear)	204
☐ Rebecca S. Duckworthy (QVC, bear)	204
☐ Redford T. Woodsbeary (bear)	204
☐ Redhead (traditional group, drake)	29
☐ Redmond Foxworthy (QVC, fox)	274
☐ Regan (Dillards, bear)	204
☐ Regena Haresford (hare)	304
☐ Reggie Foxworthy (fox)	275
☐ Regina (hare, short ears - small feet)	304
☐ Regina (hare, big ears - small feet)	304
☐ Regina (hare, big ears - big feet)	304
☐ Regina (hare, two-tone)	304
☐ Reginald (Lord & Taylor, bear)	204
☐ Regulus P. Roar (ornament)	356
☐ Reilly O'Pigg (pig)	336
☐ Remington B. Bean (QVC, bear)	204
☐ Remington Braveheart (bear)	204
☐ Remus Q. Tweeter with Zip (bear)	204
☐ Resting Swan (white group)	30
☐ Resting Swan (wooden stained group)	31
☐ Reva (bear)	205
☐ Revolutionary Santa (ornament)	37
☐ Rex (bear)	205
☐ Rhoda (GCC, bear)	205
☐ Riblet F. Wuzzie (pin)	362
☐ Richard Tee Dobbsey (Coach House Gifts, bear)	205
☐ Ricky & Lucy Bandito (raccoon)	337
☐ Riesling Beardeaux (bear)	205
☐ Riley B. Bean (bear)	205
☐ Ripple (frog)	275
☐ Rita (hare)	304
☐ Roary Maneford (ornament)	357
☐ Roberta (bear)	205
☐ Roberto (Ideation, bear)	205
☐ Robin T. Tweeter with Goldie (bear)	205
☐ Robyn (CAN, bear)	205
☐ Robyn Purrsmore (cat)	258
☐ Rochelle & Dessa (QVC, bear)	205
☐ Rockie Mountberg (SLE, bear)	205
☐ Rockwell B. Bruin (bear)	206
☐ Rocky B. Barken (dog)	271
☐ Rodney (SLE, bear)	206
☐ Rohley (bear)	206
☐ Roland (Dillards, bear)	206
☐ Roma Applesmith (BBC, bear)	206
☐ Romano B. Grated (mouse)	318
☐ Ronald (May Company, bear)	206
☐ Roosevelt (dog)	271
☐ Roosevelt (bear, 14" mohair)	206
☐ Roosevelt (bear, 8")	206
☐ Roosevelt P. Bearington (bear)	206
☐ Rootie T. McRooster (QVC, bear)	206
☐ Roq (mouse)	318
☐ Rosalie & Celina Dubeary (QVC, bear)	206
☐ Rosalie Bloomengrows (hare)	304
☐ Rosalind (SFMB, bear)	206
☐ Rosalind II (SFMB, bear)	207
☐ Rosalynn P. Harington (hare)	304
☐ Rosalynn P. Harington II (hare)	305
☐ Rosanna duBeary (bear)	207
☐ Rosanna P. Angelbuns (QVC, hare)	305
☐ Roscoe P. Bumpercrop (hare)	305
☐ Rose (hare)	305
☐ Rose Bud (Harry & David, pig)	336
☐ Rose Mutton (lamb)	314
☐ Rosemont Bear (Rosemont, bear)	207
☐ Rosie (Yankee Candle, bear)	207
☐ Rosie B. Goodbear (Country Clutter, bear)	207
☐ Rosie O'Pigg (pig)	336
☐ Rosie O'Pigg (SFMB, pig)	336
☐ Roslyn Hiphop (hare)	305
☐ Ross Angelstar (ornament)	357
☐ Ross G. Jodibear (bear)	207
☐ Rowen Yachtley (bear)	207
☐ Rowena Prissypuss (cat)	258
☐ Roxanne K. Bear (bear)	207
☐ Roxbunny R. Hare (hare)	305
☐ Roxie and Reba DuBeary (QVC, bear)	207
☐ Royce (cat)	258
☐ Royce (bear)	207
☐ Royce Bear (bear)	207
☐ Royce Hare (hare)	305
☐ Ruddy Duck (wooden stained group)	31
☐ Ruddy Duck (traditional group, drake)	29
☐ Rudolf (bear)	207
☐ Rudolph (SLE, bear)	208
☐ Rudy McRind (bear)	208
☐ Rudy Pitoody (bear)	208
☐ Rudy Valentino (Harry & David, bear)	208
☐ Rudy Z. Mooseburg (GCC, bear)	208
☐ Rufus (bear, new face)	208
☐ Rumpus (hare)	305
☐ Rumsford Q. Bearsworth (QVC, bear)	208
☐ Rupert (bear)	208
☐ Rupert B. Shutterbear (bear)	208
☐ Rupert B. Shutterbear (QVC, bear)	208
☐ Ruskin K. Woodruff (bear)	208
☐ Russ Q. Goodfriends (QVC, bear)	208
☐ Russet (Frederick Atkins, bear)	209
☐ Rustley Leadbottoms (bear)	209

Name	Page
Rusty & Scardycrow (bear)	209
Rusty B. Autumnfest (BoydsBiz.com, bear)	209
Rusty McPunkin (bear)	209
Rusty Scaredybear (Longaberger, bear)	209
Ruth (hare)	305
Rutherford (bear)	209
Ruthie (bear)	209
Ruthy Appleton (Cracker Barrel, bear)	209
Rutledge (QVC, bear)	209
Ryan (Dillards, bear)	209
S.B. Twinklbeary (QVC, bear)	209
S.C. Northstar (bear)	210
S.C. Ribbit (frog)	275
S.K. (CAN, bear)	210
Sable B. Bearsdale (bear)	210
Sabrina P. Catterwall (cat)	258
Sabrina P. Catterwall (cat)	258
Sadie (Kirlins, bear)	210
Sadie B. Bearcountry (QVC, bear)	210
Sadie Bearyman (May Company, bear)	210
Sadie Bearymore (May Company, bear)	210
Sadie Ewe (lamb)	314
Sadie Utterburg (cow)	266
Sage Leafowitz (bear)	210
Sage Steadsbeary (Longaberger, bear)	210
Sailor Bear (ornament)	37
Sakary Millenia (Profitts, bear)	210
Salem Thumpkin (cat)	258
Sally and Harry (Lord & Taylor, bear)	210
Sally Quignapple and Annie (bear)	210
Sally Quignapple and Annie (SFMB, bear)	211
Salty (Casual Living, dog)	271
Sam Yule (Hallmark, bear)	211
Samantha (Kirlins, bear)	211
Samantha Marie & Brady (SYN, bear)	211
Samantha Sneakypuss (cat)	258
Sammi B. Thumblover (Linda Anderson, bear)	211
Sammy Slugger (bear)	211
Sammy Snicklepuss (cat)	258
Sammy Sue (GCC, ornament)	357
Sampson T. Lion (lion)	315
Samuel (bear)	211
Samuel Adams (bear)	211
Samuel Catberg (cat)	258
Samuel T. Kringlebear with George (bear)	211
Sandy Claus (bear)	211
Sandy Claus II (bear)	211
Sandy Sanditoes (bear)	211
Sangria (hare)	305
Santa Bear (bear)	212
Santa Gabriel (ornament)	37
Santa Toy (ornament, stand-up large)	37
Santa Toy (ornament, stand-up medium)	37
Santa Toy Ornament (ornament, green sack)	37
Santa with Bag Ornament (ornament)	37
Santa's Face (ornament)	37
Santa's Sleigh (ornament)	38
Sapphire S. Bearington (QVC, bear)	212
Sara (hare)	305
Sara Beth (POG, bear)	212
Sara II (hare)	305
Sarabeth Crystalfrost (bear)	212
Sarah (hare)	306
Sarah (CAN, bear)	212
Sarah Anne Bearsly & T. Foster Wuzzie (QVC, bear)	212

Name	Page
Sarah Beth Jodibear (bear)	212
Sarah Jane (CAN, bear)	212
Sarah Patchbeary (Kirlins, bear)	212
Sarina (Frederick Atkins, hare)	306
Sasha (bear)	212
Sasha Dubeary (bear)	212
Sassafrass (ornament)	357
Savannah Berrywinkle & Bentley (QVC, bear)	212
Savannah Buttercup (hare)	306
Scarecrow (bear)	213
Scarlett Bearington (bear)	213
Scoop (bear)	213
Scooter (bear)	213
Scotch (SLE, bear)	213
Scout P. Poochley (dog)	271
Scratches P. Whiskerpuss (cat)	258
Scruffy S. Beariluved (bear)	213
Sebastian (bear)	213
Sedgewick T Bruin (QVC, bear)	213
Serafina (QVC, ornament)	357
Seraphina (ornament)	357
Serena Goodnight (ornament)	357
Serendipity Wishkabibble (bear)	213
Sergei Bearskov (bear)	213
Settia (bear)	213
Seymour P. Snowbeary (bear)	213
Shane B. Bearsford (QVC, bear)	214
Shane B. Bearsworth (bear)	214
Shannon Oakley & Mr. Hoots (QVC, bear)	214
Shao Pan Yo (QVC, panda)	331
Shao Pan Yo (panda)	331
Shara Sugarcone (BtoB Website, bear)	214
Shari Beabeary (Longaberger, bear)	214
Sharona (hare)	306
Sharp McNibble (mouse)	318
Shasta (QVC, bear, with Caledonia and Humbolt)	214
Shasta Daisydew (POG, bear)	214
Shawnee Fisher (bear)	214
Shay Ann McLemon (bear)	214
Sheffield O'Swine (pig)	336
Sheila (Lord & Taylor, ornament)	357
Shelby McRind (Cracker Barrel, bear)	214
Shelby T. Sanditoes (bear)	214
Sheldon Bearchild (bear)	214
Shelly (cat)	258
Shepard Bear (ornament)	38
Sherie B. Bearican & Cliff (bear)	215
Sherlock (bear, pink paws)	215
Sherlock (bear, gray paws)	215
Shi Wong (QVC, panda)	331
Shiloh P. Poochdale (dog)	271
Shivers Snowbeary (bear)	215
Shoeless P. Clopsdale (QVC, horse)	311
Shorebird (black hills, curlew)	22
Shorebird (black hills, snipe)	22
Shorebird (black hills, stilt)	22
Sidney (Dillards, bear)	215
Siegfried Von Hindenmoose (moose)	329
Sierra Woodsbeary (bear)	215
Sigmund Von Bruin (bear)	215
Sillie Waddlewalk (penguin)	332
Silo Q. Vanderhoof (cow)	266
Silverton Snowbeary (ornament)	357
Silvia Jubilee (BBC, bear)	215
Simianne Z. Jodibear (monkey)	319

Name	Page
☐ Simon Beanster and Andy (bear)	215
☐ Simon S. Simianski (monkey)	319
☐ Simon T. Poochley (dog)	271
☐ Simone de Bearvoire (bear)	215
☐ Sinclair Bearsford (bear)	215
☐ Sinkin (bear, stark white)	215
☐ Sinkin II (bear, off-white)	216
☐ Sippy McLemon (bear)	216
☐ Sir Henry (bear)	216
☐ Sir Hugsalot (bear)	216
☐ Sir Humpsley (camel)	244
☐ Sir Lotslove (Hershey, bear)	216
☐ Sissy B. Bear (bear)	216
☐ Sissy Bearyfriend (SYN, bear)	216
☐ Skater Santa (ornament)	38
☐ Skidoo (bear)	216
☐ Skier Bear (ornament)	38
☐ Skip (bear)	216
☐ Skip B. Yachtley (bear)	216
☐ Skip Hopsey (ornament)	357
☐ Skipper T. Pattington (QVC, bear)	216
☐ Skylar and Starlynn (QVC, bear)	216
☐ Skylar Thistlebeary (bear)	217
☐ Skylar Thistlebeary (SFMB, bear)	217
☐ Sledder Bear (ornament)	38
☐ Sledding Santa (ornament)	38
☐ Slim B. Woodsley (bear)	217
☐ Slugger (bear)	217
☐ Sly Alleyruckus (cat)	259
☐ Sly Foxworthy (ornament)	357
☐ Smith Applewish (bear)	217
☐ Smith Witter 25th Anniversary (QVC, bear)	217
☐ Smith Witter II (bear)	217
☐ Smith Witter II (SFMB, bear)	217
☐ Smokey B. Pusskins (cat)	259
☐ Smokey Ninelives (cat)	259
☐ Smokie Mountberg (SLE, bear)	217
☐ Smooch & Snuggle (ornament)	357
☐ Snackers McSnoozle (mouse)	318
☐ Snackers Sneakypuss (QVC, cat)	259
☐ Sneaky (bear)	217
☐ Sneaky P. Snottypuss (QVC, cat)	259
☐ Sneekers (puppet)	364
☐ Snickersnoodle (bear)	217
☐ Sniffles (bear)	217
☐ Sniffles T. Woodsley (bear)	218
☐ Snooker T. Sootyfoot (QVC, cat)	259
☐ Snookie Snickelfritz (bear)	218
☐ Snoozer Bedoozer (QVC, dog)	271
☐ Snottie Snicklepuss (cat)	259
☐ Snow Bear (ornament, antique)	38
☐ Snow Bear (ornament, white)	38
☐ Snowball Bear (ornament, green)	38
☐ Snowball Bear (ornament, red)	38
☐ Snowbeary (ornament)	358
☐ Snowbunny (Bath & Body Works, hare)	306
☐ Snowy Crystalfrost (bear)	218
☐ Snuffy B. Barker (dog)	271
☐ Snuggems B. Joy (GCC, bear)	218
☐ Socks Grimilkin (cat)	259
☐ Socksley (QVC, bear)	358
☐ Sonja Frostbeary (bear)	218
☐ Sonny (bear)	218
☐ Sonya B. Burrbruin (QVC, bear)	218
☐ Sooty (cat)	259
☐ Sooty P. Pussyfoot (cat)	259

Name	Page
☐ Sophie (hare)	306
☐ Sophie B. Bunny (hare)	306
☐ Sophie B. Goodbear (Country Clutter, bear)	218
☐ Sophie Jane Gingerbeary (GCC, bear)	218
☐ Sparkle Q. Snowbeary (ornament)	358
☐ Sparklefrost (bear)	218
☐ Speara Mintly (bear)	218
☐ Spearmint and Peppermint Hollibeary (QVC, bear)	218
☐ Special Edition Whistling Swan (black hills, ¾ size)	22
☐ Speed Poochberg (dog, smooth fur)	271
☐ Speed Poochberg (dog, regular plush)	271
☐ Spencer (bear)	219
☐ Spike T. Lion (lion)	315
☐ Spiro T. Cattington (cat)	259
☐ Spooky Tangaween (cat)	259
☐ Springley T. Hopplebear (bear)	219
☐ Springsley Hopplebuns (QVC, hare)	306
☐ Spruce McMoose (moose)	329
☐ Spunky Boobear (bear)	219
☐ Squeek McSnoozle (ornament)	358
☐ Squeekers McPoppin (QVC, mouse)	318
☐ Squeekie (hare, white)	306
☐ Squeekie (hare, british tan)	306
☐ Squeekie (bear, nutmeg)	219
☐ Squeekie (bear, british tan)	219
☐ Squeeky (lamb)	314
☐ Squirt M. Stringalong (string along)	364
☐ Squirt McSnoozle (QVC, ornament, with Squeek)	358
☐ St. Moosekins (pin)	362
☐ St. Niklas (bear)	219
☐ Stacey B. Beansley (QVC, bear)	219
☐ Stacey Daisydew (bear)	219
☐ Stafford (GCC, bear)	219
☐ Stamford (QVC, hare, a.k.a. Stanford)	306
☐ Stanley R. Hare (hare, old face)	306
☐ Stanley R. Hare (hare, new face)	307
☐ Stanley R. Hare (hare, modern face)	307
☐ Star S. Bangles (QVC, bear)	219
☐ Star Santa (ornament)	38
☐ Star Steadsbeary (Longaberger, cat)	260
☐ Stardust Goodspeed (ornament)	358
☐ Starlight B. Bearsworth (QVC, bear)	219
☐ Starr B. Bearyproud with Sparkle (bear)	219
☐ Starr E. Night (Hallmark, bear)	220
☐ Starry (Art House, bear)	220
☐ Starstruck Santa (ornament)	38
☐ Stella (BBC, ornament)	358
☐ Stella (bear)	220
☐ Stella and Baby Mae (QVC, bear)	220
☐ Stella Goodnight (ornament)	358
☐ Stella Seamstress (bear)	220
☐ Stella Starbear (SFMB, bear)	220
☐ Stellina Hopswell (hare)	307
☐ Stephanie B. Bearyproud (BtoB Website, bear)	220
☐ Stephanie B. Learnin (QVC, bear)	220
☐ Sterling (EVENT, bear, 30")	220
☐ Sterling (bear, 16")	220
☐ Sterling Hopswell (hare)	307
☐ Sterner (Frederick Atkins, bear)	220
☐ Stevenson Q. Bearitage (bear)	220
☐ Stewart MacGregor (dog)	271
☐ Stewart Rarebit (hare)	307

Name	Page
☐ Stilton Mouseberg (mouse)	318
☐ Stonewall Bear (bear)	221
☐ Strawberry (Smuckers, bear)	221
☐ Stretch (bear)	221
☐ Stretch and Skye Longnecker (giraffe)	276
☐ Stryker Scoresalot (bear)	221
☐ Stuart McSnoozle (bear)	221
☐ Stubby McBobble (bear)	221
☐ Stumper A. Potter (bear)	221
☐ Sturbridge Q. Patriot (bear)	221
☐ Sue B. Bearkins (bear)	221
☐ Sue E. Appleton (pig)	336
☐ Sugar Beary Jam with Sugar's Bowl of Berries (f.o.b 2004)	48
☐ Sugar McRind (bear)	221
☐ Sugar Plum Beary (POG, bear)	221
☐ Summer Sanditoes (bear)	221
☐ Sunnie Dae (Longaberger, bear)	222
☐ Sunnie Rae Daisydew with Sprinkle (QVC, bear)	222
☐ Sunny and Sally Berriweather... Plant With Hope (f.o.b 1999)	45
☐ Sunny B. Goodcheer (POG, bear)	222
☐ Sunny B. Hugsworth (QVC, bear)	222
☐ Sunny Buzzbee (J.T.Webb, bear)	222
☐ Susie (Lord & Taylor, bear)	222
☐ Susie B. Bearlove (bear)	222
☐ Susie Dearfriend (GCC, bear)	222
☐ Susie Runsitall (bear)	222
☐ Sutton (bear)	222
☐ Suzella K. Bearington (QVC, bear)	222
☐ Suzie B. Spicebeary Gift Set (Country Clutter, bear)	222
☐ Suzie Purrkins (cat)	260
☐ Suzie Q. Scootenpedal, Lil' Louis & Poochkins (QVC, bear)	223
☐ Suzy Snugglepuss (cat)	260
☐ Sven (bear)	223
☐ Sven B. Frostman (QVC, bear)	223
☐ Swan (minnesota flats, preener)	27
☐ Swan (minnesota flats, sentinel)	27
☐ Swan (minnesota flats, swimmer)	27
☐ Sweetie McLemon (bear)	223
☐ Sweetpea Catberg (cat, old face)	260
☐ Sweetpea Catberg (cat, new face)	260
☐ Swiss C. Mouski (mouse)	318
☐ Sydney (CAN, bear)	223
☐ Sydney G. Bearsmark (Hallmark, bear)	223
☐ Sylvia G. Bearimore (bear)	223
☐ T. Dean Newberger III (GCC, bear)	223
☐ T. F. Wuzziewitch (ornament)	358
☐ T. Fargo Wuzzie (moose)	329
☐ T. Fargo, T. Foster & T. Fuzzball Wuzzie (QVC, moose)	329
☐ T. Farley Wuzzie (bear)	223
☐ T. Farrell Wuzzie (hare)	307
☐ T. Fodder Wuzzie (cow)	266
☐ T. Foley Wuzzie (dog)	271
☐ T. Frampton Wuzzie (bear)	223
☐ T. Frankel Wuzzie (cat)	260
☐ T. Frasier Wuzzie (bear)	223
☐ T. Fulton Wuzzie (bear)	223
☐ T. Hopplewhite (hare)	307
☐ T. Lynne Bearyproud (bear)	224
☐ T.D. Gridiron (bear)	224
☐ T.F. Buzzie Wuzzie (ornament)	358

Name	Page
☐ T.G. Trickster (bear)	224
☐ T.J. Bearheart (QVC, bear)	224
☐ T.K. Bear (CAN, bear)	224
☐ T.L.C. Sparkleheart (bear)	224
☐ Tabbie F. Wuzzie (QVC, ornament, with T. F. Wuzziewitch and Tricky)	358
☐ Tabby F. Wuzzie (cat)	260
☐ Tabitha J. Spellbinder with Midnight Sneakypuss (bear)	224
☐ Tad Northpole (ornament)	358
☐ Taddley (bear)	224
☐ Taddy (frog)	275
☐ Taffy C. Hopplebuns (hare)	307
☐ Taira (QVC, ornament)	359
☐ Taj Tigertail (tiger)	338
☐ Talbot F. Wuzzie (moose)	329
☐ Talia (SLE, hare)	307
☐ Tallulah Baahead (lamb)	314
☐ Tami F. Wuzzie (hare)	307
☐ Tami P. Rally (bear)	224
☐ Tammy (QVC, bear)	224
☐ Tangerine Thumpster (hare)	307
☐ Tanner F. Wuzzie (hare)	307
☐ Tapper F. Wuzzie (hare)	308
☐ Tara & Tia F. Wuzzie (QVC, bear, with Tilly)	224
☐ Tarragon (hare)	308
☐ Tartan Tess (Country Peddler, bear)	224
☐ Tasha B. Frostbeary (bear)	225
☐ Tasha F. Wuzzie (QVC, bear, with Tami and Tatum)	225
☐ Tassel F. Wuzzie (bear)	225
☐ Tatiana (hare)	308
☐ Tatters Beariluved (QVC, bear, with Patches)	225
☐ Tatters T. Hareloom (hare)	308
☐ Tatum F. Wuzzie (bear)	225
☐ Tawny Tweeter with Scarlet (bear)	225
☐ Taylor (Dillards, bear)	225
☐ Taylor Purrski (cat)	260
☐ Taylor Rene (Cracker Barrel, bear)	225
☐ Tea Time Brewin Bubble (f.o.b 2000, pin)	46
☐ Teal (wooden stained group)	31
☐ Ted & Teddy (QVC, bear)	225
☐ Ted Bear (bear)	225
☐ Ted E. Bear (ornament)	39
☐ Teddie Collectibear (Longaberger, bear)	225
☐ Teddy B. Bear (EVENT, bear)	225
☐ Teddy Bauer (QVC, bear)	226
☐ Teddy Beanberger (bear)	226
☐ Teddy Hare (hare, golden tan)	308
☐ Teddy Hare (hare, rust)	308
☐ Teddy Hare (hare, tan)	308
☐ Teddy Hare (hare, white)	308
☐ Teedle F. Wuzzie (pin)	362
☐ Tennyson (cat)	260
☐ Teresa D. Bestlove (bear)	226
☐ Tess (ornament)	359
☐ Tess Autumnbeary (Welcome Home, bear)	226
☐ Tess F. Wuzzie (pin)	362
☐ Tessa (Lord & Taylor, ornament)	359
☐ Tessa Fluffypaws (cat)	260
☐ Tessa, Tilden, Tori & Tessa F. Wuzzie (QVC, bear)	226
☐ Tessie T. Nibblenose (hare)	308
☐ Texanne (Dillards, bear)	226
☐ Thaddeus Von Bruin (bear)	226
☐ Thatcher (bear)	226

BoydsTracker - Alphabetical Index

Name	Page
☐ Thayer (bear)	226
☐ Thea St. Griz & Everett Elfston (QVC, bear)	226
☐ Theo F. Wuzzie (lion)	315
☐ Theodora Maria (QVC, bear)	226
☐ Theodore (bear)	226
☐ Theodore Jr. (bear)	227
☐ Theodore Jr. (SFMB, bear)	227
☐ Theodore M. Bear (QVC, bear)	227
☐ Theodore Sr. (EVENT, bear)	227
☐ Theresa Marie (Elder Beerman, bear)	227
☐ Thinkin (bear)	227
☐ Thisbey F. Wuzzie (bear)	227
☐ Thistle F. Wuzzie (pin)	362
☐ Thom (cat)	260
☐ Thomas F. Wuzzie (pin)	362
☐ Thomas T. Rugsley (QVC, bear)	227
☐ Thomasina F. Wuzzie (ornament)	359
☐ Thomasina Purrkins (QVC, cat, with Suzie)	260
☐ Thor M. Berriman (bear)	227
☐ Thoreau (cat)	261
☐ Thump (hare)	308
☐ Thurston (Clarion Bear Festival, bear)	227
☐ Tia Cherrybeary (bear)	227
☐ Tiana (Frederick Atkins, bear)	227
☐ Tibbles Q. Woodsley (hare)	308
☐ Tibbs (bear)	228
☐ Tibsley Purrsalot (QVC, cat)	261
☐ Tidbit F. Wuzzie (mouse)	318
☐ Tiffany F. Wuzzie (QVC, pin, with Tinger and Teedle)	362
☐ Tigerlily (cat, old face)	261
☐ Tigerlily (cat, new face)	261
☐ Tigger (Disney, tiger, Winter Holiday)	338
☐ Tigger (Disney, tiger, plaid hat)	338
☐ Tigger (Disney, tiger, Costume Party)	338
☐ Tigger (Disney, tiger, Cozy Holiday)	338
☐ Tigger (Disney, tiger, Holiday Caroling)	338
☐ Tigger 1999 (Disney, ornament)	359
☐ Tigger 2000 (Disney, ornament)	359
☐ Tigger Resin and Plush Set (Disney, tiger, Elf)	338
☐ Tillie (bear)	228
☐ Tilly & Toots Ribbit (QVC, ornament, with Lilly)	359
☐ Tilly F. Wuzzie (bear)	228
☐ Tilly Weedsalot (bear)	228
☐ Timmy (Lord & Taylor, ornament)	359
☐ Timothy & Tiny Jodibear (bear)	228
☐ Timothy F. Wuzzie (bear)	228
☐ Timothy T. Beansley (bear)	228
☐ Tina Autumnfest (bear)	228
☐ Tina F. Wuzzie (EVENT, pin)	362
☐ Tina Marie Hopgood (hare)	308
☐ Ting F. Wuzzie (panda)	332
☐ Tinger F. Wuzzie (pin)	362
☐ Tinker F. Wuzzie (pin)	362
☐ Tinkin (bear, stark white)	228
☐ Tinkin II (bear, off-white)	228
☐ Tinman (bear)	228
☐ Tinsel F. Wuzzie (pin)	363
☐ Tiny T. JodiBear (bear)	228
☐ Tiny Tux Waddlewalk (pin)	363
☐ Tipper (hare)	309
☐ Tippy Beartoes (bear)	229
☐ Tippy F. Wuzzie (hare)	309
☐ Tippy P. Hopplebuns (hare)	309
☐ Tipton F. Wuzzie (bear)	229

Name	Page
☐ Toby F. Wuzzie (dog)	272
☐ Toe (bear)	229
☐ Tom, Dick & Harry (QVC, cat)	261
☐ Tomba Bearski (bear)	229
☐ Tommy Kat (cat)	261
☐ Tommy Leafowitz (bear)	229
☐ Tommy Tomato (bear)	229
☐ Tony Stewart #20 (tony stewart, firesuit)	43
☐ Tony Stewart #20 (tony stewart, jacket)	43
☐ Tony Stewart #20 (tony stewart, plush ornament)	43
☐ Tony Stewart #20 (tony stewart, resin ornament)	43
☐ Tony Stewart #20 (tony stewart, sweatshirt)	43
☐ Toodles F. Wuzzie (monkey)	319
☐ Toof Beary (bear)	229
☐ Tootall F. Wuzzie (ornament)	359
☐ Tootie F. Wuzzie (bear)	229
☐ Topper F. Wuzzie (QVC, monkey, with Theo and Tumble)	319
☐ Townsend Q. Bearrister (bear)	229
☐ Travis (Banana Republic, bear, black and gold sweater)	229
☐ Travis (Banana Republic, bear, black and gold sweater)	229
☐ Travis (Banana Republic, bear, dark blue sweater)	229
☐ Travis (Banana Republic, bear, red sweater with tree)	230
☐ Travis B. Bean (bear)	230
☐ Travis B. Bean (bear, variation)	230
☐ Treat F. Wuzzie (bear)	230
☐ Tree Santa (ornament)	39
☐ Tremont (bear)	230
☐ Trevor F. Wuzzie (bear)	230
☐ Trevor T. Elfbeary (bear)	230
☐ Tricky F. Wuzzie (ornament)	359
☐ Trillium (CAN, bear)	230
☐ Trish Boombah (bear)	230
☐ Trissy Teabeary (Longaberger, bear)	230
☐ Tristan (Frederick Atkins, bear)	230
☐ Trixie (hare)	309
☐ Trixie B. Barken (dog)	272
☐ Trixsley (QVC, bear)	230
☐ Trudie Ann Hugsalot (QVC, bear)	231
☐ Trudy F. Wuzzie (ornament)	359
☐ True Luv B. Mine (bear)	231
☐ Truelove F. Wuzzie (ornament)	359
☐ Truffle D. Sweetbeary... So Much Chocolate, So Little Time (f.o.b. 2005)	49
☐ Truffleina & Twila (QVC, pig)	336
☐ Truffles O'Pigg (pig)	337
☐ Truly B. Mine (bear)	231
☐ Truly D. Bestmom (bear)	231
☐ Truman S. Bearington (bear)	231
☐ Trundle B. Bear (bear)	231
☐ Tucker Applesmith (GCC, bear)	231
☐ Tucker F. Wuzzie (pin)	363
☐ Tucker P. Woofensniff (dog)	272
☐ Tulip (SLE, hare)	309
☐ Tulla B. Bearfoot (Hallmark, bear)	231
☐ Tumble F. Wuzzie (bear)	231
☐ Tundra Northpole (bear)	231
☐ Turner F. Wuzzie (cat)	261
☐ Turner with Kris (GCC, bear)	231
☐ Tutti F. Sugarcone (bear)	231

Name	Page
Tuttle F. Wuzzie (ornament)	360
Tutu (lamb)	314
Tutu (hare)	309
Tutu (bear)	232
Tutu F. Wuzzie (elephant)	274
Tuxie Waddlewalk (penguin)	332
Twaddle F. Wuzzie (ornament)	360
Twas F. Wuzzie (bear)	232
Tweedle & Opie Waddlewalk (QVC, penguin, with Tuxie)	332
Tweedle F. Wuzzie (ornament)	360
Tweek McSnoozle (ornament)	360
Twickenham F. Wuzzie (ornament)	360
Twiddle F. Wuzzie (ornament)	360
Twigley Hopsalot (hare)	309
Twila Higgenthorpe (bear)	232
Twila Twinkletoes (ornament)	360
Twilight F. Wuzzie (bear)	232
Twink L. Starbeary (bear)	232
Twinkle B. Beansley (QVC, bear)	232
Twinkle Bear (Macy's East, bear)	232
Twinkle Crystalfrost (Country Clutter, ornament)	360
Twinkle F. Wuzzie (pin)	363
Twinkles Starbeary (Longaberger, bear)	232
Twinksley (QVC, ornament)	360
Twizzle F. Wuzzie (bear)	232
Tylar F. Wuzzie (bear)	232
Tyler (Dillards, bear)	232
Tyler Glorybear (bear)	232
Tyler Summerfield (bear)	233
Tyler T. Bear (bear)	233
Tyrone F. Wuzzie (bear)	233
U.B. Fuzzyfleece (lamb)	314
U.B. Mine with Heart (QVC, bear)	233
Uncle Ben Bearington (bear)	233
Uncle Edward O'Beary (GCC, bear)	233
Uncle Elliot (f.o.b 1996, pin)	44
Uncle Elliot...The Head Bean Wants You (f.o.b 1996)	44
Uncle Gus & Honeybunch (QVC, bear)	233
Uncle Sam (bear)	233
Uncle Zeb & Cousin Minnow (QVC, bear)	233
Union T. Jack Bear (United Kingdom, bear)	233
Ursa (bear)	233
Ursula Berriman (QVC, bear)	233
Valentina B. Bearhugs (SFMB, bear)	234
Valentina with Evalina, Caterina, & Michelina (QVC, bear)	234
Valentino (bear)	234
Valerie (Ideation, bear)	234
Valerie B. Bearhugs (bear)	234
Vance Bearsworth (bear)	234
Vanessa D. LaPinne (hare)	309
Vanessa Fluffypaws (SFMB, cat)	261
Vanessa R. Angel (Starlight, bear)	234
Vanessa V. Fluffypaws (cat)	261
Vanna Hopkins (hare)	309
Varsity Bear (bear, 16")	234
Varsity Bear (bear, 8")	234
Velma Q. Berriweather (f.o.b 1996)	44
Velma Q. Berriweather...The Cookie Queen (f.o.b 1996)	44
Venus (ornament)	360
Venus (Elder Beerman, ornament)	360
Vera W. Bearsworth (bear)	234

Name	Page
Verdeia (Frederick Atkins, bear)	234
Vermooth (QVC, moose, with Margarita)	329
Vernette (Frederick Atkins, bear)	234
Veronica (hare)	309
Veronica Angelbright (tree topper)	366
Veronica Bearskov (Platinum Paw, bear)	235
Veronica Laflame (QVC, bear)	235
Veronica Marie Bearington (QVC, bear)	235
Victoria (hare)	309
Victoria Bearybright (Yankee Candle, bear)	235
Victoria L. Plumbeary (bear)	235
Victoria Lynn Primsley (bear)	235
Vincent (bear)	235
Viola Flutterby (QVC, bear)	235
Viola Magillacuddy (gorilla)	276
Violet Dubois (hare)	309
Violet Ewe (lamb)	314
Violet Flowerflit (ornament)	360
Virginia Bluebell (SFMB, hare)	310
Virginia Dobbsey (Coach House Gifts, bear)	235
Virginia Thistlebeary (Show Specials, bear)	235
Vivian Q. Dickens (bear)	235
Wabbit McVeggie (hare)	310
Waddlekins (bear)	235
Wade N. Sanditoes with Buster the Crab (bear)	236
Waitsfield (GCC, bear)	236
Waldo Bearsworth (bear)	236
Walker (dog)	272
Walking Bunny (ornament, stand-up)	39
Wally B. Beartoes (bear)	236
Wally Fishbreath (walrus)	339
Walpole (bear, old face)	236
Walpole (bear, new face)	236
Walter Q. Fuzzberg (cat)	261
Walter, Wayne and Wilbert Tinkerbeary (QVC, bear)	236
Walton (bear)	236
Wanna B. Ladybug (bear)	236
Wannabee Ewe Too (lamb)	314
Warner Von Bruin (bear)	236
Warren (bear)	236
(The) Watermelon Stand (fruit stand)	32
Watson (bear)	236
Wayfer North (bear)	237
Wayne B. Bear (CAN, bear)	237
Weaver Bearyproud (Longaberger, bear)	237
Weaver Berrybrook (bear)	237
Webb Q. Yachtley (duck)	273
Webber Vanguard (bear)	237
Webster Hopplebuns (hare)	310
Webster T. Bearsworth (bear)	237
Wedgewood J. Hopgood (hare)	310
Weezie Flitenfly (ornament)	361
Wellington (bear)	237
Wendy S. Appleby & Anna Mae (SLE, bear)	237
Wendy Weaver (Longaberger, bear, a.k.a. Weaver Girl)	237
Werner Von Bruin (bear)	237
Wesley Bearimore (bear)	237
Wesley, Willoughby & Woodward (QVC, bear)	237
Westin Woodsley (QVC, bear)	238
Wheatley B. Barker (dog)	272
Wheaton Flatski (bear)	238
Whihley with Winkle & Pip (QVC, bear)	238
Whilley Frostifeet (bear)	238

Name	Page
☐ Whimsie T. Faeriebear (QVC, bear)	238
☐ Whiskers P. Tweeter with B.B. (cat)	261
☐ Whitaker A. Bruin (bear)	238
☐ White Bean Bear (bear)	238
☐ Whitefurd Felinsky (cat)	261
☐ Whitley B. Beariluved (QVC, bear)	238
☐ Whitney (hare)	310
☐ Whittington P. Bearsford (bear)	238
☐ Wicked Witch of the West (bear)	238
☐ Wilbur Bearington (bear)	238
☐ Wilby Beardeaux (bear)	238
☐ Wilcox J. Beansford (bear)	239
☐ Wiley P. Chatsworth (puppet)	364
☐ Wilhelm van Bruin (hare)	310
☐ Wilhelmina Q. Bearsworth (QVC, bear)	239
☐ Will (Dillards, bear)	239
☐ Willa Bruin (bear)	239
☐ William (CAN, bear)	239
☐ William Henry Bearington (QVC, bear)	239
☐ William P. (bear)	239
☐ Willie B. Bacon (pig)	337
☐ Willie B. Chillymitts (ornament)	361
☐ Willie B. Mouseking (POG, mouse)	318
☐ Willie B. Porkroast (BBC, pig)	337
☐ Willie S. Hydrant IV (ornament)	361
☐ Willie Waddlewalk (penguin)	332
☐ Willmar Flatski (bear)	239
☐ Wilma & Gracey Bearfriends (QVC, bear)	239
☐ Wilson (bear, old face)	239
☐ Wilson (bear, new face)	239
☐ Wilson with Boat (QVC, bear)	239
☐ Wilson with Pie (QVC, bear)	240
☐ Wilt Stiltwalker (giraffe)	276
☐ Windberg (moose)	329
☐ Windsor & Sarasota (QVC, bear)	240
☐ Winifred (SLE, bear)	240
☐ Winifred Witebred (bear)	240
☐ Wink (puppet)	364
☐ Winkie II (bear)	240
☐ Winkin (bear)	240
☐ Winkle B. Bumbles (ornament)	361
☐ Winnie II (bear)	240
☐ Winnie II (SFMB, bear)	240
☐ Winnie Stillwithus (bear)	240
☐ Winnie Stillwithus (SFMB, bear)	240
☐ Winnie Wuzzwhite (bear)	240
☐ Winnie Wuzzwhite (SFMB, bear)	240
☐ Winny Wimbleton (bear)	241
☐ Winstead & Pensacola (QVC, bear)	241
☐ Winstead P. Bear (bear)	241
☐ Winston B. Bean (bear, early smooth fur)	241
☐ Winston B. Bean (bear, old face)	241
☐ Winston B. Bean (bear, new face)	241
☐ Winter Mallard (wooden stained group)	31
☐ Winter Mallard (traditional group)	29
☐ Winter Mintly (bear)	241
☐ Winter Redhead (traditional group, drake)	29
☐ Wishley B. Bunnybear (QVC, bear)	241
☐ Witch-A-Ma-Call-It (bear)	241
☐ Witchy-Boo (bear)	241
☐ Wixie (hare)	310
☐ Wixie Lee Hackett (bear)	241
☐ Wood Duck (traditional group, sentinel)	29
☐ Wood Duck (traditional group, sleeper)	29
☐ Wood Duck (minnesota flats, preener)	27
☐ Wood Duck (minnesota flats, sentinel)	27

Name	Page
☐ Wood Duck (minnesota flats, swimmer)	27
☐ Wooden Angel Bear (ornament)	39
☐ Wooden Momma Cat (ornament)	39
☐ Wooden Momma Rabbit (ornament)	39
☐ Wooden Poppa Cat (ornament)	39
☐ Wooden Poppa Rabbit (ornament)	39
☐ Woodrow T. Bearington (bear)	241
☐ Woodruff K. Bearsford (bear)	242
☐ Woody Puttsalot (Longaberger, bear)	242
☐ Wookie Snickelfritz (bear)	242
☐ Woolfie P. Poorpooch (QVC, dog)	272
☐ Worthington Fitzbruin (bear)	242
☐ Wuvey B. Bear (bear)	242
☐ Xin Fu Wongbruin (QVC, panda)	332
☐ Yankee & Doodle McBear (QVC, bear)	242
☐ Yankee Doodle Doo (QVC, rooster)	337
☐ Yardley Fitzhampton (bear)	242
☐ Yeager Bearington (bear)	242
☐ Yeti A. Bominable (bear)	242
☐ Ying & Yang Bearington (QVC, ornament)	361
☐ Yippeeyo Beanster (QVC, bear)	242
☐ Yogi (bear)	242
☐ Yolanda Panda (QVC, panda)	332
☐ Yolanda Panda (panda)	332
☐ York (bear)	242
☐ You and Me (QVC, bear)	243
☐ Yowley Alleyruckus (cat)	262
☐ Yu'Kon B. Bear (CAN, bear)	243
☐ Yvette Dubeary (bear)	243
☐ Yvonne & Yvette (QVC, bear)	243
☐ Zachariah Alleyruckus (cat)	262
☐ Zack (QVC, lion)	315
☐ Zap Catberg (cat)	262
☐ Zazu (bear)	243
☐ Zeiggy and Roary Tigertooth (tiger)	339
☐ Zelda Catberg (cat)	262
☐ Zelda Fitzhare (hare)	310
☐ Zelda Fitzhare (SFMB, hare)	310
☐ Zelda Z. Witchypuss (cat)	262
☐ Zelma G. Berriweather (f.o.b 1998)	45
☐ Zenus W. Grimilkin (cat, smooth fur)	262
☐ Zenus W. Grimilkin (cat, regular plush)	262
☐ Zephyr Goodnight (ornament)	361
☐ Ziggy Bear (bear)	243
☐ Zinnia (ornament)	361
☐ Zinny Beardeaux (bear)	243
☐ Zip Catberg (cat)	262
☐ Zipp Angelwish (ornament)	361
☐ Zoe R. Grimilkin (cat)	262
☐ Zoe R. Grimilkin (QVC, cat)	262
☐ Zoom Catberg (cat)	262
☐ Zsa-Zsa Yippsalot (dog)	272
☐ Zwick (Dillards, bear)	243

BoydsTracker
Exclusive Index and Checklist
Items are listed in alphabetical order followed by page number.

Boyds Exclusives

Boyds Bear Country
- ☐ Ann I. Bearsary (bear) 57
- ☐ B.B. Country Bear (bear) 64
- ☐ Bumpkin…Country Bear (bear) 84
- ☐ C.C. Peeker (ornament) .344
- ☐ Dixon (bear) 103
- ☐ Dolly M. Bearsevelt (bear) 104
- ☐ Frazier (bear) 119
- ☐ G.B. Gingerpeeker (ornament, 10") 348
- ☐ Gettysbear (bear) 123
- ☐ Henita P. Cooper (hen) .310
- ☐ Little Twink (bear) 163
- ☐ Manley Strutencrow (rooster) 337
- ☐ Mason (bear) 172
- ☐ Muddles T. Moxley (moose) 326
- ☐ Ralph McFarmin (bear) .204
- ☐ Roma Applesmith (bear) 206
- ☐ Silvia Jubilee (bear) 215
- ☐ Stella (ornament) 358
- ☐ Willie B. Porkroast (pig) .337

Boyds Family Reunion
- ☐ Bear Lee Survivedit (bear) 70

BoydsBiz.com
- ☐ Rusty B. Autumnfest (bear) 209

BtoB Website
- ☐ Lexi Burrbruin (bear) 160
- ☐ Shara Sugarcone (bear) 214
- ☐ Stephanie B. Bearyproud (bear) 220

Canadian Exclusive
- ☐ Agnes MacBear (bear) 52
- ☐ Al'Berta B. Bear (bear) 53
- ☐ AP Gold Bear (bear) 59
- ☐ Betty Fisher (bear) 74
- ☐ Big Pig, Little Pig (pig) 333
- ☐ Brian (bear) 80
- ☐ Cindy (bear) 93
- ☐ Ewell Manitoba Mooselman (bear) 115
- ☐ GP Gold Bear (bear) 126
- ☐ Jamie (bear) 145
- ☐ Jean (bear) 145
- ☐ Joe (bear) 148
- ☐ John (bear) 148
- ☐ Lester (bear) 160
- ☐ Mary B. Mistletoe (bear) 171
- ☐ Molly R. Mistletoe (bear) 179
- ☐ Ms. Bee Beezley (bear) 186
- ☐ Pierre (bear) 199
- ☐ Robyn (bear) 205
- ☐ S.K. (bear) 210
- ☐ Sarah (bear) 212
- ☐ Sarah Jane (bear) 212
- ☐ Sydney (bear) 223
- ☐ T.K. Bear (bear) 224
- ☐ Trillium (bear) 230
- ☐ Wayne B. Bear (bear) 237
- ☐ William (bear) 239
- ☐ Yu'Kon B. Bear (bear) 243

Clarion Bear Festival
- ☐ Americus P. Bearsley (bear) 56
- ☐ Bradie B. Bearsley (bear) 78
- ☐ Thurston (bear) 227

Holiday or Retailer Special Event
- ☐ Elder with Newton (bear) 110
- ☐ Friendship Bear Pair (bear) 120
- ☐ Jack B. Twinkletune (bear) 143
- ☐ Lizzie (pin) 362
- ☐ Lizzie Wishkabibble (bear) 163
- ☐ Patriotic Bailey (bear) 196
- ☐ Sterling (bear, 30") 220
- ☐ Teddy B. Bear (bear) 225
- ☐ Theodore Sr. (bear) 227
- ☐ Tina F. Wuzzie (pin) 362

Gold Paw
- ☐ Leanne Bearsdale (bear) 159

Paw Dealer
- ☐ Janet C. Daisydew (bear) 145
- ☐ Kristen T. Beansley (bear) 156
- ☐ Letti McVeggie (bear) 160
- ☐ Lindsley Ladybug (bear) 162
- ☐ Nellie T. Bearypatch (bear) 189

Platinum Paw
- ☐ Alicia Bearsley (bear) 54
- ☐ Clark II (bear) 94
- ☐ Jeannie S. Berriman (bear) 146
- ☐ Merry Beary (bear) 175
- ☐ Veronica Bearskov (bear) 235

Rosemont
- ☐ Rosemont Bear (bear) .207

Show Specials
- ☐ Auntie Autumn and Lil' Harvey (bear) 62
- ☐ (The) Bearsleys (bear) 71
- ☐ Betty Lou, Clementine & Josie McCoy (bear) 74
- ☐ Carly Bearworth (bear) 88
- ☐ Dorinda & Donna (bear) 104
- ☐ Fawn W. Fallsbeary (bear) 116
- ☐ George Berriman (bear) 123
- ☐ Huck, Mandy, & Zack (bear) 139
- ☐ Jordan T. Fallsbeary (bear) 149
- ☐ Kaytie & Mattie with R.J. (bear) 153
- ☐ Petula P. Fallsbeary (bear) 198
- ☐ Virginia Thistlebeary (bear) 235

Special Limited Edition
- ☐ Alpine (hare) 277
- ☐ Anissa (hare) 278
- ☐ Annette Bearberg (ornament) 341
- ☐ Barrett (bear) 68
- ☐ Beauregard (bear) 71
- ☐ Betty Jane (pig) 333
- ☐ Boo-Boo (bear) 78
- ☐ Braden (lion) 314
- ☐ Brianne (lamb) 312
- ☐ Bronson (bear) 81
- ☐ Cara Sue (bear) 87

☐ Casper Cat O'Lantern (cat) 246
☐ Cass (bear) 89
☐ Chantanay (hare) 282
☐ Cher Fussberg (cat) 247
☐ Collette (bear) 96
☐ Darby (bear) 99
☐ Dean B. Bearberg (bear) 100
☐ Dion Bearberg (bear) 103
☐ Douglas (bear) 105
☐ Duncan (bear) 105
☐ Dutch (hare) 285
☐ Ellie (hare) 286
☐ Estelle (hare) 288
☐ Fletcher (hare) 289
☐ Floradora (hare) 289
☐ Frankie Bearberg (bear) .119
☐ Geneva (bear) 122
☐ Gettie Mountberg (bear) 123
☐ Gourdie Frightmare (bear) 126
☐ Grayling (hare) 290
☐ Gunnar (bear) 129
☐ Honeybee Cottontail (hare) 292
☐ Jan B. Bearberg (bear) .145
☐ Jebel Cottontail (hare) 293
☐ Katie (pig) 334
☐ Kyle (bear) 156
☐ Leslie G Catberg (cat) 253
☐ Madison (bear) 167
☐ Mallory (hare) 298
☐ Marilyn (bear) 169
☐ Mr. BoJingles (bear) 183
☐ Mrs. Mother May I (bear) 185
☐ Nana Purrington & Gouda (cat) 255
☐ Nicholas (bear) 190
☐ Parker (hare) 302
☐ Penelope (hare) 303
☐ Poppa Ted Truckingham (bear) 201
☐ Ragna (bear) 203
☐ Rockie Mountberg (bear) 205
☐ Rodney (bear) 206
☐ Rudolph (bear) 208
☐ Scotch (bear) 213
☐ Smokie Mountberg (bear) 217
☐ Talia (hare) 307
☐ Tulip (hare) 309
☐ Wendy S. Appleby & Anna Mae (bear) 237
☐ Winifred (bear) 240

Starlight
☐ Alisa R. Angel (bear) 54
☐ Ashlee R. Angel (bear) 60
☐ Jesselyn R. Angel (bear) 147
☐ Vanessa R. Angel (bear) 234

United Kingdom
☐ Union T. Jack Bear (bear) 233

York Fair
☐ Adam (bear) 51
☐ Brittney (bear) 81

Catalog Exclusives
Gift Creation Concepts
☐ Alexis Bearinsky (bear) 54
☐ Alyssa M. Punkinbeary   (bear) 55
☐ Andrea Jane (bear) 56
☐ Angel (bear) 57
☐ Annabella (bear) 58

☐ Ardyth (ornament) 341
☐ Aspen P. Ninelives (cat) .245
☐ Aubrey (bear) 61
☐ Blossom Monarch (bear) .77
☐ Brandon A. Bearski (bear) 79
☐ Bunker Bedlington (bear) .84
☐ Carly Anna   (ornament) .345
☐ Casimir B. Bean (bear) 88
☐ Constance Bearyfine (bear) 96
☐ Corrine Patchbeary (bear) 97
☐ Cranston (bear) 98
☐ Dana Marie Bearsley (bear) 99
☐ Denise Needsmoreshoes (bear) 101
☐ Destiny Angelbear (bear) 102
☐ Devon (bear) 102
☐ Diane Bearyfriend (bear) 102
☐ Drema Yawnsalot (bear) 105
☐ Edward Q. Bearston & Apopka (bear) 109
☐ Engelbert Q. Elfberg (bear) 113
☐ Evergreen Elfston (ornament) 347
☐ Gannon Bear (bear) 121
☐ Gracie C. Burrbruin   (bear) 127
☐ Guilford (bear) 129
☐ Havarti Chrismouse (mouse) 317
☐ Ingred S. Witebred (bear) 141
☐ Isabel Grizbeard (bear) .142
☐ Kimberlyn Woodsbeary (cat) 252
☐ Kortney Kringlebeary   (bear) 155
☐ Lady Flora Monarch (bear) 157
☐ Letitia T. Bearington (bear) 160
☐ Libby Bearyproud (bear) 161
☐ Mallory Witebruin (bear) 168
☐ Manfred von Merrymoose (moose) 323
☐ Marjorie Ellen Bearsley (bear) 170
☐ Mary Alice Weedsalot (bear) 171
☐ Mattie C. Bearsley (bear) 173
☐ Maxine T. Bearsley (bear) 173
☐ McCormic T. Moosleton (moose) 324
☐ Mimi & Arlene (bear) 176
☐ Mindy Witebruin (bear) .177
☐ Miss Nicole Plumbeary (bear) 178
☐ Moe Munchencrunch (moose) 325
☐ Momma McGoldberg & Cissy (bear) 181
☐ Mountie Moosletoe   (moose) 326
☐ Mr. Barnum (bear) 182
☐ Mrs. Beariwell (bear) 185
☐ Natalie Plumbeary (bear) 188
☐ Oliver (bear) 192
☐ Olivia Beariluved   (bear) 192
☐ Ottie Wilhelmina (bear) .194
☐ Petey von Pupp (dog) 270
☐ Princess Nicole Bearyspoiled (bear) 201
☐ Rhoda (bear) 205
☐ Rudy Z. Mooseburg (bear) 208
☐ Sammy Sue   (ornament) 357
☐ Snuggems B. Joy (bear) 218
☐ Sophie Jane Gingerbeary (bear) 218
☐ Stafford (bear) 219
☐ Susie Dearfriend (bear) .222
☐ T. Dean Newberger III (bear) 223
☐ Tucker Applesmith (bear) 231
☐ Turner with Kris (bear) 231
☐ Uncle Edward O'Beary (bear) 233
☐ Waitsfield (bear) 236

Ideation
☐ Chelci Robear (bear) 91

☐ Guinella (bear) 129
☐ Joyelle (bear) 150
☐ LaBelle (bear) 157
☐ Little Larson (bear) 163
☐ Roberto (bear) 205
☐ Valerie (bear) 234

Parade of Gifts
☐ Abby Grace (bear) 50
☐ Anna Belle (bear) 58
☐ Bee Mihoney (bear) 72
☐ Briana Bearlov (bear) 80
☐ Butterfly Kisses & Bear Hugs (bear) 84
☐ Gabriella (bear) 121
☐ Georgie (bear) 123
☐ Honey B. Bean (bear) .137
☐ Honey B. Elfberg (bear) 137
☐ Honey B. Growin (bear) 137
☐ Little Orchard Annie (bear) 163
☐ Mae I. Loveya (bear) 167
☐ Margaret Hollybeary (bear) 168
☐ Prince Harry B. Nutcracker (bear) 201
☐ Sara Beth (bear) 212
☐ Shasta Daisydew (bear) 214
☐ Sugar Plum Beary   (bear) 221
☐ Sunny B. Goodcheer (bear) 222
☐ Willie B. Mouseking (mouse) 318

Syndicated Catalog Groups
☐ Ava Marie (bear) 63
☐ Bobbi Frostbeary (bear) 77
☐ Casey Renee (bear) 88
☐ Kristi & Kaylie Marie (bear) 156
☐ Miranda Hollybeary (bear) 177
☐ Morgan B. Thumblover (bear) 182
☐ Samantha Marie & Brady (bear) 211
☐ Sissy Bearyfriend (bear) 216

QVC Exclusives
Quality, Value, Convenience
☐ 20th Anniversary Bear (bear) 50
☐ Abdul Duneworthy (camel) 244
☐ Aberdeen (bear) 50
☐ Abigail A. Beanster (bear) 51
☐ Abigail and Beryl Bramblebeary (bear) 51
☐ Ace Swingster (monkey) 318
☐ Adelaide & Aggie (cow) 263
☐ Agatha B. Bearington (bear) 52
☐ Albin and Tootie Whizzalong (bear) 53
☐ Aleesha Bearlet (bear) .53
☐ Alexander M. Pattington (bear) 53
☐ Alexandra and Belle (bear) 53
☐ Alley McCat (cat) 245
☐ Allison B. Beansley (bear) 55
☐ Allison Bearburg (bear) .55
☐ Alvin D. Elf (ornament) 340
☐ Amber Glorybear (bear) 55
☐ Ambrose P. Hydrant III (dog) 266
☐ Ambrosia Angelwish   (ornament) 340
☐ Amelia P. Quignapple (bear) 56
☐ Americana Angelbear (bear) 56
☐ Amos T. Woodsley (bear) 56
☐ Amy Lynn Flutterfoot (bear) 56
☐ Anais Angelwish (tree topper) 364
☐ Anastasia (bear) 56
☐ Angela (ornament) 341
☐ Angeline (bear) 57
☐ Anita Lotsalove with Basket (bear) 57

☐ Anna Eleanor Bearington (bear) 58
☐ Annabelle Z. Witebred (bear) 58
☐ Annie & Jennifer Hopkins (hare) 279
☐ Arcturus (ornament, with Aurora Goodnight) 341
☐ Aria & Astra Angelwish (ornament) 341
☐ Ariel (ornament) 341
☐ Aubry T. Autumnfest with Buckeye (bear) 61
☐ Aunt Mattie MacDolittle (bear) 62
☐ Auntie Edna with Flora & Tillie (bear) 62
☐ Auntie Esther and Theona J Doolittle (bear) 63
☐ Auntie Marguerite, Honeybruin, Beesley
    Honeybruin, and Topaz F. Wuzzie
    (bear) 63
☐ Auriella Angelfrost (tree topper) 365
☐ Autumn & Fallston (bear) 63
☐ Azalea & Jordan Rosebeary (bear) 64
☐ Azania Sparklefrost (tree topper) 365
☐ Azure Lee, Ginger. & Sunbeam P.
    Snickelfritz (bear) 64
☐ B.A. Bigfoot (bear) 64
☐ B.B. Bugsley with Lil' Lady Bugsley (bear) 64
☐ B.W. Poochley (dog) 267
☐ Baby Bailey 1999 & 2000 (ornament) 343
☐ Bailey (bear, shiny purple dress) 66
☐ Bailey (bear, lilac dress) .66
☐ Bailey with Squiggles (bear) 67
☐ Barret, Belinda & Berg Blizzard (ornament) 343
☐ Barston Q. Growler (bear) 69
☐ Bartley & Wilbur (dog) .267
☐ Beauregard (bear) 71
☐ Bebe Z. Beezley with Bizzybee (bear) 71
☐ Becca & Bethany Angelwish (ornament) 343
☐ Becky Sue, Bobbi Jo & Mary Lou (ornament) . . .343
☐ Beesley Buzzoff (bear) 72
☐ Beezer B. Goodlebear (bear) 72
☐ Benjamin F. Almanac
    (bear, with Caroline Mayflower) 72
☐ Bernadette B. Bearington (bear) 73
☐ Bernadette Bearbuck (bear) 73
☐ Betsey B. Hoofenudder (cow) 264
☐ Betsey Lou Bearyproud (bear) 74
☐ Betsy B. Bearyproud (bear) 74
☐ Betty Lou (bear) 74
☐ Bill (bear) 75
☐ Bingham (bear) 75
☐ Bingles (bear) 76
☐ Bixby B. Bear (bear) 76
☐ Blackstone (bear, big eyes) 76
☐ Blake & Ogden Wordsworth
    (cat, with Dickens) 245
☐ Blink, Hush & Shush (bear) 76
☐ Blossom DuBearvoire (bear) 77
☐ Bobbie Sue Maybeary (bear, with Betty Jane) . . .77
☐ Bobble B. Beansford (bear) 77
☐ Boo B. Bear (bear) 78
☐ Brambley B. Bigfoot (bear) 79
☐ Brandie & Madeira (bear) 79
☐ Brantley B. Beansley (bear) 79
☐ Brendon B. Beanster (bear) 79
☐ Brewster McRooster (bear) 80
☐ Brianna Angelbless (bear) 80
☐ Brianna Q. Yachtley with Mr. Waddlesworth
    (bear) 80
☐ Bridgette & Suzanne Dubeary (bear) 81
☐ Brighton, Salisbury & Somerset (bear) 81
☐ Brinsley Bruin (bear) 81
☐ Brinton S. Beansford (bear) 81

- Brumley (bear) 82
- Bruno Bedlington (bear) 82
- Bryson Beansley (bear) 82
- Buchanan J Bearington (bear) 82
- Buckley (bear) 83
- Buford B. (bear) 83
- Bumbles S. Beezley (bear) 84
- Burwell Busheytail with Bud (raccoon) 337
- Buxton B. Beansley (bear) 84
- C. Fallin' Leafowitz (bear) 85
- C.B. (bear) 85
- C.C. Beansley (bear) 85
- C.Z. Sparklefrost Sparkling (bear) 86
- Caesar Q. & Cosmo Hydrant (dog) 267
- Cameron G. & Deacon T. Bearsford
  (bear, with Jameson) 87
- Candy (ornament) 344
- Caramel, Meringue, Molasses Bearenburg
  (bear) 87
- Carina T. McBeansley with Bah-Bah (bear) 87
- Caroline (bear) 88
- Carrie B. Beansley (bear) 88
- Cassandra Purrsley (cat) 246
- Cassidy (bear) 89
- Ceylon Pekoe (bear) 90
- Chadwick (bear, with Bosley) 90
- Chanceford Q. Beansley (bear) 90
- Charlotte Tewkysbeary with Hobbes (bear) 91
- Chelsea & Cornwell
  (bear, with Bristol B. Windsor) 91
- Chris B. Trickpuss (cat) 247
- Christmas Bear (bear) 92
- Christopher T. Beansley (bear) 92
- Cimmaron (bear) 93
- Cinnamon P. Pussytoes (cat) 247
- Clara B. Bearcountry (bear) 94
- Clark (bear) 94
- Claude Q. Catberg (cat) 247
- Claudette Tatterpuss (cat) 247
- Claudia & Rowena P. Pussytoes (cat) 247
- Claudine P. Pussyfoot (cat) 248
- Claudius B. Bean (bear) 94
- Cleo P. Pussytoes (cat) 248
- Clovis Hoofheifer & Ferdinand Bullsworth
  (cow) 264
- Colleen (bear) 96
- Collin Q. Bearsworth (bear) 96
- Comfy B. Bear (bear) 96
- Corky (dog, with Clancy G. Hydrant, Jr.) ... 268
- Courtney (bear, burgundy plaid) 97
- Crackers with Roquefort (cat) 248
- Creme Bearleigh (bear) 98
- Cromwell (bear) 98
- Cubby T. Bearington (bear) 98
- Cynthia Berrijam (bear) 98
- Dana & Desiree DeBearvoire (bear) 99
- Dandy B. Doodlebear (bear) 99
- Daniel & Darbey Bearimore (bear) 99
- Danielle & Elizabieta de Bearvoire (bear) ... 99
- Darby & Drew Polartrek
  (ornament, with Douglas) 346
- Daria & Dickens Jodibear (bear) 100
- Darla May & Ann Marie (bear) 100
- Deborah Sue Bearington (bear) 100
- Delilah Higgenthorpe (bear, with Twila) 101
- Delmarva V. Crackenpot (bear) 101
- Delta (bear) 101

- Diane D. Beansford and Topsey F. Wuzzie
  (bear) 102
- Dingles (bear) 103
- Dolly & Jed (ornament) 346
- Dolly M. Bearington (bear) 104
- Doodle B. Beanster (bear) 104
- Doonuttin Buckshot (bear) 104
- Dugan B. Beansley (bear) 105
- Edam & Gouda (mouse) 317
- Edith & James Henry Maybeary (bear) 107
- Edward & Binkie LE Set (bear) 109
- Elise Frostbeary (bear) 110
- Elisia P. Bearypoppin with Ross & Darrell
  (bear) 110
- Elmo Q. Elfbeary LE Set (bear) 111
- Elmore Elf Bear (bear) 111
- Elton (bear) 112
- Emily Babbit (hare, Spring 1998 squiggles
  on hat) 287
- Emma Jean Bearsworth & Lil' Pusskins (bear) .. 112
- Emma Rose (hare) 288
- Eubie Lovedalot (bear) 114
- Evan & Sheldon Bearchild (bear) 115
- Evangeline (ornament) 347
- Fannie, Farrah & Flora (ornament) 348
- Father Kristmas Bear & Northwind P. Bear
  (bear) 116
- Felicity Merrybeary (bear) 116
- Fenton & Forrest Snowbeary
  (ornament, with Silverton) 348
- Ferguson Q. Fuzzface (bear) 117
- Fern Woodsbeary, the Woodland Guardian
  with Resin (bear) 117
- Fillmore (bear) 117
- Flopsie, Mopsie & Moxie Angelbuns
  (ornament) 348
- Florence B. Bearhugs (bear) 118
- Florimae Bearley (bear) 118
- Francine deBearvoire (bear) 119
- Fred Farfle (dog) 268
- Fritzle Farklefrost with Frostley (bear) 120
- Frostina with Kristy (bear) 120
- Fuzzy Jake Cattington (cat) 250
- G. Wilbur McSwine (pig) 333
- G.W. Bearyproud (bear) 121
- Gabriella Angelfaith (bear) 121
- Gardener B . Buzzoff (bear) 121
- Gareth (bear, with Glynnis) 121
- Garnet & Sapphire (bear) 122
- Garret T. Woodsbeary (bear) 122
- Gary B. Bean (bear) 122
- Genevieve Rose Frostbeary
  with Blizz, Maddie, and Polaris
  (bear) 122
- George (bear) 122
- George & Martha Jodibear (bear) 123
- George & Thomas Bearington (bear) 123
- George W. Bearington (bear) 123
- Geraldine & Sylvester (bear) 123
- Gideon (bear) 124
- Gimmie A. Hugster (bear) 124
- Ginger P. Purrski (cat) 250
- Girdwood & Juneau (bear) 124
- Giseppi Renaldi (monkey) 319
- Gladys Tidings (bear) 124
- Gloria and Van (bear) 125
- Glorianna Angelbear (tree topper) 365

- ☐ Gomer P. Hugsley (bear) 126
- ☐ Goober Greenwood (bear) 126
- ☐ Grandma Babbit (hare) 290
- ☐ Grandma Henrietta & Lizzie (bear) 128
- ☐ Grandmother Beatrice B. Bearhugs, Baileyanne Bearhugs & Tedley F. Wuzzie (bear) 128
- ☐ Grannie Lovedalot (bear) 128
- ☐ Granny Smith and Gala Bear (bear) 128
- ☐ Gregory G. Bruin (bear) 128
- ☐ Grosvenor Catberg (cat) 251
- ☐ Grovsnor S. Grizbear (bear) 129
- ☐ Guildford Q. Bearrister (bear) 129
- ☐ Guinevieve (bear) 129
- ☐ Guthrie and Gibbley (dog) 269
- ☐ Guthrie P. Mussy (bear) 130
- ☐ Gwennora (bear) 130
- ☐ Hannah, Henry, Herbie (bear) 131
- ☐ Hannah, Ursula, Greta, & Sarabeth (bear) 131
- ☐ Harvey (hare) 291
- ☐ Heathcliff (bear) 133
- ☐ Hedda (bear) 134
- ☐ Hefty B. Bear (bear) 134
- ☐ Heidi Thistlebeary (bear, with Bethany Thistlebeary) 134
- ☐ Herbert Harrison McBearsley (bear) 135
- ☐ Herman B. Bearsdale (bear) 135
- ☐ Hippity & Hoppity Thumpster (hare) 292
- ☐ Hiram Q. Hamhock (bear) 136
- ☐ Hobson Q. Hugmeister (bear) 136
- ☐ Hollie and Ivy (bear) 136
- ☐ Holly B. Bearsley (bear) 136
- ☐ Holly Bearberry (bear) 136
- ☐ Homer & Yukon (ornament) 349
- ☐ Honey Bunny (hare) 292
- ☐ Hopson Q. Woodsley (hare) 293
- ☐ Horace B. Hugsworthy (bear) 138
- ☐ Hoskins Q. Hugmeister (bear) 138
- ☐ Howard McBeansley (bear) 138
- ☐ Howard P. Potter (bear) 138
- ☐ Hubbard (bear) 138
- ☐ Hubbard Q. Bearsley (bear) 138
- ☐ Huett & Huntley (bear) 139
- ☐ Hugo P. Bearhugs (bear) 139
- ☐ Humphrey P. Bearhugs (bear) 140
- ☐ I Bea Lovinya & Lots (bear) 140
- ☐ Icabod Scaredbear and Midnight (bear) 141
- ☐ Ike D. Bearington (bear) 141
- ☐ Ilona B. Mooseltoes (moose) 321
- ☐ Ima Hugginya (bear) 141
- ☐ Indigo Jones (bear) 141
- ☐ Ingrid & Heidi Svenberay (bear) 142
- ☐ Ingrid & Tasha Norbruin with Toggle (bear) ...142
- ☐ Isaiah Q. Woodsley (bear) 142
- ☐ Ivana Purrkins (cat) 252
- ☐ Ivanna Hugsley (bear) 142
- ☐ Ivy M. Fuzzyfleece (lamb) 312
- ☐ Iza Basketcase (bear) 142
- ☐ J.B. Pinesley (bear) 143
- ☐ J.J. Honeypot (bear) 143
- ☐ Jack B. Frostbeary (bear) 143
- ☐ Jackie B. Beariproud (bear) 144
- ☐ Jackson B. Beanster (bear) 144
- ☐ Jacqueline K. Bearington (bear) 144
- ☐ Jake, Jay & Jette Magilla (gorilla) 276
- ☐ James & Malachi (bear) 144
- ☐ Jarvis Boydsenberry (bear) 145
- ☐ Jasper T. Fisher with Paddle (bear) 145
- ☐ Jefferson B. Beanster (bear) 146
- ☐ Jenessa T. Angelbear (ornament) 349
- ☐ Jennie Lynn & Fussypuss (bear) 146
- ☐ Jennie Marie Warmheart with Happy (bear) ...147
- ☐ Jennifer B. Bearheart (bear) 147
- ☐ Jenny McBruin (bear) 147
- ☐ Jewell & Rainbow Flowerflit (ornament) 349
- ☐ Jobie & Kibby Bearington (bear) 148
- ☐ Jocelyn Thistlebeary & Carson T. Bibbly (bear) 148
- ☐ John William (bear) 149
- ☐ Jolly B. Nick (bear) 149
- ☐ Jonathan Macbear (bear) 149
- ☐ Joy N. Goodcheer (tree topper) 365
- ☐ Jubilation P. Hambone (pig) 334
- ☐ Juilian and Justin Jodibear (bear) 150
- ☐ Juliana de Bearvoire (bear) 150
- ☐ Julianna Hugsley (bear) 150
- ☐ Julie Ann Gingerbeary and Cookie (bear) ...150
- ☐ Jupiter (ornament) 350
- ☐ Justina & Matthew (bear) 151
- ☐ Kacy Mae Sugarcone & Lil' Scoop (bear) ...151
- ☐ Kaitlin & Kendall McSwine (pig) 334
- ☐ Kandy B. Hopensit (hare) 294
- ☐ Karen B. Bearsdale (bear) 151
- ☐ Karissa Lynn Bearsdale (bear) 151
- ☐ Karl Von Fuzzner (bear) 151
- ☐ Karley & Melanie Bearibug (bear) 152
- ☐ Kassandra P. Berriwinkle (bear) 152
- ☐ Katerina Winterbeary (bear) 152
- ☐ Kathy B. Bearsley (bear) 152
- ☐ Katrinka Berriman (bear, with Thor) 152
- ☐ Kayla Bearimore (bear) 153
- ☐ Kaylie Angelfrost & Kringle's Village St. Nicholas Chapel (bear) 153
- ☐ Kelly Sue Bearican (bear) 153
- ☐ Kensington K. Braveheart (bear) 154
- ☐ Kinsey Snoopstein (bear) 154
- ☐ Kirsten DeBearvoire with Mimi DeBearvoire (bear) 154
- ☐ Kit, Bang & Kaboodle (bear) 155
- ☐ Knut C. Berriman (bear) 155
- ☐ Kringle's Retreat Set (bear) 155
- ☐ Krista Blubeary (bear, with Kayla Mulbeary) ...156
- ☐ Kristi Ann Bearibrook (bear) 156
- ☐ Kristoff (bear) 156
- ☐ Kylie & Baabs (bear) 156
- ☐ Lacey V. Hare (hare) 295
- ☐ LaDonna & Darlene DuBeary (bear) 157
- ☐ Lady Harrington (hare) 295
- ☐ Lapis (ornament) 351
- ☐ Lara (bear) 157
- ☐ Latte Lapine (ornament, with Josanna Java and Katalina Kafinata) 351
- ☐ Laura B. Bearyproud (bear) 158
- ☐ Laura P. Bradbeary (bear) 158
- ☐ Lauren B. Ladybug with Spot (bear) 158
- ☐ Lavender Q. Prissyfoot (cat) 253
- ☐ Leigh Ann Beansford (bear) 159
- ☐ Leonard S. Uproarius (lion) 315
- ☐ Leonardo B. Hartbreak (bear) 159
- ☐ Leopold Q. Roarsmore (lion) 315
- ☐ Lewis (bear) 160
- ☐ Lil' Einstein, Baby C. Corn & Gourdy (ornament) 351

- ☐ Lil' Mischief (bear) 161
- ☐ Lil' Stella with Lil' Frazier (ornament) 351
- ☐ Lil' Theodore (bear) 161
- ☐ Lindsey II & Tucker F Wuzzie (cat) 253
- ☐ Lindsey Lou with Pee-Wee (bear) 162
- ☐ Lindy & Nell Bradbeary (bear) 162
- ☐ Linsey McKenzie (bear) 162
- ☐ Linus P. Fuzzfrost (bear) 162
- ☐ Little Bangles (bear) 162
- ☐ Little Ted 100th Anniversary Mohair Bear (ornament) 352
- ☐ Liza Mae & Alex (bear) 163
- ☐ Lizzie McBee (bear, red plaid dress) 163
- ☐ Logan (bear) 164
- ☐ Lorraine P. Bearsley (bear) 164
- ☐ Louisa Catherine Bearington (bear) 164
- ☐ Lovey (bear) 164
- ☐ Lucinda D. Bearsley (bear) 165
- ☐ Lucy Bea LeBruin (bear) 165
- ☐ Lucy Belle Lambston (lamb) 313
- ☐ Lucy Lynn Beansley (bear) 165
- ☐ Ludmilla Berriman & Ludwig Von Fuzzner (bear) 165
- ☐ Lula B. Lightfoot (bear) 165
- ☐ Lulu Mae Ladybug (bear) 165
- ☐ Lyndon & Mondale Cattington (cat) 253
- ☐ M.B. Hugsley (bear) 166
- ☐ M.T. FuzzieFriend (bear) 166
- ☐ Ma Shen San (panda) 330
- ☐ Macadoo McSnoozle with Ernie (moose) 322
- ☐ Macy M. Mooselmuff (moose) 322
- ☐ Magnus P. Moosefield (moose) 322
- ☐ Malcolm Mooselfluff (moose) 322
- ☐ Malinda T. Bloomberg (bear) 168
- ☐ Mamie E. Bearington (bear) 168
- ☐ Manchester S. Bearrister (bear) 168
- ☐ Mandy Jo and Suzie (bear) 168
- ☐ Maple T. Leafowitz (bear) 168
- ☐ Margaret Q. Harington (hare) 298
- ☐ Margaux P. Pussyfoot (cat) 253
- ☐ Marissa duBeary (bear) 170
- ☐ Marshmallow Q. Furryfoot (bear) 170
- ☐ Martha T. Bearyproud with Yankee Doodle (bear) 171
- ☐ Marvin T. Luvbunny (hare) 298
- ☐ Mary Angelwish (tree topper) 366
- ☐ Mary Elizabeth, Becca & Ruth (bear) 171
- ☐ Mary Louise Bearington (bear, 10" gold mohair) 171
- ☐ Mary Louise Bearington (bear, 6" white mohair) 171
- ☐ Mary Lucinda & Marjorie Mayberry (bear) 172
- ☐ Maryanne McBeansley (bear) 172
- ☐ Mattie Frostbuns (moose) 323
- ☐ Maximillian, Thornton, & Elford (bear) 173
- ☐ Maxine von HindenMoose (moose) 323
- ☐ Maxton P. Bean (bear, with Craxton and Paxton) 173
- ☐ Maxwell (Max) Mittbruin (puppet) 363
- ☐ McKinley (moose) 324
- ☐ Melanie Lockley & Sam (bear) 174
- ☐ Melba, Mimsie & Myrtle Bahsworth (ornament) .353
- ☐ Melinda M. Milestone (bear) 174
- ☐ Melinda McRind & Dixie LE Set (bear) 175
- ☐ Merrimew McPurrsley (cat) 253
- ☐ Merrybeary Beanster (bear) 175
- ☐ Mervin Q. Rugsley (moose) 325
- ☐ Michelle B. Bearsley (bear) 176
- ☐ Mildred Q. Moostein (cow) 265
- ☐ Miller G. Mooselhuggs (moose) 325
- ☐ Milton Q. Stiltwalker (giraffe) 276
- ☐ Mindy D. Beartucket (bear) 176
- ☐ Mindy S. Basketcase (bear) 177
- ☐ Mintley (ornament) 353
- ☐ Miss Abby and Lexie Dowbunny (hare) 300
- ☐ Miss Amirella & Ripley (bear) 177
- ☐ Miss Annie Fuzzybuns (cat) 254
- ☐ Miss Flufficat (cat) 254
- ☐ Miss Isabelle Q. Bearsworthy (bear) 178
- ☐ Miss Lorriane & Abby Mae (bear) 178
- ☐ Miss Mabel & Mr. Miles Bearister (bear) 178
- ☐ Miss MacIntosh & Sarahbeth with Topsey (bear) 178
- ☐ Miss Niblers (bear) 178
- ☐ Miss Poinsley (bear) 178
- ☐ Miss Pussyfoot & Mr. McScurry (cat) 254
- ☐ Miss Sourpuss with McLemon (cat) 254
- ☐ Miss Winsalot (bear) 178
- ☐ Missy Lou & Gilbert (bear) 178
- ☐ Missy P. Pusskins and Squeekers (cat) 254
- ☐ Mistle & Taux (bear) 179
- ☐ Mitt, Muff & Puff (ornament) 353
- ☐ Mizz Buzzley & Mrs. McFlutter (bear) 179
- ☐ Mom & Baby Hugs (bear) 179
- ☐ Momma Beansford & Sweet Cheeks (bear) ...179
- ☐ Momma Bear, Alouetta, & Victor (bear) 179
- ☐ Momma Bearsworth with Mary-Margaret, Stuart & Frame (bear) 180
- ☐ Momma Bearybake (bear) 180
- ☐ Momma Berrywinkle & Woodrow (bear) 180
- ☐ Momma Hollybeary with Baby Jingles (bear) ...180
- ☐ Momma MacBeansley & Toots (bear) 180
- ☐ Momma McBear & Cedric (bear) 180
- ☐ Momma Purrsalot & Pusskins (cat) 255
- ☐ Monique de la Fleur (hare, with Giselle) 300
- ☐ Morley Moose (ornament) 354
- ☐ Morton Elfbeary (moose) 326
- ☐ Mother Bearston & Bluebell (bear) 182
- ☐ Moxley Mooselkins (bear) 182
- ☐ Mr. & Mrs. Forevermore (bear) 182
- ☐ Mr. Baxter (bear) 182
- ☐ Mr. Bojangles (bear) 183
- ☐ Mr. Chucklebeary (bear) 183
- ☐ Mr. McHootle (owl) 330
- ☐ Mr. Mufflemoose (moose) 326
- ☐ Mr. Nicholsby (bear) 183
- ☐ Mr. Peepers (bear) 184
- ☐ Mr. Stuffle (bear) 184
- ☐ Mr. Tannebaum (bear) 184
- ☐ Mr. Webster (bear) 184
- ☐ Mrs. Bearhugs (bear) 185
- ☐ Mrs. Kringles (bear) 185
- ☐ Mrs. Nestor (hen) 311
- ☐ Mrs. Plumbles (bear) 186
- ☐ Mrs. Potter & Her Lil' Sprouts (bear) 186
- ☐ Mrs. Tuttle (bear) 186
- ☐ Mrs. Tweeter and Purrsley (bear) 186
- ☐ Ms. Appleby & Olivia (bear) 186
- ☐ Ms. Magnolia (hare) 301
- ☐ Ms. Odetta & Neville (bear) 187
- ☐ Ms. Potter & Amadeus (bear) 187
- ☐ Muffles T. Toastytoes (cat) 255
- ☐ Mungo Mooselwood (moose) 328

- Myrtle MacMoo (cow) 266
- Nadia Berriman (bear) 187
- Nancy D. Bearington (bear) 188
- Nancy Jo Warmheart (bear) 188
- Nandykins (bear) 188
- Nanna O'Harea and Audrey (hare) 301
- Nettie (bear)..............................189
- Nicholas with Ansel & Fitzgerald (bear) 190
- Nicolas Bearington & Tinker (bear) 190
- Nicole (bear) 190
- Nicole & Amy Berriman with Tassel (bear) 190
- Nikali Q. Ribbit (frog) 275
- Niklas, Matilda & Trevor (bear) 191
- Noella deBearvoire with Holly (bear) 191
- Ol' MacBruin...Down on the Farm
  Auto-Delivery (bear).....................192
- Olas & Omar (panda) 331
- Olivia Q. Witebred (bear) 192
- Olivia T. Bearington (bear) 192
- Ollie B. Elf (ornament) 354
- Olympia (pig) 335
- Ophelia W. Witebred (bear) 193
- Opie Paddypasture & T. Ferdinand Wuzzie
  (bear)..................................193
- Opie V. Beanster (bear) 193
- Orabella Fitzbruin (bear) 193
- Orella Berrywinkle (bear) 193
- Oscar P. Alleyruckus (cat) 256
- Otis T. Elf (ornament) 354
- Otto Z. Elf (ornament) 354
- P.B. Punkinpaw (bear) 194
- P.B. Woodsley (panda) 331
- P.J. Bearsdale & Tink (bear) 194
- P.J. McBeansley (bear) 194
- Paigley B. Blumbeary (bear) 195
- Pamela P. Prissypuss with Nibley (cat) 256
- Pandemonium (panda) 331
- Pansey & Parsley Hopsalot (hare) 302
- Pansie P. Potter (bear) 195
- Pansley B. Bean (bear) 195
- Pansy (bear) 195
- Patrick B. Beanster (bear) 196
- Patrick Henry (bear) 196
- Paula Cherrybeary with Tart (bear) 196
- Paulina P. Punkinbeary & Tisket (bear) 196
- Pauline & Penelope (cat) 256
- Peachie P. Pussyfoot (cat) 256
- Pee Wee & Yogi (bear) 197
- Peeker of the Month (bear) 197
- Peeker P. Heartlove (bear) 197
- Percy P. Pawsley (bear) 198
- Petals P. Peeker (bear) 198
- Petey Poochkins (dog) 270
- Phoebe B. (bear) 199
- Piper Angelbuns (hare) 303
- Piper P. Plumbottom (bear) 199
- Pitty Pat Pussytoes (cat) 256
- Pittypat Pussyfoot (cat) 256
- Pookie W. Penworthy & Midnight Sneakypuss
  (cat) 257
- Port S. Mouski (mouse, with Colby) 317
- Primrose (pig) 336
- Princess Pussytoes [QVC] (cat) 257
- Proudly P. Peeker (bear) 201
- Pudgy Q. Honeypott (bear) 202
- Puff & Poof Fuzzibutt (bear) 202
- Purrcilla Pusskins (cat) 257
- Putnam & Kent (bear) 202
- Q.P. Peeker (bear) 203
- Quincy & Corliss (bear) 203
- Rachael & Phoebe Truefriends (bear) 203
- Rebecca S. Duckworthy (bear) 204
- Redmond Foxworthy (fox) 274
- Remington B. Bean (bear) 204
- Rochelle & Dessa (bear) 205
- Rootie T. McRooster (bear) 206
- Rosalie & Celina Dubeary (bear) 206
- Rosanna P. Angelbuns (hare) 305
- Roxie and Reba DuBeary (bear) 207
- Rumsford Q. Bearworth (bear) 208
- Rupert B. Shutterbear (bear) 208
- Russ Q. Goodfriends (bear) 208
- Rutledge (bear) 209
- S.B. Twinklbeary (bear) 209
- Sadie B. Bearcountry (bear) 210
- Sapphire S. Bearington (bear) 212
- Sarah Anne Bearsly & T. Foster Wuzzie (bear) ..212
- Savannah Berrywinkle & Bentley (bear) 212
- Sedgewick T Bruin (bear) 213
- Serafina (ornament) 357
- Shane B. Bearsford (bear) 214
- Shannon Oakley & Mr. Hoots (bear) 214
- Shao Pan Yo (panda) 331
- Shasta (bear, with Caledonia and Humbolt) ..214
- Shi Wong (panda) 331
- Shoeless P. Clopsdale (horse) 311
- Skipper T. Pattington (bear) 216
- Skylar and Starlynn (bear) 216
- Smith Witter 25th Anniversary (bear) 217
- Snackers Sneakypuss (cat) 259
- Sneaky P. Snottypuss (cat) 259
- Snooker T. Sootyfoot (cat) 259
- Snoozer Bedoozer (dog) 271
- Socksley (bear) 358
- Sonya B. Burrbruin (bear) 218
- Spearmint and Peppermint Hollibeary (bear) ..218
- Springsley Hopplebuns (hare) 306
- Squeekers McPoppin (mouse) 318
- Squirt McSnoozle (ornament, with Squeek) ..358
- Stacey B. Beansley (bear) 219
- Stamford (hare, a.k.a. Stanford) 306
- Star S. Bangles (bear) 219
- Starlight B. Bearsworth (bear) 219
- Stella and Baby Mae (bear) 220
- Stephanie B. Learnin (bear) 220
- Sunnie Rae Daisydew with Sprinkle (bear) 222
- Sunny B. Hugsworth (bear) 222
- Suzella K. Bearington (bear) 222
- Suzie Q. Scootenpedal,
  Lil' Louis & Poochkins (bear) 223
- Sven B. Frostman (bear) 223
- T. Fargo, T. Foster & T. Fuzzball Wuzzie
  (moose) 329
- T.J. Bearheart (bear) 224
- Tabbie F. Wuzzie
  (ornament, with T. F. Wuzziewitch and Tricky) ..358
- Taira (ornament) 359
- Tammy (bear) 224
- Tara & Tia F. Wuzzie (bear, with Tilly) 224
- Tasha F. Wuzzie (bear, with Tami and Tatum) ..225
- Tatters Beariluved (bear, with Patches) 225
- Ted & Teddy (bear) 225
- Teddy Bauer (bear) 226
- Tessa, Tilden, Tori & Tessa F. Wuzzie (bear) ..226

- ☐ Thea St. Griz & Everett Elfston (bear) 226
- ☐ Theodora Maria (bear) 226
- ☐ Theodore M. Bear (bear) 227
- ☐ Thomas T. Rugsley (bear) 227
- ☐ Thomasina Purrkins (cat, with Suzie) 260
- ☐ Tibsley Purrsalot (cat) 261
- ☐ Tiffany F. Wuzzie (pin, with Tinger and Teedle) . .362
- ☐ Tilly & Toots Ribbit (ornament, with Lilly) 359
- ☐ Tom, Dick & Harry (cat) 261
- ☐ Topper F. Wuzzie
  (monkey, with Theo and Tumble) 319
- ☐ Trixsley (bear) 230
- ☐ Trudie Ann Hugsalot (bear) 231
- ☐ Truffleina & Twila (pig) .336
- ☐ Tweedle & Opie Waddlewalk
  (penguin, with Tuxie) 332
- ☐ Twinkle B. Beansley (bear) 232
- ☐ Twinksley (ornament) .360
- ☐ U.B. Mine with Heart (bear) 233
- ☐ Uncle Gus & Honeybunch (bear) 233
- ☐ Uncle Zeb & Cousin Minnow (bear) 233
- ☐ Ursula Berriman (bear) 233
- ☐ Valentina with Evalina, Caterina, & Michelina
  (bear) 234
- ☐ Vermooth (moose, with Margarita) 329
- ☐ Veronica Laflame (bear) 235
- ☐ Veronica Marie Bearington (bear) 235
- ☐ Viola Flutterby (bear) 235
- ☐ Walter, Wayne and Wilbert Tinkerbeary (bear) . .236
- ☐ Wesley, Willoughby & Woodward (bear) 237
- ☐ Westin Woodsley (bear) 238
- ☐ Whihley with Winkle & Pip (bear) 238
- ☐ Whimsie T. Faeriebear (bear) 238
- ☐ Whitley B. Beariluved (bear) 238
- ☐ Wilhelmina Q. Bearsworth (bear) 239
- ☐ William Henry Bearington (bear) 239
- ☐ Wilma & Gracey Bearfriends (bear) 239
- ☐ Wilson with Boat (bear) 239
- ☐ Wilson with Pie (bear) .240
- ☐ Windsor & Sarasota (bear) 240
- ☐ Winstead & Pensacola (bear) 241
- ☐ Wishley B. Bunnybear (bear) 241
- ☐ Woolfie P. Poorpooch (dog) 272
- ☐ Xin Fu Wongbruin (panda) 332
- ☐ Yankee & Doodle McBear (bear) 242
- ☐ Yankee Doodle Doo (rooster) 337
- ☐ Ying & Yang Bearington (ornament) 361
- ☐ Yippeeyo Beanster (bear) 242
- ☐ Yolanda Panda (panda) 332
- ☐ You and Me (bear) 243
- ☐ Yvonne & Yvette (bear) 243
- ☐ Zack (lion) 315
- ☐ Zoe R. Grimilkin (cat) .262

SFMB Exclusives
San Francisco Music Box

- ☐ Abbey Ewe (lamb) 311
- ☐ Alexis Berriman (bear) .54
- ☐ Alison Babbit (hare) 277
- ☐ Angelina (ornament) .341
- ☐ Ariel (ornament) 341
- ☐ Ashley (hare) 279
- ☐ Aubrey T. Tippeetoes (bear) 61
- ☐ Aunt Becky Bearchild (bear) 61
- ☐ Benjamin (bear) 72
- ☐ Bestest & Buddy Truefriends (bear) 73

- ☐ Bojingles (bear) 77
- ☐ Braxton B. Bear (bear) .79
- ☐ Buckley the Fireman (bear) 83
- ☐ Bud Buzzby (ornament) 344
- ☐ Chamomille Quignapple (bear) 90
- ☐ Clarissa (bear) 94
- ☐ Claus Kringlebeary (bear) 95
- ☐ Cleo P. Pussytoes (cat) 248
- ☐ Delanie B. Beansford (bear) 101
- ☐ Dixie Hackett (bear) 103
- ☐ Duncan Doodledog (dog) 268
- ☐ Emmie Bramblebeary (bear) 113
- ☐ Eugenia II (bear) 115
- ☐ Fidelity B. Morgan IV (bear) 117
- ☐ G.P. Hugabunch (bear) 121
- ☐ Galaxy (ornament) 349
- ☐ Guinevere (bear) 129
- ☐ H.B. Bearwish (bear) .131
- ☐ Hayes R. Bearrington (bear) 133
- ☐ Heranamous (cat) 251
- ☐ Juliette (ornament) 350
- ☐ Klaus Von Fuzzner (bear) 155
- ☐ Lady Pembroke (hare) 295
- ☐ Lavinia V. Hariweather (hare) 296
- ☐ Maribel Gardenglow (hare) 298
- ☐ Marissa P. Pussytoes (cat) 253
- ☐ Momma McBear & Delmar (bear) 180
- ☐ Momma McFuzz and Missy (cat) 255
- ☐ Momma McNew with Hugsley (bear) 181
- ☐ Mooshell Patchbeary (cow) 266
- ☐ Mrs. Northstar (bear) .186
- ☐ Mrs. Petrie (cat) 255
- ☐ Mrs. Trumbull (bear) .186
- ☐ Murtaugh Moosetrax (moose) 328
- ☐ Nana Bearhugs (bear) 188
- ☐ P. Gallery Trunkster (elephant) 274
- ☐ Pendleton (bear) 197
- ☐ Poof Pufflebeary (bear) 200
- ☐ Poor Ol' Bear (bear) 201
- ☐ Prudence Berrimore (bear) 202
- ☐ Rosalind (bear) 206
- ☐ Rosalind II (bear) 207
- ☐ Rosie O'Pigg (pig) 336
- ☐ Sally Quignapple and Annie (bear) 211
- ☐ Skylar Thistlebeary (bear) 217
- ☐ Smith Witter II (bear) .217
- ☐ Stella Starbear (bear) 220
- ☐ Theodore Jr. (bear) 227
- ☐ Valentina B. Bearhugs (bear) 234
- ☐ Vanessa Fluffypaws (cat) 261
- ☐ Virginia Bluebell (hare) 310
- ☐ Winnie II (bear) 240
- ☐ Winnie Stillwithus (bear) 240
- ☐ Winnie Wuzzwhite (bear) 240
- ☐ Zelda Fitzhare (hare) .310

Store Exclusives
Alps

- ☐ Barton (bear) 69
- ☐ Cousin Murray (moose, burgundy hat) 320
- ☐ Cousin Murray (moose) 320
- ☐ Meeka (moose, green sweater) 324
- ☐ Meeka (moose, green plaid pajamas) 324
- ☐ Meeka (moose, red sweater) 324
- ☐ Meeka (moose, purple sweater) 324
- ☐ Meeka (moose, green sweater with flowers) 324

- ☐ Meeka (moose, mint green sweater) 324
- ☐ Mookie (moose, cream sweaters) 325
- ☐ Mookie (moose, navy sweater with red and white stripe) 325
- ☐ Mookie (moose, beige sweater with aztec trim) 326
- ☐ Mukluk (moose, blue sweater) 326
- ☐ Mukluk (moose, red plaid pajamas) 327
- ☐ Mukluk (moose, blue/green sweater) 327
- ☐ Mukluk (moose, 2000) 327
- ☐ Mukluk (moose, blue sweater with ribbon trim) 327
- ☐ Mukluk (moose, Weekender) 327
- ☐ Mukluk (moose, Super Mukluk) 327
- ☐ Mukluk (moose, American Mukluk) 327
- ☐ Mukluk (moose, Varsity Mukluk) 327
- ☐ Mukluk (moose, Super Mukluk III) 327
- ☐ Mukluk (moose, Cold Springs) 327
- ☐ Mukluk (moose, Holiday) 327
- ☐ Mukluk (moose, Outdoorsman) 327
- ☐ Mukluk (moose, Weekender Mukluk II) 328
- ☐ Mukluk (moose, Tobacco Weekender) 328

Art House
- ☐ Starry (bear) 220

Banana Republic
- ☐ Travis (bear, black and gold sweater) 229
- ☐ Travis (bear, black and gold sweater) 229
- ☐ Travis (bear, dark blue sweater) 229
- ☐ Travis (bear, red sweater with tree) 230

Barnes & Noble
- ☐ Benjamin W. Bear (bear) 72
- ☐ Bernard B. Bear (bear) 73
- ☐ Bernice B. Bear (bear) 73

Bath & Body Works
- ☐ Bath & Body Works Bear (bear) 69
- ☐ Bath & Body Works Dog (dog) 267
- ☐ Snowbunny (hare) 306

Bear Heaven
- ☐ Jae Lynn Jackson (bear) 144

Belks
- ☐ Benjamin Beanbeary (bear) 72
- ☐ Lindsey (bear) 161

Bon Ton
- ☐ Abigail (bear) 50
- ☐ Barney B. Keeper (bear) 68
- ☐ Clara (bear) 94
- ☐ Deirdre Rose (bear) 101
- ☐ Effie May (bear) 110
- ☐ Francesca (bear) 119
- ☐ Gatsby (bear) 122
- ☐ Heywood Bearlanski (bear) 135
- ☐ Isabella (bear) 142
- ☐ Joanne Pearl (bear) 148

Boscovs
- ☐ Alice Hopplebeary (hare) 277
- ☐ Barbara Mary (bear) 68
- ☐ Gabriella (bear) 121

Carlton Cards
- ☐ Abby & Katie Forever Friends (bear) 50
- ☐ Alexandra & Jessica Bearyfriends (bear) 53
- ☐ C.C. Cocoa Bear (bear) 85
- ☐ Cecile Bearnet (bear) 89
- ☐ Cela Bration (bear) 89
- ☐ Faye & Jennifer (bear) 116
- ☐ Hannah H. Woodsbeary (bear) 131
- ☐ Momma McBearsley with Jessica (bear) 181

Carson Pirie Scott
- ☐ Auntie Adeline (bear) 62
- ☐ Glimmer B. Snowflake (bear) 125

Casual Living
- ☐ Salty (dog) 271

Centre Gift Shoppe
- ☐ Niagra (bear) 189

Coach House Gifts
- ☐ Debbie M. Dobbsey (bear) 100
- ☐ Emily E. Dobbsey (bear) 112
- ☐ Helena Marie Boydsley (bear) 134
- ☐ Richard Tee Dobbsey (bear) 205
- ☐ Virginia Dobbsey (bear) 235

Country Clutter
- ☐ C.C. Goodbear (bear) 85
- ☐ Crystal B. Goodbear (bear) 98
- ☐ Daisy Anna Goodbear (bear) 99
- ☐ Flora Mae Goodbear (bear) 118
- ☐ Heather Goodbear (bear) 133
- ☐ Jessie Lu Goodbear (bear) 147
- ☐ Lauren Nicole (bear) 158
- ☐ Lindsey Marie Goodbear (bear) 162
- ☐ Millie Marie Goodbear (bear) 176
- ☐ Penelope Pearsley Gift Set (bear) 197
- ☐ Rosie B. Goodbear (bear) 207
- ☐ Sophie B. Goodbear (bear) 218
- ☐ Suzie B. Spicebeary Gift Set (bear) 222
- ☐ Twinkle Crystalfrost (ornament) 360

Country House
- ☐ Glory B. America (bear) 125

Country Living
- ☐ Ali Marie Beansley (bear) 54
- ☐ Artemus J. Bear (bear, a.k.a John Michael) 59
- ☐ Jeremiah (bear) 147

Country Peddler
- ☐ Tartan Tess (bear) 224

Cracker Barrel
- ☐ Caitlynn P.J. Crystalfrost (bear) 86
- ☐ Cindy Lou Bearican (bear) 93
- ☐ Hamilton (pig) 333
- ☐ Jenna Rae (bear) 146
- ☐ Maddison Bearyproud (bear) 166
- ☐ Ruthy Appleton (bear) 209
- ☐ Shelby McRind (bear) 214
- ☐ Taylor Rene (bear) 225

Dillards
- ☐ Aldina (bear) 53
- ☐ Alex Nicole (bear) 53
- ☐ Andrew (bear) 57
- ☐ Aubrey (bear) 60
- ☐ Brandon (bear) 79
- ☐ Brittany (hare) 281
- ☐ C. Elbert (bear) 85
- ☐ Caleigh (cat) 246
- ☐ Christian (bear) 92
- ☐ Debbie Claire (bear) 100
- ☐ Ella (bear) 111
- ☐ Elsbeth (bear) 111
- ☐ Erin Shaughnessy (pig) 333
- ☐ Eugenia (bear) 114
- ☐ Glenna (bear) 125
- ☐ Gracie (bear) 127

BoydsTracker - Exclusive Index

- ☐ Gunter (bear) 130
- ☐ Heather (hare) 291
- ☐ Henry (bear) 134
- ☐ Izzy (moose) 322
- ☐ Jaime Lisa (bear) 144
- ☐ Jake (bear) 144
- ☐ Jenna Kathleen (cat) 252
- ☐ Jeremy (bear) 147
- ☐ Jillian (bear) 148
- ☐ Julia (bear) 150
- ☐ Justin (bear) 151
- ☐ Katie O'Pigg (pig) 334
- ☐ Kelsey (bear) 153
- ☐ Laura Ann (bear) 158
- ☐ Lena O'Pigg (pig) 334
- ☐ Lindsey (hare) 297
- ☐ Lone Star (bear) 164
- ☐ Meg (bear) 174
- ☐ Merentha (pig) 335
- ☐ Michael (bear) 175
- ☐ Michaela (bear) 176
- ☐ Natalie (hare) 301
- ☐ Nichley (bear) 189
- ☐ Oliver (bear) 192
- ☐ Olivia (lamb) 313
- ☐ Pepper (cat) 256
- ☐ Raylee (bear) 204
- ☐ Regan (bear) 204
- ☐ Roland (bear) 206
- ☐ Ryan (bear) 209
- ☐ Sidney (bear) 215
- ☐ Taylor (bear) 225
- ☐ Texanne (bear) 226
- ☐ Tyler (bear) 232
- ☐ Will (bear) 239
- ☐ Zwick (bear) 243

Disney

- ☐ Eeyore (donkey) 272
- ☐ Eeyore (donkey, Winter Holiday) 272
- ☐ Eeyore (donkey, plaid vest) 272
- ☐ Eeyore (donkey, Costume Party) 273
- ☐ Eeyore (donkey, Cozy Holiday) 273
- ☐ Eeyore (donkey, Holiday Caroling) ..273
- ☐ Eeyore 1999 (ornament) 347
- ☐ Eeyore 2000 (ornament) 347
- ☐ Eeyore, Piglet, Pooh & Tiger [Disney] (ornament) 347
- ☐ Piglet (pig, Santa's Helper) 335
- ☐ Piglet (pig, Winter Holiday) 335
- ☐ Piglet (pig, cardigan and hat) 335
- ☐ Piglet (pig, Costume Party) 335
- ☐ Piglet (pig, Cozy Holiday) 335
- ☐ Piglet (pig, Holiday Caroling) 335
- ☐ Piglet 1999 (ornament) 356
- ☐ Piglet 2000 (ornament) 356
- ☐ Pooh (ornament, santa hat) 356
- ☐ Pooh (bear, Mohair Classic) 200
- ☐ Pooh (bear, Mohair Santa) 200
- ☐ Pooh (bear, Santa with Ornament) ..200
- ☐ Pooh (bear, Mohair Winter Holiday) 200
- ☐ Pooh (bear, Winter Holiday) 200
- ☐ Pooh (bear, plaid coat) 200
- ☐ Pooh (bear, Mohair red pajamas) ...200
- ☐ Pooh (bear, Costume Party) 200
- ☐ Pooh (bear, Mohair Cozy Holiday) ..200
- ☐ Pooh (bear, Cozy Holiday) 200
- ☐ Pooh (bear, Winter Caroling) 200
- ☐ Pooh 1999 (ornament) 356
- ☐ Pooh 1999 (ornament, stocking) 356
- ☐ Pooh 2000 (ornament) 356
- ☐ Pooh 2000 (ornament, sweater) 356
- ☐ Pooh 2002 (ornament, mohair) 356
- ☐ Tigger (tiger, Winter Holiday) 338
- ☐ Tigger (tiger, plaid hat) 338
- ☐ Tigger (tiger, Costume Party) 338
- ☐ Tigger (tiger, Cozy Holiday) 338
- ☐ Tigger (tiger, Holiday Caroling) 338
- ☐ Tigger 1999 (ornament) 359
- ☐ Tigger 2000 (ornament) 359
- ☐ Tigger Resin and Plush Set (tiger, Elf) .338

Eddie Bauer

- ☐ Bartholomew (bear) 69
- ☐ Bauer B. Bear (bear) 69
- ☐ Eddie Bauer Betty (dog) 267
- ☐ Eddie Bauer Diamond (bear) 106
- ☐ Eddie Bauer Hunter (bear) 106
- ☐ Eddie Bauer Moose (moose) 320
- ☐ Edmund (bear) 107

Elder Beerman

- ☐ Abigail (bear) 50
- ☐ Ashley Lynn (bear) 60
- ☐ Brianna (bear) 80
- ☐ Caitlin Cherry Berry (bear) 86
- ☐ Chloe (hare) 282
- ☐ Cosmos (ornament) 346
- ☐ Daphne (bear) 99
- ☐ Gretchen (hare) 291
- ☐ Hannah (bear) 131
- ☐ Holly (cat) 251
- ☐ Jamison Ann Dickens (bear) 145
- ☐ Kelby (bear) 153
- ☐ Lindy (hare) 297
- ☐ Mackenzie Alexandra (bear) 166
- ☐ Madeline (bear) 167
- ☐ Marnie (bear) 170
- ☐ Morty (ornament) 354
- ☐ Nicole de la El-bee (bear) 190
- ☐ Theresa Marie (bear) 227
- ☐ Venus (ornament) 360

Ethel M. Chocolates

- ☐ Noelle (bear) 191

Faith Mountain

- ☐ Honey Bee Bear (bear) 137

Frederick Atkins

- ☐ Adkin (bear) 52
- ☐ Attie (bear) 60
- ☐ Beatrice (bear) 71
- ☐ Bria (bear) 80
- ☐ Clementine (bear) 95
- ☐ Emma (bear) 112
- ☐ Fredrica (bear) 120
- ☐ Karmen (bear) 152
- ☐ Magdalena (bear) 167
- ☐ Meredith (hare) 299
- ☐ Monica (bear) 181
- ☐ Peyton (bear) 199
- ☐ Quinn (bear) 203
- ☐ Russet (bear) 209
- ☐ Sarina (hare) 306
- ☐ Sterner (bear) 220
- ☐ Tiana (bear) 227

441

- ☐ Tristan (bear) 230
- ☐ Verdeia (bear) 234
- ☐ Vernette (bear) 234

GoCollect
- ☐ Heidi May Patchbeary (bear) 134

Gottschalks
- ☐ Little Celeste (bear) 163
- ☐ Lucy (bear) 165

Hallmark
- ☐ Baxter T. Birch (bear) 69
- ☐ Cameron W. Bearsmark (bear) 87
- ☐ Cassidy L. Bearsmark (bear) 89
- ☐ Emma M. Sweetstuff (bear) 113
- ☐ Faith 'N Dreams (bear) 115
- ☐ Holiday (bear) 136
- ☐ Josie K. Bearsmark (bear) 150
- ☐ Mikie O'Burr (bear) 176
- ☐ Rainey Bloomengrows (bear) 203
- ☐ Sam Yule (bear) 211
- ☐ Starr E. Night (bear) 220
- ☐ Sydney G. Bearsmark (bear) 223
- ☐ Tulla B. Bearfoot (bear) 231

Harry & David
- ☐ Baby Rosebud (pig) 333
- ☐ Bearly A. Hare (bear) 70
- ☐ Bearwinkle (bear) 71
- ☐ Belle (hare) 280
- ☐ Elliot (bear) 111
- ☐ Mommie and Me (bear) 181
- ☐ Rose Bud (pig) 336
- ☐ Rudy Valentino (bear) 208

Hello Shops
- ☐ Emily Starbright (bear) 112

Hershey
- ☐ Chocolate (cow) 264
- ☐ Harry Harvest (bear) 132
- ☐ Hersh E. Kiss (bear) 135
- ☐ Hoppy E. Star (hare) 293
- ☐ Kisses (cow) 265
- ☐ Sir Lotslove (bear) 216

Hunter's Hope
- ☐ Hope & A. Future (bear) 138
- ☐ Hunter (bear) 140

J.C.Penney
- ☐ Anastasia Bearskoff (bear) 56
- ☐ Bartholomew (bear) 69
- ☐ J.C. Von Fuzzner (bear) 143
- ☐ James C. Penneybeary (bear) 144
- ☐ Kevin Kringlebeary (bear) 154
- ☐ Krystal Penneybeary (bear) 156
- ☐ Pamela Penneybeary (bear) 195
- ☐ Penny Bearsley (bear) 197

J.T.Webb
- ☐ Aunt Phiddy Bearburn (bear) 62
- ☐ Laura E. Bearburn (bear) 158
- ☐ Sunny Buzzbee (bear) 222

Kirlins
- ☐ Clara (bear) 94
- ☐ Daisy Bearylove (bear) 99
- ☐ Emily Daisydew (bear) 112
- ☐ Emma Jane Mintly (bear) 112
- ☐ Hannah B. Punkinbeary (bear) 131
- ☐ Holly B. Kringlebeary (bear) 136
- ☐ Kaitlyn Bearlove (bear) 151
- ☐ Lauren Ladybug (bear) 158
- ☐ Madeline Ann Woodsbeary (bear) 167
- ☐ Madison Glorybear (bear) 167
- ☐ Marian (bear) 169
- ☐ Megan (bear) 174
- ☐ Mitzie Mae (hare) 300
- ☐ Nadia (bear) 187
- ☐ Pauline (hare) 302
- ☐ Sadie (bear) 210
- ☐ Samantha (bear) 211
- ☐ Sarah Patchbeary (bear) 212

Linda Anderson
- ☐ Mrs. Bradley (bear) 185
- ☐ Sammi B. Thumblover (bear) 211

Little Debbie
- ☐ Ellsworth (bear) 111

Lock, Stock & Barrel
- ☐ Flora B. Lilac (bear) 118
- ☐ LeGrand Ol' Bear (bear) 159

Longaberger
- ☐ Autumn Pumpkin Patch (bear) 63
- ☐ Bea Beary (bear) 70
- ☐ Betsie L. Steadsbeary (bear) 74
- ☐ Bunnie B. Springbeary (hare) 281
- ☐ Doodle & Dandy (bear) 104
- ☐ Elli Bean (hare) 286
- ☐ Faith (bear) 115
- ☐ Flopsie Bunnyears (hare) 289
- ☐ Glory Steadsbeary (bear) 125
- ☐ Glory Steadsbeary (variation, bear) 125
- ☐ Gracie Blossombeary (bear) 127
- ☐ Grammy Quiltsbeary with Patches (bear) .. 127
- ☐ Heather Steadsbeary (bear) 133
- ☐ Holly Beary (tree topper) 365
- ☐ Holly Jolly Peeker (bear) 137
- ☐ Honey B. Beary (bear) 137
- ☐ Hope L. Bearywell (bear) 138
- ☐ Ima Bestfriend (bear) 141
- ☐ Libbee Bearamerica (bear) 160
- ☐ Lil' Love (bear) 161
- ☐ Lucky O'Beary (bear) 165
- ☐ Luvey Heartstrings (bear) 166
- ☐ Patricia L. Cooksbeary (bear) 195
- ☐ Petunia Steadsbeary (pig) 335
- ☐ Philip A. Stocking (ornament) 356
- ☐ Posie Picksabunch (bear) 201
- ☐ Rusty Scaredybear (bear) 209
- ☐ Sage Steadsbeary (bear) 210
- ☐ Shari Beabeary (bear) 214
- ☐ Star Steadsbeary (cat) 260
- ☐ Sunnie Dae (bear) 222
- ☐ Teddie Collectibear (bear) 225
- ☐ Trissy Teabeary (bear) 230
- ☐ Twinkles Starbeary (bear) 232
- ☐ Weaver Bearyproud (bear) 237
- ☐ Wendy Weaver (bear, a.k.a. Weaver Girl) . 237
- ☐ Woody Puttsalot (bear) 242

Lord & Taylor
- ☐ Ally (bear) 55
- ☐ Ally II (bear) 55
- ☐ Ambrose Q. Hydrant (dog) 266
- ☐ Athena with Holly Berries (ornament) 342
- ☐ Buckles (bear) 82
- ☐ Buzz (dog) 267
- ☐ Cissy (bear) 93

- ☐ Claudius B. Bean (bear) 94
- ☐ Comet (ornament) 345
- ☐ Edwin R. Elfstein (bear) 109
- ☐ Emily Ann (moose) 321
- ☐ Erin (bear) 113
- ☐ Felicity (bear) 116
- ☐ Guinevere (bear, with wings) 129
- ☐ Hartley (bear) 132
- ☐ Holly (bear) 136
- ☐ Jesse (bear) 147
- ☐ Katie Kat (cat) 252
- ☐ Katie Kat II (cat) 252
- ☐ Marina (bear) 169
- ☐ Matilda with Holly Berries (ornament) 353
- ☐ Max (ornament) 353
- ☐ Mortimer (moose) 326
- ☐ P.J. (bear) 194
- ☐ Reginald (bear) 204
- ☐ Sally and Harry (bear) 210
- ☐ Sheila (ornament) 357
- ☐ Susie (bear) 222
- ☐ Tessa (ornament) 359
- ☐ Timmy (ornament) 359

Macy's East
- ☐ Aunt Carole Beary (ornament) 342
- ☐ Aunt Elaine Wilbear (ornament) 342
- ☐ Aunt Jo Ann O'Beary (bear) 62
- ☐ Carlie Icebeary (ornament) 345
- ☐ Ethan B. Boyds (bear) 114
- ☐ Evan E. Elfbear (ornament) 347
- ☐ Janie Icebeary (bear) 145
- ☐ Lainie M. Elfbear (ornament) 351
- ☐ Maci E. Kringlebeary (bear) 166
- ☐ Twinkle Bear (bear) 232

Marshall Field's
- ☐ Boo Bear (bear) 78

May Company
- ☐ Beatrice Bearyman (bear) 71
- ☐ Beatrice Bearymore (bear) 71
- ☐ George (bear) 122
- ☐ Gracie (bear) 127
- ☐ Henry Bearyman (bear) 135
- ☐ Henry Bearymore (bear) 135
- ☐ Jackson (bear) 144
- ☐ Jolee (bear) 149
- ☐ Ronald (bear) 206
- ☐ Sadie Bearyman (bear) 210
- ☐ Sadie Bearymore (bear) 210

Miss Yvonne's & Sarah's Bears
- ☐ Anna Mae Bakersbear with Li'l Snap (bear) 58

My Gift Cottage
- ☐ Laura Elizabeth Yachtley (bear) 158

Norm Thompson
- ☐ Grant S. Bearington (bear) 128

Peebles/Gottschalks
- ☐ Auntie Sheila Bearisch (bear) 63

Profitts
- ☐ Carlie & Kristen (bear) 88
- ☐ Jenna (bear) 146
- ☐ Sakary Millenia (bear) 210

Rocking Horse
- ☐ Libearty C. Star (bear) 161

Sarah's Bears
- ☐ Cocoa Mousse (moose) 320

Sight & Sound Ministries
- ☐ Daniel (bear) 99

Smithsonian Institute
- ☐ Cherry Blossom Bear (bear) 91
- ☐ Cherry Blossom Kimono Bear (bear) 92

Smuckers
- ☐ Bluebeary (bear) 77
- ☐ Strawberry (bear) 221

Sparx
- ☐ CB The Skater (bear) 89

Spiegel
- ☐ Honey B. Bear (bear) 137
- ☐ Maynard Von Hindenmoose (moose) 324

Victoria's Secret
- ☐ Buffy (bear) 83

Welcome Home
- ☐ Allie Bearington (bear) 54
- ☐ Amber Woodsbeary (bear) 56
- ☐ Bess Bearman (bear) 73
- ☐ Chance Furgold (bear) 90
- ☐ Crystal & Frosty Icebeary (bear) 98
- ☐ Emily Claire (bear) 112
- ☐ Heather and Heathcliffe Plumbeary (bear) .. 133
- ☐ J.T. Jordan III (bear) 143
- ☐ Marla Mae Beary (bear) 170
- ☐ Miss Maggie & Theo (bear) 178
- ☐ Molly Maybeary (bear) 179
- ☐ Orianna (bear) 193
- ☐ Pelmon Thomas McBear (bear) 197
- ☐ Precious Plumbeary (bear) 201
- ☐ Tess Autumnbeary (bear) 226

Yankee Candle
- ☐ Muffin B. Bluebeary (bear) 187
- ☐ Rosie (bear) 207
- ☐ Victoria Bearybright (bear) 235

Younker's
- ☐ Chandler (bear) 90